RESEARCH IN THE THREE R'S

RESEARCH
in the
THREE
R's

Edited by C. W. HUNNICUTT
Syracuse University

and WILLIAM J. IVERSON
Stanford University

HARPER & BROTHERS
PUBLISHERS, NEW YORK

To LILLIE AND ADELAIDE

Contents

Preface—The Purpose of the Book

This is the century of research. The technology which makes our lives different from those of any other historical era is based on research. In education, too, the factor which is exerting the greatest influence in helping our profession grow to maturity is research. To the degree that we can move away from sole reliance upon hunch, opinion, rule of thumb and can establish our practices upon the solid ground of experimentation—to that degree we achieve maturity as a profession.

There is widespread realization of the importance of research as a primary foundation for instruction. There is also strong conviction that the more direct the contact teachers have with the research the more likely they are to be influenced in their teaching by the findings. Translating these convictions into everyday practice, however, has typically proved almost impossible. To begin with, the studies are so numerous—over 3000 in reading, 1200 in arithmetic—that few people have the time and devotion to trudge through even a small portion of them and to judge their relative value. Principals, supervisors, and many college instructors may thus be forgiven a certain lack of assurance in directing teachers or students to the best relevant studies when a particular question arises.

For generations methodology has concerned itself with the *how* of teaching. We now know that it is equally important to know the *why*. A person taught to meet specific situations only with specific techniques or "tricks" is lost when confronted with the novel. No teacher-training institution and no supervisory helper can anticipate all the myriad situations that will develop in a classroom filled with young America. Only if the teacher has a broad framework of understanding or generalizations to guide his behavior in specific situations can he meet these difficulties with full effectiveness. These understandings come at least in part from an extensive knowledge of relevant research.

A study of these experiments can have other outcomes. Some understanding of basic research procedures will be gained. This in turn can lead to a richer appreciation of the search for truth in the highly complex area of human behavior and education. It may strengthen the habit and skill of objective thought processes in judging ideas. It should encourage the critical evaluation of existing practices in education. Many indeed will be led to the realization that research is not something possible only to some strange breed of "experts" but something that can be carried on to a greater or lesser degree by *everyone* in the normal course of school operation. One outcome may be the redoing of some of these experiments by regular classroom teachers to see if they really work in their classrooms.

At present there is no ready means for many people to become acquainted with the significant research in teaching the three R's. Meeting that need is the purpose of this book. Textbooks of methodology serve a different purpose. Knowledge of relevant research forms a part of the scholarly background brought to the writing by the textbook author. His purpose, however, is to summarize and suggest desirable methodology but not to present the research as such upon which his suggestions are based. This volume can undergird and supplement such texts by enabling their readers to examine for themselves the key studies which have influenced decisions about instruction.

In recent years it has become apparent that teachers, principals, and supervisors over the country are seeking the foundation which research can give to opinion. One indication is the excellent group of pamphlets published by the National Education Association. These were written in direct response to teacher demand; each summarizes research in some curricular area. However, experiments are not quoted directly, and the reader is forced either to accept the authors' interpretation on faith or to attempt with some difficulty to obtain the original sources and check for himself. He still is not given direct contact with research and is deprived of the opportunity to evaluate and decide for himself.

Any extensive checking of research, moreover, is seldom feasible. Few libraries in the country can provide extensive research references. Most of the early studies are no longer in print. Even when these studies are available in the institution's library, an instructor hesitates to require their reading by large numbers of students. Irreplaceable references are soon worn to shreds and become unavailable to advanced scholars. Furthermore, experience in the relation between availability of materials and quantity read indicates that a book in the student's hand is worth ten in the library.

Direct contact with some of the fundamental research should be part of every teacher's training. Only in this way can we truly progress from the immature "I'm doing this because you say it's the right way" to a mature "I am doing this because I know the supporting experimental evidence." With adequate familiarity with research, teachers can outgrow both a naïve and unquestioning awe of scientific experimentation and a sophomoric distaste or contempt for the apparent contradictions of research. This may also lead more practitioners to graduate from "Research is something only other people do" to "I'm going to see what happens if I. . . ."

Teachers have another need for experimental evidence beyond the obvious one of improving instruction. The recurring wave of criticism and questioning about public-school practices often focuses on the three R's. Here argumentation or philosophic conviction is seldom as convincing as a study of the experimental evidence. Probably the latter is second only to "my child's experience" as a persuader of parents.

The studies reported here have been adapted and abridged to conserve space so that the maximum number of reports could be included. Omissions consisted chiefly of secondary findings, extended discussions of related studies done by others or of the origins of the study, routine details of the experimental methods used, and plans for further research. It is hoped that readers will want to take advantage of any opportunity to read the more complete original reports to obtain additional information or to clear up unanswered questions.

In each case an effort has been made to acquaint the reader with the key purposes or problems of the study, the methods used to try to solve them, and the important findings achieved. Where the implications for school practice are not apparent from the author's report, the editors have sometimes added a note indicating some reasonable inferences. The editors, through the use of introductions and occasional connective sentences or paragraphs, have attempted an organized and integrated presentation, not solely a scissors and paste patchwork.

The studies included were chosen because they are significant. They deal with important topics, have been influential, have been carefully done. In some cases studies equally good have been omitted since they duplicate other works which have been included. The studies included here are a small sample of the vast reservoir of accumulated experimentation. Not all areas of existing research within any one of the three R's have been represented. For some areas more studies are included than for others. This relative weighting is due to the high quality of investigation in some areas and to the degree of importance or controversy of studies in other instances.

The reports have been limited to those whose major function was to explore the three R's. It was a temptation to include ones like Sears'.[1] Her experiment showed the great effect children's success or failure experiences had upon the goals they set for themselves, and in turn upon their accomplishments in reading and arithmetic. But the prime purpose of the study was to explore learning behavior rather than any of the R's, so it was omitted.

The studies included are not all of equal levels of scientific quality. This fact characterizes all research and will be a challenge to the critical judgment of the reader.

The selection of studies inevitably reflects the special interests and biases of the editors. We have consulted with others but the responsibility remains ours. Any contribution accruing to education is of course to be credited to the original investigators.

We are deeply grateful to these experimenters and their publishers for permission to abridge and use their reports. Acknowledgment in footnote form is made throughout the book.

C. W. H.
W. J. I.

November, 1957

---

[1] Pauline Snedden Sears, "Levels of Aspiration in Academically Successful and Unsuccessful Children," *Journal of Abnormal and Social Psychology* (1940), 35:498–536.

Editor's Introduction

The three R's have been, are, and it is hoped by the writer will always be the basic elements in the program of elementary education in the nation's elementary schools. Children and adults alike require competence in the three R's to comprehend and interpret the increasingly complex phenomena revealed about our physical and social worlds. Urgently needed are more individuals capable of thinking creatively and communicating lucidly in terms of verbal and mathematical symbols.

Research in the three R's can contribute much, not only to communication but also in the teaching of the three R's. Without continuing research in the three R's, classroom practices are not likely to move forward as broadly and rapidly as is demanded. Parents, as well as teachers and children, should share in the knowledge of the results of research in the fundamental skills. Those who are registered as students, whether undergraduate or graduate, in preparation for a career in education, need assistance in locating, studying, and evaluating research in the three R's. Similarly, the staffs of local school systems also need to have easily available a collection of basic researches which have been selected with discrimination and which have vital bearing upon the daily activities of such local school staffs.

The authors of the present volume have taken upon themselves the considerable task of searching out and evaluating published research in the three R's. From thousands of investigations the authors have included those which appeared to be most significant and most promising of assistance to classroom teachers. In addition to a presentation of the title and summary of each research, the methods of study employed, bias of the study, and suggestions for possible classroom application are included. It seems probable in light of this challenging presentation that many classroom teachers will be stimulated to conduct research—pursue studies and find out for themselves.

The authors of this volume represent high competence in the three R's, since they are established practitioners as well as scholars in the language arts and social studies. The present work should prove extremely valuable to all concerned with the improvement of teaching, and therefore learning, the three R's.

JOHN GUY FOWLKES

February, 1958

RESEARCH IN THE THREE R'S

EXPLORATION SERIES IN EDUCATION

Under the Advisory Editorship of

JOHN GUY FOWLKES

Chapter I

WHY WE READ

For centuries the printed word has been the principal language reposi-
tory in which are recorded the ideas, feelings, and actions of peoples
present and past. Yet the printed word has never been the basic form
of language. The spoken word has always been preëminent in face-to-
face communication for people in whatever circumstance. Speech has
permitted stress, pitch, overtone, and immediate response to the lis-
tener, all of which are difficult and often impossible to capture in the
printed word. Furthermore, speech has always been more readily
learned than has facility with the printed word.

On the other hand, communication through the spoken word has
always been restricting until very recent years. The spoken word has
required proximity to the speaker in order to be within the range of
his voice. To be dependent upon spoken communication has meant for
the most part to have limited access to the ideas, feelings, and actions
of people.

Hence, those who could decode the printed word have enjoyed an
advantage in a wider world of communication. They have had ready
to the mind whatever has been said, by whomever, whenever it has
been recorded. To be a well-read man has always been a mark of distinction.

Gradually the ability to read has spread, more rapidly of course in
some cultures than in others. It is somewhat ironic, then, that as the
promise of widespread literacy appeared within realization in some
cultures competing channels of communication suddenly opened. The
radio and allied recording mechanisms have made the spoken word no
longer confined to the range of a speaker's voice. Television and the
motion picture have even made it possible to look at the speaker
though he speaks a thousand miles away. And electronic recording of
both the visual image of the speaker and his spoken word is already

promised in a form as economical and accessible as a phonograph record.

So the printed word can no longer be regarded as the prime conserver in language of the ideas, feelings, and actions of people. What is its place, then, in today's culture? This chapter on "Why We Read" invites consideration of that question.

WHAT DO PEOPLE READ? [1]

Henry C. Link and Harry Arthur Hopf

[As competition for people's time in today's culture continues to rise, many have speculated about the place of reading. Some speculation begins with a negative prejudice: people just don't read any more. Some speculation starts from a positive bias: people read more than they ever have. But what are the facts? This study attempted to find part of the answer.]

PURPOSES

This study was made under the auspices of the Book Manufacturers' Institute by the Psychological Corporation and the Hopf Institute of Management. The scope of the study is indicated by the following queries:

1. What are the present reading habits of the consumer? Who reads books: when, where, how many, what type?

2. What changes may there be in reading tastes in the future?

3. Are there any observable trends in present reading habits?

METHODS

THE QUESTIONNAIRE

Eight different versions of the questionnaire were listed. Each of the first seven tests was made in from one to three separate localities and comprised from twenty-five to sixty test interviews. The eighth revision was tested on a larger scale, with 300 personal interviews conducted in six cities and towns widely scattered throughout the country. The questionnaire was then submitted to a committee of the Book Manufacturers' Institute. With the help of the committee's suggestions, one more revision was made and tested.

THE SURVEY

The consumer survey of 4000 was made by a total of 235 interviewers, averaging seventeen interviews each. The interviews were made in 106 cities and towns representing a cross section of the

[1] Adapted and abridged from Henry C. Link and Harry Arthur Hopf, *People and Books*, Book Manufacturers' Institute, New York, 1946.

urban and rural nonfarm population. Follow-up interviews were made by persons not employed in the study to verify the original interviews.

THE SAMPLE

The following criteria were established as necessary to control adequately the sampling in this study:

1. Area.
2. City size (including urban versus rural nonfarm population).
3. Age.
4. Sex.
5. Socioeconomic status.
6. Day of week on which interview was conducted.
7. Place where respondents would be located, including interviews in the home and outside the home.

Area and City-Size Quotas. Quotas by areas were set up for the 4000 sample on the basis of the 1940 census, taking into account such subsequent population estimates as were provided by the Census Bureau. A comparison of the proportions used in the study with those of the 1940 census is shown in Table 1. Distribution of the sample by city size is shown in Table 2.

TABLE 1. Area Quotas

	Sample for Study		1940 Census (000 omitted)	
East	1335	33%	33,691	33%
Midwest	1220	31%	30,885	31%
South	925	23%	25,322	25%
Far West	520	13%	11,555	11%
Total	4000		101,453	
			(excluding rural farm population)	

Age and Sex Distribution. In considering the age range within which interviewing for the study would be feasible, it was decided that only persons fifteen years of age or over would be included. The distribution by age and sex is shown in Table 3 with the sample compared to the 1940 census.

It will be seen in this table that the distribution of women by age groups matches the 1940 census. However, more older men than younger men were interviewed in this study as compared to the proportion in the 1940 census. The proportions for the sample take into account the age distribution of men in the armed forces, who could not have been properly sampled and were, therefore, not included in this study.

Socioeconomic Status. In each city, areas were defined by rental value and

TABLE 2. Quotas by City Size

Sample for Study			1940 Census (000 omitted)	
500,000 and over	891	22%	22,368	22%
100,000-499,999	613	15%	15,620	15%
25,000- 99,999	588	15%	14,761	15%
2,500- 24,999	854	21%	21,675	21%
Under 2,500 (rural nonfarm)	1,054	27%	27,029	27%
	4,000		101,453	

type of home, prevailing occupations, and other characteristics denoting standard of living. On a socioeconomic basis, people of the upper 30 percent, of the

TABLE 3. Age and Sex Distribution

Sample for Study			1940 Census (000 omitted)	
Women				
15-19 years	267	12%	4,376	11%
20-29 years	544	24%	9,362	24%
30-39 years	468	20%	8,154	21%
40-49 years	400	17%	6,725	17%
50-59 years	289	13%	4,971	13%
60 and over	327	14%	5,477	14%
	2,295		39,065	
Men				
15-19 years	158	9%	4,397	12%
20-29 years	202	12%	8,573	23%
30-39 years	363	21%	7,879	21%
40-49 years	391	23%	6,816	18%
50-59 years	297	18%	5,118	13%
60 and over	294	17%	4,955	13%
	1,705		37,738	

middle 40 percent, and of the lower 30 percent were identified and interviewed.

Interviews by Days of the Week. In order to obtain a representative cross section, interviews were distributed evenly between weekdays and Saturdays and Sundays.

Interviews Away from Home. To confine interviewing to persons reached at home might bias the study by the selection of a slightly more sedentary or "stay-at-home" group than if people were approached at places of amusement, while traveling, or while actively engaged in sports, etc. The people found in their homes might represent a more active group of book readers than would be true of the population generally.

For these reasons, the interviewers were instructed to locate 30 percent of their respondents in or near places of amusement, downtown and neighborhood shopping areas, various types of retail establishments, and railway and bus terminal points. An analysis of the results indicated that this precaution might have been eliminated without serious bias.

BIASES IN THE STUDY

There are two important biases which affect the results of the study. One is the bias inherent in the prestige connected with the reading of books. People who read books are proud of the fact and glad to talk about it; people who do not read books are as a rule not proud of it and tend to resist a questionnaire such as the one we used. For this reason, the interviews tend toward the selection of people interested in books.

The second bias relates to education. In one neighborhood where a large proportion of the people had only grade-school education or less, interviewers found that more than half the persons approached would not coöperate in any way with a study which had anything to do with reading in any form. Therefore even though interviews were carefully assigned we tended to get completed interviews with the better educated.

FINDINGS

1. *Readership.* About 70 percent of all books are read by 21 percent of the population. About 94 percent of all books are read by 50 percent of the population.

2. *Borrowing and buying.* Of books read by the active readers, 57 percent are borrowed, 31 percent are bought, and 11 percent are received as gifts. In proportion to the amount of reading, the lower income groups purchased their books just about as often. The borrowed books came 51 percent from a family member or friend, 37 percent from a public library, 11 percent from a private rental library.

3. *Fiction and nonfiction.* About 58 percent of the books most recently read by the sample were fiction; 37 percent were nonfiction.

4. *Most read versus best-sellers.* The best-seller lists give no indication of the popularity of the books reported in terms of the total number of people who read them.

5. *Ownership of books.* Of the sample, 34 percent claim to have 100 or more books in the home; 22 percent could not or would not make an estimate; 41 percent say definitely that they have less than 100 books.

6. *What makes people read books?* Many factors induce people to read books, but the underlying influence among all these seems to be formal education. The higher the education the greater the frequency with which books are read.

There is also a relation between frequency of reading and income or socio-economic status. However, this relation is not so close as that between frequency of readership and years of formal education.

7. *Competitors with books for attention.* Our population spends practically twelve times as much time per day reading newspapers and magazines, listening to the radio, and going to the movies as it spends reading books. This gives a rough measure of the time people have available for the reading of books were they so disposed.

8. *Under what circumstances are books read?* Reading takes place most often in restful and relaxing circumstances.

9. *What kind of books are read?* When allowed to state more than one preference, 20 percent read miscellaneous novels, 19 percent read adventure, 19 percent read mysteries, 15 percent read biography, 13 percent read history, 10 percent read humor, 10 percent read religion, 9 percent read travel, 7 percent read romance.

10. *How do people select their books?* Thirty-one percent read their last book on the basis of recommendation, 26 percent because of interest in the subject, 20 percent because of convenience and accessibility, 14 percent because of advertising and reviews. As usually happens in studies of people's behavior, the influence of advertising is admitted by only a small number of the respondents. Because of the extent to which people rationalize their actions, it would be unwise to take the stated reasons too literally.

11. *What geographic area reads most?* Eastern and far western states have appreciably more active readers, proportionately, than the midwestern or southern states.

WHAT READING DOES TO PEOPLE [1]

Douglas Waples, Bernard Berelson, and Franklyn R. Bradshaw

[If it is granted that the role of reading in contemporary culture has changed, the question immediately arises: What is the new place of the printed word? Perhaps reading has unique capacities not possessed by other media. What may reading do which cannot be displaced? This study generates a number of hypotheses in response to this and other inquiries about the effects of reading in modern society.]

This discussion as a whole seeks to identify and to interrelate the more important of the factors or conditions presumed to determine the effects of any reading experience. Such factors may be grouped in broad classes for easier description.

A reading experience involves a person who reads a publication and who is affected by the reading in various ways and in varying degrees. How he is affected depends both upon the publication and upon what he brings to it. Hence it becomes important to distinguish the content of the publication itself from the reader's predispositions and from such other factors as may be responsible for any inferred or observed effects of the experience.

CONTENT OF PUBLICATION

The publication combines several distinguishable factors: the author's predispositions, the subjects discussed, the statements made (whether statements of fact or statements of preference), the simplicity or complexity of the idiom, the author's many psychological traits which give the work its individuality, the author's intent, and the "slanting." By slanting we mean the author's conscious and unconscious use of symbols which tend to sway the reader's sympathies and convictions in certain directions.

READER'S PREDISPOSITIONS

The reader's predispositions combine elements somewhat more difficult to identify because the predispositions may change. The predispositions that partially determine the effects of reading include the reader's sympathies with the various groups in which he is placed by his sex, age, income, education, occupation, and other—sympathies which combine to sway the reader toward or away from the direction in which the publi-

[1] Adapted and abridged from Douglas Waples, Bernard Berelson, and Franklyn R. Bradshaw, *What Reading Does to People*, University of Chicago Press, Chicago, 1940.

cation is slanted; the reader's motives for reading, or the satisfactions he expects the particular publication to furnish; his present beliefs, loyalties, opinions, prejudices, and other attitudes regarding the subjects read about, which may strengthen or weaken or completely reverse the flow of influence intended by the author; and the emotional and physical conditions in which the reading is done. Such conditions affect the quality of attention the publication receives and hence the number and character of the predispositions called into play.

The two major factors (the publication itself and the reader's predispositions) combine to produce reader responses and effects. The effects upon the individual reader extend through time, and the more remote effects are complicated by the publication's effects upon other readers, by what people are saying about it. They are also complicated, of course, by the effects of other communications (conversations, radio talks, newsreels, etc.). The range of time and space through which the social effects of a publication may be traced extends even to nonreaders: not merely to those who have not read the item in question—say, the *Federalist* papers or *Uncle Tom's Cabin*—but even to those who do not read at all. The initial effect upon a few readers may be so diffused by the currents of group interest and by the ground swells of public opinion at large that the effects of a single publication may carry far indeed.

The unrealistic character of present notions about the social effects of public communications may be due in large part to inadequate terms of description. The terms conventionally used, by popular writers and by students alike, are inadequate because they confine attention to but one or two of the many factors involved in the effect.

SOCIAL EFFECTS OF READING

Any "social effect" of reading may be attributed in part to several major factors, each of which needs to be duly considered—for example: (1) the social context (folkways and group conflicts and personal conditions), which explains the publication of some writings and the nonpublication of others; (2) the methods of distributing publications, which explain the variations between what different groups of people would prefer to read and what they do read; (3) the differences among the publications themselves, which explain why and how some are more influential than others; and (4) the different predispositions of readers, which explain why the same publication will incite one reader to revolutionary action, will be vigorously condemned by another, and will be ignored or read with apathy by a third. To these, for logical completeness, should be added a fifth, namely, the influence of other communications than reading, since the influences of radio, films, public speeches, or private conversation may either reinforce or offset the influences of reading as such.

Clarity in discussing the effects of reading demands attention to all the major factors responsible. Conclusions must not be drawn from any one factor —as when the most widely printed book, or the most accessible book, or the book with the most sensational contents, or the book which tells most of us what we most want to be told is assumed to have produced a certain social effect for any one of these reasons alone. It is entirely proper to discuss character of production, scope of distribution, slanting of the content, or predispositions of readers, provided that we are talking about factors. The impropriety consists in talking about one of several factors at work as though that one factor, if clearly established, were certain to produce a corresponding and equivalent effect. Our survey of the literature has shown not merely the layman and the popular writer but even experienced students in the field to be careless about this distinction. They discuss factors, partial factors, as though they were effects. Among the most serious offenders are those who study the reading of students. We have yet to find any comprehensive study of the effects of students' reading. But we have found many studies of isolated factors and of partial effects upon which far-reaching educational recommendations have been based.

Studies of group reading and its social effects may well be patterned after the more satisfactory studies of reading effects upon individuals. Since individuals are not studied to learn the effects of books they have not read, the case studies of individuals take due account, perforce, of the facts of relative accessibility, which the group studies so frequently ignore. The case studies also interrelate content, the reader's predispositions, and the observed responses. They bring all three to bear upon the description of effects and describe the effects over successive periods of time. The weakest element in the typical case study is its generally insufficient or naïve analysis of content, a defect easily remedied.

TYPES OF SOCIAL EFFECT

It is, of course, much harder to identify the several factors in the effects of reading upon groups. The student of group effects should therefore begin with groups so chosen that as many as possible of the factors may be safely inferred. The choice of groups, other things being equal, should be based primarily upon the type of effect which is assumed to predominate. The more easily distinguishable types of group effect might include the following: (1) the instrumental effect (e.g., fuller knowledge of a practical problem and greater competence to deal with it); (2) the prestige effect (e.g., relief of inferiority feeling by reading what increases self-approval); (3) the reinforcement effect (e.g., reinforcement of an attitude or conversion to another attitude toward controversial issues); (4) the aesthetic effect (e.g., obtaining aesthetic experience from specimens of literary art); and (5) the respite effect (e.g., finding relief from tensions by reading whatever offers pleasant distraction).

PUBLICATIONS SERVING SOCIAL EFFECTS

Typical effects of about this degree of generality offer a useful frame of reference for group studies because they suggest effects upon which the more important factors converge. It is plain that each of these five types represents a large amount of publication; for example, (1) instrumental effects are served by factual reports of all kinds; (2) prestige effects are served by sentimental fiction, as in women's magazines, with characters expressly drawn to encourage the readers to identify themselves with those they would like to resemble; (3) reinforcement effects are served by the entire range of special pleading which seeks to influence votes or purchases; (4) aesthetic effects are served by all genuinely artistic writing which helps the reader to view reality through the author's more observing eyes, by writing which is innocent of "designs" upon the reader; and (5) respite effects are served by all sorts of writing—comic strips, joke columns, human-interest stories, and other diverting items which come between the reader and his worries.

It is equally plain that the system of

distribution is well organized to supply each of these types of publication to some groups who demand them—for example, (1) textbooks to students; (2) women's magazines to housewives; (3) campaign literature to voters, journals of opinion to businessmen, and the equivalent in each occupation or special-interest group; (4) belles-lettres to the sophisticated reader; and (5) newspaper supplements to everybody.

Each of these types of publication is abundantly supplied to several groups who are known to read it constantly. Hence we can generally select one or more groups sufficiently homogeneous to exhibit certain common predispositions toward the given type of publication; e.g., (1) the students' desire to learn what textbook information will pass the course, (2) the housewives' loneliness and desire for prestige, (3) the businessmen's desire to find support for their political opinions, (4) the stimulation sought by the readers of any first-rate novel, or (5) the relaxation looked for by the readers of the *New Yorker*. In selecting housewives, for example, whose common predispositions would encourage their identification with the fiction characters of women's magazines, one would naturally seek housewives who are young, who have slender incomes, who have not attended high school, who belong to few organizations, and who for other reasons are likely to be lonely and to feel inferior. Such women are likely to seek and to obtain prestige effects from their reading.

ANALYSIS OF CONTENT OF PUBLICATIONS

A further step in describing the group effects of reading will be to identify the relevant content in each type of publication by making appropriate analyses.

The categories to be used in the analysis will naturally be determined by the effects anticipated and by the publications involved. Factual writing will require categories which distinguish differences in the veracity, organization, concreteness, etc., of the subject matter. Sentimental magazines will require categories distinguishing types of fiction characters by their social class, age, income, sophistication, deference to other characters, attitude toward authority, and the like. Controversial writing will invite attention to the symbols showing with which particular social or political interests the author sympathizes and to which he seeks to convert the reader. Belles-lettres will involve categories based on appropriate principles of aesthetic criticism. Merely diverting publications will require categories which differentiate the kinds and degrees of novelty they supply.

We should have then as our sources of evidence a group suspected of a common predisposition toward a definable literary stimulus which the agencies of distribution make easily available and which we know the group seeks with some consistency because it supplies a type of satisfaction this group wants more than most readers want it. The more important factors are thus accounted for in the situation available for study. We have then to examine the group's responses to the reading in relation to responses to other comparable experiences—e.g., other communications. While it is not possible to psychoanalyze the group, it is possible under such conditions to apportion responsibility for any assumed effects among the several factors involved. As the examples may suggest, reliable evidence concerning the several factors will serve to identify the stimuli supplied by the publications read by the group and to relate the stimuli to the personal and environmental conditions which give them meaning, which determine how much and in what directions the group is influenced by the reading experience. Analysis of such typical effects makes it easier to describe the social effects of any widely read publication when its modal readers have been identified. Such is the justification for intensive and synthetic study of the problem.

As the result of our labors, the conclusion that the social effects of reading cannot be fairly described without due attention to each of their major factors is by no means dramatic. It smacks of anticlimax. We wish the conclusion were instead a revolutionary idea, simple of statement and easy of application, from which we could confidently expect the prompt clarification of our present notions on what reading does to people. But the plain facts are that the problem has hitherto been greatly oversimplified. Hence the pedestrian qualities of our conclusion are forced upon it by the nature of the problem. If a simpler prescription could accomplish the desired results, it would doubtless have been produced long ago by the efforts of each generation's best minds to describe the social consequences of contemporary writing.

POTENTIAL VALUES OF READING

The problem of comparing and scaling the various potential values of reading is complicated by the difficulties of finding a fair perspective. One must somehow escape out of the closed circle of his own private assumptions and yet he must remain aloof from any other system of assumed values. Such difficulties are best met, perhaps, by suggesting the various aspects or uses of reading to which any system of values may be related.

One might begin, for example, by distinguishing the personalizing or individualizing effects of reading from the socializing or integrating effects. What we have called the prestige effects and the aesthetic effects would probably be classed with the former, though not exclusively; the instrumental, the reinforcement, and the respite effects might be classed with the latter or with both. To the personalizing effects of reading could thus be attached the values of self-expression. The evidence supplied by psychoanalysis and mental hygiene could be used to argue, if not to demonstrate, that the recognized psychological and neurological values of free self-expression to the individual in society are the values of any reading experience which facilitates self-expression. There is no doubt that some reading does facilitate self-expression by stating what the reader would like to say, and stating it more clearly and more effectively than he can state it himself.

On the other hand, one can argue as plausibly that the socializing effects of reading carry the values ascribed to a well-organized society as against a disorganized society. Reading can supply information and can develop attitudes which make for social tolerance, coöperative enterprise, and good government. Whether reading does carry such values to any section of the community at any given time would need to be determined.

Or again the values of reading might be classed as either instrumental or terminal, i.e., as either useful or good. If instrumental, one could proceed to specify the values in terms of the persons to whom the reading is useful. Are such persons important to society or are they unimportant, and why? Or the values might be stated in terms of the ends to which reading is the means. Such values as ends would be definable again merely by reference to normative systems. What reading is good for might be discussed in terms of the two main uses of language—the symbolic use, to convey meanings; and the rhetorical use, to stimulate emotions. But such further classifications do little to bridge the gap between evidence of an effect and the values ascribed to the effect.

GENERAL CATEGORIES OF READING VALUES

To conclude these remarks on reading values, we may attempt a rough classification of the alleged values on the basis of relevant evidence. Reading values may be helpfully classed in each of three related and progressively general categories. The categories are best visualized as three concentric circles. The innermost circle represents the reader's ability to understand and recall what he reads. Hence, the schools traditionally conceive reading values in terms of the students' abilities to remember and to criticize. The more the reader remembers, the more valuable the reading. Because of its simplicity, this notion dominates and distorts the layman's understanding of reading values. Yet this is the only assumption on which the values of the same publication to different readers can be easily and objectively compared.

The second circle represents the instrumental or "transfer" values of reading as inferred from the reader's behavior—as when by reading some books in Russian the reader has learned to read any book in Russian, or by reading about a strange city the visitor can find his way about, or by reading about children a teacher can manage them more successfully. Such "transfer values" or applications are more comprehensive than the mere ability to recall what was read, but they include other than reading factors which are hard to isolate.

The third circle represents the highly generalized or normative values of reading as they appear in traits of character associated with certain publications. Such values were widely assumed even before Francis Bacon's famous essay. Examples would include the belief that readers of philosophy or law or biology will acquire the intellectual traits of the philosopher, the lawyer, and the biologist. It is commonly assumed that such traits are more successfully acquired by reading than by other kinds of experience. For this assumption there is no supporting evidence.

The three circles of assumptions about the values of reading thus represent "values" of increasing importance. They also represent values which are increasingly hard to establish. The values of remembering what is read—and such "values" are lowly enough—can be established, of course, by making the reader recite. The transfer "values" also can be established by properly controlled experiments. But the more general "values" of reading remain to be empirically examined by procedures suggested by our approach to the description of social effects. Here the normative values must supply the content of the questions to be studied.

READING AS A FORM OF COMMUNICATION

In conclusion, our approach to reading effects deserves some relation to communication in general. We attach at least four meanings to the term "communication":

We use it to cover a single, definite message or communiqué—as delivered by a messenger, presented to an audience, printed in scientific proceedings or in a newspaper. This meaning is not important.

A second meaning derives from the verb and indicates the action of communication. Its most common use in this sense implies a one-way movement to the receiver—e.g., "the communication of sports news by radio," "communication of market reports." This usage is associated with the communication agencies.

A third use appears when two or more people are said to be "in communication." We understand at least a two-way movement, as when two rooms communicate. Each person may both give and receive ideas.

Closely related to the third usage is another which stresses the social process of communication in the sense of sharing or communizing certain attitudes and beliefs. "Developments in the arts of communication since the war have removed many social barriers." Social communication is thus used to mean popular diffusion of certain attitudes and beliefs over periods of time.

The first of the four meanings is useful because of its generality. There are few other words in English that cover all sorts of messages—whether by radio, film, print, lecture, exhibits, or other media. Its value in the present connection is merely one of convenience. The three other meanings are more important. They call attention, respectively, to three essential factors, namely, the social coverage of the various media, the individual's response to the communication, and the various conditions that determine the effects of communications upon communities.

The first two of the four aspects can be treated somewhat mechanically. The task of describing the existing varieties of communications, their relative frequency, and their relative distribution by the several agencies to different social groups is comparatively simple and straightforward.

The third aspect of communication is a two-way transmission of ideas. Sudden announcement of an interesting fact, like the election of a new pope, is largely, but not entirely, a one-way flow. Readers of the headline naming the pope are all prepared in various degrees to accept the fact when it is reported. The report accordingly is received objectively by nearly all readers, however subjectively they may later react to it. But a solid book or article commonly induces something like a state of solitary meditation. Similar mental processes might have been induced without the book—by free association, by the physical environment, by adjustment to some dominant emotion, or by the stimulation of some persistent problem. The process involved in thoughtful reading and in emotional response to belles-lettres has much in common with the associative processes involved in creative writing.

Reading differs from all other arts of communication, except the contemplation of works of art and other exhibits, in the freedom of self-expression it invites. Among popular media like the cinema, radio, lecture, and drama, reading alone proceeds at a rate of speed which the reader himself controls. He pauses whenever and as long as he likes to compare what he reads with his own experience. Unlike the other media, reading even permits him to turn back, to reread, to read again at other times and in other moods. The pace of radio, film, and lecture is consequently too slow for the satisfactory self-expression of many persons and too fast perhaps for many others. They can neither speed up, slow down, nor repeat. Yet it is to the character, intensity, and persistence of the resulting self-expression that we must look for the psychological effects of any communication.

One cannot therefore disregard the ratio of expression to impression in describing the social effects of reading.

Differences between readers and non-readers, between readers of serious and of trivial publications, and between readers of equally substantial works in different fields are generally best explained by differences in experience, personality, intelligence, and education. Such differences determine the reader's powers of self-expression and his desire to express himself in a certain direction on the subjects he reads about. Hence the third aspect of communication, that which regards the reader as "in communication" with a writer, invites primary attention to predispositions affecting the reader's self-expression.

The fourth aspect of communication, the communizing or diffusion of certain ideas within a community, likewise appears whenever reading serves to stimulate the expression of certain ideas already held by the community. Such ideas are developed largely by discussing direct experiences with one's intimate associates, partly by public communications, and hence partly by suggestions found in reading; but our evidence has never identified reading as the sole cause of a community's dispositions toward any issue, and it probably never will.

Reading clarifies, formulates, and hence helps to express the ideas born of the readers' common experience. The social effects of reading can be understood only in the social context which explains the community's hopes and fears.

In short, reading is a social process. It relates the reader to his environment, and it conditions that relationship. To some aspects of the environment the reader has a primary relationship; that is, he is in direct physical contact with them. To other aspects of the environment he holds a secondary relationship; he establishes contact only through symbols. Both sets of relationship make up his experience. Through reading the individual may extend his secondary relationships with the environment; and they may do as much to condition him, to make him what he is, as do his primary relationships. The extension of popular education, the improvements of communication methods, and the rapid increase in the scope of public communications are certain to increase the importance of such symbolic experience. In this context, reading is one channel among many through which the environment affects the individual, and the concern of research is to explain the process.

Chapter II

HOW WE READ

In a very real sense reading involves all the capacities of the reader. It involves his language capacities—his ability to use a system of symbols to communicate. It involves his physiological capacities—his ability to coördinate both the physiological receptors and the reactors to the visual stimuli provided by the printed words. It involves his psychological capacities—his ability to respond appropriately in thought and emotion to the summons of language. And it involves all of these in a nice balance always adjusting to the varying demands of the task.

In such a subtle process, the difficulties in pursuing research are considerable. Concepts about language have been drastically changed by the linguistic research of the last twenty-five years. These investigations have yet to be applied to any considerable extent to reading. Psychological research on perception in recent years has begun to indicate the intricate interplay set in action by even simple stimuli. Research in reading will one day profit from understandings and techniques of investigations only now being formulated in this field. It is in the more accessible physiological capacities that reading research has made the greatest progress.

Because the reading act is so complex there has always been a strong temptation to ignore some of the components. Yielding to temptation usually takes the form of selecting one element or another and treating it as so important that the other components are inconsequential. The studies in this section should make clear that any attempt to regard the process of reading as simple and straightforward is indeed mistaken.

DEVELOPMENTAL STAGES IN EYE MOVEMENTS [1]

Guy Thomas Buswell

[Eye movements have long intrigued those who studied the reading process. Just what do these overt actions indicate about the reading process? One of the pioneers who tried to reply to that query was Guy Thomas Buswell. He wondered whether the patterns of eye behavior changed with increasing maturity in reading. This study reports what Buswell found.]

PROBLEM

The first problem with which the present investigation is concerned is the determination of the stages of growth for three fundamental elements of eye movements in reading. These elements are, first, the span of recognition for printed material; second, the rate of recognition regardless of the size of the recognition unit; and third, the regularity or rhythmic progress of the perceptions along the printed lines. The basic data utilized in determining the growth curves were secured from the measurement of the three primary characteristics of eye movements, which are symptoms, respectively, of the fundamental elements just mentioned. These characteristics are, first, the average number of fixations per line; second, the average duration of fixations; and third, the average number of regressive movements per line.

SUBJECTS

In gathering data on this problem, photographic records were taken of the eye movements of 186 different subjects selected from all grades of the elementary school and high school and from an adult college group. (Only 179 subjects' records were used.) In selecting subjects below the high-school level for

Number of Subjects for Each Grade

Grade 1—21   Grade 4—15   Grade 7—8
Grade 2—18   Grade 5—16
Grade 3—15   Grade 6—19

High-school freshmen—11
High-school sophomores—12
High-school juniors—19
High-school seniors—12
College students—13

this part of the investigation exceptionally good and poor readers were eliminated, since the purpose was to find normal growth curves. For the most part the high-school and college group were

[1] Adapted and abridged from Guy Thomas Buswell, *Fundamental Reading Habits: A Study of Their Development*, Supplementary Educational Monographs, No. 21, University of Chicago Press, Chicago, 1922.

students of average scholarship, although in the high-school junior class some students were included who ranked superior.

SELECTIONS READ

With the exception of the first-grade pupils all subjects read the same selection. The purpose of using the same paragraphs throughout was to keep this element constant in order that the growth curves would not be affected by varying degrees of difficulty in the material. With a constant selection to be read, the degree of difficulty will vary according to the maturity of the subjects' reading habits. The first paragraphs used were easy enough to be read by pupils from the second grade up, but first-grade children found them too difficult; consequently two somewhat easier selections were used for them. The fact that the paragraphs used with the pupils in the first grade were somewhat easier would tend to reduce the steps in the growth curves between the first and second grades by just that amount.

GROWTH IN SILENT READING

DEVELOPMENT IN SPAN OF RECOGNITION

A measure of the span of recognition may be obtained from the average number of fixations per line in reading. As the number of fixations per line decreases, the width of the recognition span increases. The development of this element during the school period will be studied by ascertaining the decrease in the grade medians for the average number of fixations per line.

Figure 1 shows the growth curve for these grade medians. From this figure it is evident that there is a very rapid growth in span of recognition up to the end of the fourth grade; beyond this the rate of growth is less pronounced, with the exception of a notable increase during the sophomore and junior years in the high school.

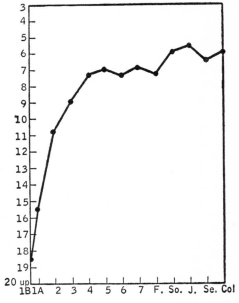

Fig. 1. Growth Stages for Average Number of Fixations Per Line in Silent Reading. School grade shown on horizontal axis; average number of fixations per 3.5 inch line shown on vertical axis.

The reader should note that the nature of the growth curve for this, as for other elements of reading, is biased by the type of training which the school has given. It cannot be assumed that the particular curves which appear are necessarily the most desirable forms of growth or even the natural forms. Different emphases upon the various elements at different levels of the school period might produce a considerable change in the rate of growth at those points. The growth curves shown represent the stages of development of the various elements of reading under the present school conditions.

A careful examination of the growth curve in Figure 1 will reveal three definite tendencies: first, a very rapid growth during the first four school years; second, a plateau extending through the fifth, sixth, seventh, and freshman years; and third, a second rise during the middle high-school years. It is clear from the figure that the chief development in span of recognition comes early in the school course. The child proceeds a long distance toward maturity in this element before he enters the fifth grade. While a small increase occurs during the fifth grade, it is only one-fourth as great as the increase during the preceding year. It is a significant fact that the fourth grade marks the turning point in this element. The radical change in the curve of growth at the end of the fourth grade demands an explanation, either in terms of the element itself or in terms of the school reading situation. It is clear that the limit of growth in span of recognition has not been reached in the fourth grade. The later rise in the curve shows that the high-school medians above the freshman year exceed the highest score up to the fourth-grade level. If mature habits of reading require a further growth in span of recognition, why does not the curve make a continuous rise up to the highest median?

A possible answer to this question is found in the nature of the school work during the fifth, sixth, seventh, and freshman years. Up to the end of the fourth grade, the principal emphasis of the school is placed upon the subject of reading. The reading which the child does is more or less of the same type and for the same purpose. Beginning in the fifth grade there is an increasing amount of time given to a variety of counter subjects. The character of the demand upon the child's reading habits

changes. A greater emphasis is placed upon a type of study quite different from the former reading, which, for the greater part, was concerned with materials easy of comprehension. As long as the reading is of the same general character, a regular increase in the elements of the process would be expected. When the purpose of reading is changed and different types of material are taken up, the attention of the pupil must be centered on these variations, while the old elements are in a measure neglected. For example, when a pupil is given a text in algebra or foreign language his previous habit of using a wide recognition unit with simple story material is entirely inadequate for the mastery of this new content. Meanings in algebra and foreign language are not as clear as meanings in descriptive geography or fiction. The change from the formal subjects of the elementary period to the varied content of the high-school course seriously interrupts the development of the span of recognition, the extent of the interference being disclosed by the plateau in Figure 1.

The rise in the curve during the sophomore and junior years suggests that the pupil has by that time become adjusted to the various types of new material and to the new study habits required for high-school work. The heavy reading requirements of literature and history stimulate the further development of a wide span of recognition. The drop in the senior year may be accidental or it may be the compensating result of some other type of adjustment. In any case, the median remains at a higher level than during the period of the plateau.

In the total complex process of reading the size of the average recognition span is a very significant element. The ultimate goal of reading is to secure meaning from the printed page in large thought units. The smallest possible unit of thought is the word, while the most common units are phrases. As long as a reader is unable to grasp these thought elements in a single recognition his mental processes are interrupted by the necessity of piecing together the material to make up meaningful elements. It is perfectly evident from an examination of Figure 2 that this first-grade reader is not dealing with thought units, since a large part of her effort is taken up with an analysis of the words.

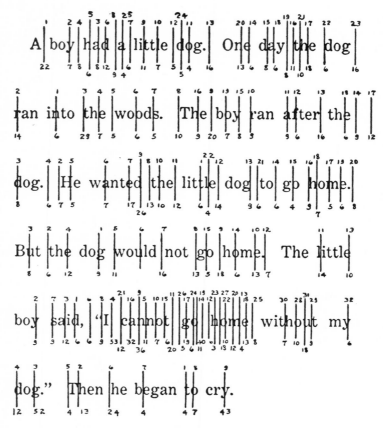

Fig. 2.   Silent Reading by Subject 17, Grade IA. In the figures showing records of eye movements the positions of the eye-fixations are indicated by the short vertical lines drawn across the lines of print. The serial numbers above the verticals indicate the order of the pauses; the number at the lower end of each vertical indicates, in twenty-fifths of a second, the duration of the fixation. A cross appearing instead of a number at the lower end of a vertical indicates that the duration of the fixation could not be determined with precision. An oblique line indicates a pronounced head movement, the exact location of the fixation being at some point between the ends of the oblique.

Until she reaches the stage of maturity where she can recognize the word or phrase as a whole and in an automatic manner, she will not be able to give her full attention to the meaning. The col- lege student in Figure 3 has a recogni- tion span which is wide enough to deal with whole thought units, making pos- sible a type of reading in which inter- pretation is the dominant element in

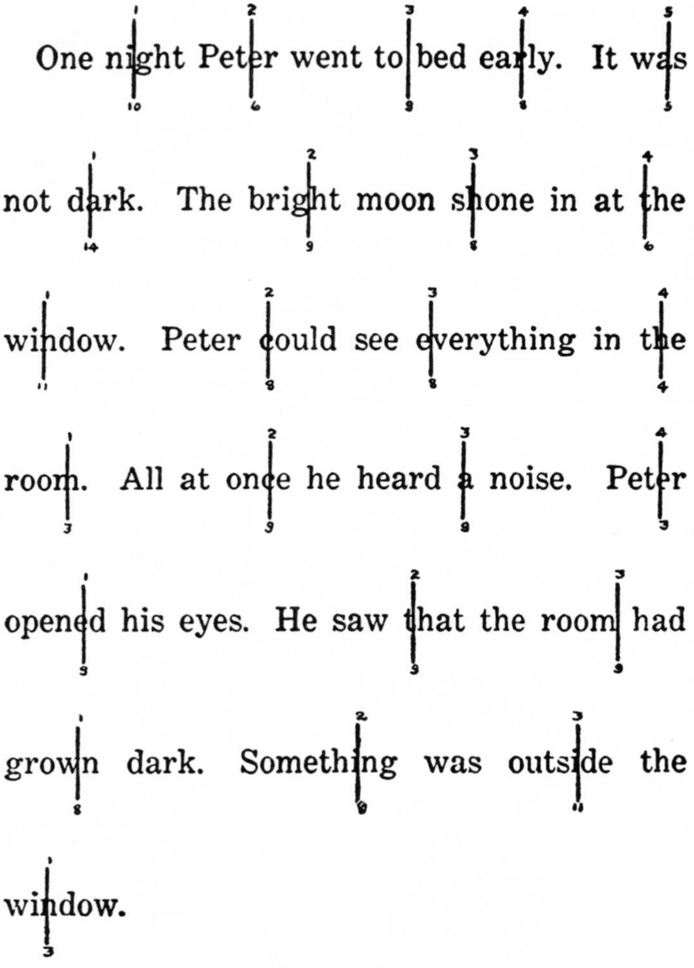

One night Peter went to bed early. It was

not dark. The bright moon shone in at the

window. Peter could see everything in the

room. All at once he heard a noise. Peter

opened his eyes. He saw that the room had

grown dark. Something was outside the

window.

Fig. 3. Silent Reading by Subject 174, College Senior.

consciousness with only a minimum of attention to the recognition process. The immature reader must piece together his small units of recognition with much the same difficulty which a pedestrian would experience in getting a general idea of the geography of a city by walk- ing up and down the streets between the skyscrapers, while the mature reader has so far mastered his recognition unit that his interpretation of reading could be compared to a bird's-eye view of the city from an airplane. The significance of a wide recognition span is that it relieves the mind of a detailed form of word analysis and makes possible the focusing of consciousness upon the process of interpretation.

GROWTH IN RATE OF RECOGNITION

It has just been shown that the width of the span of recognition increases as the reading habits become more mature. If the reader will turn again to Figures 2 and 3 he will see that the college student not only covered a larger unit of material at each pause but that the average duration of her fixations was considerably shorter than that of the first-grade pupil. The rate of recognition, regardless of the size of the recognition unit, becomes, therefore, an important factor in reading. Figure 4 presents the

grade medians for the duration of fixation pauses. The curve shows a rapid increase in rate of fixation up to the end of the fourth grade, with a continued but smaller increase on through the sixth grade. From that point no higher median is observed with the exception of that of the high-school juniors. The median for college adults is the same as that for the fifth grade.

These medians show that growth in speed of recognition proceeds in quite a different manner from growth in span of recognition. The fact is that fifty-two subjects were able to reach an average fixation time of 5/25 of a second, while only four subjects were able to make a shorter average, indicating that the limit of fixation time is about 5/25. Out of the 110 subjects in the grades above the fourth, only nine failed to raise their average fixation time to the level of 6/25 of a second. From these data it is evident that a speed of fixation of from 5/25 to 6/25 of a second satisfies the demands of maturity in reading. It is also evident that it is entirely possible to reach this level by the end of the fourth grade.

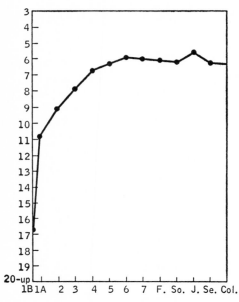

Fig. 4. Growth Stages for Average Duration of Fixation Pauses in Silent Reading. School grade shown on horizontal axis; average duration of fixation pause shown on vertical axis.

RHYTHMIC PROGRESSION ALONG
PRINTED LINES

The third element of reading for which a growth curve was determined is that of rhythmic progression along the printed lines. In the eye-movement record of a mature reader (see Fig. 3) it will be seen that the eye progressed across the lines with a rhythmic swing, making approximately the same number of fixations per line with few or no backward movements. In contrast with this the immature reader (see Fig. 2) moves forward a few fixations, then backward to refixate upon some word which was not clearly recognized, then forward and soon back again in the reverse direction.

Since regular, rhythmic progress along the lines of print is possible only through the development of habits of sure recognition, the number of regressive movements required in reading furnishes an index of another element in the recognition process.

The relationship between average number of regressive movements per line and school grade is exhibited by the data in the curve in Figure 5. The curve

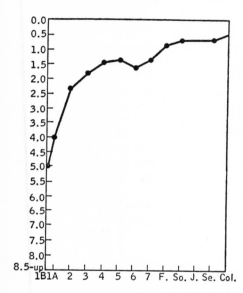

Fig. 5. Growth stages for Average Number of Regressive Movements Per Line in Silent Reading. School grade shown on horizontal axis; average number of regressive movements per line shown on vertical axis.

of growth makes a very rapid rise during the first four grades, a notable lack of progress during Grades 5, 6, and 7, and a second rise during the first two high-school years. In general form the curve is similar to that for span of recognition. The fact that all the medians for the grades beyond the seventh are distinctly higher than any medians below that

point indicates that the development of regular, rhythmic eye movements is one element of reading toward which high-school and college training directly contributes. It also shows that the possibility of increased efficiency at the upper levels of the school period is considerably greater for this habit than for that of duration of fixations.

COMPARISON OF GROWTH CURVES FOR THREE ELEMENTS OF SILENT READING

Data have now been presented relating to the three fundamental characteristics of eye-movement habits, namely, the average number of fixations per line, the average duration of the fixation pauses, and the average number of regressive movements. It has been shown that a decrease in the measure of each of these three characteristics accompanies progress through school grades. Other data obtained in this study (omitted in this abridgment) show that a decrease in the measure of each of these three characteristics also accompanies development of oral reading ability and increase in comprehension in silent reading. The significance of these facts can be seen more clearly if the curves of growth of the three different elements studied are plotted on the same graph, where their characteristics can be compared.

In order to reduce the curves for the three measures to a similar scale, the percentage of increase at the different grade levels was computed, the median for Grade 1B being taken as a base. The percentage of increase in the successive grades is shown in graphic form in Figure 6.

The presentation of the three curves upon the same background serves to emphasize the fact that the period of major development of the elements of span of recognition, speed of recognition, and regularity of eye movements across the line comes during the first four grades. A continued rise in the

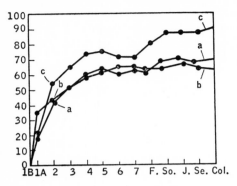

Fig. 6. Percent of Increase in Growth for Three Eye-Movement Habits—Silent Reading. School grade shown on horizontal axis; percent of increase shown on vertical axis. Curve **a** represents average number of fixations per line; curve **b** average duration of fixation pauses; curve **c** average number of regressive movements per line.

growth curves is apparent in the fifth grade, but it is relatively small in amount. The turning point in the direction of the curves appears at the end of the fourth grade. The indications are that the character of the reading process is different during the first four years and in the later period. Certainly in the fifth, sixth, and seventh grades the type of development is entirely different from that in the first four years. Evidently these stages of development are sufficiently clear to suggest a definite variation in the treatment of the school.

The later rise in the curves for regressive movements and average number of fixations per line suggests that the high school is concerned with a reading problem quite definite in character. It would be an interesting experiment to determine whether a modification of the reading course in the intermediate grades would eliminate the plateau in these two curves. If this could be accomplished one would expect a considerable improvement in the character of reading during this period.

THE EFFECTS OF CHANGES IN PURPOSE AND DIFFICULTY ON EYE MOVEMENTS [1]

Charles Hubbard Judd and Guy Thomas Buswell

[Suppose the purpose of a reader changes. Or suppose that one selection is more difficult than another. Are these changes reflected in changes in eye movements? In this study Buswell was joined by another early student of the reading process, Charles Hubbard Judd.]

This monograph is a study of some of the more complex forms of reading. In the main, the types of reading dealt with are those which are usually carried on silently. It will, perhaps, make the later discussions easier to follow if the general psychological principles which issue from this study are briefly illustrated. To this end, we may describe some of the typical results from the studies to be reported in the later pages of this monograph.

It is found that a pupil makes eye movements which are different when he is asked, on the one hand, to read a passage with special attention to certain grammatical questions which he is to answer and when he is asked, on the other hand, to repeat the passage word for word at the conclusion of the reading. The characteristically different eye movements which appear in these two cases make it certain that the demand for grammatical analysis and the demand for reproduction word for word cannot be fully met by the pupil through one and the same kind of attention. While

he is attending to grammar, he is in one frame of mind, and he makes one kind of attack on the printed page. While he is reading for the purpose of reproducing verbatim, he is in a different attitude.

A printed page turns out to be, as shown by this study, a source of a mass of impressions which the active mind begins to organize and arrange with reference to some pattern it is trained to work out. If the mind is fitting together the impressions so as to bring into high relief grammatical distinctions, the grouping of words and the distribution of emphasis will be according to one pattern. If the mind is intent on something wholly different from grammar, as, for example, the experiences which the author is trying to picture, the whole mental and physical attitude of the reader will be very different.

ADJUSTMENTS IN READING TO CHANGES IN THE CONTENT OF PASSAGES

One of the statements very commonly

[1] Adapted and abridged from Charles Hubbard Judd and Guy Thomas Buswell, *Silent Reading: A Study of the Various* *Types*, Supplementary Educational Monographs, No. 23, University of Chicago Press, Chicago, 1922.

made about passages which are assigned to be read is that they are easy or difficult. Such a statement may refer to a variety of characteristics. One type of difficult passage is made up of long words or unfamiliar words; the seat of the difficulty in such cases is the vocabulary. In other cases it may be the sentence structure which is complex or drawn out to such an extent that it taxes the reader's attention. Again, the logic of a discussion may be difficult to follow; the reader will in such a case, perhaps, know all of the words and be able to follow the sentence structure but will have difficulty with the thought.

As a first step in the analysis of the mental processes which are involved in reading difficult passages, photographs were taken of the eye movements of ten pupils in the fifth grade while they were reading Paragraphs 4, 6, 8, 10, and 12 from Gray's Standardized Reading Paragraphs. This gave fifty records for comparative study. The paragraphs are carefully standardized to measure oral reading and are known in their own field to be of equal steps of increasing difficulty. Difficulty is not here analyzed into its elements. As a matter of fact, there are changes in vocabulary, in

length of sentences, and in complexity of logic. It should be noted that the paragraphs are not standardized for the type of reading for which they were used in this experiment, namely, silent reading.

The purpose of this first inquiry was to find out what a pupil does when he is confronted with a series of passages which can be described in general terms as increasingly difficult. Before the general table of results is presented, it will be well to discuss in detail the records of several individuals and their methods of dealing with the type of increasing difficulty found in these paragraphs.

Table 1 shows the facts for Subject D. S. It will be noted that there are two ways in which this subject meets difficulties. Either he makes more fixations per line or he increases the average length of his fixation pauses. If we compare Paragraph 6 with Paragraph 4, we see that the chief change is the number of fixations. If we compare Paragraph 8 with Paragraph 6, we see that the major adjustment is in the length of the fixation pauses.

The psychological process which is going on when the number of fixation pauses increases is clearly shown in the

TABLE 1.   Record of Subject D. S. in Silent Reading of Paragraphs of Increasing Difficulty from Gray's Standardized Reading Paragraphs [a]

Paragraph	Average Number of Fixations per Line	Average Number of Fixation Pauses [b]	Number of Words Read	Average Number of Words Read per Fixation	Total Time for Five Lines [b]
4	5.2	5.4	45	1.73	136
6	6.2	5.5	49	1.58	164
8	5.8	6.4	42	1.44	186
10	5.6	6.0	34	1.21	168
12	6.8	7.4	32	0.97	225

[a] In all of the calculations of averages from eye-movement records, the first line and the last are omitted, because it has been shown in earlier investigations that these lines are of special character. The figures presented in the tables are, therefore, from the second line to the next to the last, inclusive.

[b] The time unit used in all of the tables is 1/25 of a second.

column in Table 1 which records the average number of words read per fixation. The amount of material which is recognized in a single fixation becomes smaller with increasing difficulty. The pupil has to take in such a word as "philosophers" or "statisticians" in two or more fixations, while the words "it is better" which appear in an easy passage, are taken in at a single glance.

The facts here described have led to the use of the term "span of recognition" in describing the reader's mental achievement in taking in reading matter during a single fixation.

Evidently the immature reader will have a narrow span of recognition. Correspondingly, when the content of a passage becomes increasingly difficult for a mature reader, he is thrown back by the increasing difficulty into the class of immature readers with reference to that particular passage. Each step in his mental endeavor then covers less ground, because for each impression received he must carry on a more elaborate and laborious process of interpretation.

There is, however, a second expedient which the reader can adopt in the presence of a difficulty. He may take in a considerable body of impressions and spend more time in trying to master

that which confronts the eye. If one can have more time to collect experiences which will interpret a phrase, one may be saved the necessity of cutting down the amount which one is trying to take in. This is what Subject D. S. does in the case of Paragraph 8.

Incidentally, the table shows something with regard to the structure of Gray's test. Paragraphs 4, 6, and 8 are made up of words of about the same length. The "hard" paragraphs, 10 and 12, contain long words. These are what make the passages especially hard to read orally. Evidently Subject D. S. did not find Paragraph 10 as difficult in some respects as Paragraph 8. When we consider the number of words read per fixation, however, we see that even in this case there was a contraction of the individual recognitions. This must mean that the contraction of the span of recognition was common to all of the paragraphs as compared with the first, while the longer fixation pauses in such cases as Paragraph 10, when compared with Paragraph 6, mean more complicated efforts at interpretation.

Another type of adjustment to difficulty appears when we study the detailed record of Subject M. B. This record is given in Table 2. Subject M. B.

TABLE 2.   Record of Subject M. B. in Silent Reading of Paragraphs of Increasing Difficulty Selected from Gray's Standardized Reading Paragraphs

Paragraph	Average Number of Fixations per line	Average Duration of Fixation Pauses	Average Number of Words Read per Fixation	Total Time for Five Lines
4	7.0	5.1	1.29	178
6	8.2	5.5	1.19	225
8	11.2	5.5	0.75	308
10	6.2	6.5	1.09	201
12	11.0	6.9	0.58	379

shows a sudden change in her methods of meeting difficulty. Through the first

three paragraphs she increases the number of fixations per line. In Paragraph 10 she adopts the method of lengthening the fixation pause.

It is not easy to explain this series of records. Paragraph 8 has fewer words than Paragraph 6, as shown in Table 1. We cannot, therefore, attribute the in-

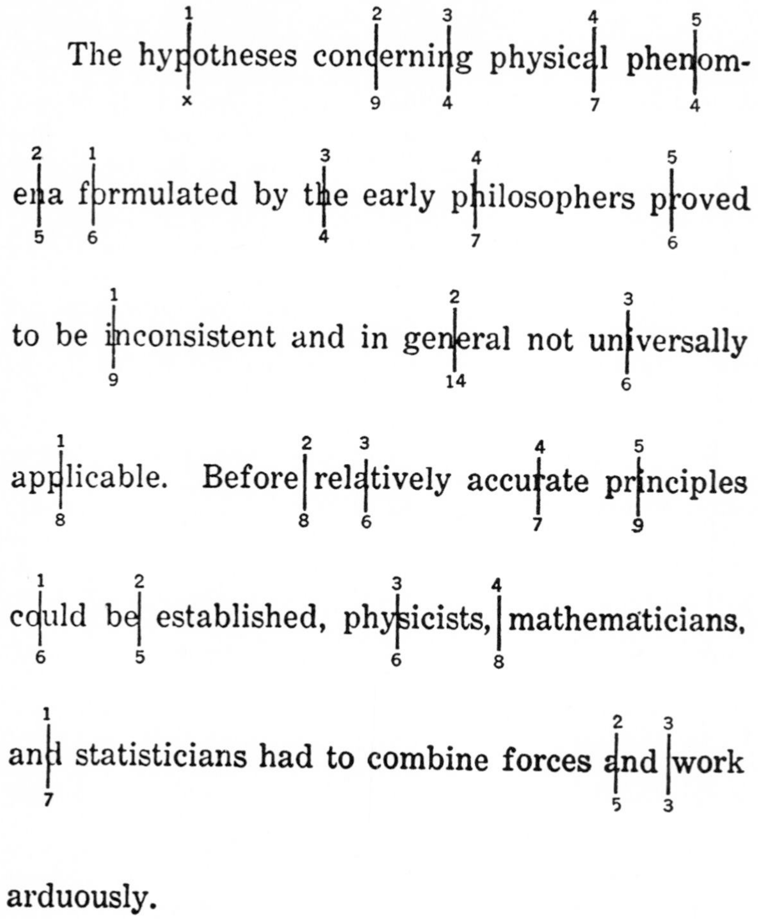

The hypotheses concerning physical phenom-

ena formulated by the early philosophers proved

to be inconsistent and in general not universally

applicable. Before relatively accurate principles

could be established, physicists, mathematicians,

and statisticians had to combine forces and work

arduously.

Fig. I. Silent-Reading Record of Subject C.W. Numerous omissions of difficult words. Each vertical line shows the position of a fixation. The numbers at the upper ends of the lines show the serial order of the fixations. The numbers at the lower ends of the lines show the length of the fixations in twenty-fifths of a second. An X at the lower end of a line indicates that the record was illegible. A crooked or oblique line means a movement during the period of fixation.

crease in number of fixations to concentration on single words. We must look for an explanation in the varying contributions which individual experiences bring to the interpretation of passages. Very striking evidence of this appears in the fact that the subjects reported in Tables 1 and 2 proceeded by wholly different modes of adjustment. If special attention is given to the last columns in the two tables, the suggestion naturally comes to mind that the differences in method of adjustment arise from the fact that Subject M. B. is a

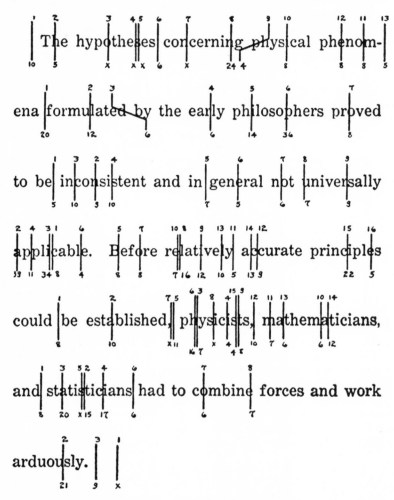

Fig 2. Oral-Reading Record of Subject C.W. Record subsequent to that shown in Fig. I.

slow reader. This fact, in turn, is illuminated by a comparison of the two columns showing the average number of fixations per line. The major reason why Subject M. B. is slow is that she makes many fixation pauses. Her adjustments to difficulty follow the line of her general habit until the number of fixations becomes excessive, as in Paragraph 8, whereupon a radically different method appears in the next paragraph.

A third interesting case is exhibited

in Figures 1 and 2. Subject C. W., who seemed on the face of the results to break all of the rules, read Paragraph 12 as shown in Figure 1. It was so evident from this record that this subject was omitting, in his silent reading, all of the words which were inconvenient that he was asked to read the same paragraph out loud, with the result shown in Figure 2.

These figures can hardly be said to show a method of meeting difficulties, but they exhibit the method of poor reading which many pupils doubtless adopt in dealing with such reading matter as they encounter in some of their lessons.

A fourth case in this series presents another type of adjustment which is worth noting. The facts are shown in Table 3. The striking feature of this table is the contrast of method shown in the different paragraphs.

Enough has been given of the details

TABLE 3. Record of Subject M. H. on Silent Reading of Paragraphs of Increasing Difficulty Selected from Gray's Standardized Reading Paragraphs

Paragraph	Average Number of Fixations per Line	Average Duration of Fixation Pauses
4	6.0	5.8
6	4.2	7.4
8	6.3	6.7
10	7.4	6.8
12	8.2	7.9

in this part of the investigation to prove, first, that an increase in the difficulty of passages results in a change in the reader's attitude toward the task which he is undertaking. There are various ways of meeting the complex situations that arise. The assumption that any single formula of simple association between words and their meanings can be made the basis of teaching is immediately discredited by an examination of such details as have been presented in these records. It is also evident, in the second place, that complex reading processes can be understood only when individual pupils are studied. General tables of median practices are suggestive, perhaps, as showing general tendencies, but they do not reveal the essential facts, because these facts are different for different individuals.

In Table 4 are presented the medians

TABLE 4. Medians of the Records of Ten Fifth-Grade Pupils. Silent Reading of Paragraphs of Increasing Difficulty Selected from Gray's Standardized Reading Paragraphs

Paragraph	Average Number of Fixations per Line	Average Duration of Fixation Pauses	Average Number of Words Read per Fixation
4	6.0	5.9	1.50
6	7.0	6.1	1.40
8	7.2	6.2	1.16
10	6.4	6.2	1.06
12	7.8	6.9	0.82

for ten pupils, including the four to the discussion of whose records the foregoing paragraphs have been devoted. This table serves to emphasize the general fact that increased difficulty of passages means new combinations of scope and duration of attention, but the series of figures presented should be interpreted also in the light of the individual variations set forth in the foregoing tables. The medians cover up the manifold variations in fact appearing in the changes, which, as we have seen, emphasize now one, now the other, mode of adjustment.

The qualifying statements made regarding Table 4 should be kept in mind throughout this monograph as ample justification for constant insistence on individual analysis. There can be little doubt that all of the more complex processes are highly individuated. They are, as was pointed out, complex patterns, not uniform mechanical structures. As complex patterns, they are more dependent on subjective factors, such as acquired tendencies with regard to frequent pauses in reading, than on any external impressions.

THE INDIVIDUALITY OF EYE MOVEMENTS [1]

William C. Morse

[For many years the early studies of Buswell and others concerning eye movement went unchallenged. Recently, however, some investigations have yielded results somewhat at variance with the previous research. Just how individual are eye movements?]

CONDITIONS OF THE STUDY

The present study has involved a comparison of the eye movements of fifty-four fifth-grade and fifty-four seventh-grade pupils reading materials of equal or corresponding difficulty. So far as possible, these subjects were selected so as to be in the proper grade with respect to chronological age, mental age, and reading age. They were so-called average

children, separated by two years in developmental level. The average reading achievement of the two groups was exactly two grades apart. The groups were matched for sex, intelligence, and school background.

Fifth- and seventh-grade subjects were used in an effort to get beyond the point where maturational changes alone might differentiate the groups. This control was necessary in order to test the hy-

[1] Adapted and abridged from William C. Morse, "A Comparison of the Eye-Movements of Average Fifth- and Seventh-Grade Pupils Reading Materials of Corresponding Difficulty," in *Studies in the Psychology of Reading,* University of Michigan Press, Ann Arbor, 1951.

pothesis that equal difficulty means equal eye movements. According to Buswell's results, maturational factors cease to be important by the fourth grade. Average fifth- and seventh-grade pupils may be said to be safely beyond this point.

Four pairs of passages were used in the experiment. The passages were selected for difficulty by the Lorge [2] and Yoakam [3] formulas for estimating the difficulty of material. One passage of each pair was used as a practice selection, the other as the test selection. One pair was standardized at the third-grade level, one at the fifth-grade, one at the

TABLE 1.   Summary of Data on Fifth- and Seventh-Grade Subjects

Measures	Grade 5 (54 Cases)			Grade 7 (54 Cases)		
	Mean	Range	SD	Mean	Range	SD
Chronological age in months	130.28	116–146	5.43	154.61	141–173	7.74
Mental age in months [a]	130.50	112–150	7.50	157.48	141–183	10.02
Intelligence quotient	100.13	88–111	5.54	101.65	91–115	5.41
Reading grade [b]	5.6	4.5– 6.5	.516	7.61	6.8– 8.3	.47

[a] California Test of Mental Maturity, Southern School Book Depository, Los Angeles, California, 1940.
[b] Stanford Reading Achievement Test, World Book Co., Yonkers, N.Y., 1940.

seventh-grade, and one at the ninth-grade. The third-grade passages were intended to represent the same difficulty for the fifth-grade pupils as the fifth-grade passages represented for the seventh-grade pupils; the fifth-grade passages the same difficulty for the fifth-grade pupils as the seventh-grade passages for the seventh-grade pupils; and the seventh-grade passages the same difficulty for the fifth-grade pupils as the ninth-grade passages for the seventh-grade pupils.

All passages were 300 words in length. Length of line and style and size of type were constant. Eye movements were photographed on the middle 100 words in order to obtain a representative sample of each child's reading. The Ophthalm-O-Graph was used to record eye movements. The fifth-grade pupils read the third-, fifth-, and seventh-grade pas-

sages; the seventh-grade pupils read the fifth-, seventh-, and ninth-grade passages. Three passages were used with each child in order to permit as many comparisons as possible as well as a measurement of change in eye movements with difficulty. Each test selection was preceded by a reading of the practice selection. The test and practice selections were administered under the same conditions except that no photograph was made in the case of the practice selection. An objective test of fifteen items always followed each practice and test selection. The questions were uniformly based on the total of 300 words.

[2] Irving Lorge, "Predicting Reading Difficulty of Selections for Children," *Elementary English Review* (1939), 16: 229–233.
[3] G. A. Yoakam, "A Technique for Determining the Difficulty of Reading Material," University of Pittsburgh, Pittsburgh, November, 1938 (mimeographed), pp. 5 ff.

VARIATION OF EYE-MOVEMENT MEASURES WITH DIFFICULTY OF MATERIAL

COMPARISON OF THE EYE-MOVEMENT RESULTS OF THE FIFTH-GRADE GROUP FROM PASSAGE TO PASSAGE

The results for the fifth-grade children on the three passages read by this group show no consistent variation with difficulty. It might be expected that the most difficult material would be read with more frequent fixations and regressions and a slower rate than the less difficult material. Actually, passage VII was read with more efficiency than either passages III or V, in so far as the eye-movement measures were concerned. With the exception of faulty return sweeps, passage III was read with greater efficiency than passage V, which is in accordance with the expectation. However, only two of the eye-movement differences in the whole table were statistically significant. These were for regression frequency and rate of reading between the results for passages V and VII, and both differences favor passage VII. The differences between the average eye-movement scores in general are not large. Expressed in words per minute, which is a composite measure of eye movements, the rate changed from 96 words per minute on passage III to 94 words per minute on passage V to 103 words per minute on passage VII. These are not large changes and they are certainly smaller than were the differences between the two grades for this measure. The surprising thing is how nearly alike the eye-movement results were from passage to passage. Children of this grade apparently tend to read materials of different difficulty in pretty much the same way. At any rate, the eye-movement results do not vary in a consistent fashion with difficulty. In the comparison of both passages III and V

with VII, the results favored the more difficult passage, whereas in the comparison of passages III and V themselves, the results favored the easier passage of the two. Such irregularities, taken together with the smallness of most of the differences, suggest that there is no real relationship with difficulty and that the differences which do exist are in the nature of chance and even when statistically significant must be attributed to some unknown outside factor.

The results for the comprehension check test favor the passage which tended to be read with the least efficient eye movements. In two comparisons, the differences on the comprehension check test are significant. Both of these comparisons involve passage VII. The point has previously been made that the comprehension check test for this passage may be relatively more difficult than the check test for passages III and V, since it was on the test for this passage that the seventh-grade children also made their lowest average comprehension score. Even so, the generalization still seems to hold that, when the eye-movement efficiency favors one passage of a pair, the comprehension check test results favor the other member of a pair. Children at this stage of development apparently do not adapt their eye-movement behavior to the difficulty of the material. The eye movements were just as efficient on passage VII as on passage III. If anything, comprehension is what is reduced on the more difficult passage.

COMPARISON OF THE EYE-MOVEMENT RESULTS OF THE SEVENTH-GRADE GROUP FROM PASSAGE TO PASSAGE

In the corresponding results for the seventh-grade children, again no consistent variation of the eye-movement results with the difficulty of the material exists. Passage V, which was the easiest of the three, was not read any more efficiently than either passage VII or passage IX. If anything, it was read less efficiently than the other two. Only two of the differences involving the eye-movement measures were significant. These were for regression frequency between passages V and VII and between passages VII and IX. One of these differences favors the more difficult passage of the pair, while the other difference favors the easier passage of the combination. There was another difference that approached statistical significance. This was for fixation frequency between passages V and VII, and the difference favors the more difficult passage. In other words, there is no consistent variation of the eye-movement scores with difficulty, either for a single measure from passage to passage or even for the different measures within a comparison. Thus, in the comparison of passage V with IX, the results for fixation frequency favor passage IX but for regression frequency passage V. Seventh-grade children are no more skillful than fifth-grade children in adapting their eye-movement behavior to changes in difficulty. To resort again to a composite measure of eye movements, the average reading rates for the seventh-grade group, expressed in words per minute, were 115, 124, and 123, respectively, for passages V, VII, and IX. None of the differences between the possible combinations of these figures is statistically significant.

For the seventh-grade group, the comprehension check test yielded significant differences in every comparison of two passages. Rather interestingly, a similar condition exists between the two grades with regard to the way average comprehension and the eye-movement measures are related; that is, while the comprehension favors one passage of a pair, most of the eye-movement data favor the other passage of that pair. The same interpretation may be given to this condition as was given before, namely, comprehension may vary but the ocular-motor patterns do not adapt readily to changes in difficulty. There is a developmental difference between the fifth- and seventh-grade readers which was apparent in all of the comparisons previously made between the two groups. In every comparison, even that in which the fifth-grade children read passage III and the seventh-grade children passage IX, the seventh-grade group performed more efficiently. The reason now seems clear: there is a certain stability of performance within each grade regardless of the difficulty of the material read. The difference in the level of this performance shows up in all of the intergroup comparisons.

CORRELATIONS BETWEEN EYE-MOVEMENT MEASURES FROM PASSAGE TO PASSAGE

While the average eye-movement results in each grade remain pretty much the same from passage to passage, there is still the question as to whether the performance of the individuals within each grade manifests a similar consistency. In order to answer this question, correlations have been computed between the eye-movement measures for every combination of two passages in each grade.

CORRELATIONS BETWEEN THE EYE-MOVEMENT MEASURES FOR THE FIFTH-GRADE GROUP

Taking first the results for Grade 5, it may be said that the correlations are in general substantially high. The correlations between the results for passages

III and V tend to run slightly higher than the correlations between the results for either other pair. The lowest correlations for this grade were obtained between the results for passages III and VII. It is doubtful whether any particular significance can be attached to the differences in magnitude between the correlations for various pairs inasmuch as the results for Grade 7 do not follow the same pattern. What can be said is that there is a distinct tendency for the individual to retain the same position within the group from passage to passage. This statement holds for every combination of two passages and all eye-movement measures. This generalization, taken together with the average group results, which show relatively little change from passage to passage for any of the eye-movement measures, implies that there was a general tendency for the individual to read all three passages in somewhat the same fashion. In some cases this tendency results in a highly similar pattern of eye movements from passage to passage.

CORRELATIONS BETWEEN THE EYE-MOVE-MENT MEASURES FOR THE SEVENTH-GRADE GROUP

Table 2 shows that the correlations for Grade 7 were in general even higher than the ones for Grade 5. These cor-

TABLE 2. Correlations Between Eye-Movement Measures for Every Combination of Two Passages in Each Grade [a]

Measure	Correlations for Fifth-Grade Readers			Correlations for Seventh-Grade Readers		
	3–5	5–7	3–7	5–7	7–9	5–9
Fixations per em	.74±.04	.66±.05	.52±.06	.84±.03	.85±.03	.85±.03
Regressions per em	.69±.05	.77±.05	.57±.06	.79±.03	.87±.02	.79±.03
Rates in ems per minute	.80±.03	.67±.05	.65±.05	.70±.05	.80±.03	.86±.02
Faulty return sweeps per line	.57±.06	.60±.06	.38±.08	.74±.04	.74±.04	.77±.04

[a] The figures are the product-moment correlations with their probable errors.

relations for Grade 7 are remarkably high correlations and indicate a strong tendency for the individual to retain the same rank in his group regardless of the passages compared.[4] Inasmuch as there was not in general a significant variation in the group performance from passage to passage, the inevitable conclusion again is that of a consistency of individual performance from passage to passage. Some children of course were more consistent in their performance than others.

[4] These correlations also speak well for the reliability of the measures.

INDIVIDUAL DIFFERENCES IN EYE-MOVEMENT PERFORM-ANCE WITHIN EACH GROUP

One question remains: How do the children within each group vary among themselves in their eye movements? This question introduces us to the problems of the individual differences which exist within each group when the children read the same passage. How do these differences compare with the group and individual variation from passage to passage?

Detailed results will be presented only for rate of reading. Since rate is a composite measure of eye movements it follows that essentially the same picture holds for the individual records which can be plotted from the total record.

Vast individual differences are apparent in each grade on each paragraph. In both grades the intrapassage individual variation is overwhelmingly greater than the interpassage group variation. For example, in the fifth grade Case 55 read eight lines in considerably less time than was required by Case 20 to read five lines.

Similarly, in seventh grade, Case 45 read eight lines in less than half the time required by Case 38 to read four lines. The first child read more than four times as rapidly as the second child here compared. No such variation occurred for the same group or child from passage to passage. The greatest difference which occurred in rate on the part of an individual fifth-grade child is Case 36, where, as he read passages III, V, and VII, the rate in ems per minute changed from 216 to 231 to 507, the greatest variation being more than double the two slowest rates. The most stable rate performance was made by Case 2, who read the same three passages at rates of 265, 270, and 270 ems per minute. For the seventh grade, the most variable rate performance was made by Case 7, who read passages V, VII, and IX at rates of 607, 616, and 838 ems per minute, respectively. The most stable performance was given by Case 24, who read the same three passages at rates of 476, 459, and 467 ems per minute. Evidence that pronounced variation in rate from passage to passage by a particular child is not typical is available by relating the stable group rates from passage to passage and the relatively high interpassage correlations previously presented.

Wide individual differences were found for fixation and regression frequency just as for rate of reading. For example, one fifth-grade child on the fifth-grade passage made 9.55 fixations per line while another fifth-grade youngster on the same passage made 29.21 fixations per line. Similarly, one fifth-grade child made .745 regressions per line on passage V while another fifth-grade subject on the same passage made 10.4 regressions. In other words there were children in this group who made as many regressions per line as other children made fixations per line.

SUMMARY

To answer now the question with which we started this section, extraordinary intrapassage individual variations seem particularly significant when one takes into account the sifting process that was used to select the subjects. The intrapassage individual variation is overwhelmingly greater than the interpassage group variation. These individual factors doubtless account for the relatively high constancy of both the group and individual performances from passage to passage.

READING AND CHILD GROWTH AND DEVELOPMENT [1]

Willard C. Olson

[Is reading primarily determined by eye movements? Or is reading principally a matter of intelligence? Or is reading dictated for the most part by the kind of reading program undertaken? Willard Olson thought that one way to seek answers to these questions would be to conduct long-term studies of children. He decided to follow the same children over a period of years measuring various facets of their growth and development. His conclusions about what factors affect reading are provocative.]

While regularly significant correlations can be obtained between mental-test data and the differential ability of children to read, the relationships are far from perfect, and many puzzling cases are always encountered where neither the status of intellectual functions nor the regimen that the child has undergone in reading seems adequately to explain certain failures to make expected progress. Recent studies of child development reveal reading achievement as an aspect of the total growth of children.

The tendency so to view reading is a result of two emphases in current research in child development. The first of these is the attempt to describe how children change through time and to be less concerned with the status of the moment. Thus the *direction* in which reading is proceeding as an aspect of growth becomes of equally great interest with the *level* of its individuation out of the total growth of the child. A second characteristic of current growth studies is an attempt to see the child as a whole and to determine the laws that govern the individuation of partial aspects of growth out of the total matrix of common protoplasm which characterized his beginning.

In attempting to describe the total growth, we must actually, of course, resort to a process of sampling, and it is difficult to know what samples to include. I shall speak of mental age and reading age but shall also translate height in inches into a height age, weight in pounds into a weight age, strength in kilograms into a grip age, and number of teeth erupted into a dental age. With the aid of a scale developed by Flory of the University

[1] Adapted and abridged from Willard C. Olson, "Reading Is a Function of the Total Growth of the Child," in W. S. Gray (ed.), *Reading and Pupil Development*, Proceedings, Conference on Reading held at the University of Chicago, Supplementary Educational Monographs, No. 51, University of Chicago Press, Chicago, 1940, pp. 233–237.

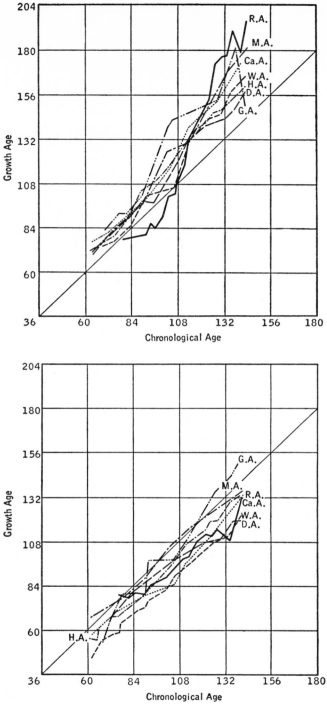

Figs. 1–4. Individual Differences in Child Growth: A Basis for Improved Practices at Home and School. (From studies by Willard C. Olson and Byron O. Hughes, Child Development Laboratories, University of Michigan.)

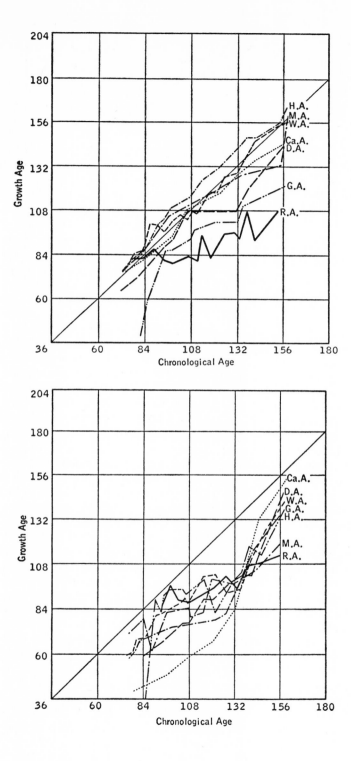

of Chicago, we translate x-rays of the hand and wrist into carpal age. In our use of the age principle there is no thought that the averages from which the ages are derived are standards in any sense of the term. The data secured should be thought of in terms of the operations which produced them, since it is questionable whether the concept of standards is serviceable in the description of growth and individual differences. If one takes a time slice of an organism based on longitudinal growth curves and secures an average of all the values attained by the child, one obtains what we have called an "organismic age." This center of gravity grows in a stable manner, while the separate attributes of the organism vary in compensatory ways.

In our current analyses we have twenty-eight boys and twenty-eight girls with longitudinal records from five to eight years in length. An interesting way to view these records in our atlases of development is to arrange them in order of organismic age as of a common period of time. We have arranged our series in the order of organismic age as of nine years of chronological age. When for purposes of contrast one views the highest boy and the highest girl and the lowest boy and the lowest girl in the series, one secures a most dramatic picture of the generalization that reading tends to be an aspect of the growth of the child as a whole. Thus in these illustrative instances, as in the whole series, reading tends to be somewhere in the pattern of the total growth of children. Former correlational studies involving two variables attempted to make a generalization on a one-to-one correspondence in children. The organism-as-a-whole approach insists only that growth is unified and that each aspect will be individuated at a level somewhere in the total matrix, but not necessarily always in the same relative pattern in all children.

There is a tendency among teachers and reading diagnosticians to define reading disability as a discrepancy between mental-test data and ability to read. The gathering of additional evidence on growth leads to the frequent conclusion that reading is in truth a consistent aspect of a total pattern in which physical functions are not so highly developed as are the intellectual functions. In other words, the child's organismic age reveals a greater immaturity than his mental age.

Do discrepancies from this generalization occur? Theoretically, only such aspects of growth are individuated as are nurtured. If, then, there has been deprivation in nurture in the area of reading experience, reading should attain less than its organismic potentiality in actual achievement. While it is easy to make this theoretical statement, it seems more difficult to say with certainty that authentic instances of reading retardation occur under present-day school conditions, for there appear to be genetic and maturational factors which frequently account even for the so-called exception. Thus one boy in the Michigan study at about nine years of age was several years below in reading as compared to his other growth values. This child had been ill frequently and had attended school in preceding periods only 72 percent of the time. A wider sampling of his growth seemed to suggest that actually he was more immature than certain values obtained for him seemed to indicate. This child became involved in a remedial-reading experiment and made gains at twice the normal rate, so that he is now reading in the area of his total growth. This case strongly suggests that, if reading is not an integral part of total growth, it can be made so by providing an adequate amount of experience. There is still an upward limiting factor based on the total growth configuration. It may be noted that we get certain instances of split growth involving delayed progress in reading in cases which are marked by hypothyroidism, delay in descent of the testicles, and similar growth retardation. The accompanying behavioral and emotional disorders are highly interesting on a clinical basis.

The longitudinal approach to the study of children permits easier sibling comparisons. We no longer need compare children of the same family separated several years in time but can examine their growth curves as of the same point in time. In the series of sibling comparisons in the Michigan study, the fidelity with which the level and patterning of growth tends to be comparable in members of the same family can be noted. This comparability extends to reading and to cases which would be superficially diagnosed as cases of reading disability.

If the philosophy and the technique of consideration of the child as a whole were generally understood and applied, workers with children would view child progress in reading against the broad background of total growth. Only when the curve of reading growth is splitting off from the other curves of growth would concern be warranted.

READING AND INTELLIGENCE [1]

U. W. Leavell and Helen Sterling

[What is the relationship between reading and intelligence? Do eye movements change with the intelligence of different readers reading the same selection? A number of researchers have been interested in these inquiries. One team, Leavell and Sterling, reports the evidence it secured.]

The type of reading one engages in, the manner in which he engages in it, and his purpose all affect his reading. However, no matter what his purpose, no matter what his material, no matter if he read orally or silently, he always makes fixations, he always has some duration of fixation, some span of recognition, he always reads with some degree of comprehension and at some rate. Usually he makes some regressions. Although some of these factors vary with different materials, purposes, or types of reading material, it seems fitting that they be compared with intelligence under controlled conditions. It is logical

[1] Adapted and abridged from U. W. Leavell and Helen Sterling, "A Comparison of Basic Factors in Reading Patterns with Intelligence," *Peabody Journal of Education* (1938), *16*:149–155.

to expect children to react in somewhat the same fashion to material of the same type.

One hundred ninety-one sixth-grade children were used in the study. One hundred three of these pupils were boys and eighty-eight were girls. All of the children were white and the large majority were American born. The group ranged chronologically from 10 years, 2 months to 15 years, 4 months, the median chronological age being 11 years, 9.5 months. The median intelligence quotient of the whole group when measured by the Kuhlmann-Anderson Test was 103.93, but when measured by Meyers Mental Measure it was 108.25. Two hundred twenty children were tested originally. Elimination was necessary if a child missed a test or if the photograph of his eyes was not usable. Records were complete on 191 children.

Three schools coöperated in the study. Two were public schools, one in a good residential section, one in a section representing both middle-class homes and a mill and factory district. The other was a private school.

The ophthalmograph was used to secure data on the number of fixations, the span of recognition, comprehension, and the rate of reading. The Monroe Silent Reading Test, Revised Edition, was used to study comprehension and speed in reading. The Keystone Ophthalmic Telebinocular was used to obtain information concerning fusion, lateral imbalance, and sharpness of image at reading distance.

The children were divided into three intelligence groups. To make this division the median Kuhlmann-Anderson IQ's and the quartile deviations were found. On this basis children of 111 and above fell in the superior intelligence group. Those with IQ's of 97 to 110 fell in the average intelligence group. Those with IQ's of 96 and below fell in the inferior intelligence group. The same division was maintained for comparing the medians when the Mey-

TABLE 1. Coefficients of Correlation of Intelligence and Basic Factors in Reading Patterns

Factor	Kuhlmann-Anderson		Meyers Mental Measure	
	r	PE	r	PE
Number of fixations	−.30	.05	.04	.05
Number of regressions	−.87	.11	−.45	.01
Rate (ophthalmograph)	.43	.04	.12	.05
Comprehension	.23	.05	.15	.66
Duration of fixation	−.30	.04	−.05	.05
Span of recognition	.36	.04	.15	.05
Rate (Monroe test)	.24	.05	.05	.05
Comprehension (Monroe test)	.13	.05	−.03	.05

ers test was the measure of intelligence.

Therefore, upon examining the data in the table we see that the Kuhlmann-Anderson Test indicated a fairly high negative relationship between intelligence and the number of regressions made per hundred words of reading. In other words, there was a fairly high degree of evidence indicating that children of inferior intelligence made more regressions per hundred words than children of high intelligence. While the Meyers test indicated less relationship, it was still evident. The Kuhlmann-Anderson Test indicated a fairly marked positive relationship between intelligence and the rate of reading as measured on the ophthalmograph. The results of the Meyers test did not substantiate this, however.

Coefficients of correlation of visual defects and intelligence were low.

According to the data in Table 2 the inferior intelligence group made significantly more fixations and regressions per hundred words of reading material than did the superior intelligence group. The superior intelligence group made significantly higher scores on rate as measured by the Monroe test, comprehension as measured by the Monroe test, and span of recognition. The superior intelligence group made significantly higher scores than the average intelligence group on rate as compared by the Monroe test. The differences between the medians of the average intelligence group and the inferior intelligence group were not significant.

According to the data in Table 3 the

TABLE 2. Median Differences of Intelligence Groups (Kuhlmann-Anderson) for Basic Factors in Reading

	Superior and Inferior Intelligence	PE Median	Superior and Average Intelligence	PE Median	Average and Inferior Intelligence	PE Median
Number of fixations	—22.41	4.30	—13.12	3.61	—8.29	4.30
Number of regressions	—7.37	1.61	—3.03	1.43	—4.34	1.53
Rate (ophthalmograph)	71.00	1.09	40.55	8.80	30.45	9.83
Comprehension	5.89	3.25	—.60	2.76	6.49	3.01
Duration of fixation	—.03	.06	—.02	.02	—.01	.01
Span of recognition	.23	.01	—.13	.04	.10	.04
Rate (Monroe test)	24.55	5.50	8.77	4.93	15.78	5.36
Comprehension (Monroe test)	3.04	.41	3.38	.39	—.34	.40

—The less intelligent group scored higher than the more intelligent group.

TABLE 3. Median Differences of Intelligence Groups (Meyers Mental Measure) for Basic Factors in Reading

	Superior and Inferior Intelligence	PE Median	Superior and Average Intelligence	PE Median	Average and Inferior Intelligence	PE Median
Number of fixations	—.07	3.14	—13.17	3.93	12.50	4.08
Number of regressions	.32	1.52	—3.43	1.65	3.75	2.00
Rate (ophthalmograph)	5.78	9.49	36.68	9.37	—30.90	10.60
Comprehension	.98	3.08	.22	2.84	.76	3.30
Duration of fixation	.01	.01	—.01	.01	.01	.01
Span of recognition	.03	.03	.17	.04	—.14	.04
Rate (Monroe test)	9.28	4.74	—.10	4.97	9.38	6.37
Comprehension (Monroe test)	1.20	.49	.47	.55	.73	.48

—The less intelligent group scored higher than the more intelligent.

only significant difference was in the span of recognition, where the superior intelligence group had a broader span than did the average intelligence group.

SUMMARY

1. The significance of the coefficients of correlation of the rate of reading and intelligence varied.

2. The coefficients of correlation in this study indicated that there seemed to be at least a marked tendency for the less intelligent children to make more regressions than the more intelligent.

3. When the Kuhlmann-Anderson Test was used as a measure of intelligence, the data indicated that there were significant differences in the median score between the superior and inferior intelligence groups in the number of fixations per hundred words of reading, the number of regressions per hundred words, the span of recognition, and the rate of reading.

4. When the Kuhlmann-Anderson Test was used as a measure of intelligence, there seemed to be significant differences in the median score of the superior intelligence group and the average group in only two factors. These were rate and comprehension. However, the significance of the median differences varied according to the tests used.

5. When the Meyers Mental Measure was used as a measure of intelligence, the data indicated that there was a significant median difference between the superior intelligence group and the average intelligence group in only one factor, namely, span of recognition. The superior intelligence group had a broader span of recognition.

Chapter III

GETTING READY TO READ

Introduction

In the American culture, children getting ready to read enjoy at least as much attention as children getting ready to walk or children getting ready to talk. Anxieties mount rapidly if children do not get ready at some arbitrary time, largely decreed by custom. Many parents indeed tend to regard "tardiness" in developing any one of these abilities as somehow a reflection on them.

Still tolerance, even though limited, is greater in the case of walking and talking than in the case of reading. For generations now in America, there has come to be a rather universal and rigid expectation that every child will get ready to read in the first grade of the elementary school. Variations in the nature of the child's endowment or in the nurture which circumstance has accorded seem to be blandly disavowed.

Yet it is clear that nature and nurture both do play a part in getting ready to read. Physiological endowments, the eyes for example, mature at quite different rates. This is apparent in physical stature but somehow ignored in reading. Psychological endowments, the intelligence for example, similarly elude neat uniformity in growth. At the same time, environment lays its omnipresent hand on malleable human substance, cherishing some and denying others. Nurture presses on such different matters as the background of experience needed to lend meaning to the printed words and the whole amalgam of attitude and desire required to tolerate the burden of learning to read.

The task of research has been to identify what kind of role nature and nurture play in getting ready to read. Inevitably, some controversy and some lingering doubt remain even in this well-studied aspect of reading.

THE IMPORTANCE OF CHILDREN'S EXPERIENCES TO SUCCESS IN BEGINNING READING [1]

Millie Corinne Almy

[Some children go to kindergarten; some do not. Some children are much interested in books even before first grade; some are not. Some children have many other stimulating experiences; some do not. Do the experiences of children before first grade affect their chances of success in beginning to read? Millie Almy's study gathered evidence on this point.]

First-grade programs in reading have varied widely, depending in part upon whether the teacher felt it necessary to devote extensive time to developing readiness. Children with "poor background" presumably have had few experiences with reading materials and may be unready for reading.

In this study an attempt has been made to explore the possible relationships between success in beginning reading and reading experiences before first grade. The hypothesis to be tested was that success in beginning reading is positively related to the number of the child's responses to opportunities for reading prior to first grade and that the kinds of activities participated in influence the child's approach to learning to read in school.

Success in beginning reading was tested at the end of the first grade with the Word Recognition and Sentence Reading Tests of the 1942 revision of the Gates Primary Reading Tests.[2] In addition, each child received ratings by his teacher on his interest in reading and his ability to understand what he read. The reading ages obtained on the Gates tests and the teachers' ratings were converted into standard scores and the average was taken as a composite reading score. The composite reading scores were treated as the criterion of reading success. The difficulties of adequately measured reading achievement at this age were apparent in the fact that a large number of the children failed to make an appreciable score on the Gates tests. The ratings of their teachers, as was expected, clustered around the middle of the scale. Consequently, the reading criterion did not discriminate very well.

[1] Abridged and adapted from Millie Corinne Almy, *Children's Experiences Prior to First Grade and Success in Beginning Reading*, Bureau of Publications, Teachers College, Columbia University, New York, 1949.

[2] *Gates Primary Reading Tests*, Bureau of Publications, Teachers College, Columbia University, New York, 1942.

The appraisal of experiences prior to first grade was made at the end of the first grade, through interviews with the parents, who were asked to give retrospective information on the children's experiences in the year prior to first grade. Questions were also asked about the children's interests at the time of the interview. Interviews were held with the children to find out how they appraised their reading ability and believed they had learned to read. It was recognized that the errors of reporting in retrospection would contribute to unreliability.

The group selected for study consisted of 106 children in five first grades in three schools in one school system. The mean chronological age for the group was 83.01 months, with all but two children falling within a range of 13 months. The spread in reading and mental ability, as would be expected, was considerably greater but the maximum did not exceed 96 months in mental age [3] or 105 months in reading age. The narrow range of ability is relevant in considering the data.

FINDINGS

A significant, positive relationship exists between success in beginning reading and the child's responses to opportunities for reading prior to first grade. This is true despite the limitations of the criterion, the unreliability contributed by retrospective errors, and the narrow range of ability in this group.

RELATIONSHIPS BETWEEN THE READING CRITERION AND EARLY READING EXPERIENCES

The score for "Free Mention Responses, Before First Grade" (variable 9

[3] *Kuhlmann-Anderson Intelligence Test,* Educational Test Bureau, Minneapolis, 1942.

in Table 1) was based on those areas in the questionnaire which offered the parent an opportunity to mention reading spontaneously. These were: "What did the children do in kindergarten?" "What were some of the things he liked to do with adults?" "What did he play?" and "What kind of playthings did he like best?" One credit was allowed for each area in which the parent's answer to the question included mention of an interest in reading, such as "looked at books" in kindergarten, or "liked to be read to," for activities with adults, or "liked to play school with his brother's books," for play activities. The highest possible score for this variable was 3. Such a score occurred only in those cases in which the parent spontaneously mentioned such interests in each of the three areas.

The intercorrelation between the reading criterion and free mention responses before first grade is .26. This is significant at the .01 level. Considering the lack of fine discrimination in the criterion, and the restricted range of the group, this relationship is most striking. There is reason to believe that the children who are reading enough to make the higher scores on the reading criterion are children whose experiences in kindergarten, in play, and with adults have had in them some elements of reading.

The score for "Directed Mention Responses, Before First Grade" (variable 11) was based on nine different items in the interview schedule. Three of these related to kindergarten: "Did they have any books?" "Did anyone read to them?" "'Did anyone try to teach them to read?" One credit was allowed for each positive indication. Four questions for which one credit was given for positive indication asked, "Did he ever pay any attention to the signs he saw?" "Did he ever use books, magazines, paper, or pencil in his play?" "Did he ask to be read to often?" "Did he ever pretend he was reading?" One item concerned the child's questions about words, letters, or numbers that he saw around him and specifically whether he noticed them on cans and packages, cards, grocery or laundry lists, letters, magazines and books, phonograph records, the radio, signs, or table games. A positive indication for each of these gave a total of nine credits. As many as six credits were allowed for positive indication of liking to "read" newspapers, magazines, comic books, adult books, children's books, or other reading material. The highest possible score for directed mention responses prior to first grade was 22.

The intercorrelation between the reading criterion and directed mention responses before first grade is .25. This is significant at the .05 level and closely approaches the .01 level. This supports the hypothesis that a positive relationship exists between reading success and response to opportunities for reading prior to first grade. Again bearing in mind the constraints in the criterion, the unreliability of the retrospective reports, and the narrow range of ability in the group, we see that the importance of this relationship becomes even more apparent. It is clear that the children who were able to make appreciable scores on the reading criterion were those who had been more interested in reading prior to first grade. Not only had they wanted to be read to, but they had exhibited interests which reached out to reading wherever they found it.

This finding has several implications for teaching beginning reading. The teachers are confronted with children whose preschool reading experiences have varied rather widely. To proceed without any knowledge of what these experiences have been may very well mean that some children repeat to the

point of boredom what they have already learned. Others struggle through the same materials with great difficulty, needing both time and richness of experience to make up for previous lack of opportunities.

In the directed mention responses prior to first grade two items were singled out for special study. The first of these is "Reading Details" (variable 6 in Table 1), referring to the child's interest in words, letters, or numbers that he saw around for non-book reading. It is interesting to find how much of a correlation there is between it and the reading criterion. The correlation, .26, is significant at the .01 level. The children who were able to make good scores on the reading criterion apparently had interests in words, letters, and numbers regardless of where they appeared.

It is well to raise at this point the question of whether these kinds of experiences may not need to be offered by the school to those children who have not yet had them. Situations in which children ask about words, letters, or numbers because they are really curious and have something which they want to find out must be contrasted with many reading readiness programs in which, too often, children are passive recipients of whatever materials the teacher hands out.

The other item of the directed mention responses prior to first grade which received special study is "Reading Likes" (variable 7 in Table 1). This measured the more conventional reading experiences, i.e., those with newspapers, magazines, comic books, adult books, and children's books. The correlation of this variable with the reading criterion is not significant. It is, however, highly correlated with "Reading Details" (.52). The correlation with the child's indication that he can read (.25) is also positive and significant at the .01 level. All of these show that the tendency toward interest in reading of one kind of material goes along with interest in other kinds. Children who indicate that they can read are children who have many interests.

The occupational level of the home was estimated by rating the father's occupation on the five-point Taussig [4] scale. No relation was found between this level and the reading criterion or with the degree of children's independent activity. Neither was there a significant relation between occupational level and free mention responses before first grade, but the correlation with directed mention responses, .22, was significant at the .05 level.

The correlation between mental age and the reading criterion, .15, showed but slight relationship. Mental age, however, was significantly related to free mention responses prior to first grade (r .23, .05 level) and to directed mention responses prior to first grade (r. 36, .01 level). Bright children appear to respond more positively to opportunities for reading prior to first grade.

Surprisingly, there was little relation (r .17) between ability to read (reading criterion) and the child's statement that he could read. There was a relation (r .29, .01 level) between his mental age and his indication that he could read. A similar relation (r .25, .01 level) existed between his statement that he could read and his report of the number of things he liked to read.

The free mention response (variable

[4] F. W. Taussig, *Principles of Economics*, New York, The Macmillan Company, 4th rev. ed., 1939, Vol. 2, pp. 235–237.

10) for the end of first grade represented the scores for two items. One, from the parent's interview, was "What does he like about first grade?" A credit of 1 was given for mention of reading. The other, from the interview with the child, was "What do you usually do right after school? in the evening? on Saturday? on Sunday?" and "When you have some time at home when you can do whatever you please, what do you like to do best?" A credit of 1 was given for mention of reading or being read to.

The correlation between variable 10 and the reading criterion is .23, significant at the .05 level. Again, the positive relationship between the child's responses to opportunities for reading and his success is maintained.

The fourth variable representing children's responses to reading opportunities which was studied in relation to the reading criterion was that of directed mention responses at the end of first grade (variable 12). Here the score was based on the parent's response to the question "Does he ever bring any books home from school?" and the child's response to the question "Do you like to have someone read to you?" with a positive indication being given a credit of 1 in each instance.

The correlation between directed mention responses at the end of first grade and the reading criterion is .08, which is not significant.

A further analysis of Table 1 reveals that nearly all of the correlations, though small, are consistently positive. The exposure to reading experiences before first grade and encouragement of reading activities outside of school during the first grade appear to be valuable.

TABLE 1. Intercorrelation Coefficients for Mental Age, Composite Reading Scores, Occupational Status, and Scores Based on Reading Experiences [a] for 106 children in Elmont, New York, at the End of the First Grade

	1	2	3	4	5	6	7	8	9	10	11	12	Mean	SD
1. CA		.10	−.02	.08	.04	.17	.01	.03	−.07	−.02	.11	.10	83.01	3.29
2. MA			.15	.17	.02	.28	.18	.29	.23	.12	.36	.14	82.04	8.97
3. Reading Criterion				−.02	.11	.26	.17	.17	.26	.23	.25	.08	63.18	44.15
4. Occupational Level					−.15	.19	.16	.20	.05	.12	.22	.15	3.15	1.23
5. Independence [b]						.19	.14	.14	.14	.01	.23	.07	3.44	1.17
6. Reading Details							.52	.15	.33	.11	.86	.03	3.35	2.05
7. Reading Likes								.25	.34	.12	.79	.16	2.71	1.40
8. Child Reads									.14	.17	.29	.19	1.08	.74
9. Free Mention Responses, Before First Grade										.27	.39	.13	.67	.75
10. Free Mention Responses, End of First Grade											.12	.19	.73	.72
11. Directed Mention Responses, Before First Grade												.10	9.86	3.76
12. Directed Mention Responses, End of First Grade													1.59	.58

[a] For description of each variable, see pp. 49–51.
[b] Refers to question on interview with parent: How much was child "on his own" before he entered first grade? Possible responses included: dressing self, errands for family, cross street alone, etc.

WHEN SHOULD CHILDREN BEGIN TO READ ? [1]

Mabel V. Morphett and Carleton Washburne

[Schools in different countries start to teach children to read at different times. Some countries begin earlier in their schools than the typical beginning time in the United States. What advantages and disadvantages accrue to different beginning times? Is there any one best time to begin? This study was one of the first to investigate these important concerns.]

The research department (of Winnetka Schools) set about the task of discovering the period in the mental development of children when, as a rule, they best learn to read readily.

In September, 1928, all Winnetka first-grade children, 141 in number, were given the Detroit First-Grade Intelligence Test. The eight first-grade teachers were not told the mental ages of the children and attempted to teach all of them to read. The method was largely individual, so that the slow children did not retard the fast ones. In February, 1929, the reading progress of these children was measured for the purpose of determining the amount of progress made by children at each mental level.

The first large teaching unit was divided into definite steps, which were measurable by the teachers. Twenty-one steps took the children through the beginning reading materials.

In addition to these progress steps the sight-word score of each child was found. The sight words are those most frequently used in primers and first readers. The children were tested individually with flash card, and the number of words recognized by each child was recorded as his sight-word score.

Thirteen progress steps and thirty-seven sight words were accepted by the first-grade teachers as the measure of the minimum degree of satisfactory progress by February.

The Detroit First-Grade Intelligence Test given in September was followed by the Stanford-Binet Test later in the year. Mental ages were calculated as of September. In this way comparison between the mental ages determined by the two tests was made possible.

Table 1 gives the correlations which were found between the sight-word scores and intelligence and between reading progress and intelligence. Since the data proved to be nonlinear, the correlation ratios rather than the correlation coefficients are given. When the relation between reading progress and intelligence was calculated, it was nec-

[1] Adapted and abridged from Mabel V. Morphett and Carleton Washburne, "When Should Children Begin to Read?" *Elementary School Journal* (1931), 31:496–503.

essary to use the rank method of figuring correlations since the intervals of progress did not necessarily represent equal difficulty. The correlations show that there is a fairly high degree of relationship between mental age and reading progress. Of the three measures of intelligence—mental age, average of mental and chronological age, and intelligence quotient—mental age shows the greatest degree of relationship and, in the calculations that follow, is used as the method of figuring intelligence.

The scores were next divided into

TABLE 1. Correlations Between Achievement in Reading of 141 First-Grade Children and Their Intelligence as Measured by Detroit and Stanford-Binet Tests

Factors Correlated	Detroit	Stanford
Sight-word score and mental age	.65	.58
Sight-word score and average of mental and chronological age as of September 1, 1928	.57	.49
Sight-word score and intelligence quotient	.56	.54
Reading progress and mental age	.59	.51
Reading progress and average of mental and chronological age as of September 1, 1928	.55	.49
Reading progress and intelligence quotient	.50	.53

groups based on the children's mental ages in September. The percentage of children of each mental age making satisfactory progress (thirteen steps or more) and the percentage making satisfactory sight-word scores (thirty-seven or more) were determined. Tables 2 and 3 show the results.

TABLE 2. Number of Children of Each Mental Age and Percentage Making Satisfactory Reading Progress

Mental Age in Years and Months [a]	Number of Children [b]		Percentage Making Satisfactory Reading Progress [c]	
	Detroit	Stanford	Detroit	Stanford
4–5 to 4–11	1	1	—	—
5–0 to 5–5	12	1	0	—
5–6 to 5–11	12	12	0	8
6–0 to 6–5	17	22	47	41
6–6 to 6–11	23	38	78	68
7–0 to 7–5	29	31	79	68
7–6 to 7–11	16	15	75	87
8–0 to 8–5	7	11	—	82
8–6 to 9–0	8	2	—	—

[a] Intervals are half-sigmas above or below the mean of the entire group as determined by the Detroit test.

[b] Because the tests were given on different dates, some children who were given the Detroit test were not given the Stanford-Binet and vice versa.

[c] No percentages were figured for groups of less than ten children.

Table 2 shows that a small percentage of children who began with a mental age of less than six years were able to achieve satisfactory reading progress but that for the group having a mental age between six years and six years and six

TABLE 3. Number of Children of Each Mental Age and Percentage
Making Satisfactory Sight-Word Scores

Mental Age in Years and Months	Number of Children [a]		Percentage Making Satisfactory Sight-Word Scores	
	Detroit	Stanford	Detroit	Stanford
4–5 to 4–11	1	1	—	—
5–0 to 5–5	12	1	0	—
5–6 to 5–11	12	12	0	8
6–0 to 6–5	17	25	71	52
6–6 to 6–11	23	43	87	77
7–0 to 7–5	31	35	84	89
7–6 to 7–11	23	18	83	94
8–0 to 8–5	10	11	90	91
8–6 to 9–0	12	3	100	—

[a] The numbers of children whose sight-word progress is compared differ from the numbers whose reading progress is compared in Table 2 because one group of children not taught by the individual method was omitted from the reading progress group.

months there was a sharp rise in the percentage making satisfactory progress.

If Table 2 were placed on a graph, the curve of the results on the Stanford-Binet would seem to indicate that chil-

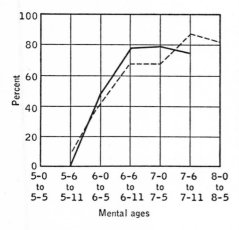

Fig 1. Percentages of Children of Various Mental Ages, as Determined by the Detroit First-Grade Intelligence Test (Solid Line) and by the Stanford Revision of the Binet-Simon Scale (Broken Line), Making Satisfactory Reading Progress in School Year 1928–29.

dren would gain considerably in speed of learning if they could wait until they had attained a mental age of seven years and six months before beginning to read. However, the curve of the results of the Detroit test shows that the children with mental ages of six years and six months made progress practically as satisfactory as that of children with higher mental ages. Since the results of the Detroit test show a higher correlation with reading progress than do the results of the Stanford-Binet test and since the Detroit test is more practicable to administer than the Stanford-Binet test, it seems reasonable to use the Detroit test as a basis for determining children's readiness for reading. The mental level of six years and six months is the point beyond which there is very little gain in postponing the teaching of reading.

If the sight-word scores were similarly graphed, they would point to the same conclusion—that it pays to postpone beginning reading until a child has attained a mental age of six years and six months. If this practice is followed, 78 percent of the children may be expected to make satisfactory general progress, and 87 percent of the children may be

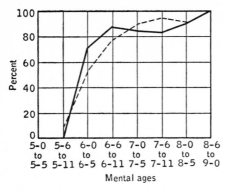

Fig. 2. Percentages of Children of Various Mental Ages, as Determined by the Detroit First-Grade Intelligence Test (Solid Line) and by the Stanford Revision of the Binet-Simon Scale (Broken Line), Making Satisfactory Sight-Word Scores in School Year 1928–29.

expected to make satisfactory progress in learning sight words.

A similar study was carried on during the school year 1929–30 to check the results of the 1928–29 experiment. All children who were mentally six years of age or more were taught reading from the beginning of the year. The previous study made it seem futile to try to teach younger children, but a few with lower mental ages were taught reading for the purpose of the experiment. Mental ages were determined this time by the Detroit First-Grade Intelligence Test and the Pintner-Cunningham Primary Mental Test.

At the end of the year (June, 1930) the children were tested on the sight-word list and the Gray Standardized Oral Reading Check Test. A child was considered to have made satisfactory progress if he knew a sight-word list of 139 words and read the Gray test in forty seconds or less with three errors or less. This standard has been set by Gray for Grade I. Table 4 gives the number of children of each mental age and the percentage of children at each mental level making satisfactory scores on both sight words and oral reading.

TABLE 4. Number of Children of Each Mental Age and the Percentage of Children Making Satisfactory Scores on Sight Words and Oral Reading

Mental Ages in Years and Months [a]	Number of Children		Percentage Making Satisfactory Progress	
	Sight Word	Oral Reading	Sight Word	Oral Reading
5–0 to 5–5	1	0	—	—
5–6 to 5–11	10	9	—	—
6–0 to 6–5	25	24	64	58
6–6 to 6–11	23	23	87	83
7–0 to 7–5	23	23	87	91
7–6 to 7–11	12	12	83	92
8–0 to 8–5	5	5	—	—
8–6 to 9–0	1	1	—	—

[a] Average of scores on Detroit test and Pintner-Cunningham test.

The percentage of children who learned to read satisfactorily is greatest at the mental ages of six years and six months and of seven years. If placed on a graph, the curve for sight-word scores breaks at the mental age of six years and six months, while the curve on the Gray Standardized Oral Reading Check Test breaks at the mental age of seven.

The second year's experiment, therefore, in which a different set of children, different teachers, a different method of determining mental age, and a different method of determining progress were used and in which a whole year's work instead of a half-year's was taken as the measure of progress, confirms the experiment of the first year.

THE NECESSARY MENTAL AGE FOR BEGINNING READING [1]

Arthur I. Gates

[Here is another answer to the problem of when to begin instruction in reading. The study, undertaken some half-dozen years after that by Morphett and Washburne, reaches a somewhat different conclusion. Wherein do the two studies differ?]

For some time the problem of determining the optimum or necessary mental-age level at which reading can be successfully introduced has been under investigation. Recently statements have been made which imply that success with typical first-grade reading programs requires a stipulated mental age, six and a half years being the age usually given. The fact remains, however, that it has by no means been proved as yet that a mental age of six and a half years is a proper minimum for learning to read by *all* school methods, or organizations, or *all* types of teaching skill and procedures. It is quite conceivable—indeed the evidence in general tends now definitely to show—that the crucial mental-age level will vary with the materials; the type of teaching; the skill of the teacher; the size of the class; the amount of preceding preparatory work; the thoroughness of examination; the frequency and the treatment of special difficulties, such as visual defects of the pupil; and other factors.

In the present article are assembled data on the relations between mental age and success in learning to read in Grade I in a number of different groups which were taught by appreciably different methods and materials. The particular classes selected for this report are taken from a somewhat larger number that were analyzed to illustrate the facts related to certain issues.

FIRST GROUP

The pupils were divided into two first-grade classes of forty-one and thirty-seven pupils, respectively. The intelli-

[1] Adapted and abridged from Arthur I. Gates, "The Necessary Mental Age for Beginning Reading," *Elementary School Journal* (1937), 37:497–508.

gence quotient of the former class was higher than that of the latter.[2] In addition to the usual equipment of books, the teachers were provided with a considerable amount of supplementary practice and teach-and-test materials made up for the purpose. Not only was the teaching rather closely supervised, but the teachers had a larger amount of easy reading and self-diagnostic material than usual. For present purposes, the pupils of the two classes have been combined into one group. The reading attainments were measured more than a month before the end of the school year by an average of three Gates Primary Silent Reading Tests.

In the group of seventy-eight pupils the correlation between mental age and the average reading grade was .62 ± .05. This figure, it will be noted, is rather high in comparison with the correlations usually obtained in similar studies. The correlation between chronological age and average reading age was .10 ± .08.

As a means of locating a possible critical mental age for success in beginning reading, these pupils were grouped according to mental age by six-month steps beginning with a step containing pupils from the lowest in the list to 5.0 years inclusive; then from 5.0 to 5.5, inclusive; and so on to the highest.

TABLE 1. Pupils in Pennsylvania Study Who Failed to Achieve Reading Grades of 1.50, 1.75, and 1.95, Distributed According to Mental Age

Mental Age	Number of Pupils	Reading Grade Below 1.50	Reading Grade Below 1.75	Reading Grade Below 1.95
		Number of Pupils		
8.5–8.9	2	0	0	0
8.0–8.4	0	0	0	0
7.5–7.9	6	0	0	0
7.0–7.4	6	0	0	0
6.5–6.9	13	0	0	0
6.0–6.4	14	0	1	1
5.5–5.9	19	0	0	0
5.0–5.4	11	0	1	3
4.5–4.9	6	2	4	5
4.0–4.4	1	1	1	1
		Percentage of Pupils		
5.0 or above	71	0	3	7
5.5 or above	60	0	2	2
6.0 or above	41	0	2	2
6.5 or above	27	0	0	0
7.0 or above	14	0	0	0

In these classes there was a range of mental age from 53 months to 102 months or approximately 2 to 1. The lowest mental age was four years and

[2] For further details, see Florence W. Raguse, "Qualitative and Quantitative Achievements in First Grade Reading," Teachers College Record (1931), 32:424–436.

five months, and the highest eight years and six months, a difference of four years and one month. It will be noted that practically half the members of the class (thirty-seven) had a mental age of less than six years on entering. An inspection of these several groups will show that practically all the near-failures fell in the group below five years.

The method of determining the minimum mental age desirable for introducing a child to reading involves certain problems. For example, what reading ability should a pupil have acquired by the end of the year to have achieved a status which may be described as a successful reading experience? Since this matter is one on which opinions may differ, the data from these pupils have been computed on three bases: (1) the percentage of the pupils who in the final test achieved a reading-grade score of 1.50 or higher, (2) the percentage achieving a reading-grade score of 1.75 or higher, and (3) the percentage equaling or exceeding 1.95. The last figure represents substantially the norm on the Gates test for the end of Grade I. It should be noted that in the population at large approximately 45 percent of the pupils would have fallen below a reading grade of 1.95 at the end of Grade I.

In Table 1 the data have been assembled showing both the numbers and the percentages of pupils with stipulated beginning mental age who failed to exceed a reading grade of 1.50, 1.75, and 1.95, respectively. Thus, of all the pupils who had a mental age of 5.0 or higher at the beginning of the year, none made a reading grade at the end of the year below 1.50; 3 percent made a reading grade below 1.75, and 7 percent made a score below 1.95. Of the children who had a mental age of 5.5 or higher at the beginning of the year, none fell below 1.50, 2 percent fell below 1.75, and 2 percent below 1.95. Of the children having a mental age of 6.0 or higher at the beginning of the year, none fell below a reading grade of 1.50, 2 percent fell below 1.75, and 2 percent below 1.95. Of those having a mental age of 6.5 or higher, none made a reading grade below 1.95.

As already stated, decision concerning the level of achievement in reading which should be considered optimum or satisfactory is arbitrary. If we assume that a program is, under practical conditions, highly satisfactory when no more than 10 percent of the pupils fall below a reading grade of 1.95, it appears that in the case of this group a mental age of 5.0 is satisfactory. Only 7 percent of the pupils with a beginning mental age of 5.0 or higher fell below a final reading grade of 1.95. Since defects in vision and in hearing, poor previous training, illness, absence from school, and many other factors, as well as inadequate mental age, are known to result in inferior reading attainments, it will be obvious that the record of the class was remarkably good. Since substantially all the seriously backward cases fell in the group with a mental age of five years or less at the beginning of the year and since very few of the seriously backward pupils appeared among the higher mental ages, the writer considers it entirely justifiable to say that a mental age of 5.0 at the beginning of the year, other things being satisfactory, is sufficient for learning to read satisfactorily.

SECOND GROUP

A second group of pupils was taught in a New York City school by teachers who were judged to be more expert than average and who used a considerable body of experimental materials developed by the writer and his colleagues. These materials consisted of various types of practice and seat work, teach-and-test materials, and supplementary easy reading material, largely limited to the vocabulary used in the basal books. The class consisted of forty-eight pupils, for forty-five of whom complete records were obtained. A summary of the pertinent data is contained in Table 2.

In this class pupils with a mental age of less than five years were not so successful as those in the first group. One out of five fell below a reading grade of 1.50, two fell below 1.75, and three below 1.95. When all the pupils who began with a mental age of 5.5 or higher are considered, it is found that only 3 percent fell below 1.50, 9 percent below 1.75, and 12 percent below 1.95. The records for pupils with a minimum mental age of 6.0 are similar. To the writer it appears reasonable to state that this

TABLE 2. New York Pupils Taught with Specially Prepared Materials Who Failed to Achieve Reading Grades of 1.50, 1.75, and 1.95, Distributed According to Mental Age

Mental Age	Number of Pupils	Reading Grade Below 1.50	Reading Grade Below 1.75	Reading Grade Below 1.95
		Number of Pupils		
7.5–8.0	2	0	0	0
7.0–7.4	3	0	0	0
6.5–6.9	8	0	1	1
6.0–6.4	9	1	1	1
5.5–5.9	10	0	1	2
5.0–5.4	8	0	1	3
4.5–4.9	5	1	2	3
		Percentage of Pupils		
5.5 or above	32	3	9	12
6.0 or above	22	5	9	9
6.5 or above	13	0	8	8
7.0 or above	5	0	0	0

program was satisfactorily adjusted— some allowance being made for practical limitations due to absence from school, uncorrected defects, and other constitutional limitations—to pupils with a mental age of 5.5 or higher. In other words, it is a program which represents a difficulty level about one-half year higher than that employed for the first group.

In this group the correlation between mental age and reading grade was .55, somewhat lower than the .62 found for the first group.

THIRD GROUP

A third group consisted of forty-three pupils in a rather superior urban public school. In this class very good teaching was conducted with a better-than-average amount of typical classroom reading matter and other equipment, but the teacher did not have any large amount of the specially prepared types of teach-and-test material employed in the two groups previously considered. Table 3 gives a summary of the data for forty pupils.

In this case poor reading appeared among the pupils with mental ages below 6.0. For the entire group with mental ages of 5.5 or above, 14 percent earned a reading grade below 1.75 and 27 percent below 1.95. When the group is restricted to those with mental ages of 6.0 or higher, only 5 percent fell below 1.50, 10 percent below 1.75, and 20 percent below 1.95. Figures for the higher mental-age groups were greatly affected by two pupils in the upper mental ages who fell below the average reading score. These represent instances of special factors contributing to reading difficulty which may, and do, appear at all levels. If some allowance is made for this possibility, it is reasonable to say that the program in this case was fairly well suited to all pupils with a beginning

TABLE 3. Urban Pupils in Superior Public School Taught Without Large Amount of Specially Prepared Materials Who Failed to Achieve Reading Grades of 1.50, 1.75, and 1.95, Distributed According to Mental Age

Mental Age	Number of Pupils	Reading Grade Below 1.50	Reading Grade Below 1.75	Reading Grade Below 1.95
		Number of Pupils		
7.5–8.0	1	0	0	1
7.0–7.4	3	0	0	0
6.5–6.9	7	0	1	1
6.0–6.4	9	1	1	2
5.5–5.9	9	1	2	4
5.0–5.4	7	1	3	5
4.5–4.9	4	2	3	4
		Percentage of Pupils		
5.5 or above	29	7	14	27
6.0 or above	20	5	10	20
6.5 or above	11	0	9	18
7.0 or above	4	0	0	25

mental age of six years or higher. In other words, the program used with this group requires a mental age a full year in advance of that used in the first group and a half-year in advance of that used in the second group.

The correlation between mental age and reading grade in this group was .44. It will be noted that, thus far, the better the program is suited to the pupils of lower mental age, the higher the correlation between mental age and reading ability at the end of the year.

FOURTH GROUP

The fourth group comprised eighty pupils from two public-school classes in

TABLE 4. Pupils in Metropolitan Schools Taught with Inferior Materials Who Failed to Achieve Reading Grades of 1.50, 1.75, and 1.95, Distributed According to Mental Age

Mental Age	Number of Pupils	Reading Grade Below 1.50	Reading Grade Below 1.75	Reading Grade Below 1.95
		Number of Pupils		
8.0–8.4	1	0	0	0
7.5–7.9	3	0	0	1
7.0–7.4	7	1	1	3
6.5–6.9	14	1	3	5
6.0–6.4	17	3	5	8
5.5–5.9	17	2	4	9
5.0–5.4	13	4	6	11
4.5–4.9	8	3	5	8
		Percentage of Pupils		
5.5 or above	59	12	22	44
6.0 or above	42	12	21	40
6.5 or above	25	8	16	36
7.0 or above	11	9	9	36

a metropolitan area. Both classes were large; the teachers were judged to be somewhat below the average of those in the system; and the reading materials and other equipment were inferior. The classes were taught largely by mass methods, with much oral instruction and little individual or self-manageable work. There was less attempt than usual to adjust instruction to individual needs.

The data in Table 4 indicate that in this group a larger proportion of the pupils fell below reading grades of 1.50 and 1.75 than in the other groups. It will be noted also that some pupils from all the mental-age categories except the two highest fell below a reading grade of 1.50. Of the pupils with a mental age above 6.5, 8 percent achieved a reading grade below 1.50, 16 percent below 1.75, and 36 percent below 1.95. Of those having a mental age of 7.0 or higher, however, only 9 percent fell below 1.75, although 36 percent fell below 1.95. It is, of course, difficult to designate a satisfactory mental-age level for instruction which was apparently of rather unsatisfactory general character. If a reading grade of 1.75 is set up as a reasonably satisfactory achievement at the end of the year, 84 percent of the pupils with a mental age above 6.5 would have been rated as successful and 91 percent of those with a mental age above 7.0. In other words, it would appear that on this rather conservative basis a mental age of somewhere between 6.5 and 7.0 would be necessary for a reasonable assurance of success in reading.

The correlation between mental age and reading grade in this group was .34.

CONCLUSIONS

These representative data point rather convincingly to certain conclusions concerning the relationship between mental age and success in reading. In the first place, they indicate clearly that statements concerning the necessary mental age at which a pupil can be expected to learn to read are essentially meaningless. The age for learning to read under one program or with the method employed by one teacher may be entirely different from that required under other circumstances.

The foregoing conclusion should not be interpreted to imply that mental age is of no significance in learning to read. Correlations between mental age and reading achievement were highest in classes in which the best instruction was done and lowest in those in which the poorest instruction was provided. More specifically, the magnitude of the correlation seems to vary directly with the effectiveness of the provision for individual differences in the classroom.

It is necessary for each teacher to understand the mental age and other qualifications required for successful pursuance of the program that she will put into effect. The study shows that the determination of the optimum mental age and other factors in reading readiness is not so simple as some recent pronouncements seem to imply. It is impossible to set up, once and for all, a stipulated list of particular requirements for successful work in beginning reading in general. Reading is begun by very different materials, methods, and general procedures, some of which a pupil can master at the mental age of five with reasonable ease, others of which would give him difficulty at the mental age of seven. It is necessary for each teacher to determine what mental age, what background of previous experience, what special aptitudes her particular program requires.

Finally, it should be made clear that the results presented in this report do not answer the question: At what age is it best to introduce reading to pupils? Although the data seem to indicate that it is *possible* to organize materials and methods to teach children to learn to read at a mental age of 5.0 or higher, they do not, in any way, imply that it is *desirable* to do so. Decision on the optimum time of introducing reading to pupils must be based upon investigation of the value of this activity at different stages of development.

FACTORS DETERMINING SUCCESS AND FAILURE IN BEGINNING READING [1]

Arthur I. Gates and Guy L. Bond

[At least one critic of current reading instruction suggests that much of the effort to promote reading readiness is unnecessary. How much does a teacher need to know about children's facility with language, visual and auditory acuity, or motor coördination? Should any effort be devoted to developing readiness? Or will time take care of it all? Two well-known figures in the field of reading submit some suggestive data.]

This article is a partial report of a study of four large classes of children who were given instruction in reading soon after entering first grade. For each of these children, the results of more than one hundred tests, examinations, and ratings of characteristics alleged to be involved in readiness for reading or ability to learn to read were obtained as soon as possible after the opening of school. Although most of the tests and examinations were repeated at the middle and end of the school year, this preliminary report is concerned primarily with the relationships of the characteristics of the pupils when they entered

school and their achievements in reading during the year.

It should be pointed out that the study is not a comparison of the success of groups of children starting reading immediately upon entering the grade with that of others starting a term or a year later. It will not give a final answer to the question whether it is better, all things considered, to begin reading on entering school or after a term or a year or several years of school experience in a nonreading curriculum.

In the classes here reported, the age range on October 1 was from 5 years 7 months to 7 years 7 months, with a

[1] Adapted and abridged from Arthur I. Gates and Guy L. Bond, "Reading Readiness: A Study of Factors Determining Success and Failure in Beginning Reading," *Teachers College Record* (1936), 37:679–685.

median of 6 years 2 months. The range of Stanford-Binet IQ was from 80 to 130, median 98.6. The range in mental age was from 4 years 11 months to 7 years 8 months (a range of nearly three years), median 6 years 2 months. During the year the pupils were taught by regular teachers in New York City schools, using a textbook with several copies of supplementary material. The teaching was mostly mass instruction, with perhaps less than average attention to individual differences.

Correlations of mental age with reading achievements at the end of the year were about .25. When one studies the mental age from the lowest to the highest in relation to reading achievement, there appears no suggestion of a crucial or critical point above which very few fail and below which a relatively large proportion fail. The ten pupils who came nearest to failure are scattered from a point just above the lowest mental age to a point just below the highest mental age. The child with the lowest mental age in the group, 4 years 11 months, got along very well. The average mental age of the poorest group is 5 years 11 months, four months lower than the average mental age of the group as a whole.

Two pencil-and-paper readiness tests yielded fairly good correlations with reading achievement as a whole, better than Binet MA or IQ; but they were by no means invariably successful in indicating either the best or the poorest readers. For example, the average score of the pupils coming nearest to failure was only slightly below the average score of the group as a whole. Some of the pupils getting the lowest ratings on these tests learned to read quite well.

Tests of naming the letters in the alphabet, reading letters, matching or comparing words, looking at a word and recognizing it in a series of more or less familiar words which contained it, and other examinations which would reveal different degrees of familiarity with printed letters and words (totaling sixteen), tended in general to give fair correlations with ability to learn to read; but they were not perfectly successful in indicating the pupils who would have maximum difficulty. A series of examinations in learning to recognize real words, nonsense words, and geometrical figures give essentially similar results. The same is true of tests of oral abilities, such as repeating letter sounds, nonsense words, and so forth, as given, telling whether two words spoken in rapid succession were the same or different, guessing the letter which represented a particular letter sound, and the like. In tests of rhyming ability and phonetic aptitude, such as giving words which begin with a stated sound, as ca in cat, or giving words which rhyme with a sample offered, the pupils who were finally nearest failure differed little, if at all, from the others. Several auditory fusion or blending tests produced about the same results.

Very careful examinations of hearing at different pitches made and repeated by an expert with the 2A Audiometer tended to show a fairly clear difference. Although the correlation with hearing loss and final reading achievement was not very high, the pupils in the near-failing group showed an appreciably greater amount of hearing loss than did the group as a whole. In fact, six out of the ten were below the average in this respect, and three of the reading failures showed rather marked hearing loss.

The Betts Telebinocular Tests of Vision were applied on three different occasions. The correlation of scores on these tests and the final reading achievement was near zero. On certain tests, particularly the test of ametropia or astigmatism, there was, however, a somewhat greater number of low scores among the ten pupils doing poorest in reading than in the group as a whole. There was little difference in average acuity, although three of the failing children scored lower than 70 percent on the acuity chart.

Tests of hand and eye dominance, motor coördination, and speech defects showed nothing to differentiate the failing group from the whole group. Ratings by experienced examiners of the degree of foreignness in the speech revealed very slight differences between the groups. Tests were also made of the pupil's ability in oral composition, as in the case of a test which required the pupil to complete a story begun by the examiner. There was little correlation between the length of the compositions or the number of ideas contained in them, but there was a fairly high correlation between the general quality of the oral composition and success in learning to read.

Data gathered concerning the pupil's home background and previous schooling were judged independently by seven different judges on each of several factors, such as the general richness and educative possibilities of the social activities in the home, amount of time spent in miscellaneous activities, and so forth. There was a correlation between the amount of previous instruction in reading given at home or in kindergarten or elsewhere and success in reading, which was slightly greater than the correlation of MA and reading success. This finding in general confirmed the results of miscellaneous tests, such as recognition tests of amount of familiarity with printed letters and words which measured the effects of previous experience in reading. The fact that the reading readiness tests measure the effects of previous learning is one reason for their value.

In addition to studying the failing group as a whole, an analysis was made of all data obtained for each of the ten children. The records of four of these children revealed nothing in the way of constitutional handicaps, previous background, or other characteristics which could easily account for the failure in reading. Each of the other six cases showed one or more defects or deficiencies.

Certain children without constitutional limitations experience difficulty in learning, such as that which results from an insufficiency of material, failure to understand a particular direction or to acquire a particular technique or the development of inappropriate ones, failure to acquire certain lessons owing to absence or other causes, and other factors which come from inability of the teachers to keep a detailed daily account of each pupil's successes and difficulties. It might be argued that such factors were largely instrumental not only in the case of those who showed no constitutional limitations but in the case of those who did, as suggested by the fact that when a teacher took these pupils in hand and adjusted her instructions and materials to their needs everyone began to read very rapidly.

It is fairest perhaps to say that the source of the difficulty is often a combination of the two circumstances.

There is, of course, another possibility, namely, that the pupil's lack of reading readiness and constitutional limitations were expressions of immaturity and that the mere lapse of time would remove them. To obtain some data on this point, practically all the tests and examinations were given at the middle and at the end of the year as well as at the beginning. Some things, of course, such as mental age, amount of experience in working in school, listening to the teacher, handling educational tools, chronological age, and the like increased. In certain other respects, such as amount of hearing loss, no changes occurred. Some types of visual difficulties got worse; some remained the same; and certain ones, noticeably ametropia, as determined by the Betts test, got better. The fact that the children when taken in hand and taught in a program adjusted to their particular needs and difficulties improved rapidly inclines us to suspect that the same satisfactory results might have been secured earlier in the year.

The present experiment does not give conclusive evidence concerning the possibility that all these difficulties would be removed by delaying the beginning of reading for one or more terms. We believe that the data point to the likelihood that certain major difficulties would not be thus removed. The study emphasizes the importance of recognizing and adjusting to individual limitations and needs before and after the beginning of reading rather than merely changing the time of beginning.

It appears that readiness for reading is something to develop rather than something merely to wait for. Most teachers interested in a "reading readiness program" will, of course, declare that they do not merely wait; they engage actively in building readiness. Many of them will declare that they do not favor delaying the beginning of reading merely to secure older beginners but primarily to provide time for a preparatory period in which readiness and equipment of interests and skills for beginning are cultivated. The indication that success in reading was most closely correlated with symptoms of earlier preparation, as shown by tests of familiarity with printed words, pencil-and-paper reading readiness tests, and

so forth, affirms the soundness of this view. The fact that these correlations were not very high suggests that there is much yet to be learned concerning exactly what type of preparatory experiences are most effective. The problem of determining how long this period should be is as yet barely touched in experimental work. These issues comprise a fundamental problem in reading. Another problem of even greater importance remains to be considered.

The determination of the optimum time of beginning reading seems to be a problem of determining the maximum general and social returns from learning to read at any given time. We believe that investigations should be made to determine the time at which reading ability will be of more general, social, and educational value than other activities which would be pursued if reading were not taught. We believe that the reading program can be organized to enable children to learn to read at this time whatever it may be. This implies that the optimum time of beginning reading is not entirely dependent upon the nature of the child himself but in a large measure determined by the nature of the reading program. We think there is no ultimate justification for assuming that materials and methods of teaching must remain forever fixed as they are, waiting upon nature to change the child through maturity until he reaches a point at which he can proceed successfully. We think, on the other hand, that techniques and materials of reading can be adjusted to teach children successfully at the time when reading is, all things considered, of optimum value to them. At least, we think that to determine the best time to begin reading it is quite necessary to conduct investigations designed to produce the best possible adjustment of the program to the child beginning early or later, and not merely to determine children's success at different times of beginning in a standardized program. To do the latter may merely tell us how difficult the materials and methods are rather than when —all things, especially social and educational values, being considered—it is best for a child to learn to read. Although there is little to indicate that constitutional or physiological factors require a postponement of reading to later than the usual ages, there is evidence that physiological, especially sensory, handicaps may interfere with beginning reading at any time. The remedy is correction of the difficulties or adjustment to them rather than merely waiting for time to cure them. Preparation for reading consists in part in discovering and correcting or adjusting to various constitutional handicaps.

Chapter IV

LEARNING TO READ

The very complexity of the reading task has made the selection of appropriate teaching materials and teaching methods subject to long-standing contention. Indeed a survey of the history of reading instruction in America demonstrates how bitter the controversy has been in every era. Obviously disagreement has not always been based on complete information.

The goal of this chapter is to make the debate better informed, not of course to end the debate. The argument will not, and should not, be terminated until the processes of teaching and learning are known in unequivocal detail. This eventuality is not likely to be realized soon.

One persisting center of contention has been located in the process by which words are recognized. It was noted earlier that much of the research in linguistics and perception has yet to be applied to reading. Perhaps when it is, word recognition will become less of a battleground. It may be, for example, that the most acrid quarrels about the importance in word recognition of the system by which English represents the sounds of speech are beside the point. Meanwhile, some pertinent research data about "phonics" are available and are offered here.

An allied facet of word recognition concerns the number of words the reader shall be called upon to recognize. Prior to this century, measures taken to restrict vocabulary, especially for beginning readers, were not very systematic. For the most part whatever limitations a writer for young children imposed on himself were based on crude "trial and error" runs with child audiences or on his own unverified familiarity with children's language. In this century researchers began to try to establish what words might be considered "basic," or of highest utility, and how many should be introduced at succeeding levels of reading instruction. Some of this research is presented in a later chapter on what has come to be called "readability."

The research affected materials—stories, articles, practice exercises—prepared for teaching reading. Vocabulary was "controlled"; that is, only a certain number of new words were allowed to appear at a given level of instruction. Moreover, a rate of introduction page by page was established. Inevitably, debate immediately began about the extent to which vocabulary control should be practiced at any given level. In some cases it was even maintained that no limitation in vocabulary was necessary at all. But more often the position was taken that, while some adjustment in vocabulary to the maturity of the reader should be made, vocabulary control as commonly practiced was far too drastic.

In recent years another thesis has been advanced by the critics. In brief, it is this: Certainly vocabulary is an important element in regulating the difficulty of ideas and feelings but it is not the sole element. The idea or feeling itself can be complex even when couched in a few simple words. The favorite illustration is Hamlet's statement: "To be or not to be, that is the question." The vocabulary is clearly controlled, but the difficulty of the idea escapes the control. What is needed in reading materials, according to these critics, is intensive research on succeeding levels of difficulty in the quality of ideas and feelings being presented, as well as some measure of vocabulary control. Research in this chapter indicates the beginnings that have been made to attempt to reduce the conflict.

Another concomitant of the increasing recognition of the subtlety of the reading process is the increasing paraphernalia that reading instruction has accreted. Publishers surround the books in a series designed for reading instruction with records, motion pictures, filmstrips, charts, slides, cards, cutouts, and practice exercises. It is the practice exercise material, the so-called "workbook," which attracts the handsomest acrimony. One point of view asserts that the workbook only provides "isolated drill" or "busywork." Usually it is claimed by those who make this assertion that the teacher herself can devise better practice work designed especially for the individual. Another position holds that the whole idea of practice in the several skills of word recognition and comprehension is an abomination. All that is necessary, this group believes, is to "read, read, read." Research on the uses of the workbook is not extensive. One example is included in this chapter.

All these disagreements about materials and methods for teaching reading have been caught up in one larger dissension which has affected the whole of education in America. There are various names for the differences of opinion and certainly there are many facets. But in reading instruction, the disagreement has focused on how much materials and methods of teaching can be preplanned. The issue is: Can an orderly progression of learning tasks be prescribed in detail and in advance with appropriate materials and methods, or must the learning tasks as well as materials and methods be determined from day to day, and hour to hour, based on an assessment of emerging "needs" of children? Semantic difficulties immediately arise over such terms as "orderly progression" and "emerging needs of children." One piece of research is included in this chapter to illustrate what kind of further study may be appropriate.

HOW USEFUL ARE PHONICS IN READING? [1]

Donald C. Agnew

[Agnew's study of the usefulness of phonetic training in increasing ability to read is quoted far and wide. Oddly enough, it is quoted both by those who favor more phonetic training and by those who say quite enough is already provided. Each reader must decide for himself which side, if either, the study in fact supports.]

PROBLEM

This investigation was an effort to determine the effects of varied amounts of phonetic training on certain reading abilities as measured by a battery of tests.

The history of phonetic instruction is one of inconsistency and controversy. Below are summarized some of the arguments for and against phonetic training.

IN FAVOR OF PHONETICS

1. Phonetic training has been used in the teaching of reading for a century and should be scrutinized carefully before being abandoned.

2. Phonetic training gives the pupils independence in recognizing words previously learned.

3. Phonetic training aids in "unlocking" new words by giving the pupil a method of sound analysis.

4. Phonetic training encourages correct pronunciation and enunciation.

5. Phonetic training gives valuable "ear training" in recognizing and differentiating sounds.

6. Phonetic training improves the quality of oral reading—for instance, in breath control and in speech coördination.

7. Phonetic training improves spelling.

8. Many cases of reading disability may be traced to deficiencies in word recognition and sound analysis.

[1] Abridged and condensed from Donald C. Agnew, *The Effect of Varied Amounts of Phonetic Training in Primary Reading,* Duke University Research Studies in Education, No. 5, Duke University Press, Durham, N.C., 1939.

9. These disabilities are often overcome by remedial procedures involving phonetic training.

THE CASE AGAINST PHONETICS

1. Phonetic training tends to isolate words from their meaningful function by emphasizing sound.

2. Phonetic training tends to lead to the neglect of context clues.

3. Phonetic training tends to sacrifice interest in the content of reading.

4. Phonetic training leads to unnecessarily laborious recognition of familiar words.

5. Phonetic training is impractical because of the nonphonetic character of English.

6. Phonetic training is unnecessary for many pupils since its advantages can be obtained without formal training.

7. Phonetic training encourages the breaking of words into unnecessarily small units.

8. Phonetic training tends to emphasize too explicit articulation.

The claims and objections listed above are inferences based largely on a priori considerations. Perhaps phonetic training is neither as bad as one group claims nor as good as the other group insists.

The study specifically attempted to answer these questions:

a. What is the comparative effect of phonetic and nonphonetic reading instructions on speed and comprehension in silent reading?

b. What are the effects of phonetic and nonphonetic training on speed and accuracy in oral reading?

c. What is the effect on eye-voice span in oral reading?

d. What are the effects of phonetic and nonphonetic training on reading vocabulary?

e. Does or does not phonetic instruction actually result in greater abilities to use phonetic methods?

PROCEDURES

The procedures fall logically into three parts: (1) those used to secure data on the pupils' phonetic experience, (2) those employed in testing, and (3) those involved in treating the results.

PUPILS' PHONETIC EXPERIENCE

Data were obtained through a Pupils' Blank and a Teachers' Blank.

The Pupils' Blank showed the schools and teachers each pupil had during the first three grades and a phonetic-experience score for each grade obtained from the Teachers' Blank.

The Teachers' Blanks were secured for all teachers who had taught in the first three grades during the immediately preceding three years. A blank was filled out for each year. The Teachers' Blank was composed of twenty-five questions, each of which had four possible answers. For instance, Item 6 read as follows: "With respect to consonant blends (tr, bl, st, etc.) I teach children (a) a very great many, (b) all the common ones, (c) only a few of the most common, (d) none at all as such." For purposes of scoring, (a) was here given a weight of 4, (b) a weight of 3, (c) a weight of 2, and (d) a weight of 1. These twenty-five item scores, therefore, constituted a scale with a possible range of 25 to 100.

It is important to note the facts represented in the scores in the Teachers' Blanks. A teacher's reaction to a single item may be no index to that teacher's general practice with respect to phonetics, but her reactions to the sum of twenty-five such items very probably do represent her instructional procedure. Differences in teachers' scores may, therefore, be taken to indicate differences in their practices.

The scores obtained from the Teachers' Blanks were transferred to the Pupils' Blanks to yield a quantitative measure of the pupils' phonetic experience.

THE TESTING PROGRAM

Group tests of silent reading abilities (Gates Silent Reading Test: Types A, B, C, and D) and vocabulary (Pressey Diagnostic Test: Vocabulary—Grades 1A–3A) and individual tests of oral reading (Gray Oral Check Tests: Sets II and III), word pronunciation (Gates Graded Word Pronunciation Test: Form II), eye-voice span (a test patterned after the Buswell Eye-Voice Span Test), and phonetic abilities (Gates Tests for Phonic Abilities: A4, A5, B2, B3) were administered. A group intelligence test (Otis Intelligence Scale) was also given. The tests were administered by the investigator and his assistants.

THE TREATMENT OF THE RESULTS

Groups of pupils were compared in terms of the scores made on various tests. The methods of comparison will be described later.

LOCALE OF THE STUDIES

One study was made in Raleigh, North Carolina, where it was supposed to be the policy not to teach by phonetic methods, and a second study in Durham, North Carolina, (1) in order to check the results obtained in Raleigh and (2) in order to provide new data on the effects of larger and more consistent amounts of phonetic experiences than those found in Raleigh.

DATA COLLECTED IN RALEIGH

Data were collected on 230 pupils in the third grade. These pupils had had all of their school training in the Raleigh schools. The pupils had all made normal progress in school; that is, they had been neither retarded nor accelerated.

DISTRIBUTION OF SCORES ON TEACHERS' BLANKS

The distribution of scores on the Teachers' Blanks is given in Table 1, which should be interpreted as follows:

TABLE 1.   Distribution of Scores on Teachers' Blanks by Grades

Scores on Blanks	Frequencies by Grades Grade 1	Grade 2	Grade 3	All Grades
75–79	0	1	1	2
70–74	0	3	1	4
65–69	2	3	0	5
60–64	7	3	3	13
55–59	3	0	3	6
50–54	0	2	2	4
45–49	1	2	1	4
40–44	8	6	5	19
35–39	0	1	2	3
30–34	3	3	2	8
Total	24	24	20	68

No teacher in the first grade taught phonetics to the extent represented by a score between 75 and 79. One teacher in Grade 2 and one in Grade 3 taught phonetics to this extent.

Since it was supposed to be the policy in Raleigh schools not to teach by phonetic methods, it is interesting to note the wide variation in scores. The scores range from between 30 and 35 to between 75 and 80. Thus, the scores represent a range of 45 points out of a possible 75. The extreme upper range of possible scores, from 79 to 100, is not represented in the distribution of scores.

DISTRIBUTION OF TOTAL PHONETIC-EXPERIENCE SCORES

Table 2 represents the distribution of the total phonetic experience scores for the 230 pupils. Each total score is the sum of the scores for each of five

TABLE 2. Distribution of Total Phonetic-Experience Scores
(3A Pupils in Raleigh)

Score	Frequency
340–349	10
330–339	0
320–329	9
310–319	18
300–309	15
290–299	21
280–289	20
270–279	15
260–269	26
250–259	15
240–249	2
230–239	3
220–229	9
210–219	13
200–209	4
190–199	15
180–189	2
170–179	22
160–169	11
Total	230
Median	267

half-grades (Grades 1A and 1B, 2A and 2B, and 3B). The lowest possible score a teacher could give was 25. Thus the lowest possible phonetic-experience score was 125. Likewise, since the highest possible score was 100, the highest possible total phonetic-experience score was 500.

The range of the scores was found to be from 160 to 349. The upper ranges of the distribution which represent extremely large amounts of phonetic experience contain no scores. Nevertheless the distribution indicates a considerable variation in amounts of phonetic experience.

TREATMENT OF THE RALEIGH DATA

The pupils were divided into groups representing different amounts of phonetic training and compared in terms of tests of reading abilities. Two methods were used for this purpose: (1) comparison of groups based on the total phonetic-experience scores and (2) comparisons of patterns of phonetic experience, the different patterns representing different amounts of training at different times in the pupil's school experience.

COMPARISON BASED ON TOTAL PHONETIC-EXPERIENCE SCORES

Comparison of the scores on the tests of reading ability between pupils who had experienced large amounts of phonetic training and pupils who had experienced little phonetc training was made possible by a process involving three steps. (1) Pupils with total phonetic-experience scores below 230 were included in a low group and pupils with scores above 290 were included in a high group. This method yielded 89 pupils in the low group and 86 pupils in the high group, and omitted 55 in the middle of the distribution. (2) Pupils in the high and low groups were paired in terms of MA and IQ. Cases that could not be suitably paired were dropped. The resulting matched groups each included 43 pupils. The range of MA was from 80 to 134 in terms of months with a mean of 112.04 and a sigma of 10 for both groups. The range of IQ was from 80 to 129 with a mean of 107.5 and a sigma of 10.15 for the high group and a mean of 108.08 and a sigma of 10.2 for the low group. (3) The scores of these matched groups on tests of reading ability were compared.

COMPARISONS OF PATTERNS OF PHONETIC EXPERIENCE

The gross scores give equal values to phonetic experiences at different grade levels. This method may yield measures so coarse that they obscure important differences. There may be, for example, a critical point in the child's educational experience that is particularly propitious for phonetic instruction. In order to bring out the effects of phonetic in-

struction at different grade levels, another method of treating the data was necessary.

The method was as follows: (1) Each grade was divided into "phonetic," "medium," and "nonphonetic" groups; (2) the medium group was omitted, and (3) the "phonetic" and the "nonphonetic" groups were equated with respect to the sum of the phonetic-experience scores for the other two grades. To illustrate, the derivation of one pair of patterns is described.

Derivation of Patterns Ap and An. To measure the effects of varying amounts of phonetic experience in Grade 1, the amounts in Grades 2 and 3 had to remain constant. Meanwhile, Grade 1 was divided into phonetic and nonphonetic groups. The possible range of phonetic-experience scores for the two half-grades of Grade 1 was from 50 to 200. Eighty cases with scores above 120 were selected for the phonetic group and 111 cases with scores below 90 for the nonphonetic group.

TABLE 3. Distributions of Phonetic Experience Scores for Grades 2 and 3 Combined Before and After Equating

Scores	Initial Distribution		Equated Distribution	
	Ap	An	Ap	An
200–209	14	8	8	8
190–199	15	1	4	1
180–189	6	1	6	1
170–179	2	23	2	22
160–169	14	3	11	2
150–159	14	9	12	7
140–149	2	0	1	0
130–139	1	2	1	2
120–129	11	13	7	9
110–119	0	15	0	0
100–109	1	24	0	0
90–99	0	11	0	0
80–89	0	1	0	0
N	80	111	52	52
Mean			167.1	166.9
Σ			26.1	25.5

In order to keep consistent the amounts of phonetic training in Grades 2 and 3, the two groups, phonetic and nonphonetic, were equated in terms of their phonetic-experience scores in these two grades. Two distributions were made of the scores for Grades 2 and 3, one for the phonetic group and the other for the nonphonetic group. In Table 3 the distributions are shown as "initial." New distributions were then obtained by elimination from one group or the other until nearly equivalent means and standard deviations were secured. In the table below these distributions are shown as "equated."

The phonetic group in Grade 1 was called Ap and the nonphonetic group An. Groups in other grades were given similar descriptions.

Other Patterns. In all, six patterns were isolated in this manner. Table 4 indicates in what grades the phonetic experience was varied and in what grades it was kept constant.

Table 4 may be read as follows: Pattern An consists of all the cases having a phonetic score below 90 in the first grade that could be equated with cases in pattern Ap, which consists of those who had a phonetics score in the first grade of more than 120. Equating was

TABLE 4. Distributions of Equated Groups

Pattern	Limits	Grades in Which Phonetics Varied	Constant Grades (Amount of Phonetics Equated)	N	Mean	Standard Deviation
An	90 and below	1	2 and 3	52	167.1	26.1
Ap	120 and above	1	2 and 3	52	166.9	25.5
Bn	90 and below	2	1 and 3	50	136.2	22.1
Bp	120 and above	2	1 and 3	50	136.2	21.2
Cn	42 and below	3	1 and 2	45	228.3	18.7
Cp	50 and above	3	1 and 2	45	229.3	20.0
Dn	130 and below	2 and 3	1	56	90.5	20.8
Dp	165 and above	2 and 3	1	56	90.4	20.5
En	129 and below	1 and 3	2	53	107.9	26.3
Ep	165 and above	1 and 3	2	53	108.4	27.3
Fn	195 and below	1 and 2	3	47	40.7	7.6
Fp	230 and above	1 and 2	3	47	40.9	7.4

done on the basis of the sum of the phonetics scores for Grades 2 and 3. The number of cases in An (and Ap) is 52, the mean is 167.1, and the standard deviation is 26.1.

COMPARISON OF TOTAL PHONETIC EXPERIENCE AND PATTERNS OF PHONETIC EXPERIENCE IN TERMS OF SCORES ON READING TESTS

The high and low total phonetic-experience groups were compared by cal-

culating the differences between the means of the reading-test scores.

Differences between each pair of patterns (in terms of the differences between the means of the scores of the various tests) were similarly calculated except that in these cases the usual formula for the critical ratio was used.

CONCLUSIONS FROM RALEIGH DATA

Before considering the results obtained in Raleigh, factors that might have influenced test scores will be considered.

1. *Lack of Homogeneity of Subjects in Age, School Experience, Etc.* All pupils selected had made normal progress, were in the same grade, and lived in the same city, where they had received all of their school experience.

2. *Biased Sampling of Schools and Teachers.* The pupils came from nine different schools. Each group or pattern was composed of pupils from at least four different schools, and in many cases from as many as six or seven schools. Because of this wide sampling, the chances are against having a difference which is due to peculiar excellences or deficiencies of teachers.

3. *Differences in Intelligence of Groups Compared.* It is unlikely that the small differences in intelligence

found between the groups compared could have been responsible, to any great extent, for the differences in test scores.

4. *Differences in Methods of Testing.* The methods were under the same supervision throughout the schools; and there is no reason to believe that the methods were causative in producing the differences in test scores.

5. *Differences in Instructional Material.* Since all schools were in the same system, there is no reason to believe materials varied significantly or, if they did, tended to favor one group more than another.

Table 5 summarizes the Raleigh data. The following are interpretive comments on the summary table.

1. *Influence of Phonetic Experience in Test Scores of Phonetic Ability.* The

TABLE 5. Summary of the Differences in Terms of the PE of the Differences [a]

| Tests | G | Groups and Patterns | | | | | |
		A (1)	B (2)	C (3)	D (2–3)	E (1–3)	F (1–2)[b]
Gates A4	1.66	.42	2.15	.71	−1.68	4.56	−2.53
Gates A5	−.84	1.12	.52	1.36	−1.15	.34	−3.69
Gates B2	1.22	−.21	.34	−1.25	−.96	1.88	−3.97
Gates B3	3.02	1.27	.75	−1.88	−.26	6.41	−5.74
Gates Word Pronunciation	−2.40	−.85	1.21	1.79	2.30	1.98	−3.72
Gates Type A	−2.50	1.68	−.89	1.22	−1.82	1.18	−8.49
Gates Type B	−2.73	−.04	−.75	.15	−3.17	1.98	−5.72
Gates Type C	−1.92	−1.40	−.61	.16	−.49	2.84	−6.35
Gates Type D	−.87	−1.23	.39	−.75	−1.35	−2.83	−6.63
Pressey Vocabulary	.12	−.26	−.90	2.03	−1.33	−8.25	3.73
Gray II (errors)	.30	−1.16	1.02	−.91	.15	1.32	−3.54
Gray III (errors)	1.43	−1.16	2.10	.48	1.40	2.55	−5.13
Gray II (time)	−.32	−.80	2.46	−.00	1.60	1.50	−3.20
Gray III (time)	.85	−.33	2.46	.02	2.11	4.52	−5.17
Eye-Voice Span	1.68	1.22	.89	1.95	−.09	3.54	−3.53
Mean	−.08	.00	.65	.33	.18	1.56	−4.17

[a] Negative differences favor the nonphonetic groups.
[b] Numbers in this row represent grades of variation.

differences that are statistically reliable, as shown in the table, are consistent for each pair of patterns, as far as the four

Gates tests are concerned, but inconsistent between patterns. Thus, the two reliable differences between the E patterns favor the phonetic group while the differences between the F patterns favor the nonphonetic group. The apparent inconsistency casts doubt on the significance of the difference obtained.

2. *Influence on Word Pronunciation.* A comparison of the high and low groups on total phonetic experience reveals a small difference in favor of the nonphonetic group. A comparison of the various patterns of phonetic experience reveals: (a) phonetic training in Grade 1 seems to have a slight detrimental effect on word pronunciation ability; (b) phonetic training in Grade 2 seems to result in a slight increase of ability to pronounce words; (c) phonetic training in Grade 3 has a slightly greater tendency to increase ability to pronounce words; (d) the differences show a general lack of reliability.

3. *Influence on Silent Reading Abilities.* In the comparison of the patterns in terms of the results from Gates Silent Reading Tests, Types A, B, C, and D, five differences appear that are greater than three times the PE of the difference. All of these favor the nonphonetic groups, one favoring pattern Dn, and four pattern Fn. The difference in the case of the D patterns (for Type B) may not be significant because it is not supported by the other measures of silent reading ability (Types A, C, D), but the large and consistent differences favoring the nonphonetic group in the F patterns appear to be more significant. If this is the case, it may be concluded that there is some evidence that large amounts of phonetic training in Grades 1 and 2 are not so advantageous to silent reading abilities (as measured by these tests).

4. *Influence on Vocabulary.* In the comparisons of patterns in terms of the Pressey test, one large difference appears to favor the nonphonetic group in the E patterns, and one fairly large difference appears to favor the phonetic group in the F patterns. It is possible that the phonetic group in pattern E was so accustomed to the phonetic attack on unfamiliar words that much time was taken in analyzing the nonsense words of the Pressey test. If this is true, the test may not have measured the actual vocabulary of the pupils in this group. However, if this were the case, there should be some evidence of this phenomenon in the comparisons of the C patterns in which phonetic training in the third grade is isolated. Unreliable differences between the C patterns favor the phonetic group. The C patterns and the F patterns are thus seen to be inconsistent with the E patterns. This inconsistency tends to reflect doubt on the significance of the differences obtained.

5. *Influence on Oral Reading.* In the comparisons of the patterns with respect to speed and accuracy on the Gray Oral Reading Check Tests (Gray II and III) there are five reliable differences. One, in the E patterns, favors the phonetic group in the speed of reading (Set III). The fact that the other differences between the E patterns on both speed and accuracy are unreliable casts doubt on the significance of the one difference found. Reliable differences are found to favor the nonphonetic F pattern as opposed to the phonetic F pattern in both the measures of speed and accuracy. However, no other comparisons bear out these conclusions, and again the differences seem to be of doubtful significance.

6. *Influence on Eye-Voice Span.* The test of eye-voice span is of questionable validity because it was necessarily short and seemed, in many cases, to involve too difficult reading material. On the other hand, although the instrument was somewhat crude, it was hoped that it might show extreme differences

in eye-voice span (if they existed). The results in no case present differences as great as four times the PE of the difference. Small differences appear within the E pattern and within the F pattern. These differences are in opposite directions so that they are of questionable significance.

7. *Influence on Battery of Tests as a Whole.* The foregoing table presents an average of all the differences. This is, of course, a crude method of summary because it is impossible to say how the tests should be weighted. Also, any isolated reliable differences are obscured by being averaged with differences of small reliability. Yet these averages may aid in bringing out some general characteristics of the table as a whole.

a. Perhaps the most striking feature of these averages, and, in fact, of the comparisons as a whole, is the paucity of reliable differences. (1) Not a single difference as great as four times the PE of the difference appears in the comparison of groups on the basis of total phonetic experience. Only one difference (Gates B3) is as great as three times the PE of the difference. (2) In the comparison of phonetic and nonphonetic groups in patterns A, B, and C only five are as great as three times the PE of the difference. (3) In the D pattern (phonetic emphasis varied in Grades 2 and 3) only one difference is as great as three times the PE of the difference. (4) In the E pattern (phonetic emphasis varied in Grades 1 and 3) five differences are as great as three times the PE of the difference, and, of those, four favor the phonetic and one the nonphonetic. Thus, in the above comparison there is no consistent evidence that the differences in phonetic training affected the test scores appreciably.

b. Only in the case of the comparisons of the F patterns (phonetic emphasis varied in Grades 1 and 2) do differences appear consistently reliable. (1) With but one exception the differences are as great as three times the PE of the difference. (2) All but one of these differences (that in vocabulary) favor the nonphonetic groups. This is true even in the phonetic tests. (3) The average of these differences is 4.17 PE. It would seem that the comparison of the F pattern in terms of the battery of reading tests presents rather consistent evidence that phonetic experience (in the first two grades) is not so beneficial to reading abilities, as measured by the tests, as is nonphonetic experience.

c. The inner consistency of the differences found in the E pattern (phonetic experience varied in Grades 1 and 3) suggests that these differences have some significance. If the difference favoring the nonphonetic group in the vocabulary test is omitted and the average of the other differences computed, the resultant mean is 2.35. This difference seems to indicate a fairly adequate advantage on the part of the phonetic group.

GENERAL CONCLUSIONS FROM RALEIGH DATA

1. The comparisons made failed to reveal a significant advantage or disadvantage (in terms of reading-test scores) arising from different amounts of phonetic experience as measured by the Total Phonetic Experience Scores.

2. The effort to find a critical grade in which phonetic experience is particularly effective for training in reading was unsuccessful.

3. There seems to be a tendency for large amounts of phonetic experience in Grades 1 and 2 (as is indicated in the F patterns) to affect the reading abilities adversely.

4. The direction of the differences

found in the E patterns suggests that large amounts of phonetic experience in Grades 1 and 3 are beneficial to most of the reading abilities measured.

DATA COLLECTED IN DURHAM

Two schools were selected with two criteria in mind: pupils with large amounts of phonetic training and pupils comparable in ability and background to those studied in Raleigh.

The Teachers' Blanks were again used to secure total phonetic-experience scores for 110 third-grade pupils who had made regular progress and had received all three years of training in the selected schools. It was possible to obtain phonetic-experience scores for all three years for all 110 pupils.

DISTRIBUTION OF SCORES ON TEACHERS' BLANKS

Table 6 shows that pupils had received consistently large amounts of phonetic training. When it is recalled that, in Raleigh, no total phonetic-experience scores excelled 350, and only a few exceeded 320, it is clear that the Durham pupils had received considerably more phonetic instruction.

TABLE 6. Frequency Distribution of Total Phonetic Experience Scores (110 Cases, Durham)

Score	Frequency
390–399	20
380–389	0
370–379	90
Total	110

TEST DATA

The same battery of tests previously administered in Raleigh was given in Durham by assistants of the investigator and under comparable conditions.

TREATMENT OF RESULTS

Raleigh pupils with low total phonetic-experience scores (160–270) were paired with Durham pupils with high total phonetic-experience scores (370–400) on the basis of MA's and nearly equivalent IQ's. The 89 pupils paired in no case differed more than two months in MA's or more than eight points in IQ's.

Table 7 presents the results of the comparison.

Comparison on Phonetic Tests. The comparative scores on the four phonetic tests indicate a definite superiority on the part of the Durham group. In every case the difference between the means is reliable.

Comparison on Word Pronunciation. The Durham pupils obtained much higher scores than the Raleigh pupils. The difference is more than eight times the PE of the difference.

Comparison on Silent Reading. In the table the test scores have been reduced to grade equivalents. The differences are the smallest of all comparisons. In Types A and B (Reading to Appreciate General Significance, and Reading to Predict Outcomes) no reliable difference appears. In Type C (Reading to Understand Directions), a small reliable difference favors Durham. A somewhat less reliable difference favors Durham in Type D (Reading to Note Details).

Comparison on Speed and Accuracy in Silent Reading. The data show no consistent evidence that large amounts of phonetics make silent reading slower but more accurate as in the case of oral reading.

Comparison on Vocabulary. A dif-

TABLE 7. Differences Between the Raleigh and Durham Groups in Terms of the Differences Between the Means of the Test Scores (89 Cases in Each Group)

Test	Group [a]	Mean	Difference Between Means [b]	PE of Differences [c]	Critical Ratio
Gates A4	D	79.50			
	R	63.31	16.19	1.61	10.05
Gates A5	D	32.17			
	R	23.85	8.32	1.17	7.11
Gates B2	D	29.29			
	R	18.11	11.18	.93	12.02
Gates B3	D	15.20			
	R	9.29	5.91	.70	8.44
Word Pronunciation	D	70.17			
	R	53.15	17.02	1.92	8.86
Gates Type A	D	4.08			
	R	4.03	.5	.09	.55
Gates Type B	D	4.18			
	R	4.18	.00	.11	.00
Gates Type C	D	4.61			
	R	4.11	.50	.12	4.16
Gates Type D	D	4.38			
	R	4.15	.23	.08	2.87
Pressey Vocabulary	D	71.85			
	R	59.26	12.57	1.21	10.39
Gray Set II (errors)	D	2.35			
	R	8.79	6.44	.76	8.47
Gray Set III (errors)	D	7.05			
	R	17.50	10.45	.83	12.54
Gray Set II (time)	D	73.04			
	R	38.78	−40.26	2.34	17.20
Gray Set III (time)	D	77.48			
	R	52.87	−26.61	3.09	8.61
Eye-Voice Span	D	37.94			
	R	31.69	6.25	.64	9.76

[a] D and R refer to Durham and Raleigh respectively.

[b] Negative differences favor the Raleigh group.

[c] The Lindquist formula for matched groups was used to determine the PE of the difference.

ference of more than ten times the PE of the difference favors Durham.

Comparison on Oral Reading. Raleigh pupils made considerably more errors but read more rapidly. Durham pupils appear to be slower but more accurate. The differences in all cases are statistically reliable.

Comparison on Eye-Voice Span. Durham is favored by a difference of more than nine times the PE of the difference.

GENERAL CONCLUSION OF THE STUDY

Earlier the arguments for and against phonetic training were summarized. The study supports arguments that phonetic training in large amounts (1) increases independence in recognizing words previously learned, (2) aids in "unlocking" new words, (3) encourages correct pronunciation, and (4) improves the quality of oral reading. No evidence on the other arguments in favor of phonetic training was provided.

There was no evidence that large consistent amounts of phonetic training tend: (1) to sacrifice interest in the content, (2) to result in the neglect of context clues, (3) to result in unnecessarily laborious recognition of unfamiliar words, and (4) to be unnecessary because the advantages attributed to phonetic training might be obtained without formal training. Some positive evidence indicated too that (5) phonetic training does not narrow the eye-voice span.

On the other hand, there are some data to show that large amounts of phonetic training tend to slow up oral reading. This is, in a sense, counteracted by greater accuracy in oral reading.

There was no evidence that phonetic training decreases efficiency in silent reading. This may be due to the fact that speed in silent reading is largely acquired in the grades above the primary level. Further investigation would be necessary to determine the effects of this early training on silent reading in the advanced grades.

WORKBOOKS, VOCABULARY CONTROL, PHONICS, AND OTHER FACTORS IN BEGINNING READING [1]

Arthur I. Gates and David H. Russell

[It is no accident that the name of Arthur I. Gates appears repeatedly in a book on research in the "three R's." Gates has had a lasting effect on the methodology of reading instruction. At the time this investigation was made, David H. Russell was Gates' pupil. Now, of course, Russell has stature in his own right in the field of reading. Gates and Russell attacked three questions which continue to plague teachers of reading: (1) What are the effects of large amounts of "workbook" material? (2) How beneficial is vocabulary restriction on early reading instruction? (3) Are "informal" methods of word analysis as effective as large amounts of drill in phonetics?]

PROBLEM

This article describes the results of an effort to evaluate the effects of several factors on the acquisition of reading

ability in the beginning stages. It is based on data obtained from 354 pupils out of a total population of 382, comprising nine classes in four schools in New York City. The pupils were fairly

[1] Adapted and abridged from Arthur I. Gates and David H. Russell, "Types of Materials, Vocabulary Burden, Word Analysis, and Other Factors in Beginning Reading," *Elementary School Journal* (1939), 39:27–35, 119–128.

representative of the population of New York City. The distribution of intelligence was approximately the mean given in the test manuals. The classes were mainly large. For most comparisons of data, the groups were equated on the basis of mental age, mainly obtained from group tests, and scores on the Metropolitan Readiness Tests,[2] which were given by the investigators in late September, 1936, about a month after the opening of schools.

In all the classes the pupils used as basal material the Gates-Huber primer[3] and the accompanying *Preparatory Book* —a loose-leaf workbook of ninety-six pages. When consideration is given to the results presented later, it must be recalled that the use of these materials was common to all classes and that other activities and materials were additional.

Classes were obtained in which practices ordinarily varied or in which teachers agreed to effect certain variations during the course of the study. In this way it became possible to determine, with reasonable validity, the effects of differences in the total size of the reading vocabulary, in the type of material read, in the amount of work-type material employed, in the amount and character of "phonics" or word analysis and word-study games, and in other features of the total program.

PROCEDURES

EFFECTS OF A LARGE ADDITIONAL
AMOUNT OF "WORKBOOK" MATERIAL

The Gates-Huber primer and the ninety-six-page *Preparatory Book* include

[2] *Metropolitan Readiness Tests,* World Book Co., Yonkers, N.Y.
[3] Arthur I. Gates and Miriam Blanton Huber, The Work-Play Books: *Peter and Peggy* (Primer), The Macmillan Company, New York, 1930.

292 different words. The two books contain 9356 running words, or approximately thirty-two running words for every different word. One factor studied was the effect of adding a large quantity of material similar to that in the *Preparatory Book.*

This supplementary practice material consisted of 173 mimeographed pages, 8½ by 11 inches in size, containing approximately 18,000 running words. These pages were of the following types: miscellaneous exercises in sentence reading and word recognition, 5 percent; directions to draw, color, etc., without any accompanying story or selection— that is, mainly sentence reading—5 percent; short selections with a picture (line drawing) and directions to color the picture, 10 percent; reading selections followed by comprehension exercises, 10 percent; and reading selections followed by comprehension exercises and directions to color the picture, 70 percent.

The supplementary practice materials were regarded by most observers as being less attractive in format and less attractive in content than the printed, basal practice book.

Three classes, totaling 138 pupils, used the materials, and four classes, totaling 157 pupils, served as control groups. The latter used the same printed basal materials but not the mimeographed matter. In each school an effort was made to secure, for experimental and control groups, classes which had about the same scores on intelligence and reading-readiness tests and which were handled by teachers of equal ability.

Analysis of the data by classes showed several variables other than the experimental factor. The classes differed in size (from thirty-six to fifty, four containing from forty-eight to fifty pupils), in proportions of boys and girls, in intelligence, and in scores on the readiness tests. When medians of the nine classes were used as the data, it was found that a coefficient of .65 existed between the scores on the reading-readiness test and scores on the final reading achievement tests (given in February), .057 between mental age and reading status, and −.017 between class size and reading achievement. The girls exceeded the boys in reading achievement by about .07 of a reading grade. These data led to the elimination of all comparisons of total classes. Instead, from the total groups were selected two smaller groups as nearly as possible equivalent in the following respects: (1) mental age, (2) intelligence quotient, (3) score on Metropolitan Reading Tests, and (4) proportion of boys and girls. We also secured approximately the same numbers in the groups from each school using the supplementary material and from classes of similar size. The final "supplementary group" contained 85 from the original 138 pupils; the "no-supplementary group," 82 from the original 157 pupils. In Table 1 the groups are reclassified according to score on the reading-readiness test, and the results are shown for these subgroups and for the "supplementary" and the "no-supplementary" groups as a whole.

The data for the entire groups show that the large amount of work-type or practice materials (in addition to the primer and the ninety-six-page *Preparatory Book*) produced no reliably greater achievement in reading during the first semester. Although all the differences are in favor of the groups using the supplementary mimeographed material, the differences are too unreliable to be taken as "significant." It should be noted that the reading attainments for both groups were very good for the time of the year

at which they were tested. The national normal for the Gates test at the time is a grade score of approximately 1.52; the four means for the present groups (1.74, 1.72, 1.71, and 1.70) are about two-tenths of a grade better. The mean reading grade based on all scores available for the entire population taking the final tests (354 children) was 1.68—slightly lower than the means of the two matched groups but nearly two-tenths of a grade above the norm.

Further study of the data showed that the effect of using the supplementary mimeographed material differed with the ability of the pupils. This fact is shown by the data in Table 1, which give the records for pupils in three classifications of high, intermediate, and low scores on the readiness tests. These data show that the reading abilities of the three groups corresponded, in general, to the mean scores on the first-grade readiness tests.

The data also show that the large amount of mimeographed material gave no advantage to the group with the highest readiness scores. Indeed, the difference between the scores on the Gates tests favored the control group not using the mimeographed materials.

In the case of the pupils with intermediate reading readiness the scores of those who used the additional materials show practically no advantage in the Gates tests and some superiority in the tests confined to the vocabulary of the basal materials.

In the low reading-readiness group no advantage for the supplementary material is shown by the standardized tests, and the slight superiority in the tests based on the vocabulary of the basal materials lacks satisfactory statistical reliability.

In the case of the results presented, several considerations should be noted.

Classification	Group Using Supplementary Material	Group Not Using Supplementary Material	Difference in Favor of Group Using Supplementary Material
Number of cases			
Reading-readiness scores of 85 and above	26	24	—
Reading-readiness scores of 70–84	31	29	—
Reading-readiness scores below 70	28	29	—
Entire group	85	82	—
Mean mental age (in months)			
Reading-readiness scores of 85 and above	83.4	83.3	0.1
Reading-readiness scores of 70–84	74.2	73.6	0.6
Reading-readiness scores below 70	63.8	65.4	−1.6
Entire group	73.8	74.1	−0.3
Mean score on Metropolitan Readiness Tests (Sept., 1936)			
Reading-readiness scores of 85 and above	93.2	93.3	−0.1
Reading-readiness scores of 70–84	78.4	78.8	−0.4
Reading-readiness scores below 70	52.5	52.2	.3
Entire group	74.4	74.5	−0.1
Mean reading grade on Gates Primary Reading Test, Type 1, Word Recognition (Feb., 1937) [a]			
Reading-readiness scores of 85 and above	1.82	1.92	−0.10
Reading-readiness scores of 70–84	1.80	1.78	.02
Reading-readiness scores below 70	1.63	1.60	.03
Entire group	1.74	1.71	.03
Mean reading grade on Gates Primary Reading Test, Type 3, Paragraph Reading (Feb., 1937) [a]			
Reading-readiness scores of 85 and above	1.75	1.81	−.06

TABLE 1.   (Continued)

Classification	Group Using Supplementary Material	Group Not Using Supplementary Material	Difference in Favor of Group Using Supplementary Material
Reading-readiness scores of 70–84	1.73	1.67	.06
Reading-readiness scores below 70	1.53	1.54	–.01
Entire group	1.72	1.70	.02
Mean score on test of vocabulary of basal materials, word recognition (Feb., 1937) [b]			
Reading-readiness scores of 85 and above	30.6	30.2	.4
Reading-readiness scores of 70–84	29.8	27.8	2.0
Reading-readiness scores below 70	26.0	24.8	1.2
Entire group	29.1	27.5	1.6
Mean score on test of vocabulary of basal materials, paragraph reading (Feb., 1937) [c]			
Reading-readiness scores of 85 and above	15.3	15.0	0.3
Reading-readiness scores of 70–84	14.8	13.4	1.4
Reading-readiness scores below 70	10.5	9.9	.6
Entire group	13.4	13.0	.4

[a] *Gates Primary Reading Tests*, Bureau of Publications, Teachers College, Columbia University, New York.

[b] This test was composed of forty items which were similar to those in the Gates test but which were based entirely on words taught in the basal books.

[c] This test was composed of forty paragraphs which were similar to those in the Gates test but which contained only words used in the basal books.

First, the primer and the *Preparatory Book* provide a relatively large number of repetitions for each new word. Some of the materials, moreover, provide for motivated rereading (as in the case of rereading of directions while they are being carried out), perhaps enough, of certain kinds at least, for most pupils. Furthermore, the additional mimeographed material was largely of the "read-to-do," or workbook, type. It is possible that additional amounts of reading of narrative and informative selections without manual directions to execute, comprehension exercises to complete, questions to answer, etc., would have been more useful and interesting. Finally, it should be noted that, when a large amount of the workbook material is used, the time thus employed may cut into the time available for personal supervision, explanation, instruction, and guidance which the teacher would otherwise provide for individual

Classification	Group A (Introduced to Largest Number of Different Words)	Group B (Introduced to Medium Number of Different Words)	Group C (Introduced to Smallest Number of Different Words)
Number of Cases			
Reading-readiness scores of 85 or above	17	17	17
Reading-readiness scores of 70–84	21	21	21
Reading-readiness scores below 70	24	24	24
Entire group	62	62	62
Mean mental age (in months)			
Reading-readiness scores of 85 and above	82.7	83.0	82.8
Reading-readiness scores of 70–84	80.4	80.7	81.1
Reading-readiness scores below 70	74.4	73.9	73.8
Entire group	77.9	78.1	78.2
Mean score on Metropolitan Tests (Sept., 1936)			
Reading-readiness scores of 85 and above	92.8	92.6	92.8
Reading-readiness scores of 70–84	78.3	78.3	78.6
Reading-readiness scores below 70	52.7	52.8	52.7
Entire group	76.1	76.2	76.3
Mean reading grade on Gates Primary Reading Test, Type 1, Word Recognition (Feb., 1937)			
Reading-readiness scores of 85 and above	1.90	1.91	1.80
Reading-readiness scores of 70–84	1.76	1.80	1.84
Reading-readiness scores below 70	1.51	1.58	1.67
Entire group	1.66	1.75	1.77
Mean reading grade on Gates Primary Reading Test, Type 3, Paragraph Reading (Feb., 1937)			
Reading-readiness scores of 85 and above	1.84	1.90	1.79
Reading-readiness scores of 70–84	1.67	1.72	1.73

TABLE 2. (*Continued*)

Classification	Group A (Introduced to Largest Number of Different Words)	Group B (Introduced to Medium Number of Different Words)	Group C (Introduced to Smallest Number of Different Words)
Reading-readiness scores below 70	1.47	1.51	1.58
Entire group	1.65	1.73	1.77
Mean score on test of vocabulary of basal materials, word recognition (Feb., 1937) Reading-readiness scores of 85 and above	29.9	30.4	30.1
Reading-readiness scores of 70–84	27.2	28.3	30.1
Reading-readiness scores below 70	22.4	25.3	26.5
Entire group	26.5	28.4	29.1
Mean score on test of vocabulary of basal materials, paragraph reading (Feb., 1937) Reading-readiness scores of 85 and above	15.1	15.3	14.8
Reading-readiness scores of 70–84	13.1	14.4	15.1
Reading-readiness scores below 70	9.1	9.6	11.0
Entire group	12.7	13.7	14.6

children. Indeed, this possibility seemed especially important in the case of the slow learners.

EXTENDED VERSUS RESTRICTED
VOCABULARY

A study of the methods and the materials [4] used in the classes showed that in some of the control groups pupils read a wide variety of books, bulletin-

[4] The methods and the materials used in a class were determined chiefly by study of the teachers' own reports and records and the information supplied by her in a questionnaire filled out after the completion of the term. Notes kept by Russell based on his observations of the teachers' own work were also consulted. The final description of a particular teacher's program, used in this and subsequent sections, is subject to such errors as commonly exist in an appraisal of this kind.

board announcements, experience stories, and other materials. In other classes the materials were selected and somewhat restricted, motivated rereading and re-use of practice-book material was employed, and in other ways the work was confined to a smaller total vocabulary. In two experimental groups reading of supplementary materials was combined with some work with the mimeographed material. The pupils were, therefore, rearranged into three groups: Group A, those introduced to the largest number of different words; Group B, those introduced to a medium number of words; and Group C, those introduced to the smallest number of words. The three groups were approximately equivalent in scores on the reading-readiness test and in mental age and contained equal numbers of boys and girls. The results are shown in Table 2.

In the case of the entire groups, the largest differences in the scores of Groups A, B, and C appeared in the two tests based on words in the vocabulary of the basal materials, which were studied by all the children. The pupils whose reading was most confined to a common vocabulary (Group C) scored higher both in word recognition and in paragraph comprehension. In word recognition the difference between the two extremes, Group A and C, was 2.6, nearly twice the standard error of the difference. In paragraph comprehension the difference between Groups A and C was 1.9, a little less than twice the standard error of the difference. In the Gates standardized test, which includes many words taught to neither group, the differences, though not highly reliable, favored the smaller vocabulary loads. The difference between Groups A and C is approximately one-tenth of the normal progress in reading during a year.

The pupils available for this comparison were divided into three groups according to initial reading-readiness scores. When consideration is given to the scores of these three groups, it appears that the pupils who had the highest reading-readiness scores were little influenced by the range of reading vocabulary offered to them. Although the differences among the test scores were unreliable, it may be noted that in all four reading tests the pupils in the high reading-readiness group who were given the medium amount of diversity in their supplementary reading obtained the highest reading scores. In the case of the pupils of medium reading-readiness scores, the highest reading scores in the four tests were obtained by those whose activities were restricted to the smallest vocabulary. In the case of the pupils of the lowest reading-readiness scores, there

was a clear tendency for reading scores to be higher as the total mass of reading activities was conducted in the smallest vocabularies. Contrariwise, those of the lowest reading readiness were less successful when they were confronted with a heavy vocabulary in a great variety of different books, bulletin-board announcements, experience stories, and other materials. It is a fair assumption that, in the case of these pupils, new words appeared more rapidly than at the optimum rate and that consequently both word recognition and comprehension suffered.

VALUE OF PHONICS AND WORD ANALYSIS

It was apparent that, although all classes used the same basal materials, there were differences in the amounts and the kinds of word analysis and phonic activities employed. At the one extreme was a class in which a fairly extensive plan of conventional phonetic drill was introduced; at the other, a class in which little work in word analysis, strictly speaking, was used. A number of the teachers employed a rather large amount of word analysis, such as discussing the general features of words (initial and final letters or phonograms), noticing common parts of words (syllables, double letters, etc.), finding little words in bigger ones, comparing the features of words which were confused with one another, having each pupil build up his own groupings or families based on some common element, and contrasting reversed words ("was" and "saw," for example). These activities differ from conventional phonics, in which the main procedure is to study isolated letters and phonograms, build upwards from these, and train diligently on translating letters into letter sounds after having studied the sound equivalents of the letters.

The pupils were assembled in three groups according to the type of training: Group D, those who received the smallest amount of phonics or word analysis; Group E, those who were given moderate amounts of informal, newer-type word analysis, comparisons, etc.; and Group F, those who had substantial or large amounts of conventional phonetic drill. The results are shown in Table 3.

In the case of the scores for the entire groups, although the differences were not marked or highly reliable, Group E (moderate amount) had the highest scores in all the tests of word recognition and comprehension, and Group D (smallest amount) exceeded Group F (large amount) slightly in two of four tests, being equal in the other two. The activities used with Group E were, in the main, examples of the more recent, informal exercises in comparing, studying, and analyzing word forms. It is significant that the scores of the pupils in that group exceeded those in the groups employing the more conventional or formal phonetic drills by slightly more than one-tenth of a grade in the Gates standardized tests of both comprehension and word recognition. A program including little or no phonetic or word-analysis activities in the first year is not so good as the informal program but is at least as good as the one containing large amounts of formal phonetic work.

In the case of the group highest in reading-readiness scores the moderate, modern program of word analysis gave the highest average scores in reading and word recognition, but it barely exceeded the minimum word-analysis program, which in turn had a very slight advantage over conventional phonics. Since the differences have low reliability the indication is that it matters little which type or how much phonics is taught to the ablest pupils during the first year but that a moderate amount of the newer, more informal types of word analysis is most promising. The average pupils (those of intermediate reading-readiness scores) appear more clearly to secure greater benefit from this type of experience and to profit least from conventional, formal phonics. The pupils of lowest reading-readiness scores show this trend still more clearly. A moderate amount of informal word analysis is helpful; very little of this type seems to be better than large amounts of formal phonetic drill.

PROGRAMS AS A WHOLE

The reading scores obtained in the nine classes showed clear differences. For example, the reading grade in the Gates paragraph reading test for the top class was 1.91 and for the bottom 1.45, a difference of almost one-half of a grade's progress—a large difference to be obtained by the middle of the first year. These differences were due to inequalities in the abilities (mental age and reading readiness) of the pupils and to variations in the teachers' skill, as well as to other factors. All such factors for a class cannot be equated nor canceled out by class comparison of the total programs, but it was possible to eliminate pupils until the nine classes were equivalent in scores on the intelligence and the reading-readiness tests.

Pupils were eliminated until the means and the standard deviations in the mental age and the reading-readiness scores of the classes differed by negligible amounts. The scores were then assembled, and the standard deviations were computed for each of the four reading tests. The mean scores for the classes given in the following summaries

TABLE 3. Comparison of Reading Achievement of First-Grade Pupils Classified According to Scores on Metropolitan Readiness Tests and According to Amount and Kind of Phonetic Instruction

Classification	Group D (Given Smallest Amount of Phonics)	Group E (Given Moderate Amount of Informal Word Analysis)	Group F (Given Large Amount of Conventional Phonics)
Number of cases			
Reading-readiness scores of 85 and above	17	42	15
Reading-readiness scores of 70–84	20	56	20
Reading-readiness scores below 70	20	48	16
Entire group	57	146	51
Mean mental age (in months)			
Reading-readiness scores of 85 and above	82	82.1	82.4
Reading-readiness scores of 70–84	80.2	80.5	80.7
Reading-readiness scores below 70	74.5	74.1	74.9
Entire group	78.0	77.9	78.3
Mean score on Metropolitan Readiness Tests (Sept., 1936)			
Reading-readiness scores of 85 and above	92.6	92.5	92.2
Reading-readiness scores of 70–84	78.2	78.4	78.5
Reading-readiness scores below 70	52.9	52.8	53.2
Entire group	76.4	76.3	76.1
Mean reading grade on Gates Primary Reading Test, Type 1, Word Recognition (Feb., 1937)			
Reading-readiness scores of 85 and above	1.88	1.92	1.87
Reading-readiness scores of 70–84	1.76	1.85	1.73
Reading-readiness scores below 70	1.55	1.68	1.54
Entire group	1.77	1.83	1.71
Mean reading grade on Gates Primary Reading Test, Type 3, Paragraph Reading (Feb., 1937)			
Reading-readiness scores of 85 and above	1.85	1.88	1.82

TABLE 3. *(Continued)*

Classification	Group D (Given Smallest Amount of Phonics)	Group E (Given Moderate Amount of Informal Word Analysis)	Group F (Given Large Amount of Conventional Phonics)
Reading-readiness scores of 70–84	1.68	1.73	1.66
Reading-readiness scores of below 70	1.54	1.56	1.47
Entire group	1.69	1.75	1.61
Mean score on test of vocabulary of basal materials, word recognition (Feb. 1937)			
Reading-readiness scores of 85 and above	29.8	29.8	28.4
Reading-readiness scores of 70–84	28.8	30.1	28.3
Reading-readiness scores of below 70	24.4	26.4	23.7
Entire group	27.6	29.6	27.7
Mean score on test of vocabulary of basal materials, paragraph reading (Feb., 1937)			
Reading-readiness scores of 85 and above	15.2	15.1	14.8
Reading-readiness scores of 70–84	14.4	14.8	13.7
Reading-readiness scores of below 70	10.2	10.4	9.2
Entire group	13.5	14.1	13.5

are standard deviations, that is, the amount (in terms of hundredths of the standard deviation) by which the mean scores for the four tests exceeded (+) or fell below (—) the mean of the total population of the nine classes. Following are brief characterizations of the instruction in these classes taken in order from the class with the highest to that with the lowest standard-deviation score on the reading tests.

Class A. Average reading score, + .40 SD.

1. Used the mimeographed material as much as seemed advisable for particular pupils.
2. Other reading materials (books, bulletin board, etc.) were rigidly selected or edited to introduce new words no more rapidly than particular pupils were able to handle them.
3. Oral reading confined to material previously read silently.
4. Moderate use of word-study games.
5. Moderate use of informal word analysis.

Class B. Average reading score, + .38 SD.

1. Almost the same program as for Class A except that Class B was a control group and did not have the mimeographed material. Employed considerable re-use of the practice-pad materials for slower learners.

Class C. Average reading score, + .28 SD.

1. Very similar to program for Class A. Used the mimeographed material more extensively and uniformly. Used

phonics rather more fully and more formal oral-reading activities, including occasional sight reading.

Class D. Average reading score, + .25 SD.

1. Very similar to program for Class B. Class D was a control group not using the mimeographed materials. Used less phonics or informal word-analysis work with more word-recognition games.

Class E. Average reading score, + .06 SD.

1. An experimental group using the mimeographed material plus other reading of varied types resulting in fairly substantial additions to vocabulary.
2. Very little phonics or word analysis.
3. Considerable time spent in related projects involving nonreading activities.

Class F. Average reading score, + .06 SD.

1. Used the mimeographed material. Very similar to Class E, except that a great deal of conventional phonics and relatively few projects were used.

Class G. Average reading score, —.24 SD.

1. Used the mimeographed material, considerable experience reading, much oral reading for practice purposes, much formal phonics.

Class H. Average reading score, —.40 SD.

1. A control group not using the mimeographed material. Employed a considerable amount of diverse reading matter.
2. Emphasis on drill in phonics and oral reading.

Class I. Average reading score, —.76 SD.

1. A control group. Children undertook supplementary books with little guidance. Considerable experience reading with little editing of material.
2. Used word and phrase cards with wall pocket.
3. Used considerable formal phonics.

CONCLUSIONS

Although study of the programs conducted in these individual classes, only briefly suggested above, was illuminating, the more general features may be suggested by grouping them.

1. *High Final Scores.* Classes A, B, C, and D may be grouped together. Certain common features of the program used by the teachers in these classes are as follows:

a. All these teachers, in order not to bewilder the pupils with too many new words, exercised restrictions on the total range of material offered. They strove to secure a generous amount of rereading of the words considered basal. In most cases words outside the vocabulary of the basal textbooks were, within limits, considered "basal." These teachers tried to make possible an abundance of reading of material which contained few or no unfamiliar words.

b. In these classes an effort was more clearly made to adjust the material, the reading, the related activities, and the vocabulary burden to the pupils. In this group were two teachers who refused to put every child through the same entire amount of supplementary mimeographed material.

c. These teachers used bulletin-board announcements; blackboard and chart work; "experience" and other oral compositions for reading; supplementary books; and artistic, dramatic, and other projects. They carefully edited or controlled the number of new words appearing in these materials and critically considered the individual pupils in the various types of activities.

d. These teachers exercised special caution before having pupils read orally before the group materials that they had not previously read. Oral sight reading was rarely or never used for mere purposes of drill.

e. These teachers used moderate amounts of word-recognition games but rarely employed word-form pronunciation drills unrelieved by correlated interest-producing features.

f. All these teachers used moderate amounts of the newer types of informal word-analysis activities, such as comparing words which have been confused or which contain common factors or tend to be read in reverse, noting features within words, finding small words in larger, and making families from words already known. In no case was word analysis omitted, and in none was the conventional, formal phonetic drill employed.

2. *Average Final Scores.* The two classes (E and F) which finished the term with average reading scores used the material of the workbook type. The programs for these two classes were similar to each other but presented the following differences from the programs characteristic of the first group:

a. They used the mimeographed material more fully.

b. They brought in other reading matter with less concern about its vocabulary, with a resulting heavier vocabulary burden.

c. There was less adjustment to individual abilities and interests.

d. They used different methods of word analysis. Class E employed a minimum of any kind, and Class F used formal phonetics.

3. *Low Final Scores.* The classes with the lowest reading ability (Classes G, H, and I) included one which used the mimeographed material and two control groups. The main distinguishing features of the work in these three classes were as follows:

a. A relatively large amount of varied reading material, that is, a large total vocabulary, was used.

b. There was greater disposition to teach the class instead of individuals or small groups of similar abilities or needs.

c. More emphasis was placed on formal phonetic drill.

d. Treatment of oral reading was more formal.

e. In two classes at least (H and I), there was a tendency to combine rather extreme devices, such as much free, undirected reading of diverse materials and oral sight reading before the class; some interesting word games and formal phonetic drill were used. These classes gave the impression of having a great variety of activities which were less well integrated and related than those used in the other groups. The main things to be taught were less clearly brought to the fore; the pupils more frequently seemed confused or uncertain concerning what, exactly, they should learn.

It must be recalled that these comparisons are relative. Even the lowest class scores were good, while the average exceeded the standards for the grade position and the highest were remarkably good.

SYSTEMATIC VERSUS OPPORTUNISTIC METHODS IN TEACHING READING [1]

Arthur I. Gates, assisted by Mildred I. Batchelder and Jean Betzner

[Here is the name of Gates again, this time assisted by Mildred I. Batchelder and Jean Betzner. Although one of his early investigations, this study is still widely cited. But it is rarely quoted with sufficient regard for the qualifications carefully interposed by the research team alongside the conclusions of the study. Unless a student of reading instruction takes the time to appraise the original studies, these important reservations are unknown to him. All too often reliance on summaries of research leads to dogmatic assertions quite unsupported by the actual investigations. This study, for example, is usually regarded as the firm foundation for the clear superiority of systematic instruction over opportunistic methods in teaching reading. But what did the Gates research team really say?]

PROBLEM

This study was designed to disclose in some measure the outcomes of a year of first-grade school work carried on in one group by a modern systematic method and in another by what we have decided to term an "opportunistic" method. During the work of the year, all relevant factors, such as attendance, time allotments to scholastic work, recesses, materials and equipment, individual attention in school and out, outside study, teacher assistance, etc., were to be kept as nearly equal as possible. For each group, one teacher only was provided. These two teachers, according to a com-

posite of judgments of several experts in education who knew them both well, were exceptionally, and about equally, able.

PROCEDURES

SELECTING PUPILS FOR THE
TWO GROUPS

From the large number of candidates for the first grade in the school, pairs of pupils who were as nearly as possible alike, in all the respects considered, were selected. Twenty-five pairs completed the year's work. How nearly equivalent the two groups were is indicated in the

[1] Adapted and abridged from Arthur I. Gates, Mildred I. Batchelder, and Jean Betzner, "A Modern Systematic Versus an Opportunistic Method of Teaching," in *Teachers College Record* (1926), 27:679–700.

accompanying averages and distributions of ability.

As far as possible equivalence in other traits was secured. About twenty of the pupils came from the junior primary division of the Horace Mann School. For these children, the combined estimates of several teachers for (1) physical ma-

TABLE 1. Mean (M) and Mean Deviation (MD) in Various Traits at the Beginning of the School Year

	Total Number	Number Boys	Age M	MD	Mental Age M	MD	Intelligence Quotient M	MD
Systematic group	25	12	6.3	.29	7.3	.55	116.3	.97
Opportunistic group	25	12	6.3	.31	7.3	.60	117.6	1.11

	Detroit Intelligence M	MD	General Information M	MD	Alphabet Test M	MD	Pronunciation Word Test M	Failures
Systematic group	37.8	15.5	37.12	9.08	129	48	1.3	20
Opportunistic group	35.8	16.1	37.04	8.38	122	50	2.7	17

	Speed of Reading Words Failures	Oral Reading Paragraphs Failures	Word Selection Test M	MD	Oral Spelling M	MD
Systematic group	all	all	5.2	2.8	0.9	0.8
Opportunistic group	all	all	5.0	2.9	1.6	1.8

	Oral Arithmetic M	MD	Writing M	MD
Systematic group	18.0	7.6	3.6	1.7
Opportunistic group	16.6	7.9	3.7	1.7

turity and fitness, (2) mental maturity and common sense, (3) social maturity and adaptability, (4) emotional maturity and stability, and (5) educational maturity and fitness for scholastic work were available. The children were matched individually in these traits and assigned to the two groups in equal number. The pupils appearing at the school for the first time were appraised as well as possible in the same traits during the first two weeks and rearranged to yield equivalent pairings. For all children, the measures of height, weight, strength, and physical fitness made by the school physicians were taken into account. We believe that, on the whole, the two groups were as nearly equivalent in traits related to possibilities for educational achievement as can be obtained at the present time.

METHODS OF TEACHING

Each of the two methods, the "modern systematic" and the "opportunistic," was followed by an exceptionally able teacher who was experienced in the method and believed it to be, on the whole, the best one. Both teachers followed the same general schedule, the same time assignments to different phases of the work, recesses, etc. Neither was given any assistance in teaching;

neither enjoyed any advantage in clerical or other help, in funds for materials, in special demonstrations, etc.

In addition to the general plans for the year, detailed records of much of the work, as it actually occurred, were made. On certain occasions visitors, whose purposes were unknown to the teachers, observed and compared the work of the two rooms, and on occasional days verbatim reports of all that was said and detailed accounts of all that was done by both teachers and pupils were recorded by an experienced stenographic reporter. From these sources the differences in the teaching methods were discerned.

The systematic method and the opportunistic differed primarily in these respects: The former adopted a course of study that was more definitely determined, outlined, and organized beforehand than that of the latter. The daily lessons were more definitely arranged, the study of definite lessons was more rigidly prescribed, the accomplishments of these particular assignments were more strictly required, and the order of the development of topics was more fully determined by the nature of the subject matter and more vigorously adhered to. The opportunistic method utilized a less definite program of studies and activities while aiming more to conform to the inclinations and interests of the pupils. To a greater extent the teacher awaited, and attempted to utilize, the self-initiated urges of the pupils to learn to read, write, spell, etc. To a smaller extent were set up lessons and projects which the pupils were encouraged or required to attack; to a greater extent the policy of awaiting special incentives or opportunities which provided a "need" for certain information or skill was followed. Given the ripe opportunity the facts or abilities were furnished as the occasions demanded. Under such a procedure, the words to be read were those found in an invitation to a party from another grade, etc. The subjects were, consequently, taught less systematically and more in accordance with the demands of such opportunities as occurred or were provided. The systematic teacher did not, of course, disregard special opportunities for motivating the teaching, although she depended less on them. The differences between the two methods were of degree, but they were appreciable. The systematic group was not required to adhere slavishly to particular texts of so many pages; nevertheless, the pupils were expected to master certain materials and skills which the teacher had herself arranged in a developmental order. The comparison, then, is not between the extreme traditional daily - lesson - in - the - book - plus - recitation method and an extreme do-as-you-like procedure but between what, for want of better terms, may be called modern systematic teaching, with considerable emphasis on pupil initiative, and a considerably less systematic procedure in which the pupils control the amount, kind, and order of learning, with the teacher taking advantage of opportunities for instruction as they are afforded.

The achievements of the pupils during the year in information and skill were measured by a battery of tests, many of them given individually and most of them constructed specifically for the purpose. All of the tests in which any of the pupils might score at all were given at the beginning of the year and utilized in equating the groups; most of them were repeated near midyear, and all, together with additional ones, were given at the end of the year. In many of the functions tested the progress during the year was determined by sub-tracting the initial scores from the final scores; in others, the initial score was demonstrably, or assumed to be, zero and the final scores were taken as representing the gains in ability. Table 2 shows the results in terms of average gains during the full year.

ACHIEVEMENT IN READING

The first nine tests measure various phases of silent and oral reading ability. The first two tests consisted of the letters of the alphabet. The pupils, in individual tests, read the letters aloud. The systematic group shows slightly higher scores but they are neither very great nor very reliable.

The third test required the oral reading of forty digits, 0 to 9 inclusive, irregularly arranged. In this test, both in time and in number of errors, the systematic group showed some superiority—the difference in time amounting to four times the PE.

The fourth test was designed to measure the speed and accuracy of recognizing words. It consisted of exercises, such as:

hat / sat pat rat bat hat

the words increasing in difficulty. The pupil encircled the word in the series which is identical with the one at the left. Score is the number of exercises right. The systematic group showed some superiority—amounting to about five times the PE—in this form of word recognition.

The fifth test was a form of the Gates Pronunciation Test which required the oral reading of 100 words ranging from words such as to and it to words such as handkerchief and affectionate. The systematic class averaged 27.5; the opportunistic, 17.7. The difference be-tween the groups was here considerable —five and a half times the PE.

The sixth test examined silent reading. It began with words such as dog and chair and later introduced phrases, the longest of which was "a mother giving her little girl some water." The pupil read silently, marking a picture to demonstrate his comprehension of the text. In this test the systematic group showed a clear superiority—difference being more than eight times the PE.

Test seven was patterned after Gray's Oral Reading Test, consisting of passages ranging from very easy to very hard. The systematic group was clearly far more advanced in this type of oral reading.

Tests eight and nine consisted of sentences of increasing difficulty to be read silently. In both, the systematic group excelled.

In all nine tests of reading skills, then, the systematic group surpassed the opportunistic. The superiority was greater in word pronunciation, in silent reading of words, phrases, and sentences, and in oral reading of passages than in the simpler tests of recognition of letters or words.

The most interesting results appear, not in the averages shown in Table 2, but in the records of the particular individuals in the two groups. For example, in the oral reading test—in which the scores are given in terms of "reading ages"—the distribution of abilities in the two groups was as shown in Table 3. Fifteen of the opportunistic group failed in this test, whereas all of the systematic group succeeded well enough to secure some score. Another significant result was the greater spread of abilities in the systematic group and the relatively large number making very high achievements—five exceeded the norms for average nine-year-old pupils. The

TABLE 2. Initial and Final Scores and Gains of Each Group and the Differences in Gains between the Two Groups

	1	2	3	4	5	6	7	8	9	10	11	12	13	14	15
	Reading [a] Capital Letters	Reading [a] Lower Case Letters	Reading [a] Digits	Word Selection	Word Pronunciation	Oglesby Silent Reading	Horace Mann Oral Reading	Hagerty Reading Test I	Hagerty Reading Test II	Spelling	Writing Quality	Writing Speed	Arithmetic Problems	Perception of Numbers	General Information
Systematic group															
Initial score	129	127	77	5.2	1.3	—	—	—	—	—	—	—	—	—	37.1
Final score	60	73	37	14.1	27.5	21.3	7.2	7.9	4.5	8.9	3.8	30	24.9	14.0	44.8
Gain	69	54	40	8.9	26.2	21.3	7.2	7.9	4.5	8.9	3.8	30	—	—	7.7
Opportunistic group															
Initial score	122	120	76	5.0	2.7	—	—	—	—	—	—	—	—	—	37.8
Final score	62	72	49	11.2	17.7	12.2	2.8	3.8	2.9	6.2	4.2	36	21.8	12.1	44.4
Gain	60	48	27	6.2	15.0	12.2	2.8	3.8	2.9	6.2	4.2	36	—	—	7.4
Difference in favor of systematic group	9	6	13.0	2.7	11.2	9.1	4.4	4.1	1.6	2.7	-0.4	6.0	3.1	1.9	0.3
PE difference	5	5	3.2	.55	2.0	1.1	0.4	0.85	0.5	0.6	0.25	4.2	1.2	0.9	2.0

[a] These tests are scored in number of seconds; hence the smaller the figure the better the score.

TABLE 3. Reading Age

	Failures	6–7 Years	7–8 Years	8–9 Years	9–10 Years	10–11 Years
Systematic	0	16	4	0	4	1
Opportunistic	15	5	4	1	0	0

systematic method achieved some reading ability with all pupils, without holding the more able to a common level. In the silent reading tests the results were similar.

ACHIEVEMENT IN SPELLING

In both groups, the training in spelling and writing was one and the same; no drills in silent and oral spelling were conducted. The differences in the methods appear in the teachers' descriptions. The opportunistic teacher gave no specific drill in spelling: only "toward the end of the year" were the words which the children could write listed, noted, checked up, and compared with "the second grade list in Pearson and Suzzalo." The systematic teacher selected the word "needed for a chart or sign or some other purpose," wrote it on the board twice, and required trials at writing it from memory. "The Pearson-Suzzalo list for Grade I guided me but did not limit what the children needed to write."

The test in spelling, given at the end of the year, consisted of words taken from the Ayres-Buckingham list. All of the words selected were taken from a longer list that had been approved by both teachers as containing no words incompatible with the verbal experiences of the children.

Tests were given individually. The average score of the systematic group exceeded that of the opportunistic by an amount equal to 4.5 times the PE. The distribution of scores is shown as follows:

Scores	Systematic	Opportunistic
18–19	1	0
16–17	2	1
14–15	0	0
12–13	2	0
10–11	4	6
8–9	8	6
6–7	2	1
4–5	3	2
2–3	3	4
0–1	0	5

As in reading, the systematic group showed no failures whereas the opportunistic group showed failure in 20 percent of the cases. The systematic group again showed a large number achieving high scores.

ACHIEVEMENT IN WRITING

In writing is found a characteristic type of difference in teaching which may be expected from the natures of the two general methods. The opportunistic teacher reports: "Writing was a great interest in this class; from my point of view, not a great need. However, I followed the interest and taught writing. The ease with which manuscript writing is acquired by little children is a great factor in their interest. All writing, at first, was on the blackboard or with crayon and large paper. I wrote the word on the board. They wrote it from memory. Sometimes we all had difficulty with the same letter. Then we had an old-fashioned drill. We wrote every day after the first six weeks from five to thirty minutes." This description epitomizes beautifully the opportunistic method, perfectly conducted. Although the teacher did not see "a great need" for writing, she seized and utilized the apparent interest, which resulted in a relatively considerable amount of training.

The systematic teacher taught writing definitely in two weekly periods, on the average, of from twenty to thirty minutes after the first of December. Words needed for some purpose or those selected from the Pearson-Suzzalo speller were used.

The test in writing given at the end of the year differed from that given at the beginning, since at the beginning very few children could write either words or letters. Both classes had been taught the printlike or manuscript writing. For a final test, the sentence *The boy saw a cat* was placed on the board in manuscript writing. After a half-minute period, the tests proper—two periods of one minute each with a rest interval between—were given. The specimens were graded on a scale corresponding in character to the Thorndike scale, independently, by two experienced judges. Speed and quality were measured separately. Both tell the same story—the opportunistic group is superior by amounts less than twice the PE. The distributions of scores are nearly identical; no complete failures appeared in either class.

ACHIEVEMENT IN ARITHMETIC

Neither teacher attempted to teach any considerable amount of arithmetic during the year. Neither used a textbook and neither assigned daily or other regular periods to this subject. Both had in mind the same objective—to establish ability to use foot rules and yardsticks, to count articles used in work, to read page numbers or dates on the calendar, to understand the calendar and clock, to use familiar coins, etc. The extent of the facts and skills held as desirable differed little between the teachers.

The test in arithmetic used at the end of the year was made up without knowledge of what was being done or taught in either class. Each child was examined orally and individually. The problems were mainly practical and realistic ones concerned with everyday affairs. A sample of the items follows:

4. If you brought 2 crackers for your lunch and someone gave you 2 more crackers, how many would you have altogether?

9. Here are 10 cents and I have some postage stamps to sell (examiner has 10 pennies and some one- and two-cent stamps).
   a. How many two-cent stamps can you buy for 10 cents?
   b. Here are 5 cents and you want a one-cent stamp. Pay me. How many cents will you have left? Etc.

14. a. What time is it now? (Examiner—Adjust your watch.)
    b. Eight o'clock. (Examiner—Turn watch hands to show this time.) Etc.

The systematic group excelled in this test of forty-one items by a trifle less than three times the PE.

A second but minor test in arithmetic, already considered under reading, consisted of the oral reading of a series of digits. In this test the systematic group proved superior by an amount equal to nearly four times the PE. A third test measured the rate of perceiving the identity of, or the difference between, pairs of numbers, such as 186, 186, 127, 137, etc. In this test the systematic group excelled by twice the PE.

On the whole, then, the differences in achievement in arithmetic favor the systematic group.

ACQUISITION OF GENERAL INFORMATION

A series of questions designed to measure acquisition of information of a practical and general sort, different, in the main, from what is typically found in systematic courses in reading, arithmetic, etc., was constructed before teaching in the groups was far under way. The examination was designed to test the claim, sometimes made, that forms of opportunistic teaching typically result in the acquisition of more information about people, practical affairs, and the surrounding environment than does systematic teaching. The questions were given orally by the examiner to each child individually.

The gains of the two groups and their final average scores were almost identical.

SUMMARY AND DISCUSSION OF RESULTS

The results of the study may be summarized as follows:

1. In the objectives of education outside of the traditional scholastic subjects, in interests, in school activities, in social and personal habits, in attitudes as they were appraised, and in general information of varied types, the groups taught by the opportunistic and the modern systematic methods were substantially equal.

2. Opportunistic teaching, following the special interests of the pupils, resulted in slightly higher achievements in the motor functions—writing (manuscript style), rather certainly, and drawing, less surely.

3. Modern systematic teaching resulted in considerably greater average achievements in the other school subjects—arithmetic, spelling, silent and oral reading.

An interesting and significant difference between the outcomes of the two methods appeared in the divergencies in the distribution of abilities in some of the school subjects. In reading, for example, in the opportunistic group, there was what a standard test in reading of simplest materials designates as "complete failure" in fifteen out of twenty-five cases, whereas in the modern systematic group there was none. In the former group there were no exceptionally high achievements, whereas in the latter there were five "reading ages" from nine to eleven years at the end of this first year.

If ability to read—if achievement objectively manifest—were the only criterion, the systematic method might lay claim to superiority, since it is in connection with such cases—those who do not learn without help but really need a teacher and teaching—that the question of method achieves any significance. Here lies the crux of the matter; here lie the inadequacies of our data. For the development of interest and enthusiasm in reading and other school activities, for the improvement of initiative, determination, and other volitional traits, for the general improvement of inappropriate habit tendencies, immaturity, and the dispositions toward inhibitive mental adjustments, for the stimulation of healthful mental and temperamental growth in general, which is superior, the method which achieves the goal of reading ability by aggressive behavior or the one which lingers to secure it by a smoother, even if delayed, route? This question we cannot fully answer. At the most, we may say that, in so far as we were able to secure evidence concerning interest, character development, and the like, the two methods produced no perceptible differences. We should hasten to admit, however, that our evidence is not as detailed and reliable as we desire. We are, therefore, unwilling to make the statement that our data indicate that one method is better than the other in any ultimate sense. The study did disclose certain facts, certain pertinent and clear differences. These findings pave the way for further much needed study. This should take the form of much more extensive and detailed study of all relevant factors in the critical cases of children upon whom the two general methods exert a differentiating effect. In other words, we should ascertain by far more searching analyses the influence of the contrasting methods upon all aspects of the maturing personality.

Chapter V

WHAT WE READ

A generation ago when reading instruction was discussed, there used to be repeated this statement: "First you learn to read: then you read to learn." Hence, in keeping with this aphorism, the primary grades were supposedly largely devoted to teaching students to read. Then, apparently believing that three years provided enough time to develop skill in reading fully, teachers did not need to offer further instruction in reading but could concentrate on using the developed reading ability to study literature, social studies, arithmetic, science, and so on.

Gradually the earlier confidence in completing reading instruction in the primary grades disintegrated. With varying degrees of resistance, still apparent in some school systems, reading instruction was extended into the intermediate grades. It seems apparent that, before very long, the years for teaching reading to all students will include at least the junior and senior high school.

At the same time that security in the period of time required to teach reading was shaken, a new kind of doubt began to assail teachers of reading. Did the ability they developed in what was called a "basic" reading program function equally well in reading any kind or quality of thought? To be more specific, could this "basic" reading ability manage with the same facility the ideas in literature, social studies, mathematics, and science—to name just four different "disciplines"? And, if "basic" reading ability did not prosper equally well in all fields of learning, what were the degrees of distinctiveness to which the reading act must be reoriented? The research answers to these searching queries have only been begun.

Particularly difficult to define have been the inquiries about just what, if any, redirection of reading ability is demanded in the "content" fields. One field, the social studies, has been included in this section to illustrate the kind of detailed definition such instruction, if needed, will require.

Paralleling the rising concern about reading in the several "disciplines" has been anxiety about the reading interests of young people. The competition of other communications media for the time of boys and girls has, of course, accentuated the attention being paid to what kinds of reading bid most likely to intrigue. Two categories of research are reproduced in this section as examples of pertinent investigations.

READING AND ACHIEVEMENT IN THE CONTENT FIELDS [1]

Eva Bond

[Eva Bond set herself the difficult task of determining the relationship between general reading ability and achievement in specific fields of learning. To explore the amount of interplay, she chose the strategic ground of the ninth grade. At this time the fields of study have usually a clearly established identity and the program of instruction in "basic" reading has usually been terminated. How well does a good general reader perform in English, Latin, mathematics, science? Does he perform equally well in all subjects or are some subjects more directly benefited than others?]

This investigation was initiated to study the relationship between various reading skills and scholastic achievement in various ninth-grade subjects. Three hundred children in a Mansfield, Ohio, junior high school were studied. The reading skills investigated were:

A. Reading comprehension, based upon a composite of reading comprehension on:

1. The Iowa Silent Reading Test, Advanced, Form B (Revised 1931).[2] The total comprehension score includes the score received on word, paragraph, and sentence meaning, organization and location of information subtests.

2. The Traxler Silent Reading Test, Form I, Grades 7 to 10 (1934).[3] The total comprehension score includes measures of story and paragraph comprehension, and word meaning.

3. The Shank Tests of Reading Comprehension, Test II, Form A,

[1] Adapted and abridged from Eva Bond, *Reading and Ninth Grade Achievement*, Contributions to Education, No. 756, Teachers College, Columbia University, New York, 1938.

[2] World Book Co., Yonkers, N. Y.

[3] Public School Publishing Co., Bloomington, Ill.

Grades 7, 8, 9 (1929).[4] The total comprehension is derived from measures of paragraph comprehension.

B. Reading rate, based upon a composite rate on the Iowa and Traxler tests.

1. The Traxler rate test is so arranged that the measure of rate is begun after the child has read three lines of a story about animal life and has had an opportunity to become interested in it. The time interval is 200 seconds.

2. Simple questions, which supposedly do not interfere with the rate of reading, are interspersed in the Iowa rate test. The students read, for two minutes, material upon the influence of the press in a democracy, answering questions as they go along.

C. Power of comprehension, based on Part III of the Traxler test. This is a measure of ability to read materials of varying levels of difficulty. The element of time is largely eliminated, twenty minutes being allowed for the reading of six short paragraphs and the answering of twenty questions.

D. Location of information, based on Part 5 of the Iowa test. The ability to locate information is measured by ten questions to be looked up in a selection from an index and twenty short questions, followed by seven words or phrases from which three key words are to be selected.

E. Paragraph organization, based on Part 3 of the Iowa test. One section of this test consists of nine short paragraphs which the student reads and, from a list of five, selects one descriptive phrase that tells the central idea of the paragraph. The other section is made up of five paragraphs which the student outlines.

F. Fifth-grade level of comprehension, based on the Modern School Achievement Test.[5] When the pu-

pils being studied were in the fifth grade, the short form of this test was administered to them. It was decided to determine the value this measure of reading comprehension might have in predicting scholastic achievement in ninth grade. The reading test is made up of thirty-four short paragraphs, from each of which two or three words are omitted and the child selects from a group of four words the words to insert in the blank space.

G. Fifth-grade speed of reading, based on the Modern Achievement Test. This five-minute test consists of fifty short paragraphs. Each paragraph contains a question.

Scholastic achievement in the ninth grade was investigated in the following areas:

A. English, based on the Cooperative English Test, Form N (1937).[6] This test measures vocabulary, spelling, and usage. The vocabulary test consists of 100 words. The spelling section consists of fifty groups of four words, one of which in most cases is misspelled. The usage test has one section testing the ability of a student to select the most coherent sentence in each of twenty groups of four sentences. A second section is composed of twenty sentences in which the student makes suggested changes in the structure of each sentence. A third section includes two short proofreading selections in which errors in punctuation, capitalization, and grammatical usage are to be deleted and corrected.

B. Literary acquaintance, based on the Cooperative Literary Test, Form N (1937).[7] This test contains 150 multiple-choice items selected on the basis of difficulty, discriminating quality, and proportionate representation of different fields and writers.

C. Latin, based on the Cooperative Latin Test, Elementary Form N

---

[4] C. A. Gregory Co., Cincinnati, Ohio.
[5] Bureau of Publications, Teachers College, Columbia University, New York, N. Y.

[6] Cooperative Test Service, New York.
[7] Cooperative Test Service, New York.

(1937).[8] Part I consists of reading three paragraphs of Latin material and answering seven questions in English about each paragraph. Part II lists fifty Latin words, each followed by five English words, from which the student selects the one which most nearly corresponds to the specific Latin word. Part III is composed of thirty-five English sentences followed by an incomplete Latin translation, which the student completes by inserting one of five words or phrases.

D. General mathematics, based on the Cooperative General Mathematics Test for High School Classes, Form N (1937).[9] This test is made up of sixty questions selected from materials incorporated in typical high school mathematics courses.

E. Algebra, based on the Cooperative Algebra Test, Form N (1937).[10] This test consists of fifty-four short questions covering the application of the basic skills and principles included in elementary algebra.

F. General science, based on the cooperative General Science Test, Form N (1937).[11] This test includes eighty questions which concern scientific developments usually stressed in a high-school general science course.

G. Composite achievement in the college-preparatory course, based on the 100 children who were enrolled in a college-preparatory course. For this group, sigma scores of achievement in each of four subjects were combined into a composite achievement score.

PROCEDURES

The study did not attempt to develop predictive equations or to determine the reliability with which individual predictions of achievements can be made. It

[8] Cooperative Test Service, New York.
[9] Cooperative Test Service, New York.
[10] Cooperative Test Service, New York.
[11] Cooperative Test Service, New York.

attempted only to determine the relationship for ninth-grade groups between reading skills and scholastic achievement. To compare the achievement of good and poor readers, some method of controlling extraneous factors, such as mental and chronological age, was needed. One way to control these extraneous factors would have been to match good and poor readers on these traits. In this case, it was decided that the matching technique was undesirable because it would have resulted in a great reduction in the number of cases available. In this attrition, groups not typical of a representative population would have been produced. So instead an analysis-of-variance technique was used. The total group of 300 was divided into six approximately equal mental-age divisions and four chronological-age divisions. Twenty-four categories resulted from the combination of the mental-age and chronological-age divisions. Each of the 300 cases was placed in one of the twenty-four categories. These categories were then treated as being homogeneous. Thus, mental age and chronological age were held constant. Then the cases within each category were divided into thirds on the basis of their achievement rank in each reading skill (composite comprehension, rate, etc.). For each reading skill, comparisons within each of the twenty-four categories were made between the upper third (good readers) and the lower third (poor readers) in relation to each scholastic achievement. For example, the category of all those with mental ages 195 to 214 (12¼ years to 16⅚ years) and chronological age 176 to 180 (14⅔ years to 15 years) was divided into a good reading group, an average reading group, and a poor reading group for the reading skill, let us say, composite comprehension. Then the good comprehenders were compared to the poor comprehenders with regard to their respective achievement in, let us say, literary acquaintance. This process was then repeated within each of the twenty-four categories for each reading skill in relation to each scholastic achievement.

The good-reader group as a whole for each reading skill consisted of the totals of the good-reader group within each category; similarly for the poor-reader group as a whole. The study was able to show what these good-reader groups ("good" in terms of a specific reading skill) as a whole and what these poor-reader groups as a whole did with relation to each kind of scholastic achievement.

FINDINGS

ENGLISH

1. A highly significant relationship existed between composite comprehension and achievement in the five aspects of English measured: usage, punctuation, spelling, vocabulary, and literary acquaintance.

2. A similar result was obtained for the relationship between power of comprehension and the aspects of English measured.

3. The relationship between skill in location of information and achievement in usage, punctuation, vocabulary, and literary acquaintance was also highly significant. The relationship to achievement in spelling was also significant but not to such a pronounced degree.

4. Skill in paragraph organization was significantly related to achievement in usage, punctuation, vocabulary, and literary acquaintance. It was not significantly related to achievement in spelling.

5. Composite reading rate was significantly related to achievement in vocabulary and literary acquaintance. It was not significantly related to achievement in usage, punctuation, or spelling.

6. Fifth-grade reading comprehension was significantly related to ninth-grade achievement in all the tested aspects of English.

LATIN

Here the number of cases was relatively small (eighty-eight) and real differences may not be revealed as significant. Composite comprehension was related to achievement in Latin in a highly significant way. Composite rate, location of information, and paragraph organization were not significantly related to achievement in Latin. Fifth-grade reading comprehension was not significantly related to achievement in Latin.

GENERAL MATHEMATICS

Skill in location of information was the only reading ability which showed a significant relationship to achievement in general mathematics. Fifth-grade reading comprehension was not significantly related to achievement in general mathematics.

ALGEBRA

Skill in location of information was also related to achievement in algebra in a highly significant way. Composite comprehension was related to achievement in algebra in a way probably significant, but power of comprehension showed no significant relationship. Composite rate and paragraph organization were probably not significantly related to achievement in algebra. Fifth-grade comprehension was not significantly related to achievement in algebra.

GENERAL SCIENCE

The relation of composite comprehension and power of comprehension to achievement in general science was highly significant. Skill in location of information was significantly related to achievement in general science. Composite rate and paragraph organization were not significantly related. Fifth-grade comprehension was not significantly related.

COMPOSITE ACHIEVEMENT IN THE
COLLEGE-PREPARATORY COURSE

Many of the previous studies of reading have been based upon some composite measure of achievement. This study demonstrates that many subtle relationships between skill in reading and scholastic achievement are obscured by such a blanket method of procedure. The summary below illustrates the point:

1. Composite comprehension was a highly significant factor in composite achievement. Yet the relationship between it and one item of composite achievement, general mathematics, was not significant.

2. Power of comprehension was a highly significant factor in composite achievement but not in Latin or general mathematics.

3. Skill in location of information was significantly related to composite achievement but was not significantly related to achievement in Latin.

4. Fifth-grade comprehension was not significantly related to composite achievement but was significantly related to achievement in English.

5. Skill in paragraph organization was not significantly related to composite achievement but was highly significant in four out of five aspects of achievement in English.

6. Speed in reading was not significantly related to composite achievement but was a highly significant factor in vocabulary and literary acquaintance. A relatively slow rate of reading was characteristic of high achievement in science, mathematics, and Latin.

GENERAL IMPLICATIONS

The data all indicate that there is no such thing as a critical level of reading ability above which added skill in reading is no longer a factor in achievement at the ninth-grade level. They indicate that any increase in reading ability will be reflected in increased scholastic achievement. The study supports the statement that "every teacher should be a teacher of reading." The study also illustrates the need for carefully planned guidance in reading throughout the ninth grade.

COMPREHENSION DIFFICULTIES IN HISTORY [1]

J. C. Dewey

[Eva Bond's study did not probe the particular problems imposed by reading in the social studies. Two investigations are included to indi-

[1] Adapted and abridged from J. C. Dewey, "A Case Study of Reading Comprehension Difficulties in American History," *University* *of Iowa Studies in Education* (1935), *10*:26–54.

cate the kind of difficulties encountered in that field. The first is a pioneer effort by J. C. Dewey and the second a recent study by Kathleen B. Rudolf. Dewey, like many before him, had wondered what elementary pupils did with the facts they learned about history. Did they draw any conclusions? Or were they just what another had called "a mind-crushing load"? And what about the abstractions which so many historical words represent?]

These problems in reading eighth-grade American history were set up for investigation:

1. What is the relationship between ability to understand factual material read and ability to propose inferences from material read?
2. What concepts do children have of the various words, phrases, and sentences in the material they read?
3. How does ability to interpret the printed page vary at different levels?
4. What is the relationship between ability to respond correctly to verbal and to nonverbal items on material read?
5. Are children's responses consistent regarding material read?
6. Do children respond in the same way in written tests as they do in oral tests on the same reading material?

PROCEDURES

SELECTION OF READING MATERIAL

Eighteen textbooks in American history in current use in public schools were investigated. The following criteria were used in selecting reading material from these texts:

1. Paragraphs or other units that contain certain meanings or concepts that require careful, inferential thinking.

2. Selections that discuss topics in political, economic, and social history.
3. Selections that lend themselves to several methods of testing.
4. Selections that are short enough to permit exhaustive testing and long enough to permit a reasonable continuity of discussion.

On the basis of these criteria, the following were chosen: Selection A (from Tryon and Lingley, *The American People and Nation*, pp. 115–116), consisting of two paragraphs (202 words) on colonial lighting; Selection B (from Barker, Webb, and Dodd, *The Growth of a Nation*, p. 581), containing four paragraphs (212 words) on the invention and development of the reaper; Selection C (from Evans, *The Essential Facts of American History*, pp. 356–357), five paragraphs (265 words) describing the Dred Scott decision; and Selection D (from Leonard and Jacobs, *The Nation's History*, p. 225), two paragraphs (243 words) on the Articles of Confederation.

In each case the selection was a unit; that is, it was a rather complete treatment of the topic in so far as the textbook gave it. All words were checked against the Thorndike Word List (1921 version). Selection A contained no words not in this list; the other selections contained a few words not in this list; Selection B contained *six-shooter* and *tractor*; Selection C used *irritation* and *recourse;* Selection D included the words *byword, currency, requisitioned,* and *unlimited.*

TESTS USED

The following types of tests were used:

1. A true-false-no data test.
2. A free-expression inference test.
3. A multiple-choice test.
4. A true-false inference test. Pupils were required to indicate the specific sentences upon which these responses were based.
5. Map test. Pupils indicated their understanding by making outline maps of the United States.
6. Picture-choice tests. Pupils were asked to identify in the pictures items they were responding to in words in the verbal tests.

Each child was also given the Kuhlman-Anderson Intelligence Test and the Iowa Silent Reading Test.

TEST CONSTRUCTION

Each item was checked by the author, by two assistants, and by a member of the History Department of the University of Iowa. The incorrect responses in the multiple-choice test were drawn from the most plausible incorrect responses given by children in a preliminary test.

TEST ADMINISTRATION

All tests were given by the writer. The tests were not used as recall tests. The selections were before the pupils and the pupils were urged to use them as often as seemed necessary. No time limit was set and each pupil was urged to try again, especially on inference tests. In School A sixty-eight eighth-grade pupils were tested on Selections A

and C and in School B eighty-eight eighth-grade pupils on Selections B and D. One school was in a city of 2000 while the other was in a city of 60,000. Both groups seemed to be living in average school situations and in typical American communities. The intelligence quotients of the pupils in the smaller city varied from 80 to 125; in the larger city from 73 to 126.

TEST VALIDITY AND RELIABILITY

The criterion of validity was the combined judgment of the investigator, the two assistants, and the member of the History Department. The tests were also correlated with scores in the Iowa Silent Reading Test with the following results:

Test	Correlation Coefficients
A	$.657 \pm .050$
B	$.553 \pm .054$
C	$.761 \pm .038$
D	$.782 \pm .031$

The reliability of the tests, calculated by the split-halves method and the result stepped up by the Spearman-Brown prophecy formula, ranged from $.68 \pm .04$ to $.86 \pm .04$.

INDIVIDUAL INTERVIEWS

As soon as the written tests were completed each child was subjected to an individual thirty-minute oral interview for the purpose of determining more accurately than the written tests could do what the children understood by what they read. The reading selections were before the children during the interview.

All interviewing was done by the investigator according to a set interview but with variations on the basis of responses of individual children. An effort was made to make each interview as concrete as possible. For example, on the material on how fire was made, the children were given flint and steel and requested to show just how fire was made.

All interviews were recorded on dictaphone records. The children did not know the responses were being recorded.

ANALYSIS OF TEST RESULTS

SELECTIONS A AND C

The distribution on Form A was fairly normal with a range of 31 to 70 (possible total 78). The mean score was 51.43 and the standard deviation 7.84. Form C also showed a normal distribution with a range of 17 to 52 (possible total 65). The mean score was 33.94 and the standard deviation was 8.60.

Test scores for corresponding groupings were correlated. The coefficient (Pearson r) was .689 ± .046. Corrected for attenuation to discover what the relationship would be if both tests were perfectly reliable, the coefficient was .807.

The next matter studied: Do children respond to similar or identical test items consistently? If pupils respond to one test item in one way and to a similar item in the opposite way, it is difficult to believe that either answer gives a true picture of their understanding. In order to study this, all similar test items were grouped together and the percentages of consistency of responses to similar items were calculated.

TABLE 1. Mean Percentages of Responses to Test Items on Form A by IQ Groups

IQ	Number of Cases	Percentage of Consistency
80–89	10	53.04
90–99	19	38.74
100–109	17	50.64
110–119	5	57.39
120–129	5	66.09

Some of this inconsistency may be due to defects in the test items themselves; but very probably much of it (how much it is impossible to tell) is due to the unreliability of any one response made by a child on a written test.

The results of this tabulation are in

TABLE 2. Mean Percentages of Responses to Test Items on Form C by IQ Groups

IQ	Number of Cases	Percentage of Consistency
80–89	10	48.82
90–99	17	47.10
100–109	18	47.05
110–119	5	55.28
120–129	5	62.36

rather close agreement with those on Form A. In a general way it appears that the more intelligent children are more consistent in their responses to similar test items than the less intelligent ones.

These data, while subject to the limitations stated, seem to advise a cautious attitude in interpreting results secured from single test items.

Inconsistencies. Picture and map tests were used to determine whether or not pupils really know the correct meanings of the words they use. For example, in test items regarding the date of the Dred Scott decision only half the children who gave the correct date were able to choose a picture of the Lincoln-Douglas debate as representing the same time in history. In a map test designed to discover whether the pupils actually understood what territory was settled in the United States by 1763, only 58 percent of the pupils were consistent in their responses between map test and verbal test.

Ability to Secure Facts and to Make Inferences. A study was made of the relation between ability to secure facts and ability to make inferences from those facts. The investigator is unable to account for the great difference in

Test	Coefficient of Correlation
A	.382 ± .075
C	.650 ± .051

the results for the two tests. It may be that the inference items on one form were more difficult than those on the other. From the coefficient it is evident that the same factors are not operating in reading for facts and reading to make inferences. This generalization is supported by examination of the mean percentages of correct responses on factual and inferential items. The very low mean percentages for inferences indicate the need for better instruction on inferential reading.

SELECTIONS B AND D

The distribution of scores on these tests is fairly normal although Form D shows a bimodal curve. Correlation between the two tests was .642, corrected for attenuation .84.

	Range	Mean	SD
Form B	22–46	32.27	7.88
Form D	15–52	32.27	7.88

Securing Facts and Making Inferences. As in Forms A and C there was a large discrepancy between the two forms in the coefficient of correlation between ability to secure facts and ability to make inferences. In neither form was the coefficient high, B having a coefficient of .435 ± .061 and D having .650 ± .051. Mean percentages of cor-

rect responses on factual and inferential items indicate that pupils do much more ineffective inferential reading.

ANALYSIS OF INTERVIEWS

SELECTIONS A AND C

The percentage of consistency of response between tests and interviews was

TABLE 3. Mean Percentages of Consistency of Responses of Test Items and Interview Items by IQ Groups

IQ	Percentage of Consistency	
	Form A	Form C
80–89	74.00	64.05
90–99	75.26	61.96
100–109	77.46	68.36
110–119	85.32	83.10
120–129	89.38	86.80

computed. If a child was consistently right or consistently wrong he was considered consistent for the item.

These tables point out that children are not consistent in their responses. It should be noted, however, that the brighter children are more consistent than the duller children.

CHILDREN'S ERRONEOUS CONCEPTS

NATURE OF THE ERRORS

In Selection A three words gave the children most of their trouble. *Primitive* proved to be the most difficult. *Tender* and *projecting* also caused difficulty.

By far the greatest amount of trouble in Selection A was found in the sentence "Aside from the fireplace, the candle was the chief source of light." Many children simply omitted *aside from the fireplace* in interpreting the sentence; others thought the phrase meant away from or beside the fireplace.

Pupils gave a great many erroneous or inadequate answers to inferential questions.

In Selection B there were twelve words that seemed difficult for the children. Of these, *cradle, mankind,* and *reaper* seemed most troublesome. The *cradle* referred to is the tool which was used for cutting grain, a scythe with attachments.

The sentence "In some cases the harvest hands have eaten biscuits for dinner made from wheat that was standing in the fields in the early morning" was not understood by a majority of the children. Some thought that the biscuits were baked in the sun while others believed that grain could not be cut, threshed, ground into flour, and baked into biscuits in so short a time.

There were twelve words in Selection C that were difficult for pupils. *Sue, recourse, Supreme Court,* and *territory* were among these.

Five words were difficult in Selection D. These included *requisitioned, byword,* and "*not worth a continental.*" Similarly, *Stuffing their pockets with printed promises to pay* was not at all clear to the children.

TYPICAL READING COMPREHENSION DIFFICULTIES

As a result of this study a number of typical difficulties appeared.

1. Inability to suppress previous knowledge which does not apply to the particular selection read. For example, a pupil evidently had heard that fire may be produced by friction but seemed unable to understand that fire in the selection read was made by striking stone against steel.
2. Ignorance of word meaning.
3. Tendency to disregard certain parts of the sentence—for example, in the sentence "Aside from the fireplace, . . ." discussed above.
4. Tendency to consider the reading process as merely memorizing words which are to be given back to the teacher regardless of what they mean. For example, a student repeated the phrase "sue for his liberty" but could not explain what he meant.
5. Personal prejudice. For example, in discussing the most important part of the Dred Scott decision, a student said, "He didn't have any right to sue for his liberty."

CONCLUSIONS

1. Children are not always consistent in responding to different types of tests on identical or similar ideas.
2. There is a marked relationship between intelligence and consistency of pupil's responses to different types of tests on the same material.

3. Children sometimes chose the correct picture in a picture-choice test but demonstrated in the oral interviews that they had inadequate or erroneous concepts of what the picture represented.

4. On the whole, the pupils make a larger percentage of correct responses on the oral interviews than on the written test.

5. The fact that the words in which any given meaning is expressed are found in well-known vocabulary lists is no guarantee that the meaning will be gained by children. Children know certain meanings for a word, but they may not know the meaning necessary for the proper understanding of a given sentence.

6. Too much confidence should not be placed in verbal responses as evidence of understanding or in verbal presentation as an adequate method of teaching. The use of concrete materials such as models, maps, charts, and pictures wherever possible will make more certain a real understanding of the meanings presented.

7. The high percentage of correct responses in factual test items as compared with the small number of correct answers in inference test items is open to two interpretations:
   a. It may be that the responses to the factual test items although correct are no indication of proper understanding of the facts, and that a part of the inability to make inferences is due to the inadequate understanding of the facts upon which the inferences are based.
   b. It may be that the ability to make inferences is, of itself, so poorly developed in eighth-grade children that, even though the facts are adequate for a thorough understanding, inferences are not easily made.

8. Children are often unable to locate in the reading context the exact sentence upon which their test responses are based.

9. Children in the eighth grade do not seem to possess sufficient backgrounds in the fields of history, civics, economics, or geography, or even in general experience, to understand and interpret such technical material as judicial decisions, problems of federal finance, governmental theory, or economic processes.

10. It is difficult to predict what meaning or element in reading selections or in test questions will not be understood by any particular pupil at any given time.

11. The presentation of ideas in historical selections in sequence other than that in which the events occurred creates special difficulties for children.

12. Many children seem to possess a very rudimentary time sense as shown by their difficulties in arranging events in their proper sequences and their inability to choose contemporary events which belong to any given date.

13. Teaching children to comprehend what they read is more than the casual explanation of difficult ideas in words. The children must receive an adequate experience regarding each idea presented in words in the reading material.

TEACHING STUDENTS HOW TO READ SOCIAL STUDIES MATERIALS [1]

Kathleen B. Rudolf

[Impressed by such studies as the early effort of J. C. Dewey, a number of researchers have tried to specify just how social studies materials should be read. One of the more successful efforts was that undertaken by Kathleen B. Rudolf. She sought her answers at the same level as J. C. Dewey did: the eighth grade. Here she tried to spell out just what reading in the social studies entailed. Then she made her experimental assessment. One group was directed toward the particular abilities which seemed to be requisite in the social studies. The other group followed the normal pattern, assuming no particular instruction was required. The results of Rudolf's study seem worthy of careful appraisal.]

Two groups of eighth-grade pupils were studied to determine the effect of incorporating reading instruction into the presentation of the prescribed social studies content. It was assumed that the result of successful teaching would be measurable improvement in social studies information, in study skills, and in reading comprehension. Performance of the experimental and control groups was compared on a series of standardized achievement tests, administered before and after the period of special instruction.

Three hundred and sixty-five pupils in three Rochester, New York, high schools were used. These were all children who had completed the seventh grade and had just entered the first year of a five-year high school.

Experimental and control classes were selected to have (1) similar socioeconomic backgrounds as judged by the assistant superintendent and the high-school principals, (2) similar range of intelligence quotients, and (3) equal representation of superior, average, and slow classes. The background variables of chronological age, intelligence, and score on the New York State Reading Progress Test were then matched statistically.

Both groups of pupils were taught by experienced social studies teachers, who followed the same courses of study, used the same textbooks, and had available

[1] Adapted and abridged from Kathleen B. Rudolf, *The Effect of Reading Instruction on Achievement in Eighth Grade Social Studies*, Bureau of Publications, Teachers College, Columbia University, New York, 1949.

the same supplementary books, films, recordings, and current events periodicals, as well as other teaching aids. Specially prepared teaching materials were used by the teachers of the pupils in the experimental group throughout the first term of the eighth grade. These teaching materials were based upon social studies content and were designed to provide specific instruction and practice in the reading skills required in comprehension, interpretation, and application[2] of social studies materials, reference work, note-taking, outlining, and summarizing.

In planning the instructional material for the pupils in the experimental group, the relevant literature was canvassed and the skills[3] recommended were specifically considered. The essen-

[2] Table 1 contains a list of the reading skills incorporated in the teaching materials used for the experimental group.
[3] See Table 1.

TABLE 1.   The Social Studies Reading and Study Skills Reported in the Literature Which Were Provided For in the Instructional Materials Used in This Experiment

I. Skills Required in Comprehension, Interpretation, and Application
   1. To read social studies material with comprehension and discrimination.
   2. To read with sufficient care and attention to remember ideas gained from reading.
   3. To read carefully enough to distinguish exact meanings of questions and problems and to select specific facts to answer them.
   4. To read carefully enough to select main ideas.
   5. To appreciate cause-and-effect relationships.
   6. To appreciate significance of a long unit read.
   7. To make deductions.
   8. To perceive relationships which involve chronology.
   9. To raise relevant questions.
   10. To interpret facts presented.
   11. To make and apply generalizations.
   12. To read with comprehension and to make maps, charts, graphs, pictograms, and tables.
   13. To skim.
   14. To read for information necessary to participate in discussion or quiz programs, to make an oral report, write a story, essay, poem, letter, or drama, to prepare an exhibit, scrapbook, map, chart, or "Who's Who" for a suggested period of history.
   15. To read to follow directions.
   16. To understand general and technical vocabulary.
   17. To read extensively in response to stimulation caused by reading or viewing a film, listening to a discussion attentively and appreciatively, suggestions indicated in material read, et cetera.
   18. To listen attentively to discussions, reports, stories, and develop criteria to appraise these activities.

II. Skills Required in Reference Work
   1. To select relevant references for the solution of a problem or completion of an activity.
   2. To develop ability to use tables of contents, title pages, indexes, lists of maps, paragraph headings, marginal headings, and footnotes.
   3. To develop ability to use the library card index.
   4. To become familiar with sources of information, such as common reference material: Who's Who, World Almanac, Dictionary of American Biography, Pageant of America, unabridged dictionary, Compton's Encyclopedia, Reader's Guide to Periodical Literature, historical atlases, et cetera, and to learn how to use these aids.
   5. To evaluate materials as to source, authenticity, and relevance.
   6. To make and use bibliographies for units studied.

III. Skills Required in Note-taking, Outlining, and Summarizing
1. To discriminate between ideas of major and minor significance in making notes.
2. To complete outlines given the major headings.
3. To make complete outlines.
4. To make summaries.

tial difference in the methods employed by teachers of the experimental and control pupils was that the former directed attention to the understanding of printed matter. The "how to read it" emphasis, used by the teachers of the pupils in the experimental group, minimized errors and provided a realistic approach within the regular framework of the social studies. The pupils were given instruction in what they would have to do. They were taken through the steps carefully and had the satisfaction of immediate knowledge of their success. The usual approach used by teachers of pupils in the control group was based upon the assumption that pupils could read the materials of the social studies course. In the discussion which followed reading, if the competent readers responded correctly the teachers may not have been aware that many pupils got the facts, not from their own understanding of what they read, but from the discussion.

The special teaching materials were organized around the subject material of the first three units [4] in the eighth-grade course. The investigator used techniques and devices [5] described by authoritative educational opinion in the fields of reading and the social studies and some described in the research literature, as well as those indicated by her own experience. The series of teaching materials for each unit was designed to attain the subject-matter objectives as well as to assist pupils to develop and perfect the reading skills. Acquisition of reading and study skills to provide for maximum efficiency in the pursuit of social studies information was recognized as of importance equal to the attainment of social studies knowledge.

The equally experienced social studies teachers who taught the control group used their customary methods to attain their subject objectives. The procedure indicated by the local course of study [6] provides for the unit organization of subject matter and involves the solution of a series of suggested problem questions. It presumes reading supplemented by teacher explanation, discussion, use of maps, use of the library, outlining, answering questions, activities, et cetera. Inasmuch as there was no attempt to standardize methods of instruction, each control teacher was free to utilize his own experience in adjusting instruction to the individual needs of his pupils.

Data for the comparison of pupil achievement before and after the experiment were secured from results on the following tests:

The Kuhlmann-Anderson Intelligence Test.

The New York State Reading Progress Test.

The Thorndike-Lorge Reading Test, Forms 1, 3, 5.

The Cooperative Test Service Social Studies Test, Forms R and S.

The Cooperative Test Service Contemporary Affairs Test, Forms 1941 and 1942.

[4] Course of Study in Eighth Grade Social Studies, *An Epochal History of the United States*, Board of Education, Rochester, N.Y., 1938, p. 11.

[5] Strang, Ruth, *Study Type of Reading Exercise*, Bureau of Publications, Teachers College, Columbia University, New York, 1935, pp. 1–89; Gibbons, Alice N., *Directed Study Guide in the Origins of Contemporary Civilization*, Ginn and Company, Boston, 1934, pp. 250–253.

[6] Course of Study in Eighth Grade Social Studies, *op. cit.*

The Iowa Every-Pupil Tests of Basic Skills, Test B, Forms M and N.

The Rochester, New York, Term-End Examination in Eighth Grade Social Studies.

The data were analyzed by using M. Tappan's technique, "Partial Multiple Correlation Coefficients in a Universe of Manifold Characteristics," in combination with R. A. Fisher's "Discrimination Function." These statistics permit discrimination into two groups on the basis of multiple measurements. Tappan's treatment uses only that part of the score which is unrelated to the background variables to predict whether an individual belongs in the experimental group or the control group.

FINDINGS

Analysis of the data secured in this study reveals the following findings:

1. Statistically significant gains in social studies knowledge, study skills, and reading comprehension were made by all classes in the experimental group.

2. The mean score gains made by four of the experimental classes on the Cooperative Social Studies Test exceeded those made by the comparable control classes by 5.95, 6.13, 14.3, and 13.3 score points respectively.

3. The mean score achieved by the experimental classes on the city Term-End Examination was 10.6 score points higher than that of the control group.

4. On the Contemporary Affairs Test both experimental and control groups made gains in excess of expectancy.

5. The mean score gains made by five of the experimental classes on the Iowa Every-Pupil Tests of Basic Skills exceeded those made by control classes by 2.60, 10.97, 17.73, 31.89, and 24.57 score points respectively.

6. All of the experimental classes made marked gains in study skills, whereas both control slow classes actually incurred losses. The gross mean score gains in study skills [7] made by the experimental classes exceeded those made by the control classes by 2.6, 10.9, 17.8, 31.9, and 24.7 score points respectively. The normal mean score gain suggested by the authors of the test was 9.0 score points.

7. The reading gains made by the experimental classes were not only retained but increased during the subsequent term. (The control classes incurred losses in reading ability during both semesters.)

8. The mean score reading gains made by the experimental classes exceeded those made by the comparable control classes by three, twenty-two (superior classes), six, seven (average classes), six, fifteen (slow classes) months respectively.

EDUCATIONAL IMPLICATIONS

1. This study demonstrates the desirability of providing reading instruction in social studies classes in order that the pupils may more adequately master the social studies.

2. A corollary or by-product of this training is that pupils also improve in reading skills and increase their reading comprehension.

3. As a result of receiving this reading instruction pupils improve in those skills required for reference work, note-taking, outlining, and summarizing as well as ability to comprehend written materials.

4. This study shows that special reading instruction can be given in the regular social studies class without additional class time or additional expenditure for instruction, or any change in

---

[7] One experimental superior class made a slightly smaller mean score gain (4.6) than that of the comparable control class.

the regular departmental organization of the secondary school.

5. The difference in achievement of the pupils in the experimental and control groups indicates the need for consciously planned practice for the reading skills required in the social studies in the secondary school.

6. The failure of the pupils in the control group to equal the achievement of the pupils in the experimental group on measures of social studies information indicates the inadequacy of the usual approach used in teaching social studies for the development of the needed reading skills.

7. It is believed, as a result of the findings of this study, that it would be possible for teachers to apply this reading-emphasis approach to any course in the social studies.

THE READING INTERESTS OF BRIGHT, AVERAGE, AND DULL CHILDREN [1]

May Lazar

[Reading instruction in American schools, like instruction in most other areas, proceeds on the thesis that there are common bases from which teaching can proceed. Individual differences are recognized, but few schools attempt completely individualized instruction. Instead, some kind of grouping is attempted. But in order for any grouping to succeed, some mutuality must be discovered. May Lazar has investigated one frequent basis for grouping: intellectual capacity. Suppose children are sorted out on this basis: do they have interests in common? Can teachers find bases from which instruction can proceed?]

PURPOSES

An investigation involving 4300 pupils in New York City schools was undertaken to determine significant differences between retarded and non-retarded pupils in various factors: Are there significant differences in the reading interests of bright, average, and dull children? Do dull and retarded children have home surroundings not conducive to achievement in reading or to literary interests? Are there marked sex differences in reading interests?

About half the group of 4300 was selected for intensive study. The data for this group may be summarized as follows:

[1] Adapted and abridged from May Lazar, *Reading Interests, Activities and Opportunities of Bright, Average and Dull Children,* Bureau of Publications, Teachers College, Columbia University, New York, 1937.

	Boys	Girls	Total
Number of cases	1,039	989	2,027
Mean IQ [a]	102.0	101.3	101.6
Median IQ	99.3	98.0	98.6
Quartile deviation—IQ	14.2	13.7	14.0
Percentage of bright pupils	33.3	29.4	31.4
Percentage of average pupils	36.5	39.0	37.8
Percentage of dull pupils	30.2	31.6	30.8
Median chronological age in years	11.4	11.4	11.4
Quartile deviation—age	.55	.55	.55

Grades: 2A-8B
School progress: retarded, 40 percent; non-retarded, 60 percent
Racial make-up: white, 96.4 percent; Negro, 3.4 percent; yellow, 0.2 percent
Foreign-born parents: 60 percent of cases
Foreign language spoken at home: 40 percent of cases

[a] All IQ's according to Stanford-Binet Scale.

HOME BACKGROUND

It was found that the bright group had in general better environmental opportunities than either the average or the dull group, and the average group had better opportunities than the dull group.

1. More than 60 percent of the parents were foreign born. The predominating nationalities of the children's parents were American, Italian, Russian (Jewish); forty different countries were represented; the predominating foreign languages spoken in the homes were Italian and Jewish (about 44 percent).

2. About 52 percent of the fathers were classified as skilled and unskilled laborers. In the dull group 75 percent of the fathers were in these groups. In the bright group 40 percent of the fathers were in the professional and clerical groups. The dull group showed the largest percentage of unemployed fathers. The results of correlations showed a marked relation between the occupational status of the parents and the intelligence of the pupils; also between the home background status and the intelligence of the pupils.

3. A substantial correlation was found between the number of books in the homes and the intelligence of the children, and an even closer association between books in the home and socio-economic status.[2] Even when the effect of intelligence was eliminated there still remained a significant relation between these factors. Schools showing the largest percentages of foreign-born parents reported the largest percentages for no books in the homes.

4. As indicated by the correlations for number of magazines in the home, there was a decided association between this item and the IQ of the children and a slightly higher association with socioeconomic status. When the effect of each of these factors was eliminated, there still remained a significantly positive relationship. The "better" types of magazines were found in the homes of the bright pupils to a much greater extent than in the homes of the dull pupils. Children's magazines were found mostly in the homes of bright pupils. The correlation (contingency method) between IQ of pupils and kinds of magazines, although significant, was not so high as that between IQ and number of books in the home. The "better"

[2] Verner M. Sims, *Sims Score Card for Socio-Economic Status*, Public School Publishing Co., Bloomington, Illinois, 1927.

types of magazines were found in the homes of higher socioeconomic status.

5. The newspaper most frequently mentioned was one of the tabloids. The "better" types of papers were reported chiefly by the bright pupils; the tabloids were mentioned chiefly by the dull pupils. The lowest average IQ was shown for those who reported no newspaper read. Correlations by the contingency method showed a close relationship between the quality of the newspapers and the intelligence of the pupils.

6. An analysis of the responses of bright pupils rating lowest in socioeco-

nomic status showed that these pupils were interested in reading but that the quality of the material was inferior. There were too few dull pupils with high socioeconomic ratings to include in the study.

READING INTERESTS

PERCENTAGE OF PUPILS OWNING LIBRARY CARDS

Only 57 percent of the whole group reported "Yes." Table 1 shows the percentage of pupils having library cards according to IQ levels. These data show

TABLE 1. Pupils Having Library Cards

	130 and Above	120–129	110–119	100–109	90–99	80–89	Below 80
Percent boys	83	71	61	55	45	37	26
Percent girls	83	78	69	65	53	51	46

that the higher the intelligence level, the larger the percentage of pupils having library cards. The girls at each intelligence level, except the very highest, show a much larger percentage than the boys at the same level.

NUMBER OF BOOKS READ PER MONTH

Table 2 shows the median number of books for each IQ level. At each level except IQ 110–119, the girls showed a higher number than the boys for the

TABLE 2. Median Number of Books for Each IQ Level

	130 and Above	120–129	110–119	100–109	90–99	80–89	Below 80	All Levels
Boys, median number	4.4	4.4	3.7	3.1	2.6	1.7	1.0	2.7
Girls, median number	5.1	4.5	3.3	3.2	2.9	2.4	1.2	3.0

number of books reported as read. The ranks in number of books read agree closely with the ranks in intelligence ratings.

KIND OF BOOKS LIKED BEST

In response to the question "Check

twice the one kind you like best of all," it was found that mystery stories were the first choice of both boys and girls. The choices in rank order are summarized in Table 3.

Bright boys, however, preferred adventure and ranked mystery second. Average boys reported mystery as first choice and adventure second; dull boys preferred mystery stories with detective stories as second choice. Fairy tales re-

TABLE 3.   Kind of Book Liked Best According to Frequency of Mention

Rank	Kind	Boys Number	Percent	Kind	Girls Number	Percent
1.	Mystery	250	24.4	Mystery	269	27.5
2.	Adventure	227	22.1	Fairy tales	239	24.4
3.	Detective	206	20.1	Adventure	138	14.1
4.	History	99	9.6	Home and school	74	7.6
5.	Invention	69	6.7	History	55	5.6
6.	Science	66	6.4	Detective	53	5.4
7.	Nature and animal	48	4.7	Novels	47	4.8
8.	Fairy tales	24	2.3	Nature and animals	36	3.7
9.	Biography	16	1.6	Biography	25	2.6
10.	Novels	13	1.3	Poetry	25	2.6
11.	Home and school	7	.7	Science	12	1.2
12.	Poetry	1	.1	Invention	5	.5

ceived the highest number of votes from dull girls, with mystery ranking second. The percentage of dull girls who preferred fairy tales was more than twice the percentage of bright girls, and almost twice as large as the percentage of average girls. Average girls preferred mystery stories, with fairy tales ranking second; bright girls gave mystery as first choice and adventure as second. Fairy tales ranked third in order of choice for bright girls, second for average, and first for dull.

The five kinds of books liked best by bright, average, and dull boys are shown in Table 4.

The choices can also be ranked according to median IQ, as in Table 5.

TABLE 4.   Five Kinds of Books Liked Best by Bright, Average and Dull Boys

Percent Bright		Percent Average		Percent Dull	
Adventure	33.0	Mystery	23.4	Mystery	30.8
Mystery	19.7	Adventure	22.1	Detective	29.2
Detective	14.2	Detective	18.1	Adventure	9.8
Science	10.4	History	13.6	History	7.9
History	7.0	Invention	8.2	Nature and Animal	7.9

TABLE 5.   Books Liked Best by Bright, Average, and Dull Girls

Percent Bright		Percent Average		Percent Dull	
Mystery	27.1	Mystery	32.3	Fairy tales	38.3
Adventure	21.0	Fairy tales	21.1	Mystery	21.8
Fairy tales	14.4	Adventure	14.1	Detective	8.6
Novels	9.6	Home and school	7.0	Adventure	7.6
Home and school	9.3	History	6.2	Home and school	6.6

For "kinds of books liked best" the ranks in average Socio-Economic Index were very similar to the ranks according to intelligence. Novels, science, and adventure were among the highest for both intelligence and socioeconomic status. "Fairy tales" were chosen by the lowest in socioeconomic status for boys and girls; poetry and detective stories also were chosen by those low in socioeconomic status as in the case of intelligence.

When responses to the two questions ("books I liked" and "books I liked best of all") were analyzed according to ages, it was found that nature and animal stories, fairy tales, home and school life, poetry, and biography were mentioned more frequently by ten-year olds than by eleven- and twelve-year-olds. Novels, adventure, invention, and science were mentioned more often by the older pupils.

The findings for this item seem to warrant the following conclusions:

1. There are marked sex differences in choices of books. Although both boys and girls like mystery stories, adventure, and history, there are decided preferences in the case of other types. Girls show a definite preference for fairy tales.

They also choose novels, poetry, and stories of home and school more often than boys do. Boys are less interested in fairy tales and poetry or stories of home and school. Girls have little interest in detective stories or in books dealing with science and invention.

2. There seems to be a definite relationship between intelligence ratings of pupils and types of books liked best. According to intelligence ratings, novels, science, and adventure ranked highest. Fairy tales, detective stories, nature and animal stories and poetry ranked lowest.

3. Socioeconomic ratings and quality of books were shown to be associated. The types ranking highest and lowest according to intelligence showed similar ranks according to socioeconomic ratings.

KINDS OF MAGAZINES LIKED BEST

The five kinds of magazines most frequently mentioned by bright, average, and dull boys respectively are shown in Table 6, which indicates that all groups of boys showed preference for the same five types of magazines but in slightly different order.

Of the five kinds of magazines liked

TABLE 6. Books Liked Best According to Median IQ

Kind	Boys Median IQ	Number	Kind	Girls Median IQ	Number
Novels	123.0	13	Novels	121.8	47
Science	112.1	66	Adventure	106.9	138
Adventure	110.1	227	Home and school	100.9	74
Biography	103.3	16	Science	100.0	12
Invention	101.6	69	Mystery	99.4	269
History	97.3	99	History	98.8	55
Mystery	96.0	250	Nature and animal	97.8	36
Detective	93.2	206	Poetry	96.4	25
Nature and animal	90.0	48	Biography	95.5	25
Fairy tales	88.6	24	Fairy tales	90.7	239
			Detective	90.5	53

TABLE 7. Magazines Liked Best by Bright, Average, and Dull Boys

Percent Bright		Percent Average		Percent Dull	
Science and mechanics	37.3	Detective and mystery	29.0	Detective and mystery	28.4
Detective and mystery	30.1	Science and mechanics	23.2	Science and mechanics	7.7
Children's	19.1	Children's	11.1	General story	7.7
Adventure	18.8	General story	8.4	Adventure	6.7
General story	11.8	Adventure	8.2	Children's	5.1

TABLE 8. Magazines Liked Best by Bright, Average, and Dull Girls

Percent Bright		Percent Average		Percent Dull	
Children's	39.5	Movie and theater	22.5	General story	20.2
Movie and theater	19.9	General story	20.7	Movie and theater	12.8
General story	18.9	Detective and mystery	14.8	Detective and mystery	8.7
Science and mechanics	14.1	Serious-popular	10.4	Serious-popular	6.4
Literary	10.3	Household	9.8	Household	5.4

best by bright, average, and dull girls the two types common to all groups were movie and theater and general story magazines. The average and the dull girls liked the same five types in practically the same order of preference.

TABLE 9. Newspaper Sections Liked Best by Bright, Average, and Dull Boys

Percent Bright		Percent Average		Percent Dull	
Comics	73.0	Comics	82.2	Comics	85.8
Sport	37.1	Sport	21.6	Sport	6.6
News	12.8	Crimes	4.1	Stories	5.6

PART OF THE NEWSPAPER ENJOYED MOST

The three sections of the newspaper mentioned most frequently by bright, average, and dull boys and the three sections mentioned most frequently by bright, average, and dull girls are shown in Tables 8 and 9. The same three sections were liked by all three groups of girls.

TABLE 10. Newspaper Sections Liked Best by Bright, Average, and Dull Girls

Percent Bright		Percent Average		Percent Dull	
Comics	87.0	Comics	91.7	Comics	88.2
News	13.7	News	5.6	News	4.4
Crossword puzzles	8.4	Crossword puzzles	5.3	Crossword puzzles	3.0

IMPLICATIONS

The emphasis in reading programs should be on how to improve the quality of reading for all types of pupils. We must begin to devise methods for interesting pupils in other than purely narrative materials. Pupils should be trained to read thoughtfully and therefore it will be necessary to include more factual material. This cannot be done if we emphasize only "make-believe" literature. Children should be taught to read some material dealing with the realities of life in order to arouse a desire for knowledge. How can we expect thoughtful reading in adults if the habits are not begun sometime in childhood?

DIFFERENCES IN BOYS' AND GIRLS' READING INTERESTS [1]

George W. Norvell

[Unlike most educational systems in the rest of the world, American schools are largely coeducational at the upper-grade and high-school levels. How large a problem does this pose for reading instruction? It has been noted that most reading instruction depends upon finding some common bases for teaching. Do preadolescent and adolescent boys and girls have enough interests in common to permit instruction out of the same materials? George W. Norvell's study is certainly the most comprehensive investigation to date attempting to answer this query. To obtain his data, Norvell surveyed over 50,000 boys and girls in grades seven to twelve.]

The factors influencing children's reading interests will be considered through regroupings which bring together all selections dominated by a single interest factor (for example, humor) whether the selections are poems, stories, or essays. We will conclude with a section presenting specific suggestions on selecting reading materials for boys and girls.

To undertake a grouping by special interests raises a question to which at present there seems no satisfactory answer: Among the special-interest factors, which are the most significant? The only procedure that seemed defensible in the current study was to attempt to discern the factors of interest which the data themselves suggested were significant and to employ them tentatively. There are, unquestionably, other interest factors. According to the plan just described, the data were grouped under the following nineteen headings: grim physical adventure; adventure without grimness; love; sentiment (not romantic love); home and family life; the supernatural (not religion); religion; obvious humor; subtle humor; animals; form, technique, word choice; didacticism; reflection and philosophy; description; pa-

[1] Adapted and abridged from George W. Norvell, *The Reading Interests of Young People*, D. C. Heath & Co., Boston, 1950.

triotism; nature; narration; male characters; and female characters.

Two interest factors instead of one may be found throughout certain groupings. For example, adventure, whether grim or mild, involves narration. However, "narration" is found in selections where adventure is absent. Further, it appears helpful to make possible a comparison of selections which are narrative with other groupings which are not, since the contrast, as will be discussed later, is significant.

ADVENTURE

Boys enjoy adventure stories and poems of all types except when the selections are alloyed with disliked elements such as love and the supernatural. Even in such cases the story or poem may be ranked high provided the alloying interest factor is found in moderation and other factors (e.g., humor, animals) support a stirring adventure. Boys favor in particular physical encounter, war, and violent games.

Girls enjoy many types of adventure stories almost as well as boys do, provided only that the element of grim physical struggle is absent. Violent physical activity may be entirely acceptable to girls, as shown by their enjoyment of stories of school games and poems about sports, so long as the struggle remains sport. Noteworthy is girls' approval of the detective story, the mystery (provided the supernatural is not markedly involved), and indeed almost all kinds of adventure stories which omit fierce, grim, or gory struggle.

HUMOR

Both boys and girls enjoy humor of the simple, obvious type, though girls rank such selections 3.4 points higher than do boys. Neither boys nor girls rank subtle humor high, though here again girls rank it higher by 5.5 points than do boys.

In this study "subtle humor" includes not only humor which calls for mental acumen for its understanding but in addition humor which depends upon allusion, parody, and other devices making a demand (even slight) upon the erudition of the reader. It seems possible that the true division between classifications of humor so far as children's favorable and unfavorable reactions are concerned might well be: humor, understood; and humor, not understood.

ANIMALS

Of all the special factors causing boys and girls to rate reading materials high, the factor "animals" ranks at or near the top. This would be clearer except for certain technicalities of the tabulation. If, for example, the two classifications of selections of adventure had been combined (as were the two for "wild" animals and "domestic" animals), the ranking for adventure as a whole would have fallen several points under the ranking for animals as a factor. Or, had the score for domestic animals been kept separate from the score for wild animals, the former would have been higher by several points than the combined results tabulated under "animals."

PATRIOTISM

Both boys and girls show marked interest in patriotic selections. Whether the interest factor patriotism appeals more to girls than to boys, as the tabulation suggests, or whether the 2.9 points higher score given by girls is due to other interest factors in the selections merits further investigation.

SENTIMENT

The interest factor sentiment (excluding romantic love) is shown by the tabulation to be definitely more influential with girls than with boys. An examination of the 105 selections where sentiment is a prominent factor reveals that a large proportion of them are calculated to arouse sympathy in the reader. Previous studies of reading interests agree that girls are more strongly influenced than are boys by the gentler emotions.

LOVE

The dominance of the factor love in a selection, even a story, places it beyond the pale with the great majority of boys. Love stories rate on the average 54.5 points with boys, and love poems 51.1 points. Girls rate selections dominated by love 16.5 points higher on the average than do boys. The spread between boys' and girls' ratings on selections dominated by sentiment other than romantic love is 10.0 points. The only classification rivaling love poems in unpopularity with boys is nature poetry (51.7 points). It should be stated, too, that one-third of the love poems used in the tabulation present more or less of a story (a favorable interest factor), while in the nature poems the narrative element is very largely absent.

In view of the great spread of 16.5 points between boys' and girls' ratings of selections dominated by love, it would be easy to assume that this factor rates higher with girls than it actually does. Contrast the rating girls give love stories (76.4) with their ratings of the following kinds of stories: school games, 76.7; detective, 78.4; domestic animals, 81.2; humor, 78.9; school life (not games), 76.8; and patriotism, 77.2. Likewise, contrast girls' ratings of love poems (66.0) with their scores on certain other types of poems: sentimental, 71.2; religious, 67.0; supernatural, 70; didactic, 69.7; patriotic, 78.7; obvious humor, 78.0; and home and family life, 78.4.

This evidence suggests that while dominance by love is sufficient to bar a selection with most boys, it requires more than the factor love to insure high popularity with girls.

HOME AND FAMILY LIFE

The spread of 17.2 points between boys' and girls' scores for selections relating to the home emphasizes the much greater fondness of girls for such stories. Also important is the fact that both boys and girls place these stories approximately ten points higher than they place love stories.

RELIGION; THE REFLECTIVE AND PHILOSOPHICAL; NATURE

The poems relating to religion and to philosophy bear out the findings in previous studies that girls in general are more strongly influenced by these factors than are boys. Nature, as represented by flowers, birds, bees, and trees, has a greater appeal for girls than for boys. Yet even with girls nature divorced from narrative stirs little enthusiasm.

THE SUPERNATURAL; THE DIDACTIC

The supernatural and the didactic are similar as interest factors in two respects: (1) neither boys nor girls find these elements attractive; (2) the spread between boys' and girls' ratings in the case of each factor is small.

It is interesting to note that while boys and girls give evidence of liking stories of the supernatural almost equally well, when individual stories are concerned there are considerable differences that appear to be assignable to the influence of other factors. For example, boys show a preference for "The Gray Champion" (fighting) and for "The Masque of the Red Death" (bloody death). The girls may be influenced by the element of romantic love in approving "The Specter Bridegroom." Of the eight poems of the supernatural, girls prefer all but one, "The Skeleton in Armor," which, in spite of a minor love element, is predominantly a ballad of adventure. Preferences for myths and legends are almost equally divided between boys and girls. Yet here, too, we find the boys preferring fighting and grim adventure ("Adventures of Thor," "Hercules," "King Arthur Stories"), while the girls choose love and the other soft emotions ("The Weaver Maiden and the Herdsman," "Persephone," "The Other Wise Man").

DESCRIPTION

That description alone is unattractive to boys and girls in almost equal degree is indicated by the narrowness of the spread (2.2 points) and the low average interest score (58.9 points). An examination of boys' and girls' preferences among descriptive selections strengthens this conclusion by suggesting that such divergences as exist result from the presence of interest factors already recognized as influencing children's choices. Each of the three descriptions preferred by boys ("Description of Little America," "Jungle Night," "Trees at Timberline") reveals nature in a challenging mood. By contrast, girls prefer "Sunday in London" and "Sunrise in Louisiana."

FORM, TECHNIQUE

The evidence is strong that selections which depend upon artistry rather than upon content seldom make a hit with secondary-school children. This does not mean, of course, that children are totally unaffected by the beauties of form and technique. It does mean, probably, that children, like most adults, insist upon content as the touchstone of interest.

MALE CHARACTERS; FEMALE CHARACTERS

The 106 selections in which male characters predominate show beyond reasonable doubt that girls are almost as ready as boys to read with interest of the doings of boys and men, the only serious exceptions being, apparently, selections in which grim or deadly physical struggle is a factor. It is just as evident that boys refuse to be concerned with most selections in which female characters play the dominant roles. The evidence: the spread between boys' and girls' ratings of selections dominated by male characters, 3.2 points; the spread between boys' and girls' ratings of selections dominated by female characters, 17.7 points. Terman and Lima report: "From the reading records of our children it was found that 18 per cent of the girls' reading was in the field of boys' books, but only 2 per cent of the boys' reading was the human interest story of home or school life that girls so much enjoy." [2]

NARRATION

An examination of the data for the various types of narrative indicates that both boys and girls enjoy all types of narrative material with one exception: boys reject narratives in which girls or women play the leading roles. A further examination of the table presented reveals that there are only two of the special-interest factors potent enough, without benefit of narrative, to cause the selections in which these factors predominate to be rated well-liked on the average by both boys and girls: obvious humor and patriotism.

TWO INTEREST FACTORS PROMINENT

The current study affords a number

[2] L. M. Terman and M. Lima, *Children's Reading*, D. Appleton and Co., New York, 1925.

of selections in which two of the special-interest factors instead of one are prominent. The ratings of such selections by boys and by girls in the main are what would be expected from a knowledge of the scores given to selections where one only of the special-interest factors is important. It appears that while selections combining adventure and sentiment are fairly well liked by both boys and girls, the combining of romantic love with adventure causes a noticeable divergence. Girls like the combination of love with adventure even better than they like sentiment and adventure. On the other hand, boys, in accord with their revealed dislike of the factor love, rate stories of adventure and love on the average 2.7 points lower than stories of adventure and sentiment, while poems of adventure and love are rated, on the average, 6.6 points lower than poems of adventure and sentiment. Further, when humor and love are combined, boys' unfavorable reactions become even more marked. It is unfortunate that we have only three poems combining adventure and patriotism (both well-liked factors) in marked degree. However, the fact that both boys and girls rank these poems higher than they rank selections dominated by one of these two factors suggests what would seem reasonable: that a multiplication of favorable factors raises the popularity of a selection above the level it would have achieved had reliance been placed upon a single factor.

CHOOSING INTERESTING READING MATERIALS FOR CHILDREN

Since the differences in the reading interests of boys and girls are marked, the appraisal of the suitability of a selection should be made separately for boys and for girls of the secondary school. Then, if the object is to determine the suitability of a certain selection for both boys and girls, it is necessary only to answer one further question: Does it rank high by both analyses?

In examining a selection for interest factors attractive to boys we may well look first for narration. If the selection fails to tell a story, its chances with boys, except where obvious humor or patriotism is a dominant factor, are poor. A second factor equally to be insisted upon, if human characters are present, is that male rather than female characters be dominant. With these two requisites present we may then balance the favorable against the unfavorable interest factors.

If the selection is dominated by any one or a combination of the following (assuming certain adverse factors enumerated below to be absent), we may be reasonably confident that the selection will rank well with boys: adventure (including war), animals, obvious humor, and patriotism. Sentiment (except romantic love) and the supernatural may be considered neutral factors if they are not obtrusive. The same may be said of didacticism, with the added caution that the "lesson" must be very well concealed. Factors that lower the ranking of the selection (the degree of lowering depending upon the prominence of the factor) are: romantic love, home and family life, and religion. Perhaps it should be added that there are certain factors which appear to have no adverse effect when they are minor accompaniments yet will not be tolerated as major factors: form or literary finish; "nature" in quotation marks; description. Two interest factors are sufficiently powerful to recommend a selection to boys even without the component narration: obvious humor and patriotism.

As with boys, the first characteristic to look for in appraising selections for girls' reading is narration. Perhaps girls

Special Factors Influencing Reading Interest

Factors, with Subgroups	Total Number of Selections	Percent of Liking—Boys	Percent of Liking—Girls	Percent Liked—Average	Difference Girls—Boys	Level of Significance t Ratio [a]
Adventure without grimness						
Outdoor adventure (mild): short stories 8; poems 7						
Games (outdoor, school): short stories 6; poems 3						
School life (not games) 4						
Mystery (detective stories) 12						
Mystery (non detective stories) 6	46	78.5	75.3	76.9	—3.2	2%
Adventure, grim: short stories 12; poem 21	33	74.7	64.1	69.4	—10.6	1%
Humor, obvious: essays 27; poems 33	60	73.7	77.1	75.4	3.4	1%
Humor, subtle: poems	17	62.0	67.5	64.9	5.5	1%
Animals						
Domestic animals: short stories 17; poems 9						
Wild animals: stories 24	50	79.0	74.6	76.8	—4.4	1%

Patriotism: short stories 4; poems, 15	19	75.3	78.4	74.9	3.1	2%
Narration: short stories 214; narrative poems 73; story essays 10; novels 47; plays 62; biographies 50	456	71.9	73.9	72.9	2.0	1%
Male characters	106	75.5	72.3	73.9	−3.2	1%
Female characters	27	59.1	76.8	68.0	17.7	1%
Love (romantic): short stories 11; poems 35	46	52.0	68.5	60.3	16.5	1%
Sentiment (not romantic love): short stories 17; poems 88	105	61.5	71.5	66.5	10.0	1%
Home and family life: short stories 14; poems 8	22	59.2	76.4	67.8	17.2	1%
The supernatural: stories 13; poems 8; myths and legends 12; folk tales 4	37	66.0	68.6	67.3	2.6	10%
Didacticism: essays 45; poems 14	59	60.3	63.6	62.0	3.3	1%
Religion: poems	23	56.6	67.0	61.8	10.4	1%
Form, technique, word choice: poems	26	56.9	63.3	60.1	6.4	1%
Reflective, philosophical: poems	59	57.4	65.9	61.7	8.5	1%
Description: essays	9	57.8	60.0	58.9	2.2	1%
Nature: poems	65	51.7	63.8	57.8	12.1	1%

[a] At the 1 percent level of significance not more than one sample in 100 would show a difference as large as the observed difference merely because of chance sampling errors when there was no difference in population values. At the 2 percent level not more than two samples in 100; etc.

are a little more insistent on this factor than boys. At any rate, it ranks very high. Characters may be either male or female, though girls rank selections whose chief characters are girls or women 4.5 points higher on the average. Several of the special factors that are favorable to popularity with boys influence girls in a similar way. However, some of these favorable factors are more influential with girls, some less. Somewhat more interesting to girls than to boys are the factors humor and patriotism; less interesting, but still promoting interest, are the milder forms of adventure and animal stories. Sentiment, which may have a neutral effect on boys' reading choices, is a markedly favorable factor where girls are concerned. Favorable, too, are romantic love, and home and family life. Certain interest factors which are approximately neutral with boys (for example, the supernatural) also appear to have little effect either way with girls, though girls accord them a somewhat higher rating than do boys. As with boys, there are interest factors which will not be tolerated by girls as dominant factors that appear to be accepted by them in moderate amounts: form, or literary finish; "nature"; description. As a general rule we may say that the neutral factors and those which are rejected when present in large amounts are tolerated to a greater degree by girls than by boys.

To repeat in effect what was said earlier: If a selection is to be satisfactory for reading by girls and boys in common, it must meet the separate standards for girls' and for boys' reading materials.

The reading materials generally used in literature classes are better liked by girls than by boys in a ratio of more than two to one, and on the evidence of the data collected in this study seven of eight literary types are better liked by girls than by boys. The question arises, then, whether these figures are true with respect to boys' and girls' reactions toward literature in general or whether they apply only to the materials chosen by educators for classroom use. Since the question is posed most strongly with respect to poetry (1) because of the marked divergence in the attitudes of boys and girls toward it and (2) because poetry constitutes such a large part of the literary material offered to high-school children, a minor investigation was made. The results suggest a tentative answer.

The plan was to compare the list of several hundred poems afforded by the current study with a standard anthology of poetry prepared for sale to the general public. If this collection included a better proportional representation of poems better liked by boys than by girls than did school classrooms, it might be expected that among the poems common to both the anthology and our list a somewhat higher proportion would prove to be better liked by boys than the proportion shown by our total list of poems. The results, whatever they showed, should help to determine the relative attitudes of boys and girls toward poetry. This comparison would throw light also on the question as to whether the poems commonly used for class study were better liked, as a whole, than selections found in more representative collections.

To insure that the general anthology of poetry to be compared with our list should not be unconsciously skewed by feminine preferences, it seemed desirable to choose a collection edited by a man. *What I Like in Poetry*, by William Lyon Phelps, was selected. Every poem found in this book and also included on our lists was tabulated. Of the 150 poems thus secured, only 10 percent were better liked by boys, compared with 19 percent for our list of 446. Boys gave the 150 poems an interest score of 57.6 (our 466 poems, 60.7); girls rated the 150 poems 67.5, compared with 68.3 for the list of 466. The spread between boys and girls for the 150 poems of Phelps' collection was 9.9 points; for the 466 poems, 7.6 points.

If Phelps' collection is a fair sample of the poetry read by the general public and is representative as to literary quality, the comparisons made tend to confirm certain findings presented elsewhere in this study:

1. That girls like poetry decidedly better than do boys.
2. That girls' tastes in poetry are more literary than boys' tastes. (The assumption is made that the Phelps collection is of good literary quality.)
3. That if boys are to enjoy poems in the classroom as much as girls do, teachers and curriculum specialists must make a major revision in the poetry offered as a basis for class instruction.

Chapter VI

IMPROVING UNDERSTANDING AND TASTES

Introduction

"Reading is thinking," says Thorndike in one of the studies printed in this chapter. Viewed in this light, the central task of reading instruction is to improve understanding, not merely to sound out words or even just to retain ideas uncriticized. This places the domain of teaching considerably beyond such narrow provinces as eye movements, recognition spans, and reading speed.

But not everyone does view reading in this light. There is by no means universal approval of the concept that the assessing and appraising of ideas is as basic a component of the reading process as the recognition of words. To many, the task of teaching is done if the ideas can be reiterated intact.

This concept of reading also bears directly on what is involved in increasing speed of reading. Can there be such a development as "speed" *per se* or must this development always be thought of as speed of comprehension? There is, of course, a subsidiary issue: Is speed of reading dependent upon the number, scope, and depth of ideas encountered? And still another subordinate problem: Can speed of reading be divorced from the intent of the reader—casual, analytical, cursory, or detailed—whatever his purpose be? One example of the research of a long-time student of these and allied issues is included for study.

The whole problem of vocabulary and its relationship to understanding needs to be broached, too, in this chapter. Each field of learning has its own technical vocabulary. That is, each field employs words with specific significances for the kinds of ideas with which the field deals. The issue at once arises: Can vocabulary be taught best by direct instruction or should vocabulary be learned incidentally? One of the best-known figures in reading research together with a co-worker has provided one answer.

One final area of investigation is of concern in this chapter. It is the matter of improving tastes. This is the aesthetic concomitant of intellectual appraisal. Some have called this kind of reading "enjoying the creative satisfactions of language." Such satisfactions presumably include the sounds, the rhythms, the images of language as well as its capacities to evoke highly individual feeling responses by allusion, comparison, and suggestion. "Appreciation" in any one of the arts has been difficult to define and hence difficult to foster. Two primary foci of conflict in reading as an art have concerned "free" reading and the "comics." "Free" reading refers to the practice of giving students a kind of carte blanche to read on their own time whatever they choose. The assumption behind this practice seems to be that selectivity will naturally grow out of freedom to explore many kinds of books. The assumption has, of course, drawn attack. The other focus of disaffection, the "comics," recurrently makes a book like Seduction of the Innocent certain to enjoy wide circulation. In particular, so-called "comic books" are regularly charged with inducing delinquency, facilitating immorality, and, in general, ruining the taste of young people for "better" reading. The research evidence included in this chapter on "free" reading and the "comics" may be a spur to other investigators who will furnish additional data to quiet some of the more exaggerated fears.

READING TO SOLVE PROBLEMS [1]

Roma Gans

[American educators have long been fascinated with the possibilities of the scientific method as a way of studying and learning. Since this approach involves the systematic analysis of problems, "problem solving" has been a recurrent term in educational literature. In almost any kind of problem the printed word is a potent resource. How should records of data be managed by an effective reader? Is his responsibility largely to be able to reproduce what he reads accurately? Or should

[1] Adapted and abridged from Roma Gans, A Study of Critical Reading Comprehension in the Intermediate Grades, Contributions to Education, No. 811, Teachers College, Columbia University, New York, 1940.

reading instruction also be concerned with developing readers who select and reject as they read?]

Emphasis on reference reading in the intermediate grades makes critical comprehension in reading a prerequisite for the pupil in these grades. What is the difference between the common type of reading usually measured by reading-comprehension tests and critical comprehension which requires selection or rejection of content for use in solving a problem?

PROCEDURES

A reliable criterion of reading comprehension as commonly measured was derived from the Thorndike-McCall Reading Scale, Form 5; the Gates Silent Reading Test, Types A, B, and D; and the California Test of Mental Maturity, Elementary Series, Tests 5, 14, 15, and 16. The investigator designed a Test of Selection-Rejection as a criterion of critical comprehension in reading. This test included (1) descriptions of classroom situations in which problems arise, (2) reading material written to represent the style and content of books commonly used in the intermediate grades, (3) opportunities to select or reject paragraphs in the light of their relevancy to a problem, (4) checks on the pupil's understanding of the problem, and (5) checks on pupils' ability to mark sentences (which either stated some important element in the paragraph or were "joker" sentences) with three alternatives: B, believe this statement; T, states an item included in the paragraphs; H, includes information relevant to the problem.

The Test of Selection-Rejection was examined for readability. As an index, the scores where the child indicated that the ideas had or had not been included in the paragraph were used. The percent of correct responses of these scores was 71.4, which indicated that the paragraph and sentence test items were to a practical degree comprehended by the pupils.

The data on the responses designed to check the pupils' understanding of the problem also confirmed readability.

In a study of reliability the scores on the paragraphs to be chosen for relevancy to the problem were examined. Odd-numbered items were correlated with evens and the obtained coefficients corrected for double length by use of the Spearman-Brown formula. The results show the following coefficients of reliability for each type of paragraph: r (directly relevant paragraphs) $= .73$; r (remotely relevant paragraphs) $= .67$; r (fanciful-irrelevant paragraphs) $= .81$; r (encyclopedic-irrelevant paragraphs) $= .87$; r (sheerly irrelevant paragraphs) $= .90$.

By computing bi-serial coefficients between the scores of each of the seventy items of paragraph selection and the reading criterion (obtained from the usual reading-comprehension tests), additional evidence was obtained concerning the inner consistency of each type (i.e., directly relevant paragraphs, remotely relevant paragraphs, etc.) and also the variation from type to type. Not one item has a high bi-serial coefficient. The scores on the remotely relevant type of paragraph show least community of function with the reading criterion.

In a further study of the variations within the test, the scores made on the five types of paragraphs were intercorrelated to ascertain the degree of sameness revealed between type and type. These results showed the reading of directly relevant paragraphs to be independent of the abilities demanded by the other four types; the abilities needed to select fanciful, encyclopedic, and irrelevant paragraphs revealed great uniformity; and the abilities used in selecting remotely relevant paragraphs showed no significant relationship with those used in the directly relevant, but revealed a high negative correlation with the abilities used in the other three types.

The intercorrelations of the five subtests seem to indicate that a *pattern* of selecting or rejecting rather than a *process* of evaluating and weighing dominates the reading selection-rejection in the test. In general, the pupil who rejects fanciful paragraphs tends to reject remotely relevant ones, the pupil who rejects encyclopedic tends to reject remotely relevant, and the pupil who rejects irrelevant tends to reject remotely relevant—the factor of rejection operating consistently; whereas the pupil who accepts fanciful or encyclopedic or irrelevant tends to accept remotely relevant—the factor of acceptance operating consistently.

CONCLUSIONS

The coefficients of correlation of all the five types of selection-rejection (directly relevant, remotely relevant, fanciful, encyclopedic, sheerly irrelevant) in critical comprehension indicate that these abilities are not closely related to the abilities usually measured in reading comprehension.

A study of the relation between paragraph and sentence selection revealed that the two abilities have great community. Sentences from directly relevant paragraphs have a high positive relationship with sentences from remotely relevant paragraphs but a significant negative relationship with sentences from fanciful, encyclopedic, or sheerly irrelevant paragraphs.

Factor analysis showed that reference reading is a composite ability with reading ability as most potent, selection-rejection pattern as next most potent, and some function of the type of delayed recall measured by sentence selection-rejection as third most potent.

Pupils encountered the greatest difficulty in selecting the remotely relevant and next greatest difficulty in selecting the fanciful. In these difficulties, the conjecture which seems most reasonable to the investigator is that the factors of authenticity of content and relevancy of content are not dealt with in the teaching of reading. Pupils acquire or do not acquire discernment independently of their reading instruction.

Further investigation of the problem of critical comprehension is needed for all age groups, because gullibility in reading functioning conjointly with high ability in reading comprehension is an incongruity which should not be tolerated in a process directed toward education.

READING AS REASONING [1]

Edward L. Thorndike

[Thorndike was among the first to examine the relationship between reading and mental processes. His efforts profoundly influenced later investigators of reading comprehension. Particularly useful was his description of the difference between recognizing words as independent elements and recognizing words in their proper relationships. Much controversy about word recognition could be resolved if this Thorndike study were adequately brought to bear upon the issue.]

It seems to be a common opinion that reading (understanding the meaning of printed words) is a rather simple compounding of habits. Each word or phrase is supposed, if known to the reader, to call up its sound and meaning, and the series of word or phrase meanings is supposed to be, or be easily transmitted into, the total thought. It is perhaps more exact to say that little attention has been paid to the dynamics whereby a series of words whose meanings are known singly produces knowledge of the meaning of a sentence or paragraph.

It will be the aim of this article to show that reading is a very elaborate procedure involving a weighing of each of many elements in a sentence, their organization, the proper relation to one another, the selection of certain of their connotations and the rejection of others, and the coöperation of many forces to determine final response. In fact we

shall find that the act of answering simple questions about a simple paragraph like the one shown below includes all the features characteristic of typical reasonings.

Read this and then answer the questions 1, 2, 3, 4, 5, 6, and 7. Read it again as often as you need to.

In Franklin, attendance upon school is required of every child between the ages of seven and fourteen on every day when school is in session unless the child is so ill as to be unable to go to school, or some person in his house is ill with a contagious disease, or the roads are impassable.

1. What is the general topic of the paragraph?
2. On what day would a ten-year-old girl not be expected to attend school?
3. Between what years is attendance upon school compulsory in Franklin?
4. How many causes are stated which make absence excusable?
5. What kind of illness may permit a

[1] Adapted and abridged from E. L. Thorndike, "Reading as Reasoning: A Study of Mistakes in Paragraph Reading," *Journal of Educational Psychology* (1917), 8:323–332.

boy to stay away from school, even though he is not sick himself?

6. What condition in a pupil would justify his non-attendance?

7. At what age may a boy leave school to go to work in Franklin?

Responses were obtained from 200 pupils in Grade 6. The responses do not fall into a few clearly defined groups. We can, however, progress toward an explanation by using the following facts and principles:

In correct reading (1) each word produces a correct meaning, (2) each such element of meaning is given a correct weight in comparison with the others, and (3) the resulting ideas are examined and validated to make sure that they satisfy the mental set or adjustment or purpose for whose sake the reading was done. Reading may be wrong or inadequate (1) because of wrong connections with the words singly, (2) because of over-potency or under-potency of elements, or (3) because of failure to treat the ideas produced by the reading as provisional, and so to inspect and welcome or reject them as they appear.

With regard to (1) a word may produce all degrees of erroneous meaning for a given context, from a slight inadequacy to an extreme perversion.

Thus in the responses the word *Franklin* varies from its exact meaning as local unit through degrees of vagueness to meaning a man's name (as in "Franklin attends to his school" as a response to question 1), or to meaning a particular personage (as in "It was a great inventor" as a response to question 1).

In particular, the relational words, such as pronouns, conjunctions, and prepositions, have meanings of many degrees of exactitude. They also vary in different individuals in the amount of force they exert. A pupil may know exactly what *though* means, but he may treat a sentence containing it much as he would treat the same sentence with *and* or *or* or *if* in place of *though*.

With regard to (2) a very large percentage of mistakes are due to the over-potency of certain elements or the under-potency of others.

As an illustration of over-potency, consider the first question: "What is the general topic of the paragraph?" *Paragraph* when over-potent produces responses ranging from "A group of sentences making sense" through "A group of sentences" and "A few sentences" to "The sentence," "Subject and predicate," "Begin with a capital," "A letter," and "Commas and periods."

As an illustration of under-potency, the second question was: "On what day would a ten-year-old girl not be expected to attend school?" We find the under-potency of *not* resulting in answers like "When school is in session" or "Five days a week."

In 500 responses to this same test given in Grades 5 to 8, ten words were so over-potent as to appear clearly influential in the response to each of the first three questions (and in seven of the cases to the fourth question as well). These words were: *Franklin, attendance, ill, contagious, disease, impassable, school, seven, fourteen, every.*

Inspection of the mistakes shows that the potency of any word or word group in a question may be far above or far below its proper amount in relation to the rest of the question. The same holds for any word or word group in the paragraph. Understanding a paragraph implies keeping these respective weights in proper proportion from the start or varying their proportions until they together evoke a response which satisfies the purpose of the reading.

Understanding a paragraph is like solving a problem in mathematics. It consists in selecting the right elements of the situation and putting them together in the right relations, and also with the right amount of weight or influence or force for each. The mind is assailed as it were by every word in the paragraph. It must select, repress, soften, emphasize, correlate, and organize, all under the influence of the right mental set or purpose or demand.

Reading may (also) be wrong or inadequate because of failure to treat the responses made as provisional and to inspect and welcome or reject them as they appear. Many of the very pupils who gave wrong responses to the questions would respond correctly if confronted with them in the following form:

Is this foolish or not?
The day when a girl should *not* go to school is the day when school is in session.
The day is fourteen years.
Impassable roads are a kind of illness.

They do not, however, of their own accord test their responses by thinking out their subtler or more remote implications.

It thus appears that reading an explanatory or argumentative paragraph in his textbook on geography or history or civics and (though to a less degree) reading a narrative or description involve the same sort of organization and analytic action of ideas as occur in thinking of supposedly higher sorts.

It appears likely also that a pupil may read fluently and feel that the series of words are among appropriate thoughts without really understanding the paragraph. In such cases the reader finds satisfying solutions to those problems which he does raise and so feels mentally adequate; but he raises only a few of the problems which should be raised and makes only a few of the judgments which he should make.

This paragraph, for example, may be read in different ways:

Nearly fifteen thousand of the city's workers joined in the parade on September seventh, and passed before two hundred thousand cheering spectators. There were workers of both sexes in the parade, though the men far outnumbered the women.

One may read the paragraph with something like the following judgments:
Fifteen thousand did something—there was a parade—September seventh was the day—there were two hundred something—there was cheering—workers were in the parade—both sexes in the parade—the men outnumbered the women.

Contrast these with the following, which may be in the mind of the expert reader:
Nearly fifteen thousand—not quite, but nearly—of the city's workers—people who worked for a living—joined in the parade—a big parade of nearly fifteen thousand—on September seventh—the parade was in the fall—they passed before two hundred thousand cheering spectators—two hundred thousand saw the parade—they cheered it—there were workers of both sexes—there were men workers and women workers in the parade—the men far outnumbered the women—many more men than women were in the parade.

In educational theory, then, we should not consider the reading of a textbook or reference as a mechanical, passive, undiscriminating task, on a totally different level from the task of evaluating or using what is read. While the work of judging and applying doubtless demands a more elaborate and inventive organization and control of mental connections, the demands of mere reading are also for the active selection which is typical of thought. It is not a small or unworthy task to learn "what the book says."

THE RELATION OF SPEED OF READING TO COMPREHENSION [1]

Miles A. Tinker

[The present rather wide utilization of various devices to force a reader to increase his reading rate raises some important issues. Can rate of reading be independent of the content of material being read? Can it be unaffected by the kind of response required of the reader? Can it be free from restrictions imposed by the difficulty of the material? Miles Tinker offers some data in response to these inquiries.]

Through the years there have been many studies of the relation between rate and comprehension in reading. In many early studies the materials used to measure rate were different from those used to measure comprehension. It became apparent that any true measure of this relation should be based upon the same materials. Furthermore, the question arose whether the relation found would differ if the materials read were easy from that found if they were difficult.

In an initial study, (1) a correlation of — .80 was found between speed of reading and power of comprehension when the Iowa Silent Reading Test (Advanced) was administered to *university sophomores*. This test should obviously be easier for them than it would be for *high-school freshmen*. The purpose of the present study was to discover the relation between rate and comprehension with the latter, less mature readers.

The standardized test used was Form A of the revised Iowa Silent Reading Test (Advanced). Only the first five parts and the total of these were employed. All subtests yield comprehension scores. This Advanced Test is designed for high-school students and college freshmen.

The subjects in this experiment were 100 high-school freshmen. Each student was tested individually. The standard time limits listed for parts of the test were used. Empirical check revealed that only a few of the fastest workers just about completed the tests within these time limits. The readers were instructed to work rapidly and consistently, but not to sacrifice accuracy for speed. Each subject was allowed to work on a sub-

[1] Adapted and abridged from Miles A. Tinker, "Rate of Work in Reading Performance as Measured by Standardized Tests,"

Journal of Educational Psychology (1945), 36:217–228.

test until the standard time had elapsed. At that point he was interrupted and a line drawn across the page below the last item attempted. Instructions were then given to complete the test and when the last item was finished the total time required for the whole subtest was recorded.

Four scores were derived from the data: (1) the number of items done correctly in the standard time, called the "power of comprehension score"; (2) the number of items done correctly in unlimited time, termed the "level of comprehension score"; (3) the number of items attempted in standard time; (4) the total time taken to complete the whole subtest, yielding a "rate of work score" for the material read. It is probable that the term "rate of work" is more accurate in this situation than "rate of comprehension."

In the present experiment comprehension is defined in terms of how it is measured in the Iowa Silent Reading Test (Advanced); that is, the number of items completed correctly within a

set time limit is assumed to be the power of comprehension score. Similarly, the number of items completed correctly when an opportunity to attempt every item is provided is assumed to be the level of comprehension score. Although some may not agree with the method of measuring power or level of comprehension in a particular test, that question does not need to be considered here.

The reliabilities of the power of comprehension scores cited for the Iowa Silent Reading Test (Advanced) are relatively high when computed by the chance-half method. For the subtests the coefficients range from .59 to .95; for the total comprehension score, .95 to .96. The basic data of this investigation are given in Table 1. The mean number attempted in standard time is well below the number of items in each subtest. Differences between score in standard time and score in unlimited time show that the average level of comprehension is not achieved in standard time except possibly in Subtest 4.

TABLE 1. Means and SD's for Iowa Silent Reading Test:
Advanced Form A
(N = 100 High-School Freshmen)

Test	Number Correct Standard Time		Number Attempted Standard Time		Score in Unlimited Time		Total Time in Seconds	
	M	SD	M	SD	M	SD	M	SD
1. Paragraph Meaning	25.7 a	11.2	18.7	5.3	39.9 a	10.5	936.6	252.5
2. Word Meaning	36.7	8.7	55.8	10.6	41.0	7.9	541.4	165.2
3. Paragraph Organization	8.1 a	3.4	25.1	7.0	11.3 a	3.9	507.1	182.0
4. Sentence Meaning	18.2	7.7	33.2	7.2	18.6	7.9	271.1	78.0
5. Location of Information	15.9 a	5.4	19.5	4.3	21.0 a	6.2	478.8	126.0
Total score	104.6	28.8	152.4	26.3	131.8	28.4	2735.1	703.3

a Weighted score.

The correlations between rate of work and comprehension are given in Table 2. The correlations between number attempted in standard time and time to complete the test—Row (e)—reveal that the number attempted in standard time is a fair measure of rate of work with the exception of Subtest 4, which deals with

TABLE 2. Correlations Between Rate of Work and "Comprehension"
Measures on the Iowa Silent Reading
Test: Advanced Form A
(N = 100 High-School Freshmen)

Row	Measures Compared	r for Subtests and Total					
		1	2	3	4	5	Total
(a)	Score standard time vs. number attempted standard time	.80	.63	.47	.29	.43	.55
(b)	Score standard time vs. score unlimited time	.72	.88	.68	.97	.81	.84
(c)	Score standard time vs. total time [a]	−.59	−.56	−.32	−.23	−.41	−.51
(d)	Number attempted standard time vs. score unlimited time	.23	.26	−.11	.20	−.06	.09
(e)	Number attempted standard time vs. total time [a]	−.78	−.90	−.80	−.45	−.89	−.90
(f)	Score unlimited time vs. total time [a]	−.08	−.21	.24	−.10	.04	−.03

[a] Total time refers to total time in seconds to attempt all items on a test.

sentence meaning. The latter is only —.45, while the remaining coefficients range from —.78 to —.90. Nevertheless, greater emphasis should be placed upon total time than upon number attempted in standard time as a rate of work measure.

The power of comprehension score correlates fairly high with level of comprehension. This is shown by comparing score in standard time with score in unlimited time—Row (b). The coefficients range from .68 to .97. The two subtests in which power and level show least correspondence are on paragraph meaning and paragraph organization, where the coefficients are .72 and .68, respectively. The very high correlation of .97 for Subtest 4, which deals with sentence meaning, is conditioned by the fact that the readers had pretty much reached their level of comprehension within the standard time limit. For the total test, correlation between power and level of comprehension was .84.

In Row (d) of Table 2 are shown the correlations between power of comprehension and number of exercises attempted in standard time. For the subtests the coefficients range from —.11 to .26; for the total test, r = .09. Obviously there is little or no relationship present. When score in unlimited time is correlated with total time—Row (f)—to show the relation between level of comprehension and rate of work, the coefficients for the subtests range from —.21 to .24; for total test, r = —.03. Again there is little or no relationship evident.

When score in standard time is correlated with number attemped in standard time—Row (a)—the coefficients for subtests range from .29 to .80; for the total test, r = .55. Thus, except for Subtest 1, there is only a small to moderate degree of relationship between power of comprehension and number of exercises attempted within a set time limit.

The correlations between score in standard time and total time yield the relationship between power of comprehension and rate of work. They are shown in Row (c) of Table 2. Coefficients for the subtests vary from —.23 to —.59, for the total of $r = $ —.51. Thus there appear to be, under the conditions of this experiment, significant correlations ranging from a slight relationship to a moderate one between rate of work and power of comprehension. The relationship is considerably less for paragraph meaning and word meaning.

Intercorrelations between the subtests for each type of scoring are given in Table 3. Power of comprehension (score in standard time) varies considerably from subtest to subtest. The coefficients range from .24 to .61 with a median of .46. Level of comprehension (score in unlimited time) shows a similar trend.

The coefficients range from .28 to .62 with a median of .48. This is also true for number of items attempted in standard time. For rate of work (total time to complete test), however, the picture is somewhat different. The coefficients range from .56 to .81 with a median of .72. The three lower correlations (.56, .57, and .67) occurred between paragraph comprehension vs. paragraph organization, sentence meaning, and location of information. We have evidence from these intercorrelations that there is a rather prominent tendency toward a general relative rate of work for the subtests of the Iowa Silent Reading Test (Advanced).

TABLE 3. Intercorrelations of First Five Subtests of Iowa Silent Reading Test: Advanced, for Each Type of Scoring
(N = 100 High-School Freshmen)

Measure	Range of r's	Median r
Score in standard time	.24 to .61	.46
Score in unlimited time	.28 to .62	.48
Number attempted in standard time	.30 to .66	.48
Total time to complete test	.56 to .81	.72

In studying the relation between speed and comprehension in reading situations, the terminology employed should be carefully defined. Earlier workers claimed to be investigating the relationship between speed of reading and comprehension in reading. Speed of reading, however, was measured in various ways, and views concerning the relation between rate and comprehension were contradictory (1, 4). As pointed out by Anderson and Tinker (1), the important problem is the amount of relationship between rate of comprehension and degree of comprehension in a specific reading situation. Rate of comprehension was in terms of time to complete the reading task and comprehension in terms of exercises completed correctly within set time limits. This technique was also employed by Tinker (5) in a later study. He laid down the principle that rate of comprehension and degree of comprehension should be measured on the same or on strictly comparable material. Blommers and Lindquist (2) have accepted this principle but have insisted that rate of comprehension be based exclusively upon those exercises in which comprehension reaches the level set by the authors (i.e., exercises answered correctly) rather than upon time to complete the test. Although Blommers and Lindquist present data to show that rate of work on "incorrectly" done exercises is not identical with that on "correctly" done exercises, they also show that rate of work for total test is equivalent to rate of work on "correctly" done exercises. Their findings may be accepted as validating rate of work on the total test as a rate of comprehension score. This finding facilitates discussion of relationships between rate and comprehension in reading in practical situations where one is concerned with time spent on a reading task in relation to the degree of comprehension achieved. Nevertheless, it is more accurate to designate total time spent on a reading task as rate of work rather than rate of comprehension.

Although the number of exercises attempted during a set time which permits the fastest workers to just about complete the test is intimately related to rate of work in terms of time taken to complete the whole test (r = —.90), it is possible that the number of exercises attempted in standard time is not entirely adequate as a measure of rate of work or rate of comprehension. The relationship between number attempted in standard time and total time fluctuates considerably from one kind of reading to another.

Conclusions concerning the relation between rate of work and comprehension in reading must be confined to the specific reading situation investigated. This means that the reading level of the subjects as well as the kind of reading material used must be considered.

In this investigation high-school freshmen read the Iowa Silent Reading Test (Advanced). The test is designed for high-school and college students. The plan was to employ a reading situation that would be fairly difficult for the readers. In a previous study (1), university sophomores found this test rather easy.

As noted above, the correlations between rate of work and power of comprehension in this study ranged from —.23 to —.59 for the subtests, and r was —.51 for the total score. These coefficients reveal a tendency for the faster readers to comprehend more. Although the coefficients are not high, they are substantial except for parts 3 and 4 of the test. In earlier investigation (1), where university sophomores read the same test, the correlations between rate of work and power of comprehension ranged from —.48 to —.85 for the subtests, and r was —.80 for total score. Again parts 3 and 4 yielded the lower correlations. For the other parts and for the total test there was, however, a marked tendency for the faster readers to comprehend more. It is reasonable to assume that the Iowa Silent Reading Test (Advanced) was a more difficult reading situation for the high-school freshmen than for the university sophomores. It follows, then, that the relation between rate of work and power of comprehension is determined in some degree by the level of difficulty of the reading material. In other words, in relatively easy reading this relation is fairly high, but in more difficult material the relation is still significant but only low to moderate in size.

Blommers and Lindquist (2) found the relation between rate of comprehension and comprehension to be approximately .30. They used specially prepared reading material with high-school juniors and seniors as subjects. To judge from the sample cited, the material required a single response for each exercise. There could be considerable comprehension of the material and a reader might still miss the response required to reach the standard set by the authors. As suggested by Tinker (5), the nature of the material and the type of response required of the reader may influence the relation between rate of comprehension and power of comprehension.

The failure in this study to discover any significant correlation between rate of work and level of comprehension (comprehension score in unlimited time) is of interest. This finding appears to be due partly to the fact that some of the subjects were at or nearly at their level of comprehension at the end of the standard time limit. Others improved their scores markedly with extended time. In spite of such variations, however, power of comprehension and level of comprehension were fairly closely related.

How are the different findings for relations between speed of reading and comprehension to be evaluated? The earlier results, as analyzed by Tinker (4), may be dismissed as not valid because they are derived from inadequately conceived experiments. Sample conclusions and views from more recent reports follow: (1) Blommers and Lindquist (2), "The relationship between rate of reading comprehension and power of reading comprehension is significant but low . . ."; (2) Tinker (5), "The data warrant the conclusion that there is an intimate relationship between speed and comprehension in reading when the textual material is within the reader's educational experience." (3) Stroud (3)

notes that educational psychologists have been teaching that a "moderately high correlation exists between reading rate and comprehension." (4) In the present experiment a medium-sized correlation was found between rate of work and power of comprehension in reading.

Examination of the backgrounds from which these views were derived indicates that each view has a degree of validity. There are many reading skills which are somewhat independent of each other. The relationship between rate and comprehension need not be the same in any two reading situations if there are differences in textual content, nature of response required from reader, purpose for which the material is read, and difficulty. Furthermore, the conclusions in any study probably can be applied only to the reading of groups like the one measured.

In general, the trend of results from various sources indicates that there is a significant relationship between rate and comprehension in reading. This tendency of good comprehension to accompany fast reading varies from a slight relationship to a moderately high relationship. Factors affecting the size of this relationship have been discussed above.

References

1. Anderson, V. L., and Tinker, M. A., "The speed factor in reading performance," *J. educ. Psychol.* (1936), 27:621–624.
2. Blommers, P., and Lindquist, E. F., "Rate of comprehension of reading: its measurement and its relation to comprehension," *J. educ. Psychol.* (1944), 35:449–473.
3. Stroud, J. B., "Critical note on reading," *Psychol. Bull.* (1942), 39:173–178.
4. Tinker, M. A., "The relation of speed to comprehension in reading," *School and Society* (1932), 36:158–160.
5. Tinker, M. A., "Speed versus comprehension in reading as affected by level of difficulty," *J. educ. Psychol.* (1939), 30:81–94.

SHOULD VOCABULARY BE TAUGHT DIRECTLY OR INCIDENTALLY? [1]

William S. Gray and Eleanor Holmes

[Among William S. Gray's many research contributions to reading instruction, probably none has been more influential than his studies of vocabulary. His work with Leary in *What Makes a Book Readable?* showed the role of vocabulary in appraising the difficulty of reading materials. The study with Holmes reproduced here examined carefully under what circumstances vocabulary development occurred most efficiently. Is it better to focus instruction on vocabulary or should teaching rely on the impetus vocabulary growth gained while study was directed to other ends?]

The practical value of a wide meaning vocabulary is obvious. It is an essential means of interchanging ideas or acquiring new experience. Unless children attach clear, accurate meaning to words, their oral and written language is often inaccurate and ineffective. Furthermore, they are unable to acquire readily, either through listening or through reading, new ideas which the school may contribute. This is the case even in activities relating to situations which are very familiar. The need for a rich meaning vocabulary becomes increasingly evident as the ideas, concepts, and information involved depart from the everyday experiences and language activities of children.

PROCEDURES

In this experiment, the merits of direct and incidental methods of promoting vocabulary growth were compared. The factors which were held constant, insofar as possible, were the vocabulary achievement and mental capacity of the groups taught, the general purposes of teaching during the course of the experiment, the teaching materials used, the purpose or mind-set of the pupils while reading, the total amount of time given to each teaching procedure, and the personality and efficiency of the teacher.

TESTS USED

Four measures were used, namely, mental age as determined through the use of the Stanford-Binet Intelligence Tests; mental alertness as represented by the intelligence quotient; general vocabulary mastery as indicated by scores on

[1] Adapted and abridged from W. S. Gray and Eleanor Holmes, *The Development of Meaning Vocabularies in Reading: An Experimental Study*, Publications of the Laboratory Schools of the University of Chicago, No. 6, University of Chicago Press, Chicago, 1938.

147

the vocabulary section of the Stanford Reading Examination; and specific vocabulary mastery as indicated by scores on a vocabulary test composed of key words selected for use during the experiment.

The specific vocabulary test included 100 words selected in about equal numbers from the materials of two units taught during the experimental period, namely, "Primitive Man" and "Ancient Egyptians." In order to determine reliability of the test as a whole, the scores on Part I were correlated with those on Part II. Since there were fifty items in each part and since both parts were administered separately but with the same directions and under similar conditions, it was believed that the proposed correlation could be used in place of the usual even-and-odd-items correlation. When the Pearson product-moment formula was applied, a correlation of .84 ±

.03 was found, indicating a high degree of reliability for the test as a whole.

EQUIVALENCE OF GROUPS

All students were in the fourth grade of the University Elementary School of the University of Chicago. An effort was made to reorganize the pupils into three equivalent groups. Because of the nature of the distribution of the scores, it was impossible to do this satisfactorily. Accordingly, it was decided to organize one (control) group which would include pupils distributed somewhat evenly from the highest to the lowest in specific vocabulary mastery. The remaining pupils were assigned to two experimental groups, those of higher vocabulary achievement being assigned to the one and those of lower achievement to the other.

In order to insure exact comparisons,

TABLE 1.   Means of Groups

	Specific Vocabulary	General Vocabulary	Mental Age	Intelligence Quotient
Control	65.2	67.9	134.6	119.4
Experimental Groups Combined	67	68.4	137.2	123.5
Experimental (1)	73.9	76.9	147	133.7
Experimental (2)	59.2	63	126.2	112.2

TABLE 2.   Range of Groups

	Specific Vocabulary	General Vocabulary	Mental Age	Intelligence Quotient
Control	34–91	47–93	109–177	94–158
Experimental Groups Combined	25–90	47–97	107–189	94–171
Experimental (1)	43–90	52–97	125–189	107–171
Experimental (2)	25–81	47–82	107–140	94–122

it seemed desirable to pair pupils from the control and experimental sections in respect to specific vocabulary mastery.

Twenty reasonably comparable pairs were selected, using the scores on the specific vocabulary test as the chief basis of selection. The means scores of the two groups were practically the same on each of the four measures.

CONTROL OF OTHER FACTORS

The general aims of teaching were the same for both the experimental and the control groups. The materials of instruction were the same for both groups. The same teacher taught both groups.

METHODS OF TEACHING

Common procedures for all groups were used to introduce the unit: a canvass of interests and related experiences, efforts to enlarge background, attempts to open new problems and arouse keen interest. No effort was made in any of the groups at this time to lay a vocabulary foundation. In all groups the teacher explained to the pupils that they were going to read several selections and would be asked to write answers to questions after reading. She then placed mimeographed guide sheets in their hands and directed attention to the questions. She also read the directions and questions so that all would know clearly what they were to do. Up to this point the procedure was the same for all groups.

After the directions were clearly understood, the pupils engaged for several days in assimilative reading. *In the control group* the teacher provided no further guidance except as individual children came for help. She never offered such help unless the child first asked for it. When a child believed that he was prepared to answer the assigned questions, he did so and handed them to the teacher. She examined his paper for general correctness of content, legibility, neatness, and spelling and either accepted or returned it for correction, ad-

ditions, or other changes.

In the experimental classes the teacher provided specific vocabulary help before and during the reading period: (1) to form clear, vivid associations between word meanings and their oral and written symbols; (2) to promote the development of the habit of using the context in deriving the meaning of words and phrases; and (3) to provide opportunity for pupils to use the new words appropriately in either oral or written form.

In order to form clear, vivid associations between meanings and symbols, the teacher made use of specific words in meaningful connections, using illustrations, pictures, and other devices. In case the form of a word was new and unfamiliar, she wrote it on the blackboard, pointing to it only when the word was actually pronounced in order to avoid associating its form with the wrong word.

Students were encouraged to say the word softly to themselves as the teacher used it in sentences or pointed to it. Sometimes they said it aloud together. As soon as meaning and pronunciation were reasonably well known, the pupils and teacher began to use the word informally in class discussion. Those pupils who mispronounced words or used them inaccurately were given special help. Sentences were written on the blackboard and read together by pupils and teacher to help derive the meaning from context.

Following the directed study on a given day, the pupils read to prepare answers to the guiding questions. In writing the answers, they were encouraged to use as many of the new words as they needed. When a pupil brought his paper to the teacher it was criticized in the same manner as in the control group.

In all groups, when a pupil's paper had been accepted, he went to the bookshelves to select a supplementary reference to read. Then followed a period lasting from two to three days in which the pupils organized their ideas relating to the unit and engaged in various types of creative activity.

CONCLUSIONS

ACHIEVEMENT OF GROUPS

The average amount of progress as measured by a retest on the *specific vocabulary* is shown below:

	Mean Gain	Percent of Gain
Control	8.9	13.6
Experimental (1)	17.6	23.7
Experimental (2)	25.2	42.6

Greater gains were made by both groups given specific help. But the greater progress of experimental group (2) indicates that specific guidance is of relatively more value to pupils of limited initial achievement and of limited mental ability. However, pupils of superior ability who received specific help on new words made greater progress than those of similar achievement and ability who received no such help.

ACHIEVEMENT OF PAIRED PUPILS

If the twenty pairs of pupils are treated as groups, the pupils who received specific help gained twice as much as the pupils in the control group.

In the case of the ten pupils ranking highest in each group, the percent of gain of those in the experimental group (20.4 percent) exceeded somewhat that of the pupils in the control group (12.0 percent). In the case of the ten pupils ranking lowest in each group, the percent of gain of those in the experimental group (57.5 percent) was notably greater than that of those in the control group (16.1 percent).

Further evidence of the effect of the method of instruction on growth in vocabulary was obtained by teaching the words in three different ways. In Method I, sixty-five words were taught to the experimental group but not to the control group. Method II employed fifteen words which were taught directly to the experimental group and incidentally made meaningful to the control group. Method III used twenty words which were not taught to either group. The results of the three methods are shown in the table.

The findings of Method I emphasize the value and importance of teaching directly the meanings of words. The percent of gain for both groups in Method II is noticeably less. Apparently the words presented more difficulty than did

TABLE 3. Mean Gains of Paired Pupils

	Gain in Score	Percent of Gain
Method I		
Control	6.6	16.5
Experimental	18.5	47.9
Method II		
Control	1.3	10.9
Experimental	2.8	24.1
Method III		
Control	1.2	8.0
Experimental	1.3	9.1

those of Method I. The fact that the difference in the percent of gain between the two groups was not as great as that for Method I suggests that even incidental emphasis upon the meanings of words is productive in promoting vocabulary growth. In Method III the percent of gain was approximately the same.

INFLUENCE ON READING EFFICIENCY

The study next considered the effect of the direct and indirect methods of promoting vocabulary growth on (1) accuracy of word recognition in oral reading, (2) the basic habits involved in silent reading as revealed by eye-movement records, and (3) efficiency in comprehension as measured by verbal reports of the content of what was read.

Fourteen pupils—six from the control group and eight from the experimental group—were selected for intensive study. The methods of teaching were the same as those adopted in the earlier study reported above. The pupils of each group differed widely in mental ages (control: 109–177; experimental: 114–189), intelligence quotients (control: 94–158; experimental: 94–177), and reading ages

(control: 115–146; experimental: 119–149). On the other hand, the two groups did not differ radically on the average in these respects.

	Control	Experimental
Mental age	138.7	142.1
Intelligence quotient	121.5	129.1
Reading age	136.5	135.5

ACCURACY OF WORD RECOGNITION

Two selections, one at intermediate grade level and one at high-school level, were used for testing oral reading. In general, their content was similar to that in the basic reading material assigned to both groups. Reading was checked in accordance with the directions which accompany the Gray Oral Reading Check Tests. The tests were given at the beginning and at the end of the unit.

A comparison of the scores reveals a series of significant facts. Notably greater *individual* gains were made by most of the pupils in the experimental group. In addition, a greater average gain was made by the pupils of the experimental group.

TABLE 4. Percent of Decrease in Errors

	Selection A (Intermediate)	Selection F (High School)
Control	21.3	9.4
Experimental	63.6	47.2

Mispronunciations outnumbered any other type of error made at the beginning of the experiment. A notably greater decrease in the number of such errors made by pupils of the experimental group at the end of the experiment was recorded.

EYE MOVEMENTS IN SILENT READING

Records were obtained at the beginning and end of the same unit as above. Four short passages were selected from materials assigned to both groups during the unit. An appropriate reading attitude was stimulated by asking the pupil to read each passage once with care so that he could answer a question about its content at the conclusion of his reading. The responses required by the questions were such as to reflect the pupil's mastery of the important word and sentence meanings.

The meanings of important words in the selections were taught directly to the students of the experimental classes during class periods devoted to the study of the unit.

Because of technical difficulties reasonably comparable records at the beginning and end of the experiment were secured for only four pupils, as shown in Table 5. Greater improvement accom-

TABLE 5. Records for Four Control and Experimental Pupils

	Mental Age	Intelligence Quotient
Control		
Pupil 38	177	158
Pupil 34	134	119
Experimental		
Pupil 58	189	171
Pupil 12	114	94

panied the use of the direct method. Pupils showed marked decrease in total number of fixations, average duration of fixation, total reading time for each selection, total number of regressions.

COMPREHENSION IN SILENT READING

In order to determine the immediate effect on comprehension of the indirect and direct methods of promoting vocabulary growth, the pupils whose eye movements were photographed were asked to reproduce orally and to answer questions about the content of the selection read.

The direct method gave the pupils greater command of essential words in the oral reports and thus enabled them to express ideas more clearly. Both word meaning and general comprehension were corrected and enriched. As one approaches the level of average ability or below, the superiority of direct vocabulary instruction, as revealed by pupils' responses, becomes more and more pronounced.

The relative merits of the two methods were further studied by determining their influence and comprehension after some time had elapsed between direct instruction and reading. The intermediate-grade selection used in testing for accuracy in word recognition in oral reading was also used for this aspect of the study. In both the initial and final tests the pupils were permitted to reread the selection if they wished.

The recognition, meaning, and use of the various difficult words in the test passage were taught the experimental group soon after the initial test had been given. Help in these words was given to members of the control group only as they asked for it.

The results are illustrated with specific pupils from both groups:

Control

Pupil 38: Inability to recognize key words resulting in indiscriminate recall of ideas and rambling type of language response.

Pupil 23: In second test more wordy than in first. More vague and inaccurate in respect to ideas.

Experimental

Pupil 58: Clear improvement in ability to recognize key words. More fluent reproduction of details. Greatly improved sentence structure. Rapid progress in ability to grasp relationship of ideas and to organize them effectively for presentation.

Pupil 56: In second test more explicit, accurate, well organized.

The results of this analysis support the conclusion that the direct method of vocabulary development is far more effective in improving the comprehension of what is read than the indirect.

INFLUENCE OF CONTEXT ON SPECIFIC WORD MEANINGS

Two selections were chosen, one with context explaining the meaning of a key word and one with context not explaining. Prior to reading the test passages each pupil was given a sheet of paper on which the key word was written. He was directed to read the word silently and write down all that the word meant or suggested to him. After two or three days, he was asked to tell orally what the word meant to him. In this pretest the key word was in general unfamiliar.

Sixteen pupils were tested. In the selection in which context did not illuminate meaning, the more capable pupils were as a rule able to identify the fact that the paragraph gave them no help. The child of average ability could not identify specific difficulties so accurately.

In the selection in which the key word was explained, the explanation did not insure mastery on the part of all pupils. The need is obvious for materials which are simply and clearly written and in which the author has used various devices for helping the reader to derive appropriate meanings. In addition, the need is urgent for both individual and group guidance which will help pupils (1) acquire a clear, accurate understanding of essential meanings, (2) develop power in using the context where it is of value in deriving meanings, (3) recognize when the context does not aid in the acquisition of specific meanings, and (4) develop the initiative and skills essential in finding the meanings of new words when they are not disclosed by the context.

INFLUENCE OF CONTEXT ON WORDS HAVING GENERAL MEANING

Two passages were used. In one, a clear grasp of the important ideas depended on an abstract word. In the other, the important ideas were not dependent on this kind of word.

The pupils who participated were the same as those included in the study of the influence of context on words with specific meaning. The procedure differed only slightly from that in the previous study.

The fact was observed during the course of this investigation that pupils are unlikely to be conscious of the limitations in their understanding of general meanings, partly because children deal only in a limited way with abstractions. Such meanings also fail as a rule to challenge the child's interest and to enlist critical evaluation. Furthermore, it is possible for him to ignore the meaning of many such words as he reads, to base his interpretation on the meaning of familiar words in the selection, or indeed to associate wrong meanings with general terms.

CONCLUSIONS

A large majority of the pupils in the middle and upper grades are in urgent need of help in acquiring the meanings of many of the words in the reading materials assigned to them. This is due largely to the fact that they lack the specific experiences essential in attaching clear, vivid meanings to many new words. Furthermore, they are often unconscious of their limitations and fail to exert effort to overcome them. The direct method of vocabulary development is far more effective in enriching and clarifying meanings than the indirect; it also leads to more rapid improvement in reading efficiency.

AN EVALUATION OF FREE READING [1]

Lou L. LaBrant

[Lou L. LaBrant, former president of the National Council of Teachers of English, has long championed greater participation by students with teachers in the planning of instruction. This study reports the testing of that conviction. Like so many other often-quoted pieces of research, this investigation needs to be read thoroughly. In particular, the amount of teacher guidance provided during the study should be assessed carefully.]

PROBLEM

The following is a study of the reading program at University School, Ohio State University, over a three-year period, for Grades 10, 11, and 12. The class averaged fifty-seven pupils. There was continuous three-year attendance for fifty pupils, and two-year for nine others. Five of the fifty, all remedial reading cases, have incomplete records. Of the fifty-nine students, twenty-seven were boys and thirty-two girls.

Reading scores on the Iowa Silent Reading Test showed a median score of 118, above eleventh-grade ability (score of 118 norm for sixtieth percentile). Ten, however, were very low and on the Thorndike-McCall Reading Scale tested seventh grade or lower. They were given special remedial work. The curves of mental ability (Terman Group Test of Mental Ability, Form A) and reading ability were slightly flattened and bimodal. (Editorial note: No further data on the characteristics of the pupil population are reported in the study.)

PROCEDURES

In the tenth grade, each half of the class studied drama for one semester (under a teacher of speech) and had a diversified reading and free writing experience the other semester (under the investigator). In the eleventh year, the work was arranged by quarters, and one quarter was given especially to speech work. In the twelfth year all work was under the investigator, except for ten pupils with difficulties in personal adjustment who were under the special instruction of a separate teacher.

During the first year the pupils were urged to discuss in class the books they had read in previous courses and for pleasure. Discussion was also initiated by the teacher concerning the aims of reading and the possible lines of class development. Pupils naturally presented conventional terms—"development of

---

[1] Adapted and abridged from Lou L. LaBrant, *An Evaluation of the Free Reading in Grades Ten, Eleven, and Twelve*, Ohio State University Studies, Contributions in Education, No. 2, Ohio State University Press, Columbus, 1936.

good habits and of appreciation." From this the instructor called for an analysis, and pupils suggested a discussion of plots as a means for development of appreciation. During the semester the students discussed the meaning of a plot and illustrated from their own experiences what they meant, finally developing the idea that plots are conflicts whose solution or impossibility of solution is the problem of the writer.

Discussion of plots included analysis of both narratives and drama. This, with the unit in dramatics under the speech teacher, led naturally to the criterion set up at the beginning of the eleventh year. Pupils at this time decided that their reading was limited and that they should expand it by securing greater facility with a variety of forms: essays, poetry, biography, and further novels and plays. During the second quarter they expanded their aims to include facility with books written in a variety of periods and by writers of many countries.

At the beginning of the twelfth year the instructor introduced the suggestion that the class was sufficiently mature for each member to undertake some fairly complete study: a title, a writer, a period, a problem. After two weeks of discussion the group agreed that each person would choose either a writer or a group of writers for a quarter's study. In addition a free program of reading was continued but the particular problem remained a major study. These individual problems were finally arranged in chronological order and reported to the class. They ranged from a study of Greek drama and an investigation of Old Testament literature to a study of modern books on social planning.

No book lists were supplied during the three years, and after private conferences pupils were always permitted to examine and sample any books suggested before deciding to check them out for reading. They were also permitted to decide whether a book should be finished. They made their own records and were not required to write book reports. All reports, so called, were informal either in class discussion or in conference with the teacher. Not all books were reported orally in any manner. The teacher and the pupils in conference frequently agreed to disregard certain readings and talk at length about others.

The records were kept by the pupils. Each pupil wrote down on filing cards the name of the book read, the author, and the quarter when the reading was done. Proof of understanding and interest was felt to lie in further reading, and in ability to utilize the experience in suitable situations. Thus, when drama was discussed, those who had read appropriate plays contributed illustrations. In conferences reference was made to readings reported at any time; that is, the book just read might be compared to one read two years previously.

Lists of summer readings were requested. Some students kept records regularly during the summer, and others depended upon memory. There is consequently good reason to believe that the total list is incomplete.

The honesty of the records may be questioned by some. The investigator has little doubt as to the general accuracy. Pupils made note of rereadings, books skimmed, and books read in part. These are not included in the present study. The frequent conferences, the lack of pressure, and the general nature of the class procedure all tended to establish an air of confidence and hence of honesty. Chief proof lies in the growing quality in the lists. A student who is not reading cannot, if he would, make up a list of books indicative of a growing understanding and interest, in a situation in which such lists are individual and greatly varied.

FINDINGS

In three school years and two summers a total of 3974 readings of entire volumes is recorded, including 1947 different titles. During the first year, pupils were unaccustomed to free reading and inclined to wait for teacher pressure. Since the enrollment varied and changes occurred in the personnel of the class, average reading is not accurate nor is it highly significant. Roughly, the average record per pupil is seventy books. The books range from long volumes such as Ludwig's biography of Napoleon to Sara Teasdale's *Strange Victory*. The relative size of these in no way indicates relative value or difficulties, and the investigator is not aware of any device for comparison. The range of materials covered cannot be rated as to literary quality by any established techniques.

The study is confined to those readings which covered entire books. In certain fields—especially in poetry—much reading is thus disregarded. No attempt is made to picture the entire reading of the class.

For convenience, the pupils' reading was classified according to types: (1) biography and autobiography, (2) drama, (3) essays and other prose discussion, (4) narrative fiction, (5) poetry, (6) science, and (7) social science and history. For further study, notation was made concerning the nationality and period of the writer and the time and place of the setting of the book.

PUPIL-DEVELOPED CRITERIA TO GUIDE READING

These criteria did not develop suddenly and were at no time superimposed by the teacher. Parenthetical statements are by the investigator.

1. Is my reading varied as to types? (Am I free to find answers to personal needs regardless of the form in which the author has framed his contribution?)
2. Is my reading varied as to subject matter? (Am I finding aid through reading in all suitable areas of thinking?)
3. Is my reading varied as to nationality? (Am I free to find answers to personal needs regardless of the nationality of the author or of the scene in which the situation of the book is placed?)
4. Is my reading varied as to time? (Am I free to find answers to personal needs regardless of the time or place in which the author has lived and written?)

DISTRIBUTION OF READING ACCORDING TO TYPES

One year's work (the eleventh) centered on the characteristics of types. Instead of requiring reading to supplement class discussion, the investigator depended largely upon the fact that the unit itself, based upon pupil need and interest, must of necessity serve as a stimulant to wider investigation. The level of investigation was determined by individual ability. Private conferences on pupil progress supplemented class stimulation, but chief dependence was upon the books themselves rather than upon the teacher, and pupils varied greatly in their choices. A certain amount of reading in the more mature forms may be thought of as the result of group pressure. The criteria discussed in class were also considered by individuals in evaluating their reading from time to time, and thus acted as guides. There was, however, room for enough freedom beyond this minimum to suggest that the distribution according to types represents real interests. It should be remembered in this connection that tenth-grade criteria emphasized problems and twelfth-year class procedure was built around periods. Within these subjects great liberty in selection was possible.

Table 1 shows the distribution of the three years' reading according to types. In examining the table the reader should remember that the third year's record does not include the four months of summer reading recorded for the other two years. There is also to be considered the fact that during the last six weeks of a senior's high-school course there is little time for leisure reading. Consequently the third year's record in reality represents only approximately seven calendar months of reading against twelve for the other two.

TABLE 1. Distribution of Number and Percentages of Volumes Read According to Type

Type	1932–33 (Three Teaching Quarters, One Summer)		1933–34 (Three Teaching Quarters, One Summer)		1934–35 (Three Teaching Quarters)	
	Number	Percent	Number	Percent	Number	Percent
In English						
Narrative fiction	654	72.9	1002	46.8	321	34.1
Drama (including books on technique)	61	6.8	336	15.7	226	24.0
Biography and autobiography	77	8.5	224	10.5	76	8.1
Social science and history	18	2.0	167	7.8	97	10.3
Essay and other prose discussion	29	3.7	88	4.3	69	7.2
Science	13	1.4	53	2.4	24	2.5
Poetry	39	4.3	242	11.3	113	12.0
In French						
All types, chiefly fiction and drama	5	.5	25	1.1	15	1.5
Totals	896	100.1	2137	99.9	941	99.7

The table indicates important trends. The number of volumes read is not large —3974 reported volumes for a class averaging fifty-seven. The numbers must, however, be considered in relation to the total school program, in which no reading subject was based on assigned texts but instead upon reference reading, which often included whole or large parts of entire volumes. Unless the pupil felt that the reading was separate from reported work, he did not make the record on the English card.

The data seem significant in that they indicate decreasing, persevering, or growing interests. Although approximately 75 percent of the reading during the tenth grade was fiction, this type occupied less than half that importance (34 percent) in the reading program of the twelfth year. On the other hand, notable increases were made in drama (from 6.8 to 24.0 percent), in social studies (from 2.0 to 10.3 percent), in essays (from 3.7 to 7.2 percent), and in poetry (from 4.3 to 12.0 percent).

On the whole, the table gives evidence of increasing reading maturity. The decided change in balance of types would seem sufficient proof that the free reading program has provided pupils with skills and understanding sufficient to enable them to read all of the major types of writing. The shift from narrative to more abstract forms gives indication of increasing maturity.

DISTRIBUTION OF READING AS TO SUBJECT

The emphasis upon books dealing with science, social science, and history, upon essays, and upon biography indicates a widening range of subjects. These types increase in importance from 15.6 percent in the tenth year to 28.1 percent in the twelfth. It is probable also that the growth in reading of the drama indicates a similar expansion. Classic drama presents varied culture patterns and philosophies; modern drama offers many pictures of social problems. Almost without question we may conclude that increased interest in drama includes increased acquaintance with a variety of subjects. The growth in reading of poetry, coupled with the increased interest in drama, may without undue interpretation be held indicative of an expanding feeling for art forms. On the whole, therefore, the recorded reading answers affirmatively the question of whether the free reading program leads to a reading with wide interests on a variety of subjects.

DISTRIBUTION OF READING ACCORDING TO CULTURES REPRESENTED: TIME AND PLACE

The third pupil criterion concerns ability to read books written by foreign writers or placed in a foreign setting. Table 2 presents an analysis of the pupils' reading according to nationality of writer and to nationality of setting.

Striking is the consistency of the percentages from year to year, whether nationality of author or of scene is con-

TABLE 2. Distribution of Reading According to Nationality of Authors and Setting

| Nationality | Percentage 1932–33 | | 1933–34 | | 1934–35 | |
	Author	Setting	Author	Setting	Author	Setting
American	53.0	35.8	53.8	34.2	51.5	30.7
English	27.5	20.2	27.3	18.9	28.6	19.3
European	18.7	23.7	18.0	21.5	19.0	23.9
Others	0.6	20.4	0.8	25.3	0.7	26.0
Totals	99.8	100.1	99.9	99.9	99.8	99.9

sidered. In spite of the fact that the importance of understanding foreign countries was emphasized in both English and social science classes, there appears at first glance little effect of this emphasis. Throughout the three years approximately 50 percent of the books read are by American authors, and the distribution of the other 50 percent remains almost constant.

Certain changes in emphasis are, however, covered by the total figures. More detailed examination of the data by types indicates a shift of emphasis.

Table 3 compares the percentages of American books of various types read in the tenth grade to the percentages of similar American books read two years later. A smaller proportion of novels appears in the twelfth than in the tenth year, but these include an increasing percentage by American authors. This shift may in part be accounted for by the students' growing concern with the social problems of the present, and by the fact that these social problems are dealt with by many American novelists. On the other hand drama, which in-

TABLE 3. Percentage of Books of the Various Types by American Authors, Read by Pupils in Grades 10 and 12

Types	Percentage of Books by American Authors	
	1932–33 (Tenth Grade)	1934–35 (Twelfth Grade)
Narrative fiction	44	57
Drama	33	17
Biography and autobiography	54	54
Social science and history	61	75
Essay and other prose discussion	72	72
Science	77	75
Poetry	41	59
Total reading	53	52

creases in importance from 6.8 to 24 percent of the total reading, increases its emphasis on European writers from 67 to 82.3 percent. There is no noticeable change in the proportion of American authors of biography, essay, or other prose discourse. It is interesting to note that the markedly increased reading of poetry, also, is accompanied by greater attention to American poets, who rise in relative importance from 41 to 59 percent in the total poetry reported. This fact again points to an active interest of the individual in his own situation, especially significant in the emotionally colored experiences presented through poetry.

In the matter of setting, the pupils hold less to the American scene and with increasing maturity show increased interest in foreign lands. This trend is significant when we consider the accompanying decrease in narrative fiction, which includes adventure books. Not only are the pupils becoming more concerned with the foreign country, but their investigation is through more serious forms of writing.

Settings for the 1947 books represent 62 general areas. America is the scene for 700 books; England for 294; vague unidentified lands for 232; changing scenes, as in travel books, 148; France for 105; Russia for 63. It is of course apparent that availability of books is an important factor in determining choices.

The fourth criterion deals with the time element, the period in which the author wrote or the period about which he wrote. The question is analogous to the consideration of nationality. The piece written in a period other than our own brings an interpretation which a book by a modern writer may not give; on the other hand, a modern writer may, through knowing the modern's mind, present his picture or idea more effectively to his contemporary.

Table 4 shows the distribution of the reading according to (1) period during which the book was written and (2) period in which the scene was laid. The twentieth century is cut to separate earlier books from those written or placed during the life of the pupils themselves.

As might have been anticipated, the modern writer is increasingly preferred. There is greater interest also in the modern scene. There is probably most significance in the fact that 60 percent of the books read in the twelfth grade were written after 1920, that 51 percent were

TABLE 4.   Distribution of Books as to Period in Which They Were Written
and as to Period in Which Scenes Are Laid

| Period | 1932–33 | | 1933–34 | | 1934–35 | |
	Written	Scenes	Written	Scenes	Written	Scenes
			Percentage Read			
Adam–299 A.D.	.6	4.4	1.3	5.5	1.3	5.5
300–999	—	.2	.1	.8	.2	.6
1000–1399	.5	2.3	.9	2.5	.9	3.3
1400–1699	.7	6.4	2.5	6.1	6.6	7.3
1700–1799	1.3	8.9	2.1	7.8	3.6	5.9
1800–1899	20.3	32.5	18.1	25.4	13.6	23.4
1900–1919	24.2	27.0	18.3	24.5	13.7	19.2
1920–1935	51.9	18.3	56.0	27.6	60.0	34.2
Totals	99.5	100.0	99.3	100.2	99.9	99.4

by American authors, and that 31 percent dealt with the American scene.

DISTRIBUTION OF READING ACCORDING
TO SEX

Of the total 3974 volumes, boys read 1205 and girls 2769. Of the fifty-nine pupils, twenty-seven were girls, thirty-two boys; ratio of the total number of boys to total number of girls was 1.0 (girls) to 1.2 (boys). Correction to ac-count for attendance and record losses gives a ratio of 1.0 (boys) to 1.2 (girls). The ratio of number of books read by boys to those read by girls was 1.0 to 2.3.

Scores in standardized reading tests show no advantage for girls in the initial scores. Table 5, which shows the distribution by sexes according to percentile norms, suggests slight advantage for the boys.

The final table offers an analysis of

TABLE 5.   Distribution According to Percentile Norms of Scores on
Iowa Silent Reading Test, Form A, by Sexes

Percentile Rank Based on Norms	Girls	Boys	Total
99	3	5	8
90	7	5	12
80	4	3	7
75	5	4	9
70	2	2	4
60	2	0	2
50	1	1	2
40	0	0	0
30	3	1	4
25	2	3	5
20	0	1	1
10	1	2	3
1	2	0	2
Totals	32	27	59

the reading of boys and girls by types. In only two areas, drama and poetry, do girls show an interest markedly out of line with their general tendency to read more extensively. Of these types the girls read three times as much as do the boys. The boys, on the other hand, partly balance this by reading more (proportionately) science than do the girls.

TABLE 6. Reading Ratio of Amount Read by Boys to That Read by Girls

	Boys	Ratio	Girls
Enrollment	1	to	1.2
Volumes read			
Fiction	1	to	2.4
Drama	1	to	3.3
Essay	1	to	1.8
Biography	1	to	2.0
Social science	1	to	1.1
Science	1	to	0.6
Poetry	1	to	3.8
French	1	to	1.5
Total	1	to	2.3

EVALUATION

There appears evidence that the program has to a considerable degree met the needs, interests, and abilities of the students.

The pupils set as their first criterion the development of facility with a variety of forms. The increase of non-narrative forms indicates that this criterion is met through the free reading program, probably to a higher degree than through the set or prescribed course.

As their second criterion pupils asked that their reading be varied as to subject matter. The term "varied" is vague. Increased interest in such arts as drama and poetry and growing emphasis on materials dealing with social problems indicate growth in variety of subject matter. The degree of growth, either desirable or achieved, is indefinite and open to question.

As third and fourth criteria the students stated that their reading should represent cultures varied as to nationality and as to time. While interests in foreign and previous cultures persevered, the interest in the modern and American dominated. This appears to the writer desirable and to be expected, not undesirable as long as the reading of past and foreign cultures perseveres. There is no evidence that these latter interests are not continuing.

HOW "FREE" SHOULD READING BE? [1]

Bertha Handlan

[A logical concomitant of LaBrant's study is this investigation in which teacher guidance in selecting books for students was deliberately eliminated. Handlan's research is an effort to see whether students left completely free to choose what they read showed increasing ability to improve in their selection. Is the best advice to students just "read, read, read"?]

During the semester of September, 1941, through January, 1942, a study was made of the reading reported by 161 students in Grade 10 in two schools. Provided for the students in each school was a library of 443 different titles, which had been chosen to meet the predicted interests and abilities of tenth-grade boys and girls and to represent, in miniature, a typical collection of the readable books that students could find in a school library. No students were required to read any of the books; no direction was consciously given to their reading except that provided by an annotated list of the titles in the collection. The list was divided into twenty-five sections, supposed to represent topics of general interest to tenth-grade students. As a student reported the reading of a title, he was asked to take a short objective test, which covered some of the main points of the content of the book. The tests were designed only to

measure whether students had read the books they reported.

By tests, check lists, questionnaires, interviews, and observation, a mass of information about students' abilities and interests was collected. Information about the books was secured by measuring the following characteristics of a book as objectively as possible: structural difficulty, maturity, students' ratings of difficulty, and students' ratings of interest. In addition, students furnished information concerning their reasons for reading the books which they selected. A careful, but admittedly subjective, analysis was made of the "experiences" which can be found in every book in the classroom library.

Among the many conclusions that one can draw from the results of the study, the following seem most immediately important as far as a program for the guidance of reading is concerned:

1. In general, students read the books

[1] Adapted and abridged from Bertha Handlan, "A Comparison of the Characteristics of Certain Adolescent Readers and the Qualities of the Books They Read," unpublished dissertation, University of Minnesota, 1945.

which are most easily accessible. The conclusion suggests that present programs of reading in high schools have not succeeded in developing students to whom reading is so significant that they will go to some trouble to get books which they want.

2. Students' interests in reading cannot be described by general labels, but instead must be analyzed closely in terms of the characteristics of books which boys and girls choose to read.

3. Students' general interests and reading interests are not the same. Possibly teachers and librarians who are eager to help a student find books which will "meet his interests" will be advised to interpret his general interests, not read them directly or take them at face value as an infallible clue to the kind of books a student will enjoy.

4. Although capable students from privileged homes surpass less favored students in quantity, maturity, variety, and difficulty of reading choices, it seems clear that very bright students are not reading up to capacity.

5. The distinct patterns of interest obvious in boys' and girls' choices are probably not desirable and suggest that teachers and librarians—as well as the home and the school in general—might well be concerned with creating among both boys and girls some interest in reading about subjects that should be a concern of both sexes.

6. Teachers and librarians who are eager to help students find a variety of pleasure and profit in books will have to help boys and girls from limited backgrounds develop an interest in the foreign scene, in the past, and in humor; and they will have to help all students develop some interest in reading about current affairs, special hobbies, or fields of study.

7. One of the problems teachers and librarians probably should face squarely is that, as early as Grade 10, many students are reading contemporary books for adults. Probably senior high-school students should be given more help than they are in setting up standards for evaluating the mass of contemporary fiction and nonfiction available.

8. As far as a program in reading is concerned, possibly the "forgotten students" in a high school are (a) the very bright boys and girls who are too young to have decidedly adult tastes and (b) the overage students who are too mature to enjoy adolescent books and yet are not capable of reading many of the adult books that are available.

The superficial character of the books which were the favorites in the present study, the fact that tenth-grade students are beginning to abandon juvenile literature, the immaturity of the books read by bright students and older boys and girls suggest some problems for teachers and librarians who direct programs of reading. In the following concluding statement, some of the problems suggested by the present study will be discussed.

PROBLEMS OF GUIDANCE IN READING

The reading choices of students whose ages range from about fourteen to sixteen show that many such boys and girls are beginning to tire of juvenile books. The heartiness, cheerfulness, and general tone of the books for young readers are no longer attractive. Particularly is the fact true for bright students, for boys and girls whose background of experience has made them more mature than their years, and for older boys and girls. At this time when juvenile books begin to pall, students generally adopt one of three courses: (1) they virtually stop reading; (2) they turn to inferior adult magazines; (3) they make a quick jump from *Sue Barton* to *The Grapes* of *Wrath*—or to *Forever Amber*. Rarely do they turn promptly from juvenile books to standard adult classics, for many of the latter seem slow, hard, and remote from their interests. Some boys and girls, of course, make a satisfactory transition to highly reputable adult materials by way of adult adventure or love stories. A few students in the present study seemed launched upon this course. For the bulk of students, however, the transition from juvenile books to adult reading is not successful and, consequently, the general level of adult reading is lower than one would hope.

Examination of the books ordinarily supplied for older adolescents suggests one reason that the transition is not successful. There are available few books which can be used to introduce students to adult materials. When the classroom libraries in the present study were being organized, little fiction could be found that was not either distinctly juvenile or adult. Books by such writers as Edna Ferber, Bess Streeter Aldrich, James Hilton, Walter Edmonds, and Kenneth Roberts make reasonably good stepping stones from children's books to adult fiction, but the number of such books is seriously limited. Practically no biographies were available. The little fictionized biographies written for young readers are sometimes an unfortunate mixture of juvenile tone and adult subject matter. It was impossible to find many travel books that seemed to have "transition" value. Especially difficult to locate were any books—fiction or nonfiction—about foreign countries. On the market are a number of excellent juvenile books about young people of other lands, but there is almost nothing in this field that will serve as a bridge to carry older boys and girls to the great literature of foreign countries or to good, but difficult, contemporary books about foreign lands.

Equally unavailable were books about contemporary American life in which the problems of individuals or of society are treated realistically, seriously, and artistically. Most teachers and parents would agree that a fourteen- or fifteen-year-old girl is not ready to plunge freely into the realistic American novels that stem from the 1920's or 1930's; into many of the much-advertised novels of the last two or three years; into the work of serious students of American thought; or into the writing of such masters of technique as Henry James and Edith Wharton. Yet there are in print very few books suitable to the age and experience of adolescents, who undoubtedly should break away gradually from the too-pretty picture of life which they get in books for juveniles.

It was difficult to find books of information that apparently had been written with older boys and girls in mind. Too many of the craft-and-hobby books have a juvenile tone that displeases older boys and girls. Such little books as those by Floherty look juvenile and are almost too simple in style to have much appeal to bright students. There was practically no suitable nonfiction about current affairs, science, or history. Even the books about "manners and behavior"—a subject of real concern to many older students—failed to come to grips with the problems of fifteen- and sixteen-year-old boys and girls. It is interesting that the only book about "behavior" that was at all popular was *Letters to Susan*, which was read by 10 percent of the girls in the study. In this book, unlike all the others of comparable subject matter, no attention was paid to such "problems" as writing invitations, answering letters, using the right fork, and so on. Rather, in it were discussions of smoking, drinking, relations between boys and girls, and similar subjects close to the questions with which modern boys and girls are really concerned.

Surely no one would doubt that older boys and girls "need" books which touch upon their problems, give them information about important social issues, help them to understand people different from themselves, and present a realistic picture of life. And if one notes what the young people in this and other studies read—plus what they say about books—there seems no question that older adolescents are searching for the "real" in books. Many students in this investigation concentrated upon books which gave them a feeling of reality—no matter how absurdly far from the real their favorite titles actually were. Girls who read the Sue Barton stories said over and over that they liked the books because they were so true; boys who read historical novels claimed as one reason for their choice that the books were about "real history"; the readers of school and sport stories stated that the books seemed "true to life." The expression "true to life" is one of the most frequently repeated comments which students make about the books they read. In previous studies of children's interests in reading one can find ample evidence that students like books which seem real.

The fact that students read so many books which to adults seem divorced from reality is no indication that young people are not interested in life. Rather, it demonstrates their inexperience, their lack of information, their distorted point of view. Little children have trouble distinguishing between outright fantasy and reality; older boys and girls have difficulty distinguishing the pseudo-real from the real. But one wonders when young people should stop confusing life-as-they-want-it-to-be and life-as-it-is. If students as old as those in the present investigation honestly think that such books as Sue Barton, Will to Win, and

Mutiny at Midnight are "true to life," then the fact is cause for alarm. Their problem becomes less one of guidance in reading than one of education in general; and schools, homes, and social agencies may well consider whether they have done young people a disservice by failing to make them see life less romantically, more realistically. The bright sixteen-year-old girl who scorns The Connecticut Yankee in King Arthur's Court because it is untrue to life and turns to Rebecca because it is, is demonstrating not merely poor literary taste but a twisted sense of values. A boy who likes dog stories because they seem so real and dislikes Tom Sawyer because Tom's experiences "couldn't have happened" is revealing distorted ideas not just about books but about life.

Certainly no one cares to deny students—or adults—the pleasures of escape into romantic fiction. No teachers would withhold from young people the light, cheerful, or exciting books which have no more serious purpose than to entertain. The reading of such books becomes questionable only when in them students find a substitute for life or fail to see that the stories are fancy, not reality. They can be questioned only when they are the only reading which students do and when students come to value them more highly than they should.

If it can be admitted that older students honestly want to read about real life, that they are sincere in their assertion that the sentimental and adventurous books which they read seem true, and that the supply of books which bridge the gap between the juvenile and the adult is limited, then four courses of action can be suggested.

First, teachers, librarians, and parents possibly should recognize that a student is not one day a child, to be sheltered from the realities of life or of life in books, and the next day an adult, to be scorned because he does not see life clearly and because he does not read the great books. Just as we recognize that the process of physical growth extends over a long period of time, so should we realize that probably the process of growing up to great and good books is a long and gradual one.

Second, schools and homes need to revise their notion of when students are ready to face life squarely and realistically. It is unreasonable to expect students who are treated as though they were children to do anything except turn to the juvenile in books. If an individual's reading reflects anything it is his degree of maturity, and older students who are consistently regarded by home and school as immature will necessarily turn to books which correspond to their status in society. The very fact that students are kept in school as long as they are necessarily keeps them children. How teachers and parents can make older students aware of their responsibilities as young adults and still exercise the control which school and home imply are difficult problems. But they are worth working on—and only incidentally, of course, for the effect which increased maturity would have upon students' reading interests. Possibly students who are treated as adults will behave as adults—and their choices of books will reflect their new-won maturity. Teachers and librarians can certainly help students toward assumption of more mature attitudes by recognizing the real reading interests of older boys and girls and planning their work accordingly. At a time when students in senior high school are becoming very much interested in sex, their program of reading studiously avoids any books in which sex is dealt with in a forthright fashion. At a time when they are most rebellious against home ties, they are given either little stories about home

life of the past or stories in which boys nd girls neatly and unrealistically escape from home.

Not just the program of reading but the general atmosphere of school and home keeps young people from assuming adult tastes and attitudes. At a time when young people are most eager to take over realistic responsibilities, they are denied such opportunities, because schools and homes find it easier and more efficient to do the jobs themselves. At a time when boys and girls should be living life to the full, they are eternally preparing for the future. By no means can it be denied that a school is a preparation for the future; it does not exist as an entity outside the course of society. But perhaps teachers and parents have not realized that students may need help in finding joy and pleasure in the immediate job, in understanding that life is exciting at the moment. Perhaps students to whom a good day's work is a pleasure, to whom each day in itself seems "lifelike"—instead of preparation for the future—will be less inclined to escape so consistently to the South Seas with Howard Pease, or into the pseudo reality of the career books, or to the frozen North with Jack O'Brien. Students who enjoy life as it is may be less ready to find in books life as they should like to have it.

Third, schools and homes should cull the lists of available adult books for titles that will help students slide from the juvenile to the mature in books. Possibly easy contemporary adult material makes the best bridge between juvenile books and the great books of the past and the best books of the present. Contemporary fiction or nonfiction written for adults is not too difficult for most senior high-school students. And it is considerably easier to guide a student into some of the worth-while books of other centuries by way of current adult materials than directly from children's books. In the present study some adult books were used. Many more could have been added to the classroom collection if students' reading choices were to have been directed.

In any high-school library should be included a large number of easy, contemporary books written for adults. A library collection which jumps from Howard Pease to Melville and Hardy will not be highly useful to many students in the senior high school. Nor will one which admits only those contemporary writers of adult books which are so innocuous that they fail to touch upon matters with which many intelligent young adults are concerned.

Fourth, teachers, librarians, and parents should make known to publishers the need for books written especially for young adults—or older adolescents. A fifteen-year-old girl who is interested in race relations may well be shocked and horrified by *Strange Fruit* or *Native Son*. She may not be ready to read many of the serious studies of race problems that are now available. But the juvenile books about racial problems are limited in number and too simple in tone to appeal to older students. A girl who wants to read a love story may not be ready for the great love stories and poetry of the world, but she becomes dissatisfied

with the tepid little romances which she finds in books for adolescents. A student who no longer insists upon a strong narrative element in books needs some biographies and books of information which are midway between children's book and standard adult titles. One might suspect that the greatest single need in the field of books for adolescents is for titles appropriate for and interesting to older boys and girls, books that are "fun to read"—by which students mean simply easy and pleasurable—and at the same time written around subjects of interest to the young adults who are enrolled in the tenth, eleventh, and twelfth grades of our schools. Although adult books that are easy enough to read can be used with some students, for many others "transition" titles are necessary.

To help older students acquire mature reading tastes it may be suggested that teachers, librarians, and parents possibly should recognize that the development of such interests is a matter of slow growth, not sudden change; they should help students develop mature attitudes in general before they expect them to be "mature readers"; they should include in young people's libraries suitable adult books; and they should make known to publishers the need for books written especially for older boys and girls.

READING THE COMICS [1]

Paul A. Witty

[Recurrently comic books and comic strips are charged with contributing heavily to juvenile delinquency as well as debauching the tastes of

[1] Adapted and abridged from Paul A. Witty, "Reading the Comics: A Comparative Study," *Journal of Experimental Education* (1941), *10*:105–109.

young readers. Witty has conducted a number of investigations into the validity of these accusations. One representative study is included here. Evidence is presented about what kind of comic books and comic strips are most widely read. An attempt is also made to discover in a sampling of youth whether a relationship can be established between the reading of comics and tendency toward delinquency.]

Three hundred thirty-four boys and girls in Grades 4, 5, and 6 of the Evanston, Illinois, schools were recently interviewed. The investigation disclosed a genuine interest in comic books, magazines, and strips in all grades. The average number of magazines read was about thirteen; three were read regularly, an additional three were read often, and six were read occasionally. Reading the comic strips was also a popular pursuit; an average of twenty-five comic strips were read. Of these, thirteen were read regularly and four were examined often. Finally, about 60 percent of the pupils reported that they enjoyed making their own comics. These data attest unequivocally to a general interest in comics among middle-grade children, and they suggest the validity of the statement that the comics represent children's major reading interest.

The purpose of this further investigation is to study the interests of children selected at random from 2500 public-school youngsters on the same points as those covered by the preceding investigation. Children in Grades 4, 5, and 6 of eight schools in Chicago and vicinity were interviewed. Samples of 100 each were made at random by including the reports of every twentieth child in the first sample, and proportionate numbers in other samples. Eliminations and additions were made until the samples were constituted in the manner shown in Table 1. The samples showed remarkable agreement. Hence, it seemed that

TABLE 1. Number of Pupils in Random Sampling

Grade	Number of Schools [a]	Number of Pupils		Both Sexes
		Girls	Boys	
4	3	18	15	33
5	4	17	16	33
6	5	16	18	34
All grades	7	51	49	100

[a] Names of schools: Seward, Hammond, Falconer, Motley, Haven, Anderson, Field. Names of towns: Evanston, Chicago, Illinois; Milwaukee, Wisconsin.

the method provided a reliable picture of the entire group of 2500 boys and girls.

Table 2 shows the number of comic magazines read by these boys and girls. It will be noted that the average number is slightly above fifteen, and that the boys read a considerably larger number than the girls. The Evanston group read a somewhat smaller number (thirteen), and differences between the sexes were similar to those in the random sampling.

Table 3 shows that an average of four

TABLE 2. Mean Number of Comic Magazines Read
(Random Sampling)

Grade	Mean Number Read		
	Girls	Boys	Both Sexes
4	16.33	15.80	16.09
5	14.94	16.87	15.87
6	11.81	16.89	14.50
All grades	14.45	16.55	15.48

TABLE 3. Mean Frequency of Reading of Comic Magazines
(Random Sampling)

Grade	Number Read Regularly			Number Read Often			Number Read Sometimes		
	Girls	Boys	Both	Girls	Boys	Both	Girls	Boys	Both
4	6.05	4.06	5.12	4.44	4.20	4.33	5.83	7.53	6.61
5	2.11	3.62	2.84	5.82	4.75	5.30	6.88	8.50	7.66
6	3.06	4.11	3.62	3.12	5.44	4.06	5.62	7.33	6.53
All grades	3.80	3.93	3.87	4.49	4.84	4.66	6.12	7.77	6.93

magazines were read regularly; four and one-half, often; and about seven, occasionally. This study is similar to others in showing that boys read comic magazines somewhat more frequently than girls. But the differences are neither large nor consistent from grade to grade.

The favorite comic magazines are given in Table 4. In general, there is considerable similarity in the choices of

TABLE 4. Rankings Given by Girls and Boys to the Thirteen Comic Magazines
Given Highest Ranking by Both Sexes
(Random Sampling)

Name of Magazine	Rank		
	Both Sexes	Girls	Boys
Batman	1.0	2.0	1.0
Superman	2.0	1.0	2.0
Jungle	3.0	3.0	9.0
Famous Funnies	4.0	4.0	9.0
Flash	6.0	10.5	4.0
Ace	6.0	5.0	11.0
Magic	6.0	6.0	6.5
Action	8.0	13.0	4.0
Detective	9.0	a	4.0
True	10.0	13.0	9.0
Green Mask	12.0	8.0	a
Shadow	12.0	8.0	a
Wings	12.0	a	6.5

a Listed by one person.

the boys and the girls. The titles of favorite magazines are very similar to those in the Evanston group. Yet in the random sampling there is a somewhat larger range, with a higher frequency of magazines which appear only once.

Magazines favored in the different grades are listed in order in Table 5. The similarity in the choices of these grades is the essential feature of this table. Close inspection shows that the magazines *Jungle*, *Magic*, and *Famous Funnies* oc-

TABLE 5. Favorite Comic Magazines by Grades
(Random Sampling)

Grade 4	Rank	Grade 5	Rank	Grade 6	Rank
Batman	1.0	Batman	1.0	Batman	1.0
Superman	2.0	Superman	2.0	Superman	2.0
Famous Funnies	3.5	Jungle	3.5	Flash	3.0
Magic	3.5	Ace	3.5	Action	4.5
Jungle	5.0	Action	5.5	Famous Funnies	4.5
Flash	6.5	Detective	5.5	Jungle	6.5
Shadow	6.5	Crack	7.5	Ace	6.5
Green Mask	10.5	Adventure	7.5	Detective	10.5
Planet	10.5	Flash	10.5	Mystery	10.5
Ace	10.5	Famous Funnies	10.5	True	10.5
True	10.5	Fantastic	10.5	Magic	10.5
Wings	10.5			Tip Top	10.5
Blue Beetle	10.5			Wings	10.5

cupy somewhat different positions in the three grades. Despite this discrepancy, we must conclude that the most popular magazines have a rather general and similar appeal in every grade.

Table 6 presents the average number of comic strips which the children read. It will be observed that the average number both for the boys and for the girls is about twenty-six. Moreover, this

TABLE 6. Mean Number Comic Strips Read
(Random Sampling)

Grade	Mean Number Read		
	Girls	Boys	Both Sexes
4	27.67	25.73	26.79
5	26.05	24.25	25.18
6	27.00	26.00	26.47
All grades	26.92	25.34	26.15

number is found in the fourth grade and persists through the sixth grade. Thus the intense interest which is evident in the fourth grade is not lessened during the ensuing two grades.

Table 7 shows that these girls read

the comic strips more frequently than the boys. This somewhat contradictory finding probably reflects the fact that sex differences are not as pronounced or consistent in reading the comics as in other reading pursuits. In several of our

TABLE 7.   Mean Frequency of Reading of Comic Strips
(Random Sampling)

Grade	Number Read Regularly			Number Read Often			Number Read Sometimes		
	Girls	Boys	Both	Girls	Boys	Both	Girls	Boys	Both
4	15.83	13.07	14.57	6.77	2.73	4.93	3.66	9.93	6.51
5	16.06	13.00	14.57	4.00	4.18	4.09	6.00	6.12	6.36
6	14.87	14.61	14.73	4.56	6.44	5.56	7.31	4.77	5.97
All grades	15.60	13.61	14.63	5.16	4.57	4.87	5.59	6.79	6.28

tabulations, boys have been found to read the comics more frequently than the girls. But, in all these tabulations, the differences between the sexes are neither consistent nor highly significant. The only justifiable conclusion seems to be that boys and girls are generally attracted to the comics. The attraction occurs in the early grades and continues with great consistency throughout the middle grades.

Table 8 presents the most popular comic strips. It may be seen that the preferred strips are popular in Grades 4, 5, and 6. The differences between the sexes are relatively insignificant. It is apparent that certain strips have strong appeal in all grades. The fact that reading the comics has general rather than specific appeal may be gathered from observing that grade differences are small, sex differences are insignificant, and differences in locality appear to influence the amount and nature of this type of reading to a small degree only. The latter may be seen by noting the similarity in the nature and extent of reading the comics between the random sample and

TABLE 8.   Rankings Given by Grades 4, 5, and 6 to the Comic Strips
Given Highest Ranking by All Grades
(Random Sampling)

	Rank			
	All Grades	Grade 4	Grade 5	Grade 6
Blondie	1.0	1.0	2.5	1.0
Dick Tracy	2.0	13.0	1.0	2.0
Smiling Jack	3.0	2.0	2.5	5.0
Lone Ranger	4.0	5.0	8.0	3.0
Donald Duck	5.0	3.0	13.5	5.0
Mickey Mouse	6.0	13.0	5.0	5.0
Brenda Starr	7.0	7.5	13.5	13.0
Henry	11.0	5.0	13.5	c
Toots and Casper	11.0	b	13.5	8.5
Dixie Dugan	11.0	13.0	13.5	13.0
Captain and the Kids	11.0	b	8.0	13.0
Winnie Winkle	11.0	b	4.0	c
Terry and the Pirates	11.0	c	8.0	8.5
Scarlet O'Neil a	11.0	13.0	8.0	b

a Not listed on questionnaire. Added by children in space provided for others.
b Listed as a favorite by only one person.
c Not listed as a favorite by any child.

the Evanston group. This similarity is vividly shown by comparisons of Tables 8 and 9, which present the favorite comic strips of the two groups.

The general interest of boys and girls in the comics is revealed also by their inclination to make comics. In fact, exactly half of these boys and girls report a fondness for making their own comics. Again, a relatively greater interest of the

boys is revealed; 55 percent of the boys and only 45 percent of the girls indicated that they enjoyed this activity.

It is of interest that Evanston boys and girls read a somewhat smaller number of comic magazines and comic strips than the unselected group; however, they make their own comics more frequently and turn to the comics early in the grades and persist in reading them.

TABLE 9. Rankings Given by Grades 4, 5, and 6 to the Comic Strips Given Highest Ranking by All Grades (Evanston)

Name of Comic Strip	All Grades	Rank		
		Grade 4	Grade 5	Grade 6
Dick Tracy	1.0	1.0	1.0	1.0
Smiling Jack	2.0	3.0	2.0	2.0
Blondie	3.0	2.0	3.0	3.0
Donald Duck	4.0	6.0	4.0	4.0
Captain and the Kids	5.0	11.5	5.0	7.0
Brenda Starr [a]	6.0	20.0	7.0	5.0
Nancy [a]	7.0	4.0	6.0	12.5
Terry and the Pirates	8.5	15.5	16.5	6.0
Mickey Mouse	8.5	20.0	9.0	8.0
Henry	10.0	8.0	9.0	11.0
Superman	11.0	8.0	12.5	17.0
Li'l Abner	12.0	15.5	14.5	10.0

[a] Not listed in questionnaire. Added by children in space provided for others not listed.

TABLE 10. Number and Percentage of Children Who Like to Make Original Comics (Random Sampling)

Grade	Girls		Boys		Both Sexes	
	Number	Percentage	Number	Percentage	Number	Percentage
4	8	44	8	53	16	48
5	8	47	11	68	19	57
6	7	44	8	44	15	44
All grades	23	45	27	55	50	50
Mean	7.66	45	9	55	16.66	49⅔

During the past two years a number of dogmatic statements have been made concerning the baneful influence of reading the comics upon the development of boys and girls. The practice is sometimes condemned with such finality that parents and teachers are inclined to

believe that reading the comics should be discouraged or actually forbidden. In an effort to study the validity of these strictures, the 10 percent of the pupils who read comics most in one school were compared with the 10 percent who read them least. The average IQ of the two groups was in the interval 105–110 (most 107; least 105).

The boys and girls in the two groups received almost the same average marks and were considered by their teachers to be about equally well adjusted and effective in social relationships. When the general reading of the children who turn to the comics most frequently was compared with that of the group reading the comics least often, it was found that the patterns were quite similar.

Case studies also revealed that some children who read the comics very often were following reading programs which were varied, rich, and generally commendable. Thus, one sixth-grade boy, who reported that he read twenty-eight comic magazines occasionally and more than twenty strips regularly, listed thirty books which he had read voluntarily during the few months preceding the investigation. In this list were four new volumes dealing with South America, two Story Parade Adventure Books, several good biographies, and a fair assortment of exciting stories such as *Cowboy in the Making* by Will James. In addition, he had read recently a number of magazines and a considerable amount of poetry including *Peacock Pie and Other Poems* by De la Mare, *Rainbow in the Sky* and others by Lindsay, and several poems by Sandburg.

On the other hand, a boy and girl who read very few comics and two children who read a very large number were generally inadequate. Although their intelligence quotients were average, their reading patterns were distinctly impoverished.

In dealing with the pupils who were preoccupied with the comics, the coöperation of the home was sought in an effort to make other types of reading matter equally satisfying and enjoyable. The first step involved ascertaining rather fully the varied interests and leisure pursuits of these children. A number of books, magazines, and pamphlets were then made available. These were selected to satisfy or extend the children's interests. Since these children had become habituated to exciting, adventurous books, radio programs, and movies, an effort was made to capitalize on these interests and to introduce them slowly and progressively to good literature. Among the materials that were advantageously used in transitional stages were the Disney books, the Story Parade Adventure Series, and twenty volumes on aviation and sports. Reading the Disney books constituted the first new reading experience for these children. Another phase of the program included the cultivation of other inchoate interests. One child found her interest in music happily satisfied by hearing *Peter and the Wolf* and other records which caused her to appreciate new possibilities in records and in the radio; and books about music and musicians provided an easy introduction to more worth-while reading.

One boy who read very few comics displayed great originality and considerable skill in making his own comics. This interest was directed into closely related types of artistic endeavor, and it was associated with books which contained information about these new pursuits. With every pupil, the procedure was similar. First, there was a careful study of the child's interests and needs; and second, there was an effort to find worthy reading material to satisfy every child's interests. In some cases it was necessary to create new interests through an enrichment and extension of experience. But in every instance the results were gratifying.

SUMMARY

Strictures are often made concerning

the dire effects of reading of the comics. The data in this section do not afford a basis for these diatribes. In one school, two groups of children were studied intensively—those who read comics extensively and those who seldom read them. Reading patterns of the two groups disclosed little difference in amount or nature of reading. Case studies indicated that one could not generalize concerning the needs of children from a single tendency such as maximum or minimum amount of reading in this area. Instead, the problem of creating desirable reading habits can be met only by appraising each child's entire reading pattern. For some children an amount of reading in the field of the comics may seem excessive. However, when it is viewed in terms of an otherwise well-rounded and balanced program of reading, it can scarcely be considered harmful.

Similarly, a small amount of reading of comics may be associated with a desirable or with an undesirable total pattern. It seems that a child's tendency to read the comics should not be used independently as a basis for appraising his needs. Guidance should be based upon a more extensive and far-reaching attempt to understand each child's needs for reading and his efforts to satisfy them through different avenues. Finally, since reading the comics is actuated by the same motives which are satisfied by the radio and the movie, the problem is one which apparently cannot be dealt with singly. Nevertheless, appraisal and guidance of this fundamental reading habit are responsibilities of every teacher.

POSTSCRIPT [1]

Paul A. Witty and Robert A. Sizemore

Studies indicate that over 90 percent of the boys and girls between eight and thirteen years of age regularly read comic books. Fourth-, fifth-, and sixth-graders appear to be the most avid readers. Many of these children read five or six comic magazines weekly; in addition, they may read ten or more other comic books. In several of the studies, boys were shown to read the comics more frequently than girls. But in all our studies, the differences between the sexes were neither consistent nor highly significant. The only justifiable conclusion seems to be that boys and girls are generally attracted to the comics. The attraction increases in the early grades and continues with great consistency throughout the middle grades. In the seventh and eighth grades, interest in the comics continues. Children here are attracted somewhat less frequently to the comic magazines, although many of the favorites of the middle grades are still read. However, interest in the comic strip is maintained with the same in-

[1] Abridged and adapted from Paul A. Witty and Robert A. Sizemore, "Reading the Comics: A Summary of Studies and an Evaluation III," *Elementary English* (1955) 32:109–114.

tensity as in the lower grades. The average number of comic magazines read by the high-school students is distinctly lower than the average obtained in the study of junior-high-school pupils. Moreover, there is a decrease from Grade 9 through Grade 12. It became clear that at the junior- and senior-high-school level, as well as in the middle grades, reading the comics is a favorite leisure pursuit of boys and girls—a general interest affected to a relatively small degree by differences in age, sex, or locality.

Several studies show that the amount of comic book reading is unrelated to marks in school and to attainment as revealed by standard tests. Our own studies lend support to these investigations. In 1942, we found that the average educational attainment of pupils who were in the upper fourth in amount of comic book reading was almost identical with the average for those who were in the lower fourth. Repeatedly, each year thereafter, teachers in the classes of one of the writers have arrived at the same conclusion from their own studies. Similarly, these teachers report little difference between children who are in the upper quarter and those in the lower quarter in the frequency of behavior problems. Several other studies reviewed in this section show little difference between delinquent and typical pupils in the amount or nature of comic book reading.

Is one justified, therefore, in dismissing Dr. Wertham's strictures? [2] We believe not, for it may be shown that many comic books (perhaps one-fourth or more) present to the child recurring instances of violence, hate, and aggression. Such a reading diet, unbalanced by the presentation of stories and illustrations disclosing more humane and democratic values, may lead to the acceptance of violence and aggression as a *normal* way of life.

Regardless of the merits of the charge that crime comics contribute to delinquency, a further question remains as to whether we really want children to read such material. Is this good reading matter for children? Even though we could state with assurance that crime comics do not cause or aggravate antisocial behavior, it would still seem obvious that the portrayal of crime and brutality in these magazines does not constitute worth-while reading for children. It is our responsibility as adults, educators, and parents to provide children with better reading materials, as well as with real experiences to foster worth-while, engrossing interests. We should seek also to help children distinguish between fantastic representations in comics and real-life situations, and we should aid them in forming sound concepts of desirable human behavior. We should help them to recognize the difference between good and poor content, art work, writing, and printing in comic magazines. It is our job to guide children to discriminate among these magazines. We should recognize the value of some comic books, improve and apply the comic method in education, and advocate moderation in reading the comics rather than total abstinence.

[2] Frederic Wertham, *Seduction of the Innocent*, Rinehart & Co., 1953. The book charges comic books cause "moral disarmament."

Chapter VII

WHAT MAKES IT READABLE?

Introduction

In order to secure consistent and orderly development of reading ability, the student needs to proceed toward levels of increasing difficulty in the material he reads. This principle has been understood for a long time, and careful efforts have been made to provide graded material. But how is difficulty determined? Must one rely on subjective judgment? Until very recently, individual opinion has been the only appraisal mechanism available. Authors made estimates, librarians made estimates, teachers made estimates, and readers made estimates. And, of course, all were different.

It was only with the appearance of such pioneer inquiries as Gray and Leary's *What Makes a Book Readable?* that objective assessment began to be attempted. Gray and Leary uncovered the basic factors which demonstrated consistent relationship to reading difficulty.

Subsequently a number of formulas were evolved which by statistical refinement were able to rely on only a few of the long list of factors uncovered by Gray and Leary. Three of the most useful formulas are reproduced in this chapter. Complete instructions are included so that the formulas can be used by the reader at the level to which they appear to be best suited.

But before the reader becomes unduly sanguine about the kind of appraisal these formulas permit, a few cautions are in order. Perhaps the best statement of the limitations of reading formulas is by the coauthor of one of them:

First, readability formulas should be critically used. Too often the grade-placement indexes are accepted as true measures of difficulty when they should be considered only as first approximations of difficulty.

Second, readability formulas as prescriptions for writing should be approached with extreme caution. The formulas were *not* devised as rules for writing. They consider only limited aspects of difficulty.

Third, validation studies are needed to show the differences in actual reading comprehension as a result of changes effected by typical readability campaigns in journalism and industry.

Fourth, validation studies on textbooks are needed to throw light on the degree of confidence that can be placed in the grade-level indexes of the various formulas and the extent of agreement among them.

Fifth, there is a need for better exchange of results of readability appraisals, especially in education. Since the time and effort involved in appraising a book is still considerable, some provision should be made for exchange of information among publishers, teachers, school systems, and librarians.[1]

If the formulas are used with these sensible admonishments in view, they render valuable service.

[1] Jeanne Chall, "This Business of Readability: a Second Look," *Educational Research Bulletin* (1956), 35:93.

A READABILITY FORMULA FOR PRIMARY READING MATERIALS [1]

George Spache

In recent years, there has been considerable interest in and use of formulas for judging the reading difficulty of printed materials. Most of this interest has dated from the original Flesch formula offered in 1943 (3). This formula and the later studies of Dale and Chall (1) have been used extensively in the evaluation of industrial communications, books, magazines, and government publications.

An examination of these formulas and studies reveals that the interest has been focused largely on the evaluation of materials written for adults. None of the three leading formulas, the Flesch, Lorge (6) or Dale-Chall, is applicable to materials written for individuals reading on levels below the fourth grade. Because of the obvious values in having objective measures of reading difficulty, we have attempted to devise a formula that would be useful with primary reading materials.

There are a number of elements which may be used to estimate reading difficulty. Among these are word length, sentence length, percentage of personal

[1] Adapted and abridged from George Spache, "A New Readability Formula for Primary Materials," University College, University of Florida, Gainesville, Florida. Mimeographed.

words or personal sentences. In addition, the number of syllables, of affixes or of prepositional phrases, and the proportion of difficult words by comparison with various word lists have been used. Dale and Chall have reviewed the relationship of these various elements to reading difficulty. They find that the best prediction of reading difficulty is obtained from a number of difficult words (those outside a list of 3000 words known to 80 percent of fourth-graders) and average sentence length. Two other elements of almost equal predictive value are the number of affixes and the number of words outside the Dale list of 769 words (2). This is a list of the words found both in the International Kindergarten Union List and in the first 1000 of the Thorndike Teacher's Word Book.

We have followed the example of Dale and Chall in choosing average sentence length as a predictive measure. In addition, we employ the Dale List of 769 words, judging all words outside this list as hard words. The two other elements which, by reason of the evidence of Lorge, Flesch, or Dale-Chall, might have been employed were the number of affixes and the Dale 3000-word list. In our opinion, the simplicity of the vocabulary found in primary reading materials makes both of these measures inappropriate.

We secured 224 samples of 100 words each from 152 books in common use in the first three grades. These were texts used for basal reading instruction except for twenty-three social science, health, and science books. We assigned a grade level to each book according to the level of its classroom use. Thus pre-primers were designated 1.2; primers, 1.5; first readers, 1.8; second readers, 2.1; and third readers, 3.3. Where two or three books were offered for a grade level, the second-level books were graded 1.9, 2.4, 2.7, and 3.7, respectively.

The intercorrelations of these elements of reading difficulty and the grade levels assigned to the reading materials are presented in Table 1.

TABLE 1.   Intercorrelations of Style Elements and Graded Textbooks

	2	3	Means	SD
1. Sentence length	.563	.751	8.52	3.31
2. Percent hard words		.683	5.24	3.76
3. Grade level of texts			2.49	.856

The multiple correlation coefficient obtained by combining sentence length and percent of hard words to predict grade level of texts is r = .818. The accuracy with which these two elements predict reading difficulty of primary texts compares very favorably with the Dale-Chall multiple coefficient of .70 or that of .7047 in the Flesch formula for "reading ease."

Our data differ from the findings of Lorge, Flesch, and Dale-Chall in indicating that sentence length is slightly more closely related to reading difficulty than is the percent of hard words. In the three other studies, the measure of vocabulary load was the most important factor in reading difficulty. Apparently editors of primary reading materials exercise more control over sentence length than over the introduction of hard words. Above the primary grades, sentence length is less controlled and perhaps less significant in reading difficulty since the child has acquired a modicum of reading skill.

For those who wish to use this readability formula, the complete regression equation is: Grade level of text = .141 average sentence length per 100 words + .086 percent of words outside Dale 769 Easy Word List + .839.

Certain rules guiding the word count were evolved as they appeared necessary. They are:

1. Count all letters as familiar, i.e., A, B, C.
2. Count regular verb forms *ing, ed, es* as familiar. Count irregular verb forms as unfamiliar, unless formed from familiar word, as *stop, stopped.*
3. Count plurals and possessive endings of nouns as familiar.
4. Count adjectival or adverbial endings *ly, er, est* as unfamiliar. (This differs from the Dale-Chall procedure but is supported by the fact that such endings do not appear except at higher levels in primary materials.)
5. Count first names as familiar.
6. Count an unfamiliar word only once even though it appears again or with variable endings later in the sample. (This rule was adopted to prevent a single hard word from distorting the estimation of grade level in these primary materials, which tend to be highly repetitive.)
7. A group of words, consisting of repetition of a single word, as *oh, oh, oh; look, look, look;* etc., is counted as a single sentence regardless of punctuation.
8. Count family names or family relationship words (*aunt, uncle*) as unfamiliar except where name is a noun on the Dale list.

We have applied the formula to popular books, readers, and other primary materials used in our Reading Clinic. We find that the estimates of reading difficulty by means of the formula agree markedly with our observations of children's reading performances and the observations of experienced classroom teachers.

References

1. Dale, E., and Chall, J. S., "A Formula for Predicting Readability," *Educational Research Bulletin,* Ohio State University (January 11 and February 17, 1948), 27:11–20, 37–54.
2. Dale, Edgar, "A Comparison of Two Word Lists," *Educational Research Bulletin* (December 8, 1931), 18:484–488.
3. Flesch, R. F., *Marks of Readable Style: A Study of Adult Education.* New York: Teachers College, Columbia University, 1943.
4. Hotchkiss, Sanford N., and Paterson, Donald G., "Flesch Readability Reading List," *Personnel Psychology* (Autumn, 1950), 3:327–344.
5. Lewerenz, Alfred S., "A Vocabulary Grade Placement Formula," *Journal of Experimental Education* (March, 1935), 236.
6. Lorge, Irving, "Predicting Readability," *Teachers College Record* (1944), 45:404–419.
7. Wilkinson, M. S., Weedon, V., and Washburne, Carleton, *The Right Book for the Right Child.* New York: John Day, 1936.

Worksheet for Application of the New Readability Formula for Grades 1–3

Reading Laboratory and Clinic
University College, University of Florida

Title .... Date ....

Author .... Publisher ....

	Page .... From .... To	Page .... From .... To	Page .... From .... To	Page .... From .... To ....
1. Number words				
2. Number sentences				
3. Number words not on Dale 769 Easy Words List				
4. Average sentence length (Divide 1 by 2)				
5. Dale score (Divide 3 by 1, multiply by 100)				
6. Multiply (4) by .141				
7. Multiply Dale score (5) by .086				
8. Constant	.839	.839	.839	.839
9. Estimated grade placement (Add 6, 7, and 8)				

Average grade placement of .... samples ....

Analyzed by ....

Date ....

PROCEDURE

1. Count off about 100 words in the first few pages of the book.
2. Begin count at the beginning of a sentence and end with the last word of the sentence in which the 100th word occurs. Enter number of words in #1 above.
3. Count number of sentences in entire sample. Enter number of sentences in #2 above.
4. Determine how many words in the selection are not in the Dale list. Write this number under #3 above.
5. Divide number of words (#1) by number of sentences (#2). Enter answer in #4 above.
6. Divide number of words not on Dale list by number of words (#3 by #1). Multiply answer by 100 by moving decimal point two places to right. Enter answer in #5, Dale score above.
7. Multiply figure entered opposite #4 by .141. Enter under #6 above. (See table on page 184.)
8. Multiply figure entered opposite #5 by .086. Enter under #7 above. (See table on page 184.)
9. Add figures entered opposite #6, #7 and .839.
10. The sum is an estimate of the grade level of difficulty of the reading selection.
11. Repeat entire procedure, steps 1 to 10, twice more with samples from middle and rear of book.
12. Determine average grade placement by adding the three estimates and dividing by 3. This is the final estimate of the grade level of difficulty of the entire book. Drop last figures or round them off, as 2.367 = 2.4. This figure designates a book as being equal in difficulty to readers commonly used in the fourth month of the second grade.

Dale List of 769 Easy Words

a	behind	cap	dance	family	glass	hurry
about	being	captain	dark	fancy	go	hurt
above	believe	car	day	far	God	
across	bell	care	dead	farm	going	I
act	belong	careful	dear	farmer	gold	ice
afraid	beside	carry	deep	fast	golden	if
after	best	case	did	fat	gone	in
afternoon	better	cat	die	father	good	Indian
again	between	catch	different	feed	got	instead
against	big	cause	dinner	feel	grain	into
ago	bill	cent	do	feet	grass	iron
air	bird	center	doctor	fell	gray	is
all	bit	chair	does	fellow	great	it
almost	black	chance	dog	felt	green	its
alone	bless	change	done	fence	grew	
along	blind	chief	door	few	ground	jump
already	blood	child	double	field	grow	just
also	blow	children	down	fight	guess	
always	blue	choose	draw	fill		keep
am	board	Christmas	dream	find	had	kept
American	boat	church	dress	fine	hair	kill
an	body	circle	drink	finger	half	kind
and	bone	city	drive	finish	hall	king
animal	book	class	drop	fire	hand	kiss
another	born	clean	dry	first	hang	knee
answer	both	clear	dust	fish	happy	knew
any	bottom	clock		fit	hard	know
anything	bow	close	each	five	has	
apple	box	cloth	ear	fix	hat	lady
are	boy	clothes	early	floor	have	laid
arm	branch	cloud	earth	flower	he	lake
around	brave	coal	east	fly	head	land
as	bread	coat	easy	follow	hear	large
ask	break	cold	eat	food	heard	last
at	breakfast	color	edge	foot	heart	late
away	bridge	come	egg	for	heavy	laugh
	bright	coming	eight	forget	help	lay
baby	bring	company	either	found	her	lead
back	broken	cook	eleven	four	here	learn
bad	brother	cool	else	fourth	herself	leave
bag	brought	corn	end	fresh	hide	left
ball	brown	corner	England	friend	high	leg
band	build	cost	English	from	hill	lesson
bank	building	could	enough	front	him	let
basket	built	count	even	fruit	himself	letter
be	burn	country	evening	full	his	lift
bear	busy	course	ever		hold	light
beat	but	cover	every	game	hole	like
beautiful	butter	cow	everything	garden	home	line
because	buy	cried	except	gate	hope	lion
bed	by	cross	expect	gave	horse	lips
bee		crowd	eye	get	hot	listen
been	cake	crown		gift	house	lit
before	call	cry	face	girl	how	little
began	came	cup	fair	give	hundred	live
begin	can	cut	fall	glad	hunt	load

long
look
lost
lot
loud
love
low

made
mail
make
man
many
march
mark
market
matter
may
me
mean
measure
meat
meet
men
met
middle
might
mile
milk
mill
mind
mine
minute
miss
money
month
moon
more
morning
most
mother
mountain
mouth
move
Mr.
Mrs.
much
music
must
my
myself

name
near
neck
need
neighbor
neither
nest

never
new
New York
next
nice
night
nine
no
noise
none
noon
nor
north
nose
not
note
nothing
now
number

oak
ocean
of
off
office
often
old
on
once
one
only
open
or
other
our
out
outside
over
own

page
paint
pair
paper
part
party
pass
path
pay
pen
people
pick
picture
piece
place
plain
plant
play
please

point
poor
post
pound
present
press
pretty
pull
put

quarter
queen
quick
quiet
quite

race
ran
rather
reach
read
ready
real
reason
red
remember
rest
rich
ride
right
ring
river
road
rock
roll
roof
room
rose
round
row
run

said
sail
salt
same
sand
sat
save
saw
say
school
sea
season
seat
second
see
seed
seem

seen
self
sell
send
sent
serve
set
seven
several
shake
shall
shape
she
sheep
shine
ship
shoe
shop
short
should
shoulder
show
shut
sick
side
sign
silk
silver
sing
sir
sister
sit
six
size
skin
sky
sleep
slow
small
smile
smoke
snow
so
soft
sold
soldier
some
something
sometime
song
soon
sound
south
space
speak
spot
spread
spring
square

stand
star
start
station
stay
step
stick
still
stone
stood
stop
store
storm
story
straight
street
strike
strong
such
sugar
suit
summer
sun
suppose
sure
surprise
sweet

table
tail
take
talk
tall
taste
teach
teacher
tear
tell
ten
than
thank
that
the
their
them
then
there
these
they
thick
thin
thing
think
this
those
though
thought
thousand
three

through
throw
tie
till
time
tire
to
today
together
told
tomorrow
tongue
too
took
top
touch
town
trade
train
tree
true
try
turn
twelve
twenty
two

uncle
under
until
up
upon
us
use

valley
very
visit

wait
walk
wall
want
war
warn
was
wash
waste
watch
water
wave
way
we
wear
weather
week
well
went
were

west
what
wheat
wheel
when
where
whether
which
while
white
who
whole
whom
whose
why
wide
wild
will
win
wind
window
wing
winter
wish
with
without
woman
wonder
wood
word
work
world
would
write
wrong

yard
year
yellow
yes
yesterday
yet
you
young
your

TABLE 2. For Quick Computation of the Readability of a Selection as Measured by the Spache Readability Formula [a]

Dale Score *	Average Sentence Length																	
	5	6	7	8	9	10	11	12	13	14	15	16	17	18	19	20	21	22
0	1.5	1.7	1.8	2.0	2.1	2.2	2.4	2.5	2.7	2.8	3.0	3.1	3.2	3.4	3.5	3.7	3.8	3.9
1	1.6	1.8	1.9	2.1	2.2	2.3	2.5	2.6	2.8	2.9	3.0	3.2	3.3	3.5	3.6	3.7	3.9	
2	1.7	1.9	2.0	2.1	2.3	2.4	2.6	2.7	2.8	3.0	3.1	3.3	3.4	3.5	3.7	3.8		
3	1.8	1.9	2.1	2.2	2.4	2.5	2.6	2.8	2.9	3.1	3.2	3.4	3.5	3.6	3.8	3.9		
4	1.9	2.0	2.2	2.3	2.5	2.6	2.7	2.9	3.0	3.2	3.3	3.4	3.6	3.7	3.9			
5	2.0	2.1	2.3	2.4	2.5	2.7	2.8	3.0	3.1	3.2	3.4	3.5	3.7	3.8	3.9			
6	2.1	2.2	2.3	2.5	2.6	2.8	2.9	3.0	3.2	3.3	3.5	3.6	3.8	3.9				
7	2.1	2.3	2.4	2.6	2.7	2.9	3.0	3.1	3.3	3.4	3.6	3.7	3.8					
8	2.2	2.4	2.5	2.7	2.8	2.9	3.1	3.2	3.4	3.5	3.6	3.8	3.9					
9	2.3	2.5	2.6	2.7	2.9	3.0	3.2	3.3	3.4	3.6	3.7	3.9						
10	2.4	2.5	2.7	2.8	3.0	3.1	3.3	3.4	3.5	3.7	3.8							
11	2.5	2.6	2.8	2.9	3.1	3.2	3.3	3.5	3.6	3.8	3.9							
12	2.6	2.7	2.9	3.0	3.1	3.3	3.4	3.6	3.7	3.8								
13	2.7	2.8	2.9	3.1	3.2	3.4	3.5	3.6	3.8	3.9								
14	2.7	2.9	3.0	3.2	3.3	3.5	3.6	3.7	3.9									
15	2.8	3.0	3.1	3.3	3.4	3.5	3.7	3.8										
16	2.9	3.0	3.2	3.3	3.5	3.6	3.8	3.9										
17	3.0	3.1	3.3	3.4	3.6	3.7	3.9											
18	3.1	3.2	3.4	3.5	3.7	3.8												
19	3.2	3.3	3.5	3.6	3.7	3.9												
20	3.3	3.4	3.5	3.7	3.8													
21	3.4	3.5	3.6	3.8	3.9													
22	3.4	3.6	3.7	3.9														
23	3.5	3.7	3.8															
24	3.6	3.7	3.9															
25	3.7	3.8																
26	3.8	3.9																
27	3.9																	

[a] Prepared by Reading Laboratory and Clinic, University of Florida.

* % of Words Not in Dale 769 Word List.

NOTE: This table eliminates the need for the arithmetic computations necessary in applying the weights in the formula. Having found the percent of words not in the Dale list, and the average sentence length, enter the table directly. The figure found at the intersection of the two facts will be the grade level of the selection.

Table for Use with Spache Formula Reading Laboratory and Clinic
University College, University of Florida

.141 x				.086 x	
	1.	.141		1.	.086
	2.	.282		2.	.172
	3.	.423		3.	.258
	4.	.564		4.	.344
	5.	.705		5.	.430
	6.	.846		6.	.516
	7.	.987		7.	.602
	8.	1.128		8.	.688
	9.	1.269		9.	.774
	10.	1.410		10.	.860
	11.	1.551		11.	.946
	12.	1.692		12.	1.032
	13.	1.833		13.	1.118
	14.	1.974		14.	1.204
	15.	2.115		15.	1.290
	16.	2.256		16.	1.376
	17.	2.397		17.	1.462
	18.	2.538		18.	1.548
	19.	2.679		19.	1.634
	20.	2.820		20.	1.720

PREDICTING READABILITY [1]

Irving Lorge

What a person understands of the material he reads depends upon his general reading ability and the readability of the text he is reading. His reading ability, moreover, depends upon his intelligence, education, environment, and interest and purpose in reading. The readability of a text depends upon the kind and number of ideas it expresses, upon the vocabulary and its style, and upon format and typography.

Reading comprehension must be viewed as the interaction between reading ability and readability. Reading ability can usually be estimated by a person's success with an adequate reading test. Readability, however, must be measured in terms of the success that large numbers of persons have in comprehending the text. In measuring the readability of texts, the material is presented to a random sample of persons whose reading ability is known. The readability of a text is assigned the average reading ability score of the sample. In assigning the average readability score as an estimate of the readability

[1] Adapted and abridged from Irving Lorge, "Predicting Readability," *Teachers College Record* (1944), 45:404–419, including revisions by Professor Lorge, dated September, 1951.

of a text, one must assume, of course, that the variations in people's interests and purposes in reading are balanced.

THE CRITERION OF READABILITY

In terms of the definition of readability the criterion must be the measure of success that a large number of readers would have with the text. Such a criterion may be obtained by judgment or by more objective methods of appraisal. The method of judgment utilizes ratings of estimated difficulty of texts. Recently Flesch,[2] using the method of judgment, assumed that the text in magazines like *The American Scholar, Foreign Affairs,* and *The Yale Review* was more difficult (less comprehensible to a random sampling of readers) than the text of magazines like *True Confessions, Modern Screen,* and *Romantic Story.* Therefore, on the assumption that magazines are written on different levels of readability, he assigned criterion level scores to groups of magazines. More objective measures of readability, however, have been used. Vogel and Washburne's [3] criterion for the readability of a book was the average paragraph meaning score on the Stanford Achievement Test of children who had read and *liked* that book. Gray and Leary [4] used the criterion of the average reading comprehension test score of a group of adults as an estimate of readability.

[2] Rudolf Flesch, "Estimating the Comprehension Difficulty of Magazine Articles," *Journal of General Psychology* (1943), 28:63–80.

[3] Mabel Vogel and Carleton Washburne, "An Objective Method of Determining Grade Placement of Children's Reading Material," *Elementary School Journal* (1928), 28:373–381.

[4] William S. Gray and Bernice E. Leary, *What Makes a Book Readable?* University of Chicago Press, Chicago, 1935.

VARIABLES USED TO PREDICT READABILITY

The variables used to predict readability are aspects of the text, e.g., vocabulary load, sentence structure and style, and interest. One or more measures of vocabulary load are used as a predictor in every study of readability. The more usual measures are the following:

a. Number of running words.
b. Percentage of different words.
c. Percentage of different infrequent, uncommon, or hard words.
d. Percentage of polysyllabic words.
e. Some weighted measure of vocabulary difficulty.
f. Vocabulary diversity (related to b).
g. Number of abstract words.
h. Number of affixed morphemes (prefixes, inflectional endings, etc.).

Most studies also predict readability on the basis of one or more measures of sentence structure or style, e.g.,

i. Percentage of prepositional phrases.
j. Percentage of indeterminate clauses.
k. Number of simple sentences.
l. Average sentence length.

Less frequently, the prediction of readability is based on some measure of human interest, e.g.,

m. Number of personal pronouns.
n. Number of words expressing human interest.
o. Percentage of colorful words.
p. Number of words representing fundamental life experiences.
q. Number of words usually learned early in life (related to b).

Essentially, the prediction of readability requires calculation by means of an empirical formula relating specific variables of readability to the criterion for readability. Vogel and Washburne developed their equation predicting the average grade level equivalent of the paragraph meaning score of these children who read and *liked* specified books from four predictors: percentage of different words, percentage of different uncommon words, number of prepositional phrases, and relative number of simple sentences.[5]

Gray and Leary, after relating more than forty different predictors to their criterion, empirically chose five variables to predict readability: the number of different words, the percentage of uncommon words, the relative number of personal pronouns, the relative number of prepositional phrases, and the average sentence length.[6] Gray and Leary's predicted readability score was a number which was transmitted into a letter representing areas of difficulty of readability from A (very easy) to E (very difficult). Lorge, basing his work on that of Gray and Leary, tried to obtain a prediction in terms of grade level of reading. The sample of materials chosen for analysis was the 376 passages in the four books of McCall and Crabbs' *Standard Test Lessons in Reading*.[7] The criterion was the grade level score equivalent for a group of readers who would get half of the test questions right on each passage. The predictors studied by Lorge were the five used by Gray and Leary, a weighted score for vocabulary based on

Thorndike's 20,000-word list,[8] and four elements used by Morriss and Holversen[9] (percentage of elemental words, percentage of simple localisms, percentage of concrete word-labels, and percentage of abstract word-labels). Later, Flesch's two factors (affixed morphemes and human interest) were also used.[10]

The sample three-factor prediction equation of Lorge's was modified by the addition of a constant to give an estimate of the grade level score equivalent to passing three-quarters of the questions in a given passage. The formula is given on the work sheet (see pp. 193–194) for computing the readability index. A reasonably good prediction of readability can be obtained by using a weighted composite of vocabulary and sentence structure. Of these, the most important is some measure of vocabulary load. It should be recognized, however, that such elements as the number of abstract words, the number of uncommon words,

[5] The multiple correlation between the criterion and the weighted composite of the predictors was .845. Subsequently, Washburne and Vogel reported a multiple correlation of .869 on the basis of certain modifications.

[6] The multiple correlation between the five predictors and the criterion used by Gray and Leary was .644.

[7] William A. McCall and Lelah M. Crabbs, *Standard Test Lessons in Reading*, Books II, III, IV, V, Bureau of Publications, Teachers College, Columbia University, New York, 1926.

[8] Edward L. Thorndike, *A Teacher's Word Book of the Twenty Thousand Words*, Bureau of Publications, Teachers College, Columbia University, New York, rev. ed., 1932.

[9] Elizabeth C. Morriss and Dorothy Holversen, "Idea Analysis Technique," unpublished manuscript, Teachers College, Columbia University, New York, 1938.

[10] The multiple correlations were obtained predicting the criterion from various combinations of these factors. Empirically, the best prediction using the fewest factors was obtained with three factors (also used by Gray and Leary): the average sentence length, the relative number of prepositional phrases, and the relative number of different words not common to Dale's list of 769 words. The multiple correlation coefficient between the average grade score on the Thorndike-McCall Reading Test and the three predictors was .77. Adding as predictors the weighted index for word frequency and/or the number of personal pronouns, and/or the four factors of Morriss and Holversen, separately or in combination, and/or the two factors of Flesch, separately or in combination, did not increase the multiple correlation significantly.

the number of polysyllabic words, and the weighted index of difficulty of vocabulary are all intercorrelated. Any one of them could be used in place of any other, provided suitable adjustment were made in the empirical formula. Certainly some aspect of vocabulary load must be used as a predictor.

Structural elements of the passage provide the second most important basis for estimating the readability of the text. As in measures of vocabulary, most measures of sentence structure are interrelated, so that little additional information is yielded by several measures of sentence structure.

Lorge's formula, as described in the following section, uses as predictors the factors of uncommon words (vocabulary) and the factors of average sentence length, and the relative number of prepositional phrases (sentence structure).

FORMULA FOR JUDGING READABILITY

The Lorge formula, therefore, is a means of judging the relative difficulty or readability of either read or spoken passages. Readability is based upon the comprehension of passages by school children. Comprehension is judged by the correctness and completeness of responses to questions about a passage. Such questions usually deal with specific details, general import, appreciation, knowledge of vocabulary, and understanding of concepts.

It is obvious that the purpose of the reader in reading and the kinds of questions asked in estimating reading comprehension will influence greatly the estimate of reading difficulty. Since the Lorge formula is based on a criterion derived from responses to questions of the five types listed above, it tends to overestimate the difficulty of passages to be read primarily for appreciation or for general import and to underestimate the difficulty of passages to be read primarily for specific details or for following directions. Nevertheless, the formula provides an overall estimate which should be useful in grading reading materials. As an estimate, it should not be considered definitive or used blindly. The readability index is an estimate, not a rigorous determination.

As developed in the work sheet, the readability index is an estimate of the reading grade at which the average school child will be able to answer with adequate completeness and correctness about 55 percent of the questions concerning detail, appreciation, import, vocabulary, and concept. The reading grade so obtained may be thought of in terms of reading-grade scores on a test of reading comprehension. A readability index of 5.2 for a passage may be considered indicative of the material of the fifth grade; it may be thought of in terms of placement of the material as within the reading comprehension of average fifth-grade children. Such placement, however, should consider the interest of pupils, the suitability of subject matter, and other factors.

THE READABILITY INDEX

The Lorge formula, in addition to its use for estimating the reading difficulty of passages for children, may be used to advantage in estimating the difficulty of reading oral passages for adults. The formula yields a readability index which places materials in relative order. A reading passage with an index of 5.2 can be considered less difficult than a reading passage with an index of 7.1, etc. Moreover, the suitability of texts for adults can be interpreted in terms of the reading-grade scores of adults on acceptable reading tests.

Teachers of adults, or, indeed, any person choosing texts for specific audiences, might give a reading test to a sample of adults to determine the average reading-grade score (as well as the range of such scores). They then could choose texts within the demonstrated range of comprehension of such adults.

In actual practice, the formula has proved to be very serviceable in the simplification of texts for adult use. The grade placement of the text may be compared with the average highest grade reached by adults for whom it is designed. The median highest grade reached for adults twenty years old and over is reported by the Bureau of the Census for the year 1940. For the adult population "20 years old and over" the median highest grade (number of years of school completed) was 8.8. In writing for such an average population, it may safely be assumed that the reading ability as measured by grade score on a reading test will be somewhat lower—let us say, about eight-tenths of a year. Hence, in writing for a population with an assumed grade level score or a reading-test score of 8.0, steps should be taken to select vocabulary, simplify sentence structure, and reduce the number of prepositional phrases. *The Teacher's Word Book of 30,000 Words* by Thorndike and Lorge should be of considerable help, since it gives separate evaluation for vocabularies found in adult magazines, e.g., *Saturday Evening Post, Ladies' Home Journal, Woman's Home Companion, True Story,* and *Reader's Digest.*[11]

COMPUTING THE LORGE READABILITY INDEX

The following are directions for computing the readability index.

[11] Edward L. Thorndike and Irving Lorge, *The Teacher's Word Book of 30,000 Words,* Bureau of Publications, Teachers College, Columbia University, New York, 1943.

A. Selecting the sample.
  1. Short passages of 300 words or less. When a short passage is to be appraised, it is advisable to analyze the entire passage.
  2. Longer passages. When longer passages are to be appraised, it is advisable to analyze samples of the material. Select a sample near the beginning, another sample near the middle, and another sample near the end of the passage. Each of these samples should be approximately 100 words in length. Of course, if the passage is less than 300 words in length, the entire passage should be analyzed.

  A good procedure might be to number the lines of the text serially and then count the number of words per line (about ten lines) to get an estimate of the number of words. For instance, a passage has 141 lines; ten lines chosen at random have 12, 12, 13, 13, 13, 11, 12, 12, 16, and 16 words, or an average of 13 words to the line. The passage thus has approximately 1833 words. A sample of 100 words would then be approximately eight lines in length. The three samples could be chosen in a variety of ways: e.g., beginning at or near line 3 through line 11; at or near line 53 through line 61; and at or near line 103 through line 111. In this way, a sample is chosen in each third of the passage. It should be noted, moreover, that each sample should start with the beginning of a sentence and should stop at the end of a sentence. When the samples have been located with beginning and end points, the remainder of the analysis can be made.
  3. Books. When books are to be appraised, it would be advisable to analyze samples of the book, say, from 5 percent to 10 percent of the book (but never less than five

samples). These samples should be chosen throughout the book. For instance, a book has 92 pages of text with an average of 195 words per page. This indicates an approximate wordage of 18,000 words. A 5 percent sample would be 900 words; a 10 percent sample would be 1800 words. For the 5 percent sample this would require approximately five pages; for the 10 percent sample, approximately nine pages. Thus, every eighteenth page should be chosen for the 5 percent sample; every tenth page, for the 10 percent sample. Thus, the sample might be pages 3, 21, 39, 57, 75 in the one instance; or 4, 14, 24, 34, 44, 54, 64, 74, 84 in the other. Of course, a sample must start with the beginning of a sentence and stop at the end of a sentence.

B. Labeling the work sheet.
1. Fill out the information about title, author, edition, publisher, and date of publication (latest copyright year listed).
2. Carefully identify the location of the sample, thus: "p. 14, line 2, The answer . . . to p. 14, line 26, ever after."

C. Counting the number of words.
1. Begin with the beginning of the sample and count (or number serially) each word in the sample. Observe the following rules:
   a. Hyphenated words are counted as one word. When in doubt about uncommon hyphenations, follow Webster's unabridged dictionary (2nd edition): if listed in dictionary as hyphenated, count as one word; if not listed, count as two words.
   b. Words separated at the end of a line to the beginning of the next line are counted as one word.
   c. Numbers are counted as words; e.g., in "January 3,

1940," 3 is counted as one word and interpreted as the word *three*, and *1940* is counted as one word and interpreted as *nineteen-forty*.
   d. Compound words like place names or persons' names are counted as one word, e.g., *New York, United States, Van Loon, Santa Claus, St. Nicholas.*
   e. Contractions are counted as one word; e.g., *don't, he's, they'll, they'd,* etc., are each counted as one word.
2. Record the count under Basic Data, 1.

D. Counting the number of sentences.
1. Begin at the beginning of the sample and count the number of complete sentences.
2. Record the count under Basic Data, 2.

E. Counting prepositional phrases.
1. Count each prepositional phrase in the sample. Observe the following rules:
   f. A phrase is made up of a preposition and a noun, or a preposition and a pronoun, or a preposition and a gerund, e.g., *to the house* (noun), *for him* (pronoun), *in skating* (gerund).
   g. Some common prepositions are:

about	during
above	except
across	for
after	from
along	in
among	inside
at	into
before	of
behind	off
below	on
beneath	onto
beside	outside
between	till
beyond	to
by	under

until   with
up   within
upon   without

h. Less common prepositions are: despite (the opinion), concerning (the idea), notwithstanding (the opposition).

i. Infinitive phrases are not to be counted. An infinitive phrase is made up of the word *to* and a verb, e.g., *to swim, to sing, to answer.*

j. If a preposition word is followed by a clause, it is a conjunction and hence is *not* counted, e.g., "*After* the storm had passed" is *not* counted.

2. Record the count under Basic Data, 3.

F. Counting hard words.

1. Use the Dale list of 769 easy words [12] to cross out in the sample every word on the Dale list, regardless of its meaning. The Dale list of easy words is made up of words which are common to Thorndike's first thousand most frequent English words and the first thousand most frequent words known by children entering the first grade.

2. Since the count is the number of different hard words, each hard word is counted only once. For instance, if in the passage *reliability* occurred three times, it still would be counted only once. Observe the following rules:

k. Nouns. Separate counts are not made of plurals and possessives in *s*, plurals in *es*, or plurals in which *y* is replaced by *ies*: e.g., *boys, churches, berries* are counted with *boy, church, berry*; however, *knife* and *knives, goose* and *geese, man* and *men*, etc., are all counted as different words.

[12] Edgar Dale, "A Comparison of Two Word Lists," *Educational Research Bulletin* (1941), 10:484–489.

l. Special cases. An *s* added to a word in the text not forming a plural or possessive forms a different word from the root form: e.g., *Robert* and *Roberts* are two different words. Proper nouns which seem to be composed of root and derived forms are not tabulated with the root form: e.g., *Wheeling*, the proper name, is not counted with *wheel*. *Browning*, the proper name, is not counted with *brown*. Nouns formed by adding *r* or *er* to the other nouns or to verbs are not counted with the original word: e.g., *own* and *owner* are two different words.

m. Adverbs. Separate counts are not made of adverbs formed by adding *ly*: e.g., *badly, sadly* are counted with *bad, sad*. Adverbs from an adjective in *e*, as *gently* from *gentle, truly* from *true*, are counted as different words.

n. Adjectives. Separate counts are not made of adjectives formed by adding *n* to proper nouns: e.g., *Austrian, Bavarian* are counted with *Austria, Bavaria*.

o. Special cases. An adjective formed by adding *ly* to a noun is counted as a different word from the noun: e.g., *home* and *homely* are two different words.

p. Comparatives and superlatives of adjectives and adverbs. Special counts are not made of comparatives and superlatives formed by adding *er* or *r* and *est* or *st*, or by changing *y* to *ier* or *iest*: e.g., *longer, prettier, bravest* are counted with *long, pretty, brave*.

q. Special case. The rule applies to adjectives doubling the final consonant and adding *er* and *est*: e.g., *red, redder, reddest* are counted as one word.

r. Verbs. Special counts are not made of verb forms ending in *ing* and in *s, d, ed,* or of forms changing *y* to *ies* and *ied*, or of past participles formed by adding *n*: e.g., *plays, playing, played* are counted with *play*.

s. Special cases. Verb forms which drop the final *e* and add *ing* are counted with the root form: e.g., *pace* and *pacing* are counted as one word. Verb forms which double the final consonant and add *ing* or *ed* are counted as one word: e.g., *drip, dripped,* and *dripping* are counted as one word. Past participles formed by adding *en* to a verb are counted as different from the verb: e.g., *eat* and *eaten* are two different words.

t. Hyphenated words. In case of uncommon hyphenated words, follow Webster's unabridged dictionary (2nd edition). Any hyphenated word is considered one word if it is listed in the dictionary; otherwise it is counted as two words.

u. Compound names. Compound names of persons or places like *New York, United States, St. Louis, Santa Claus,* and *Van Dyke,* count as one word.

v. Contractions. Count contractions as different words from those from which they are derived: e.g., *because* and *'cause* are two different words. *He's* is not counted with *he* or with *is*.

w. Words which may be both common and proper. In the case of words which may be both common and proper

nouns, count the proper noun as being the same word as the common: e.g., *Jack* and *jack* are the same word.

x. Miscellaneous special cases. Words formed by adding *y* to a word in the list are counted as different from the root word: e.g., *snow* and *snowy* are different words. *German* and *Germany* are different words. Words of different spelling listed in the dictionary as one word are counted as the same word: e.g., *honor* and *honour* are the same word; *Frankfort* and *Frankfurt* are the same word. If a word is formed by adding two or more suffixes to a listed word, one of which when added to the listed word is counted with it, that word is different from the root word: e.g., *happen* and *happening* are the same word but *happenings* is a different word. *Excite* and *excited* are the same word but *excitedly* is a different word. Words formed by adding *en* are counted as different from the original word: e.g., *wool* and *woolen* are two different words; *bit* and *bitten* are two different words; *gold* and *golden* are two different words.

3. Record the count under Basic Data, 4.

G. Proceed to computation. Watch decimal points carefully. Check all computations.

H. Record the index at the upper portion of the page as R.I.

I. Make sure that analyst, computer, and checker have signed the record blank and dated their entries.

J. If a book or a long passage has had several samples selected from it, the average of the R.I.'s is the rating for the passage or the book.

PASSAGE ILLUSTRATING THE ESTIMATION OF THE READABILITY INDEX

Lincoln's Gettysburg Address

Four score and seven years ago our fathers brought forth upon this continent a new nation, conceived in Liberty, and dedicated to the proposition that all men are created equal. Now we are engaged in a great civil war, testing whether that nation, or any nation so conceived and so dedicated, can long endure. We are met on a great battlefield of that war. We have come to dedicate a portion of that field, as a final resting place for those who here gave their lives, that that nation might live. It is altogether fitting and proper that we should do this. But, in a larger sense, we cannot dedicate—we cannot conse-crate—we cannot hallow—this ground. The brave men, living and dead, who struggled here, have consecrated it far above our poor power to add or detract. The world will little note, nor long remember, what we say here, but it can never forget what they did here. It is for us, the living, rather, to be dedicated here to the unfinished work which they who fought here have thus far so nobly advanced. It is rather for us to be here dedicated to the great task remaining before us—that from these honored dead we take increased devotion to that cause for which they gave the last full measure of devotion—that we here highly resolve that these dead shall not have died in vain—that this nation, under God, shall have a new birth of freedom—and that government of the people, by the people, for the people, shall not perish from the earth.

Readability Index for First Revision of Gettysburg Address
Illustrations of Listing of Hard Words

A	altogether add advanced	3
B	battlefield birth	2
C	continent conceived/ created civil cannot// consecrate(d)/	6
D	dedicate(d)///// detract devotion/	3
E	equal engaged endure	3
F	forth final fought freedom	4
G	government	1
H	hallow honored	2
I	increased	1
J		
K		
L	Liberty	1
M		
N	nation//// nobly	2
O		
P	proposition portion proper power perish	5
Q		
R	remaining resolve	2
S	score sense struggled	3
T	testing thus task	3
U	unfinished	1
V	vain	1
WXYZ		

Basic Data

1. The number of words in the sample   269

....

2. The number of sentences in the sample   10

....

3. The number of prepositional phrases in the sample   26

....

4. The number of hard words in the sample   43

....

Computation

Item 6, average sentence length: Divide 1 by 2 = 26.9000 ×   .06 = 1.6140

....

Item 8, ratio of prepositional phrases: Divide 3 by 1 =   .0967 × 9.55 = .9235

....

Item 2, ratio of hard words: Divide 4 by 1 =   .1599 × 10.43 = 1.6678

....

Constant = 1.9892

....

Add 6, 8, 2, and C

Readability Index = 6.1945

....

R.I. =

Revised
Lorge Formula for Estimating Grade Placement of Reading Materials

Work Sheet

Title of book or article: ....   Edition: ....

Name of author: ....

Magazine: ....   Volume and No.: ....

Publisher: .... Date of publication: ....

Location of sample in text: ....

Basic Data

1. The number of words in the sample   ....
2. The number of sentences in the sample   ....
3. The number of prepositional phrases in the sample   ....
4. The number of hard words in the sample   ....

Computation

Item 6, average sentence length: Divide 1 by 2 =   .   ×   .06 =   .

Item 8, ratio of prepositional phrases: Divide 3 by 1 =   .   ×   9.55 =   .

Item 2, ratio of hard words: Divide 4 by 1 =   .   × 10.43 =   .

Constant = 1.9892

Add 6, 8, 2, and C

Readability Index =   .

Notes:

Name of analyst: _____   Date of analysis: _____
Name of computer: _____   Date of computing: _____
Name of checker: _____

A FORMULA FOR PREDICTING READABILITY [1]
Edgar Dale and Jeanne S. Chall

The war period made us realize more than ever the importance of reaching large audiences. More people had to fill out tax forms; more people had to be appealed to to buy war bonds; more people had to coöperate in numerous activities to help win the war. Because a larger audience had to be reached, the writers had to use a style that could be understood by more persons than the usual book readers. They could no longer afford to hit or miss with printed materials.

Along with the growing need for more scientific means of verbal communication there was a growing fund of prac-

[1] Adapted and abridged from Edgar Dale and Jeanne S. Chall, "A Formula for Predicting Readability," *Educational Research Bulletin* (Jan. 21, 1948), 27:11–20, 28; (Feb. 18, 1948), 27:37–54.

tical objective measurement of readability. The Lorge formula was one of the first easy-to-apply readability formulas.[2] By the use of this formula we could predict in a fairly short time how difficult it was to read and understand a piece of material. It was no longer necessary to guess. By counting the relative number of different uncommon words, the average sentence length, and the relative number of prepositional phrases, we could get a good index of readability in terms of grade scores.

In 1943 Rudolf Flesch produced his readability formula.[3] He presented a convincing argument for the superiority of his formula over previous ones, especially for use with materials for adult readers. With numerous correlation tables he showed that the Lorge formula, in its use of the Dale List of 769 Easy Words as a measure of vocabulary difficulty, failed to discriminate satisfactorily between materials that were above the eighth-grade level in difficulty. Since the average adult has approximately eighth- or ninth-grade reading ability, he thought that another technique was needed to predict the readability of materials for adult readers. In his formula, Mr. Flesch used three factors: average sentence length, relative number of affixed morphemes (prefixes, suffixes, inflectional endings), and relative number of personal references.

On the whole we found the formula adequate. However, we also found some shortcomings. The most serious shortcoming was the count of affixes, which

we found to be rather arbitrary, in the sense that two people making a count on the same sample would usually come out with a different number of affixes. If we were all extremely careful and consulted a dictionary to be certain that all affixes were included and that no non-affixes were included, we found that the work was too time-consuming.

Mr. Flesch's reasons for using affixes as a count of difficulty are very well stated, with statistical evidence, in both his books.[4] His logic was that word recognition, although an important factor in reading for beginning or poor readers, is of practically no importance for mature readers. For the better readers, it is the relationship between the words and the abstractness of the words that contribute to difficulty. He actually computed the affixes (as a measure of verbal relationship) and the abstract words contained in five levels of magazines and found that both of these factors were a good measure of difficulty. He dropped the count of abstract words in his formula because the magazine experiment "had shown that the count of affixes was a practically equivalent measure of abstractness ($r = .7849$), and the latter method was far less cumbersome."[5] In fact, in another section of his book, he refers to the count of affixes as a "simple short cut to the count of abstractions."[6]

If Mr. Flesch used a correlation of .7849 to justify his calling the affixes a "simple short cut to the count of abstractions," could we not also call the Dale List of 769 Easy Words a short cut to the count of abstractions, since Mr. Lorge found a high correlation between affixed morphemes and words outside this list? Or could we not argue

[2] Irving Lorge, "Predicting Reading Difficulty of Selections for Children," *Elementary English Review* (1939), 16:229–233, and "Predicting Readability," *Teachers College Record* (1944), 45:404–419.

[3] Rudolf Flesch, *Marks of Readable Style*, Contributions to Education, No. 807, Teachers College, Columbia University, New York, 1943.

[4] *Ibid.*, and *The Art of Plain Talk*, Harper & Brothers, New York, 1946.

[5] Flesch, *Marks of Readable Style*, p. 32.

[6] *Ibid.*, p. 24.

that Mr. Flesch's count of affixes is just another way of counting hard words?

In his article "Predicting Readability," Mr. Lorge makes the following statement about measuring vocabulary load:

It should be recognized that such elements as the number of abstract words, the number of uncommon words, the number of polysyllabic words, and the weighted index of difficulty of vocabulary are all intercorrelated. Any one of them could be used in place of any other, provided suitable adjustment were made in the empirical formula.[7]

If all counts of vocabulary load, whether abstract words, affixed morphemes, or number of uncommon words, are interrelated, why use a less exact and more cumbersome method when a simpler one can be used?

From the evidence given, we believed that there was value in using a word list to measure vocabulary load. Mr. Flesch's main objection to the use of the Dale list of 769 words was that it did not differentiate between the higher levels of difficulty. What would happen if a larger word list were used? Such a list would not be a discriminating instrument at the easy levels of writing since it would not contain words not known to some of the readers. But by using a list which included most of the words well known to fourth-grade readers, a more discriminating instrument would be devised for the upper levels of reading ability.

The second shortcoming of the Flesch formula was the count of personal references. In our numerous analyses we found that the personal-reference count was not a reliable index of difficulty. For example, when we speak of *John* and *Mary* and *he* and *she*, referring to

[7] Lorge, "Predicting Readability," *Teachers College Record* (1944), 45:406.

John and Mary, there is a justification for subtracting from difficulty. This is because in writing about John and Mary we usually say things that are not abstract or general. However, subtracting from difficulty for personal references such as *R. J. Thomas* of the automobile industry, or *Senator Austin*, when we are writing about atomic energy or the United Nations, does seem to us a bit inaccurate. If the reader does not know these persons, the difficulty of the written material is not decreased. In fact, these individuals are no longer personal; they are abstractions. Flooding printed materials with personal references to these "abstract" persons will add little to "human interest" and ease of comprehension.

In view of the shortcomings of the Flesch counts of affixes and personal references, we undertook to find a more efficient means of predicting readability. Our hypotheses were these:

First, a larger word list would predict as well as, if not better than, the count of affixes. It would avoid the pitfalls of lack of discrimination at the upper levels of difficulty.

Second, a count of personal references does not add very much to the prediction of readability.

Third, a shorter, more efficient formula could be evolved with the use of a word factor and a factor of sentence structure.

For our sample passages, we used the McCall-Crabbs *Standard Test Lessons in Reading*,[8] the same passages used by Mr. Lorge and Mr. Flesch. These are a series of 376 passages of children's readings, already graded in difficulty on the basis of comprehensibility of questions at the end of each passage. This mate-

[8] W. A. McCall and Lelah Crabbs, *Standard Test Lessons in Reading*, Bureau of Publications, Teachers College, Columbia University, New York, 1926.

rial, it should be noted, has serious deficiencies as a criterion, but it is the best we have at the present time. The writers, however, checked their findings against other passages as noted later. Following these authors, our criterion was the grade-level score equivalent for a group of readers who would get half of the test questions right on each passage. Mr. Lorge made his data sheets available to us.[9] These data sheets also included the Flesch counts of affixed morphemes and personal references.

Our word count was based on the Dale list of approximately three thousand words. This list was constructed several years ago by testing fourth-graders on their knowledge in reading of a list of approximately ten thousand words. This larger list included the most common words in the Thorndike,[10] Buckingham and Dolch,[11] and other word lists. Words such as *milkman, carrot, candlestick, catbird,* and so on, which appeared in the high thousands on the Thorndike list, were also tested with fourth-graders to see whether they knew them. An attempt was made to include all words that fourth-graders would possibly know. A word was considered known when at least 80 percent of the fourth-graders checked it as known.

This list differs from the Thorndike lists in that it is a measure of familiarity in reading rather than a measure of frequency of appearance in printed materials. Words such as *bracelet, water-*

melon, and *cabbage,* appearing in the high thousands in the Thorndike lists, are included in the Dale 3000 list. In that respect it is less artificial than the Thorndike lists. No claim is made that all the words actually known in reading by at least 80 percent of fourth-graders are on this list. Some may have been left out. The testing method used is crude. But it does present a fairly complete list of familiar and simple words.

We went through the 376 passages in Books II to V of the McCall-Crabbs test lessons. In each passage, we counted the relative number of words not on the Dale list of 3000 words.

We punched this information on Hollerith cards, along with the information made available by Mr. Lorge. The intercorrelations appear in Table 1.[12]

From Table 1 the reader can see that the highest correlation with the criterion is the relative number of words outside the Dale list of 3000 words. The correlation is .6833. The two next highest factors are the Lorge hard-word count (based on the Dale list of 769 words) and the Flesch affixed-morphemes count. The intercorrelations among these three factors are high; between the Dale score and the Flesch morphemes, .7932; between the Flesch morphemes and the Lorge hard-word count, .7441; and between the Dale score and the Lorge hard-word count, .7988. This table corroborates Mr. Lorge's findings that a measure of vocabulary load is the most important factor in reading difficulty, and that all the measures of vocabulary are highly intercorrelated.

The next highest measure of difficulty is average sentence length—which correlates .4681 with the criterion.

After making several combinations of factors, we found that the following two,

[9] The authors wish to thank Mr. Lorge for making the data sheets available and for permission to publish the intercorrelations of his factors.

[10] Edward L. Thorndike, *A Teacher's Word Book of Twenty Thousand Words,* Teachers College, Columbia University, New York, 1931.

[11] B. R. Buckingham and E. W. Dolch, *A Combined Word List,* Ginn & Co., Boston, 1936.

[12] We wish to thank Mr. Flesch for permission to use his factors and to publish the intercorrelations of his factors.

Table 1.   Intercorrelations Between Four Style Elements and Grade Score of a
Pupil Who Answered One-Half the Questions on McCall and Crabbs

	Dale Score (3000 List)	Flesch Affixed Morphemes	Flesch Personal References	Lorge Hard Words (Dale— 769)	Criterion C_{50}	Mean	Standard Deviation
(1)	(2)	(3)	(4)	(5)	(6)	(7)	(8)
Average sentence length	.5108	.4428	—.2201	.4913	.4681 [a]	16.8037	5.3813
Dale score (words outside 3000 list)		.7932	—.4033	.7988	.6833	8.1011	6.3056
Flesch affixed morphemes [b]			—.3254	.7441	.6017	25.2819	11.0668
Flesch personal references [b]				—.3422	—.3675	7.8245	5.5439
Lorge hard words (outside Dale 769 list)					.6148	17.4165	7.1659
Criterion C_{50}						5.7492	1.6565

[a] The correlation coefficient reported here between the average sentence length and the criterion is much lower than the one reported by Mr. Lorge and later by Mr. Flesch. They reported a correlation coefficient of .6174. We checked with Mr. Lorge. He went over his data and found that an error had been made in the computation.

[b] The intercorrelations of the two Flesch factors here reported are slightly different from those presented by Flesch in *Marks of Readable Style*. These differences are not significant and were probably caused by our using gross scores on Hollerith cards while Flesch used grouped data for his correlations.

plus a constant, gave the most efficient empirical formula:

$$X_{C_{50}} = .1579X_1 + .0496X_2 + 3.6365$$

When $X_{C_{50}}$ = reading-grade score of a pupil who could answer one-half the test questions correctly

X_1 = Dale score (relative number of words outside Dale list of 3000 words)

X_2 = average sentence length
3.6365 = constant

The multiple-correlation coefficient of these two factors with the criterion is .70. Adding the factor of human interests (personal reference) of Mr. Flesch raises the multiple-correlation coefficient to .7025, an insignificant increase.

Because of the correction in the sentence-length factor, we recomputed the multiple-correlation coefficients on the Lorge and Flesch formulas. The corrected Lorge formula also has a multiple correlation of .66. The corrected Flesch formula also has a multiple correlation of .66. We see that the one factor, words outside the Dale list of 3000 words, alone, has a greater prediction than the three-factor Flesch and Lorge formulas.

Does this new two-factor formula work in predicting the difficulty of reading materials other than the McCall-Crabbs reading passages? We conducted several experiments comparing the formula predictions with the judgments of experienced teachers, the judgments of readability "experts," and the actual comprehension scores of readers on passages.

On fifty-five passages of health education materials, we found that our two-factor formula predictions correlated .92 with the judgments of readability experts, and .90 with the reading grades of children and adults who were able to answer at least three questions out of four on thirty of these passages. They ranged from the extremely easy to the very difficult.

On seventy-eight passages on foreign affairs from current-events magazines, government pamphlets, and newspapers, the correlation between the predictions of the formula and judgments of difficulty by expert teachers in the social studies was .90.

As a result of these various experiments, we set up the following table of estimated grade levels:

Formula Score	Corrected Grade Levels
4.9 and below	Grade 4 and below
5.0 to 5.9	Grades 5–6
6.0 to 6.9	Grades 7–8
7.0 to 7.9	Grades 9–10
8.0 to 8.9	Grades 11–12
9.0 to 9.9	Grades 13–15 (college)
10.0 and above	Grade 16– (college graduate)

The formula devised by the writers is a simple, two-factor formula that is easy to apply. With the use of a factor of vocabulary load (relative number of words outside the Dale list of 3000 words) and a factor of sentence structure (average sentence length), we have a good prediction of readability. The additional validation on health and social studies materials shows that it compares favorably with judgments of experts and with actual reader comprehension.

The corrected grade levels help interpret the scores obtained by the formula and give a more usable means of placing materials within the comprehension of the various grades. For example, a given piece of material having a formula score of 5.2 (corrected grade level of Grades 5–6) should be within the comprehension of children who have fifth- to sixth-grade reading abilities. By this we mean that these children will be able to answer approximately one-half to three-fourths of the questions asked on the material, concerning specific details, general import, appreciation, knowledge of vocabulary, and so on.

For adults, the corrected grade levels may be interpreted to mean the number of years of schooling required to read the material with ease and understanding. For example, if an article or book has a formula score of 6.3 (corrected grade level of Grades 7–8), it should be within the comprehension of the average adult who has had about eight and one-half years of schooling.

We do not claim that the formula developed here is definitive. The nature of the multiple-correlation coefficient makes this point rather obvious. We do believe, however, that it is a short cut in judging the difficulty of written materials.

The formula can also be used as an aid to text simplification. When a text has an undesirably high score according to the prediction of the formula, it may be simplified by substituting more concrete, familiar words for the unfamiliar and abstract words. Perhaps sentences can be shortened and made clearer. Writing should not be any harder to read and understand than it needs to be. Some writing, however, is hard to understand because the ideas are hard and complicated. It may be impossible to simplify this type of writing. On the other hand, a good deal of writing is hard because the words used are unnecessarily abstract and the sentence and paragraph structure needlessly complex.

But we must be cautious about "writing for a readability formula." We must remember at all times that a formula is a statistical device. It means that, on the whole, longer sentences make comprehension more difficult. This does not mean that all long sentences are hard to read and understand. There are some very short sentences that may be harder to comprehend than longer ones. The same holds true for the use of familiar words. On the whole, the more unfamiliar the words used, the harder the material will be to understand. But sometimes familiar words are used in a symbolic or metaphoric sense. "To be or not to be" is not an easy idea although the sentence is short and the separate words used would usually be called simple and familiar ones. Readability formulas are not sensitive to such subtle variations in meaning.

Furthermore, the nature of the difficulty of a given piece of writing depends to a great extent upon what we expect a reader to get out of the material. If we ask difficult questions on a passage, even if the passage is fairly simple, the reader may not be able to answer the questions asked and therefore will not understand it by our set criterion.

The reader's purpose in reading and his interest and background in the subject matter must also be considered by anyone using a readability formula. To say that a given article on chemistry is comfortable reading for average adults because it has a predicted grade level of 7–8 is giving an incomplete picture. For those readers who have no interest or no background in chemistry, the article will probably not be comfortable reading and they may get very little meaning from it. For other readers who are interested in chemistry and do considerable

reading in the subject, the same article will probably be most comfortable reading. This difference in ease of reading and comprehension may exist even though both groups of readers have completed approximately eight and one-half years of schooling and have the same general reading ability on a standardized reading test.

Taking account of differences in background is especially important in writing and selecting materials for persons who have a specialized understanding of a field. Thus, in material written for farmers, the inclusion of such words as *barley, flax, hybrid, husk, fertilizer, mulch* will increase the predicted grade level of the material. But if these words are in the common vocabulary of the farmer, they may not offer any special difficulty in comprehension. This factor, therefore, must be taken into account in dealing with materials having a specialized vocabulary. Thus the direction "Hand me that Stillson" is perfectly clear to any mechanic but not very meaningful to the layman.

Keeping these cautions in mind, we have found that this formula can be a useful tool in selecting and preparing reading materials that can be understood by specified audiences.

The formula is based on two counts —average sentence length and percentage of unfamiliar words (words outside the Dale list of 3000 words). Rules for selecting samples of a text to be analyzed and for computing the average sentence length and percentage of unfamiliar words are presented in this section. As each count is made, it is recorded on a work sheet where detailed steps are given for arriving at the grade level of reading difficulty.

A Work Sheet Filled in for the Samples Taken from the Pamphlet "Your Baby"

Article: Your Baby

Author:

Publisher: Nat'l TB Assoc.   Date: 1945

	Page No. 2	Page No. 7	Page No. 12
	From "A happy . . ."	From "Diphtheria . . ."	From "The germs . . ."
	To . . . prevented."	To . . . often given."	To . . . or boiled."
1. Number of words in the sample	132	131	111
2. Number of sentences in the sample	7	9	6
3. Number of words not on Dale list	6	20	17
4. Average sentence length (divide 1 by 2)	19	15	19
5. Dale score (divide 3 by 1, multiply by 100)	5	15	15
6. Multiply average sentence length (4) by .0496	.9424	.7440	.9424
7. Multiply Dale score (5) by .1579	.7895	2.3685	2.3685
8. Constant	3.6365	3.6365	3.6365
9. Formula raw score (add 6, 7, 8)	5.3684	6.7490	6.9474

Analyzed by J. S. C.   Date 1/28/48

Checked by C. D. C.   Date 1/28/48

Average raw score of 3 samples   6.35

Average corrected grade level   7–8

The directions to guide the various steps in filling out the work sheet follow.

I. Selecting samples.

Take approximately 100 words about every tenth page for books.[13] For articles, select about four 100-word samples per 2000 words. Space these samples evenly. For passages of about 200 to 300 words analyze the entire passage. Never begin or end a sample in the middle of the sentence.

II. Labeling work sheet.

Enter such information as title, author, publisher, date of publication, etc., regarding the sample to be appraised.

III. Counting the number of words:

A. Count the total number of words in the sample.

B. Count hyphenated words and contractions as one word.

C. Count numbers as words: *10* is one word; *1947* is one word.

D. Count compound names of persons and places as one word; *St. John*, *Van Buren*, and so on, are each counted as one word.

E. Do not count initials which are part of a name as separate words; *John F. W. St. John* is counted as two words—*John* and *F. W. St. John*.

F. Record the number of words under 1 of the work sheet.

IV. Counting the number of sentences.

A. Count the number of complete sentences in the sample.

B. Record this under 2 of the work sheet.

V. Counting the number of unfamiliar words.

Words which do not appear on the Dale list [14] are considered unfamil-

---

[13] When a more exact grading of books is desired, 200-word samples every tenth page will probably give a more reliable measure. See Bertha V. Leifeste, "An Investigation of the Reliability of the Sampling of Reading Material," *Journal of Educational Research* (1944), 37:441–450.

[14] See the Dale list on pp. 206–212.

iar. Underline all unfamiliar words, even if they appear more than once. In making this count, special rules are necessary for common and proper nouns, verbs, and other parts of speech. These are given in the section which follows.

A. Common nouns:

1. Consider familiar all regular plurals and possessives of words on the list; *boy's* is familiar because *boy* is on the list (possessive); *girls* is familiar because *girl* is on the list (plural by adding s); *churches* is familiar because *church* is on the list (plural by adding es); *armies* is familiar because *army* is on the list (plural by changing y to *ies*).

2. Count irregular plurals as unfamiliar, even if the singular form appears on the list; *oxen* is unfamiliar, although *ox* is on the list. Several irregular plurals, however, are listed in the word list. When the plural appears as a separate word or is indicated by the ending in parentheses next to the word, it is considered familiar; *goose* and *geese* appear on the list and both are considered familiar.

3. Count as unfamiliar a noun that is formed by adding *er* or *r* to a noun or verb appearing on the word list (unless this *er* or *r* form is indicated on the list); *burner* is counted as unfamiliar, although *burn* is on the list. *Owner* is considered familiar because it appears on the list as follows: own(er).

B. Proper nouns:

1. Names of persons and places are considered familiar. *Japan*, *Smith*, and so on, are familiar even though they do not appear on the word list.

2. Names of organizations, laws,

documents, titles of books, movies, and so on generally comprise several words.

    a. When determining the number of words in a sample, count all the words in the name of an organization and the like. *Chicago Building Association* should be counted three words. *Declaration of Independence* should be counted three words. SPECIAL RULE: When the title of an organization, law, and so on is used several times within a sample of 100 words, all the words in the title are counted, no matter how many times they are repeated.

    b. For the unfamiliar word count, consider unfamiliar only words which do not appear on the Dale list, except names of persons or places. *Chicago Building Association* is counted one unfamiliar word—*Association*. *Building* and *Chicago* are familiar. *Declaration of Independence* is counted as two unfamiliar words—as *of* is on the list. SPECIAL RULE: When the name of an organization, law, document, and so on is used several times within a sample of 100 words, count it only twice when making the unfamiliar word count. *Security Council*, if repeated more than twice within a 100-word sample, is counted as four unfamiliar words.

3. Abbreviations:

    a. In counting the words in a sample, an abbreviation is counted as one word. *Y.M.C.A.* is counted one word. *Nov.* is counted one word. A.M. and P.M. are each counted as one word.

    b. In making the unfamiliar word count, an abbreviation is counted as one unfamiliar word only. *Y.M.C.A.* is considered one unfamiliar word. *Nov.* is considered familiar because the names of the months are on the word list. *U.S.* is considered familiar. A.M. and P.M. are each considered familiar. SPECIAL RULE: An abbreviation which is used several times within a 100-word sample is counted as two unfamiliar words only. *C.I.O.* is counted two unfamiliar words if repeated five times in a 100-word sample.

C. Verbs:

    1. Consider familiar the third-person, singular forms (*s* or *ies* from *y*), present-participle forms (*ing*), past-participle forms (*n*), and past-tense forms (*ed* or *ied* from *y*), when these are added to verbs appearing on the list. The same rule applies when a consonant is doubled before adding *ing* or *ed*. E.g., *ask, asking, asked* are considered familiar, although only the word *ask* appears on the word list; *dropped* and *dropping* are familiar because *drop* is on the list.

D. Adjectives:

    1. Comparatives and superlatives of adjectives appearing on the list are considered familiar. The same rule applies if the consonant is doubled before adding *er* or *est*. E.g., *longer, prettier,* and *bravest* are familiar because *long, pretty,* and *brave* are on the

list; *red, redder,* and *reddest* are all familiar.

2. Adjectives formed by adding *n* to a proper noun are familiar. For example, *American, Austrian.*

3. Count as unfamiliar an adjective that is formed by adding *y* to a word that appears on the list. But consider the word familiar if *y* appears in parentheses following the word. E.g., *woolly* is unfamiliar although *wool* is on the list; *sandy* is familiar because it appears on the list as *sand(y).*

E. Adverbs:

1. Consider adverbs familiar which are formed by adding *ly* to a word on the list. In most cases *ly* will be indicated following the word. E.g., *soundly* is familiar because *sound* is on the list.

2. Count as unfamiliar words which add more than *ly*, like *easily.*

F. Hyphenated words:

1. Count the hyphenated words as unfamiliar if either word in the compound does not appear on the word list. When both appear on the list, the word is familiar.

G. Miscellaneous special cases:

1. Words formed by adding *en* to a word on the list (unless the *en* is listed in parentheses or the word itself appears on the list) are considered unfamiliar; *sharpen* is considered unfamiliar although *sharp* is on the list; *golden* is considered familiar because it appears on the list *gold(en).*

2. Count a word unfamiliar if two or more endings are added to a word on the list; *clippings* is considered unfamiliar, although *clip* is on the list.

3. Words on the list to which *tion, ation, ment,* and other suffixes not previously mentioned are added are considered unfamiliar, unless the word with the ending is included on the list; *treatment* is unfamiliar although *treat* is on the list; *protection* is unfamiliar although *protect* is on the list; *preparation* is unfamiliar although *prepare* is on the list.

4. Numbers:
Numerals like *1947, 18,* and so on, are considered familiar.

H. Record the total number of unfamiliar words under 3 of the work sheet.

The number of words in the sample (1 on the work sheet) have now been recorded, as well as the number of sentences in the sample (2) and the number of words not on the Dale list (3). The next steps can be followed easily on the work sheet.

VI. Completing the work sheet.

1. The average sentence length (4) is computed by dividing the number of words in the sample by the number of sentences in the sample.

2. The Dale score or percentage of words outside the Dale list is computed by dividing the number of words not on the Dale list by the number of words in the sample and multiplying by 100.

3. Follow through Steps 6 and 7 on the work sheet.[15]

4. Add 6, 7, and 8 to get the formula raw score.

5. If you have more than one sample to analyze, get an average of the formula raw scores by adding all of these and dividing by the number of samples.

6. Convert the average formula raw

[15] Copies of the table of multiplications may be obtained from Edgar Dale, Bureau of Educational Research, Ohio State University.

score to a corrected grade level according to the Correction Table given on page 199.

The corrected grade level indicates the grade at which a book or article can be read with understanding. For example, a book with a corrected grade level of 7–8 is one which should be within the reading ability of average children in Grades 7–8. For adults, the 7–8 grade level can be compared to the last grade reached. If materials are being selected for persons who have had an average of eight grades of schooling, passages with a corrected grade level of 7–8 should be within their ability. The corrected grade levels corresponding to the raw scores obtained from the formula are given on page 199. These will serve to determine the grade level of materials being appraised with the use of the Dale list.

The Dale list of approximately 3000 familiar words represents words that are known in reading by at least 80 percent of the children in Grade 4. It is presented primarily as a list which gives a significant correlation with reading difficulty. It is not intended as a list of the most important words for children and adults. It includes words that are relatively unimportant and excludes some important ones. To use the list for more

than an overall statistical device which gives a good prediction of readability would be out of harmony with the purpose for which it was constructed.

The technique used for constructing the list was crude. When 80 percent of the fourth-graders questioned indicated that they knew a word, that word was included in the list. This arbitrary cutting off at the 80 percent point and the lack of any measure of the importance of these words make exceedingly dubious the wisdom of using individual words in appraising the ease or difficulty of material. For purposes of computing a level of difficulty, however, the percentage of words outside this list is a very good index of the difficulty of reading materials. The terms *familiar* and *unfamiliar* describing words are therefore used here in a statistical sense.

There is, however, a real place for a list of important familiar words, graded in about four levels, for use in the preparation of materials for adults of limited reading ability. At the present time we are experimenting with such a list. It will include such words as *nation*, and so on, which tested slightly below the 80 percent criterion on children, but are important, and for all practical purposes are probably familiar, to adults.

Dale List of 3000 Familiar Words

a	amount	away	beautify	bit	bow	burn
able	an	awful(ly)	beauty	bite	bowl	burst
aboard	and	awhile	became	biting	bow-wow	bury
about	angel	ax	because	bitter	box(es)	bus
above	anger		become	black	boxcar	bush
absent	angry	baa	becoming	blackberry	boxer	bushel
accept	animal	babe	bed	blackbird	boy	business
accident	another	baby(ies)	bedbug	blackboard	boyhood	busy
account	answer	back	bedroom	blackness	bracelet	but
ache(ing)	ant	background	bedspread	blacksmith	brain	butcher
acorn	any	backward(s)	bedtime	blame	brake	butt
acre	anybody	bacon	bee	blank	bran	butter
across	anyhow	bad(ly)	beech	blanket	branch	buttercup
act(s)	anyone	badge	beef	blast	brass	butterfly
add	anything	bag	beefsteak	blaze	brave	buttermilk
address	anyway	bake(r)	beehive	bleed	bread	butterscotch
admire	anywhere	bakery	been	bless	break	button
adventure	apart	baking	beer	blessing	breakfast	buttonhole
afar	apartment	ball	beet	blew	breast	buy
afraid	ape	balloon	before	blind(s)	breath	buzz
after	apiece	banana	beg	blindfold	breathe	by
afternoon	appear	band	began	block	breeze	bye
afterward(s)	apple	bandage	beggar	blood	brick	
again	April	bang	begged	bloom	bride	cab
against	apron	banjo	begin	blossom	bridge	cabbage
age	are	bank(er)	beginning	blot	bright	cabin
aged	aren't	bar	begun	blow	brightness	cabinet
ago	arise	barber	behave	blue	bring	cackle
agree	arithmetic	bare(ly)	behind	blueberry	broad	cage
ah	arm	barefoot	believe	bluebird	broadcast	cake
ahead	armful	bark	bell	bluejay	broke(n)	calendar
aid	army	barn	belong	blush	brook	calf
aim	arose	barrel	below	board	broom	call(er)(ing)
air	around	base	belt	boast	brother	came
airfield	arrange	baseball	bench	boat	brought	camel
airplane	arrive(d)	basement	bend	bob	brown	camp
airport	arrow	basket	beneath	bobwhite	brush	campfire
airship	art	bat	bent	body(ies)	bubble	can
airy	artist	batch	berry(ies)	boil(er)	bucket	canal
alarm	as	bath	beside(s)	bold	buckle	canary
alike	ash(es)	bathe	best	bone	bud	candle
alive	aside	bathing	bet	bonnet	buffalo	candlestick
all	ask	bathroom	better	boo	bug	candy
alley	asleep	bathtub	between	book	buggy	cane
alligator	at	battle	bib	bookcase	build	cannon
allow	ate	battleship	bible	bookkeeper	building	cannot
almost	attack	bay	bicycle	boom	built	canoe
alone	attend	be(ing)	bid	boot	bulb	can't
along	attention	beach	big(ger)	born	bull	canyon
aloud	August	bead	bill	borrow	bullet	cap
already	aunt	beam	billboard	boss	bum	cape
also	author	bean	bin	both	bumblebee	capital
always	auto	bear	bind	bother	bump	captain
am	automobile	beard	bird	bottle	bun	car
America	autumn	beast	birth	bottom	bunch	card
American	avenue	beat(ing)	birthday	bought	bundle	cardboard
among	awake(n)	beautiful	biscuit	bounce	bunny	care

careful	childhood	cocoon	cramps	dart	do	dwarf
careless	children	cod	cranberry	dash	dock	dwell
carelessness	chill(y)	codfish	crank(y)	date	doctor	dwelt
carload	chimney	coffee	crash	daughter	does	dying
carpenter	chin	coffeepot	crawl	dawn	doesn't	
carpet	china	coin	crazy	day	dog	each
carriage	chip	cold	cream(y)	daybreak	doll	eager
carrot	chipmunk	collar	creek	daytime	dollar	eagle
carry	chocolate	college	creep	dead	dolly	ear
cart	choice	color(ed)	crept	deaf	done	early
carve	choose	colt	cried	deal	donkey	earn
case	chop	column	croak	dear	don't	earth
cash	chorus	comb	crook(ed)	death	door	east(ern)
cashier	chose(n)	come	crop	December	doorbell	easy
castle	christen	comfort	cross(ing)	decide	doorknob	eat(en)
cat	Christmas	comic	cross-eyed	deck	doorstep	edge
catbird	church	coming	crow	deed	dope	egg
catch	churn	company	crowd(ed)	deep	dot	eh
catcher	cigarette	compare	crown	deer	double	eight
caterpillar	circle	conductor	cruel	defeat	dough	eighteen
catfish	circus	cone	crumb	defend	dove	eighth
catsup	citizen	connect	crumble	defense	down	eighty
cattle	city	coo	crush	delight	downstairs	either
caught	clang	cook(ed)	crust	den	downtown	elbow
cause	clap	cook(ing)	cry(ies)	dentist	dozen	elder
cave	class	cooky(ie)(s)	cub	depend	drag	eldest
ceiling	classmate	cool(er)	cuff	deposit	drain	electric
cell	classroom	coop	cup	describe	drank	electricity
cellar	claw	copper	cupboard	desert	draw(er)	elephant
cent	clay	copy	cupful	deserve	draw(ing)	eleven
center	clean(er)	cord	cure	desire	dream	elf
cereal	clear	cork	curl(y)	desk	dress	elm
certain(ly)	clerk	corn	curtain	destroy	dresser	else
chain	clever	corner	curve	devil	dressmaker	elsewhere
chair	click	correct	cushion	dew	drew	empty
chalk	cliff	cost	custard	diamond	dried	end(ing)
champion	climb	cot	customer	did	drift	enemy
chance	clip	cottage	cut	didn't	drill	engine
change	cloak	cotton	cute	die(d)(s)	drink	engineer
chap	clock	couch	cutting	difference	drip	English
charge	close	cough		different	drive(n)	enjoy
charm	closet	could	dab	dig	driver	enough
chart	cloth	couldn't	dad	dim	drop	enter
chase	clothes	count	daddy	dime	drove	envelope
chatter	clothing	counter	daily	dine	drown	equal
cheap	cloud(y)	country	dairy	ding-dong	drowsy	erase(r)
cheat	clover	county	daisy	dinner	drug	errand
check	clown	course	dam	dip	drum	escape
checkers	club	court	damage	direct	drunk	eve
cheek	cluck	cousin	dame	direction	dry	even
cheer	clump	cover	damp	dirt(y)	duck	evening
cheese	coach	cow	dance(r)	discover	due	ever
cherry	coal	coward(ly)	dancing	dish	dug	every
chest	coast	cowboy	dandy	dislike	dull	everybody
chew	coat	cozy	danger(ous)	dismiss	dumb	everyday
chick	cob	crab	dare	ditch	dump	everyone
chicken	cobbler	crack	dark(ness)	dive	during	everything
chief	cocoa	cracker	darling	diver	dust(y)	everywhere
child	coconut	cradle	darn	divide	duty	evil

exact	fiddle	follow(ing)	gain	gown	ham	hello
except	field	fond	gallon	grab	hammer	helmet
exchange	fife	food	gallop	gracious	hand	help(er)
excited	fifteen	fool	game	grade	handful	helpful
exciting	fifth	foolish	gang	grain	handker-	hem
excuse	fifty	foot	garage	grand	chief	hen
exit	fig	football	garbage	grandchild	handle	henhouse
expect	fight	footprint	garden	grandchildren	handwrit-	her(s)
explain	figure	for	gas	granddaughter	ing	herd
extra	file	forehead	gasoline	grandfather	hang	here
eye	fill	forest	gate	grandma	happen	here's
eyebrow	film	forget	gather	grandmother	happily	hero
	finally	forgive	gave	grandpa	happiness	herself
fable	find	forgot(ten)	gay	grandson	happy	he's
face	fine	fork	gear	grandstand	harbor	hey
facing	finger	form	geese	grape(s)	hard	hickory
fact	finish	fort	general	grapefruit	hardly	hid
factory	fire	forth	gentle	grass	hardship	hidden
fail	firearm	fortune	gentleman	grasshopper	hardware	hide
faint	firecracker	forty	gentlemen	grateful	hare	high
fair	fireplace	forward	geography	grave	hark	highway
fairy	fireworks	fought	get	gravel	harm	hill
faith	firing	found	getting	graveyard	harness	hillside
fake	first	fountain	giant	gravy	harp	hilltop
fall	fish	four	gift	gray	harvest	hilly
false	fisherman	fourteen	gingerbread	graze	has	him
family	fist	fourth	girl	grease	hasn't	himself
fan	fit(s)	fox	give(n)	great	haste(n)	hind
fancy	five	frame	giving	green	hasty	hint
far	fix	free	glad(ly)	greet	hat	hip
faraway	flag	freedom	glance	grew	hatch	hire
fare	flake	freeze	glass(es)	grind	hatchet	his
farmer	flame	freight	gleam	groan	hate	hiss
farm(ing)	flap	French	glide	grocery	haul	history
far-off	flash	fresh	glory	ground	have	hit
farther	flashlight	fret	glove	group	haven't	hitch
fashion	flat	Friday	glow	grove	having	hive
fast	flea	fried	glue	grow	hawk	ho
fasten	flesh	friend(ly)	go(ing)	guard	hay	hoe
fat	flew	friendship	goes	guess	hayfield	hog
father	flies	frighten	goal	guest	haystack	hold(er)
fault	flight	frog	goat	guide	he	hole
favor	flip	from	gobble	gulf	head	holiday
favorite	flip-flop	front	God(g)	gum	headache	hollow
fear	float	frost	godmother	gun	heal	holy
feast	flock	frown	gold(en)	gunpowder	health(y)	home
feather	flood	froze	goldfish	guy	heap	homely
February	floor	fruit	golf		hear(ing)	homesick
fed	flop	fry	gone	ha	heard	honest
feed	flour	fudge	good(s)	habit	heart	honey
feel	flow	fuel	good-by(bye)	had	heat(er)	honeybee
feet	flower(y)	full(y)	good-looking	hadn't	heaven	honeymoon
fell	flutter	fun	goodness	hail	heavy	honk
fellow	fly	funny	goody	hair	he'd	honor
felt	foam	fur	goose	haircut	heel	hood
fence	fog	furniture	gooseberry	hairpin	height	hoof
fever	foggy	further	got	half	held	hook
few	fold	fuzzy	govern	hall	hell	hoop
fib	folks		government	halt	he'll	hop

hope(ful)	ink	kettle	leap	lonesome	matter	mop
hopeless	inn	key	learn(ed)	long	mattress	more
horn	insect	kick	least	look	may(M)	morning
horse	inside	kid	leather	lookout	maybe	morrow
horseback	instant	kill(ed)	leave(ing)	loop	mayor	moss
horseshoe	instead	kind(ly)	led	loose	maypole	most(ly)
hose	insult	kindness	left	lord	me	mother
hospital	intend	king	leg	lose(r)	meadow	motor
host	interested	kingdom	lemon	loss	meal	mount
hot	interesting	kiss	lemonade	lost	mean(s)	mountain
hotel	into	kitchen	lend	lot	meant	mouse
hound	invite	kite	length	loud	measure	mouth
hour	iron	kitten	less	love	meat	move
house	is	kitty	lesson	lovely	medicine	movie
housetop	island	knee	let	lover	meet(ing)	movies
housewife	isn't	kneel	let's	low	melt	moving
housework	it	knew	letter	luck(y)	member	mow
how	its	knife	letting	lumber	men	Mr., Mrs.
however	it's	knit	lettuce	lump	mend	much
howl	itself	knives	level	lunch	meow	mud
hug	I've	knob	liberty	lying	merry	muddy
huge	ivory	knock	library		mess	mug
hum	ivy	knot	lice	ma	message	mule
humble		know	lick	machine	met	multiply
hump	jacket	known	lid	machinery	metal	murder
hundred	jacks		lie	mad	mew	music
hung	jail	lace	life	made	mice	must
hunger	jam	lad	lift	magazine	middle	my
hungry	January	ladder	light(ness)	magic	midnight	myself
hunk	jar	ladies	lightning	maid	might(y)	
hunt(er)	jaw	lady	like	mail	mile	nail
hurrah	jay	laid	likely	mailbox	milk	name
hurried	jelly	lake	liking	mailman	milkman	nap
hurry	jellyfish	lamb	lily	major	mill	napkin
hurt	jerk	lame	limb	make	miller	narrow
husband	jig	lamp	lime	making	million	nasty
hush	job	land	limp	male	mind	naughty
hut	jockey	lane	line	mama	mine	navy
hymn	join	language	linen	mamma	miner	near
	joke	lantern	lion	man	mint	nearby
I	joking	lap	lip	manager	minute	nearly
ice	jolly	lard	list	mane	mirror	neat
icy	journey	large	listen	manger	mischief	neck
I'd	joy(ful)	lash	lit	many	miss(M)	necktie
idea	joyous	lass	little	map	misspell	need
ideal	judge	last	live(s)	maple	mistake	needle
if	jug	late	lively	marble	misty	needn't
ill	juice	laugh	liver	march(M)	mitt	Negro
I'll	juicy	laundry	living	mare	mitten	neighbor
I'm	July	law	lizard	mark	mix	neighborhood
important	jump	lawn	load	market	moment	neither
impossible	June	lawyer	loaf	marriage	Monday	nerve
improve	junior	lay	loan	married	money	nest
in	junk	lazy	loaves	marry	monkey	net
inch(es)	just	lead	lock	mask	month	never
income		leader	locomotive	mast	moo	nevermore
indeed	keen	leaf	log	master	moon	new
Indian	keep	leak	lone	mat	moonlight	news
indoors	kept	lean	lonely	match	moose	newspaper

next	orchard	partner	pit	present	rainbow	ring
nibble	order	party	pitch	pretty	raise	rip
nice	ore	pass	pitcher	price	raisin	ripe
nickel	organ	passenger	pity	prick	rake	rise
night	other	past	place	prince	ram	rising
nightgown	otherwise	paste	plain	princess	ran	river
nine	ouch	pasture	plan	print	ranch	road
nineteen	ought	pat	plane	prison	rang	roadside
ninety	our(s)	patch	plant	prize	rap	roar
no	ourselves	path	plate	promise	rapidly	roast
nobody	out	patter	platform	proper	rat	rob
nod	outdoors	pave	platter	protect	rate	robber
noise	outfit	pavement	play(er)	proud	rather	robe
noisy	outlaw	paw	playground	prove	rattle	robin
none	outline	pay	playhouse	prune	raw	rock(y)
noon	outside	payment	playmate	public	ray	rocket
nor	outward	pea(s)	plaything	puddle	reach	rode
north(ern)	oven	peace(ful)	pleasant	puff	read	roll
nose	over	peach(es)	please	pull	reader	roller
not	overalls	peak	pleasure	pump	reading	roof
note	overcoat	peanut	plenty	pumpkin	ready	room
nothing	overeat	pear	plow	punch	real	rooster
notice	overhead	pearl	plug	punish	really	root
November	overhear	peck	plum	pup	reap	rope
now	overnight	peek	pocket	pupil	rear	rose
nowhere	overturn	peel	pocketbook	puppy	reason	rosebud
number	owe	peep	poem	pure	rebuild	rot
nurse	owing	peg	point	purple	receive	rotten
nut	owl	pen	poison	purse	recess	rough
	own(er)	pencil	poke	push	record	round
	ox	penny	pole	puss	red	route
oak		people	police	pussy	redbird	row
oar		pepper	policeman	pussycat	redbreast	rowboat
oatmeal	pa	peppermint	polish	put	refuse	royal
oats	pace	perfume	polite	putting	reindeer	rub
obey	pack	perhaps	pond	puzzle	rejoice	rubbed
ocean	package	person	ponies		remain	rubber
o'clock	pad	pet	pony	quack	remember	rubbish
October	page	phone	pool	quart	remind	rug
odd	paid	piano	poor	quarter	remove	rule(r)
of	pail	pick	pop	queen	rent	rumble
off	pain(ful)	pickle	popcorn	queer	repair	run
offer	paint(er)	picnic	popped	question	repay	rung
office	painting	picture	porch	quick(ly)	repeat	runner
officer	pair	pie	pork	quiet	report	running
often	pal	piece	possible	quilt	rest	rush
oh	palace	pig	post	quit	return	rust(y)
oil	pale	pigeon	postage	quite	review	rye
old	pan	piggy	postman		reward	
old-	pancake	pile	pot	rabbit	rib	sack
fashioned	pane	pill	potato(es)	race	ribbon	sad
on	pansy	pillow	pound	rack	rice	saddle
once	pants	pin	pour	radio	rich	sadness
one	papa	pine	powder	radish	rid	safe
onion	paper	pineapple	power(ful)	rag	riddle	safety
only	parade	pink	praise	rail	ride(r)	said
onward	pardon	pint	pray	railroad	riding	sail
open	parent	pipe	prayer	railway	right	sailboat
or	park	pistol	prepare	rain(y)	rim	sailor
orange	part(ly)					

saint	sent	shout	slipped	speak(er)	sting	surprise
salad	sentence	shovel	slipper	spear	stir	swallow
sale	separate	show	slippery	speech	stitch	swam
salt	September	shower	slit	speed	stock	swamp
same	servant	shut	slow(ly)	spell(ing)	stocking	swan
sand(y)	serve	shy	sly	spend	stole	swat
sandwich	service	sick(ness)	smack	spent	stone	swear
sang	set	side	small	spider	stood	sweat
sank	setting	sidewalk	smart	spike	stool	sweater
sap	settle	sideways	smell	spill	stoop	sweep
sash	settlement	sigh	smile	spin	stop	sweet(ness)
sat	seven	sight	smoke	spinach	stopped	sweetheart
satin	seventeen	sign	smooth	spirit	stopping	swell
satisfactory	seventh	silence	snail	spit	store	swept
Saturday	seventy	silent	snake	splash	stories	swift
sausage	several	silk	snap	spoil	stork	swim
savage	sew	sill	snapping	spoke	storm(y)	swimming
save	shade	silly	sneeze	spook	story	swing
savings	shadow	silver	snow(y)	spoon	stove	switch
saw	shady	simple	snowball	sport	straight	sword
say	shake(r)	sin	snowflake	spot	strange(r)	swore
scab	shaking	since	snuff	spread	strap	
scales	shall	sing	snug	spring	straw	table
scare	shame	singer	so	springtime	strawberry	tablecloth
scarf	shan't	single	soak	sprinkle	stream	tablespoon
school	shape	sink	soap	square	street	tablet
schoolboy	share	sip	sob	squash	stretch	tack
schoolhouse	sharp	sir	socks	squeak	string	tag
schoolmaster	shave	sis	sod	squeeze	strip	tail
schoolroom	she	sissy	soda	squirrel	stripes	tailor
scorch	she'd	sister	sofa	stable	strong	take(n)
score	she'll	sit	soft	stack	stuck	taking
scrap	she's	sitting	soil	stage	study	tale
scrape	shear(s)	six	sold	stair	stuff	talk(er)
scratch	shed	sixteen	soldier	stall	stump	tall
scream	sheep	sixth	sole	stamp	stung	tame
screen	sheet	sixty	some	stand	subject	tan
screw	shelf	size	somebody	star	such	tank
scrub	shell	skate	somehow	stare	suck	tap
sea	shepherd	skater	someone	start	sudden	tape
seal	shine	ski	something	starve	suffer	tar
seam	shining	skin	sometime(s)	state	sugar	tardy
search	shiny	skip	somewhere	station	suit	task
season	ship	skirt	son	stay	sum	taste
seat	shirt	sky	song	steak	summer	taught
second	shock	slam	soon	steal	sun	tax
secret	shoe	slap	sore	steam	Sunday	tea
see(ing)	shoemaker	slate	sorrow	steamboat	sunflower	teach(er)
seed	shone	slave	sorry	steamer	sung	team
seek	shook	sled	sort	steel	sunk	tear
seem	shoot	sleep(y)	soul	steep	sunlight	tease
seen	shop	sleeve	sound	steeple	sunny	teaspoon
seesaw	shopping	sleigh	soup	steer	sunrise	teeth
select	shore	slept	sour	stem	sunset	telephone
self	short	slice	south(ern)	step	sunshine	tell
selfish	shot	slid	space	stepping	supper	temper
sell	should	slide	spade	stick(y)	suppose	ten
send	shoulder	sling	spank	stiff	sure(ly)	tennis
sense	shouldn't	slip	sparrow	still(ness)	surface	tent

term	tin	trouble	valentine	weed	wish	youngster
terrible	tinkle	truck	valley	week	wit	your(s)
test	tiny	true	valuable	weep	witch	you're
than	tip	truly	value	weigh	with	yourself
thank(s)	tiptoe	trunk	vase	welcome	without	yourselves
thankful	tire	trust	vegetable	well	woke	youth
Thanks-	tired	truth	velvet	we'll	wolf	you've
giving	'tis	try	very	went	woman	
that	title	tub	vessel	were	women	
that's	to	Tuesday	victory	we're	won	
the	toad	tug	view	west(ern)	wonder	
theater	toadstool	tulip	village	wet	wonderful	
thee	toast	tumble	vine	we've	won't	
their	tobacco	tune	violet	whale	wood(en)	
them	today	tunnel	visit	what	woodpecker	
then	toe	turkey	visitor	what's	woods	
there	together	turn	voice	wheat	wool	
these	toilet	turtle	vote	wheel	woolen	
they	told	twelve		when	word	
they'd	tomato	twenty	wag	whenever	wore	
they'll	tomorrow	twice	wagon	where	work(er)	
they're	ton	twig	waist	which	workman	
they've	tone	twin	wait	while	world	
thick	tongue	two	wake(n)	whip	worm	
thief	tonight		walk	whipped	worn	
thimble	too	ugly	wall	whirl	worry	
thin	took	umbrella	walnut	whisky	worse	
thing	tool	uncle	want	whisper	worst	
think	toot	under	war	whistle	worth	
third	tooth	understand	warm	white	would	
thirsty	toothbrush	underwear	warn	who	wouldn't	
thirteen	toothpick	undress	was	who'd	wound	
thirty	top	unfair	wash(er)	whole	wove	
this	tore	unfinished	washtub	who'll	wrap	
tho	torn	unfold	wasn't	whom	wrapped	
thorn	toss	unfriendly	waste	who's	wreck	
those	touch	unhappy	watch	whose	wren	
though	tow	unhurt	watchman	why	wring	
thought	toward(s)	uniform	water	wicked	write	
thousand	towel	United	watermelon	wide	writing	
thread	tower	States	waterproof	wife	written	
three	town	unkind	wave	wiggle	wrong	
threw	toy	unknown	wax	wild	wrote	
throat	trace	unless	way	wildcat	wrung	
throne	track	unpleasant	wayside	will		
through	trade	until	we	willing	yard	
throw(n)	train	unwilling	weak(ness)	willow	yarn	
thumb	tramp	up	weaken	win	year	
thunder	trap	upon	wealth	wind(y)	yell	
Thursday	tray	upper	weapon	windmill	yellow	
thy	treasure	upset	wear	window	yes	
tick	treat	upside	weary	wine	yesterday	
ticket	tree	upstairs	weather	wing	yet	
tickle	trick	uptown	weave	wink	yolk	
tie	tricycle	upward	web	winner	yonder	
tiger	tried	us	we'd	winter	you	
tight	trim	use(d)	wedding	wipe	you'd	
till	trip	useful	Wednesday	wire	you'll	
time	trolley		wee	wise	young	

Dale-Chall Formula Multiplication Table of Weights

Average Sentence Length				Dale Score			
.0496 x	1– .0496	26–	1.2896	.1579 x	1– .1579	26–	4.1054
	2– .0992	27–	1.3392		2– .3158	27–	4.2633
	3– .1488	28–	1.3888		3– .4737	28–	4.4212
	4– .1984	29–	1.4384		4– .6316	29–	4.5791
	5– .2480	30–	1.4880		5– .7895	30–	4.7370
	6– .2976	31–	1.5376		6– .9474	31–	4.8949
	7– .3472	32–	1.5872		7– 1.1053	32–	5.0528
	8– .3968	33–	1.6368		8– 1.2632	33–	5.2107
	9– .4464	34–	1.6864		9– 1.4211	34–	5.3686
	10– .4960	35–	1.7360		10– 1.5790	35–	5.5265
	11– .5456	36–	1.7856		11– 1.7369	36–	5.6844
	12– .5952	37–	1.8352		12– 1.8948	37–	5.8423
	13– .6448	38–	1.8848		13– 2.0527	38–	6.0002
	14– .6944	39–	1.9344		14– 2.2106	39–	6.1581
	15– .7440	40–	1.9840		15– 2.3685	40–	6.3160
	16– .7936	41–	2.0336		16– 2.5264	41–	6.4739
	17– .8432	42–	2.0832		17– 2.6843	42–	6.6318
	18– .8928	43–	2.1328		18– 2.8422	43–	6.7897
	19– .9424	44–	2.1824		19– 3.0001	44–	6.9476
	20– .9920	45–	2.2320		20– 3.1580	45–	7.1055
	21– 1.0416	46–	2.2816		21– 3.3159	46–	7.2634
	22– 1.0912	47–	2.3312		22– 3.4738	47–	7.4213
	23– 1.1408	48–	2.3808		23– 3.6317	48–	7.5792
	24– 1.1904	49–	2.4304		24– 3.7896	49–	7.7371
	25– 1.2400	50–	2.4800		25– 3.9475	50–	7.8950

A BASIC VOCABULARY FOR ELEMENTARY-SCHOOL CHILDREN [1]

Henry D. Rinsland

[To date the most comprehensive study of the words actually used by children, Rinsland's research covered more than 200,000 individual writings by children involving over six million running words. The writings represented a national sampling of public, parochial, and private schools. The reader will be especially interested in Rinsland's discussion of the proper uses of this vocabulary.]

NEED FOR STUDY OF CHILDREN'S VOCABULARY

Numerous studies show that authors do not agree with any degree of reasonableness in either the number of words or which words to use in even basal subjects in any one grade. Probably the

[1] Adapted and abridged from Henry D. Rinsland, A Basic Vocabulary of Elementary School Children, The Macmillan Company, New York, 1945.

simplest subject in which to make such comparisons, because of the simplest use of words, at least the basic word list, is spelling. The study of Betts [2] (1940) in this subject reveals a tragic—or is it simply ridiculous?—situation. Seventeen authors agreed unanimously on only 6.26 percent of the total words used, and in grade placement they unanimously agreed on one word.

A study by Hockett [3] (1938) shows a wide disagreement in the number both of running words and of different words in elementary readers for Grades 1 to 4. Obviously experts do not agree on the number of words, whether total or different, which should be used where fewest words are given, that is, in the lower grades. Their disagreement shows that the problem is not one of enrichment or variety of vocabulary but a lack of knowledge of the difficulty and usage of words. Perhaps there is no such thing as a first-grade reading list or a first-grade vocabulary. Vocabulary knowledge and vocabulary problems are not so simple. Nor would anyone want perfect agreement, even for spellers or basal readers in Grades 1 to 8; but certainly there should be closer agreements than these studies show.

TWO APPROACHES TO VOCABULARY STUDIES

Two general approaches to determine vocabulary lists have been used: first, the determination of adults' usage, and second, the determination of children's usage. The widely known studies of Thorndike [4] (1921 and 1931) and Horn [5]

(1926) have made valuable contributions to our knowledge of the writings of adults. The Thorndike study offers our best information of the words used primarily [6] in books, and the Horn study offers our best information of the words used primarily in the writing of letters, although his study sampled other material.

The second approach claims that children, especially in the elementary school, do not use words with the same frequency as adults, and that adult usage is therefore a more or less invalid criterion. Children's writings for children's consumption seems to be a criterion to follow with certain safeguards or conditions in choosing the words and using them. Many words from many children, widely and wisely sampled from the whole country, will furnish most of the words needed for the average child and his textbooks. A broad sampling will not give all the words needed, nor will it give the correct grade placement for all words, if such a thing is possible, because successive samplings of, say, five million words each will give variations in words and frequencies. A sampling as broad as this should give reliable data for many words and their placement. Such a list will not inhibit growth, because so many more words would be found than any one child can learn, and it would not be suggestive of philosophy

[2] Emmett A. Betts, *Spelling Vocabulary Study*, American Book Co., New York, 1940.

[3] John Hockett, *The Vocabularies and Contents of Elementary School Readers*, Department of Education, State of California, Bulletin No. 3, May 1, 1938.

[4] Edward L. Thorndike, *The Teacher's Word Book of 10,000 Words*, Teachers College, Columbia University, New York, 1921, and *The Teacher's Word Book of 20,000 Words*, Teachers College, Columbia University, New York, 1931.

[5] Ernest Horn, *A Basic Writing Vocabulary—10,000 Words Most Commonly Used in Writing*, University of Iowa Monographs in Education, First Series, No. 4, State University of Iowa, Iowa City, 1926.

[6] The word *primarily* is somewhat inaccurate. The writer finds no single word that can apply. Each list is rather heterogeneous; the words come from many different types of writing, but primarily from the sources mentioned.

or reason to confine a child's learning to this list only.

There is no study, in the first place, that has broadly sampled the writings of children from all sections of the United States in all grades in large numbers that is comparable to the counts of Thorndike (1931) and Horn (1926). Second, no study gives continuous data for all eight grades. Third, no published study gives raw frequency, that is, actual number of times a word occurs in each grade. Fourth, no published study groups words in each grade into groups of practical sizes for general use, such as the first hundred, the first five hundred, and so forth. Fifth, no study gives a measure of comparable frequency of occurrence from grade to grade, such as per cent, per mill, or per hundred thousand running words (the unit used in this study).

The present study attempts to remove these objections, as far as is possible within the time and financial resources at hand, and present all obtained data.

SOURCE OF MATERIAL

In the fall of 1936, the University of Oklahoma requested a grant of funds from the Works Projects Administration of Oklahoma to carry on an extensive, nation-wide study of the words written by children who are in Grades 1–8. Requests were made on the basis of sampling a minimum of six million running words from at least five hundred schools in all states.

In order to make the children's writings obtained representative of the United States, two factors of sampling were involved. The first factor had to do with obtaining a true cross section of all types of schools; the second had to do with obtaining a true cross section of all types of writing of children. Letters were addressed to the superintendents of fifteen hundred selected schools in all

kinds of geographic, economic, and social areas. Requests were made to schools in rural communities and in cities of different sizes. Coastal, inland, agricultural, mining, lumbering, and manufacturing regions were all sampled. Public, parochial, and private schools and training schools in universities were requested to send writing.

The letters addressed to school officials requested original and genuine material written by children. With this request were sent a few paragraphs describing the project and its value. The letters stated that *all* kinds of children's writings, representing their freest and most natural compositions, were desired. It was suggested that such writings as the following should be included: personal notes, stories, poems, compositions in many school subjects, examinations in nontechnical subjects, articles for school papers that were not corrected by the teachers, and reports on projects, trips, and observations. It was necessary to depend upon the judgment of teachers that these writings represented, as nearly as they could determine, children's own work and not copying.

The number of schools in different geographical areas is given in Table 1, the grand total of which is 708, which is a 47.2 percent response. This is usually considered a very satisfactory response. It well represents all types of schools from the original selection. Evenness of sampling cannot be judged by the number of schools in any area, as many factors were involved in the original sampling, and geographical sections represented only one factor. Responses were poorest from metropolitan centers and thickly populated sections in the East. However, the high percentage of replies, involving considerable labor and trouble, attests the keen interest and faith in this problem on the part of teachers and administrators.

TABLE 1. Number of Cities, Training Schools in Colleges, and Counties by Geographical Areas Contributing Samples of Children's Writings

Geographic Area	Number of Cities	Number of Training Schools in Colleges	Number of Counties	Total
New England States	37	2	11	50
Middle Atlantic States	62	8	21	91
Southern States				
Eastern Section	53	7	10	70
Western Section	85	9	86	180
Central States				
Eastern Section	41	6	13	60
Western Section	63	13	76	152
Northwestern States	31	4	8	43
Southwestern States	44	7	11	62
Total	416	56	236	708

The number of individual papers received was more than 200,000, which is about 1 percent of the approximately twenty million elementary-school children in the United States.[7]

A comparison between the sampling of this study (6,012,395 running words) and that of others can be made by quoting the extent of sampling of several other studies, such as the 238,654 words from Grades 2 to 8 by Smith (1935);[8] the 460,907 words from Grades 4 to 6 by Fitzgerald (1934),[9] the 120,000 words from the 2225 children in Grades 2 to 7 by Francis (1934),[10] the five million adult words by Horn (1926),[11] and the ten million adult words from 279 sources by Thorndike (1931).[12]

One should remember that adults write a great deal more than children, and the total available writings from adults is perhaps several thousand times as great as the total available writings from children who are in elementary schools in the United States. The present sampling is therefore the richest from the writings of children and comparable to the largest count from the writings of adults.

SELECTING MATERIAL

In selecting material for word counting, all papers were carefully examined and marked to show grade and school. Each paper was read by a number of

[7] Education in the United States of America, Bulletin, Miscellaneous No. 3, Office of Education, Washington, 1939, p. 7, gives the population for Grades 1 to 8 for 1936 as 20, 392, 561. The collection of writings was made in the spring of 1937.

[8] James Smith, The Vocabulary of Children, Bulletin of State Teachers College, Vol. 29, No. 139, Oshkosh, Wisconsin, 1935.

[9] James A. Fitzgerald, Letters Written Outside of School by Children in the Fourth, Fifth, and Sixth Grades; A Study of Vocabulary, Spelling Errors and Situations, Studies in Education, Vol. 9, University of Iowa, 1934.

[10] Mary E. Francis, "A Survey to Determine Writing Vocabulary and Spelling Ability in Grades II to VII, Inclusive," unpublished doctor's thesis, University of Texas, 1934.

[11] Op. cit.

[12] The Teacher's Word Book of 20,000 Words.

experienced teachers familiar with children's work in the respective grades to determine authenticity or naturalness of the children's compositions. Where doubt was expressed by two readers, each paper was reread by another without knowledge of the previous readings. In order to eliminate duplications of papers coming from one school or one classroom, where a number of children's compositions were on the same subject and in which similar words and forms were used many times, only one and sometimes two papers were chosen for counting. These were judged independently by at least two teachers, and in case of disagreement the final deciding vote was made by a third teacher. After reading all compositions and classifying them under several headings, eliminating duplications and questionable children's writings, 100,212 compositions in the eight grades were used. Table 2 gives the number. Only one composition from each child was used; therefore the sampling represents the writings of approximately 100,212 children. (Writings in Grade 1 are only partially written pages; see Table 2.)

Because of the limited writing ability and experience of the first-grade children, it was necessary to secure written reports of their conversation, in school and outside. The works of Fry (1931) [13] and Trent (1931) [14] were both used. They furnished 4630 pages of conversation material. It is recognized that previous research has indicated a much larger oral vocabulary than written vocabulary. For this reason there is some justification in raising the question of consistency of source material in Grade 1.

[13] Rhey Fry, "The School Vocabulary of First Grade Children," unpublished master's thesis, University of Oklahoma, 1931.
[14] Bess M. Trent, "Vocabulary of First Grade Children Outside of School," unpublished master's thesis, University of Oklahoma, 1931.

Whether or not this is a serious difference is shown later by the number of different words in the material for Grade 1 as compared with other grades.

THE METHOD OF TABULATING WORDS

The lexical unit employed by Thorndike is not used in this study. Instead, the inflectional unit as used by Horn is used; that is, plurals, contractions, abbreviations, and so forth are tallied separately. Since children experience some difficulty in learning derivatives and since this list is to be used in teaching children, it was necessary to give due consideration to all forms of occurrences.

To assume uniformity of treatment, the following rules for tabulation were used:

1. Count all words—roots, derived forms, abbreviations, and contractions—just as they occur.
2. Tally separately run-together words.
3. Delete baby talk unless terms are found to be good English words.
4. Delete illegibles.
5. Count the correct forms intended when words are spelled unusually or wrongly.
6. Delete slang, provincialisms, colloquial expressions, as determined by the dictionary, as well as trade names and proper names of persons and places, except very well-known terms.
7. Do not tally separately words that may be written in two ways, but consider them the same for purposes of tabulation. Examples are today and to-day.
8. Tabulate the correct forms intended when errors occur in the use of homonyms. Two, too, and to are to be tabulated separately.
9. Tabulate separately words that are compounded if the compounding is incorrect or is used for running composition.

TABLE 2. Number and Kinds of Writings for Each Grade

Grade	Personal Letters	Expositions	Original Stories	Poems	Examination Papers	Conversation Pages	Projects	Others	Total
1	383	1,321	327	50	4,630		512	371	7,594
2	1,463	1,978	486	102		110	493	6,570	11,202
3	3,057	3,136	398	160		39	441	9,921	17,152
4	3,374	4,615	1,335	202		218	436	4,010	14,190
5	3,736	2,418	824	146		61	234	3,618	11,037
6	1,994	2,439	1,178	89		585	728	6,002	13,015
7	1,975	3,060	1,824	237		3,284	1,758	3,521	15,659
8	868	3,559	1,021	160		2,206	843	1,706	10,363
	16,850	22,526	7,393	1,146	4,630	6,503	5,445	35,719	100,212

FINDINGS

RELATION OF RUNNING WORDS
TO DIFFERENT WORDS

One of the most striking facts discovered after all tabulations were completed was the very large number of different words in each grade. There was a total of 25,632 different words from a count of 6,012,359 running words. This is somewhat larger than was expected from the suggestions and findings of other workers. In Table 3 is given a large group of sampling data. In Grade 1, 5099 different words would be expected, while it is very probable that 17,930 different words out of a total of 1,088,343 running words in Grade 8 are a much larger count than would be expected.

Many questions have been raised by writers concerning the contributions of the first 100, the first 500, or the first 1000 most frequently used words to a total writing list. The findings of this study in regard to this issue are given in detail in Table 3. For instance, in Grade 1, the first 100 most frequently used words contributed a total of 221,489 running words, or 63 percent of a total of 353,874 words, while in Grade 8 the first 100 most frequently used words contributed 618,417 or 57 percent of a total of 1,088,343. The first 2000 most frequently used words in Grade 1 make up 98 percent of the total writing vocabulary, but in Grade 8 the first 2000 words make up only 90 percent of the total writing vocabulary. There is a fairly consistent and graduated increase of percentage from the first 100 most frequently used words in Grade 1 to the first 2000 words in Grade 8. These percentages offer evidence of uniform sampling from grade to grade. This first story of these differences in contributions of different words to total running words will bring suggestions for further research and perhaps suggest revisions to certain educational practices, but it will answer a number of questions already raised.

At the beginning of the study no one knew just how many words to count in each grade, although Thorndike (1937) has suggested that the count of five million will determine the first five thousand words for ordinary purposes and be very helpful for the next few thousand, but this suggestion was made for a total vocabulary written in the first eight grades and not for a count in each one of the eight elementary grades. From Table 3 it will be seen that 353,874 words were counted in Grade 1 and 1,088,343 were counted in Grade 8. The number of running words sampled from grade to grade was not according to any given formula of sampling. There are several factors that have brought about an apparently uneven distribution. First of all, materials were made available by voluntary service of hundreds of teachers and school officials from hundreds of schools, and there is a limit to what teachers and administrators can do, free of charge, for the research worker. A definite number of compositions for each grade could not have been "ordered." The ideal number of different words to be secured from a sampling of each grade of course was unknown. Since this number could not be known before actual counting was done, no estimate of labor to do this task could have been made. But a general estimate had to be made in the application for a grant of funds.

The difficulty of securing adequate sampling of writings in Grades 1 and 2 is obvious; and therefore the total number of running words in these grades is not proportional to those in Grades 3 to 7. The additional sampling secured in Grade 8 was unexpected in terms of the original request, but it was decided to use a considerable amount of this ma-

TABLE 3. The Number and Percentage of Running Words Which Are Accounted for by Each 100 Within the First 1000 and by Each 500 Within the Second 1000, the Total Number of Running Words, and the Total Number of Different Words in Each Grade

Number of Running Words and Percentage for Each Grade

Different Words	Grade 1		Grade 2		Grade 3		Grade 4		Grade 5		Grade 6		Grade 7		Grade 8	
	Per-cent	Running Words	Running Words	Per-cent	Running Words	Per-cent	Running Words	Per-cent	Running Words	Per-cent	Running Words	Per-cent	Running Words	Per-cent	Running Words	Per-cent
100	63	221,489	267,265	65	458,670	60	484,787	61	513,840	62	498,954	58	531,182	58	618,417	57
200	73	258,298	308,863	76	535,944	70	571,333	72	602,268	72	583,476	68	614,869	68	719,786	66
300	79	278,415	331,109	81	578,175	75	612,470	77	645,817	77	627,504	74	658,258	72	771,171	71
400	82	291,510	346,042	85	607,197	79	640,294	81	673,986	81	656,313	77	688,540	76	807,420	74
500	85	301,056	356,294	87	627,943	82	660,900	83	695,018	83	677,985	79	711,881	78	835,255	77
600	87	308,296	364,251	89	645,568	84	676,672	85	711,345	85	695,169	81	730,402	80	856,976	79
700	89	314,398	370,662	91	657,801	85	689,681	87	724,278	87	709,635	83	745,502	82	875,000	80
800	90	319,149	375,697	92	668,795	87	700,594	88	734,858	88	721,922	85	758,284	83	889,960	82
900	91	323,237	380,164	93	677,804	88	709,440	90	743,770	89	732,263	86	769,562	84	903,040	83
1000	92	326,524	383,731	94	686,869	89	716,821	90	751,630	90	741,099	87	779,261	86	914,360	84
1500	96	339,342	393,823	96	714,511	93	742,275	94	777,211	93	772,988	91	813,070	89	956,131	88
2000	98	345,756	399,502	98	730,912	95	756,977	96	792,819	95	793,396	93	834,951	92	983,383	90
Total Running Words		353,874	408,540		770,019		792,326		835,130		853,409		910,754		1,088,343	
Total Different Words		5,099	5,821		8,976		9,976		11,449		11,304		14,820		17,930	

terial to increase the richness of vocabulary obtained at the upper level, as this may give some idea as to what the vocabulary in Grade 9 might be. However, the lack of proportional sampling in Grades 1 and 2 yielded an extremely large number of different words for each grade—over 5000.

USES OF THE WORD LIST

It is fairly certain that the number of different words in this study is more than is needed for a basic or major vocabulary for the average group of children in each grade—say the middle 80 to 90 percent. Since books are written for this average group, the use of this vocabulary should be emphasized for this purpose. It is again repeated that the writer does not suggest that the list be used as a *total* vocabulary of learning for the elementary school, but only as the *basic, general,* or *major* vocabulary. It seems reasonable to conclude from the data given and the frequencies of the words that this vocabulary should furnish much more than 90 percent of the words for Grade 8 and perhaps more than 98 percent of the words for Grade 1—with the percentages for the other grades falling below these limits. Such percentages would allow more than enough words per hundred running words of written materials for additional words from subject matter of varying kinds of interests, degrees of technicality, and social changes, even total war. When the vocabulary of the present study is used for each grade in some percentage as suggested here, the vocabulary load will not be too heavy. Neither will the use of this list tend to produce a static writing vocabulary, because many more words with known measures of usefulness are given than are ordinarily used in any grades except possibly the two highest.

A distinctive contribution of this study for use of the writer and student of children's words is the frequency of each word beyond the first thousand. Rankings from several other published counts of the first 100 or even the first 500 most frequently used words by children would probably be fairly consistent, but rankings of the second 500 by each grade would not be in high agreement. Knowledge of words beyond these low frequencies is scarce and almost unattainable, and rankings disagree sharply. Beyond a simple beginning and sustaining vocabulary of very common words, these rarer words should be of real value to any writer. Definiteness of knowledge about each word in this list varies of course with the frequency of occurrence; but even words of three frequency carry *just that much more information about their use than no count or a writer's estimate.* This is true of words of one frequency. Several writers have suggested that even words of one frequency should be published.

Writers of books from the third grade on seldom give any information concerning vocabularies, because little is known. However, lists and explanations of the vocabularies of pre-primers, primers, and first-grade readers are often given. But the problem of vocabulary knowledge above these levels is just as important. The large number of words given in this list beyond the first few thousand should be a useful vocabulary for the middle and advanced grades. Besides, the words of lower frequencies are of some value, because for each of these we have some knowledge of occurrence.

Perhaps writers should list, in basic readers and basic texts, at least all words with a frequency of three or less in this study and all words not listed. Page locations should be given so that teachers may assign these rarer or harder words for study in order to lessen reading difficulty. This list would contain important technical terms and give some measure of vocabulary load occasioned by these words. It would be a "study" list of great value to pupils.

The general method of using this list would follow the plan described by Buckingham and Dolch (1936); that is, one first decides how many words would be considered a word load at the lowest grade level in which the writing is accomplished. Then a definition as to what constitutes a distinct word must be decided. Certain derived forms—as *cats*, *dogs*, and *chairs*—at even lower levels may not be counted as different words from the roots. But in lower grades forms ending in *ing*, *er*, or *est* would be counted as separate words.

A factor that would help the writer make estimates of the number of roots, or lexicographical forms, to count from the inflectional forms given here is the fact that the ratio for the words given in this list to the root form is 1.68; that is, for each root form there are 1.68 derived forms. Obviously, the most useful ones only should be counted. Thorndike (1941) has studied the frequency of these derived forms taken from his list of 20,000 most frequently used words. Counting every derived form listed by Thorndike which contributes to 100 or more of these words, we find that there are over thirty-five. Only these derived forms are counted in the above ratio.

After this decision, the most frequently used words, in terms of raw frequencies, would be used, and/or some words of a rarer frequency in the next higher grade, and/or some words of a higher frequency in the next higher grade. As writings are done at each successively higher grade, high-frequency words not already used would have first preference, and so on through the grades. As progress is made from grade to grade the decision as to whether or not roots and derived forms would be counted or not counted for certain words must be made. The use of words in different subjects would vary. In the same grade the number of words presented in spelling is not as great as that presented in reading; and in reading a word may have different meanings, but in spelling it has only one form. However, derived forms in the lower grades in spelling might offer considerable difficulty. Thus selection depends on many other unknown but measurable factors and many factors of philosophy or opinions about which we have no measurable knowledge. Even the number of words for each grade in spelling is not a number agreed upon by authors, although there is a fairly close agreement as to the number of words to be included in a basal spelling list. Though there are still many unknowns concerning vocabulary problems, the data on frequency of words for each grade and all grades in this study give a basis for decisions by writers never before available.

There is a practical use of the word lists in writing not only textbooks but also stories, pupils' magazines, and reference books. Certainly many of these fields need additional knowledge of word difficulty or placement, as their grading is usually not so carefully done as in textbooks. Writers in these fields are not so close to the daily use of words by children as those who teach and write textbooks. In the field of educational and mental measurements the data in this study should be invaluable.

VARIATIONS IN OCCURRENCE OF WORDS

Although the rules of counting were closely followed, certain exceptions of slang widely used by children—and perhaps adults in the vernacular speech of the street and county—and certain forms of slang and provincialism not uniformly listed in standard dictionaries were recorded. In the complete list these words are all indicated with accompanying footnotes.

The "life histories" of the use of words, as shown by their frequencies of occurrence in different grades, present many interesting variations.

Some words that are rare for the lower grades become much commoner for the higher grades. A few words are rather common in the lower grades and become much rarer for children in the higher grades. Many words remain constant in frequency from grade to grade and probably on into adulthood.

But there are other variations not expected by one unacquainted with sampling thousands of different words from thousands of compositions on many different topics. First, there are certain omissions of frequencies in some grades for certain words; and second, there are irregular variations of frequencies of some words from grade to grade. These are the result of certain shortcomings in an apparently rich sampling dealing with many thousands of running words (6,012,359) in thousands of writings covering hundreds of topics. These gaps could be filled in only by sampling many times the number of writings used in this study. Irregular variations in frequency of occurrence of words from grade to grade are also a resultant of sampling, but many variations are due to differences in the use of words by children as they grow from grade to grade and change interests and topics about which they write. The 145 fewer words in Grade 6 than in Grade 5 from a slightly larger sampling (18,279) is another illustration of uneven sampling.

Many readers may have preconceived ideas as to which words are common and which are rare. This list may present many disagreements with these ideas. The only answer is that the frequencies here are actual counts, and, as in other well-established comparisons between counts and notions, the counts must be accepted as the nearest approach to facts.

Every effort was made in gathering samples of children's writing to obtain a broad sampling by asking for every kind of writing. However, it is obvious that a child in one school may write on a topic common to his immediate interests (as in the use of the word *operetta*) that is strange to the majority of children in the country and thus supply the final list with rare words. But even this is important. It shows what a wide range of words may be used by children. That a word has been used with some degree of understanding (as far as judgment can determine) by a child in the elementary school is a fact worth knowing. Finding a number of such words of three or more frequency is a strong indication, as pointed out earlier, that almost any word might be used by children if its meaning is understood and if it comes within the range of the subject of writing. It raises questions as to what factors affect intrinsic difficulty for certain children. It is definitely consistent with the psychology of individual differences and the common scientific observation that ranges objectively determined are almost always wider than those subjectively estimated. Certainly, from previous word lists, few students of children's vocabulary would have predicted the finding of as many as 25,632 different words or 14,571 words occurring with a frequency of three or more in any one grade.

HOW LARGE IS CHILDREN'S VOCABULARY?[1]

Mary Katherine Smith

[Without doubt this study is the most controversial current investigation of children's vocabulary. Mary Katherine Smith's research was completed under the direction of the late R. H. Seashore of Northwestern University. The study seemed to indicate a general vocabulary of children much larger than previous estimates. Seashore's own interpretation of the study is included as a postscript.]

PROCEDURE

The *English Recognition Vocabulary Test* by Seashore and Eckerson [2] was given to pupils from first grade through high school in two schools [3] and through the first eight grades in a third school.[4]

The Seashore-Eckerson test was constructed from a sampling of Funk and Wagnalls' *New Standard Dictionary of the English Language*, two-volume edition of 1937. The test includes "basic" words, which in the dictionary are printed in heavy type as separate entries, and "derived" words, which are compound terms or words formed from the basic word printed in medium type and usually indented under the basic word. Neither additional meanings for a word nor variant spellings are counted as separate words, but the same stem used in different parts of speech, when listed separately, and compound terms are counted as separate words.

There are three parts to this test. The first part consists of 173 multiple-choice items made up of basic general terms, arranged in approximate order of difficulty. The second part contains 158 words which are either proper nouns or rare words. The third part has 46 "derived terms," also arranged in order of difficulty. For part three as well as in part two the subject must write out the meaning of the words. Since relatively few words are ordinarily known in parts two and three of the test, this written portion of the test is rather brief.

For work with children, and especially investigating the absolute size of vocabulary, it is necessary to use the test without time limits, as a power test. By "absolute" we mean the total number of words in one's vocabulary as estimated from a representative sampling of all the words to be found in the dictionary.

[1] Adapted and abridged from Mary Katherine Smith, "Measurement of the Size of General English Vocabulary Through the Elementary Grades and High School," *Genetic Psychology Monographs* (1941), 24:311–345.

[2] Published by the authors, Evanston, Illinois.

[3] New Concord, Ohio, and Northbrook, Illinois.

[4] Niles Center, Illinois.

In order to measure absolute size of vocabulary, the method of testing must be adapted to the purpose at hand, which is to ascertain *for how many of the words in the test-sampling the child knows some correct meaning.* It would be relatively easy to adopt one criterion of knowledge and to measure the children's performance upon the vocabulary test in accordance with that criterion and thus secure rankings in vocabulary ability. However, in measuring absolute size of vocabulary we do not want mere ranking; we desire an adaptable measuring method which will allow the child to show what he knows about the test. This means the eliminating as far as possible of the influence of such factors as the child's ability to read and to spell, because we are interested only in measuring the number of words for which the child has some effective knowledge and not in his expression of that meaning.

Preliminary testing indicated that a combination of several criteria of knowledge would best accomplish this purpose, especially in testing at the lower elementary levels. In fact, there is an increasing stringency of the criteria of knowledge of a word with increase in the chronological age of the subject. This difference in criteria at the two age levels cannot be equated or legitimately ruled out except through individual testing throughout the grade range, because children simply do improve in both the quality and the quantity of words known. It was our purpose to discover those methods of testing at the different grade levels which would give the most accurate picture of the growth of vocabulary.

Preliminary tryouts showed that there were three main administrative groups into which the subjects fell: (1) early elementary, Grades 1, 2, and 3, requiring individual, oral testing; (2) middle elementary, Grades 4, 5, and 6, requiring aid in reading; (3) late elementary and high school, requiring only opening directions and occasional supervision and aid in reading. However, the change from one method to another in testing different grade levels is gradual and adaptations for exceptional individuals must be made at all levels.

In late elementary and high schools the test was administered to groups of from twenty-five to forty students. The examiner always introduced the work by telling the students that the test was part of a study which was for the purpose of finding out how many words high-school and grade-school people knew. They were assured that the results of the test would have no bearing on their school grades. They were told the test was one which could be used from first grade through college; that, accordingly, it began with easy words and gradually became harder. They were cautioned against carelessness on the easy words and encouraged to guess on any words which seemed at all familiar.

The first part of the test was scored on the basis of the number of words which the pupil attempted to define. From the number attempted were subtracted the errors corrected for guessing, and the resulting score was multiplied by a constant which gave the basic number of words known. Scores on parts two and three were the number of words correctly defined multiplied by constants. In scoring parts two and three credit was given only for definitions which indicated the meaning of a compound term *as a whole* and not definitions of the separate parts. Half-credits were used liberally. The sum of these three scores represented the total vocabulary.

For parts two and three the children in Grades 5 and 6 were requested to write the meanings of the words as in the upper grades.

In Grade 4 additional precautions were taken. Only four to six children were tested at a time on part one, in the manner described. And for parts two and three, each child was taken individually. The examiner gave the child an unmarked test booklet and then asked the child to define the words on parts three and two. The examiner wrote the child's reply as he gave it, encouraged him to attempt all the items he could, and asked whatever questions were necessary to clear up ambiguous replies.

In addition, the children were told that some of the words in part one had two meanings and that for some of them the examiner wanted examples. The examiner then asked the child to give examples, to use in sentences, and to define in his own words, and in some cases to give additional meanings for those words which the child had marked incorrectly, but which most third-grade pupils could define. Similar follow-up questioning was used with certain fifth- and sixth-graders who had missed words which children in the first three grades answered correctly.

In Grades 1, 2, and 3 the children were tested individually. The examiner asked the child to define the word. If the child could not reply at once or if he did not make his meaning clear, the examiner read the choice words. Preliminary tryouts showed that these four alternate responses if read in a series made too great an amount of material for the child's memory span. The younger child could not comprehend such a complicated question. For this reason the alternate responses were phrased in separate short questions which repeated the test word with each alternate response. These could be read one right after the other without exceeding the child's memory span. The questions which were used by the examiner were prepared in a manual and kept standard for each child.

In some instances the child's initial response to the word alone was incorrect, but when the alternate responses were presented he corrected his first response and chose the correct answer. In this case he was given full credit for the word, allowing of course for chance.

The child sometimes gave stereotyped answers to the alternative responses on the basis of position cues; that is, he would always choose the last of the four alternative responses or the first, without regard to their meaning. In such a case or if the child did not respond to the multiple-choice question at all, he was asked to describe the object in his own way or to tell something about it, or to use the word in a sentence and then to explain his sentence. If his reply to such questions was correct the choice of an incorrect alternative response was disregarded and he was given credit for that word.

When all other questions failed, leading questions were asked and only half-credit was given for correct replies to such questions.

For all of the words, any correct meaning which the child could give was credited. For some words the child might choose the wrong alternative responses or say that he did not know the word and yet be able to define the word correctly in terms of another meaning, in which case he was given full credit. For example, the child might not know "poker" as a game but might know it as a fire-tool.

RESULTS AND DISCUSSIONS

Before examining quantitative differences it is well to remember that the qualitative criteria of knowledge become increasingly stringent with progress through the grades and that to this extent the scores are not strictly comparable. However, one would scarcely expect the quality of meanings to be the same at widely different ages, and no statistical allowances would seem to be called for. It is simply an observed fact that vocabulary grows both qualitatively and quantitatively.

The number of pupils tested were: 44 in first grade, 40 in second, 59 in third, 73 in fourth, 61 in fifth, 66 in sixth, 69 in seventh, 71 in eighth, 114 in ninth, 111 in tenth, 95 in eleventh, and 64 in twelfth; making a total of 867 pupils tested.

The average size of vocabulary whether analyzed for basic words alone or by a total score including derived words is numbered in the tens of thousands. When we give the child an opportunity to show what he knows about an adequate sampling of words and avoid restricting his performance by inadequate testing methods or by a sampling which imposes an artificial ceiling, the child gives evidence of knowing a great many more words than we have hitherto estimated that he knew. Absolute size of vocabulary throughout the grade distribution greatly exceeds past estimates.

One of the striking characteristics of these distributions is the variability in scores within one grade. The range of individual differences in raw scores, especially for the total vocabulary, is very great.

There is much overlapping of scores from one grade to another. The overlapping of basic vocabulary scores is so great that only Grades 1 and 2 are completely outside the total range of individual differences in Grade 12. This is true only if the grades are compared within any one school system. Comparing all the schools together there is overlapping of even Grades 1 and 12. Within any one school system the highest first- and second-graders knew more basic words than did the poorest student in every other grade level up to and including the eleventh grade! In the scores for total vocabulary the overlapping is as great. The twelfth grade's lowest score exceeds the highest scores in only first and second grades in the Northbrook school, while first and twelfth grades overlap in the New Concord school. However, in the Niles Center School the highest first-grader does not equal the lowest eighth-grader in total vocabulary scores although the two grades overlap in basic scores; such fluctuations are, of course, greatly influenced by a few extreme scores.

This extreme overlapping is reduced somewhat when we compare quartiles rather than total ranges. In scores on basic vocabulary, Q_1 of the high-school seniors exceeds Q_3 of the first six grades, while Q_1 of the eighth grade exceeds Q_3 of the first three grades. It is much the same for total vocabulary; Q_1 of the eighth grade exceeds Q_3 of only the first two grades, while Q_1 of the high-school seniors is higher than Q_3 of the seventh grade in the New Concord and of the sixth grade in the Northbrook school. *It seems we have underestimated the ability of our better students and overestimated the ability of the poorer students all through the school.* There is a progressive growth in the average size of vocabulary from grade to grade although the rate of increase is not very regular.

In the two schools New Concord and Niles Center, the mean for the fifth grade fell below the mean for the fourth grade. This is not true of the fourth- and fifth-grade scores of the Northbrook school, although there too, the difference in the two means is not as great as the difference in the means of most other two adjacent grades. There may be several reasons for this discrepancy.

One obvious explanation would be a

difference in the ability of the children. At Northbrook and Niles Center schools the two grades were given the Kuhlmann-Anderson group test, and the mean IQ scores for both grades were slightly over 100. Likewise the Stanford Achievement Test scores from the Niles Center school show the fourth and fifth grades both to be above their grade norms, the fifth a little more so than the fourth. For these two schools at least there is apparently no difference in the general intellectual ability of the children. At New Concord no intelligence or achievement scores were available, although the fifth grade contained many more repeaters than the fourth did, and it was the feeling of the principal of the school that the fourth grade was a superior group for that school.

Another explanation may be in the change of the method of administration of the test at the fifth-grade level. The fourth grade was allowed to give definitions for the words in parts two and three orally, with the examiner recording their answers. From fifth grade on the children were asked to write out the meanings of the words. There are two disadvantages to having the children write out the definitions. In the first place, the children are not facile enough in spelling and general written expression to be able to write all they know or to make their definitions exact and clear. The duller child at the fifth- and sixth-grade levels may turn in a paper with only two sketchy attempts at definition on it. If this same pupil is taken individually and asked to give oral explanations for the words he may succeed in defining five or six of the terms; he is certain to be better than his written work indicated.

In the second place, it requires much encouragement from the examiner to persuade some of the children to attempt more than one or two of the words. Some of the children were so greatly impressed by the number of unfamiliar and difficult words that they gave up on the lists as a whole and failed to attempt the ones they did know. Particularly if the student was growing at all tired toward the end of the test, it was easy for him to overlook words for which he could give at least a partial meaning when questioned specifically on those words.

Table 1 presents the proportion of derived terms in the total vocabulary. There is a gradual increase in this proportion from first grade to twelfth. The older children not only know more words but are better able to handle words in general.

It is apparent that the three schools tested in this study, on the elementary grade level at least, are not equal. The

TABLE 1. Percentage of Derived Words in Total Vocabulary at the Different Grade Levels

School Grade	Percent	School Grade	Percent
1	29	7	37
2	33	8	35
3	36	9	37
4	44	10	38
5	34	11	40
6	36	12	41

three communities are of about equal size, ranging from a population of a little over 1000 at New Concord and Northbrook to 5000 at Niles Center. There were greater differences in the size of the surrounding communities and in the occupations of the parents than in the size of the school communities themselves. At New Concord there are no great cities nearer than Cleveland, Ohio, and Wheeling, West Virginia, which are respectively 100 miles and 60 miles away. City life and even town life do not affect many of these children very much. Children at Northbrook and Niles Center, on the other hand, live on lines of direct transportation to the city of Chicago and, at Niles Center particularly, are in contact with the city frequently. The parents of the children in the New Concord school include some professional men as the town is a college community, but the greater part of the children in the early elementary grades come from farm homes. The parents of the children at Northbrook are also farmers, artisans, and sub-professional men to a great extent. Niles Center is more of a residential suburb for the city, and a good many of the parents commute to Chicago for their work.

Thus the differences in the scores of the three schools may be due to differences in the cultural background of the pupils. These differences disappear at the upper grade levels. There the two schools involved sample about the same type of population, with the Northbrook High School students still having the advantage in the amount of contact with city life. It is not claimed that these three schools represent a normal sampling of American schools, but there is nothing to indicate that they are in any way atypical. Consequently it seems justifiable to average the scores at each grade level from all three schools.

The mean and quartile scores from

the three schools combined were plotted. Alongside these obtained means and quartiles were plotted smooth curves, representing the score for each grade averaged with the two adjacent grades; e.g., the score at Grade 2 on this curve represents the average of scores for Grades 1, 2, and 3. Using these two curves as a guide, another set of curves has been drawn, fitted by inspection, and shown in Fig. 1 and Fig. 2. Tenta-

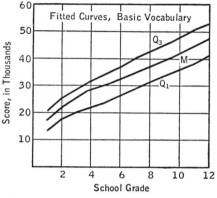

Fig. 1.

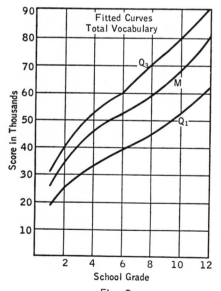

Fig. 2.

tive grade norms should be read from these fitted curves.

A child's score may be interpreted either in terms of the variability within his school grade or in terms of the averages of grades above or below his own.

For example, the score of a fourth-grader may be interpreted to mean that he ranks in the upper fourth of his class or that he has a vocabulary which is equal to the size of the average in the fifth grade.

POSTSCRIPT

R. H. Seashore

[The foregoing study was directed by the late R. H. Seashore of Northwestern University. In the April, 1949, issue of *Elementary English*, Dr. Seashore replied to a series of questions about the Smith study posed by J. C. Seegers of Temple University. Since these questions and answers amplify the findings of the Smith study, they are reproduced here in abridged form.]

ON TYPES OF DEFINITION

1. What kind of definition is considered satisfactory? Why should there be no distinction? In Binet testing the quality of the definition is quite important. If we do not consider quality of definition we may formulate very glib assumptions.

In order to measure size of vocabulary it is necessary to set up a minimal criterion of "knowing a word." It is recognized by most investigators that an individual usually enriches his knowledge of a word, as he grows older, (a) by being able to recognize additional instances of the same initial meaning (generalization), (b) by learning additional meanings of the same word, and (c) by learning finer differentiations among similar words. In our vocabulary studies the aim has constantly been to define our

experimental concepts, e.g., "knowing a word," in accordance with everyday usage insofar as possible. Thus we have distinguished "basic" from "derived" terms because many people believe that only basic words should be considered separate units. However, we have also measured derived words separately so that we could report these too, and have given our figures separately for basic words and derived words, as well as for total vocabularies, so that each reader could select the figures in which he is interested.

In the study by Lovell,[1] it was shown that individuals who made the highest scores on the Seashore-Eckerson recognition vocabulary test, i.e., who knew

[1] G. D. Lovell, "Interrelations of Vocabulary Skills: Commonest Versus Multiple Meanings," *Journal of Educational Psychology* (1941), 32:67–72.

the largest number of words by at least a single meaning, also tended to know proportionately larger numbers of additional meanings of these same words. Although size of vocabulary and richness of meaning for the separate terms are separate factors which may develop at different rates, Lovell showed they are nevertheless closely related by the time a student reaches college. Furthermore, a study by Olson [2] showed that school children who scored high on the Seashore-Eckerson recognition vocabulary test for knowledge of at least a single meaning of a word also tended to score proportionately high on a test of *diction*, in which they were to select from a list of five to ten approximate synonyms the one word which would give the most appropriate connotation for a blank in a sentence. In addition these students with large vocabularies tended to score high on the avoidance of *common errors* in the choice of words often confused in everyday usage.

In summary, we agree that the quality of a definition is important, but when we have measured this "richness of meaning" factor among adults, we have found it to be closely related to size of vocabulary in terms of at least minimal knowledge of words. In no way do our experimental results indicate that size of vocabulary is ordinarily achieved at the expense of richness or quality of meaning.

2. The claim is that depth of understanding and simple recognition are closely related.[3] Does this apply to young children also? If not, why not? Is not the test equally applicable at all ages? If not in this one particular, how can we assume applicability in any particular?

The claim is correct but refers only to college students because, to my knowledge, no experiments similar to Lovell's have ever been tried at earlier age levels. The experiment presumably could be tried at least in the middle primary grades, but it would be the writer's guess that the youngest school children rarely know more than a single meaning of many words.

The Seashore-Eckerson test has been successfully administered orally by M. K. Smith [4] to even first-grade children as a basis for estimating vocabulary size. Furthermore, Mandell [5] has constructed a pictorial form of the easier basic words on the test which is suitable for children from age four and on up to the third grade. In another experiment, by Fox, the verbal form of the Seashore-Eckerson test has been used for people in their seventies. These uses demonstrate its applicability over a very wide age range.

3. The average child at end of first grade has only primer reading ability. Knowledge of words as measured by Seashore's test and reading ability are quite different. Assuming that many first-graders do have 35,000-word vocabularies, does that mean they should be reading that many words?

If, as stated, the average child at the end of first grade has only primer reading ability, it may be due to our failure to provide earlier and additional oppor-

[2] Anne Westrom Olson, "The Measurement and Analysis of Individual Differences in Fine Discriminations of Word Meanings," unpublished master's thesis, Northwestern University, 1941.

[3] Charles C. Fries and A. A. Traver, *English Word Lists*, American Council on Education, Washington, 1940.

[4] Mary Katherine Smith, "Measurement of the Size of General English Vocabulary Through the Elementary Grades and High School," *Genetic Psychology Monographs* (1941), 24:311–345.

[5] Florence Mandell, "The Preliminary Standardization Evaluation of a Pictorial Vocabulary Test for Young Children," unpublished master's thesis, Northwestern University, May, 1947.

tunities for wider reading, and to make it interesting to the child to try additional materials. Certainly some first-grade children do read more than primers even now.

Auditory recognition knowledge of words as measured by the Seashore-Eckerson test is indeed quite different from reading knowledge of these words at the level of the first grade, though M. K. Smith's study indicates that children's reading vocabularies are large enough by about the seventh grade so that they rarely have to have words pronounced for them on the test. Evidently the discrepancy between auditory and reading recognition of words decreases quite rapidly during these early grade-school years, even though our formal reading programs are often intentionally restricted in the number of new words introduced each year. Olson's experiment on the enrichment of reading opportunity for fifth-graders and a parallel experiment on the group construction of a pictorial dictionary for new words indicate that it is possible to greatly accelerate the growth of vocabulary by such motivational and training devices during even a single year.

ON STATISTICAL PROCEDURE

1. Is it assumed that the use of the unabridged dictionary insures knowledge of technical terms?

The unabridged dictionary gives a very considerable sampling of technical terms for nearly every special field of human knowledge, so that everyone is likely to have a chance to exhibit some knowledge of his special fields of interest. It is true, however, that if we could also sample technical dictionaries and eliminate the overlapping with general dictionaries, the estimated sizes of individual's vocabularies should be still larger. Samples from a dictionary of

slang terms did add appreciable numbers of words, and the slang vocabularies were *positively*, not negatively, correlated with the size of general English vocabularies. Parallel studies by Ryden showed that American students who had never studied French or Latin nevertheless knew several thousand French words, which is not too remarkable considering the number of cognate and similar forms in English and French.

2. Is it safe to assume a one-to-one relationship between the .002 sample and the whole? Has straight-line relationship been determined?

As mentioned previously, the four samples studied by Annen did show equivalent estimated sizes of English basic vocabulary terms. The Seashore-Eckerson test showed an average variation of plus or minus 3 percent when scores on odd-numbered items were compared with those on even-numbered items on the test. The principle of representative sampling of a total group of phenomena (in this case all of the words in the dictionary) is a fundamental procedure of all scientific experimentation. Representativeness of the *kinds* and *proportions of kinds* of words in a sample is even more important than the size of the sample, and this was demonstrated by two findings, (a) the proportions of parts of speech in our samples (see later questions on this point) and (b) the similarities in average difficulties of Annen's four samples of a dictionary, which employed methods similar to ours.

A one-to-one relationship between our test sample and the whole dictionary implies perfect measurement, which we have never claimed. The significant thing in vocabulary research is not merely that we have a 3 percent probable error of measurement for one-half of the Seashore-Eckerson test but that the general order of sizes of vocabularies estimated in this way are usually at least ten times as large as previous estimates based upon measures which fail to give an individual an opportunity to show a knowledge of all (or nearly all) of the words which he is likely to know. The 3 percent error of measurement on our test certainly does not greatly limit the general significance of our findings as to the size of vocabularies.

3. Is a .002 sample adequate? A first-grader could attain reported scores on the basis of thirty to forty words. Is that enough?

Mandell's study on the pictorial form of the Seashore-Eckerson test showed a reliability coefficient of .90 for ages four to eleven, with mean scores similar to those of M. K. Smith. Again, note that the significant finding is the general order of size of these estimated vocabularies, which certainly cannot be explained by chance errors in a test having this degree of reliability for as narrow a range of talent. A longer sample would obviously be more accurate up to the point where fatigue or loss of interest interfered. However, these findings are definitely in keeping with the results on larger numbers of words with older children in successive primary and secondary grades (which indicate that scores obtained on the basis of a very small sample of the total dictionary are reliable indices of total vocabulary size).

4. Derivatives are more numerous, and as one grows older his command of derivatives increases. Why, then, do "we not count multiple meanings of the same basic word" in preparing our sample? Or, why are derivative terms practically ignored? It is stated: "We used .002 of all the basic words in the dictionary." Does knowledge of a basic word guarantee knowledge of derivatives? Is not that the assumption?

a. Derivatives, e.g., changes in parts of speech and compound terms with special meanings such as *Loyal Legion* (a Civil War veterans' organization), were measured separately and reported by Seashore and Eckerson for adults and by M. K. Smith for children.

b. Seashore and Eckerson did not count multiple meanings of the same basic word as separate words because this procedure would be misleading to most readers. Lovell, however, did measure the multiple meanings of these same words in case other readers wish to consider them as additional words known. Note that these separate interpretations give the reader the option of analyzing or combining measurements as he sees fit. Our own original interpretation was the more conservative procedure but was not misleading because it gave the bases used.

c. Knowledge of a basic word is correlated with, but does not guarantee, knowledge of derivatives. However, knowledge of derivatives is measured separately by the test.

5. If a word has many meanings, the chances of its inclusion in the sample are greatly enhanced. This obviously affects the sample, especially with reference to the inclusion of highly specific or technical words. Such words are much harder to define.

Since we took as our sample the third basic word (marginal entry in heavy type) from the top of the left-hand column of every eighth page of the F & W unabridged dictionary, I cannot see that the number of meanings listed for a word has any significance in possibly distorting our sample. If there is such a systematic sampling error, I should, of course, be greatly interested to have it demonstrated.

6. Does the method of sampling care for the fact that relatively more words begin with certain letters, fewer with others?

The above-described method of sampling employed by us in our test provides a number of words beginning with each letter of the alphabet which is proportionate to the entire number of words beginning with each alphabetical letter for the dictionary as a whole.

7. What proportion of those test words happen to be words of high frequency in terms of use?

This fact has not yet been determined, though it could be by simply looking up each word on our test in a frequency list such as Thorndike's most recent revision.

8. Nouns are easier; adverbs harder. What proportions of each are in the 331?

Seashore and Eckerson showed that a sample analysis of every hundredth page in the F & W unabridged dictionary gave the percentages of the various parts of speech which are listed in the left-hand column of Table 1. A similar analysis of the test list used in our vocabulary test (drawn from the same dictionary) is listed in the right-hand columns.

9. Suppose we use the Oxford dictionary instead of the F & W? Would we then arrive at even larger estimates?

Presumably the Oxford dictionary, containing many more words than the Funk and Wagnalls unabridged, would give the person being tested a still wider opportunity to show his knowledge of words. Note, however, that each increase

TABLE 1.   The Percentages of Parts of Speech of Basic Words in
Samples from the Dictionary

Parts of Speech	Twenty-Seven Pages at 100-Page Intervals		One Word Every Other Page (Our Large Sample)	
	Percent	Percent	Percent	Percent
Nouns	70		68	
Proper nouns		23		21
Common nouns		39		40
Abstract nouns		8		7
Pronouns	0		0	
Verbs	11		10	
Particles	18.2		22	
Adjectives		16		19
Adverbs		2		3
Prepositions		0.2		0
Conjunctions		0		0
Interjections	0.8			0
Totals	100		100	

in size of a dictionary usually includes the addition of words which have been judged by the editors of the smaller volume as likely to be used less frequently by readers because of being obsolete, provincial, technical, etc. However, our comparisons of various abridged volumes in a single series of dictionaries do not indicate that the editors have judged very accurately as to frequency of use, since first-grade children were found to know some words which were included only in the unabridged volume of the series.

Note again that our figures based on the F & W volume are more conservative than would be expected from one of the larger dictionaries. The F & W volume was chosen in the mid-thirties because it was new at that time, was completely alphabetical in word order (a slight advantage in sampling), and had various-sized abridgments which we (erroneously) thought might be useful in judging the difficulty of words used as multiple-choice answers in the recognition test.

10. Seashore reports correlations between preliminary form of the test as follows: (a) With speed of reading, .02 to .04; (b) With Otis advanced intelligence test, .49; (c) With reading comprehension in psychology, .6. What does this tell us about the significance of vocabulary as measured by the test? Would one not expect higher correlation? Does this mean that our ideas of the relationship are wrong, or does it reflect upon what is measured by the test?

a. Speed of reading has elsewhere been shown by Seashore, Stockford, and Swartz [6] to be almost totally unrelated either to reading comprehension or to size of vocabulary, although vocabulary and reading comprehension are closely correlated. These terms have been greatly confused by earlier writers, as explained in the above-mentioned article.

b. Scores on so-called "general intelligence" tests usually include sections on general information and on quantitative reasoning, etc., as well as various types of vocabulary tests. Since Thurstone has shown that so-called intelligence tests really consist of a variety of little-related factors called "primary mental abilities," it is not unusual to find that vocabulary does not correlate higher with a mixture of several such types of primary abilities.

c. About the only test which corre-

[6] R. H. Seashore, L. B. O. Stockford, and B. K. Swartz, "A Correlation Analysis of Factors in Speed of Reading Tests," *School and Society* (1937), *46*:187–192.

lates as closely with reading comprehension in psychological materials is a much longer (and hence more reliable) test such as the Ohio College entrance test, or a technical psychological vocabulary test. The reliabilities of both the measuring instruments limit the size of intercorrelations which may be obtained between them. When corrected for the effects of attenuation (unreliability of tests), the relationship is even higher than it appears to be from the uncorrected figures. A correlation of .6 between such tests is about as high as most statisticians would expect. There is no reason to believe that grades on objective reading examinations should depend exclusively on general vocabulary size, since other special abilities, e.g., information on a single field, may also be involved.

11. If children know so many words why did Rinsland, with 100,000 children, find only 25,632 different words used?

The question does not concern the reliability of the test, but rather what the test measures. Any specific type of "use" test tends to employ words appropriate to that type of use situation and is less likely to call for the use of other words which might appear if a different type of use situation were analyzed. Children acquire different vocabularies on trips, at the beach, on the playground, at a farm, in stores, etc., and the children would have to be tested in a variety of situations to find how many words they *could* use if necessary.

12. Does the test indicate the relative frequency of common words under different initial letters? Has the validity of the list been studied in comparison with longer lists?

a. The test could be so analyzed by comparing its terms with a frequency list such as the Thorndike revision, but I have not done so. It might be possible that high-frequency words tended to be distributed somewhat differently under different initial letters in comparison with all other words. However, high-frequency words are a small fraction of the total number of words in the dictionary and I do not see how this could seriously influence our findings.

b. The Seashore-Eckerson test is designed to be a representative sample of words in general from the unabridged dictionary. It was never intended to be a frequency list in itself.

13. Have correlations between the Seashore test, IQ, mental age, and reading been computed with children? Or between test results and vocabulary used in writing? Olson found moderate to close correlations between the S-E note test and intelligence test scores, achievement test scores, etc., of children.

I do not know of any experiment correlating the S-E test with children's vocabularies used in writing.

14. Why do all of the other studies vary so much from this one? Why did Serenius say that a test of 500 words was the minimum he would trust?

No method other than representative sampling from an unabridged dictionary can give as large an estimated vocabulary size for individuals, because no other method permits an individual to show all of the kinds of words which he may know. In the table given by Seashore and Eckerson [7] it is clearly shown that the larger the number of words in the dictionary from which the sample is taken, the greater will be the estimated size of vocabularies.

Any specific length of vocabulary test could be chosen, depending upon the size of probable error of measurement

[7] R. H. Seashore and Lois D. Eckerson, "The Measurement of Individual Differences in General English Vocabularies," *Journal of Educational Psychology* (January, 1940), 31:14–38.

which is permissible for the purpose at hand. Accuracy is purchased at the expense of time spent by the person being tested. The error of measurement of a test sample decreases in proportion to the *square root* of the number of words in the test. Serenius evidently decided that a particular probable error of measurement was desirable. Our error of 3 percent for ½-½ analysis of the Seashore-Eckerson test does not seem excessive to us.

15. If first-grade children know up to 42,000 words and there is an increase of 5000 words a year, what are those words which they know? It is freely admitted that *The Teacher's Word Book* does not list words according to difficulty. It is simply a listing of words as they were found in the sources stated. But it is also true that there is a high degree of community between that listing and ordinary use. The following words were selected almost at random from the latest edition, of 30,000 words:

From the sixth thousand: confederacy; degradation

From the seventh thousand: booty; dialect

From the ninth thousand: abdication; graduation; dialogue; vagrant

From the tenth thousand: saffron; sacrament; elemental

From the eleventh thousand: grovel; viceroy; bailiff; cater

From the thirteenth thousand: category; scrutinize; sacrilegious; qualm

From the fourteenth thousand: schismatic; waive; addiction; scullion

Would anyone who has worked with first-graders expect that the average first-grade child knows many—or any—of these? This list could be expanded very greatly with little difficulty. The question is: If children do not know these and similar words, what are the 24,000 words the average first-grader "knows," or the 40,000 plus which are alleged to be known by the top-ranking children in Grade 1?

a. The Thorndike-Lorge frequency list represents the commonest 30,000 words (*omitting* all less common words) found in a *restricted* sample of written materials drawn from a limited number of persons, ages, and socioeconomic groups, and dealing with a limited variety of situations. It showed what words these people did use in these situations, not what they could use if necessary, in these and still other situations.

b. The Seashore-Eckerson English Recognition Vocabulary Test employed by M. K. Smith in her study of children's vocabularies is a *systematic* and *representative* sampling of all the 167,-000 basic plus 204,000 derived terms in the F & W unabridged dictionary. Only such a sample as this can give a person full opportunity to show his knowledge of all of the words with which he has become acquainted or which he can analyze if new.

c. The T-L word list is thus a relatively small proportion of all the words in the dictionary, so there are plenty of other words to be learned.

d. The words which were most likely to be known by first-grade children on the S-E test are those near the beginning of the test, e.g.:

Basic Words

adhesive	cocoon	cheer
quick	chilling	weighty
loyal	mouse	creation
kill	percolator	falsehood
pulse	assure	winged
cowardly	constructive	reposeful
shout	devotion	centering
legal	gain	hearten
pen	lead	skill
clear	aged	ailment
	barking	

Derived Words
for mercy's sake
sea blue
gurgling
wingedly

e. As mentioned by Dr. Seegers, the frequency rating of T-L words is related to but not the same as the order of difficulty in which young children could learn them. Thus a child may not encounter a semi-legal term such as "waive" from the T-L list until he becomes an adult and becomes interested in court proceedings. On the other hand, he may easily learn terms such as "FM" (radio), "television," "convertible"(car) around his home and countless other terms from the many specialized experiences during travel to farms, cities, airports, museums, and from reading by parents and from radio and television. The T-L list combines under a single word a great many of the common variations in parts of speech. For this reason the Thorndike-Lorge vocabulary estimates would tend to be somewhat smaller than those in Seashore-Eckerson, which accepted common dictionary practice in distinguishing separate words.

In conclusion: The studies cited in this analysis raise serious questions as to the accuracy of several very widely held educational beliefs, e.g., (1) that the initial vocabularies of school children are very small, (2) that the rate of growth of their vocabularies is proportionately small and difficult to improve without pushing the children, and (3) that it is therefore necessary to carefully control the nature and number of new terms presented by texts and curricula at each grade level.

Would it not be equally fair to ask that readers who may still be skeptical of our newer findings should answer several questions about alternative beliefs?

1. What are the experimental evidences that children starting to school actually know only a few hundred or several thousand words and must have their book limited to a few hundred new words each year?

2. Since the newer estimates of vocabulary sizes and rates of growth are on the order of ten times as large as previously believed, what are the implications of these findings for continuing to control so strictly the nature and number of new words presented by texts and curricula at each grade level?

3. Even if children are apparently building vocabularies much faster than could be accounted for by present controlled vocabulary programs, what could they do if they were given a combination of enriched reading opportunities, more systematic methods of analyzing new words, and a systematic emphasis upon watching for the meanings, pronunciation, and spelling of all new words encountered in or out of school?

Certainly the informal experiments of Olson showing that the fourth, fifth, and sixth grades could double their annual rate of vocabulary growth should encourage us to analyze critically our old assumptions and to test empirically our new methods on enriching vocabulary development.

Chapter VIII

REMEDYING OUR WEAKNESSES

One of the very difficult problems to solve in reading instruction has been adjusting to the great differences of rate with which students progress. It has long been clear that for various reasons, in reading instruction as in other fields, students do not all reach the same level of achievement in the same length of time. An older solution to this problem was to retain a student at a given school grade until his achievement in reading reached the level considered adequate for that grade. In the days when compulsory school attendance into adolescence was not customary, retention caused many students to drop out of the school system. Thus, while the problem of spread in level of achievement has always been present, it used to be ": lved" in great part by dropping out those who fell well behind the others of their age group.

When students began to persist longer in school, because of the enforcement of attendance laws and for other reasons, retention proved less effective in reducing the spread in level of achievement. There is a tolerance level, soon reached, beyond which it is not feasible to keep a student with younger age groups. Nor did separation of these students into so-called "opportunity rooms" prove entirely satisfactory. Other schemes were tried, but, for the most part, school systems gravitated into what is usually called "social promotion," with students remaining with their own age groups regardless of level of achievement.

Such a scheme means, of course, that the greater the number of years the age group is kept intact, the larger the spread in level of achievement. School systems have permitted themselves some ambivalence in facing this spread realistically. On the one hand, by the way reading is actually taught, they have followed the practice of trying to overlook the existence of the spread. That is to say, everyone in the fifth grade is taught at what is regarded as approximately fifth-grade level. Of course, no one espouses this way of teaching in theory, but in practice it is certainly to be found. On the other hand, school systems have followed the practice of trying to meet every level of the spread within the same classroom. That is to say, everyone in the fifth grade is taught at what is regarded as first-grade level, or second grade, third grade, fourth grade, fifth grade, sixth grade, seventh grade, eighth grade, and so on, depending upon what spread is actually present. This way of teaching is often espoused in theory but in fact it is extremely difficult to practice.

To state the ambivalence in this manner is, of course, to polarize the differences. Actually school systems vary on a continuum from one position to the other. Indeed, within school systems or even within individual school buildings, practice in teaching reading could be located at different positions on the continuum.

But whatever position schools and school systems in fact do occupy, the spread in level of achievement is not adequately handled in regular classroom instruction. Hence interest in "remedial" reading provisions continues to grow. There have been semantic difficulties in securing an appropriate name for services to those students who require diagnosis and instruction in reading beyond what it is feasible for a regular classroom teacher to provide. If a student is progressing at what appears from competent appraisal to be his capacity, and yet is considerably below the average level of achievement of his age group, should he be called a "remedial" reading case? The instruction to be offered in such instance would certainly not be qualitatively different from "developmental" or regular reading instruction, albeit more individualized. If a student is *not* progressing at what appears from competent appraisal to be his capacity, and is considerably below the average level of achievement of his age group, is he more properly called a "remedial" reading case? The instruction to be offered in such instance could certainly be qualitatively different from "developmental" or regular reading instruction, depending upon what kind of factors seem to interfere with the exercise of capacity.

In any event, services to students considerably below the average level of achievement of their age groups in reading, under whatever name, are obviously here to stay. The real research questions to be answered are: What kind of reading disabilities exist, what causes these disabilities, what kind of services are appropriate for these disabilities, and how should such services be provided? The research evidence presented in this chapter by no means answers all of these proper queries. But the directions in which efforts are now being extended are indicated.

KINAESTHETIC METHODS FOR HELPING NONREADERS [1]

Grace M. Fernald and Helen Keller

[Grace M. Fernald was the principal proponent of using kinaesthetic methods in attacking reading difficulties. For many years in the Reading Clinic at the University of California at Los Angeles she demonstrated what she regarded as a relatively untried avenue of remediation. This report with Helen Keller represents an early date in her clinical studies but indicates clearly her point of view and methods of treatment.]

The cases reported in this section are all those of children of normal mentality who have failed to learn to read after three or more years in the public schools. In all cases but one the vision was normal. The method described here was used only after the child had been given several weeks of individual instruction by recognized methods and had failed to make any improvement.

Many children who have been brought to us as nonreaders learned to read quite easily by ordinary methods when they were given individual instruction and proper motivation; others proved to be mentally deficient. In five years we have found only seven cases of actual nonreaders, even though children have been brought to us from all parts of the state. In all seven cases the presumption of mental deficiency had been made as the explanation of the reading failure. In all but one case, however, the intelligence quotient was found to be at least 100 by the Stanford Revision.

METHOD

1. *Learning First Words.* The child was asked to tell some word he would like to learn. The word was written in large script on the blackboard or with crayola on cardboard. The child looked at the word, saying it over to himself and tracing it if he wished to do so. The tracing was done with the first two fingers of the right hand (or of the left hand if the child was left-handed) resting on the copy. It was never done in the air or with pencil. When the child was sure he knew the word, the copy was erased and he attempted to write the word, *saying the syllables to himself* as he wrote them. If he was unable to write the word correctly, the entire process was repeated until the word could be written without the copy. At no stage of the performance was he allowed to copy the word. After a few words had been learned in this way, he was shown

[1] Adapted and abridged from Grace M. Fernald and Helen Keller, "The Effect of Kinaesthetic Factors in the Development of Word Recognition in the Case of Non-Readers," *Journal of Educational Research* (1921), 4:355–377.

the word in print as well as in script. The next day he was shown the word in print only. If he failed to recognize it, it was written for him. If he still failed to recognize it, it was written for him. If he still failed to recognize it, it was retaught as on the first presentation.

2. *Spontaneous Sentences.* After the first few days the child began to ask for sentences instead of words. A sentence was then written and he learned the words comprising it, finally writing the entire sentence as many times as he wished—always from memory, never from copy.

The sentences the child had requested were then printed on cardboard or typewritten. These sentences and others, made of the same words, were read by the child. The same words were repeated in different sentences from day to day.

3. *Words in Context or Story Selected by the Child.* As soon as the child was able to make out simple sentences, he was taken to the library and allowed to select a book. The first paragraphs read were worked over in the following manner. Before the reading, each word which had not already been learned was exposed through an adjustable slit in a piece of cardboard. If the child failed to read the word it was pronounced for him. He pronounced and then wrote the word (as before without looking at the copy). If he had difficulty in writing the word after seeing it in print, it was written for him and taught from the script as in the case of the first words.

4. *Appreciation of Phrases.* After the words in the new paragraph had been taken up in this manner, brief exposures of the words were given until the child was sure of them. When recognition was immediate for every word, the slit was adjusted to phrases, and

flash exposures of the various phrases were given. The exposures were never long enough to permit the phrases to be read word by word. As many successive exposures as were necessary for recognition were given. After the entire paragraph had been worked over in this way, the child was told to read the paragraph to himself and report what he had read.

5. *Silent Reading for Content.* As soon as possible the child was encouraged to read to himself. There was no difficulty in any of our cases in getting him to do this after his progress had gone into the fourth phase.

DESCRIPTION OF CASE— BOY (FRED)

Seven cases have been successfully treated to date. One of these is described in the following pages.

Age, 9–2; mental age (Stanford Revision), 9–3; IQ, 100. Vision: right, normal; left, two-thirds normal.

SCHOOL HISTORY

Fred attended the public schools in Riverside, California, where he entered the kindergarten at the age of five. He spent three years in the first grade. He entered the University Training School, September, 1920, and was placed in the second grade but made no progress during the first month. He was unable to read words of one syllable and consequently was too poor to be tested by any formal test. He was sent to the Psychology Department for a mental test with the definite suggestion that he be transferred to one of the public-school rooms for the mentally deficient. The child had so much the appearance of a mental defective that we were surprised at the results of the mental tests.

FIRST PHASE—LEARNING FIRST WORDS

Fred spent the morning learning to write the four words *will, you, am, boy,* all of which he had asked for. The words were taught one at a time, each being written by the teacher on the board. Fred said each word over and traced it with his fingers until he was sure he could write it. It was then erased, and he attempted to write it. If the first attempt was not successful, the entire process was repeated until the word was spelled correctly.

Fred succeeded in writing each of the words correctly in the course of the morning. In the afternoon he attempted to rewrite the same words with the following results: W (for *will*); Yo (for *you*); ow (for *am*); b (for *boy*). The words were retaught and then written correctly. He then asked for the word *I,* and wrote: *I am o boy.* He wrote this sentence with his left hand, then with his right. There is little difference in the performance with the two hands, but Fred says he likes the left hand better. He usually writes on paper with his left hand and on the board with his right.

October 7. He wrote correctly from memory the first four words which he had learned the previous day, then asked for *door* and *box.* After working for some time on these words, he asked for *open,* adding, "Then I'll learn *the* next and I can write *open the door.*" When the word *open* was written by the teacher, Fred said, "Erase it quick so I can write it." He next asked for the sentence *Open the box till the mouse jumps out.* The word *mouse* had to be presented four times before Fred could write it correctly. By "presented" is meant that the word was written by the teacher and traced by the pupil until the pupil felt sure he could write it.

For the next three weeks Fred went through an orgy of writing. He wrote blackboards full of words, then he began to write sentences, and finally he wrote the letter to his father that is shown below:

Dear Daddy
    I want you to come up sometime because I want you to give me $3.00
    I want to stay up here because I like this school
    I want mama to come up here and stay with me
    I send my love this is Fred's writing.
November 10 Write me a letter
                    Freddie

This letter is only one specimen of the spontaneous compositions with which the boy occupied himself by the hour. He was constantly asking for new words, which he learned and wrote from memory. For over a month after writing his first sentence, Fred seemed to care little about subject matter, so absorbed was he in mastering the mechanics of writing. He worked so constantly and so hard that it was necessary to force him to leave the room at recess and at the close of school. He looked up one day after working for two hours at new words and exclaimed, "You know I scarcely ever used to get promoted and now just look at all I am learning." As soon as we attempted to teach him new words without having him write them, his interest was lost. He would try to learn them by saying them over and looking at them but would soon become discouraged and would fail to recognize the words after repeated presentation. This attitude in the early stage of the experiment is particularly interesting, because at the present time (March, 1921) Fred no longer wishes to write unless he has something special to say, but is reading everything he can get hold of. He is as eager over making out new words without writing them as he ever was over the writing process.

Words for which Fred asked were written for him on the typewriter or were shown him in print after he had written them. Simple reading exercises were given, using the words he had written.

The printed word was first shown the boy and then written for him. He studied it on first presentation but he was not asked to write a word a second time unless he failed to recognize it on later presentations.

THIRD PHASE—WRITING THE WORD FROM MEMORY AFTER LOOKING AT THE PRINTED COPY AND HAVING THE WORD PRONOUNCED

Within six weeks after the experiment was started, it was never necessary for Fred to have the word written for him. He was able to look at printed words of several syllables, say them over to himself, and write them correctly from memory. On November 17 he wrote *disappointed*, *department*, *training*, and *university*, after seeing the words once in print. A week later he recognized all of these words without any hesitation, and without having seen them in the interval.

DEVELOPMENT OF PROJECTS IN CONNECTION WITH READING AND WRITING

November 17. Fred suddenly decided that he wanted to draw, and was allowed to do so as long as he wished. He drew a picture of a cannon and then of a house and garage with heating system. It was then suggested that he label his pictures, and this idea pleased him greatly. He learned to write the following seven words and used them as labels: *cannon, shells, pipe, steps, window, garage, furnace.*

November 18. He wrote correctly without presentation the following words which he had previously learned: *you, ride, bicycle, furnace, hide, pipes, rope, because, garage, cannon, want, Riverside, December, October, will, live.* He then wrote above the words on the blackboard, "These words are saved."

November 19. He was taken to the library and allowed to select two books: Lynde's *Physics in the Household* and a book on plumbing. From November 19 till December 6 Fred drew and labeled diagrams, finding the words in physics and plumbing books. He was still unable to recognize new words, after he had been told what they were, unless he wrote them. One writing even of very difficult words was usually all that was necessary for word recognition.

November 22. Fred read the following paragraph without being told any words except those enclosed in parentheses:

The cooler water in the radiator (being heavier) sinks from the radiator into the furnace (boiler) and (forces) the hot water from the (boiler) into the radiator. This hot water gives up its heat to the air in the room and (thus) cools (contracts) and becomes heavier. It then sinks back into the boiler and forces more hot water into the radiator.

This paragraph was read just one and a half months from the time when the boy could not read the simple sentence "I am a boy." He stumbled over a simple word like *thus*, which he had never written, but had no difficulty in reading any of the much harder words which he had written. He was told *thus* each time he failed to read it, but was quite unable to recognize it on later presentations until he had written it, after which he recognized it whenever it occurred.

December 6. Fred suddenly stopped drawing and labeling diagrams and began writing on the blackboard sentences which he would sometimes illustrate with pictures. These sentences and others containing the same words were then typewritten and given him to read. For example, the following sentences with a picture of a racing machine at the top of the sheet were written after a visit to the automobile machine shop.

A Racer

This is a fine automobile.
It has four wheels on it. They have tires and mud guards.
It has a steering gear, and a crank on the front.
It has a windshield. It has a radiator.
It is a Mack and it is a racer.
It runs awfully hard.
Gasoline runs the engine.
The radiator has water in it to cool the engine.
The engine has eight cylinders.
This machine has United States tires.
The engine is a fine one.
The fan helps keep the engine cool.
This machine can turn corners going very fast and it won't wreck.
                              December 13, 1920.

December 22. Fred began to ask for new words and to remember them without writing them. *December twenty-fourth-January fourth*—Christmas vacation.

FOURTH PHASE—ABILITY TO PRONOUNCE NEW WORDS IF THEY RESEMBLE WORDS ALREADY WRITTEN

January 25. Fred sounded out the word *mother*, then said it over several times. He was quite excited over being able to say the word without being told,

and began to attempt the same thing with other words.

February 4. He worked out, without writing or any help, the following words: *surprised, roar, fright, noise, thirsty, dirty, middle.* He had to be told *dreadful,* pronounced *toward* "towards" and *vines* "vi-nes." He read the fable of the Fox and the Lion to himself and told the story, giving every detail. He had never heard or read the story before.

March 3. Words were given to Fred from the pages of the third reader. The longer words on various pages were given out of context to see whether he could read them without having them pronounced. All the words were new to Fred so far as we know. He read all the words, mispronouncing only eight.

At the date of writing this paper (March, 1921) Fred's progress is so rapid that it is difficult to keep records. He takes library books home, reads to himself, and has to be told only such words as might trouble any child of his age. He has been in the regular third grade for two weeks and is having no difficulty with the work. If his progress continues at the present rate, he should be able to make up the one year necessary to put him in the grade appropriate to his chronological age.

SUMMARY OF CASE

In October, 1920, Fred could not read or write even monosyllabic words. He failed completely in all tests for reading, spelling, and phonics. His school report showed steady attendance with failure of promotion in the city schools of Riverside, California. It was taken for granted that he was mentally deficient until mental tests proved him normal.

At the beginning of the experiment

his progress was very slow. He seemed wholly dependent on tracing the words first learned and continued to trace for over two months. His development went through well-marked stages, with the transition from one stage to the next apparently quite sudden.

In March, 1921, five months after the experiment was started, he was reading and writing (spelling) well enough to go into the regular third grade. He was taking library books home to read to himself and could read any ordinary story and give its content.

GENERAL CONCLUSIONS

In all but one of the cases studied, progress seems to have taken place in four distinct phases, as follows:

LEARNING TO WRITE WORDS

In all cases the children were at first lacking in ability to write words as well as in ability to read. The development of ability to write words is very slow at first. It is necessary for the child either to trace or to articulate the word many times while looking at the written copy, and finally to articulate it as he writes it from memory. The need for tracing gradually disappears, but he continues indefinitely to articulate in learning to write a new word.

ASSOCIATING THE WRITTEN WITH THE PRINTED WORD

The child sees the word in print, has it written for him, and then writes it himself, often tracing difficult words before writing them. He soon reaches a point where he can generally recognize a word in print after he has written it. He must still have the word written for him before he is able to write it himself.

ABILITY TO WRITE A NEW WORD FROM MEMORY AFTER LOOKING AT THE PRINTED COPY AND REPEATING THE WORD TO HIMSELF

The word must, of course, be pronounced for him before he is able to say it to himself. He is still unable to recognize short, easy words on subsequent presentation if they are taught him in the usual way and if he does not write them. At this stage he will often write from twenty-five to fifty words a day. He rarely fails to recognize a word after he has once written it.

ABILITY TO PRONOUNCE NEW WORDS IF THEY RESEMBLE WORDS HE HAS ALREADY LEARNED

The end of this stage is normal ability to read. The progress at the end is so rapid that it is almost impossible to keep track of the child's development. He seems suddenly to read and is able to enter regular classes in all work involving reading. In the first three cases the children not only developed normal ability to read but became incessant readers.

EFFECT OF INTELLIGENCE ON METHOD AND LEARNING RATE

The method of learning was practically the same with cases of varying degrees of intelligence, except that there was no tendency to trace in the case of the two children with the highest intelligence quotients. In all cases the articulation and the writing of the word seemed essential for developing word recognition. The progress was much more rapid in the cases of better mentality than in those of lower mentality.

PERSISTENCE OF KINAESTHETIC FACTORS

Children who have to trace words in the early learning stages continue to make slight hand and arm movements in attempting to recall difficult words or to learn new words. All the children make marked movements of articulation during the process of learning a new word, even after reading has been well developed.

ACQUIRING SKILL IN PENMANSHIP AND PHONICS

Although there has been no drill in penmanship or in phonics, the children who trace words in their early learning stages write a clear, free hand; and all acquire incidentally a good working knowledge of phonics.

In all of our cases any digression which directed the child's attention from the word itself seemed to confuse him rather than to hasten the learning process. The introduction of phonics, formal penmanship drill, oral spelling, or even spoken directions during the writing of the word seemed to hamper the learning process.

INDIVIDUAL DIFFERENCES

The cases studied differed somewhat in the exact kinaesthetic content necessary for the development of word recognition, the difference being in the amount of hand and arm kinaesthetic experience necessary before the word was written. Case IV did not go through the first and second stages as described above. Although, in this case, the word was not traced before it was written and did not have to be presented in script, it was necessary for the child to write the word before he could recognize it.

GENERAL SIGNIFICANCE OF RESULTS

It may be well to note here that, although only extreme cases are reported in this paper, the results of certain experiments now under way seem to indicate that these general principles hold true in many cases in which the child simply had difficulty in learning to read. It seems that, at least in many of these cases, the progress will become normal if the proper kinaesthetic content is supplied.

THEORETICAL

Perhaps we can go no further in theory than to say that, in the specific cases studied, lip and hand kinaesthetic elements seem to be the essential link between the visual cue and the various associations which give it word meaning. In other words, it seems to be necessary for the child to develop a certain kinaesthetic background before he can appreciate the visual sensations for which the printed words form the stimulus. Even the associations between the spoken and the printed word seem not to be fixed without the kinaesthetic links.

The motor tendency is still obvious after the children become fluent readers. They seem far to outclass other children in the same grades in their ability to look at new words, say them to themselves, and write them. All of these children still make pronounced lip movements of saying the words (not the letters) when learning a new word, even after they have reached a point where they never trace a word or speak it aloud. The children who traced in the beginning tend to make arm and hand movements in learning a new word or attempting to recall a difficult one. They are hopelessly confused as soon as they attempt to spell orally or to write a new word without saying it to themselves.

It would seem that the methods of teaching reading have always neglected the kinaesthetic factors, except those which in no way express the word as written or printed. It has been taken for granted that, in the case of all children, the visual cue is adequate to arouse those associations which make this cue stand for word meaning.

WHY PUPILS FAIL IN READING [1]

Helen Mansfield Robinson

[The most widely sold popular writings on reading usually seize upon a single, simple method of instruction. All and sundry are assured that, were this method followed, all reading problems would disappear. As an added fillip, it may be implied that only crass conspiracy has kept the system from being used. Helen Robinson's study is, in effect, a reply to those who persist in merchandising elixirs.]

PROCEDURES

This study has three major divisions. First, a summary of previous studies was grouped under the following headings: (1) visual difficulties; (2) intellectual and maturational status; (3) neurological and dominance factors; (4) auditory, speech, and language factors; (5) physical difficulties; (6) emotional reactions, and (7) social and environmental conditions.

Second, thirty severely retarded readers were each examined by the following specialists: a social worker, a psychologist, a pediatrician, a neurologist, three ophthalmologists, a speech-correction specialist, an otolaryngologist, an endocrinologist, a reading specialist, and the investigator, who acted as psychologist and reading technician. The investigator summarized all the data concerning a child. A conference of all the specialists evaluated separate findings in the light of the total picture. Recommendations for treatment were prepared. An attempt was made to determine the significance of each factor as a cause of reading fail-

ure by providing therapy and measuring progress or estimating changes.

Third, an interpretation of the findings led to tentative conclusions and the statement of problems for further study.

SUMMARY OF PREVIOUS STUDIES

Many hypotheses and theories have been set forth to explain children's failure to learn to read adequately. No single cause has ever been isolated; and, as many investigators have concluded, an attempt to isolate single causes would probably be an oversimplification.

Visual anomalies have been related to reading failures by some research investigators and denied by others. However, most investigators agree that the visual anomaly should be considered in individual cases. Visual acuity, per se, was not believed to be related to reading success in the studies reviewed. Hyperopia, hyperopic astigmatism, binocular incoördination, inadequate visual fields,

[1] Adapted and abridged from Helen Mansfield Robinson, Why Pupils Fail in Reading, University of Chicago Press, Chicago, 1946.

and aniseikonia seemed to be most closely related to reading failure. However, it appeared that many of these visual anomalies were measured by rough screening tests and were not interpreted in terms of other findings. It is possible, then, that many of the anomalies studied are symptoms rather than abnormalities themselves.

A neurological basis for reading failure has been assumed by many. Various explanations to account for this inefficiency in reading have been advanced by one or more writers, only to be criticized by others. Many eminent neurologists have felt that, although the specific area involved could not be completely localized, there might be a physical inadequacy in the brain which accounted for some retarded readers. The condition has been referred to as word blindness, alexia, congenital alexia, developmental alexia, or diplexia. Direct methods of examining the brains of children who have failed to learn to read have not been possible in many cases. Therefore, indirect methods have been used, and none have proved very satisfactory. In general, alexia has been the diagnosis in many cases in which no other cause seemed apparent. Thus for many years the term "alexia" has been used in referring to many cases of failure to learn to read. Newer methods of indirect investigation and controlled studies of children whose difficulties have been diagnosed as alexia should aid in clarifying the exact function of cerebral defects in preventing reading growth.

Conflicting views prevail concerning the role of dominance in reading. After much theoretical discussion and research on the part of specialists in the field of reading, there is still little agreement. The dominance tests most commonly used have been questioned as to validity, and the most desirable combination of preferences to expedite reading has not been established. It appears, however, that dominance should not be entirely neglected as a cause for reading failure until further research has been done.

Inadequate auditory acuity has been considered a cause of poor reading by a few investigators. The results of studies of auditory acuity of good and poor readers, while few, indicated that the latter had slightly poorer auditory acuity than the former, although both appeared to be within the normal range. Adequate auditory acuity did not appear to guarantee adequate hearing, since poor auditory discrimination and insufficient auditory memory span were found to be possible causes of reading failure. Howes' findings, indicating that a small percentage of undetected hearing loss was serious in its effect on school achievement, showed the need for further research in this area.

Articulatory defects have been considered as a cause of poor reading or as a possible concomitant of it. Little critical research, however, was found in this field, and standards of judging articulatory defects were not given. On the basis of the evidence available, articulatory defects may be conceded to be important in oral reading but of little significance in silent reading.

General physical conditions were included among most lists of causes of reading disabilities. Malnutrition, infections, and endocrine disturbances were the three most commonly recognized, although no conclusive evidence of their relationship to reading failure has been established.

Intelligence was conceded to have a positive relationship to reading success. However, since many children who are not mentally retarded fail to learn to read, lack of sufficient intelligence is only one of the many causes of severely retarded readers. At the time of writing, the Binet intelligence test was considered the best single measure of expect-ancy, although some preferred to sup-plement it with performance tests. Thus it is probable that, when the primary abilities are isolated, and a profile is made of intelligence instead of a single composite measure, reading expectancy can be more accurately estimated.

Emotional and personality maladjust-ments in children who failed to learn to read properly seemed to be very com-mon. Emotional maladjustments ap-peared to be either a cause or a result of reading failure, or each might interact on the other, intensifying both. The data secured indicated that emotionally immature children might fail to learn to read when starting school. It was like-wise stressed that neurotic children should be carefully studied before read-ing training is provided. Children who failed to read either accepted their fail-ure and lost confidence or explained away or refused to accept failure. The latter groups tended to become aggres-sive, to withdraw, or to lose emotional affectivity. The evaluation of children's emotional responses is such a complex problem that few studies have been made in this field, although most inves-tigators recognize the problem.

Several investigators believe that de-linquency is associated with reading fail-ure, since a number of delinquents stud-ied appeared to be retarded in reading. However, this relationship could not be evaluated without more controlled stud-ies.

A number of other social factors have been investigated, among which are par-ents' education, their reading ability, physical health, and emotional reactions, as well as their economic status, the lan-guage spoken in the home, neighbor-hood conditions, and ordinal position of the child in the family. Two studies showed that the ordinal position in the family appeared to be the only factor

which is related to reading failure. An effort should therefore be made to ex-plain why such a factor should be opera-tive. Many other subtle environmental problems may not have been considered, or it may not have been possible to de-termine their relationship to reading dis-ability.

The school itself might be a very im-portant cause of reading failure. Admin-istrative policies, materials, size of classes, training and personality of teachers must all be taken into consideration and, if possible, evaluated as causes of severe retardation in reading.

The following statement by Monroe and Backus should be cited in conclu-sion:

Reading disabilities are usually the re-sult of several contributing factors rather than one isolated cause. Studies of the causes of reading disabilities reveal no clear-cut factors which occur only in poor readers but never in good readers. Some children who possess the imped-ing factors appear to be able to read in spite of them. . . . A few good readers are found who have poor vision, poor hearing, emotional instability, who come from environments detrimental to read-ing and who have had inferior teaching. . . . We may conclude that in most cases one factor alone is not sufficient to inhibit the act of reading, if compen-sating abilities are present, and if the child's reaction to the difficulty is a fa-vorable one.[2]

THE PRESENT STUDY

GENERAL INFORMATION

The thirty cases ranged in chronolog-ical age from 6 years 9 months to 15 years 3 months. The mental ages, on the New Stanford Binet Intelligence Test,

[2] Marion Monroe and Bertie Backus, *Remedial Reading: A Monograph in Charac-ter Education*, Houghton Mifflin Co., Boston, 1937, p. 12.

Form L, showed that all the group rated above 7–0 years, a level considered adequate for learning to read. The IQ range was between 85 and 137. The range of reading retardation was from 0.9 grade to 6.4 grades, median 3.9 grades. This was obtained by subtracting the average achievement in reading from the expected grade when the chronological age alone was considered. In the case of very bright children, mental age must also be considered as a basis for determining expectancy in reading. The difference between mental age expectancy and average reading achievement showed a range from 0.9 grade to 7.5 grades, with a median of 3.7 grades.

Following the individual examinations, the specialists met and attempted to evaluate the anomalies and to identify possible causes of reading retardation operating in each case. An intensive remedial program for twenty-two of the thirty cases was undertaken to secure evidence of the potency of each of the possible causes. The results of the study of these twenty-two cases follow.

SOCIAL FACTORS

Maladjusted homes or poor interfamily relationships were found to be contributing causes in 54.5 percent of the cases studied. This percentage is definitely higher than any reported in the literature, few other studies having considered more basic and detailed interfamily problems.

The unusual significance of these factors is not only that organic and emotional problems of the child influence his learning to read but also that problems apparently remote from the school exert considerable influence. They emphasize the importance of the home and of the social environment on the total adjustment of the child. Such findings show that a child's failure to learn to read may be due to factors far beyond his own control and, not infrequently, beyond the control of those charged with responsibility for his progress.

VISUAL FINDINGS

Visual anomalies were found in 73 percent of the twenty-two cases which were studied fully, but were considered to be contributing causes of reading failure in only 50 percent of these cases. This percentage is higher than reported by some examiners but lower than reported by others. Visual examinations were made by ophthalmologists. Corrective procedures were administered to determine whether or not the diagnosis was accurate.

The types of visual difficulties exhibited are of special interest. Glasses were recommended as a corrective procedure for hyperopia in 28 percent of the cases. Hyperopic and myopic astigmatism were each found in 10 percent of the children. Binocular incoördinations of significance were reported in 48 percent of the cases.

Both refractive errors and binocular incoördination were present in some cases, while in others only one difficulty or the other was exhibited. Enlarged blind spots and restricted visual fields were reported in no cases.

The full significance of visual difficulties can be appreciated only when studies of peripheral interferences and perception are combined. Visual perception involves many of the higher mental processes and consequently may be associated with intelligence, previous experiences, language facility, and bodily well-being. The full import of visual interferences with reading necessitates a broader study than is called for when only peripheral interferences are involved.

EMOTIONAL FINDINGS

The psychiatrist found significant emotional problems in 41 percent of the twenty-two cases studied. However, emotional difficulties were found to be the causes of reading failure in only 32 percent of them. The percentage of cases showing emotional problems is lower than reported by some investigators.

Of large importance is the fact that emotional reactions of children may be created by family problems or by attitudes within the home. In this connection, emotional and social factors are so closely related in some cases that they cannot be disentangled.

Unfortunately, emotional difficulties may also develop at school. Probably no comprehensive list of school experiences contributing to emotional difficulties has ever been compiled. One reason is that children seldom relate them unless they have a great deal of confidence in the person to whom they are told.

It should also be added that emotional reactions may aid in learning to read as much as they may interfere with it. Some children become highly motivated when confronted with failure while others withdraw and are afraid to try to learn. The effects of emotional disturbances are so diverse and their manifestations so varied that they should never be overlooked during the examination of a poor reader.

SCHOOL METHODS

Inadequate methods of teaching reading appeared to be a cause of reading failure in 18 percent of the twenty-two cases. This incidence is lower than usually reported in the literature. Since a large number of these severely retarded readers improved, it seems logical to assume that better adaptation of methods of teaching reading to some of the devi-

ating cases has greater value than the number of such cases reported in this study indicates.

NEUROLOGICAL FINDINGS

Alexia or some other neurological difficulty was considered a cause of reading failure in 18 percent of the twenty-two cases. Previous studies have not reported the proportion of seriously retarded readers so diagnosed. These findings do not solve the controversial issues concerning alexia as a factor in reading disability. They do show that some cases diagnosed as alexia may learn to read satisfactorily if given sufficient time and if special remedial techniques are used. Perhaps all of them could be taught to read to some extent if enough were known about the relationships of various symptoms to causes, so that appropriate remedial methods could be applied.

SPEECH AND FUNCTIONAL AUDITORY FINDINGS

Speech and functional auditory factors were found to be contributing causes of reading disability in 18 percent of the twenty-two cases; dyslalia was considered one of the causes in 14 percent of them; and the remainder were accounted for by inadequate auditory discrimination and insufficient auditory memory span for sounds. This finding agrees in general with the findings reported by most investigators, although the actual percentage of cases can be compared in only a few studies.

ENDOCRINE FINDINGS

Mild hypothyroidism was the only endocrine disturbance found by the endocrinologist. Such a difficulty was found in about a third of the thirty children examined but was considered a cause of reading difficulty in only 9 percent of the twenty-two cases studied in detail. This investigation shows, for the first time, the approximate number of severely retarded readers who exhibit endocrine deficiency. Of particular importance is the fact that, when endocrine disturbances were present, they not only retarded progress in learning to read but also had much wider significance. For example, in one case this difficulty interfered with orthoptic treatment, social adjustment, and physical well-being.

AUDITORY ACUITY FINDINGS

Insufficient auditory acuity was found as a cause of poor reading in only 9 percent of the cases. The present study reinforces the general opinion that insufficient auditory acuity is relatively unimportant as a cause of reading retardation.

GENERAL PHYSICAL FINDINGS

Among the various difficulties not included in the preceding sections but which might be classed as physical, malnutrition was the only one that proved to be a cause of reading failure, and it was present in only one case. The results of the present investigation indicate that physical anomalies be studied carefully before assuming that they are causes of severe reading retardation.

DOMINANCE FINDINGS

This study made no contribution to dominance as a cause of reading failure. Tests of dominance were given to the cases. However, dominance was not included among the causes of reading disability because the group of specialists coöperating in this study was unable to interpret the test results.

INTELLIGENCE

Similarly, no contribution was made by this study to an understanding of the relationship between intelligence and reading failure. The cases in this study were purposely selected so that they would be sufficiently intelligent to indicate that there must be interferences in some other area or reading progress would be normal.

MAJOR CONCLUSIONS

First, the pupils who were seriously retarded in reading also exhibited numerous anomalies. In fact, those most seriously retarded evidenced the greatest number of anomalies, whereas those least retarded presented fewest.

There are two possible interpretations of this finding. The first is that difficulty in reading may be a part of the general deviation from the normal pattern. The second possible interpretation is that the large number of anomalies act as hampering defects, thus causing more severe reading retardation. Conclusions presented later favor the first interpretation.

Second, when the group of specialists attempted to evaluate the anomalies for each child, it appeared on the basis of all evidence available that certain of the anomalies had no direct relationship to the reading deficiency.

This conclusion is important because it shows that specialists can readily identify anomalies in isolation, but, when such anomalies are considered in conjunction with all available data on each case examined, the examiners can only conclude that some anomalies are coincidental and are not causes of reading failure.

Third, a number of factors that appeared to be possible causes of reading failure, in the opinion of the specialists, did not prove experimentally to be so.

For example, the group believed visual difficulties to be one of the causes of reading failure in 63 percent of the cases, while, after appropriate treatment, this cause appeared to operate in only 50 percent of the cases.

This finding assumes large significance when evaluating long lists of anomalies reported for poor readers by many investigators. It shows that the mere presence of anomalies does not justify the conclusion that they are causes of reading failure.

Fourth, the experimental evidence in this study indicated that certain types of anomalies operated as causes more frequently than others. Social, visual, and emotional difficulties appeared most frequently as causes of poor progress or failure in learning to read. Inappropriate school methods, neurological difficulties, and speech or functional auditory difficulties appeared less frequently as causes of deficient reading. Endocrine disturbances, general physical difficulties, and insufficient auditory acuity appeared to be least important, in so far as they contributed infrequently to reading failure among the particular children included in this study.

EYE-MOVEMENT TRAINING IN THE ELEMENTARY SCHOOL [1]

Eloise B. Cason

[Because the eyes alone indicate overtly considerable physiological activity as reading is undertaken, it has always been a marked temptation to try to manage the process through them. Reading literature still abounds with phrases inviting readers to take "bigger eyefuls." Tacitly, at least, the assumption seems to be that the eyes control the mental and allied perceptual processes. Hence, training of eye movements should enhance reading efficiency. Two reports testing this kind of assumption follow: One by Cason uses elementary-school children as clientele; the other by Westover employs college freshmen.]

This was an experiment designed to measure the efficacy of two short-term reading programs to increase the speed of reading. The programs were as follows:

1. In School A a group of twenty-five upper-third-grade children used materials specially prepared to emphasize phrasing by means of underlining, vertical marks, or spaces. Considerable opportunity was provided for the transfer of new skills to the reading of ordinary

[1] Abridged and adapted from Eloise B. Cason, *Mechanical Methods for Increasing the Speed of Reading*, Bureau of Publications, Teachers College, Columbia University, New York, 1943.

materials. Speed was emphasized in several ways. Supplementary study devices were employed, such as timing the reading and finding the answers to questions, and checks were made on comprehension of the materials read. The results were compared with those obtained by an equated group in the same school spending an equal amount of time in free library reading. The program ran for a period of five days a week for four weeks.

2. In School B a group of twenty-six upper-third-grade children were trained with the Metron-O-Scope. Reading materials at several levels of difficulty were used, and supplementary study devices were employed. Speed of reading was stressed throughout the training. The program was developed for purposes of the experiment but certain important suggestions given in the manual for the Metron-O-Scope were carried out. The results were compared with those obtained by an equated group in the same school spending an equal amount of time in free library reading. The experiment ran for five days a week for a period of four weeks.

Although the programs for the groups receiving the special training differed in many ways, an analysis of the procedures used would suggest the following similarities:

1. The materials used in both schools called attention to phrasing. In School A this was accomplished by means of spaces, vertical marks, or underlining. In School B attention was called to phrasing by the action of the Metron-O-Scope, which exposed one-third of a line of reading material at a time.

2. The phrasing was artificial in the sense that divisions between phrases were marked off for the children and presented to them as training material.

3. The training materials might be considered as artificial models of good reading habits superior to those of a majority of the children using them.

4. Both programs emphasized speed of reading.

5. In both programs an attempt was made to motivate all reading and to check comprehension.

6. In both programs there was a degree of emphasis on the direction of eye movements. This was far greater in School B, where the Metron-O-Scope was used.

Some of the important differences between the procedures used with the groups receiving special training were as follows:

1. In School A the reading materials used were of more uniform difficulty than those used in School B.

2. In School A two short selections were usually read during each practice period, whereas one roll of material was usually read for two practice periods in School B.

3. The reading was paced by the Metron-O-Scope in School B, whereas verbal suggestions to read more quickly were given in School A.

4. In School A class discussion directed the attention of the children to eye movements, fixation pauses, and other aspects of the mechanics of reading. In School B speeding up was emphasized and the mechanics of eye movements were not mentioned.

5. Specific opportunities for the transfer of skills to ordinary reading material were provided in School A, whereas only general verbal suggestions were given in School B.

The directions given to the Library Groups in both schools were identical, and with a few exceptions the same reading materials were available to the children in both groups. The records kept by the children indicated that the quantity of reading material covered by both groups was substantially the same. The following considerations seem to be of importance:

1. In School A the Library Group remained in the room with the Phrase Material Group during the practice periods, whereas the two groups were separated in School B.

2. In both schools the children in the Library Groups apparently obtained suggestions or hints on procedure from the groups receiving the special training, although they had no opportunity to participate in the special training.

The results of free library reading in the two schools cannot be compared without careful interpretation.

A battery of tests was given in both schools before and after the experimental training. A standardized reading test, nonstandardized tests of phrase reading, a test of phrasing in oral reading, and observations of eye movements were included. The purpose of the test program was to evaluate in a variety of ways improvement in speed and an increased ability to read by phrases. The standardized reading test was repeated after the summer vacation.

The main results of experiment were as follows:

1. There were no important differences between the groups having the opportunity for special practice in reading phrases and for eye-movement training provided especially by the Metron-O-Scope and the equated groups in the same school spending an equal amount of time in free library reading. This was true of the standardized reading test, which measured speed, level of comprehension, and accuracy on the speed test, of the special tests of ability to read phrases, of the measurement of eye movements, and of the test on the Metron-O-Scope. In the groups studied, and under the conditions of the experiment, the measurements made did not show that any clear-cut gains were produced in the reading process by the reading programs stressing the mechanics of reading that were not secured by free library reading.

2. The programs featuring training in phrase reading tended to show different effects on the good, medium, and poor readers in the groups studied. Certain trends were, on the whole, consistent but not in all cases statistically reliable. The reliable differences were as follows:

a. In the Phrase Material Group in School A there was a reliable difference between the upper and middle third of the group when the children were arranged in order of their average scores on the Gates Reading Survey. The upper third lost in speed when compared to the middle third.

b. In the Metron-O-Scope Group in School B there was a reliable difference between the upper and lower thirds of the group when the children were arranged in order of their average scores on the Gates Reading Survey. The use of the Metron-O-Scope increased the comprehension scores of the upper third more than the comprehension scores of the lower third.

There was a somewhat consistent trend, though not a statistically reliable one, for both programs using the mechanical approach to increase the speed of the middle third of readers the most.

The following are some of the considerations that are of importance in evaluating a teaching method:

1. The improvement that may be directly attributed to the use of the method.

2. A comparison of the effectiveness of the method with other methods that might attain the same objective.

3. The expense involved in using the method, including the expenditure of the time of the teacher.

When group differences are considered, the mechanical approach was not effective in either of the schools coöperating in this experiment, in the sense that comparable results were obtained with equated groups spending an equal amount of time in free library reading, which is a far simpler method. An analysis of the different effects of the mechanical approach on the good, medium, and poor readers would perhaps justify the recommendation that an evaluation of the reading status of the individual child be made before a decision is reached to use either of the methods studied in this experiment.

EYE TRAINING VERSUS PRACTICE EXERCISES IN READING [1]

Frederick L. Westover

PROBLEM

The purpose of this study has been to find out the comparative effectiveness of three methods of improving the reading performance of college freshmen. Entering college freshmen whose speed-of-comprehension scores on the Cooperative English Test, C-2, Reading comprehension, Higher Level,[2] fell in the lowest 40 percent of national norms composed the subjects of this study. Those who participated took two initial tests of reading and two initial tests of intelligence,[3] on the basis of which three

[1] Abridged and adapted from Frederick L. Westover, *Controlled Eye Movements versus Practice Exercises in Reading*, Bureau of Publications, Teachers College, Columbia University, New York, 1946.
[2] *Cooperative English Test, C-2, Reading Comprehension, Higher Level*, Form R, Cooperative Test Service, New York, 1940.
[3] *American Council on Education, Psychological Examination for College Freshmen*, American Council on Education, Washington, 1941; *Otis Self-Administering Tests of Mental Ability, Higher Examination*, Form A, World Book Co., Yonkers, N.Y., 1928.

equivalent groups were arranged. The two reading tests were the Cooperative Test, mentioned above, and the Traxler High School Reading Test.[4] From the Cooperative Test three measures of reading were taken: (1) vocabulary, (2) speed of comprehension, and (3) level of comprehension. From the Traxler Test two measures of reading were taken: (1) rate of reading and (2) total comprehension.

Group I, composed of forty-five lower freshmen, was given two fifty-minute periods of practice a week for five weeks in reading and taking tests on the *Study Type of Reading Exercises*.[5] Group II, also composed of forty-five lower freshmen, was given the same amount and kind of work on the same exercises, but the exercises were read by means of a device for controlling eye movements. Group III, composed of fifty lower fresh-

[4] *Traxler High School Reading Test*, Form B, Public School Publishing Co., Bloomington, Ill., 1938.
[5] *Study Type of Reading Exercise*, Bureau of Publications, Teachers College, Columbia University, New York, 1935.

men, attended college but received no special exercises in reading.

At the end of the five-week training period the students were tested on alternate forms of the two reading tests. Six months later they were retested on the same form of the Cooperative Test as that given in the initial test eleven months earlier. The grade points earned by the students in each group during the term in which training was given and during the term following training were computed. The gains in reading-test scores and in grade points of each group and the differences in the gains of each group were calculated.

FINDINGS

It was found at the end of the five-week training period that:

1. Group I, the practice-exercise group, made significant gains in speed of comprehension and in rate of reading.
2. Group II, the controlled-eye-movement group, made significant gains in speed of comprehension, in level of comprehension, and in rate of reading.
3. Group III, the no-exercise group, made significant gains in speed of comprehension and in level of comprehension.
4. Groups I and II combined, the instructional groups, made significant gains in all measures.
5. At the close of the term in which the training was given, there were no significant differences in the grade points earned by the three groups.

Comparing the gains made by each group, it was found that Group I, Group II, and Groups I and II combined each made significantly greater gains in rate of reading than Group III, but there

were no significant differences between the two instructional groups.

On a readministration of the Cooperative English Test six months after the training period, it was found that the gains made by each of the three groups, and by the two instructional groups combined, were significant for each of the aspects of reading retested—vocabulary, speed of comprehension, and level of comprehension.

Comparing the gains made by each group on the retest, it was found that there were no significant differences between Groups I and II, but that Group II and Groups I and II combined were each significantly better in vocabulary, as measured by the test, than Group III.

At the close of the term following training there were no significant differences in the grade points earned by the three groups.

Each group showed an increase of variability following training, but Group I made a greater increase in variability than either Group II or Group III.

In the two instructional groups there were significantly more students with good scholarship marks and fewer students who withdrew from college than in the no-exercise group.

CONCLUSIONS

In immediate results produced by training, it was discovered that:

1. Speed of comprehension in reading, as measured by the Cooperative English Test, may be improved (a) by ordinary practice on the *Study Type of Reading Exercises*, (b) by practice on these exercises under conditions of controlled eye movements, and (c) by college work without special practice on reading exercises.
2. Rate of reading, as measured by the Traxler Test, may be improved by

ordinary practice on the *Study Type of Reading Exercises* under conditions of controlled eye movements, and such improvements are greater than those secured by college work alone.

3. Level of comprehension in reading, as measured by the Cooperative English Test, may be improved by reading the *Study Type of Reading Exercises* under conditions of controlled eye movements, or by college work without special exercises in reading, but such gains are not reliably greater than those made by ordinary practice on the reading exercises.

4. There are no significant differences in the effectiveness of the two instructional methods, as far as this study shows.

5. There are no significant differences in the grade points earned under the three methods, as far as this study shows.

6. Use of each method is followed by an increase in variability, but ordinary practice on the reading exercises is followed by a greater gain in variability than follows the use of either of the other two methods.

After the immediate effects of training had worn off it was found that:

1. Application of the three methods is followed by significant improvement in all aspects of reading retested—vocabulary, speed of comprehension, and level of comprehension.

2. Reading under conditions of controlled eye movements is followed by significantly greater gains in vocabulary than follow college work alone, but there are no significant differences in the gains made under the two instructional methods.

3. There are no significant differences in the grade points earned under the three methods.

4. Special exercises in reading, as compared with no special training in reading, is accompanied by better scholarship and fewer withdrawals from college.

In brief, the mechanical control of eye movements by means of a specially constructed machine did not show significantly better results in the achievements tested than the same reading exercises used alone. From the short training periods employed in this study, not only were no significant differences found in the effectiveness of the two experimental methods, but, after a lapse of six months without training, all three methods showed significant gains in reading, with no significant differences between the trained and the untrained groups in speed and comprehension in reading.

PART TWO

The Second "R"

The second "R" has arbitrarily been interpreted to include handwriting, spelling, and certain aspects of grammar and composition. There is a smaller body of significant research in these fields than in either reading or arithmetic. Nevertheless, much crucial research has been in progress and our accustomed ways of teaching have been challenged.

The rather restricted skills of handwriting and spelling lend themselves fairly readily to neat problems for experimentation. What words shall the children learn to spell? What learning methods are better? Shall we teach manuscript and/or cursive writing? How can they be learned most efficiently? All of these problems can be attacked with rather clear-cut experimental rationales and techniques.

When dealing with grammar and composition, on the other hand, we are confronted with far more complex issues. What is good usage? How can we change accustomed patterns of usage? What is the grammar of our language that we should teach? These problems were once thought to be rather simple. During the past quarter of a century, however, careful investigation has been unearthing revolutionary answers. Our growing, changing, dynamic English language does not fit the neat pattern we once believed it did. We are beginning to understand better why we typically have been so unsuccessful in our efforts to improve children's language operation. In turn we are seeing better how we can achieve our purposes.

A reference [1] highly important for elementary-school methodology was not included. This book did not meet our criteria as "research" even

[1] Alvina Burrows and others, *They All Want to Write*, Prentice-Hall, Inc., New York, 1952.

261

though it described a deliberate pattern of teaching by which several elementary-school teachers succeeded in helping children learn to write effectively. Among other things, they consciously separated the mechanics of writing—spelling, handwriting, punctuation, capitalization, grammar, etc.—from the act of putting ideas down on paper. During the time any child was engaged in "creative writing" of a story, poem, or essay he was encouraged to concentrate only upon the ideas being expressed. Later, the child would edit the paper for others to read and at that time would concentrate upon the various mechanics of good writing. The quality of ideas and expression that ensued indicated high merit for the approach.

Because of the complexity of the problem there is as yet little significant and clear-cut research dealing with composition as such. Much remains to be done.

Chapter IX

HANDWRITING

Introduction

From earliest civilized times schools have necessarily been concerned with handwriting; written language and civilization have been almost synonymous. With the advent of printing and later the typewriter, handwriting as an art form began to recede in importance. Today we are primarily concerned with but two aspects of writing skill: legibility, as a social courtesy to anyone who must read one's writing; and fluency, so that one may write without undue strain.

The goal today is to reach an adequate standard in these two respects while using but a minimum of precious school time. The school curriculum in today's complex civilization requires so much to be learned that any way to reduce the time to be devoted to this pure skill is most welcome. Fortunately, great progress has been made toward this goal.

The first three studies deal with the issue of manuscript writing. The first is representative of studies showing the overall advantage of children beginning their handwriting with the printed form. This form requires only mastery of short discontinuous lines (either straight, or arcs of circles) and is obviously easier for small children to master. A study [1] not presented here revealed that most public schools (84.3 percent in 1945) are now starting children with this form. While a change-over to cursive is usually made when the children are a little older (96 percent by the end of the third grade), a few schools continue manuscript throughout, presenting cursive writing only for purposes of learning to read it. The next two studies offer some experimental justification for this practice.

The majority of our schools will probably continue to teach cursive

[1] Frank N. Freeman, "Survey of Manuscript Writing in the Public Schools," *Elementary School Journal* (1946), 46:375-380.

writing indefinitely. The other three studies should prove of great help in focusing teaching attention upon spots where attention is needed. Generalized teaching of writing as a whole to children as a total class is much less efficient than pinpointed teaching. The rationale of the final study might equally well be used in polishing children's manuscript writing.

WHY START WITH MANUSCRIPT? [1]

Prudence Cutright

[Studies such as this one have exerted great influence upon elementary schools. The evidence has strongly favored starting children with manuscript rather than cursive writing not only for the sake of the writing skill alone but because of the effect upon other areas of the curriculum. This concise study is an interesting example of the matched-group technique in experimentation.]

Many claims have been made for manuscript writing. Just a few of these are: (1) It is easier to learn. (2) It is more rhythmical to write. (3) It can be written as rapidly as cursive. (4) It is more legible and, therefore, more easily read. (5) It facilitates the learning of reading and of spelling. (6) It satisfies the young child's desire to write.

A study made in 1935 in Minneapolis by Gertrude Drohan, principal of the Cleveland School, showed that 58 percent of a group of 2B pupils who had been taught only manuscript achieved a significantly higher score on the Metropolitan Reading Test than did the matched cases who had been taught only cursive. This 58 percent of the manuscript group had an average reading level six months in advance of the cursive group. In the 2A grade, Miss Drohan found that 52 percent of the 142 pupils who had been taught manuscript not only achieved higher reading scores but read on a level six and a half months in advance of their matched cases in a cursive group. She found, quite as Voorhis found, that manuscript not only aided dull children but also greatly speeded the task of learning to read for children in the upper quartile in intelligence.

The evidence in the case of manuscript writing in relation to reading is about as conclusive as anything to be found in the field of educational research. There seem to be no studies of any weight which would discredit the statement that manuscript writing is a

[1] Adapted and abridged from Prudence Cutright, "Script-Print and Beginning Reading and Spelling," *Elementary English Review* (1936), 13:139–141.

distinct aid to young children who are learning to read print.

The claim is made that manuscript satisfies a child's desire to write and facilitates the learning of spelling. As yet very little evidence is available on either of these points.

Last year Minneapolis conducted a study of the comparative effect of cursive and manuscript writing on second-grade children's ability to spell and on the spread of their vocabularies in written composition. The 2B children in the schools where only cursive writing was used and the 2B children in eight schools where only manuscript was used were made the subjects of the study. These children were given group intelligence tests. Later they were asked to write a short composition under controlled conditions.

The schools used were located in highly similar socioeconomic districts and the children had had about the same quality of teaching. The children in the schools using cursive were matched with those using print on the bases of sex, intelligence, and chronological age. When the matchings were completed there were fourteen matched groups of girls. These matched groups included fifty-six girls from cursive schools and seventy-six from print schools. In each group, the girls in the cursive schools were matched with the girls in manuscript schools on the bases of intelligence and chronological age. Thus in the first group there were two girls from cursive schools and three from manuscript schools all having IQ's between 120 and 125 and chronological ages between 7 years and 7 years 5 months. The other thirteen groups of girls were similarly matched.

There were fifteen groups of boys, including fifty-two from cursive schools. They were matched in the same way as were the girls. The children from manu-script schools and those from cursive schools were compared (1) as to the number of different words written in their composition (illegible and misspelled words as well as correctly spelled words were counted) and (2) as to the number of words spelled correctly.

When compared as to the number of different words written, it was found that, in nine out of the fourteen matched groups of girls, the girls in manuscript schools had a higher average number of different words than did the girls in cursive schools. In the boys' groups, in ten out of the fifteen groups the boys in manuscript schools had a higher average of different words than did the boys in cursive schools and in one group the average number of different word was the same. If the ability to write a larger number of words is an indication that a form of writing aids in satisfying a desire for expression, then it would seem that children who are taught manuscript have a better tool than have those who are taught cursive.

When compared as to the number of misspellings, in eight of the fourteen groupings of girls, the girls in the manuscript schools misspelled a smaller average number of words than did their matched groups in cursive schools, and in one matching the average number of misspellings was the same for both groups.

In the matchings of boys, the difference in the spelling of children in the cursive and manuscript schools was even more decidedly in favor of the manuscript writing. In eleven out of the fifteen matchings of boys, the boys in manuscript schools misspelled a smaller average number of words than did the boys in cursive schools.

While this study of the spread of vocabulary and of spelling ability in relation to manuscript and cursive writing is not of sufficient scope to permit the drawing of conclusions, the trend is so much in favor of manuscript as to suggest certain comments.

First, children who begin their writing experience with print seem to write more freely, that is, use a larger number of different words than do children who begin with the cursive form of writing.

Second, children who begin their school writing experiences with print seem to spell a larger number of words correctly than do children who begin with cursive writing.

Supervisors and classroom teachers frequently ask those engaged in research this question: What are the findings of research which are sufficiently well established to justify me in putting them into practice? From evidence reviewed, we would seem justified in introducing manuscript in the primary grades for all pupils.

ARE CHILDREN HANDICAPPED WHO LEARN TO WRITE ONLY MANUSCRIPT? [1]

Carleton Washburne and Mabel Vogel Morphett

[It has become common practice to start children with manuscript rather than cursive writing. It is common practice, also, to "change over" to cursive writing at the second- or third-grade level. The authors present striking evidence that questions the wisdom or necessity of teaching a child the second method, especially before the first has become thoroughly established. This issue is distinctly controversial, even though there is little experimental evidence to support the present teaching of cursive writing.]

Manuscript writing has made its way into the primary grades so positively and with such a weight of scientific evidence in its favor that a discussion of its merits at that level is no longer necessary. Until recently, however, evidence has been very meager on the question of whether children should change from manuscript to cursive writing and, if so, at what time and by what means.

The present section sets forth investigations organized to answer the following questions: (1) How does the rate of writing manuscript under test conditions compare with national norms for the writing of cursive at the various levels? (2) What is the difference in rate of writing by high-school pupils who have been taught manuscript writing and who use it habitually and that of pupils who have always used cursive writing? (3) Are children who are taught to write manuscript handicapped in the reading of cursive after they reach eighth grade and

[1] Adapted and abridged from Carleton Washburne and Mabel Vogel Morphett, "Manuscript Writing—Some Recent Investigations," *Elementary School Journal* (1937), 37:517–529.

high school? To these questions this section gives statistical answers.

There are three other questions which it will attempt to answer in terms of experience: (1) Is there a lack of individuality and personality in manuscript writing? (2) If a child is going to transfer from manuscript to cursive writing, when can the transfer best be made and by what means? (3) Are manuscript-writing signatures valid in business transactions?

Manuscript writing has been taught in the Winnetka public schools since 1924. At that time the children entering first grade and many of the children in second grade were taught manuscript. Each year, as these children moved up a grade, manuscript writing moved up with them, until it was the only kind of writing taught throughout the schools. The children who were in that first class have now graduated from high school, and all children who have gone through the Winnetka schools since that time have been trained in manuscript writing the majority of them using this kind of writing right through their high-school life.

To check the relative rates of manuscript and cursive writing at the various grade levels has therefore been a comparatively simple matter in Winnetka, but we wished to compare with other schools as well. A list was therefore secured of schools in various parts of the United States that taught manuscript writing, and each was asked to give a timed test by having the children write "Mary had a little lamb" for two minutes continuously.

Figure 1 shows the results in comparison with the Ayres Handwriting Scale. It will be noted that at the second-grade level Winnetka children are very much slower than the Ayres standard and that the children in the other schools are slightly slower. This difference is probably due to an effort on the part of the Winnetka teachers to emphasize form rather than speed when the children are learning to write. By the end of the third grade the Winnetka children are almost equal to those of the other schools, but both groups are below the Ayres standard. The same situation is found at the end of the fourth grade. At the end of the fifth grade Winnetka children have overtaken the children in the other schools but are still distinctly behind the Ayres standard. This situation still holds, but to a lesser degree, at the end of the sixth grade. By the end of the seventh grade, however, both the Winnetka children and the children in the other schools have exceeded the Ayres standard and continue to do so at the end of the eighth grade.

Apparently, therefore, the development of speed in manuscript writing is, under current practice, somewhat slower than in cursive writing. We say "under current practice" because we believe it is the tendency (we know it is true in Winnetka) for teachers to be much more meticulous about letter formation in manuscript writing than they were in cursive writing. They seem to feel that, once the manuscript forms are well established, the speed will take care of itself. The results in the seventh and the eighth grades seem to vindicate this point of view.

The second question has to do with the rate of writing after children reach high school. Children from Winnetka attend the New Trier Township High School, together with children from three neighboring communities and a sprinkling of children from a variety of other elementary schools. The majority of children not trained in Winnetka have had the usual courses in cursive writing and continue this kind of writing in the high school. The majority of Winnetka children have had training in manuscript writing throughout their elementary-school careers and continue to use it right through high school. It was therefore a simple matter to give a speed test in writing to several hundred children at New Trier High School, in which each child would write according to his custom. Each child was asked to

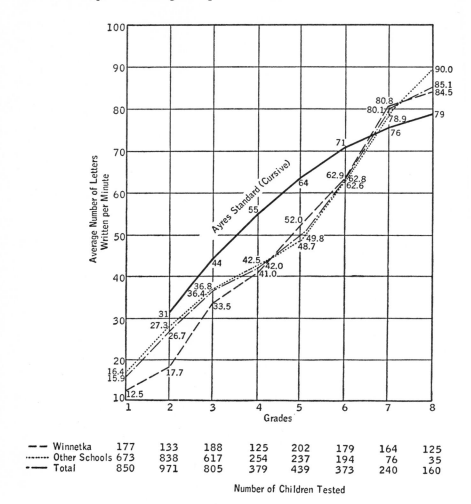

Fig. I.

indicate on his paper whether he wrote manuscript all the time or part of the time or never. The records of children who wrote manuscript part of the time were disregarded, as there were no data to indicate whether "part of the time" meant occasionally or most of the time or whether the pupils had been trained in manuscript or cursive writing.

The data in Table 1 bear out the seventh- and eighth-grade data and indicate that, once the children have learned manuscript and have used it consistently through their school work, it tends to be slightly faster than cursive; certainly not slower.

Our third question is whether children trained in writing manuscript can read cursive as well as do children trained in writing cursive. Again children at the New Trier Township High School were used as subjects.

In order to get a sample of cursive writing that would be more or less typical, we asked all the members of the Winnetka Rotary Club to write in their ordinary handwriting the first part of the song "America." The samples were rated on the Ayres Handwriting Scale by four teachers independently. The paper receiving the median rating happened to be that of the man who supervises physical education in the Winnetka schools. We asked this man to copy Test Six of the Iowa Silent Reading Test, Form A. We then reproduced his paper photostatically, with the permission of the

Table 2 is in favor of the cursive writers but is not serious enough to be a handicap since there are few times in life when the ability to read one more line in two minutes is vital. Nevertheless, on the basis of such studies the Winnetka public schools have introduced a definite course in the reading of cursive at the end of the fifth grade. The children who have had this course had not yet reached high school when these studies were made, but they have been tested in eighth grade and compared, on the same test, with children of the same age in a neighboring community who always write cursive. The results are shown in Table 3. Apparently a little training in the reading of cursive completely wipes out the small handicap shown in Table 2.

There would seem, consequently, to be no evidence to indicate the necessity for changing from manuscript to cursive

TABLE 1. Comparison of Rates of Writing of High-School Pupils Who Habitually Use Manuscript or Cursive Writing

	Manuscript Writers	Cursive Writers
Number of children	78	214
Number of letters written per minute		
Lower quartile	104	99
Median	116	113
Upper quartile	131	126

publishers, and gave this test to the children at New Trier High School, having each child indicate on the test whether he had always used manuscript writing or had always used cursive. It was on the back of this same reading test that the children wrote their speed samples in manuscript or cursive.

The results of this test are shown in Table 2, the scores being in accordance with the directions for the Iowa Silent Reading Test. The slight difference in

TABLE 2. Comparison of Rates of Reading Cursive Writing by High-School Pupils Trained in Writing Manuscript or Cursive

	Manuscript Writers	Cursive Writers
Number of children	80	215
Reading-test score		
Lower quartile	14.0	14.6
Median	16.9	18.1
Upper quartile	21.8	23.5

TABLE 3. Comparison of Rates of Reading Cursive Writing by Eighth-Grade Pupils Trained in Writing Manuscript or Cursive, the Manuscript Writers Having Had a Course in Reading Cursive

	Manuscript Writers	Cursive Writers
Number of children	69	75
Reading-test score		
Lower quartile	12.2	12.8
Median	16.1	16.1
Upper quartile	22.9	18.3

writing. The advantage of manuscript from the standpoint of superior legibility has never been challenged by anyone who has any acquaintance with the product.

In the Winnetka schools, partly to silence the criticism of some parents, we offer an elective course in cursive writing any time after a child has his manuscript well established, preferably in the junior high school but permissibly in the fifth or the sixth grade. Since there are few children in each room whose parents want them to make this change or who want to do so themselves, regular class work in cursive is not practicable. Consequently we have developed a self-instructive workbook, and it has been our experience that children, with little help from the teacher other than a general supervision of their work, are able to transform their manuscript into a very acceptable cursive in from six to twelve weeks of practice, using a writing period of approximately twenty minutes a day. The transition has caused no difficulty whatever, and, if the manuscript writing has been well developed and the letter forms have been made up to standard, the cursive writing tends likewise to be clear and legible and well formed. When, on the other hand, children try to change from manuscript into cursive writing before the manuscript has become thoroughly a part of them, we find that the cursive writing tends to be poor.

Without statistical evidence we would say out of our experience of a number of years that, if a child is to change from manuscript to cursive writing, the later he makes the change the better, up to junior-high-school age. Our reason for this statement is partly our observation and partly the obvious fact that, when the coördinations are first being made and have not become thoroughly established as automatic, there is a great deal of confusion in changing styles of writing. When, however, the coördinations are adequately made, the cursive writing can be developed from the manuscript without breaking down the established habits.

With respect to the question of whether manuscript writing has individuality, best answer lies in an examination of any collection of children's manuscript writing or the manuscript writing of adults. When a member of the Winnetka Board of Education raised this question, we simply fastened up on the walls of the room where the board met, thirty or forty samples of the junior-high-school writing in the Winnetka schools. This demonstration completely disposed of the question, as a similar observation must to any open-minded observer.

Finally, there is the question of the legality of manuscript-writing signatures. We have taken this question up with local banks and find that the signature placed on file by the depositor is the legal signature no matter in what form it is written.

There thus seems to be no sound reason for changing from manuscript to cursive.

DO UNJOINED STROKES SLOW THE WRITER? [1]

Gertrude Hildreth

[This study presents additional and relevant evidence on the issue raised in the preceding report on manuscript writing. Most people would agree that the two major objectives of handwriting methodology are legibility (as a social courtesy to the reader) and fluency (for personal efficiency). Few question the normally superior legibility of manuscript; many question its fluency. To many it seems counter to "common sense" that interrupted lines with "wasteful" raising and lowering of the pen could be made as rapidly as a continuous line. The issue is here subjected to experimentation.]

Is cursive wrirting with its continuous line inherently faster than manuscript, in which pencils must be lifted so often? Which can be written the faster, joined or unjoined strokes? To check on this point the following experiment was conducted.

Seventy eighth-grade pupils were given tests to determine the number of joined and unjoined "up-and-down" pencil strokes they could make on a line in a short time interval. Such a test measures motor skill and manual dexterity similar to that required in writing but obviates the training effect due to having practiced a certain style of writing. The subjects were twenty-seven boys and forty-three girls with a median chronological age of 13–0 years and a median IQ of 123 on standard tests. Each was tested individually in the school psychological laboratory.

The pupil was first shown either a row of unjoined strokes (like matches laid parallel to each other across the sheet) or a row of joined strokes (in which the pencil continues on paper from the bottom of each stroke to the top of the next). He was told to make a similar row of strokes on his paper, beginning when the stop watch clicked and stopping at the final click fifteen seconds later. The same directions were given for the other stroke test. To equalize the practice effect from the first to the second test, the examiner alternated which one he started with for each succeeding child. The pupils were told that they might make the strokes vertically or slant them in whichever direction seemed most natural. As a "warming up" device the pupil first made a row of X's across the page for fifteen seconds.

Although all writing was done with pencil, there is every reason to suppose that comparable results would be obtained with fountain pens. The children

[1] Adapted and abridged from Gertrude Hildreth, "Comparative Speed of Joined and Unjoined Writing Strokes," *Journal of Educational Psychology* (1945), 36:91–102.

were greatly interested in the tests and coöperated well.

Preceding the stroke tests a two-minute sample of each child's handwriting was taken in which he copied certain typed material at his usual rate and in his accustomed style.

RESULTS OF THE TESTS

In the stroke tests, the median for unjoined strokes was 44.3; for joined strokes, 40.7. With a critical ratio of 3.2, there is considerable assurance that this is a true difference. Variability was wider in the joined-stroke test than in unjoined, although the highest scores were made in the latter. The difference was negligible between boys and girls, and between those who wrote habitually by cursive or by manuscript style. The practice effect from the first stroke test to the second also seemed to be negligible; there appeared to be little difference in results due to order of presentation.

In their handwriting samples, these pupils did well. Their speed was above normal: the median number of letters written per minute by the manuscript writers was 80.17; by the cursive writers, 85.5. The Ayres norm for their grade level was 77 letters per minute. Of those writing more than 100 letters a minute, six were manuscript writers and eight wrote cursive style—about the same proportion as the total number of pupils who used each style, twenty-eight and forty-two respectively. The sixty-eight seventh-grade pupils in the school were given the same test. Half were manuscript, half cursive writers and they scored respectively 70.5 and 70 letters a minute.

The cursive writers were normal in quality on the Ayres standards, and while there were no comparable standards for rating the quality of the manu-

script writing, the latter in general surpassed the former in legibility. Letters were neatly made and evenly spaced. There was good spacing between words, direction of strokes was consistent, and alignment was even. The manuscript writers appeared to work as smoothly as the cursive-style writers and with no more effort.

Most of the cursive writers were children from public schools who had received systematic handwriting instruction through the upper grades; no more than half the manuscript writers had been given writing instruction beyond the third grade.

The poorest writers proved to be "change-over" cases who had had insufficient drill in cursive writing to establish good habits. Within the same writing sample they often showed combinations of the two styles. Some told of their struggles in learning to write. Several left-handed children, half changed over, and those who had fluctuated between manuscript and cursive-style writing had experienced the most difficulty. One child not only had been shifted from left to right hand but had been required to change his style of writing at the same time.

CONCLUSIONS AND RECOMMENDATIONS

Since the test results show that making unjoined strokes is at least as rapid as making joined strokes, it is reasonable to infer that with equal amounts of practice and equally thorough teaching throughout the elementary-school grades manuscript writing can be as fast as, if not faster than, joined-letter writing.

Of course neither manuscript nor cursive writing consists merely of joined or unjoined up-and-down strokes. Letters such as s, e, f, and z require horizontal strokes in manuscript writing. It is these letters requiring sharp angles that Gray [2] found to be more time consuming compared with the corresponding letters in cursive-style writing. The remaining letters of the alphabet, however, require similar direction of strokes in the two styles.

We are not concerned solely with the question as to whether one style is faster than the other, but must inquire: (1) How fast can handwriting that employs the Roman alphabet be done and still be highly legible? (2) Can the standards that are set up for speed and quality be attained with manuscript writing?

These results suggest that manuscript

[2] William H. Gray, "An Experimental Comparison of the Movements in Manuscript and Cursive Writing," *Journal of Educational Psychology* (1938), 21:259–272.

writing can be fast enough in the upper grades for all practical purposes and that children who first learn manuscript writing in the primary grades would do well to continue in that style.

In the busy world today business people, ticket agents, salespeople, and others are required to "print" the papers they fill out. Manuscript writing, which is superior in all ways to printing in capital-letter style, meets the requirement for high legibility and is sufficiently rapid.

To achieve economy in learning it is recommended that all children who are to learn to read and write material employing the Roman alphabet be taught manuscript writing. Then the material they write by hand and on the typewriter will correspond with the handwritten and printed material they read.

WHAT ARE THE MOST COMMON CURSIVE ERRORS? [1]

T. Ernest Newland

[This early study has been a classic in the field. From this one can determine the kind of errors that are likely to appear at various stages of development. It is encouraging to discover how few errors account for so great a proportion of the total illegibility. Appropriate teaching should thus be able to prevent or alleviate much difficulty fairly readily.]

INTRODUCTION

The problem of illegibilities is essentially a social one; correspondence of all sorts is illustrative of this, whether it be in terms of confusions on personal checks or in terms of undecipherable

[1] Adapted and abridged from T. Ernest Newland, "An Analytical Study of the Development of Illegibilities in Handwriting

parts of social correspondence. In spite of the fact that this problem is of such importance, illegibilities have not attracted sufficient scientific attention. That they are deserving of such consideration should be apparent to anyone

from the Lower Grades to Adulthood," *Journal of Educational Research* (1932), 26:249–258.

who will recall instances in which errors have occurred on account of confusions.

This study is an attempt to answer the following questions: (1) What letters are most frequently illegible? (2) In what way or ways do these illegibilities occur? That is, are certain letters illegible in one or more ways? Do the different forms appear with approximately the same frequencies? Are any differences apparent in the comparison of results at different age levels? And (3) do the answers to these questions suggest any remedial or preventive measures?

MATERIALS AND METHODS

The material used for this analysis consisted of regular periodic papers collected from a total of 1500 pupils in the eight grades of the elementary school, from 452 students in the four grades of the high-school level, from 297 college students represented mainly by sophomores, but including also juniors and seniors, and letters written by 132 adults to editors of two city newspapers. The schools from which the specimens were collected were in widely separated states and can reasonably be considered typical of the general school situation. Both city and country schools supplied material. No one system of handwriting instruction contributed an overwhelming portion. No papers were prepared expressly for this study. Some of them were done with pencil and some with pen. In all, 341,315 words, or 1,344,905 letters, written by 2381 different persons provided the basis for this analysis.

Some twenty-four different persons contributed their analyses to one or more parts of this study. They were instructed to record each time they encountered something in their reading of the specimens which made them stop and look a second time at what they

were reading in order to determine what the writer meant.[2] Specific directions were given to the effect that they were not to let such things as misspellings, rewritings, crowdings, or erasures enter their results as illegibilities. Such things as these were recorded, but separate from the specific illegibilities. If the readers were unable to record the illegibilities in some such category as "a like o," "g like cj" or "e closed," they copied as best they could the specific form of the illegibility and entered a tally mark opposite the reproduction.

RESULTS

A total of 42,284 specific illegibilities were tabulated. These included 499 different forms of illegibilities. Only 16 percent of this total were common to all three of the major age groups used—the elementary, the high school, and the adult. An additional 20 percent were common to only two of these three groups.

Table 1 shows the frequencies per 100,000 running letters with which the letters of the alphabet appeared illegible and the extent to which each letter contributed to the total number of illegibilities at each level, as expressed in

[2] This procedure may seem to have been unreliable, but quite the contrary was found to be the case. Not only the gross correlational method of comparison but also a minute analysis of the particular forms of illegibilities showed a high agreement, for this type of study. In the case of the former method, a rank correlation between the frequencies of letter illegibility as recorded by one person, and the frequencies of letter illegibility as recorded by two other persons working together on the same set of over 400 high-school papers, was found to be +.80 ±.05. Similar computation on the results of one person's analyzing twice the same set of forty-five high-school English papers, without his knowing the purpose of the duplication of the work, gave +.96 ± .01.

percentages. It can be seen that the illegibilities of the four letters a, e, r, and t
were among the first five in importance
in each major age group and that they
together contributed 45, 46, and 47 percent to the elementary, high-school, and
adult groups respectively. Taking all the
letters together, the high-school students
wrote 136 percent more illegibly than
did the elementary-school children but
were surpassed 52 percent by the adults.
It is interesting to note that the adults
wrote more than three times more illegibly than did the elementary-school children.

When one considers the most frequent forms of illegibilities, which accounted for approximately one-half of
all the illegibilities among lower-case letters, as shown in Table 2, one is impressed by two things, namely, the small
number of forms, as compared with the
total number recorded at each level, and
the degree of consistency with which
certain forms appeared at the different
levels. Of particular interest is the fact
that, of the nine forms of illegibilities
which accounted for 50 percent of all
the illegibilities recorded for the adult
level, six were common to all three lev-

TABLE 1. Frequencies per 100,000 Running Letters with Which Each Letter Appeared Illegible and the Percentages of the Totals the Illegibilities of Each Letter Represented

Letter	Elementary		High School		Adult		Total	
	Fr.	%	Fr.	%	Fr.	%	Fr.	%
a	153	11	277	9	377	8	269	8
b	89	6	278	9	180	4	172	5
c	16	1	47	1	70	1	44	1
d	126	9	260	8	266	5	214	7
e	167	12 a	392	12	904	18	495	16
f	39	3	120	4	155	3	102	3
g	31	2	53	2	66	1	50	2
h	80	6	154	5	235	5	157	4
i	57	4	158	5	362	7	195	6
j	1	— b	2	—	1	—	1	—
k	19	1	49	2	30	1	31	1
l	34	2	49	2	100	2	62	2
m	16	1	10	—	27	1	19	1
n	55	4	63	2	457	9	205	6
o	73	5	181	6	185	4	143	5
p	15	1	113	3	84	2	65	2
q	1	—	3	—	1	—	1	—
r	167	12	290	9	440	9	302	9
s	47	3	132	4	273	6	152	5
t	134	10	515	16	600	12	402	13
u	23	2	8	—	15	—	17	1
v	11	1	22	1	35	1	23	1
w	22	2	47	1	35	1	34	1
x	—	—	—	—	—	—	—	—
y	10	1	25	1	31	1	22	1
z	1	—	4	—	2	—	2	—
Total	1,387		3,252		4,931		3,179	

a This shows that the letter e was found illegible 167 times in every 100,000 running letters written by the elementary group and contributed 12 percent of the total number of illegibilities of that group.

b The dashes indicate percentages of less than 0.5.

TABLE 2. The Most Frequent Forms of Illegibilities Accounting for Approximately 50 Percent of All Illegibilities Among Lower-Case Letters, Their Frequencies, and the Percentages They Contributed to All llegibilities

Elementary			High School			Adult			Total		
Fr.	%	Form	Fr.	%	Form	Fr.	%	Form	Fr.	%	Form
145	11	e closed [a]	373	11	e closed	882	18	e closed	473	15	e closed
81	6	d like cl	265	8	t like l	363	7	n like u	155	5	n like u
56	4	a like o	152	5	a like u	216	4	d like cl	148	5	d like cl
47	3	a like u	146	4	d like cl	200	4	i, no dot	131	4	t like l
45	3	a like ci	120	4	r like i	188	4	a like o	114	4	r like i
42	3	t, cross above	94	3	i, no dot	185	4	r like i	111	4	i, no dot
41	3	r like i	91	3	o like a	182	4	t, cross above	103	3	a like o
36	3	b like li	84	3	h like li	151	3	k like li	102	3	a like u
35	3	t like l	63	2	r like s	148	3	t, cross right	93	3	t, cross above
35	3	i, no dot	55	2	t, cross right	—			88	3	h like li
34	2	r like half n	53	2	r like half n	51			68	2	b like li
33	2	o like a	52	2	t, too short				—		
30	2	h like li	50	2	n like u	(9 of 220 forms)			51		
27	2	n like u	50	2	d like cl						
—			—						(11 of 498 forms)		
50			53								

(14 of 279 forms)   (14 of 264 forms)

[a] This means that "e closed" occurred 145 times in every 100,000 running letters written at the elementary level and accounted for 11 percent of all illegibilities at that level.

els. The illegibility "e closed" accounted for nearly twice as many illegibilities in the elementary and adult groups and practically 50 percent more than its nearest competitor in the high-school group. With one exception, the other five, "d like el," "r like i," "i not dotted," "h like li," and "n like u," showed no marked tendency either to increase or to decrease in relative importance going from the elementary grades to the adult group. This exception, "n like u," had a percentage from four to five times greater among the adult illegibilities than among those in the lower age groups.

As for the analysis of capital-letter illegibility, out of a total of 753 illegibilities tabulated for these letters, 439 of them were recorded for the letter I. The malformation of I accounted for at least 55 percent of the capital-letter illegibilities in the elementary group and for no less than 43 percent of all the illegibili-

ties at the high-school level. At the adult level failure to close D's accounted for at least 30 percent of the illegible capitals.

A grouping of the different illegibilities with respect to common types of errors in the writing process provided very interesting possibilities remedially and preventively. For instance, the failure to close letters, Type 1, Table 3, was found to be the most consistently serious illegibility habit, as indicated by the percentages of 24, 20, and 16 for the elementary, high-school, and adult groups respectively. The tendency to loop strokes unnecessarily fluctuates from a 12 percent importance in the elementary group to one of 27 percent in the high school, and goes back to 12 percent for the adults. While Types 20 to 24 contribute less than one-half of one percent to the total of the illegibilities recorded, they are included here as interesting negative findings.

TABLE 3. Analysis of Letter Malformations

Type	Percentages Contributed			
	Elementary	High School	Adult	Total
1 Failure to close letters (a, b, f, g, j, k, o, p, q, s, y, z)	24	20	16	18
2 Top loops closed ("l like t," "e like i")	13	14	20	18
3 Looping non-looped strokes ("i like e")	12	27	12	16
4 Using straight up-strokes rather than rounded strokes ("n like u," "c like i," "h like li")	11	10	15	13
5 End stroke difficulty (not brought up, not brought down, not left horizontal)	11	6	9	9
6 Difficulty crossing t	5	5	9	7
7 Difficulty dotting i	3	5	5	5
8 Top short (b, d, f, h, k, l, t)	6	7	3	5
9 Letters too small	4	5	4	4
10 Closing c, h, r, u, v, w, y	4	3	3	3
11 Part of letter omitted	4	4	3	3
12 Up-stroke too long	2	3	1	2
13 Letters too large	2	1	— a	1
14 Beginning stroke off line	—	3	1	1
15 Bottom short (f, g, j, q, y, z)	2	1	—	1
16 Using rounded up-strokes instead of straight ones ("i like e," "u like ee")	—	1	2	1
17 Down-loop turned incorrectly	1	1	1	1
18 Excessive flourishes	—	1	1	1
19 Part added to letter	—	—	1	1
20 Down-stroke too long	1	1	—	—
21 Up-loop turned incorrectly	—	—	—	—
22 Down-loop closed	—	—	—	—
23 Printing	—	—	—	—
24 Palmer r	2	1	—	—
25 Unrecognizably recorded	2	1	3	3
26 Unclassified	10	9	9	9

a The dashes represent frequencies which accounted for less than one-half of one percent of the total.

The upshot of this phase of the work seems to be that concentration on three or four types of difficulties would focus attention on those groups of faulty habits which account for about one-half of the total illegibility problem. Each of the 8 illegibility habit groupings shown in Table 3 contributed 5 percent or more of the 42,284 illegibilities. The possibilities of recombining the twenty-four groupings in this table are numerous, and the remedial and preventive implications of these new types of difficulty should be of great importance to those interested in the teaching of handwriting.

Preventive and corrective work in handwriting can be not only quite definite but also highly concentrated on a very few aspects of the total problem. Any one of at least three lines of evidence would seem to substantiate this. It will be recalled that the illegibilities of only the four letters a, e, r, and t contributed no less than 45 percent of all the illegibilities recorded at any age level. The fact that only a very small number of forms of illegibilities occurred so frequently that they represented one-half of all the illegibilities found is at once suggestive of the specificity of the preventive or remedial measures. And then it will be remembered that the prevention or correction of only four types of bad writing habits would improve legibility at least 50 percent. It does not seem unreasonable to hazard the guess that preventive and remedial efforts directed along a combination of all three of these lines might eliminate three-fourths of all illegibilities encountered.

WHAT FACTORS MAKE WRITING HARD TO READ? [1]

Leslie Quant

[This study neatly supplements the foregoing study by Newland. In this the author tested various types of handwriting each with a consistent characteristic to see how readily it could be read in comparison with "normal handwriting" or with the printed page. Several factors stood out as significant barriers to rapid communication. Others, upon which much teaching time is likely to be concentrated, proved to be of negligible influence. Obviously the former should receive more teaching attention than the latter.]

The investigation here reported is an attempt to show how various factors modify the legibility of handwriting. The data are derived from an objective study of the eye movements of subjects as they read paragraphs of handwriting. In this study legibility is considered as synonymous with readability. Legibility is not considered as a unitary characteristic but is regarded as a composite made up of simpler elements. Dr. Frank N. Freeman in his Chart for Diagnosing Faults in Handwriting has selected five characteristics for measuring the quality of handwriting: (1) letter formation, (2) spacing, (3) alinement, (4) slant, and (5) quality of line. The present study will be organized around these characteristics.

In the present study each factor is considered separately from the other factors, in an attempt to determine the relative importance of each in the total composite which is called good writing or poor writing on the basis of legibility. The ease with which the handwriting can be read is to be considered through an attempt to answer the following questions:

1. What effect, if any, do variations in letter formation have on legibility of handwriting?

2. What effect, if any, does variation in spacing have on legibility of handwriting?

3. What effect, if any, does irregularity of alinement have on legibility of handwriting?

[1] Adapted and abridged from Leslie Quant, "Factors Affecting the Legibility of Handwriting," *Journal of Experimental Education* (1946), 14:297–316.

4. What effect, if any, does irregularity of slant have on legibility of handwriting?

5. What effect, if any, does the quality of line have on legibility of handwriting? (*Quality* is used here in a restricted sense, and refers to the weight of the line of writing.)

The author selected a paragraph, designated in this study as Selection 2, produced in his habitual style of writing, with a medium-point fountain pen. After a period of intensive practice the writer found it possible to modify his own handwriting so that other selections could be written similar to Selection 2 in all respects but one. For example, one paragraph was written in which the letter formation was poor, but in all other respects (spacing, slant, etc.) the writing was of the same quality as the original paragraph (Selection 2).

In order that the difficulty of the content of the selections would remain constant throughout the study, the standardized paragraphs "Peter's Dream" were used.

The following selections were read by the subjects participating in this investigation:

Selection 1—a printed paragraph.

Selection 2—a paragraph of normal handwriting in the author's habitual style of writing.

Selection 3—handwriting with poor letter formation.

Selection 4—normal handwriting, but with reduced spacing between letters and between words.

Selection 5—normal handwriting with reduced spacing between letters, but with normal spacing between words.

Selection 6—normal handwriting, but with the spacing reduced to ¼ inch between the lines of writing.

Selection 7—normal handwriting, but with increased spacing between letters and between words.

Selection 8—a paragraph written with uneven alinement of letters (not properly meeting the horizontal line of writing).

Selection 9—a paragraph written with irregular slant.

Selection 10—a paragraph written with a heavy line (heaviest writing pen available).

Selection 11—a paragraph written with a light line (finest writing pen available).

Examples of poor letter formation were failure to close the loop of the *a*, *d*, or *o*; *m* and *n* not rounded at the top of the strokes; failure to complete the loop of *b*, *g*, *h*, *j*, *l*, and *y*; incorrect formation of *r*, *w*, *v*; and confusions of *i* and *e* or of *a* and *o*. Selections 4 to 7 had deviations in spacing established by the use of dividers. Selections 10 and 11 are considered "quality of line."

The degree of legibility was measured by the rate and accuracy with which thirty-five adults (eleven women, twenty-four men) could read the selections at a given distance while their eye movements were being photographed. They were asked to read through the paragraph once, silently, in their accustomed manner of reading any material that they wished to remember. They were told that at the end of the reading of each paragraph simple questions would be asked to test how well the reading had been done. The questions were not standardized but were designed only as an incentive for the subjects to read the selections with care. No comment was made, either favorable or unfavorable, on the answers that the subjects gave to questions, since the experimenter did not wish to influence the performance of the subjects by introducing any factors extraneous to the reading of the material.

Before beginning the reading of each paragraph the subject was asked to "close your eyes as soon as you have finished the last line." The precaution precluded the possibility of additional eye movements back over the material which had already been read.

The developed films were placed in a projector, and the enlarged image of the eye movements was adjusted exactly to fit the length of the line of handwriting of each selection. The eye movements for each subject for each selection were plotted. In this manner an exact record was obtained for each subject of the number, location, and duration of every eye pause during the reading of each paragraph.

RESULTS

Some major findings are shown in Table 1.

1. Analysis of the data for the selection of print and the selection of normal handwriting shows that handwriting is less legible than print. The relationship is consistent, measured by the average number of words per fixation, average duration of fixations, and average number of words read per regressive movement.

2. *Good letter formation* is the most important factor in determining the legibility of handwriting; poor letter formation reduces legibility more than any other single factor considered in this investigation.

When handwriting has poor letter formation the reader must pause frequently in the line, because the words are not recognized in large wholes. Words are perceived when the eye is at rest, and the eye pauses in the line in order that perception may take place.

At each pause the reader perceives groups of letters. If the letters are poorly formed he recognizes them less easily; consequently the units of recognition become smaller, and the number of fixations per line increases. The table shows clearly the effect of poor letter formation, with 0.8 word read per fixation for Selection 3, characterized by poor letter formation.

Other evidence of the reduction of legibility when poor letter formation is found in handwriting is furnished by the duration of the fixations. The duration of the fixations is an index to the speed with which the reader recognizes the words. If the reader has rapid recognition the pauses are short in duration. In reading the selection with poor letter formation the duration of fixations is longest for all the handwriting selections used in this study. The subjects recognize the words least rapidly in this selection.

If material is legible the reader can recognize the written words in the lines with few fixations, and the movement of the eye is from left to right, without the necessity of backward movement. When the handwriting has poorly formed letters the number of words recognized per regression decreases. The table shows that Selection 3 has the smallest average number of words read per regression. The data in the table show clearly that poor letter formation reduces legibility of handwriting.

3. The compactness of handwriting affects its legibility. Reduction of spacing between letters and between words appears to improve legibility, but the evidence is not conclusive. The reduction of space shortens the line of writing and results in a decrease in the number of fixations necessary in reading the shortened line. The average number of words read per fixation is increased

TABLE 1. Average Number of Words Read per Fixation, Average Duration of Fixations, and Average Number of Words Read per Regression for Selections

Selection	Average Number of Words Read per Fixation	Average Duration of Fixations (in 1/25 sec.)	Average Number of Words Read per Regression
1 Printed	1.4 [a]	6.5 [a]	19.4 [a]
2 Normal handwriting	1.0	6.0	10.1
3 Poor letter form	0.8 [b]	6.4	4.3 [b]
4 Reduced space between letters, words	1.1 [a]	6.0	9.2
5 Reduced space between letters only	1.0	6.1	9.7
6 Reduced space between lines	1.0	5.8	8.0
7 Increased space between letters, words	0.8 [b]	6.2	4.4 [b]
8 Uneven alinement—not meeting horizontal line properly	1.1	5.9	11.4
9 Irregular slant	1.0	5.9	7.8 [b]
10 Heavy line—heaviest pen available	1.0	5.8	8.6
11 Light line—finest pen available	1.1 [a]	6.0	8.8

[a] This differs with statistical reliability (.01 level of confidence) from data on normal handwriting (Selection 2), indicating more legibility.
[b] This differs with statistical reliability (.01 level of confidence) from data on normal handwriting (Selection 2), indicating less legibility.

significantly. The average duration of fixations is decreased, but the decrease is not significant in amount. The average number of words read per regression shows a slight increase, but not enough to be significant.

Reduction of spacing between letters only, with no reduction between words, shows the same tendency as reduction of spacing between words and between letters. Reduction of spacing from ⅝″ to ¼″ between lines does not noticeably affect the legibility of handwriting.

Increasing the spacing between words and between letters reduces legibility. The increase in spacing results in a longer line, which in turn increases the number of fixations. The number of words per fixation is perceptibly and significantly decreased. The average duration of fixations remains exactly the same as for normal handwriting. The average number of words read per regression is significantly decreased. The selection with wide spacing between letters and between words ranks next to the selection with poor letter formation in illegibility.

4. Evenness of alinement apparently is not an important factor in legibility.

5. The regularity of slant of letters is important; when the slant becomes irregular, legibility is decreased. There was little change in the duration of fixations or in the number of words read per fixation. But there was a decrease in the number of words read per regression, and since regressions occur only as an index of difficulty for the reader, it is evident that legibility was lessened.

6. The influence of weight of line on legibility was inconclusive, though a

light line apparently increased the average number of words that could be read per fixation.

IMPLICATIONS

1. No one characteristic of handwriting exists separately from other characteristics, but they are interrelated in the handwriting process. In any attempt to improve the quality of handwriting it is necessary to keep clearly in mind the fact that one characteristic is dependent on others. Letter formation is closely related to spacing, slant, alinement, and weight of line. Any change in one characteristic is accompanied by a corresponding change in the others.

2. Since letter formation is the most important factor in determining the legibility of handwriting, this aspect of writing should receive the greatest emphasis in teaching children to write.

In recent years handwriting instruction has emphasized the use of simplified letter forms, free from flourishes and extra strokes, containing only the essentials of the letters. The results of this study indicate that, from the point of view of legibility, this emphasis is correct.

In teaching children to write, the development of good letter formation should be the chief outcome, and the development of other characteristics—slant, alinement, spacing, quality of line—is important only as they contribute to good letter formation.

3. Pupils should be taught to use a compact type of writing, though not at the sacrifice of good letter formation. A medium or narrow spacing between letters is desirable. There need be no concern regarding the size of paper ruling (⅝″ and ¼″) in its effect upon legibility, nor does evenness of alinement demand much emphasis.

4. Teachers should emphasize regular slant as an important aspect of correct letter formation for increasing legibility.

5. Since there is no clear-cut case for either the heavy or the light pen, it is probably best to use a pen of medium weight.

6. Handwriting has social value only as it provides a more or less permanent record which can be read by someone. Children should be made aware of the need for producing a legibly written record and of the factors contributing to legibility.

TEACHING HANDWRITING DIAGNOSTICALLY [1]

Hilda Lehman and Luella C. Pressey

[This early study is particularly significant in offering a clear-cut method for efficient teaching of a skill. Direct diagnosis of an individual's own characteristic errors enables him to concentrate in turn upon each of his most pressing ones until high legibility becomes habitual. "Editing committees" of children at early grade levels can learn to do this diagnosing, thereby saving teacher time and themselves becoming more observant of handwriting form. Illegible writing is not necessary.]

It is a curious circumstance that work on the handwrriting problem to date has concerned itself almost entirely with the general appearance or comeliness of the writing, without reference to its major function, the ease with which it can be read. Pragmatically this last consideration is obviously the important one, and as a matter of actual observation it is clear that handwriting is often good looking and still baffling to the reader. Specific investigation of those forms which interfere with reading would thus seem desirable. And it would seem desirable also to determine whether drill in handwriting to eliminate illegibility might not produce more gain in legibility than the type of drill to obtain better form, which is now common. It is conceivable that such concentration upon specific malformations of letters might be very effective in improving general appearances also.

The experiment reported in this section is based upon an investigation to determine specific factors interfering with legibility which has already appeared in print.[2] This study shows that certain few specific malformations (for example, d written like el, n like u, r like undotted i, h like li) account for the great majority of difficulties which readers find in reading handwriting samples. As a matter of fact, the twenty-seven most frequent specific illegibilities accounted for approximately 80 percent of all the "holdups" in reading. On the basis of this investigation a chart was made exhibiting these most common errors and providing place for the tabulation of the illegibilities made by each child in a class.

The present experiment has to do

---

[1] Adapted and abridged from Hilda Lehman and Luella C. Pressey, "The Effectiveness of Drill in Handwriting to Remove Specific Illegibilities," *School and Society* (1928), 27:546–548.

[2] L. C. and S. L. Pressey, "Analysis of Three Thousand Illegibilities in the Handwriting of Children and Adults," *Educational Research Bulletin* (1927), Vol. 6, No. 13.

with the efficacy of drill to increase the legibility of handwriting, based on the diagnosis of each child's illegibilities by means of this chart.

THE EXPERIMENT

The children worked with were twenty-three youngsters in a 4B class. The experimenter (Miss Lehman) first "diagnosed" the illegibilities of each pupil and then met the class one-half hour twice a week for nine and a half weeks for remedial work. The gains made by this group were compared with a control group of nineteen 3A children who had the regular handwriting drill usual in the school. Both of these classes were under the same teacher and therefore (except for the special help given the twenty-three 4B children) were subject to the same general instructional and classroom influences. The question then is as to the effects of the special procedure used by Miss Lehman as contrasted with the advances made by the nineteen children in 3A during the same period.

At the beginning, the handwriting of both groups was appraised from handwriting samples obtained in two different ways. In the first place both groups wrote for two minutes the sentence "The mail was late yesterday," and then the sentence "Write a letter to him tomorrow." These samples were judged as to quality on the Ayres-Gettysburg scale, the median rating of five judges working independently being used as the final statement of quality on each sample, and the samples being so mixed that the judges did not know from which group a given sample came. The speed of writing, in terms of number of letters per minute, was also determined.

The children were next asked to write an original composition on an interesting theme. The handwriting of the compositions was also rated as to quality on the Ayres scale. Most important, however, was the measure of "readability." Each composition was read by three different readers, each reader timing himself with a stop watch, to determine the total time taken. The figures were then made comparable by expressing legibility in terms of average number of letters read per second, on each composition. As will be seen from Table 1, the two groups were essentially the same as regards handwriting, by both determinations.

Remedial work was then started with the experimental group. First the compositions were gone over, and all instances of the twenty-seven illegibilities generally most common were tabulated on the diagnostic chart. The experimenter then pointed out to each child the illegibilities which he frequently made, and showed him how they could be corrected. She also adopted various practice procedures. Thus there was special practice for each child in writing those letters most commonly formed wrongly and lists of words containing these troublesome letters. Lists were also prepared illustrating to each child how his common illegibilities might cause confusion —such pairs as "dean" and "clean" to show how failure to close the loop on a "d" might cause misreading. After this more formal work the children wrote dictation exercises and original compositions, the writing in all cases being gone over for illegibilities and made the basis for further remedial work. The program thus continued for the nine and a half weeks' period—nineteen half-hour meetings in all. The same end tests were then given to both experimental and control groups; both groups wrote two different timed dictation exercises and an original composition assigned without reference to handwriting. Table 1 shows the outcome.

As will be seen from this table, the control group gained twelve letters per minute in speed of writing, while the experimental group gained eighteen; in quality the control group gained three points on the Ayres scale, whereas the experimental group gained fourteen. In other words, although in the work with the experimental group there was no emphasis on either speed or quality, distinct gains were made in speed and rather striking gains in quality also. In terms of the Ayres norms the gain is one grade in speed and one and one-half grades in quality, in the nine and one-half weeks' period.

TABLE 1. Median Standings of a Class Before and After 12 Weeks of Drill in Legibility, Compared with Results from a Class Not so Drilled

| | Dictation Exercise | | | | Composition | | | |
| | Speed | | Quality | | Quality | | Legibility | |
	Control	Experimental	Control	Experimental	Control	Experimental	Control	Experimental
Beginning	46	51	31	32	30	32	17	19
End	58	69	34	46	30	41	14	29
Gain	12	18	3	14	0	9	-3	10

Speed is in terms of number of letters per minute, quality in terms of values on the Ayres-Gettysburg scale, legibility in number of letters read per second.

On the compositions the gain in quality as rated by the Ayres scale was nine points. In readability, the figures show the control group to have lost slightly in the number of letters of their writing which could be read per second (the loss is probably so small as to be of no significance). For the experimental group, however, ten more letters per second could be read at the end of the training than at the beginning. To put it another way, the readers were able to read the writing of the experimental group about 50 percent faster at the end of the experiment than before.

THE GENERAL SIGNIFICANCE OF THE FINDINGS

The findings perhaps are so obvious as not to need comment. It deserves to be emphasized, however, that by directing teaching effort straight at specific faults of legibility, not only was legibility strikingly increased, but both speed and quality of handwriting were also very definitely increased. The educational moral seems obvious. The specific nature of educational problems and the need for a direct and specific attack upon these problems are clear.

Chapter X

SPELLING

In our culture spelling has assumed an especially high importance. To a surprising degree it has become a symbol of education. Even in this era of teacher shortages, a misspelled word in a letter of application might jeopardize employment—unless a secretary could readily be blamed. Perhaps this is due to the amount of phonetic irregularity in our language. In a phonetically regular language like Spanish a partially educated person can spell almost any word he can pronounce, and spelling achievement carries little status.

Whatever the cause, the problem of teaching spelling is probably with us to stay. The many and varied efforts to rationalize English spelling have had little effect as yet and will probably have little effect in the foreseeable future. Hence our children will probably continue to face the chore of learning to spell, and any means we can use to help them be more efficient should prove valuable.

A first problem is the selection and grade placement of words to be learned. Obviously it is both unwise and impossible to attempt to teach children the many hundred thousand words found in our language. Only words they are likely to use in their *writing* are worth the effort of learning. Fortunately for the teaching of spelling, a relatively few words do most of the work of our language. There have been many excellent studies of the frequency of words in our language. The classic *Teacher's Word List* prepared by Thorndike shortly after World War I based upon several million words of print led to Ernest Horn's *A Basic Writing Vocabulary* (1926), and to the Thorndike and Lorge *The Teacher's Word Book of 30,000 Words* (1944). Horn [1] points out that 2000 "words with their repetitions make up 95.05 percent of the

[1] Ernest Horn, *Teaching Spelling*, National Education Association, Washington, 1954.

286

running words in adult writing; 3000, 96.9 percent; 4000, 97.8 percent; and 10,000, 99.4 percent." With these facts in mind it is difficult to justify very extensive lists.

Light is shed upon the grade placement of words to be learned by Rinsland's A Basic Vocabulary of Elementary School Children, a section of which is presented in this book in the chapter on readability. Most spelling lists today take the above factors into account in their selection of words.

The first two studies reported below are concerned with factors in children which contribute to their ease or difficulty in learning to spell. The remainder are concerned with methods that are most effective in helping children learn.

WHY ARE SOME CHILDREN POOR SPELLERS? [1]
David H. Russell

[Assuming children have reached a stage of readiness for learning to spell, what other factors are related to good or poor spelling ability? This study throws light on this question and suggests implications for teaching.]

This study attempts to help answer such questions as the following:

1. What is the relation of spelling disability to (a) functional auditory factors such as auditory perception, acuity, and discrimination; (b) functional visual factors such as visual perception and acuity; (c) organic visual handicaps such as astigmatism and muscular imbalance?

2. To what extent is spelling disability associated with (a) speech handicaps such as bilingual background and mispronunciations; (b) certain academic abilities such as silent reading, speed and quality of handwriting?

3. What are the most frequent types of spelling error made by each of the visual, auditory, and speech handicapped groups—omissions, transpositions, insertions, additions, phonetic, etc.?

4. How do the two groups of spellers (the normal and the retarded) differ in such factors as attitude toward spelling as a school subject, methods of studying new words in spelling, utilization of imagery, etc.?

The method of the study is to compare group differences between individually matched normal and retarded spellers, supplemented by further analy-

[1] Adapted and abridged from David H. Russell, Characteristics of Good and Poor Spellers, Contributions to Education, No. 727, Bureau of Publications, Teachers College, Columbia University, New York, 1937.

ses of individual cases of disability. Disability as used here does not imply that children are incapable of learning to spell but that they are so far below their grade standards that they are definitely hampered in free expression and logical arrangement of their ideas.

The Modern School Achievement Test in spelling was given to 1185 pupils of Grades 3, 4, and 5 in four New York City public schools. On the basis of available records sixty-nine pairs of children were matched individually as to school, sex, grade, terms (half-years) in school, chronological age, and IQ. The maximum variation allowed was six months in chronological age, five points in intelligence quotient, and one term in school (two terms were allowed for upper fifth-graders). One of each pair was normal or better in spelling; the other was one year or more retarded. The difference in spelling grades for the sixty-nine pairs ranged from one to three years, with a mean difference of over two years.

In addition to the intelligence and spelling tests, each child was given sixteen different tests of constitutional and academic status. These included tests of handwriting, a battery of nine diagnostic spelling and reading tests, tests of vision, hearing, speech, and silent reading. All were given individually except spelling, handwriting, and the group intelligence tests for certain of the pairs. Case studies were made using these test data and any other available and relevant information to discover possible syndromes associated with spelling disability.

RESULTS

Spelling Disability and Constitutional Factors (intelligence, vision, hearing, kinaesthesis, and attitude toward spelling).

1. The correlations between spelling grade and mental age for the normal and retarded groups, with the influence of terms in school eliminated, were .39 and .27 respectively, showing little relationship.

2. The Betts Telebinocular Series showed no reliable (critical ratio 3.00 or higher) differences between the normal and retarded groups on any of the fifteen subtests. This does not preclude an important effect of defective vision in individual cases; a case study reveals that visual factors may be important in an individual disability.

3. A reliably greater number of retarded than normal spellers made errors on the Gates Reversals Test. Poor spellers should be examined for reversal tendencies.

4. A reliably greater number of normal spellers than retarded were "good" in attitude toward spelling and the diagnostic tests.

5. The tests of hearing acuity on the 2A Audiometer showed no educationally significant or statistically reliable differences in the hearing acuity of the groups of normal and retarded spellers.

6. The types of error (additions, substitutions, etc.) made by thirteen of the subjects with greatest hearing loss did not differ significantly from the types of error made by the individuals with whom they were matched or from the types of error made by the whole normal group.

7. On the test of auditory discrimination of pairs of words of similar sound the normal group made a reliably better score than did the retarded group.

8. Disabilities in auditory acuity and discrimination may affect spelling achievements in individual cases.

Spelling Disability and Academic Achievement (silent reading, handwriting, speech and oral reading, giving letters for letter sounds, spelling of non-sense syllables, and word pronunciation).

1. The types of errors made on the Modern School Achievement Test were analyzed as to additions, insertions, omissions, substitutions, transpositions, and phonetic errors. The differences in types of errors made by each group did not exceed 3 percent.

2. The retarded group made a reliably higher percentage of additions in their errors than did the normal group. The normal spelling group tended to make a higher percentage of phonetic errors than did the retarded group.

3. The mean grade score of the normal group was reliably higher than that of the retarded group on the Gates Silent Reading Tests, Grades 3 to 8, Types A and D.

4. The mean speed and mean accuracy of reading scores of the normal group were reliably higher than those of the retarded group.

5. In the normal group there is a suggestion that speed and accuracy of reading for general comprehension are not so closely related to spelling grade as is reading to note details. In the retarded group little difference was found on the different types of reading.

6. The normal spellers are reliably better in quality of handwriting as measured by the Thorndike Scale than are the retarded spellers. The difference in speed of writing between the groups is insignificant educationally and statistically.

7. Within the limits of the method used, the retarded spellers made more errors in speech than did the normal spellers except in vowel sounds, where the difference was negligible. The differences are statistically reliable for total mispronunciations and total types of errors, and tend to be reliable on other items.

8. The normal spellers are rated reliably higher in "rhythm" than the retarded spellers on the basis of oral reading of poetry.

9. The commonest types of speech errors are the same as the commonest spelling errors on the Modern School Achievement Spelling Test—omission and substitution. Further studies are needed to investigate the relationships between speech and spelling errors.

10. The reliability of the results obtained by comparing the records of errors obtained by two different listeners suggests the need of an improved test of speech.

11. A case study illustrates that a speech handicap, combined with certain related factors, may be a cause of spelling disability.

12. The normal spelling group had reliably higher scores than did the retarded group on each of the following tests: oral spelling, word pronunciation, giving letters for letter sounds, spelling nonsense words of one and two syllables.

13. Inability to turn sounds into letters, phonograms, or syllables is probably a basic cause of poor spelling.

14. The rather striking agreement between these tests and others involving language usage suggests the possibility of a general linguistic ability, evidenced by facility in handling words well in various ways.

15. The data indicate that spelling disability is often caused by failure to acquire in the primary grades techniques of handling letter sounds, syllables, word analysis, similarities and differences in words, and other basic language skills. Within certain limits of ability, the failure is pedagogical.

Spelling Disability and Methods of Study.

1. When asked to study as they usually do the pupils of both the normal

and the retarded groups used an average of only 3.68 different techniques of study. This was from fifteen techniques noted by the examiner and is considerably less than the nine techniques suggested by Horn, Breed, and other writers.

2. The normal and retarded groups repeated their techniques approximately the same number of times, i.e., used the same number of "efforts"—about ten—per word.

3. The normal and retarded groups differed considerably in the kinds of word study techniques they used. More retarded spellers pronounced the word oftener than the normal spellers and the group tended to spell orally letter by letter more than the normal group. More of the normal spelling group tended to write the word without looking at the original and to spell by syllables looking at the original than did the retarded group. In general the retarded group used somewhat inactive approaches such as saying the word and spelling by individual letters while the normal spelling group used active approaches such as syllabication and checking their written trials.

4. The pupils of both groups used few techniques, and more inactive than active ones, and many showed that they had not mastered a technique of studying new words.

5. The normal spelling group utilized the "auditory" method and tended to use the "visual" method better than the retarded group. On the "kinaesthetic" method the groups showed little difference, with a slight trend in favor of the retarded group.

6. Fifty-eight percent of the normal spelling group and 29 percent of the retarded group (a reliable difference) showed definite preference for and capacity in one of the visual, auditory, or kinaesthetic methods to the exclusion of the other two.

7. In oral spelling a reliably higher percentage of the retarded group than of the normal group spelled letter by letter.

8. On the pronunciation test a reliably higher percentage of the normal group than of the retarded group were good at blending and analyzing words by syllables. A reliably higher percentage of the retarded spelling group than of the normal group guessed the words as a whole on the same test. Ability to blend word parts and to syllabicate seems to be positively associated with spelling ability.

The above report of factors associated with disability might imply that they are unitary, independent factors; actually, we find that such is rarely the case with real boys and girls. A broad division of constitutional, academic achievement, or study method seldom contains all the sources of difficulty for any one child. Analysis of the individual case studies indicates that a syndrome tends to be connected with spelling disability.

Since certain skills fundamental to most spelling can be determined, it follows that (1) any diagnostic program will include a testing for these skills and (2) the school's best work will be preventive—the building up of these skills in the earlier school years. Undoubtedly most pupils will acquire such skills in the regular course of their school career. But just as children fail occasionally to get the language skills necessary for reading they may also fail to get the needed tools (probably some of the same ones) for spelling success. The important thing becomes a knowledge of the child's probable limitations (as determined by tests on entering school and observation by the teacher), the prevention if possible of linguistic failures, and the correction of difficulties as soon as they arise.

The accumulated evidence seems to

indicate that for the present, at least, some definite training in word study is needed by most children. It would seem to be a possibility, then, that the reading period could be devoted to reading for pleasure and information and that the spelling period could be devoted to word study. For those having difficulty, this would include practice in basic skills such as those mentioned above. In addition to studying letter sounds, combining syllables, seeing similarities and differences in words, etc., the pupils would write some words, learn to spell others, know something of the interesting history of some of our English words, get special help in dictionary and library techniques, and in general acquire word skills. This work of necessity would be carefully correlated with reading, spelling, and oral and written language needs and would provide a basis for a richer variety of school and home activities.

It is apparent that the members of the poor spelling group do not, as a rule, use the most effective techniques. The teaching of spelling has been unable to impose on the members of either of the groups studied the set, formal system which prevails in most classrooms. When asked to study words as they usually do they select only three or four steps, and the chief difference seems to be that the normal spellers have acquired the most adequate steps. A reliably greater number of the normal spellers showed definite preference for a method of study which stressed one type of imagery, but there was some evidence that they varied their procedure somewhat with the form of the different words. The evidence is clear that the poor speller seldom develops an efficient attack on new words. One of the most important outcomes of the present study is its demonstration of the fact that poor spellers have not acquired adequate techniques of word study; it would seem that elementary-school spelling programs should place less emphasis on acquiring a spelling vocabulary of four or five thousand words and more emphasis on developing in their pupils techniques for the mastery of new words they need to use.

In a later study [2] approximately 250 children in Grades 5 and 6 were given a series of tests to measure their visual and auditory abilities in relation to spelling. Vocabulary, reading ability, and mental ability as measured by parts of the SRA Primary Mental Abilities Test were also investigated. The results appear in the Table 1.

Comparisons were made between the children who scored in the top and bottom 27 percent on the spelling test of the Progressive Achievement Test. The results indicate that the group of good spellers exceed the group of poor spellers in the same grades on fourteen out of fifteen of the measures used, the t score indicating that the differences are significant at the .01 level. Only on the Space test of the Primary Mental Abilities Test is there no significant difference between the good and poor spellers. (This is a test of recognition of letter-like and geometric figures which have been rotated or otherwise shifted in position.) The results indicate that good spellers at the fifth- and sixth-grade levels tend to have superior auditory and visual perception, that they score higher in reading comprehension and a wide variety of vocabulary tests, and that they are superior in perception, reasoning, and the total scores of the Primary Mental Abilities Test. Although this superior spelling ability is associated with superior mental ability as measured by the Thurstone test, a number of studies

[2] David H. Russell, "A Second Study of Characteristics of Good and Poor Spellers," *Journal of Educational Psychology* (1955), 46:129–141.

TABLE 1. Differences Between Good Spellers (Upper 27 Percent) and Poor Spellers (Lower 27 Percent) of Approximately 250 Children in the Fifth and Sixth Grades

Measure	Mean Upper	Mean Lower	Differ- ence	D	t	r $_{x.sp}$
Auditory	43.82	27.76	16.06	1.96	8.19	.54
Visual	36.88	27.09	9.79	.91	10.76	.50
A + V	80.70	54.85	25.85	2.02	12.80	.66
California Reading						
Comprehension	71.20	41.58	29.62	6.17	4.80	.45
Vocabulary	72.06	23.47	48.59	4.48	10.84	.60
Experimental Vocabulary Tests						
Mathematics	41.24	29.79	11.45	3.72	3.08	.42
Miscellaneous 1	74.66	35.62	39.04	4.75	8.22	.31
Miscellaneous 2	41.10	25.76	15.34	3.04	5.05	.48
Miscellaneous T	115.00	62.88	52.12	6.91	7.54	.66
Social Studies 1	30.57	18.05	12.52	2.54	4.93	.49
Social Studies 2	83.76	62.67	21.09	5.06	4.17	.42
Primary Mental Abilities						
Perception	62.11	37.05	25.06	4.86	5.16	.29
Reasoning	63.83	30.89	32.94	6.03	5.46	.51
Space	66.17	63.26	2.91	4.68	.62	.14
Total	60.81	27.05	33.75	5.96	5.66	.58

t = Fisher's t = difference between means divided by the standard error of that differ-ence, sample size being taken into account in the computation equation.
r $_{x.sp}$ = Pearson r = correlation between spelling grade and the measure shown.

have shown that the correlation between spelling ability and general mental abil-ity is not high, usually ranging between .20 and .55. Even the relatively high correlation obtained in the present study (.58) suggests that factors of perception and word meaning as well as general mental ability contribute to spelling ability. The highest correlations with spelling scores are those of the combined auditory-visual test and a total miscel-laneous vocabulary score.

Further analysis of the relation of the auditory and visual perception abilities to spelling was of interest, so scatter-grams showing the relationships were constructed. The eta test of curvilinear-ity of regression was applied and eta was found to differ significantly from the Pearson r in predicting spelling from auditory plus visual (A + V) score or auditory and visual scores alone. The re-sults suggested that the Pearson r's of Table 1 somewhat underestimated the relationships and also that there is a somewhat lower correlation between spelling ability and auditory discrimina-tion than there is between spelling abil-ity and visual discrimination. Further, the results suggested that the relation-ship between spelling score and A + V score decreases as spelling score in-creases. Since the mean spelling score of the lowest 27 percent was 3.9 (in terms of grade) and of the highest 27 percent was 7.8, it may be stated that spelling ability was more closely related to audi-tory and visual abilities around the third-and fourth-grade levels of ability than around the seventh- and eighth-grade levels of ability. Put another way, poor spelling ability in the fifth and sixth grades is closely related to poor discrim-ination of auditory and visual differences, but high spelling ability at these levels is not closely related to superior discrimination. It may be that for children spelling at the average seventh- or

eighth-grade level of achievement a number of factors other than auditory and visual discrimination abilities affect spelling ability.

SOME FACTORS IN SPELLING READINESS [1]

David H. Russell

[When are children ready to learn to spell? If there is an identifiable period in a child's life after which he can learn to spell with far less expenditure of time and energy than before, the potential savings are obvious. A recent study by Bradford [2] suggests a physiological base for one possible aspect of spelling readiness. His results indicated that there is marked growth from the first to the second grade in ability to discriminate between sound elements in spelling words used at these grade levels. If children learn to spell in part by building phonetic generalizations regarding sounds and their written symbols, then a prerequisite is the ability to differentiate among these sounds when heard. It may become possible to identify the minimum level of sound discrimination sufficient for spelling readiness. The present study investigates several other factors associated with readiness for spelling.]

This study is an attempt to discover some factors associated with "readiness" for spelling, or ability to learn English spelling in the primary grades. It explores the relation of spelling ability to other language skills in the high first and low second grades and studies some effects on early spelling ability of two types of reading programs, one involving

early and large amounts of phonetic analysis, the other later and less emphasis on phonetic procedures.

PROCEDURES

This investigation involves four classes and 116 pupils of the greater Vancouver, British Columbia, area who were studied in the first grade in May and June of 1941, and in the second grade in November of 1941. Each pupil's abilities were measured by six group tests and seven individual tests. The group tests used were: (1) a group intelligence test—the Detroit First Grade or the Pintner-

[1] Adapted and abridged from David H. Russell, "A Diagnostic Study of Spelling Readiness," *Journal of Educational Research* (1943), 37:276–283.

[2] H. F. Bradford, "Oral-Aural Differentiation Among Phonemes as a Factor in Spelling Readiness," unpublished dissertation, Stanford University, 1952.

Cunningham Primary Mental Test; (2) an informal spelling test of twelve words (given in June); (3) the dictation test of the New Stanford Achievement Test: Primary Examination (given in November); (4) Gates Primary Reading Test, Type I, Word Recognition; (5) Gates Primary Test, Type III, Paragraph Reading; (6) a mimeographed visual perception test of like and unlike word-pairs (which had a split-halves reliability stepped up by the Spearman-Brown formula of 0.89). The individual tests taken from the Gates Reading Diagnosis Tests were: (7) Word Recognition Test—Visual Presentation (VIII 2); (8) Naming Capital Letters (IX 10); (9) Naming Lower Case Letters (IX 11); (10) giving letters corresponding to letter sounds (X 2); (11) giving words ending with a stated sound (Rhyming Words) (X 4); (12) Spelling Nonsense Syllables (B_2); and (13) Visual Perception (B_2). In summary, each pupil was given one group intelligence test, two spelling tests, four reading and letter recognition tests, three visual perception tests, and three auditory perception tests.

The four classes used in the study came from "average" districts as determined by the opinion of school officials. They were selected on the basis that two of the teachers used much phonics and two used little phonics in their primary reading programs. The original division on the basis of method of instruction was made by the Primary Supervisor of the Vancouver Schools and verified further by classroom visits and interviews with the teachers. In regard to their methods the two teachers who stressed the use of phonetic methods with their pupils (hereinafter called the "phonics group") said, "Phonics should be so integrated with reading activities that they are in perpetual use" and "The very first week some child remarks on words beginning with the same sound; right

then attention is directed to the similarity of sound. After that, day by day a new sound is found, always related to their reading work." The two teachers who did little work in phonics with their pupils (hereinafter called the "little-phonics group") put more stress on an informal reading-readiness program in the early months and suggested that they started a little work in phonics "often in January" and "when the children read little library books independently." The two groups also differed in their approach to handwriting. Both teachers of the phonics group said that they began some handwriting "the first week of school" while the teachers of the "little-emphasis" group made it much more incidental in their programs. None of the pupils had formal spelling lessons in the first grade, but all had them in the second grade. In promoting pupils to the second grade in June, none of the teachers took spelling ability into account, but the two teachers of the phonics group used phonetic ability "as it affects reading attack" as one criterion of promotion. In general, then, the "much-emphasis group" had early and rather direct instruction in reading, phonetic analysis, and handwriting, while the "little-emphasis group" had somewhat later and less direct practice in these language skills. The average IQ of the phonics group was 104 and of the little-phonics group was 105. The four teachers concerned were not rated formally but all are considered in their school systems above average or superior in teaching ability.

RESULTS AND IMPLICATIONS

The results shown in Table 1 reveal consistent and, in all but one instance, reliable differences favoring the "much-emphasis group" in the spelling, reading, visual perception, and auditory perception tests given in the study. The only differences not reliable are those in mental age, on which the groups were matched, and in (12) the rhyming test, which seems unimportant since pupils in each group scored, on the average, only 3 (out of a possible 9). The table reveals clearly that the early and rather direct type of instruction in the phonics group has a favorable influence on achievement in spelling, reading, as measured by the Gates primary tests, and some related visual and auditory abilities as here measured. This influence persists at least into the following semester in the case of spelling as measured by the New Stanford dictation test.

In comparing scores in spelling with other factors, low correlations were found with mental ages (0.41), with chronological ages (0.16), with rhyming (0.26), and with perception of paired words (0.59): but all other correlations were 0.80 or higher.

CONCLUSIONS

1. Spelling readiness seems to be acquired in the high first grade by most of the pupils involved in this study. Practically all of the pupils studied can spell ten words and their teachers estimate that two-fifths to one-half of them can spell fifty words by the end of their first-grade careers. This ability is acquired without any formal work in spelling as such, but undoubtedly it is dependent upon a type of language arts program in the first grade that places considerable emphasis upon several types of language skills.

2. A first-grade program of direct instruction in reading that includes early instruction in handwriting and phonetic analysis (with emphasis on both appearance and sound of words, syllables, and letters) produces better achievement in English spelling than a more incidental first-grade program involving little "phonics." (This study, however, does

TABLE 1. Verbal, Visual, and Auditory Abilities of 61 "Phonics Group" Pupils and 55 "Little-Phonics Group" Pupils in Four High First Grades of Greater Vancouver, Canada

	Phonics Group Mean	Little-Phonics Group Mean	CR of Difference
1. Primary Mental Tests—mental ages (mos.)	88.52	86.06	1.3
2. Spelling (June)	8.88	5.06	7.8
3. Spelling a (November)	23.94	9.06	9.3
4. Gates Primary Reading—Word Recognition	37.74	9.86	17.4
5. Gates Primary Reading—Paragraph Reading	19.38	7.60	13.4
6. Naming Capitals (Gates IX 10)	22.21	14.44	5.2
7. Naming Lower Case Letters (Gates IX 11)	22.03	12.95	6.5
8. Recognition of Word Seen (Gates VIII 2)	16.46	11.47	7.2
9. Multiple Choice Word Recognition (Gates B_2)	14.36	7.98	24.6
10. Perception Paired Words	22.51	18.70	3.7
11. Giving Letters for Letter Sounds (Gates X 2)	22.52	9.70	7.5
12. Giving Words Ending with Stated Sounds (Gates X 4)	3.23	3.11	0.3
13. Spelling Nonsense Syllables (Gates B_2)	5.64	1.01	9.4

a This test was given in the following semester when the pupils were in the low second grade.

not offer evidence of spelling achievement beyond the second grade or compare growths in desirable social and emotional attitudes developed in the two programs.)

3. It seems probable that habits of attention directed to parts of words, of seeing similarities and differences in words, of recognizing "word families," or other habits developed in a program emphasizing "phonics" are conducive to initial success in English spelling.

4. Spelling ability in the second grades studied is closely related to abilities in word recognition and paragraph reading, to abilities in recognition of capital and lower-case letters, to visual perception abilities such as distinguishing a word seen from other similar words or recognizing small differences in words, and to auditory perception abilities such as giving the names of letters sounded or spelling nonsense syllables.

5. The closeness of the relationship between spelling ability in the second grade and the other abilities mentioned in 4 above is partly determined by the type of primary language program in which the children have participated. In the "phonics group," spelling ability is more highly correlated with reading ability than in the "little-phonics group"; in the "little-phonics group" spelling ability seems more closely related to chronological age and mental age. Differences between the two groups in the correlations between spelling ability and other abilities tested are negligible.

6. A spelling-readiness test as such is probably not needed in the primary grades because the beginnings of spelling ability can be tested directly and because spelling ability is closely related to reading ability as measured by the tests used in this study. Diagnosis of individual difficulties and preventive measures are, of course, still necessary.

7. There exists a constellation of skills which can be taught and which seem basic to success in the language arts at least in the primary grades. Systematic instruction in these skills seems to have a favorable influence, not so much on separate subject-matter achievements as in the general area of language arts development.

GENERALIZATION IN SPELLING [1]

Arthur I. Gates

[At the time of this study, Dr. McConnell (see below) had made his significant investigation of generalization in arithmetic. He had shown that children learned more efficiently when they were encouraged to think and generalize than when they depended upon drill and rote memory. In this study, Dr. Gates investigated a similar problem in the field of spelling and reached some interesting conclusions.]

[1] Adapted and abridged from Arthur I. Gates, *Generalization and Transfer in Spell-* *ing*, Bureau of Publications, Teachers College, Columbia University, New York, 1935.

The writer undertook the task of determining whether one fairly comprehensive program of teaching spelling would prove superior to another. The one differed from the other only in the employment of rules and groupings, of demonstrations of applications and common factors, as well as exceptions and differences. Would it result in more or less immediate efficiency in learning the daily lessons, in greater or less retention, and in increased or decreased power in meeting new spelling problems? In other words, the purpose of the experiments was to determine the value of a program which employed a variety of generalization devices as compared with one which

made no effort to encourage or guide rationalization or transfer.

The study reports the results of two comparisons of teaching spelling—by a method designed to foster generalizing and by the method of specific study of words treated as isolated items. The experimental period comprised a full school term in each investigation. Grades 2 to 8 were included. The subjects comprised 3800 pupils in 106 classes in Public School 210, Brooklyn, New York. The same basal list of words was used for both groups. The weekly lists contained the same number of words. The amount of time spent in study and review was identical.

TABLE 1. Number of Words Taught per Week in the Several Grades of the Non-Generalization or Control Group

Words	Grade													
	2A	2B	3A	3B	4A	4B	5A	5B	6A	6B	7A	7B	8A	8B
Words per week	12	12	15	16	20 19	20 19	20	20	20	20	20	20	20	20
Total for 16 weeks	192	192	240	256	312	312	320	320	320	320	320	320	320	320

For the generalization group, the weekly lists consisted of words grouped according to some common element, such as those comprising derived forms with the suffix s and es or d and ed or ing or those falling under the ei and ie rule or those containing some common visual or phonetic element, such as in, eep, able, ly, tion, and so forth. For example, the following are some of the words studied by both groups: suffixes—ing: answering, interesting, bathing, becoming, changing, beginning, letting, lying; suffixes—d and ed: decided, filed, hoped, failed, formed, canned, fitted, satisfied; suffixes—s and es: buildings, crops, prices, problems, slipper, slippers, stands, themselves; ie rule: parties, earlier, eighteen, freight, friendly, niece, priest, review, view.

The method of teaching comprised activities designed to lead to the observation of the common factors, to the search for such factors in new words, to the association of words according to common characteristics, and, in some cases, to the rationalization of the characteristics or procedures. As an aid in the process of rationalizing or generalizing, the familiar rules for adding the suffixes s and es, d or ed, and ing, for deciding between ei and ie, and for the use of the final silent e in certain cases were introduced. For example, the following familiar rule was taught: "i before e, except after c, or when sounded as a in neighbor and weigh." Each rule or set of rules for a given suffix (s and es, and so forth, being treated as one) was introduced and taught during a single week early in the term and formally reviewed but once. The rules were, in other words, not taught long or rigorously. In fact, they were introduced rather than taught. Efforts to encourage pupils to see similarities and differences and to generalize their experiences were made during each week. The generalization method, then, consisted of a variety of devices in which learning rules was but one, and a minor, feature.

For the specific learning or non-generalization method, words were not grouped according to "word-form" characteristics but were arranged in lists on the basis of a combined difficulty and frequency-of-use criterion according to a practice now well known. In the teaching of these groups, no rules were introduced and attention was not called to common word characteristics. Each word was treated as a specific spelling problem.

The main results of the comparisons of the two methods in general are as follows:

1. The two methods produced practically the same ability to spell the words studied during the term. This fact was determined by giving an initial and final test of 100 words selected at random from the words taught. Although the mean gains were in favor of the generalization method, the differences were so small as to be of uncertain statistical reliability and of no practical significance.

2. The two methods produced practically the same ability to spell words selected from those taught during the term to which rules taught to the generalization group could be applied. Although the scores for the generalization group in these tests were slightly greater than for the specific learning group, the differences were too small to be significant.

3. The generalization method produced greater ability than the specific learning method to spell representative "new" words, that is, words not previously studied in the spelling class, from the same and higher grade levels. The superiority of the generalization group in this test was estimated as 6 or 8 per cent.

TABLE 2.   Ability to Spell New Words

	Grade									
	2		3		4		5		6	
	N	Mean	N	Mean	N	Mean	N	Mean	N	Mean
Generalization	138	12.2	136	21.2	115	27.8	138	33.5	126	39.5
Control	138	10.2	136	19.4	115	25.4	138	31.4	126	37.6
Difference		2.0		1.8		2.4		2.1		1.9
SD difference		1.1		1.2		1.3		1.3		1.4

4. The generalization method produced greater ability to convert unstudied base forms into derived words by adding the suffixes *s*, *es*, *d*, *ed*, or *ing*, and to write words containing *ei* and *ie* and other common elements like *in* or *tion*. The superiority in the test of applying the specific generalizations which were introduced to the generalization group was estimated to be about 9 per cent.

On the whole, then, it may be said that a broad and varied program of generalization, while it does not increase ability to spell the words studied during the term more than the specific learning

TABLE 3. Ability to Apply Rules to New Words

		3A		3B		4A		4B		5A		5B
	N	Mean	N	Mean	N	Mean	N	Mean	N	Mean	N	Mean
Generalization	58	15.1	61	15.7	60	18.5	65	23.5	46	25.2	56	26.8
Control	58	12.6	61	12.7	60	15.1	65	18.4	46	20.0	56	21.3
Difference		2.5		3.0		3.4		5.1		5.2		5.5
SD difference		1.6		1.7		1.7		1.8		1.5		1.7

		6A		6B		7A		7B		8A		8B
	N	Mean	N	Mean	N	Mean	N	Mean	N	Mean	N	Mean
Generalization	54	27.2	34	27.7	81	28.7	75	30.2	61	32.4	42	32.9
Control	54	23.1	34	22.6	81	24.4	75	24.1	61	27.4	42	27.0
Difference		4.1		5.1		4.3		6.1		5.0		5.9
SD difference		1.8		2.0		1.4		1.4		1.4		1.4

method, does tend to increase to some extent the power to spell new words and especially to handle the specific derivatives and other elements to which the generalization program was especially directed.

5. Some rules are more difficult to learn than others, especially in the lower grades, where the discrepancies seem to be greatest. Probably the best general

indication of the relative difficulty of the several "type" rules is to be secured in the data from the second experiment, which gives the percentage of pupils in the grade who gave the rule correctly either in its general form or in the form of a statement illustrated in terms of the concrete problem offered for solution. These figures appear in Table 4.

Of these, the three suffix rules are

TABLE 4. Percent of Pupils Giving Satisfactory Statements of Rules

Rule	Grade					
	3	4	5	6	7	8
1. Silent *e* (suffix)	42	64	70	76	84	86
2. y to i (suffix)	38	60	65	72	78	85
3. Double consonant (suffix)	15	37	45	72	78	85
4. *ei* and *ie*	—	—	68	74	79	78

fairly comparable because they were introduced in the same way and because the test situations calling for them were of the same type. The "silent *e*" rule is, at the most, only slightly easier than the "y to i" rule. Both are stated "satisfactorily" in either general or concrete form by 60 percent of the pupils in Grade 4 and by larger percentages in higher grades. The double consonant rule is not given, under the conditions of this study and test, by 50 percent of the pupils until Grade 4 is passed. While it lags behind the two other rules in Grades 6 and 7, it is given as well as any in Grade 8.

6. The data indicate that a suffix rule of a given type (e.g., the "y to i" rule) is about equally well learned and stated in connection with the three suffixes *ed*, *es*, and *ing*.

7. Tests of ability to write the derived forms when the primary form is given in the case of words in which both primary and derived forms are "new" in the sense of being from grade lists higher than those studied show that

pupils taught by the generalization method excel those taught by the specific learning method. The superiority of the pupils trained by the generalization method is about the same for the three types of derivatives. As computed, the advantages in "percentage of the total number possible" which are successfully given are for s and es 18.5 percent, for *ing* 18 percent, and for *d* and *ed* 17 percent. It should be realized that these advantages are due not merely to teaching rules but to all of the generalization influences combined.

8. The generalization pupils excelled the specific learning pupils in writing words containing *ie* and *ei* by about 7 percent.

9. In writing words by analogy with some of the type words introduced in "families" to the generalization group —such as writing words spelled with *sion* as in *mansion*—the generalization method showed an advantage over the specific learning method of approximately 15.7 percent. A speculation offered in the monograph is that, since in

this case no rules or verbal formulas were used as in the case of the suffixes, the difference between an average superiority of 18 percent for the latter and 15.7 or roughly 7.5 percent of the advantage given by the whole generalization process as used in the study may be attributed to the rule itself; the remainder to all other generalization factors.

SELF-STUDY IN SPELLING [1]
C. W. Dupee

[Studies in arithmetic and in other subject areas have shown the advantage of student responsibility and initiative in the learning process. This study indicates that the principle is also true when applied in teaching spelling.]

THE PROBLEM

The purpose of this study was to compare by means of experimentation the pupil-self-study method and the modern-systematic method of teaching spelling with regard to (1) the amount of learning achieved; (2) the rate at which learning is achieved; (3) the extent to which learning acquired by each of the two methods is retained; and (4) the use pupils make of the time saved through exemptions.

SOURCES OF DATA

Third-, fourth-, fifth-, and sixth-grade pupils and teachers in five different school systems in the northeastern part of the state of Pennsylvania furnished the data. In the third grades there were 305 pupils and 9 teachers for an average enrollment of 33.9; fourth grade, 346 pupils, 10 teachers, and 34.6 average enrollment; fifth grade, 299 pupils, 9 teachers, and 33.2 average; sixth grade, 298 pupils, 8 teachers, and 37.2 average —for a total of 1248 pupils and 36 teachers. It is apparent that the classes were not unusually small. The teachers were, according to the teacher-training standards of Pennsylvania, well trained.

EQUATING PUPILS AND TEACHERS

The alternate method was used in equating such variable factors as initiative, mental capacity, attitudes, home environment, etc., on the part of both pupils and teachers. That is to say, a teacher and his or her pupils proceeded by the pupil-self-study method for a period of twenty days; during the next twenty-day period said teacher and pu-

[1] Adapted and abridged from C. W. Dupee, "A Comparative Experimental Study of the Pupil-Self-Study Method and the Modern-Systematic Method of Teaching Spelling," *Journal of Experimental Education* (1937), 6:1–6.

pils alternated methods and proceeded by the modern-systematic method.

As a precaution against any advantages one of the methods might have over the other because of initial use, approximately one-half of the teachers in each of the four grades participating, together with their pupils, used the pupil-self-study method as the initial or beginning method. The remaining teachers and pupils used the modern-systematic method as the initial method. Thereafter the groups alternated methods with each successive twenty-day period.

Approximately half the pupils in each grade began with the pupil-self-study method while the other half were using the modern-systematic method. The experiment continued for four learning periods of twenty days each, with each group alternating the method of learning during successive periods. The daily time allotment was twenty minutes; each group had 100 words during the four-week period.

PUPIL-SELF-STUDY METHOD

1. Teachers using the pupil-self-study method proceeded on the first day of a twenty-day learning period as follows: (1) gave a pre-study test (written form) on the 100 words in the contract for the twenty-day period; (2) collected test papers; (3) supplied each pupil with a printed copy of the 100 words in the contract for that period; (4) advised the pupils that they were to do their own studying when the pupil-self-study method was used, that they would be tested daily (written form) on the 100 words in the contract, and that a pupil would be exempt from spelling, except for the final test, when he or she made a perfect score on two successive tests.

2. From the second to the nineteenth day inclusive the teachers used the twenty minutes for giving non-exempt pupils a written test on the 100 words.

3. On the final day all pupils took the 100-word test.

4. When a pupil became exempt, he was asked to note in diary fashion the use he made of the spelling period on the days on which he was exempt.

5. All test papers were scored and returned to their owners at the earliest possible convenience.

6. A chart was posted on the bulletin board at the beginning of each twenty-day learning period. The number of words misspelled or the learning status of such pupil was recorded on the chart daily.

The primary teacher duties were group testing, analyzing results, diagnosing individual cases, and helping each pupil work to capacity, but refraining from mass instruction.

MODERN-SYSTEMATIC METHOD

1. The twenty-day period was divided into four periods of five days each. The 100-word contract was likewise divided into four units of twenty-five words each.

2. The teachers proceeded on the first day as follows: (1) gave a pre-study test, written form, on the 100 words; (2) collected test papers; (3) gave pupils printed copies of the twenty-five words; (4) informed the pupils that they would all study spelling together during the regular spelling period each day, that none would be exempt from spelling, and that spelling could be studied at home or outside of the regular spelling period if the pupils so desired.

3. The general procedure on the first and the last day of the twenty-day period differed to the extent that the pre-study test and the final included the entire list of 100 words.

4. The duties of the teacher on a given day of the week, except for the first and the last day of the twenty-day period, were: Monday, give a pre-study test on the twenty-five words; use the balance of the period for teaching the pupils the correct spelling of some of the twenty-five words in the week's assignment. Tuesday and Wednesday, use the twenty minutes for teaching with his favorite technique. Thursday, give an after-study test on the twenty-five words taught during the week; use the remainder of the period for reviewing or re-teaching purposes. Friday, conduct a review lesson with the class as a whole for the purpose of fixing in the pupils' minds the troublesome or unlearned words in that portion of the contract studied to date.

5. On the twentieth day all pupils took the 100-word test.

6. The teachers recorded the results of the pre-study tests on Monday and the after-study tests on Thursday of each week on a chart posted on the bulletin board for that purpose.

With the modern-systematic method, the primary duty of the teacher was methodically directing the learning of the pupils *en masse.*

One month after the date of the final tests a retention test of 200 words (half the total) was given each grade.

FINDINGS

1. The mean number of words learned per pupil per contract period by each of the four grades was greater when they studied by the pupil-self-study than by the modern-systematic method: Grade 3, 39.79 to 33.06; Grade 4, 35.64 to 28.59; Grade 5, 35.47 to 28.68; and Grade 6, 36.31 to 28.26, respectively. These differences are reliable at the 0.001 level of confidence.

2. The mean number of words learned by each pupil during each twenty-minute period actually devoted to spelling was likewise greater for the pupil-self-study method: Grade 3, 2.5 to 1.6 words; Grade 4, 2.4 to 1.4; Grade 5, 2.6 to 1.4; and Grade 6, 2.8 to 1.4 words, respectively.

3. There was no significant difference between the two methods in percentage retained a month later.

4. The total number of twenty-minute spelling periods saved by pupils exempted from spelling in the pupil-self-study method was 11,845, which was nearly 4000 clock hours of school time or nearly 30 percent of the total time allotted to this method.

5. During this time saved, pupils "did homework"—prepared next day's arithmetic, geography, etc.—for 38.84 percent of the time; "read a library book" for 38.46 percent; "drew pictures" for 15.13 percent (total of these three, 92.43 percent); and scattered over many activities the small balance.

The large amount of time saved, together with the use pupils make of their exemption periods, is conclusive evidence that the pupil-self-study method has great possibilities for meeting individual differences and for varying and enriching the curriculum.

DO THEY LEARN FROM TESTS? [1]

Thomas D. Horn

[Knowledge of results as an important stimulus to learning has long been recognized. One form of knowledge of results is the corrected test. This study has attempted to measure the size of the contribution of the corrected test to the total learning of spelling. The results were rather surprising. Incidentally, in a later study [2] Horn found that presenting words to children in syllabified form is apparently no help to them in their learning to spell.]

The purpose of this investigation was to determine the effect of a corrected test upon learning to spell when the test is corrected by the pupils under the direction of the teacher. The study is concerned with this test as a learning device in addition to its role as an instrument of measurement. Basically in this experiment the spelling learning of children during one week when they studied the words in accordance with the test-study procedure outlined in their spelling books and also used test correction was compared with their learning when they did no regular study of the words but used the corrected test alone.

The subjects for this study were 268 sixth-grade pupils in six schools, three schools in each of two school systems. Since it was not desired to introduce an additional factor of specially prepared

[1] Adapted and abridged from Thomas D. Horn, "The Effect of the Corrected Test on Learning to Spell," *Elementary School Journal* (1947), 47:277–285.
[2] Thomas D. Horn, "Learning to Spell as Affected by Syllabic Presentation of Words," *Elementary School Journal* (1949), 49:263–272.

study materials, the lessons in the books in regular use by the participating schools were selected for the experiment. The words in the lessons were approximate, but not equal, in difficulty. Only complete data were used; that is, the scores of pupils who missed one or more tests were not included in the results. The regular teachers of the participating pupils administered the tests.

Each spelling lesson consisted of twenty-five words, five of which were review words from the new words studied four weeks previously. The difficulty of the lessons in the experimental week was either equal to or greater than the difficulty of the lessons in the preceding week, with which comparisons are made. Since these comparisons are based essentially on the results of one week in which the test-study method was used and the results of the following week in which all study was omitted, it was necessary to make the word lists as completely comparable as possible.

An attempt was made to eliminate all study of spelling except that incidental to taking and correcting the tests for the period of one week. During the preceding week the pupils' attention was directed to the importance of the corrected test in order that they should be able to receive maximum benefit from it during the experimental week. It should be noted that the corrected test plays an important role in both the preceding and the experimental weeks. This study is an attempt to measure the size of the contribution of the corrected test to the learning of spelling.

Three experimental groups were set up: Group A, including 85 pupils who (1) took a test over the words, (2) corrected the test, and (3) took another test immediately after the correction of the first test on Monday, Wednesday, and Friday of the experimental week; Group B, including 87 pupils who (1) took a test over the words, and (2) corrected the test only, on Monday, Wednesday, and Friday of the experimental week; and Group C, whose procedure was identical with Group B's except that a pronunciation exercise was included in the Monday lesson.

Because of the nature of such elementary-school subjects as spelling, where 100 percent mastery is the goal of teaching and learning, the test scores ordinarily pile up at the top of the frequency distribution. The usual statistical descriptions of experimental results have, therefore, been modified somewhat in an attempt to give an accurate picture of what took place in the experiment.

In every group the scores for the preceding week (test, corrected test, and study) were superior to those for the experimental week (test, corrected test) by statistically significant differences.[3]

[3] The difference was considered statistically significant when the level of confidence was 3 percent or higher, indicating that this great a difference would occur by chance alone fewer than three times in a hundred testings.

Group A showed a mean difference of .84 words, significant at the 2.2 percent level of confidence; Group B, 1.06 words, .86 percent level of confidence; and Group C, 2.42 words, .01 percent level of confidence, all three favoring the preceding week. These differences will later be considered from the standpoint of practical significance. Since the purpose of this study was not to establish the superiority of any method over another but rather to measure the effect of the corrected test on the learning of spelling, comparison of the methods used (test and corrected test versus test, corrected test, and study) is made mainly to determine what part of the total learning may be ascribed to the corrected test.

CONCLUSIONS AND RECOMMENDATIONS

1. The corrected test alone will contribute from 90 percent to 95 percent of the achievement resulting from the combined effect of the pronunciation exercise, corrected test, and study.

2. In some classes the corrected test alone is sufficient for mastery or near-mastery of the typical spelling lesson by the upper third of the class.

3. The corrected test appears to be the most important single factor contributing to achievement in spelling.

4. Since the time spent on the formal study of spelling results in a relatively small increase in achievement over the effect of the corrected test alone, it might be well to consider the practical significance of spending additional time for spelling study to achieve such limited additional results.

5. Since the corrected test has been shown to be such a potent factor in learning to spell, it should be used during the spelling period in such ways as to insure its maximum effect.

6. Time allotted for the study of spelling in excess of sixty minutes a week may be spent more advantageously in other areas, and, in classes of pupils with better-than-average ability, the time allotted to the study of spelling may be further reduced.

WHAT METHODS ARE BETTER? [1]

Claire Zyve

[This early investigation tried the varied effects of several methods in teaching spelling. The study had considerable effect upon teaching practice.]

The problem of the present study was to give additional data on some of the problems in method on which previous results have been conflicting or meager. The factors considered here are:

1. Teacher-directed study compared with individual study.
2. Study of words solely from lists compared with the writing of words in sentences during study (list-context method).
3. Effect of homework review compared with the effect of teacher-directed review.
4. Efficiency of blackboard use compared with that of a lantern-slide projector for the presentation of words.
5. Effect of emphasis on the form of the word before study by identification among similar forms, combined with more careful attention to the form of the word in the child's own writing. Hereafter this method is referred to as "other factors in form."
6. Results of limiting the study of new words to four days a week, using the fifth day for systematic review.

The above methods were studied individually and in combination with each other.

Participating in the study were the children of ten classes, Grades 3 through 7, of a school accustomed to good teaching. Appropriate tests in intelligence, arithmetic, reading, and spelling given before the study and at its end indicated that there had been consistent teaching both before and during the study—the experiment did not subject the children to radically different drill. Throughout the study the spelling words used were appropriate to the grade level of each group.

The study was divided into eight five-week periods, each week containing five spelling periods of fifteen minutes each. An initial test was given at the beginning of each five-week period, covering the next eighty words in the spelling list. This test was a regular procedure in each of the grades in question. Results showed twenty-eight as the nearest mean

[1] Adapted and abridged from Claire Zyve, An Experimental Study of Methods, Contributions to Education, No. 466, Bureau of Publications, Teachers College, Columbia University, New York, 1931.

number of words incorrect throughout the groups. A few times during the study, when these grade lists proved to be too easy or too difficult for the grade, other unstudied portions of the grade lists were selected until the list in question was equalized with the others. The equalization of the groups was thus essentially one of equalization of the learning load.

A final dictation test covering the eighty words was given at the end of the five-week teaching period. These results were then a combination of immediate- and delayed-recall. They include immediate-recall for the words studied in the fifth week; a one-week's delayed-recall for the words taught in the fourth week; a two-weeks' delayed-recall for those taught in the third week; a three-weeks' delayed-recall for those taught in the second week; and a four-weeks' delayed-recall for the words that were taught in the first week.

In *teacher-directed study*—the taking up of each new word in turn by the teacher—the children worked together, spending a uniform amount of time on each word missed by any individual in the class. The word was written on the board as a whole and in syllables in the presence of the class. The children worked at the same time but not in unison; that is, each child said the word and spelled it softly and at his own rate of speed. The children who did not miss any words in the preliminary test of the words for the week were excused from study. The words to be studied included all those missed in the sixteen-word list for the week.

In the *individual-study plan* the child studied the words which he himself missed on the preliminary Monday test. The same study method was carried out as that used by the teacher-directed groups, with the exception of a con-trolled division of time on the various words.

In the factor "*study of words from lists*" the children studied on Tuesday the words they missed on the Monday test. Another test was given on Wednesday; on Thursday they studied again words missed on Wednesday; and on Friday another test was given, followed by further study on the words missed. This testing was list testing, the words being studied entirely apart from context.

In the factor called "*list-context method*" the preliminary testing and the Tuesday studying were carried on in the same way. On Wednesday, instead of another test, each child wrote the words missed in his own sentences. In the case of individual study, he wrote the words he himself had missed; in the case of teacher-directed study, he wrote the total list missed by the class. On Thursday in the list-context method, the teacher dictated all words for the week in sentences to be written by the children. The entire list was again dictated as a list on Friday, and the words missed were restudied. As will be noted, the words were studied in isolation on one day and written in sentences on two other days. All the words missed on any day were studied in isolation under the teacher's direction.

To study the effect of *homework review*, during two testing periods the children were asked to take work home on Tuesday and Thursday nights. They were to use whatever study method was then being used in their room. This resulted in about a half-hour of additional time on the week's words. In classes using teacher-directed review, the words missed on Friday were retaught on Tuesday and Thursday of the following week and were given with the words of the week in the Friday test. The use of blackboard or lantern-slide projector for presenting new words is self-explanatory

In the methods using "*other factors in form*" three additional factors emphasing word form were included. Onè was the identification of the word in a group of similar but not identical forms before detailed study. (Underline *six* in: *fix, mix, six, sift, sing, sixes*.) The second element was writing the word once in syllables before writing it as a whole. The third was to correct the word the first time it was written as a whole, then to cover this word and the following times to compare the words as they were written during study with the previous ones in the subject's own writing.

RESULTS

1. Teacher - directed study proved more efficient than individual study.

2. The use of sentences as an element in method when combined with the use of lists gave better results than the use of lists alone.

3. Additional home study was of little value in the learning of words when the teacher-directed, list-context method was used. It helped to equalize results, however, when used with the less efficient methods.

4. The use of a lantern for the presentation of words gave better results than the use of the blackboard when a method which was the same in other respects was used.

5. The use of teacher-directed review gave better results than no review.

6. Increased emphasis on form of the word before study by identification among similar forms, when combined with the child's close observance of the word in his own writing, as used in this experiment, did not give a measurable difference in results.

7. Four fifteen-minute periods a week for study on the new words with the remaining fifteen-minute period for systematic review gave the same gain as did five fifteen-minute periods for study when two reviews of the words missed on the Friday test were included.

8. Each of the factors, the list-context method, teacher-directed study, lantern presentation of words, and teacher-directed review, seemed about equally significant in increasing the mean number of words gained.

9. A method which combined these favorable elements was significantly better than a method which did not include them.

These results are also shown in Table 1.

TABLE 1. Factors in Method Favored, with Approximate Chances That the True Difference Is Above Zero

Factors Compared	Difference in Number of Words in Final Mean Gain	Sigma of Difference	Approximate Chances
A	2	1.24	20 to 1
B	2	1.25	18 to 1
C	1	1.02	5 to 1
D	1	1.85	2 to 1
E	4	1.61	155 to 1
F	2	1.17	24 to 1
G	2	1.44	11 to 1
H	6	1.66	6,700 to 1
I	8	1.81	Highly significant
J	0	—	
K	2	1.44	11 to 1

Saxon verbs and is, therefore, in the grammatical sense not a true tense. Like all the Germanic languages, English expresses the idea of future by the use of the present tense (I go tomorrow), by the present progressive form (am going tomorrow), and by a large number of various phrases, including I shall go, I will go, I hope to go, I plan on going, and so forth. To insist that a certain fixed arrangement of *shall* and *will* constitutes the future tense in English is to perpetuate an error originally derived from Latin influences.

From time to time efforts have been made by earnest but poorly informed teachers to make the grammatical terminology of English coincide with that of Latin. Not many years ago a formal report recommended the use of such terms as nominative, genitive, and accusative cases. In addition to confusing English grammar with Latin grammar such terms tend to obscure the real functions of English forms which are described by the terms subjective, possessive, and objective. Even these terms apply chiefly to pronouns. Except for a series of devices for signaling the possessive, the English noun has no case distinctions remaining.

The fact is that English grammar, as it is generally taught, is far from being a satisfactory explanation of English as it is actually used. The tradition of the eighteenth century has carried forward to our day an unscientific and not even fully rational scheme of English grammar.[1]

What, then, *is* the truth about our language that we should teach?

The first study, by Marckwardt and Walcott, reveals the striking contrast between the assumptions held by many reasonably well-informed students of English usage and the true reality. This knowledge can save much unnecessary effort now spent attempting to eradicate usage that need not be eradicated.

The second, by Fries, discloses much of what is the true grammar of English in contrast with the Latinized version. The third, by Greene and others, reveals the futility of attempting to improve language structure in student writing by the use of certain accustomed teaching methods.

The final three are studies of methods that apparently prove successful in improving student usage.

[1] National Council of Teachers of English, *The English Language Arts*, Appleton-Century Co., New York, 1952, pp. 279–280.

FACTS ABOUT CURRENT ENGLISH USAGE [1]

Albert H. Marckwardt and Fred G. Walcott

[What constitutes acceptable English usage? Few areas of scholarship arouse more bitter controversy; in few do otherwise rational people argue more vehemently from emotion and prejudice rather than from knowledge of fact. In the final analysis, the only valid criterion of acceptability must be not someone's rule or opinion but actual usage by reputable writers and speakers. Fortunately, a vast body of scholarship dating back through many decades makes available the knowledge of such usage. The unique contribution of the present study has been the contrasting of the *judgment* by well-educated users and teachers of English usage regarding acceptable usage with the *facts* of usage. Reputable usage is far more inclusive and flexible than has been generally recognized. This means that teachers need no longer waste effort trying to eliminate the many, many usages which they have assumed were not acceptable, but can concentrate with greater effectiveness upon a more restricted group.]

In an earlier study [2] a list of 230 expressions "of whose standing there might be some question" was submitted to 229 judges, composed of 30 linguistics specialists, 30 editors, 22 authors, 19 businessmen, and about 130 teachers of English and of speech. The judges were asked to "score according to your observation of what is actual usage rather than your opinion of what usage should be," but many nevertheless reported their own likes and dislikes. They were asked to place the various expressions into one of the following three categories:

1. Formally correct English, appropriate chiefly for serious and important occasions, whether in speech or writing; usually called "literary English."
2. Fully acceptable English for informal conversation, correspondence, and all other writing of well-bred ease; not wholly appropriate for occasions of literary dignity; "standard, cultivated colloquial English."
3. Popular or illiterate speech, not used by persons who wish to pass as cul-

[1] Adapted and abridged from Albert H. Marckwardt and Fred G. Walcott, *Facts About Current English Usage*, Monograph No. 7 of the National Council of Teachers of English, D. Appleton-Century Co., New York, 1938.

[2] Sterling A. Leonard, *Current English Usage*, Monograph No. 1, National Council of Teachers of English, Chicago, 1932.

tivated save to represent uneducated speech or to be jocose; here taken to include slang or argot, and dialect forms not admissible to the standard or cultivated area; usually called "vulgar English," but with no implication necessarily of the current meaning of vulgar; "naïf, popular, or uncultivated English."

Those items which at least 75 percent of the judges agreed upon as being cultivated colloquial English were labeled *established*. Those items disapproved by at least 75 percent of the judges were labeled *illiterate*. Those approved by more than 25 percent but fewer than 75 percent of the judges were labeled disputable. The 230 items were ranked in the order of their acceptance by linguists.

Examples

Item No.

Established usages (107 items)
10. You *had better* stop that foolishness.
20. *Under these circumstances* I will concede the point.
30. *As regards* the League, let me say . . .
40. The New York climate is *healthiest* in fall.
50. We cannot discover *from whence* this rumor emanates.

Disputable usages (80 items)
110. Sam, who was then in town, was with me *the three or four first* days.
120. I *expect* he knows his subject.
130. *Neither* of your reasons *are* really valid.
140. *Leave* me alone, or else get out.
150. Everybody bought *their* own ticket.

Uncultivated or *illiterate* usages (43 items)
190. The engine was hitting good this morning.
200. He *begun* to make excuses.

210. I *have drank* all my milk.
220. You *was* mistaken about that, John.
230. They *swang* their partners in the reel.

In contrast with this above study which surveyed *opinion* about usage, the present study attempts to compile the recorded *facts* of usage concerning the same 230 items. The most authoritative single compilation of linguistic fact is the Oxford dictionary together with its supplement. Accordingly, the Oxford dictionary was consulted in respect to each of the test expressions, to discover what record there was of its use on the formal literary level, on the informal or colloquial level, in dialect, at the present time, or in any earlier period. In a great many instances the information given in the Oxford dictionary was deemed sufficiently complete for the purposes of this investigation. Since this monumental work was a long time in the making, some of the earlier volumes are based on less complete evidence than those in the second half of the alphabet. Thus, it was felt desirable, at times, to add to the Oxford dictionary data information supplied by the second (1934) edition of *Webster's New International Dictionary*. This was especially true in the case of words or expressions whose status in usage is not the same in Great Britain and America. Horwill's *Modern American Usage* was also consulted in respect to suspected Americanisms. In some instances the dictionary was not the most satisfactory source for a record of usage, and the grammars of Jespersen and Curme were used to supplement the dictionary findings.[3] These gram-

[3] O. Jespersen, *A Modern English Grammar*, Heidelberg, 1928-31, 4 vols.; G. O. Curme, *Syntax*, D. C. Heath & Co., Boston, 1931, and *Parts of Speech and Accidence*, D. C. Heath & Co., Boston, 1935.

mars have the weight of scholarly authority behind them, and in them illustrative citations from modern writings and from earlier periods are extensively employed to support the observations which are made. Likewise Hall's *English Usage*,[4] a record of usage based upon 75,000 or more pages of literary English, was consulted at various points. In a few other instances articles in the scholarly journals were employed.

If the expression was recorded without a limiting label in the collections of usage consulted and if a citation was recent, the expression was considered.

If an expression was given in any of the sources with the limiting label "U.S." and the citations illustrating it were drawn from serious or formal writing, it was classified as American *literary English*. The categories colloquial English and American colloquial English are self-explanatory. It must be emphasized, however, that the term *colloquial*, as it is employed in reputable dictionaries and by sound scholars, is not used in a derogatory sense. It merely means that the expression or word is to be found in spoken or informal written rather than in formal written English.

The *dialect* category needs but one bit of explanation. Since the Oxford dictionary recorded only dialectal words or expressions that had formerly been in general use, not those that had begun as dialect here and remained so, the same qualification must apply to what is listed as dialect here. Any words or expressions for which no citations after 1800 were found in the Oxford dictionary were listed as archaic unless one of the other sources indicated that they were still in use. If a word was labeled both *dialect* and *archaic* by the dictionaries, it was placed in the *dialect*

⁴ J. Leslie Hall, *English Usage*, Scott, Foresman & Co., Chicago, 1917.

category on the ground that it was still in use somewhere at the present time.

The authors wish to make it clear at this point that in this study they are not advocating any one usage, a group of usages, or a level of usage. With advocacy of any kind we have absolutely no concern. We are only reporting the facts of the English language as they appear in the work of universally recognized authorities. We have conscientiously given all of the sources of our information so that our findings may be verified. The subjective element has been eliminated as far as was humanly possible, that is, except for placing the items in their respective categories, and in performing this task we have attempted to lean neither to right nor to left.

Examples

Item No.

Established usages

10. You *had better* stop that foolishness. LE (literary English). Oxford dictionary from 971 on, including Shakespeare.
30. As *regards* the League, let me say . . . LE. Oxford, 1824 on. Jespersen, Vol. 3, p. 178, characterizes this as a "frequent combination."
40. The New York climate is *healthiest* in fall. LE. Oxford, 1552 on.
50. We cannot discover *from whence* this rumor emanates. LE. Oxford, 1377 on.

Disputable usages

110. Sam, who was then in town, was with me *the three or four first* days. LE. Oxford, 1340–1781, "This still survives, though it is now rarely used when numbers above 3 or 4 are concerned." Webster, "May otherwise follow numbers."
"May otherwise follow numbers."

120. I *expect* he knows his subject. CE (colloquial English). Oxford, 1592 on, "Now rare in literary use; is often cited as an Americanism but is very common in dialectal or colloquial speech in England." Webster, "chiefly colloquial."

130. *Neither* of your reasons *are* really valid. LE. Oxford, 1611 on, citing Shakespeare, Dryden, Newman, and Ruskin.

140. *Leave* me alone or else get out. LE. Oxford, 1400 on.

150. Everybody bought *their* own ticket. LE. Oxford, 1530 on, citing Sidney and Ruskin.

Uncultivated or illiterate usages

190. The engine was hitting *good* this morning. Archaic. Oxford, 13– 1887, "Obsolete, rare except in vulgar or slang phrases."

200. He *begun* to make excuses. CE. Oxford, 1563–1793, Pope cited. "An alternative from the old plural *begun* has also come down to the present day." Curme (*Parts of Speech, etc.*, p. 307) marks it as an older literary form and comments that it survives in popular speech.

210. I *have drank* all my milk. Archaic. Oxford, 1704–1819, "From 17th to 19th century *drank* was intruded into the past participle, probably to avoid the inebriate associations of *drunk*."

220. You *was* mistaken about that, John. Dialect. Oxford, 1340–1837, "Still dialect in all persons." Webster, "Widely used in the 18th century, often by standard authors, now regarded as grammatically incorrect or illiterate."

230. They *swang* their partners in the reel. LE. Oxford, 1000–1912, "rarely swang." Curme (*Parts of Speech, etc.*, p. 318) marks it as older literary form. Webster, "Archaic past tense."

Of the 107 *established* usages of Leonard's study (literary and acceptable colloquial), only fourteen were found in this study to be restricted to reputable colloquial and informal written English; three items appear to be in acceptable colloquial use in America but not in England; one appears to be dialect; and one is literary in America but not in England.

Of the eighty *disputable* usages of Leonard's study, this study found twenty-six to qualify as literary English; ten literary in America but not in England; sixteen colloquial English; fifteen colloquial in America but not in England; five dialect; and for eight there was no evidence available—they had not been recorded.

Of the forty-three *uncultivated* or *illiterate* usages of Leonard's study, this study found five to qualify as literary English; four literary in America but not in England; three reputable colloquial English; five colloquial in America but not in England; twelve dialect; eight archaic, formerly but not now acceptable; for six there was no evidence.

Of these forty-three usages rejected by the opinions recorded in Leonard's study, more than a third (seventeen) are recorded in reputable literary or colloquial use, either in England or in America. The extreme conservatism of opinion about usage, as compared with the factual record of usage itself, is strikingly demonstrated.

It is also noteworthy that all but six of the forty-three items were recorded in the sources employed, and furthermore, that all of those for which any record was found appeared in the Oxford dictionary or its supplement. Thus we find that not only the disputable but even most of these condemned expressions were in accepted usage at some former period, but that nearly half of them (the twelve dialectal and the eight archaic) are now confined to particular regional or social dialects, that is to say, to limited, nonstandard spheres of usage. We are reminded again how much of nonstandard, "incorrect," or questionable language has a continuous history and tradition behind it; it is not created on the spur of the moment but, to indulge in a simile, is like an underground stream which pops up into the light of day where it is least expected and frequently not welcome.

There is one final observation to be made on this group of expressions. This is in connection with the type of error or supposed error condemned as illiterate. According to the classification employed in the body of current English usage, these illiterate items represented sixteen different types of errors. Yet no less than twenty-one of the expressions were concentrated in those categories which dealt with forms and uses of verbs. There were eight items which were concerned with past-tense forms alone. Of the expressions involving questions of verb form and use, seven were found to be standard English, two archaic, and the remaining eleven were dialectal forms.

All of this would seem to suggest that in respect to matters of verb formation and use, our prejudices are heightened. This is particularly true of the past tenses of strong verbs. As a matter of fact, even the past-tense form sung, given equal rank with sang by all of the factual sources, was rated as literary English by two English teachers, as colloquial English by fourteen, and as illiterate by sixteen. This particular verb eventually ended up in the "disputable" category, but there is no overlooking the fact that 50 percent of the judges considered a fully accepted verb form to be illiterate. The past participle awoken, still in literary use in England, was voted "illiterate," and it is particularly ironic that the very last item on the list, the most discredited, was the form swang, not at all uncommon in British speech.

WHAT GRAMMAR SHOULD BE TAUGHT? [1]
Charles C. Fries

[The effect of Latin influence upon systematic English grammar has been described above. If as indicated the grammar customarily and traditionally taught in our schools is not a true picture of our language, what is? This crucial study presents important evidence on the topic and suggests conclusions regarding what should be taught.]

Anyone who cannot use the language habits in which the major affairs of the country are conducted, the language habits of the socially acceptable of

[1] Adapted and abridged from Charles C. Fries, *American English Grammar*, Monograph No. 10 of the National Council of Teachers of English, Appleton-Century Co., New York, 1940.

most of our communities, is under a serious handicap. The schools, therefore, have assumed the burden of training every boy and girl, no matter what his original social background and native speech, to use this "standard" English, this particular social or class dialect. To some pupils it is almost a foreign language; to others it is their accustomed speech. Many believe that the schools have thus assumed an impossible task. Certainly the widespread and almost unanimous condemnation of the results of their efforts convinces us that either the schools have not conceived their task adequately or they have chosen the wrong materials and methods to accomplish it. We shall find, I think, that seldom have school authorities understood the precise nature of the language task they have assumed and very frequently have they directed their energies to teaching not "standard" English, realistically described, but a "make-believe" correctness which contains some true forms of real "standard" English and many forms that have practically no currency outside the classroom.

1. All considerations of an *absolute* "*correctness*" in accord with the conventional rules of grammar or the dicta of handbooks must be set aside, because these rules or these dicta very frequently do not represent the actual practice of "standard" English but prescribe forms which have little currency outside the English classroom. We assume, therefore, that there can be no "correctness" apart from usage and that the *true* forms of "standard" English are those that are actually used in that particular dialect. Deviations from these usages are "incorrect" only when used in the dialect to which they do not belong. These deviations suggest not only the particular social dialect or set of language habits in which they usually oc-

cur but also the general social and cultural characteristics most often accompanying the use of these forms.

2. It is the assumed obligation of the schools to attempt to develop in each child the knowledge of and the ability to use the "standard" English of the United States—that set of language habits in which the most important affairs of our country are carried on, the dialect of the socially acceptable in most of our communities.

3. The first step in fulfilling that obligation is the making of an accurate and realistic survey and description of the actual language practices in the various social or class dialects. Only after we have such information in hand can we know what social connotations are likely to attach to particular usages.

This study was designed to identify the inflections and syntax—the grammar —of present-day American English. The ideal material would be mechanical records of the spontaneous, unstudied speech of a large number of carefully chosen subjects. The practical difficulties prevented collecting this.

The use of any kind of *written* material for the purpose of investigating the living language is always a compromise but at present an unavoidable one, and the problem becomes one of finding the best type of written specimens for the purpose in hand. The stenographic reports of evidence given in our courts are usually worthless for linguistic study, for almost invariably the stenographers, in transcribing their notes, not only use their own spelling but normalize the language forms as well. Business correspondence is much too limited in respect to its range of situation. Informal letters, if carefully handled, can provide at least the basis of a valuable tentative sketch to serve as a chart to guide methodical observation in the field. Certainly to check and to verify the conclusions of such a tentative sketch is a much more feasible undertaking than to make an original study without such a chart. Through the efforts of the Modern Language Association of America with the support of the Linguistic Society there were made available for this investigation about 3000 letters from certain files of informal correspondence received by the United States government.

Any correspondence to be so used must satisfy certain requirements:

1. It must be certain that the language used in the particular letter or letters is really the language of the subject whose usage we are attempting to investigate. For that reason we included no typewritten letters; we took only those in the original handwriting of the persons selected as suitable subjects. At the time of examination we tried to make sure that there was always some item of evidence in connection with the letter that would justify the conclusion that the language used was actually that of the writer.

2. It must be possible to procure sufficient and reliable information concerning the writer. In respect to the writers of the letters here gathered we had at hand the following information:

a. Place and date of birth of the writer.
b. Place and date of birth of both father and mother.
c. Present address of each.
d. A record of the writer's schooling.
e. A record of the occupations in which he had been engaged.
f. In some cases (not in all, and chiefly in those classed in the "vulgar" or "popular" English group) a confidential report on the family.

3. There must be enough material from each subject to be a fair sample of

his language—not, of course, of his vocabulary, but of the language forms and structures.

4. The correspondence must cover a wide range of topics. The material here used was largely made up of intimate descriptions of home conditions (family activities, family needs, domestic troubles, financial difficulties, sicknesses, ambitions, accidents), all offered as reasons for appeals of one kind or another. This material was limited, however, by the fact that all the letters were very serious in tone. Nowhere was there anything of a light or humorous feeling.

We were seeking to record as completely as possible the methods used by the English language to express grammatical ideas and to discover the precise differences in these methods as employed by the various social dialects. The outlines of our grouping quite naturally settled themselves. The facts gathered all fitted into a classification made up of three general types of devices to express grammatical ideas: *word forms, function words,* and *word order.*

WORD FORMS

Word forms or inflections include prefixes and suffixes as well as more drastic changes.

A. The major uses are number (singular or plural) and tense (past or present).

    1. Number (*table, tables; go, goes; man, men; this, these;* etc.).
    2. Tense: The forms to distinguish the preterit (or past) tense of the verb from the present tense provide the second important use in Modern English of the forms of words to express grammatical ideas. The simple past tense is the only one of the time distinctions expressed in Present-day English that is still distinguished by inflection or the form of the

words. The others are shown by function words in periphrastic combinations and will be treated below. The participles distinguished from the present tense form by inflections—the present participle with the ending -ing and the past participle with a form (in most cases) like that of the simple past tense (preterit). Within the preterit there is now no distinction of form for number or for person except in the verb to be, in which was is used with singulars and were with plurals. The preterit form, therefore, does duty as a tense form only, and in all except eighteen verbs clearly distinguishes the past tense from the present. These eighteen verbs are: beat, bet, burst, cast, cost, cut, hit, hurt, let, put, rid, set, shed, shut, spit, split, spread, thrust.

Most verbs now form the past tense "regularly" by adding -d or -ed to the present tense. Of the many hundred which formerly formed the past tense by a change of stem vowel (e.g., begin, began, begun) all but sixty-six now follow the regular pattern and, of the sixty-six, only forty-two maintain a difference between past tense and past participle.

B. There are four minor inflections of words.

1. Genitive: In pronouns the inflectional genitive (my, mine, his, her, etc.) still predominates (98.4 percent) in comparison with the periphrastic with of. With nouns the reverse is true: only 4.3 percent of usage is with the inflectual genitive; 95.7 percent of usage is with of.

2. The six dative-accusative forms (me, us, him, them, her, whom) are all that are left of the many distinctive forms that existed in Old English.

3. Comparison. The inflections -er and -est have been supplanted in about half of Standard English with the function words more and most. The former tend to be used largely with simple (one syllable) and common words, the latter with longer, more learned words. The use of the superlative for two, ignoring a dual as distinct from plural, is a fact of Standard English and not just of Vulgar English.

4. Person (I, we, you, he, she, it, they; am, is; and the -s of the third singular present indicative verb ending) and mood (subjunctive, which has tended to disappear from use, replaced by function words). The subjunctive is still used somewhat (a) after demand, ask, recommend, etc.; (b) in conditions—"If I were you . . ."; and (c) in wishes—"God bless you."

FUNCTION WORDS

Function words are those having little meaning apart from the grammatical ideas they express. They appear to be growing in usage.

A. Function words with substantive (prepositions) express a great and growing variety of relationships, often with other function words or adjectives (due to). Nine of them (at, by, for, from, in, of, on, to, with) occur in about 92 percent of the instances.

B. Function words with verbs fall in two categories. Those used with the infinitive are to, do, shall, will, be, have to, get, used to, may, can, must, might, could, would, should, ought. Those with the participles are be, get, keep, and have.

C. Function words used with adjectives are numerous. They include the comparatives more and most; the intensifiers very good, pretty good, mighty good, real good, etc.; the -ly intensifiers: duly grateful, fairly large, hardly able, etc.: the intensifiers without -ly ending; far distant, quite sure, *so* glad, etc.; and *enough*: good *enough*, old *enough*, large *enough*.

D. Function words used with word groups are the so-called conjunctions. Of the thirty-two most common words of this category, seven (*and, that, which, if, as, who, but*) account for 84.9 percent of the instances and five more (*when, while, what, where, so*) raise the percentage to 92.2.

E. Three miscellaneous function words, *it, there*, and *one*, complete the category. "I know *it*." "*It* turned me gray." "*It* appears *that*." "*It* is hard to . . ." "*There* is no other way." "The home is a good *one*." "Do not mistake my position for *one* of criticism." "No *one* ever told me."

WORD ORDER

Word order has come to be a major concern in Modern English; many grammatical ideas depend upon word order for expression. In contrast with the "dispensable or secondary" relational concepts of word form and function words, word order deals with "essential or unavoidable" relational concepts. If, for example, one is to say anything about a bear and a man in connection with the action of killing, it is essential and unavoidable that he indicate which one did the killing and which one was killed. All known languages express this sort of relationship (the so-called subject-object relationship) unmistakably. On the other hand, whether the killing took place in the past, the present, or the future; whether it was instantaneous or long drawn out; whether there were several bears, or two bears, or but one bear; and whether the speaker knew this fact of his own firsthand knowledge or only from hearsay—these matters are of the "dispensable or secondary" type and may or may not be expressed.

We have seen the particular grammatical ideas expressed in English by inflections or the forms of words. These are, in Present-day English, chiefly number and tense—grammatical concepts that are clearly of the dispensable or secondary type. Function words indicate especially precise times for the action or attitudes of the speaker toward the action, and therefore, also, in large measure, express grammatical ideas of the dispensable or secondary type. The grammatical ideas expressed in English by word order are almost completely those that must be classed with the essential or unavoidable relational concepts. They are primarily those of the so-called "subject" and "object" relation and those that we include under the term "modification." As a matter of fact, it might almost be fair to say that the history of the English language in respect to its grammar has in some large measure been a steady progress away from that type of language in which both "dispensable or secondary" grammatical concepts and "essential or unavoidable" ones are expressed by inflections or word forms, toward a type of language in which inflections are used for only the "dispensable or secondary" grammatical ideas and word order for the "essential or unavoidable" grammatical relationships.

The first of the essential grammatical relationships that all languages express are the "subject and object" relations. If we wish to speak of a thing and an action we must know whether the thing is conceived as the "starting point" or the "end point" of the action. The first we call "subject"; the second, "object." In Old English practically all grammatical relationships were expressed by inflections; apparently none by word order. The "subject" relationship was expressed by the nominative case form and the "object" relationship was expressed by the accusative or dative inflection. The meaning was the same regardless of the word order of the sentence. "The man the bear killed. The bear the man killed. Killed the bear the man. Killed the man the bear." Because of case endings the reader always understood that the bear was the "end point"—was killed. In writings of 1000 A.D. the accusative-object occurred before the verb 52.5 percent of the time; in 1300 40 plus percent; in 1400 14.3 percent; and by 1500 only 1.87 percent of the time. By 1500 the position following the verb had become as now the fixed position for the accusative-object. In similar fashion by the early part of the fifteenth century, the position of a noun as dative-object had become fixed in a position after the verb but before an accusative-object.

In general, then, in respect to the expression of the subject and object relations, the development in English has been away from inflectional devices which made it grammatically possible for subjects and objects to stand in any position among the words of a sentence, to the use of grammatically functioning fixed word-order patterns which made the position before the verb "subject" territory and the position after the verb "object" territory.

The word-order pattern found for the nouns of the actor-action-goal construction:

1. A single noun preceding the verb —a noun that has the full characteristics of a substantive (i.e., with possible determiners as well as inflection for number), that is not preceded by an accompanying function word or inflected for genitive case—is the subject or the starting point of the actor-action construction. "The *man* stood by the sentinel box."

2. Two such nouns preceding the verb—nouns that are equivalent or refer to the same person or thing—are the subject and an appositive, the first in order being the subject. "The *sentinel*, a man, stood by the box." "The *man*, a sentinel, stood by the box."

3. Two or more such nouns preceding the verb—nouns that do not refer to the same person or thing but are leveled by similar accent and/or function words —constitute a compound subject (two or more subjects). "The *sentinel* and a man stood by the box."

4. If two nouns precede the verb, stand next to one another, and are not leveled by accent and/or function words, but with only one possible determiner and that before the first noun, the second noun is the subject and the first a modifier of the subject. "The sentinel *man* stood by the box." "The man *sentinel* stood by the box."

5. A single noun following the verb —a noun that has the full formal characteristics of a substantive and is not preceded by an accompanying function word or inflected for genitive case—if this noun refers to the same person or thing as the subject noun, is an identifying noun, a so-called "predicate nominative." "The man stood a *sentinel* by the box."

6. Such a single noun following the verb, if it does not refer to the same person or thing as the subject noun, is the end point of action or object. "A man hit the *sentinel*."

7. Two such nouns following the verb—nouns that do not refer to the same person or thing as the subject noun but do themselves each refer to the same person or thing as the other— are a "direct" object and a "result" object or a so-called "object complement" after such verbs as *call, make, elect, appoint, consider*. After other verbs they are "direct" object and appositive, the first in order being the direct object. "The captain made the *man* a sentinel."

8. Two or more such nouns following the verb—nouns that do not refer to the same person or thing as the subject noun and do not themselves each refer to the same person or thing as the

other but are leveled by accent and/or function words—are a compound accusative ("direct") object, i.e., several objects. "A man hit the *sentinel* and the *captain.*"

9. Two such nouns following the verb—nouns that do not refer to the same person or thing as the subject noun and do not themselves each refer to the same person or thing as the other, and are not leveled by accent and/or function words—are a dative object ("indirect" object) and an accusative object ("direct" object), the first in order being the dative or indirect object. "The men made the *sentinel* a box."

10. If two nouns follow the verb, stand next to each other, and are not leveled by accent and/or function words, but with only one possible determiner and that before the first noun, the first noun is a modifier of the second and the second may be either 5 or 6 above. "A man hit the *sentinel* box."

The second essential relationship in the direction of modification—we must know what modifies what. Was it utter darkness or a dark utterance? Does the photographer have a dark green room or a green dark room? In Old English this relationship was indicated primarily by word endings in which articles and adjectives "agreed" with the nouns they modified. Through case endings the word order "in any other monastery's things" could mean in our terminology "in any other things of the monastery." Today "other" can be made to modify "things" only by being placed immediately before it. In Alfred's time (around 900 A.D.) the inflected genitive modifying a noun like an adjective occurred after its noun 47.6 percent of the time; by 1250 A.D., less than 1 percent of the time; and by 1300, none of the time. Single word modifiers of nouns in any position other than preceding the noun tended to be eliminated or to use a function word.

In fact, in Present-day English, position alone indicates modification, and nouns, both singular and plural, are freely placed before others as modifiers. The nature of the modification may be of the widest variety and often is extremely vague: "flood control projects," "the present Works Progress Administration system," "war threat," "state jobs," etc.

On the other hand, word-group modifiers such as prepositional phrases, and clauses introduced by relative pronouns, have become fixed in positions immediately following the nouns they modify. "The undersigned was given a physical examination for promotion by a Medical Board." This usage rose from 0.5 percent in 900 A.D. to 84.4 percent in 1300. By now this position is so fixed that there has appeared an increasing number of modifying clauses with the introductory function word relative no longer necessary. "This is the boy we spoke of." "Those people I stayed with."

Both in respect to the grammatical relation of modification just discussed and in respect to the subject-and-object relation dealt with earlier in this study, the development in English has been away from grammatically functioning inflectional devices and a variety of accompanying positions in the sentence to a loss of inflections with grammatically functioning fixed word order.

The most noteworthy facts concerning the uses of word order in the modifier-noun (character-substance) relation are the following:

1. As a pattern, single-word modifiers precede the nouns they modify.

2. If two nouns stand next to one another, and are not leveled by accent and/or function words, but with only one possible determiner and that before the first noun, the first noun is a modifier of the second: "a *school* teacher,"

"*sea* level," "a *home* visit," "*army* life," "the *bread* bill," etc.

3. There may be two or more modifier-nouns for a single noun.

    a. These may be leveled or operate as do single word modifiers: "*strong and beautiful* children," "a *robust, active* physique."

    b. Where not leveled each tends to modify the unit immediately following where word meaning permits: "*high moral* character," "*more varied* service"; but: "a *little* rented house."

4. Word group modifiers of nouns (prepositional phrases, subordinate clauses) in general modify the noun immediately preceding: "a reconciliation *between him and his wife*," "a journey *by transport*," "people *who know the father*," "the only decision *I can find*."

CONCLUSION

It is the point of view of this report that *a study of the real grammar of Present-day English has never been used in the schools* and that the conclusions concerning its effectiveness relate only to the type of "grammar" that has been tried. The "grammar" hitherto used in the schools has been either the logical analysis of sentences and "parsing," most often illustrated by the various methods of diagraming, or a learning of rules and definitions which were assumed to be the measures of correct language. This use of grammar has assumed that the problem of language usage is a simple one of *correct* forms and *mistakes*, which can easily be separated according to the rules. The teaching efforts that have been devoted to this type of grammar have therefore been directed toward making pupils "conscious of the rules" by which to determine correctness.

In the light of the principles which underlie our investigation this customary use of "grammar" is fundamentally unsound. First, language usage cannot thus be separated into two simple classes. Instead, our usage presents a complex range of differing and changing practices which must be understood in relation to the feelings of an indefinite number of social groups. Second, sensitiveness to usage—a richness of assimilated experience through which one becomes aware of the suggestions attaching to words and constructions because of the circumstances in which they are commonly used—is the only condition upon which good English can be won. All the effort which goes to make one *conscious* of "rules of grammar" serves to deaden this sensitiveness to one's speech environment and to turn one's attention away from the only source of real knowledge.

This study, therefore, presents a grammar of Present-day American English that differs from any that has been tried in the efforts to deal with the language practices of students. It contains no rules and definitions of correct English and it is not a closed handbook of usage. It does, however, attempt to provide the starting point for a workable program in English language for the schools by its method and materials.

1. In method it presents an outline of the three important grammatical devices which Present-day English uses (forms of words, function words, word order) and the purposes for which they are employed. This grammatical outline is in reality a sketch to guide observation and to furnish a basis for the classification and interpretation of the language phenomena observed.

2. In method, too, this sketch attempts to give some proportion to the description of the grammar of Present-day English by the use of quantitative information. Many of the generaliza-

tions appearing in English grammars actually express or imply quantitative judgments—judgments of absolute or relative frequency. Most of these depend upon general impressions rather than upon an attempt carefully to calculate the frequency of actual instances in any body of material. Here every example of each grammatical item discussed was recorded so that its relative frequency in the body of material here examined could be indicated. For a teaching program it seems worth while to know, for example, the nine words that account for 92 percent of all the instances of prepositions used and the twelve words that account for 93 percent of all the instances of conjunctions, and to know that only forty-two verbs have different forms for the past tense and past participle, and that less than 5 percent of the instances of plural nouns have forms other than the "s" pattern.

Finally, (1) we must agree upon the kind of English which it is the obligation of the schools to teach. The experience of at least 200 years shows that we cannot hope to change the practices of a language; we can only help students to learn what those practices are. Social pressure will necessarily support a particular set of speech habits, and a language program to be effective must have the active support of real social pressure. But it cannot be an imaginary social pressure as has so often been the case in the attempt to foster a school-mastered speech; it must be the vigorous social pressure of a living speech, the forms of which can be constantly verified upon the lips of actual speakers. For our schools we can muster real social pressure for the learning of actual, living *informal* Standard English.

(2) We must agree to base our teaching upon an accurate, realistic description of the actual practices of informal Standard English and eliminate from our language programs all those matters of dispute for which there is any considerable usage in informal Standard English.

(3) We must agree to stimulate among our pupils observation of actual usage and to go as far as possible in giving them a practical equipment for this purpose. Even if the subject of English could command much more of the pupil's time than it does now, *it would be impossible* to train the pupil in all the specific language items he would need throughout his life. To be really effective a language program must prepare the pupil for independent growth, and the only possible means of accomplishing that end is to lead him to become an intelligent observer of language usage. If we would have him observe intelligently the facts of the language usage about him, he must acquire the necessary tools; he must become thoroughly familiar with the three types of devices which our particular language uses to indicate grammatical ideas. He must know the usual grammatical uses in English of word forms or inflections, of function words, and of word order. It is upon *grammar* in this form that is new in the schools that the hope of a workable program of English language teaching rests.

FORMAL METHODS? [1]

Harry A. Greene, Claire J. Butterfield, and James Reece Stewart

[Extensive research in arithmetic has shown that teaching adult rules or generalizations to children and then drilling is far less effective than helping children discover relations for themselves—that is, teaching meaningfully. Somewhat similar studies in the language arts have indicated a similar futility in formal teaching compared with meaningful teaching. Among the most convincing are the present studies dealing with punctuation and sentence diagraming conducted under Dr. Greene's direction.]

In recent years the teaching of English has been tossed back and forth between two conflicting points of view—the formal-grammatical and the direct-associational. Up to 1850 the language curriculum was almost entirely dominated by grammar. During the next sixty years grammar held an important place among the disciplinary subjects, and instruction in formal grammar gained many supporters as a method of teaching English. Many well-intentioned educators still hold that belief today, as is shown by the division of opinion among authors and editors of English textbooks. Perhaps much of the difficulty arises because of the lack of a clear statement of what is meant by grammar.

In his last book, Ward presented a very helpful statement of the functions of grammar. First, grammar is conceived by some to be largely a study of the forms and classifications of single words. This type of grammar is now conceded to be obsolete and almost worthless. The second conception of the purpose of grammar is that it improves the thought processes. Perhaps grammar could be a help toward straight thinking, but thus far no curriculum has shown the way to this achievement. The third is that grammar aims at correct idiom by a study of rules. This may be a legitimate objective but it appears to operate most effectively from the adult and editorial angle. Ward himself placed great emphasis on the fourth conception of the purposes of grammar: *to attain*

[1] Adapted and abridged from Harry A. Greene, "Direct versus Formal Methods in Elementary English," *Elementary English Review* (1947), 24:273–285; Claire J. Butterfield, "The Effect of a Knowledge of Certain Grammatical Elements on the Acquisition and Retention of Punctuation Skills," unpublished dissertation submitted for the Ph.D. degree, University of Iowa, 1945; and James Reece Stewart, "The Effect of Diagraming on Certain Skills in English Composition," unpublished dissertation submitted for the Ph.D. degree, University of Iowa, 1941.

an *understanding of sentences.* As a matter of fact, those who defend formal grammar do so primarily on the basis of that purpose. It implies that grammar should be taught, not for the sake of grammar as the science of language, but for the purpose of developing a knowledge of sentence elements which are necessary for the improvement of composition.

If the importance of that function of grammatical instruction may be assumed, then there is reason to expect that systematic instruction on the recognition of such definite elements of the sentence as the complete subject or the complete predicate should result in a definite improvement in sentence mastery. Surprisingly enough, this does not seem to follow. Numerous studies have failed to show any important relation between the amount of grammatical information possessed by children and their ability to read and comprehend the meaning of sentences or their ability on English usage tests. Pupils making high scores on grammatical information tests make low scores on related usage exercises. The reverse is equally true.

DOES FORMAL GRAMMAR IMPROVE LANGUAGE?

The long history of experimental research in transfer of training fails almost uniformly to reveal any significant relationship between the study of formal grammar and the development of skills in English expression. The most significant result thus far is that many exaggerated claims for grammar have been modified. In recent years the trend among students of English methods has been to emphasize only those aspects of grammar which are said to be functional. In spite of the fact that practically every authoritative report since 1913 has stressed functional grammar rather than

structural, there is still no very exact agreement on a definition of "functional." Newsome has perhaps come as near to defining the issues as anyone in her sliding scale of grammar values, in which she classifies grammatical elements as functional, formal, useless, and pernicious. Rivlin defined "functional" as "that application of the knowledge of a grammatical item which will prevent the commission of an error in English or will assist in the correction of an error already made." This definition obviously presumes the omission of much formal grammar, predicates a change in grammar teaching from a memory to a thought process, and places grammar in its rightful place as a highly valuable editorial instrument. It seems reasonable to conclude that any element which helps in recognizing, interpreting, or constructing sentences may be said to be functional. While this definition may not be universally accepted it does express quite closely the consensus of opinion of most grammarians and many teachers of English. Moreover, it provides an excellent basis for planning some much-needed research in the field of English methods.

The recognition of the sentence as the focal point of language instruction raises definitely the question of the methods by which this mastery of the sentence may best be obtained. One school of thought holds that such mastery is best secured through the analysis and diagraming of sentences. The other believes just as firmly that correct language habits are developed in accordance with the general laws of habit formation, and that the way to mastery of the sentence is through extensive experience in the formulation of sentences. The latter procedure is what is meant in this discussion by the term "direct" method.

DOES DIAGRAMING HELP?

Diagraming of sentences was widely used as a method of teaching in the language-composition area from early records in educational methods until well into the 1920's. Then, for no apparent reason based on research, it was discarded almost entirely from the textbooks for use in elementary and high schools. Within the past ten years diagraming has returned for no more reason apparently than it disappeared. Probably because it was traditional, some schools used the method continuously. Those who seek evidence that the practice of diagraming is regaining popularity need only examine the current methods books and upper-grade language textbooks. Since 1935 there has been a frank return to the use of simple diagrams to aid pupils in understanding sentence structure. Moreover, many of the authors and editors feel that there is no educational malpractice in making a diagram of a sentence. They point out that sentence diagrams serve a useful purpose if through their visual appeal they make clear the construction of sentences and thus aid the pupil in understanding these sentences and later in constructing sentences of his own on similar patterns. They hold that if the pupil cannot express in some graphic way the structure of sentences he does not understand sentences.

In view of the rather widespread belief in diagraming as an effective method of developing sentence mastery, it would appear to be legitimate to expect to find considerable experimental evidence supporting it in the professional literature. A careful search of all available compilations of investigations in the field of language composition from 1900 to 1941 was made. There was no indication that diagraming of sentences had been subjected to experimental attack.

Two studies were made to discover the effect of improvement in one field upon skill in another, those by Dr. J. R. Stewart and by Dr. C. J. Butterfield. The purpose of Dr. Stewart's investigations was to evaluate experimentally sentence diagraming as a method of teaching certain phases of language composition, namely, usage, capitalization, punctuation, grammar information, and sentence structure. The subjects included approximately 1000 pupils enrolled in ninth-grade English classes in twenty-two Iowa, Illinois, and Minnesota school systems. Each of the pairs of classes was taught by the same teacher, was not grouped according to ability, and was from a school in which little or no diagraming had been taught during the past five years. On a random basis one of the two classes in each school was designated as a control group and the other as an experimental group. An initial testing program composed of tests of the five phases of language composition named above was carried out. Immediately after the initial testing, all classes began an eight-week period of intensive study of certain concepts in English from special instructional booklets prepared by the investigator. The experimental classes devoted their time almost exclusively to learning by diagraming sentences. The control classes expended exactly the same amount of time in learning identical concepts by the use of composition exercises. That is, the exercise books used by the control classes presented exactly the same language skills as were taught to the experimental groups but were taught by extensive exercises in the writing of original sentences and in the rewriting of poor sentences.

The usage, capitalization, and punctuation sections of the 1940 Iowa Every-Pupil Test in English Correctness were used in the initial testing program. The three comparable sections of the 1939 Iowa Every-Pupil Test in English Correctness were used in the final testing program. A seventy-item grammar information test composed of certain critical items selected from Forms A and B of the Iowa Grammar Information Test and thirty-two new items was used in both the initial and final testings in this study. Since diagraming is concerned with the structure of the individual sentence it was apparent that a special criterion device was needed which would measure the ability of the pupil to construct sentences. A survey showed that no existing measuring devices quite met this need. Accordingly, it was decided to attempt to produce an instrument which would evaluate the quality of sentences as constructed by the pupils. The actual construction and validation of this novel instrument was a contribution in itself. In this experimental sentence-structure test ideas were supplied in short simple statements and the pupils were asked to organize them into the most interesting

and effective sentences possible. The operations necessary to combine these ideas into effective sentences constituted the point score on the test. Twenty different grammatical factors involved in sentence structure were tested in the final sentence-structure test. A special diagraming test was constructed for use in the final testing program. This test covered approximately two-thirds of the concepts taught during the eight-weeks instructional period. These tests, being the criterion measures for this study, were carefully analyzed for statistical evidences of validity, item discrimination, and reliability.

The data for this experiment were treated by the method of analysis of covariance, which, by the use of initial measures, secures the same increase in precision as does the exact matching or equating of groups. The results appear in Table 1. At no point were the differences between the two groups sufficiently great to indicate anything but chance differences.

TABLE 1. Final Means Adjusted to Allow for Chance Differences in Initial Ability

	Control Groups	Experimental Groups (Studied Diagraming)	Differences
Language usage	39.27	39.26	0.01
Capitalization	42.36	43.16	0.80
Punctuation	52.09	50.52	1.57
Grammar information	50.46	49.71	0.75
Sentence structure	55.43	54.75	0.68

Subject to certain inescapable limitations, such as the teacher's personal attitude toward one method or the other, unidentified faults in the evaluating devices, or the length of the experimental period, the following conclusions were stated by Dr. Stewart:

1. The learning of capitalization, punctuation, and English usage is no

more pronounced under the instructional program composed largely of diagraming exercises than it was under the one emphasizing composition exercises.

2. The diagraming of sentences is no more effective in teaching grammar information than is a direct emphasis on composition as such.

3. Sentence structure is developed as

effectively by a composition method as it is by the diagraming of sentences.

GRAMMAR AND PUNCTUATION

The second of the major studies in this research program was designed to determine how much the teaching of certain grammatical elements affects the skill with which sixth-, seventh-, and eighth-grade pupils are able to use certain selected punctuation skills which are said to depend upon them. In order to accomplish this purpose it was necessary (1) to isolate the punctuation variants which have been found to be essential to an effective language program and (2) to identify the elements of functional grammar which are said to be basic to an understanding and a mastery of these specific mechanical skills.

Since the purpose of this study was to determine whether or not these grammatical elements were functional when applied to the development of punctuation skills, the identity of these punctuation skills was next established. Fifty punctuation variants were selected from an analysis made by Dr. J. W. Evans, in which he determined the punctuation skills carrying the major burden of usage in five types of compositions written by pupils in grades four to eight. The following criteria were used in selecting these variants: (1) the difficulty index, (2) the index of discrimination, (3) the unit frequency of each at the sixth-, seventh-, and eighth-grade levels, and (4) the relationship that exists between the variants and the thirty-five functional elements of grammar described below. Of these punctuation variants, one dealt with the period, thirty-nine with the comma, four with the apostrophe, four with the semicolon, one with the interrogation point, and one with the colon.

Since the determination of the elements of grammar that are functional is largely a matter of opinion, three separate criteria were followed. First, grammar items were selected from lists which were reported in research studies as having specific functional applications in composition. Then each item was further verified by checking the content of representative courses of study, textbooks, and workbooks. As a final determining factor, three well-qualified teachers of English were asked to point out independently the specific functional application of each grammatical item to the punctuation skills involved. Thirty-five elements of grammar meeting these three criteria were finally selected.

Two sets of instructional materials were prepared and used under controlled conditions with 831 pupils from nineteen midwestern city school systems. Two groups of pupils were selected from each of the schools participating in the experiment. The classes consisted of approximately the same number of pupils and each pair in a given school was taught by the same teacher. One set of the teaching materials was adapted from a recent commercial textbook in which instruction in grammar and in punctuation is integrated in such a manner as to emphasize the functional relationships which are thought to exist between them. The other set of instructional materials was adapted from a textbook that used the "thinking" approach to punctuation. This approach holds that a knowledge of grammar is a very incidental part of punctuation problems, and stresses the importance of reading the marks correctly as well as putting them where they will aid the reader.

Under experimental and statistical conditions quite similar to those followed in the Stewart study, initial and final tests of established validity and reliability were administered and interpreted. Table 2 gives the gist of the results.

TABLE 2. Average (Mean) Gains Made Between Initial and Final Tests

	Group Taught Grammar	Group Taught "Thought" Method
Grammar information	5.3	2.8
Punctuation skill	4.5	7.0

F score: Grammar, 11.83; Punctuation, 10.17. F required for significance at 1% level, 8.40.

Fewer than one time in a hundred would differences in gain as great as these occur by chance if there were no true differences between the learnings of the two groups. The reader can have great confidence that these differences are real. Subject again to such inescapable limitations as the possibility that the grammatical elements selected might not have the expected high degree of relationship to the punctuation variants, or the existence of a definite prejudice on the part of the teachers favoring one method or the other, or the limited validity of the measuring devices used, the following conclusions seem to be statistically defensible:

1. The students who were taught grammar as such revealed, as might have been expected, significantly higher accomplishment in knowledge of grammar than students who were taught by the other method, but grammatical knowledge did not appear to transfer into the area of skill in punctuation to any appreciable extent in spite of the fact that the two were supposed to be functionally related.

2. Significantly superior results in punctuation were obtained by the direct method.

GENERAL CONCLUSIONS

The results of educational research are valuable only to the degree that they affect practice. The implications of the studies just reported are of practical significance. The studies dealing with sentence diagraming indicate uniformly that diagraming is a skill which can be developed but has little or no value in itself. It does not lend itself to correlation with other subjects or projects or the program of the school. There is little point in training the pupil to graphically portray sentences except for the improvement which it brings to his ability to write effectively. The evidence shows that this is slight. There is considerable question, therefore, of the advisability of employing sentence diagraming as a method of developing language mastery. In the light of the data secured by Butterfield, there is reason to expect superior results in the teaching of punctuation by direct methods rather than by methods which are based upon a knowledge of related grammatical elements. Punctuation is a function of meaning rather than a function of grammar. Furthermore, the description of the grammatical elements of a sentence often must be deferred until the punctuation is completed according to the meaning intended, as in the sentences "Take that coat off George" and "Take that coat off, George." A comma has changed the meaning and the grammar. Students learning to write should be taught to associate the three functions (separating, connecting, and tacking-on) with the proper marks. The following simple rules meet most needs.

1. Separate sentences from each other by a period or other end-mark.
2. (a) Use a comma or the word *and* to connect items that are working together in lists of two or more things.
(b) If two statements are to be combined in one sentence, use both the comma and the word *and* (, and) to prevent any possible misreading. (*But, yet, or,* or *nor* may take the place of *and* if the meaning requires it.)
3. Use a comma, or a pair of commas, to warn the reader of a turn in the thought.[2]

   [2] Quoted in Butterfield's dissertation from

The results of the experiments presented here are believed to be convincing. They all point in the same direction. Evidently the indirect methods by which we have been attempting to teach pupils to write the English they will need in life have largely failed to function. The evidence shows that repeated and spaced habit-forming experiences are productive of mastery and should be substituted for formal rules and exercises whose values as a part of teaching method are at least open to question. Let us reserve the grammar for later adult editorial use.

Rachel Salisbury, "The Psychology of Punctuation," *The English Journal*, December, 1939.

THOUGHT APPROACH IN SENTENCE STRUCTURE [1]

Ellen Frogner

[The section on arithmetic presents extensive research showing the superiority of insightful, meaningful learning over drill-type learning in which facts or generalizations are presented, applied, and practiced. The present study pursues a similar hypothesis in the field of the language arts and reaches similar conclusions.]

The contribution of grammar to ability in sentence structure has long been emphasized. A survey of literature on the subject since 1900 reveals a decided tendency to think of sentence mastery as the primary purpose in the study of grammatical principles. The importance of submitting the assumption to investigation is evident, especially in consideration of the fact that sentence structure contributes so much to the total effect of the composition.

The author carried out an extended study of the relative effectiveness of a grammatical and a thought method in the teaching of sentence structure. The experiment was conducted for one semester with forty-seven pairs in Grade

   [1] Adapted and abridged from Ellen Frogner, "Grammar Approach Versus Thought Approach in Teaching Sentence Structure," *English Journal* (1939), 28:518–526.

9 and sixty pairs in Grade 11. The aim was to compare the improvement made by pupils who were directed to approach problems of sentence structure entirely from the standpoint of the adequate expression of thought with the improvement made by pupils who, besides having their attention directed to the clear expression of thought, were also given the drill needed to insure an understanding of the grammatical construction of the sentence. In other words, the important point is that while some of the thought approach was included in the grammar classes, no grammar was used in the classes taught according to the thought method, where the underlying principle was the clear, effective expression of ideas.

AN ILLUSTRATION OF THE TWO METHODS

An example from the units taught will indicate the differences between the two methods.

UNIT II. SUBORDINATION OF IDEAS IN PHRASES

The classes in which the grammar method was used began Unit II with examples of subordinating ideas by means of different kinds of phrases: prepositional, appositive, participial, gerund, and infinitive. Pupils differentiated phrases according to their kind and their use in the sentence. Ideas from short, choppy sentences were combined into a more effective expression of the thought by means of phrases. In all probability, if this last step had been omitted, the procedure would have been more typical of grammar teaching today. With the inclusion of this step, however, grammar should contribute to the acquiring of more effective sentence structure, if knowledge of grammar is essential to accuracy and clarity of ex-

pression. The pupils then proceeded to the discussion and correction of errors in the use of phrases, such as the misplaced prepositional phrase or the dangling participle.

The thought approach was less involved. Pupils started out by noticing the various ways of subordinating ideas. Illustrative sentences were written on the board, and in combining ideas pupils were urged to try as many of these sentence patterns as possible. There was, however, no pointing out that certain kinds of phrases had been used. For instance, a composition contained such statements as the following: "Mr. White is our class adviser. He grasped the seriousness of the situation. He immediately called a meeting of the officers." How could the ideas be combined to avoid the monotonous childish sentences? Several possibilities were suggested, one of which was: "Having grasped the seriousness of the situation, Mr. White, our class adviser, immediately called a meeting of the officers." Pupils improved the expression of the thought by means of subordinating ideas in a participial and an appositive phrase; yet they were not drilled in the recognition of the grammatical constructions used. The classes taught according to the thought method also went on to the correction of errors in the use of phrases, but from the standpoint of meaning only. In a sentence like "Waiting on the corner for a bus, the accident occurred," there was no labeling of "waiting" as a dangling participle. The test was: Did the writer say what he evidently meant to say?

RESULTS OF THE EXPERIMENT

The effectiveness of the two methods was compared in results for three general tests of sentence structure, tests for each of the seven units, and two tests of knowledge of technical grammar. Following are the major conclusions based on many specific comparisons for 107 pairs of pupils in Grades 9 and 11:

1. The pupils in the grammar classes definitely learned more grammar than did those in the group using the thought method. All of the differences in gains, for instance, made on the two tests of grammar were in favor of the grammar classes. Five of the twelve possible differences satisfied the upper level of statistical significance. Other comparisons evidenced a like superiority on the part of the pupils in the grammar classes.

2. In spite of this fact, the thought method brought about superior results in sentence structure, as measured by general tests covering the work of the semester. All of the eighteen possible differences in gains favored the classes taught according to the thought method. Three of these differences satisfied the upper level of statistical significance.

A comparison of the thirty-three pairs in the ninth grade in Bemidji illustrates the fact that knowledge of grammar is evidently not essential to improvement in sentence structure: In gains made on the general test in sentence structure especially constructed for the experiment seventeen pupils in the grammar class surpassed their mates by a total of 148 points, while sixteen pupils taught according to the thought method surpassed by a total of 217 points. Yet in gains made on the test measuring knowledge of the grammar involved in the items of sentence structure, thirty-one pupils in the grammar class surpassed their mates by a total of 1489 points, compared with two pupils in the thought class who exceeded their mates by a total of only 10 points.

3. Results of the unit tests in individual elements of sentence structure given immediately at the close of each unit did not, in general, favor either group. Comparison of these figures with those for the long-time tests at the end of the experiment suggests that, when a test calls for the application of grammatical rules recently learned and practiced, little difference is evident between the grammar and thought methods, but that the thought approach makes for longer retention of the fundamental abilities involved.

4. The thought method in both Grades 9 and 11 was definitely superior to the grammar approach for all pupils with an IQ below 105. Evidence for this statement is found in the fact that all of the differences in gains made by the pupils of average and below average intelligence favored the thought method, and in every instance the difference more than satisfied the lower level of statistical significance. There was little difference between the two methods among superior pupils, except for a tendency on the part of those of the highest range of intelligence (IQ from 114 to 129) to profit more from the thought than from the grammar method.

5. The thought approach required approximately 80 percent of the time required by the grammar method; thus a saving of the equivalent of one day out of five could be effected.

6. A study of the reasoning used by the pupils revealed that those in the thought classes made use of the thought method predominantly. In the grammar classes more pupils used thought aids along with grammatical reasoning than confined themselves to a strictly grammatical approach.

Results of the study, therefore, lend no support to the claims made for grammar as being essential to improvement in sentence structure. On the contrary, since the experiment demonstrates that an emphasis upon thought is effective in improving details of usage and style, it makes evident the value of such an approach in the whole problem of fostering ability in speaking and writing —an approach wherein the major emphasis in the improvement of ability in language coincides with the inherent purpose of language as a means of expressing ideas.

SOME WAYS TO IMPROVE LANGUAGE USAGE [1]
Prudence Cutright

[This study was less restricted than the immediately preceding research in language methodology. The merits of several teaching approaches were investigated to discover their relative values. Attention might be directed to two points: (1) the method showing the greatest superiority was the one giving direct practice with the types of choices that were called for on the test used to measure improvement; (2) the importance of building correct auditory images that forms the basis of Moyer's study below is glimpsed in this report.]

Studies that reveal the specific errors children make in speaking and writing are numerous, but studies dealing directly with method are few. This study compared the effectiveness of six methods in securing correct usage in Grades 4, 5, and 6. The methods were (1) games, (2) practice on the incorrect form with knowledge of the correct (hereafter called Beta), (3) proofreading of prepared paragraphs, (4) choice of written constructions (writing the selected form in a blank), (5) all methods with one week on each, (6) choice of written and oral constructions (writing the selected form plus oral reading of all sentences). (7) A control group carried on the usual work without special attention to correct usage.

The general plan of the study included the following features.

1. A group intelligence test was given to all groups, and eliminations were made until all pupils were within ten points of one another in average intelligence.

2. Pretests were made of the children's ability to use twenty selected expressions. Two measures were used: a written test, patterned after Charters' Diagnostic Language Test, and an oral test, patterned after Webster's oral tests.

3. Teachers were provided with guide sheets describing the method for each group. The number of practice periods, the number of minutes of practice, and

[1] Adapted and abridged from Prudence Cutright, "A Comparison of Methods of Securing Correct Language Usage," Elementary School Journal (1934), 34:681–690.

the amount of outside work were carefully controlled.

4. Pupils' practice materials were prepared for each method with the exception of the method using games, where it was necessary merely to supply the teachers with descriptions of the games to be used.

5. At the end of a six-week teaching period the initial tests were repeated to measure growth immediately after teaching.

6. The same written and oral tests were repeated two weeks after the close of the experimental period as a measure of retention.

The mean scores of each group at each grade level were noted on both pretest and final testings, oral and written, to discover average decreases in errors made. Thus each method was compared with some other method thirty-six times. The method employing choice of constructions with both written and oral responses showed superiority in all thirty-six comparisons; the all-methods group, in twenty-nine comparisons; the Beta group, in twenty-one; the group using choice of constructions with written responses and the proofreading group, in seventeen comparisons each; the games group, in only six; and the control group in none.

Not all of these differences had a sufficiently high critical ratio (3 or above) to indicate statistical reliability; many may have been due to chance. When the latter were eliminated, the method using choice of constructions both written and oral still showed a superiority with a statistically reliable difference in twenty-three comparisons; the all-methods group in fourteen; the Beta group in thirteen; the written constructions group in nine; the proofreading group in eight; the games group in six; and the control group in none. If the total number of reliable positive differences is taken as an index of the effectiveness of the various methods, then obviously the first three methods above stand out in their superiority.

IMPLICATIONS

Undoubtedly, each method was more effective for some individual child than any other method would have been. Still, the problem of this study was to ascertain the effectiveness of certain methods with groups of children, and the evidence presented here seems to justify the following conclusions.

1. If errors in usage are to be eliminated, some definite attempt toward that end is necessary. The control group, or that group which carried on only the ordinary work of the language lesson, showed but little growth during the six-week period.

2. Games were of but slight assistance in securing better usage as measured either by oral or by written tests.

3. The Beta method ranks third in effectiveness and seemed somewhat more effective with the older pupils (Grades 5A and 6A) than with the younger pupils (Grade 4A).

4. Proofreading was more effective than the use of games but ranks fifth among the six methods in the number of reliable and positive differences.

5. Choice of constructions with written responses ranks fourth in the number of positive and reliable differences. The improvement secured by this method on the written test was consistently greater than the improvement secured on the oral test. It is apparent that, if teachers hope to improve oral usage through drill, they must provide oral drill. The group employing choice of constructions with written responses and the group employing choice of constructions with both written and oral responses used the same practice ex-

ercises; the only variation was the addition of the oral response to the one method. The greater effectiveness of the latter method, that using responses of both types, gives reliable evidence of the value of practicing the type of response which we hope to improve; that is, if improvement in oral usage is desired, oral practice must be provided.

6. The all-methods group ranks second in the number of positive reliable differences. The effectiveness of this method may have been caused by the motivating effect of the use of new materials and procedures each week. On the retention test, which was given two weeks after the close of the practice period, this group showed a greater loss than was shown by any other group, with the possible exception of the games group. (The results of the retention tests are not presented in this limited report.) This loss suggested that, while many methods may have stimulated great interest, they may have resulted in some confusion.

7. The method employing choice of constructions with both written and oral responses ranks first in effectiveness. It seemed slightly more effective in securing correct oral usage than in improving written usage.

8. Much of the commercialized and homemade practice materials on correct grammar usage is of the choice-of-construction type. Teachers using such materials would do well, according to the implications of this study, not only to have the pupils write their choices in the proper blanks, but also to provide some type of chorus drill or oral practice.

DOES "EAR TRAINING" HELP? [1]

Haverly O. Moyer

[Occasionally a mechanical invention arrives that has great teaching potentiality. The motion picture was an obvious example. The sound recorder is another tool appearing theoretically to have almost unlimited promise in all forms of oral communication. Adults who first hear their own voices recorded realize with a shock that people seldom hear themselves as others hear them. This study, dealing largely with an oral methodology, is included here because of its relevance to the basic problem of improving written usage. Do children normally write things in the way that "sounds right" to them? The foregoing studies have indicated that stress upon grammatical rules and most formal methods are not highly effective. The present study attempted to see whether helping things "sound right" would improve recognition of correct written usage. If so, much time now given to written drills can be used more effectively in social communication.]

[1] Adapted and abridged from Haverly O. Moyer, "The Effect of Ear-Training on Certain Aspects of Children's English Usage," unpublished doctoral dissertation, Syracuse University, 1950, under the direction of C. W. Hunnicutt.

A guiding principle often stated is that the speech level of a child is most effectively altered by training the ear, building appropriate auditory images. As here used, the term "ear training" means helping children to listen to their classmates and themselves with the intent to understand that which is communicated and also with the awareness of the correctness and adequacy of the spoken word. It implies that teachers will help individual pupils to hear themselves and through self-evaluation develop higher-level modes of expression where higher-level modes would be more adequate. The term is used to stand for the kind of experiences which can be provided by any elementary teacher without special training in the field of speech.

This principle has had little research to substantiate it. The present study sought an answer to the question "If two groups are taught correct English usage, one by the conventional method and the other by an ear-training method, would the latter progress as well on standardized tests of usage?" A corollary problem was to discover which group would gain more in quality of oral expression and oral composition.

The results would affect the support of the ear-training principle and would influence the use of stereotype exercises. It might help change the whole elementary-school language program to center more on real language problems of importance to the needs and interests of children.

The study was carried on in a laboratory school of a state teachers college and in the public schools of the same city. The experimental periods were for sixteen weeks, September, 1948, to January, 1949, and for a second sixteen weeks, September, 1949, to January, 1950. The experimental groups were the fourth, sixth, and eighth grades (seventy-three children) of the laboratory school; the control groups were the fourth, sixth, and eighth grades (seventy-five children) of the public schools. These were their grades during the first experimental period; during the second period a year later only those then in the fifth and seventh grades were available for study.

No attempt was made to match individual pupils of the experimental and control groups since it was administratively impossible. Instead, an analysis of covariance was used to secure the results that would ordinarily necessitate larger groups and more precise controls.

The students in the control groups had advantages over the experimental groups in that they were taught by experienced teachers, while the experimental groups were taught by student teachers under supervision. The experimental groups had a change of student teachers at the midpoint of each sixteen-week period, which necessitated an adjustment by the pupils to new teachers and the orientation of the student teachers to the ear-training program.

Three standardized tests were administered at the start and finish of each experimental period: Language Usage (Public School Publishing Company), Metropolitan Achievement Tests (World Book Company), and Every Pupil Test of Basic Skills: the Language Usage Test (Houghton Mifflin Company).

The variable factor was the method of instruction in the respective groups. In the control groups the teachers continued their regular pattern of teaching, following a textbook in English and doing the written corrective usage drills found in the text.

The experimental groups had ear training through the use of tape recorders. No written drills or formal exercises were used. Nearly all of the lesson periods were given to recording and analyzing the effectiveness of the language in the stories, reports, or language games of the children. Every attempt was made to have the procedure as natural and functional as possible. Teacher-prepared materials were used only when a child did not have something which he wanted to have recorded. Discussion of language as it is used and interest in language as a social tool were encouraged. A critical but friendly attitude about language usage was fostered. The children learned to listen to each other, which helped promote ear training in the usual or natural situation. This was thought to be as important to improvement as the recording experiences.

The children were induced to think of language as a medium of self-expression with which they could experiment to discover the effectiveness of one way of saying something as contrasted with another.

At the beginning and at the end of the second sixteen-week experimental period, tape records were kept of talks by all experimental and control children. These records, carefully coded for anonymity, were later evaluated by a jury competent to judge the quality of the oral expression and oral composition. At no time did a judge know whether the voice he was listening to belonged to the experimental or to the control group, to a member of the fifth grade or of the seventh grade, or whether it had been recorded at the beginning or at the end of the experimental period. Quality of expression included enunciation, rhythm in speaking, voice quality, pronunciation, vocabulary, and correct usage. Quality of oral composition included importance and interest to listeners, logical organization, unified and coherent sentences, proper build-up to climax, and style appropriate to the purpose.

As might have been anticipated, the children in the experimental groups at both the fifth- and the seventh-grade levels made strikingly greater gains than those of the control groups in their oral expression and composition. In each variable the difference was at the 0.1 percent level of confidence, implying little doubt of the reality of the difference.

An analysis of covariance of the standardized test scores revealed the following information:

1. There was no significant difference in gain between boys and girls.

2. There was no definite relationship between the ability to do well on a standardized test of correct usage and oral correctness or between the ability to improve on a standardized test and the ability to improve in oral expression.

3. There were four concomitant improvements among the ear-training groups: the number of run-on sentences was reduced, many mispronunciations were corrected, ease and fluency were improved, and better use of volume and tempo seemed to result.

4. The number of usage errors was greatly reduced by both methods.

5. At each grade level and during both experimental periods the experimental groups made greater progress than the control on the Public School Publishing Company test of Language Usage.

From observing the children in action the author and coöperating teachers believe the following to be true:

1. Ear training through the use of recordings has a high motivating value.

2. Ear training through the use of recordings helps to develop wholesome attitudes about language as a tool.

3. Ear training improves the pupils'

ability to express themselves with poise and confidence.

The implications of this study may be far-reaching. Ear training through the

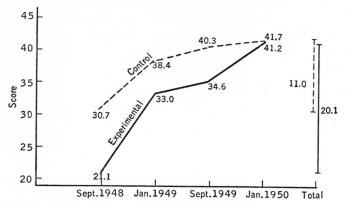

Fig. 1. Gains of Fifth Grades, Public School Test. The control group line shows a gradual improvement throughout the three periods. The experimental group line shows a definite improvement during both periods of ear training and very little improvement during the period January, 1949, to September, 1949, when the experimental procedures were not being used.

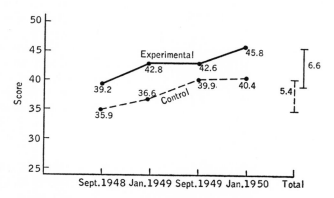

Fig. 2. Gains of Seventh Grades, Public School Test. The control group line shows a gradual improvement throughout the three periods. The experimental group line shows a definite improvement during both periods of ear training but indicates a slight loss during the period January, 1949, to September, 1949, when the experimental procedures were not being used.

use of some kind of recording device apparently can alter greatly the speech level of children and help establish the habits which need to become automatic for effectiveness in social communication. It may eliminate some criticisms of contemporary English teaching. Much, if not all, of the drill on correct usage in which the pupils fill in blanks or cross out alternate forms apparently can be omitted. Such practice does not seem to have the power to alter speech habits that ear training does, presumably because it is silent and thus detached from genuine communication.

The conventional methods do not generally have the motivating force for self-improvement that the ear-training method seems to provide. Unless a child really wants to improve his speech, drill is probably wasted. The ear-training approach, in which recordings are made of those things which are important to the child, gives motivation that is not normally so easily produced by other methods. The child hears himself as others hear him and has the privilege of immediate knowledge of results and of self-evaluation.

It would seem that an English program should include ear training as the method for improving oral communication combined with instruction in written expression which should grow out of pupils' needs to record actual experiences, feelings, or ideas. If both phases of communication were properly balanced and activities were provided that arose from pupil experiences, a much more vital language program should result.

PART THREE

The Third "R"

Today's civilization is based largely upon our ever-advancing science and technology. These in turn are founded upon the basic science of mathematics. As never before in history, it is essential that America have an adequate reservoir of mathematically competent citizens. This is especially important in the light of Russian practice. There the top priority in the school curriculum is given to science and mathematics.

In America, mathematics may well be the weakest subject in the curriculum. While children today on the whole are better in arithmetic than were children in previous generations, they still are inadequate to the needs of today. All too often their teachers dislike arithmetic, fear it, and are incompetent to teach it well. Few teachers have a modern knowledge of effective arithmetic teaching. Children are likely to come from homes where parents have passed on to the children their own remembered dislike of arithmetic. Many factors thus militate against children's having the kind of arithmetic satisfactions that lead to a desire to study mathematics in high school and college.

All of this can and must be changed. The accumulated research offers many clues to improvement.

There is no attempt here to cover all questions in arithmetic planning and teaching upon which there has been experimentation. An inexpensive pamphlet [1] which may well be used to supplement this volume used the findings of research to answer thirty-seven key questions asked by several hundred teachers and supervisors. No research studies were quoted there directly—that was not its function—but the variety of issues

[1] Vincent J. Glennon and C. W. Hunnicutt, *What Does Research Say About Arithmetic?* Association for Supervision and Curriculum Development, National Education Association, Washington, 1952.

347

treated was wider than here. In the present volume a sampling of the most significant research is quoted at sufficient length to permit the reader to judge for himself the evidence upon which conclusions have been drawn.

Certain issues, such as the function of drill, the problem of readiness, and the grade placement of arithmetic topics, are of so crucial a nature that they have attracted extensive and penetrating study. Much of the best experimentation is in these areas, and hence they occupy what to some may seem an excessive portion of the available space in this volume. The major controversy of the last two decades has been over "drill versus meaning" in teaching. Its outcome has revolutionized arithmetic teaching and has made some of the earlier experimentation less important. Almost incidentally and in passing, an investigation of a major problem may furnish rather conclusive evidence on some minor problem such as the use of "crutches" or of "checking."

Complex studies, such as certain of Brownell's monographs, have a tendency to overflow the bounds of any narrow categorization. Nevertheless, an effort has been made to cluster these reports in a few related groups. Typically, the arrangement is chronological within each group, furnishing a glimpse of the dynamic growth of research, and of the way in which one investigation may stimulate another.

In the first chapter, "Insight Versus Connectionism," the evidence against much dependence upon repetitive drill seems so conclusive that there should no longer be an issue. However, common practice in our schools is heavily weighted with this outmoded methodology and one can only conclude that the implications of research have not yet penetrated very deeply.

Closely related are the problems of children's readiness for learning and of the selection and placement of topics. What arithmetic should children learn? When should they begin? What should be the sequence of topics? Should they be presented in a mathematically logical order or in the order of their complexity and difficulty? At what stage of mental development can each major type of learning be learned most efficiently? What arithmetic do children know before they start formal arithmetic in school or before they start school itself? These are some of the kinds of questions confronting those responsible for planning arithmetic programs. Some aid in answering them was obtained from these various studies, though much research still must be done before definitive answers are possible.

The third chapter treats selected other areas of methodology. These range from the rather simple problem of upward versus downward direction in column addition to the complex question of whether any organized program of arithmetic is necessary or whether it may be left to a more mature form of the incidental learning that functions in the preschool years. In many of the areas reported the results are reasonably convincing, but most areas of methodology still await thorough investigation.

Chapter XII

INSIGHT VERSUS CONNECTIONISM—
THE ROLE OF DRILL

Introduction

Thorndike's early studies of S-R bond psychology had an influence upon his followers far beyond what he would have liked. Inspired by this apparently clear-cut and simple answer to the problems of teaching, unnumbered thousands flocked to this methodology in arithmetic. Bonds or connections could be made by repetitive drill.

Presumably it would be dangerous for children to attempt to make discoveries for themselves since they might make mistakes and thus make erroneous bonds difficult to eradicate. So adults analyzed arithmetic computation into thousands of component parts ($3 + 2$ is different from $2 + 3$) and drilled away at children. Whether children saw meaning or purpose seemed unimportant; the important thing was to achieve mastery. "Let him learn; then sometime when he is older he will be able to use the learning." This machine-like operation was obviously authoritarian, assuming children were incapable of thinking for themselves and must be told by their elders.

Strongly opposed to the connectionists were those supporting a field or insightful theory of learning. This more democratic theory assumed child intelligence and stressed the importance of understanding and insight as the foundation of rapid and permanent learning. The implications for school practice are apparent: Must we insure, for example, that children shall discover relationships for themselves, or is it enough simply to tell them a fact and then drill?

Significant research soon began to appear. Several of the more influential are presented here in a roughly chronological order. Their cumulative effect is to build convincing support for the meaningful teaching of arithmetic.

DISCOVER OR BE TOLD? [1]

T. R. McConnell

[Dr. McConnell's investigation of the learning of the primary addition and subtraction facts contains a wealth of data carefully obtained. This is one of the first important studies of this problem of drill as opposed to understand, though it will be seen later that one conclusion in Brownell's *The Development of Children's Number Ideas in the Primary Grades*, published in 1928, anticipated the later discrediting of repetitive drill. In this study a major start was made toward undergirding the use of insightful learning.]

This investigation deals with a controlled experiment in the learning of the 100 basic addition and the 100 basic subtraction facts continuing for more than seven months in the second grades of selected schools in Toledo, Ohio. More particularly, it is designed to reveal the relative effectiveness of two procedures for learning these 200 facts as laid down in two arithmetic learning books. Hereafter, these two procedures will be referred to as "Method A" (used with 441 pupils) and "Method B" (used with 422 pupils). The two methods purport to use describably different theories of learning.

Method A rests its case primarily on repetition of stimulus-response connections "authoritatively identified" with no attempt to invest them with meaning. The number combinations are to be learned by sheer repetition, each number combination being considered

as a specific bond, or S-R connection. Each fact (e.g., 8 plus 5 is 13) is identified in the abstract form without meaning, dogmatically and autocratically. There is a studious effort to keep the child from either discovering or verifying the answers to the number relations. In case of error during practice he does not discover either the error or the correct response; the teacher does it for him. He must never experiment, never find out for himself, but must always "ask the teacher."

Method B, on the other hand, stresses the discovery of truth and meaning; it assumes that learning is the process of achieving insight, rather than of sheer repetition. The number combinations are presented in a manner designed to bridge the gap between concrete number and abstract number, introducing all combinations in concrete or pictured situations. It assumes that to discover meaning is to learn. A general halo of meaning is not enough;

[1] Adapted and abridged from T. R. McConnell, *Discovery vs. Authoritative Identification in the Learning of Children*, University of Iowa Studies in Education, Vol. 9, No. 5, 1934, pp. 11–62.

learning implies insight and does not proceed without it. Meaning is the essence, the absolute essential of learning. Through an active, self-initiated process of discovery and verification the child learns, for example, that 5 plus 3 is 8. In case of error, he never asks the teacher but goes back to the illustrated number patterns and discovers the truth for himself. Specific characteristics of Method B follow:

1. All of the 200 addition and subtraction facts are developed in from three to five concretely pictured situations, some leading to more definite imagery than others.

2. The abstract forms are tied closely to the concrete presentations.

3. The number relation is presented in a variety of different particulars.

4. Repetition of the abstract symbols occurs only after their concrete development.

5. The specific number facts are organized into a variety of patterns and systems, and generalization of the principles involved in these systems is facilitated.

6. These number configurations are progressively extended until the child may see comprehensive aspects of the arithmetical systems involving the addition and subtraction combinations.

7. For authoritative identification is substituted the active process of self-discovery, of seeing the truth of the facts.

8. The child works in the direction of a definite goal, which is not that of pleasing the teacher but that of finding the answers for the number facts and of seeing their relationships. This is a situation demanding "closure"; the tension (or motivation) is created by the inherent demands of the task or goal. The interest is intrinsic rather than extrinsic. The goal is real and meaningful, not artificial.

Evaluation of these two programs was made primarily from the results of seven interpolated and seven final tests. Preliminary data for each child included chronological age; intelligence quotient based on the *Pintner-Cunningham Primary Mental Test*; reading score, reading age, and reading grade on three forms of the *Gates Primary Silent Reading Test*, combined; and scores on an arithmetic pretest.

The Interpolated Tests. To secure some insight into the comparative achievement of the two groups during the period of learning, seven tests were administered at three intervals during the experiment. They included tests of ability to respond to number facts with speed and accuracy (two tests each), and tests of transfer to untaught combinations (three tests).

The Final Tests. At the close of instruction seven tests were administered, one each day, followed by a pupil questionnaire designed to reveal pupil attitudes to arithmetic and to the learning method used.

SUMMARY OF RESULTS

(Group A was taught by Method A, Group B by Method B.)

1. Group A is definitely superior to Group B on Interpolated Test Four and Final Test Two, both training tests with speed instructions.

2. Group B is superior to Group A on Interpolated Test Six, on transfer to untaught combinations, and on Final Test Seven, maturity of manipulation of the number facts.

3. Five of the observed mean differences on the interpolated tests are in favor of Group B, and two are in favor of Group A.

4. Five of the observed differences on the final tests are in favor of Group B, and two are in favor of Group A.

5. The results of the interpolated and final tests are internally consistent. That is, Group A excelled on immediate and automatic response to the number facts as measured by tests with limited administration time and speed instructions; Group B excelled in tests which put a premium on deliberate and thoughtful responses, and those with generous administration times. The only possible exception to this trend is the observed difference in favor of Group A on the error-recognition test, a difference, however, which is not sufficient to be statistically significant.

6. Within the limits of the experiment, the necessary conclusion is that, time consumed in learning being taken into consideration, the method of mechanical repetition is the more forthright means of attaining automatic and immediate responses to the number facts.

7. In terms of practicality, none of the differences revealed in the experiment will be likely to impress the person concerned with the technique of instruction.

8. Coefficients of correlation between intelligence and scores on final tests are uniformly larger for Group A than Group B, not only when the entire distributions are considered, but also when the correlations are computed for the pupils in the upper one-quarter of IQ distributions for each group.

9. The correlations between arithmetic pretest scores and final test scores are all higher in the case of Group A than of Group B, although none of the differences are statistically significant.

10. There are no important functional differences between the two groups in the way they responded to the flow of specific items within Final Tests One and Two. On Test Three, however, Group B made all of its observed superiority (which is not statistically significant) on the first thirty-five of the forty-seven test items. This margin was cut down by the larger percentage of correct responses for Group A in the last twelve items. The implication again is that Group B pupils were somewhat slower and probably more deliberate about their responses.

11. The percentage of pupils who checked arithmetic as the best liked against the field of second-grade subjects is practically the same for both groups. There is likewise no significant difference in the frequency with which the two groups checked arithmetic as the least-liked subject.

12. The pupil questionnaire failed to reveal pronounced consciousness on the part of the pupils in Group B of the major dynamics of learning supposedly employed by their method of instruction.

GENERALIZATION IN LEARNING [1]

C. Louis Thiele

[Dr. Thiele went somewhat further than McConnell in providing freedom for children to think out for themselves their own generalizations in number relationships. Moreover, he attempted to measure their ability to apply their generalizations in novel situations. This study further strengthened support for meaningful teaching.]

In this experiment were two groups of Detroit beginning second-graders total- ing 512 who were roughly equivalent in intelligence (see Fig. 1). Four weeks

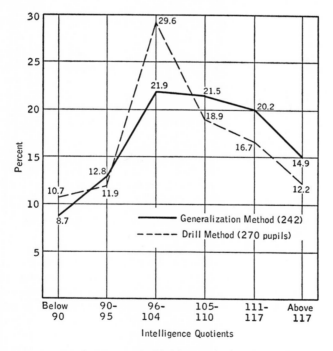

Fig. 1. Percent of Children of the Two Experimental Groups in Each Level of Intelligence.

[1] Adapted and abridged from C. Louis Thiele, *Contribution of Generalization to the Learning of the Addition Facts*, Contributions to Education, No. 673, Bureau of Publications, Teachers College, Columbia University, New York, 1938.

were devoted to the same "number readiness" instruction for both groups. During the ensuing fifteen weeks one group was taught the addition facts by the "generalization" method; the other group by the "drill" method. The drill method stressed repetition of the number facts, each considered as a separate entity. This should not be construed to mean that the activities of the drill-method pupils were confined to repetitions of abstract number facts. The drill-method pupils did find authority for the addition facts through the manipulation of concrete objects; they did illustrate and dramatize addition facts. They also prepared statements about many of the addition facts and

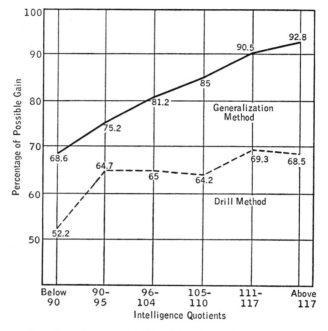

Fig. 2. Percent of Possible Gain Between Initial and Final Tests Made by Pupils of the Same Intelligence Ratings.

dealt with the facts in the solutions of word problems. However, no attempt was made to cause the drill-method pupils to perceive and utilize number generalizations. Their purpose was to commit to memory the number facts.

In the course of instruction followed by the generalization-method classes, speedy and accurate recall of the addition facts was also sought. The process was a slow one in which the pupils were stimulated and led to abstract likenesses and differences in number situations to the end that they perceived generalizations or laws common to many number facts. Reactions to subsequent number situations which required the knowledge of number facts were in terms of generalizations. In other words, the children taught by the generalization method did not depend upon their memories but instead thought things out for themselves. This principle was applied even to the practice on abstract number facts. Furthermore, those teaching by the generalization method did not aim to teach a list of predetermined generalizations; their chief concern was that children should generalize. If certain generalizations were generally perceived, it was in a large measure due to the order and manner in which the addition facts were presented.

The children were given an initial test at the end of the readiness program and prior to the instructional program, and a final test at the end. The progress made by the two groups between these tests appears in Figure 2. At each IQ level children in the generalization group made greater progress. Of the thirty items on this "Transfer of Training Test" the generalization group averaged 10.00 correct; the drill group, 6.07 correct. The superiority of the generalization method was especially great in the learning of the harder addition facts. All of these differences are too large to be readily attributed to chance.

CAN CHILDREN TEACH THEMSELVES? [1]

D. Banks Wilburn

[Dr. Wilburn branched off from the foregoing studies to see whether children of various age levels could use furnished materials to discover appropriate learnings for themselves with a minimum of teacher guidance. In addition to his own studies he presents evidence from those of others associated with him. Again, the evidence further supports the treatment of children as thoughtful, intelligent, purposeful humans rather than as animals to be "trained."]

During two school years Peter Melford Rider taught a total of sixty pupils in Grade 6 a method by which they could develop for themselves seemingly adequate understanding and use of the various operations in the division of common fractions. He organized the work into five teaching units, providing one unit for each of the five steps in the division of fractions. The method of instruction was designed to have the pupils find the answer for an example, such as $3\frac{1}{2} \div \frac{1}{4}$, by constructing three and one-half rectangular figures and then dividing the rectangles into fourths. By counting the fourths, the pupils determined the answer. All sixty pupils learned to use the method of instruction well enough to teach themselves the five operations in the division of common fractions.

In another experiment three elementary-school principals (Paul G. Michael, Merton V. Givens, and Wil-

[1] Adapted and abridged from D. Banks Wilburn, "Methods of Self-Instruction for Learning Arithmetic," *Arithmetic 1949*, Supplementary Educational Monographs, No. 70, University of Chicago Press, Chicago, pp. 35–43.

bur P. Cunningham) together with teachers in Grades 3, 4, 5, and 6 directed pupils in using a method of self-instruction for learning the thirty-nine multiplication facts with products from 21 to 81. The children discovered the multiplication facts by combining a number of equal groups into groups of ten. For 9 x 4 one thought, "Four 9's are how many 10's?" Blocks or sticks were arranged in four groups of nine objects, then rearranged into groups of ten. By counting the groups of ten and the remaining objects, they determined the answer, "Four 9's are three 10's and 6; four 9's are 36." They then made and practiced with cards illustrating the facts learned. All 134 pupils who previously had failed to retain multiplication facts taught by other methods learned to use this method well enough to teach themselves.

Paul J. Stevers found that all forty-two pupils of a second grade succeeded in learning the twenty-three division facts with dividends from 4 to 18. By first recognizing that $3\overline{)15}$ asks the question "How many 3's are in 15?" the children could arrange fifteen objects into groups of three, count groups, and find "Five 3's are 15."

In an earlier study Wilburn demonstrated that first-grade children can teach themselves addition facts with sums of 10 or less and their corresponding subtraction facts by taking groups apart and putting the parts together. They later made and practiced with cards having dot arrangements illustrating the facts. At the end of six months sixty-five (of seventy-two) pupils in a group test answered correctly forty or more addition combinations and sixty-three gave correct answers for forty or more subtraction facts. It thus appears that pupils at each grade level, 1 through 6, can learn appropriate units of arithmetic by methods of self-instruction.

The next question was whether pupils can move forward year by year, Grades 1 through 3, in the elementary school, learning the appropriate arithmetic by such methods. Of 556 pupils who entered Grade 1 in twenty-one rural schools, 295 moved through Grade 2 and 112 participated through all three grades. Group tests, the records of individual interviews, and other recorded observations seemed to indicate that they learned methods of self-instruction well enough to teach themselves effectively a selection of the arithmetic content appropriate for each of the three primary grades.

HOW TEACH FOR MEMORY AND APPLICATION? [1]

Esther J. Swenson

[Dr. Swenson's significant study investigated three types of teaching: a rather rigorous drill type, a somewhat advanced meaning type, and

[1] Adapted and abridged from Esther J. Swenson, "Organization and Generalization as Factors in Learning, Transfer and Retroactive Inhibition," *Learning Theory in* *School Situations*, University of Minnesota Studies in Education, No. 2, University of Minnesota Press, Minneapolis, 1949, pp. 9–39.

an intermediate type of teaching that presumably more nearly approximated characteristic school situations. She sought to discover the effects of each upon learning effectiveness, upon transfer of training, and upon retroactive inhibition. How well do children learn, and, of even greater significance, what is the effect of later learnings upon their ability to remember and apply what they have learned by these various methods? The answers are obviously important in planning instruction.]

The purpose of this investigation is to study learning, transfer of training, and retroactive inhibition as they appear in the learning of the 100 addition facts by 332 typical second-grade children taught by three different methods of instruction. The chief variable among the methods is the degree of emphasis upon organization and generalization in the learning process. There was no control group; instead, an experimental group's own performances were compared at different times during the study to get measures of transfer and retroactive inhibition.

Transfer here was measured by *gains* in performance of any group in their knowledge of a certain set of facts during instruction on another set. It was also checked by any gain in performance during a vacation period. *Retroactive inhibition* was measured by *losses* in performance in similar circumstances. The 100 addition facts were divided into three sets; original (O) taught first, interpolated (I) taught next, and final (F) taught last. During the time when any one set was being taught, no teaching was done on any of the others. Time spent: preliminary number readiness instruction, two weeks; interval between first number test and teaching of original facts, one week (allowing time for scoring intelligence and addition tests and for stratified randomization of classes among methods); teaching of interpolated facts, five and a half weeks;

Christmas holidays, two and a half weeks; teaching of final facts, four weeks; total, twenty weeks.

Three teaching methods, *generalization*, *drill*, and *drill-plus* were used with respective groups to form the experimental variables. The generalization method was similar to that of Thiele (see p. 355 above) with the children allowed to continue relatively immature methods of arriving at answers (counting, etc.) so long as needed for understanding. They were encouraged to short-cut roundabout procedures as soon as they could do so without sacrificing understanding. Practice exercises were introduced *after* generalizations had been developed, and *during* rather than *before* their development.

The drill method used was similar to those of McConnell and Thiele above. Little time was spent on developmental aspects and much on "effective drill": interesting, varied exercises, avoidance of practice in error, special repetition of the most difficult facts.

The drill-plus teachers gave children the experience of verifying each new addition fact by counting and manipulating concrete objects prior to drill. They also grouped together all facts yielding the same answer. Thus while pupils were discouraged from making generalizations of number relations, they could hardly fail to notice that reversal of addends makes no difference in the sum ($6 + 2$ and $2 + 6$ come together in the 8 group). The drill-plus method, then, was a drill method with enough concessions to concrete meaning and organization to approximate wide practice.

In all three situations a normal classroom situation was maintained, the time used was uniform, teachers were assigned a method without choice, children had similar instruction in verbal problems and in social uses and applications, and teachers were instructed to make no reference to subtraction facts or processes or to more advanced types of addition examples.

Tests on the addition facts were administered on the last day of the readiness instruction (Test 1), the last day of original fact instruction (Test 2), the last day of interpolated fact instruction (Test 3), the day after the Christmas vacation (Test 4), and the last day of final fact instruction (Test 5). On the next school day, a test was given on the hundred untaught subtraction facts (Transfer Test A); on the ensuing day was given Transfer Test B consisting of decade facts (two-digit plus one-digit examples); and finally, on the following day, Transfer Test C, with a variety of addition possibilities of one-, two-, and three-digit numbers. A gain between Tests 1 and 2 is shown by a positive score on 2 — 1.

These scores would show *learning during instruction*: 2 — 1 increase in O (original) fact score; 3 — 2 increase in I (interpolated) fact score; 5 — 4 increase in F (final) fact score. *Transfer from known to unknown and untaught facts* would be shown by: 2 — 1 gain on I facts, F facts, and combined I and F facts; and 3 — 2 gain on F facts. *Retroactive inhibition* would be shown by: 3 — 2 loss on O facts; 4 — 3 loss on O, I, and combined O and I facts; and 5 — 4 loss on O, I, and combined O and I facts. If positive scores were found in spaces where negative scores would have indicated retroactive inhibition, these positive scores would represent transfer. Total scores on the three transfer tests (A, B, and C) would also show relative transfer. The groups of children were equated for mental age as revealed by the Kuhlmann-Anderson Test.

Some significant findings, that actually ensued with intelligence and appropriate initial scores controlled, include the following:

LEARNING

1. The generalization group made the highest net achievement record for the original (O) facts, interpolated (I) facts, and final (F) facts.

2. The advantage of the generalization group on net results for O facts was highly significant in comparison with the drill-plus group and significant in comparison with the drill group.

3. The generalization group earned a highly significant advantage over the drill group and a near-significant advantage over the drill-plus group for net achievement on F facts, while the drill-plus group achieved a highly significant advantage over the drill group for the same facts.

4. The generalization group made the highest net total achievement for every period of the study and for every combination of adjacent periods that was analyzed.

5. The advantage of the generalization group over each of the other groups was statistically significant in eight comparisons (seven of these highly significant).

6. In no case did any group except the generalization group have a significant net total advantage over any other method group.

7. The generalization group was significantly superior to both of the

other groups on the net total achievement for all periods combined.

RETROACTIVE INHIBITION

1. Interpolated learning of other addition facts did not seem to result in retroactive inhibition of previously learned addition facts when both original and interpolated learning periods extended over a few weeks of time.

2. Interpolated learning of other addition facts seemed to result in less interference with previously learned addition facts than did a two-and-a-half-week vacation from school.

3. The subject's degree of learning, measured in terms of number of facts known at the end of the original learning period, seemed in most cases to be significantly related to susceptibility to retroactive inhibition. The relationship was such that the more facts one knew, the greater were the amounts of retroactive inhibition.

4. For those inter-test changes that resulted in net losses for the groups being studied, there seemed to be a significant positive correlation between the mental age of the learner and his resistance to retroactive inhibition, when the immediately preceding test score was held constant.

5. There seemed to be a tendency for retroactive inhibition to appear more frequently and in greater amounts for groups of children taught by drill methods that discouraged organization and generalization among the number facts. Children taught by a method that organized facts by size of sum but otherwise ignored generalization of number relationship took an intermediate position in amount of retroactive inhibition.

TRANSFER

1. The amounts of transfer among the addition facts, except for the vacation period, usually were significant for all method groups.

2. The generalization group was significantly superior to the drill-plus group five times compared with but once that the drill-plus group was significantly superior to the generalization group.

3. The generalization group was significantly superior to the drill group six times compared with but once that the drill group was significantly superior to the generalization group.

4. The drill-plus group transferred significantly more than the drill group in two situations.

5. There was a significant difference among method groups in their knowledge of subtraction facts after study of addition facts.

6. The order of performance was, from highest to lowest, generalization, drill, and drill-plus.

7. Learning of various sets of addition facts seemed to result in significant amounts of transfer to other untaught and previously unknown facts.

8. Learning of an interpolated set of addition facts resulted in most cases in significant amounts of transfer to previously taught but unlearned addition facts. The only cases in which significant amounts of transfer did not seem to occur were those in which the possibility of transfer was restricted by previous high achievement.

9. The study of the 100 addition facts seemed to be accompanied by a significant amount of transfer to ability to use those combinations in more difficult, complex addition examples.

10. Learning of addition facts seemed to be accompanied by transfer to knowledge of subtraction facts.

11. Most transfer to untaught addition facts occurred for groups taught to organize addition facts around number generalizations. The intermediate posi-

tion in amount of transfer was held by groups who learned addition facts organized by size of sum but had no other instruction in organization and generalization, and the least transfer occurred in drill groups who were discouraged from attempting to organize their number learning.

12. When transfer to other facts and processes was considered, the general trend of advantage for the generalization groups was similar to that for transfer among the 100 addition facts, but the number of statistically significant differences was fewer. On transfer to knowledge of subtraction facts, the group taught to generalize their number learning seemed to be significantly superior to both of the other groups. On transfer to ability to do advanced types of addition problems, the generalization group seemed to be significantly superior to the group that learned facts in sets determined by size of sum, but not to the drill group. On knowledge of higher decade facts, the generalization group had the highest average score but was not significantly superior to other groups that depended chiefly upon drill instruction.

QUANTITATIVE THINKING [1]

G. Lester Anderson

[Dr. Anderson explored the effect of drill-type and meaning-type teaching upon the development of quantitative or mathematical thinking. He found differing effects upon two types of students and extended still farther our understanding of children's learning.]

In another study contrasting drill method with meaning method of teaching fourth-graders, 208 taught by drill were compared with 181 in the meaning group. Against arithmetical processes analyzed into a large number of relatively discrete elements learned through formal repetition were pitted arithmetical processes as a highly organized system of ideas and principles learned from the beginning in meaning-ful practice *after* rather than before rationalization.

The children were equated statistically on appropriate measures. The results indicated little advantage to either method if efficacy of learning is to be judged by recall of knowledge and skill in a situation relatively unchanged from that in which learning took place. If, however, it is judged by the extent to which it can be applied in appropriate

[1] Adapted and abridged from G. Lester Anderson, "Quantitative Thinking as Developed Under Connectionist and Field Theories of Learning," *Learning Theories in* *School Situations,* 1949, University of Minnesota Studies in Education, No. 2, Minneapolis, University of Minnesota Press, Minneapolis, 1949, pp. 40–73.

situations which differ, not in principle but in detail, from those in which it was originally acquired, the advantage lies with the meaning method. These tests of quantitative thinking placed a premium, not upon ability to recall learning directly, but upon ability to adapt learning to new situations. For example, pupils had been taught how to divide with a one-number divisor; in a new situation they were asked to divide with a two-number divisor. Pupils were asked to detect relations among numbers and among processes. Could they discover in the series 3 10 18 15 9 that 10 did not belong because all the other numbers contained 3 as a factor? Did pupils understand that 2×4 and $4 + 4$ were different representations of the same fact?

In these types of test situations those instructional procedures which emphasized relational learning, discovery, and generalization were more productive, especially for children of high ability but of inferior achievement. There was evidence that drill procedures might be better for children of low ability and high achievement.

One of the chief contentions of those who have discussed the application of field principles of learning to arithmetic instruction has been that these instructional procedures would cultivate the "higher mental processes." That is, children who were subjected to methods in arithmetic that emphasized meanings, understandings, relations, and generalizations would come out better thinkers, reasoners, or problem solvers in quantitative situations than pupils subjected to more traditional drill procedures. This investigation adds substantially to the evidence supporting this hypothesis.

Probably the most interesting finding of the investigation is the evidence that the two methods have a differential effect for pupils of different abilities and initial achievements. There is recurring evidence that the drill procedures were superior for pupils who scored relatively low on the Minneapolis School Ability Test and relatively high on the pretest of arithmetic achievement. Conversely, meaningful procedures of instruction tended to be superior for pupils who scored relatively high on the test of school ability and relatively low on the test of initial achievement in arithmetic. Remedial activities ordinarily are assigned to pupils who are achieving below their ability levels. In this investigation, the trend of evidence was that this group learned more under a meaning method than under a drill method of instruction. This type of pupil can profitably spend time on getting an understanding of the number system, on discovering the relationships among numbers and among the fundamental processes. Instructional procedures that emphasize discovery, formulation of generalizations, and seeing meaning in number would be useful in remedial situations.

A second educational implication, closely related to the one just given, is that successful arithmetic instruction must be individualized instruction. All pupils do not profit equally from a particular procedure. The evidence indicates that what is best for pupils of one pattern of ability and achievement may not be best for pupils of other patterns.

An interesting psychological implication of the hypothesis is this: If there are significantly different ways in which learning can take place—for example, by rote practice procedures, by trial and error, by insight—it may be that attention to meanings, relations, or understanding of materials being learned is more important during early stages of learning, and that practice procedures are more important in late stages.

Pupils who are not working up to their abilities may be actually in an early stage of learning. Pupils who are achieving beyond the levels expected of them may be in late stages of learning. For the first group, the trend of evidence was that instruction based on field principles was better; for the second group, instruction that provided abundant practice was superior.

PREMATURE DRILL [1]

William A. Brownell and Charlotte B. Chazal

[What is the function of drill? At what stage in learning is it of value? Are there stages where it is a waste of time? Repetitive drill has occupied such a large portion of time typically devoted to the learning of number combinations that answers to questions of this type are important. An early and important experiment shedding some light on these questions is reported here.]

As used in this section "drill" refers to those activities on the part of the teacher which are designed to set up comparatively unvaried practice on the part of the pupil; it relies upon repetition for its effect upon learning.

The usual measures of efficiency (accuracy and rate) tell *how well* but not *how* one performs. Two boys required to give the sum of 5 and 4 may each respond correctly at the end of .6 second. They were equally "efficient" though one counted while the other thought "5 and 5 are 10 so this is 9." The latter demonstrated a much more advanced type of quantitative thinking. If growth in arithmetic is conceived to be the development of expert quantitative thinking, instructional procedures must be evaluated in terms of children's

thought processes. An important question, then, and the one treated here is "What contribution, if any, does drill make to raising the level of children's performance in arithmetic, to promoting growth in mature forms of quantitative thinking?"

In the fall of 1932, sixty-three children entering Grade 3 were studied. In the two previous grades these children had been taught the 200 addition and subtraction combinations through drill. There had been the least possible opportunity to discover answers for themselves; "learning" consisted of repeating the appropriate verbal formulas with flash cards, games, and simple one-step problems.

Ten days after the start of Grade 3 the children were given a group test on

[1] Adapted and abridged from William A. Brownell and Charlotte B. Chazal, "The Effects of Premature Drill in Third-Grade Arithmetic," *Journal of Educational Research* (1935), 29:17–28.

the 100 addition facts (Test A), timed to the nearest quarter-minute. On the basis of the accuracy scores on this test thirty-two children were selected for immediate individual interviews: the nine making the poorest scores, thirteen making average, and ten making the highest scores. The interviews (Interview I) were designed to ascertain how these thirty-two children thought out or obtained answers to sixteen addition combinations: the ten hardest on Test A and six of average difficulty.

During the next school month five minutes a day were devoted to drill on the addition combinations, so distributed that each combination was presented at least forty times. At the end of this time the timed group test on the addition facts (Test B) was repeated, and the thirty-two selected children were given a second interview (Interview II) on the same sixteen facts of the first interview. Following this by a month, during which no particular drill was given on the addition facts, Test C and Interview III were administered.

The results of the group tests showed the usually found improvement in efficiency: on the average Test A required seventeen minutes with eleven errors; Test B required eleven minutes, and four errors were made; Test C required seven minutes, and the errors remained at four. The drill and later incidental use of the addition facts increased both speed and accuracy. But what of level of performance in quantitative thinking?

The interview data furnished a striking contrast. Methods of solution used by children were grouped into four categories: counting, indirect solution, guessing, and immediate recall. "Counting" (3 + 4: "1, 2, 3 . . . 7" or "3, 4, 5, 6, 7,") was reported if a child dealt with any number as so many ones. "In-

direct solution" involved such processes as "3 and 3 are 6, and this is one more" or "4 and 4 are 8, and this is one less," etc. "Guessing" was reported if at once he replied wrongly and did not correct it. He was said to use "immediate recall" if he replied promptly and correctly.

The three sets of interviews each involved thirty-two children with sixteen combinations to provide 512 responses for categorizing. In Interview I after two years of drill only 39.5 percent of the combinations were known in the way combinations are assumed to be known when taught by drill. See Figure 1. After a month of drill (Interview II) and an additional month of incidental use of the number facts (Interview III) mature usage had risen only to 48.5 percent and 52.5 percent respectively.

Immature methods of thought still abounded. In the three interviews "counting" was used for 22.7, 17.4, and 19.3 percent of the responses respectively; "guessing" was reduced from 23.8 to 18.2 to 15.4 percent; while "indirect solution" was little modified (14.1, 15.6, and 12.7 percent). Counting and guessing combined still accounted for 66 percent as many responses as did immediate recall. Children persisted in using the same immature methods of solving particular combinations in spite of drill designed to stop them. Children who after two years of drill in Grades 1 and 2 "counted" to get answers to facts continued in general to "count" after a month or more of drill in Grade 3. Children who at the start of Grade 3 tended to "solve" the facts continued to "solve" them after a month's drill.

Several inferences seem warranted. (1) Drill, as here administered, does not guarantee immediate recall of combinations. (2) Despite long-continued drill children tend to continue whatever procedures they have found to satisfy their number needs. (3) Drill makes little, if any, contribution to growth in quantitative thinking by supplying maturer ways of dealing with numbers.

These data are interpreted to show the dangers of premature drill, drill on verbal statements or formulations be-fore children have reached mature pro-cedures in thinking about facts. Effec-tive teaching must *precede* drill. "Pre-mature" does not imply that Grade 3 is too soon for drill on the facts; an earlier level is not too soon if children's thought procedures on particular facts have developed to the point where their procedures on those facts should be habituated.

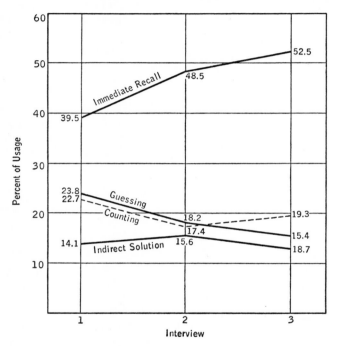

Fig. 1. Percent of 512 Responses (32 Children, 16 Addition Combinations) Based upon Each Method of Solution During Three Interviews.

ARE WE TEACHING MEANINGS? [1]

Vincent J. Glennon

[Traditionally, much teaching has been by rote: "This is the way to do it; now you do it." "Don't ask why—just invert the divisor and multiply the way I showed you." During the past two decades, however, increasing attention has been directed to the importance of teaching "meaningfully," basing the learning of skills upon a clear understanding of the underlying reasons. The following study sought to determine the degree to which products of our schools had learned these reasons. Furthermore, it sampled people who were training to become teachers and who were already teachers to see whether they themselves had the understanding that they should be expected to teach.]

This study was an attempt to discover the degree to which persons above the level of Grade 6 have possession of the meanings and understandings basic to the several computational skills commonly taught in Grades 1 through 6. A test of basic mathematical understandings was prepared that eliminated in so far as possible the effect of rote computational ability. By refining each question in personal trial with individual seventh-graders, the author prepared a test of eighty multiple-choice items covering these basic mathematical meanings: (1) the decimal system of notation, (2) basic understandings of integers and processes, (3) basic understandings of fractions and processes, (4) basic understandings of decimals and processes, and (5) basic understandings of the rationale of computa-

tion. The test was administered without time limit.

Sample item: In this example you multiply by the 6, then by the 3. How do the two results (partial products) compare?

A. The second represents a number one-half as large as the first.

$$749 \times 36$$

B. The second represents a number twice as large as the first.
C. The second represents a number five times as large as the first.
D. The second represents a number ten times as large as the first.
E. The second represents a number twenty times as large as the first.

The test was administered to a total of 1139 people on seven educational

[1] Adapted and abridged from Vincent J. Glennon, "Testing Meanings in Arithmetic," *Arithmetic 1949*, Supplementary Educational Monographs, No. 70, University of Chicago Press, Chicago, 1949, pp. 64–74.

levels as follows: Grade 7, 168, Grade 8, 157; Grade 9, 163; Grade 12, 175; teachers' college freshmen, 144; teachers' college seniors, 172; and teachers in service, 160. The seventh grade is the lowest grade at which we can be certain all the fundamental processes have been taught.

The average percents of achievement of basic mathematical understandings for each grade level were as follows: Grade 7, 12.5 percent; Grade 8, 14.0 percent; Grade 9, 18.0 percent; Grade 12, 37.0 percent; teachers' college freshmen, 44.3 percent; seniors, 42.7 percent; teachers in service, 54.8 percent. The slight growth from Grade 7 to Grade 8 did not exceed chance and indicates little growth in understanding during the seventh grade. The growths between the eighth and ninth and between the ninth and twelfth grades were significant and might be accounted for by (1) direct learning during the period,

(2) a selective factor in entering or in finishing high school, (3) added maturity, or (4) a combination of these. The teachers' college freshmen and seniors scored somewhat higher than the high-school students, indicating the selective factor of admission to college. However, these teachers-to-be knew fewer than half of the understandings and apparently learned few if any of them during college. Teachers on the job had apparently learned some more, yet still knew but slightly more than half of the understandings they might be presumed to be teaching.

The entire study indicates that the level of grasp of the basic understandings underlying arithmetic computation among the people sampled in this study was not high. The evidence does not lend much support to the argument often heard that "we are already teaching meanings."

MEANINGFUL VERSUS MECHANICAL LEARNING [1]

William A. Brownell, Harold E. Moser, and others

["In view of the abundance of rhetoric in modern education on the importance of meaningful experience in learning, the dearth of competent relevant research stands in strange contrast. In both oral and written discussion all sorts of claims are advanced for instructional programs based on meaningful experience; but few indeed are the research studies in any area of the curriculum to support these claims. This discrepancy is particularly striking in arithmetic" [2] and in part is lessened by this study. In the course of the experiment important light was also focused upon the value and alleged danger of children's use of "crutches," and upon the relative merits of teaching the two

[1] Adapted and abridged from William A. Brownell, Harold E. Moser, and others, *Meaningful versus Mechanical Learning: A Study in Grade III Subtraction*, Duke University Research Studies in Education, No. 8, Duke University Press, Durham, N.C., 1949.

[2] Quoted from this study.

principal types of subtraction procedures used in this country. In an earlier study John T. Johnson [3] had shown that when children are taught in a mechanical fashion pupils who use the equal additions method are somewhat faster and more accurate. Other studies have been less conclusive and none compare the methods in subtracting mixed numbers and decimals. The most convincing study dealing with subtraction methodology is the one reported here.]

The subjects of the experiment were approximately 1400 third-grade children enrolled in forty-one classrooms of four school systems. These children were equated in four experimental groups. Half of the classes in each center learned to borrow by decomposition (D); half, by equal additions (EA). Each half was divided again, so that one part learned their subtraction procedure meaningfully (R, rationally); the other part, mechanically (M). Thus, there eventuated the four experimental sections: DM, DR, EAM, EAR.

According to D, the child is taught to think: "Four from 12, 8; write 8; 5 from 6, 1; write 1."

$$\begin{array}{r} 72 \\ -54 \\ \hline 18 \end{array}$$

According to EA, the child thinks: "Four from 12, 8; write 8; 6 from 7, 1; write 1."

The term "equal additions" is appropriate because a ten is added to both terms in the example, as 10 ones to the 2 of 72, and as 1 ten to the 5 of 54. Likewise, "decomposition" is appro-priate because the minuend, 72, is "de-composed" (made equivalent) to $60 + 12$.

The mechanically taught pupils (DM and EAM) were taught to borrow in a purely rote fashion. At no time was the slightest hint offered concerning the rationale of the procedures. Children's questions which probed into such mat-ters were dismissed outright or with "explanations" which explained noth-ing. For example, EAM classes with the above were taught this verbal pattern: "I can't take 4 from 2, so I think of 2 as 12. Then I think '4 from 12 is 8,' and I write 8. Since I thought of 2 as 12 I must think of 5 as 6. Then I think '6 from 7 is 1,' and I write 1." Next the children were to shorten the verbal pat-tern to "Four from 12, 8; 6 from 7, 1."

The rationally taught pupils (DR and EAR) had carefully developed steps making use of crutches to clarify the meanings. DR classes, for example, fol-lowed this type of pattern:

Step 1.

(1)	(2)	(3)
$64 = 6$ tens $+ 4$ ones,	or 5 tens $+ 14$ ones	$\begin{array}{r} 5\ 1 \\ 6\ \ 4 \\ -\ 2\ \ 8 \\ \hline 3\ \ 6 \end{array}$

Item (3) illustrates the crutch.

Step 2. Have pupils copy examples

using the crutch, calling them "number pictures." Develop this verbal pattern: "I cannot take 8 from 4, so I borrow ten from the six tens. I cross out the 6 and write a little 5 to show that I borrowed a ten. I write a little 1 in front of the 4 to show that I now have 14 instead of 4. Then I subtract 8 from 14, 6, and I write 6 in the ones' place; '2 from 5, 3,' and I write 3 in the tens' place." Insist that the crutch be used in every example with borrowing.

Step 3. The children shorten the verbal pattern to a minimum but continue to use the crutch.

All classes were taught to borrow for a period of fifteen school days. (1) Midway of the three-week period class papers were collected from the R subjects only, to determine the extent to which the crutches taught were being used. (The M sections were taught no crutches.) (2a) At the end of the fifteen days a computational test was administered. Part I of this test was restricted in content to the kind of subtraction just taught. Part II was similar in content to Part I, but the R subjects were denied use of the crutch. It was designed to provide measures of transfer. Part I supplied data on the use of the crutches in R classes. (2b) Immediately after the End Test had been given, all subjects were interviewed, to ascertain relative "smoothness" in computation and degree of understanding of the process. (3) About three weeks later R subjects took a subtraction test again, to discover the degree to which the crutches were being used. (4a) Six weeks after the close of the experimental period proper a retention test was administered, intended to show progress or retrogression in the kind of subtraction taught and the extent of use of crutches by R children. (4b) Immediately thereafter the second interviews were held with all subjects available, for the purposes mentioned in (2b) above.

SUMMARY OF RESULTS IN A TYPICAL CENTER

1. If the D procedure is to be taught, it had best be taught meaningfully. In the sixteen comparisons between DR and DM (column 1 of Table 1) DR was ahead in thirteen. DM excelled in rate of computation in two cases (one reliable), but its inferiority at other more significant points negates this advantage.

2. If EA is taught, it too had best be taught meaningfully. In practically all significant ways (column 6), the EAR children surpassed the EAM children.

3. The last statement would seem to indicate that the EA procedure may be rationalized with full benefits to children with limited arithmetical backgrounds. But this inference loses weight when the records of the EAR subjects are compared with those of the DR subjects. According to column 2, the DR section outscored the EAR section in fourteen cases, seven times by reliable amounts.

4. The meaningfully taught sections rather consistently excelled the mechanically taught sections.

5. There is some evidence that rational instruction produced greater uniformity in accuracy of computation than did mechanical instruction.

6. If the D and the EA procedures are to be taught mechanically (column 5), there is not a great deal to choose between them.

7. It is clear that smoothness of performance is a poor criterion of learning. The mechanically taught sections had of course an initial superiority at this point, but this superiority was merely in glibness of pattern, and it was soon lost. The meaningfully taught sections were somewhat "rough" in their processes at the outset, as might be expected from their more involved language patterns; but in time they overcame their initial inferiority. The educational implications of this finding should be clear to the classroom teacher.

TABLE 1. Summary of Experimental Comparisons in One Center

Function Measured	DR vs. DM (1)	DR vs. EAR (2)	DR vs. EAM (3)	DM vs. EAR (4)	DM vs. EAM (5)	EAR vs. EAM (6)
I. Process Taught						
A. Accuracy						
1. End Test, Part I						
As a whole	DR	DR	DR	EAR	dm	EAR
Borrowing	DR	dr	DR	EAR	DM	EAR
Nonborrowing	dr	dr	dr	ear	dm	ear
2. Retention Test						
As a whole	DR	DR	DR	ear	dm	EAR
Borrowing	DR	dr	DR	ear	dm	EAR
Nonborrowing	DR	DR	DR	ear	eam	ear
B. Rate						
1. End Test, Part I	dm	dr	DR	DM	DM	ear
2. Retention Test	DR	ear	DR	EAR	EAM	EAR
C. Smoothness of performance						
1. Interview I	DM	ear	EAM	DM	eam	EAM
2. Interview II	dr	dr	dr	ear	eam	eam
D. Degree of understanding						
1. Interview I	DR	DR	DR	EAR	dm	EAR
2. Interview II	DR	DR	DR	EAR	dm	EAR
II. Untaught Process						
A. Accuracy, End Test, Part III						
As a whole	DR	DR	DR	dm	DM	EAR
Borrowing	DR	DR	DR	dm	DM	EAR
Nonborrowing a	dr	dr	dr	dm	dm	ear
B. Rate, End Test, Part III	DM	dr	dr	DM	DM	eam

a C.R.'s not computed, since the test included only three or four examples of this type. The letters indicate the *direction* of the advantage only.

Explanation of symbols:
dr = difference in favor of DR, but C.R. smaller than 1.5.
dr = difference in favor of DR; C.R. 1.6–2.9.
DR = difference in favor of DR; C.R. 3.0–4.9.
DR = difference in favor of DR; C.R. 5.0, or larger.

8. Rate of computation is also, by itself, an inadequate criterion of learning, particularly when it is accompanied by a tendency to error, and by absence of understanding.

9. "Understanding" is of course a relative term. The EAR children, for example, manifested much more understanding of borrowing than did the DM children at the times when they were interviewed. Yet the understanding of the EAR children was relatively limited, for in accuracy on the Transfer Test they showed no superiority over the DM children. Apparently the EAR children understood fairly well just what they were taught, but they could not carry over this understanding to new types of borrowing.

10. Most students of arithmetic now

advocate meaningful instruction in arithmetic (though they do not always agree on details). They admit that extra time may be required for such instruction in the early phases of learning and that accordingly the pace of instruction at first may have to be relatively slow. But they insist that, even so, time is not actually lost; for, once children understand what they are to learn, the pace of instruction may be speeded up in later phases of learning. Moreover, they insist that the effects of meaningful instruction are cumulative. Understanding is said to facilitate learning at later points. Support for these claims is to be found in the record of the DR section, which, unlike the EAR section, really saw sense in borrowing from tens. Because of their relatively large success on the Transfer Test it can be inferred that the children in this section would encounter little difficulty in extending their subtraction skills into more complicated types of borrowing. On the other hand, the DM and the EAM children, as well as the EAR children, would need considerable attention in mastering these types of computation.

11. There is inferential evidence that the crutches taught the DR and the EAR sections helped rather than hindered the learning of borrowing.

12. The crutches were pretty well abandoned after shorter algorisms were put into use, but there was some persistence. The seriousness of this amount of persistence is conjectural, but to the authors it appears to be of relatively little consequence.

Chapter XIII

WHAT AND WHEN IN ARITHMETIC

Introduction

In this chapter are to be found a few studies dealing with what obviously are among the most fundamental questions in education. The first study, "Useful Fractions," is included as an example of a whole theory of curriculum selection which says we should teach children what they later will need as adults. Few other studies of this nature have been so clear cut in their findings. Most efforts to determine content through experimentation have proved inconclusive; the decisions have had to remain largely philosophical.

Experimentation in sequence has proved more fruitful in its efforts to discover what children of various maturity levels are capable of learning. Most of these have dealt with the preschool or primary grade levels, where results have more easily proved conclusive. Studies of the extensiveness of children's arithmetic understandings prior to entering school gave support to those who wished arithmetic to continue being taught incidentally without any organized sequence of learnings. This approach, however, has never gained many adherents, since it ignores the whole internal logic and mathematical structure of arithmetic itself. Too many learnings, moreover, are likely to be omitted or skimped. Incidental may become accidental. These studies of early learnings gave support also to those who wished children to be taught formally at an early level, since they appeared to be capable of much learning.

In striking contrast were the widely publicized findings of the Committee of Seven, which indicated that rather advanced mental ages were necessary for learning many areas of arithmetic. Influenced by these findings and by a faulty interpretation of Benezet's dramatic report, the leaders of numerous school systems in all parts of the country adopted a "stepped-up" curriculum. They kept the same general pattern of sequence but delayed the teaching of each part by a semester, or a year, or more. From Chicago, in 1940, came an indication that this approach was fruitful.[1]

Arithmetic topic placement was shifted upward about one year for 350,000 children. Three survey tests given at semester intervals to random samples of 1000, 3000, and 10,000 pupils in each of Grades 3 to 8 showed increases in accuracy in terms of percent based on points gained each semester.

Percent Gain in Norms

Grade	3B	3A	4B	4A	5B	5A
Sem. I	3.0	18.5	10.0	31.0	5.5	6.1
Sem. II	27.2	0.0	6.1	16.1	16.5	10.2

Percent Gain in Norms

Grade	6B	6A	7B	7A	8B	8A	Average
Sem. I	13.4	6.8	18.8	15.4	20.0	15.5	13.7
Sem. II	14.8	1.2	41.0	22.4	42.5	25.0	18.6

"The above gains in so short a period coupled with the fact that teachers and pupils are better satisfied because getting better results than formerly are here offered as one share of the bit of evidence contributed by better grade placement of arithmetic topics in the elementary school.

"It should be added that no sacrifice of topics was made in the seventh or eighth grade. Instead, two new topics were added."

Continued research (Brueckner and Melbye, and especially studies under Brownell's direction) indicated, however, that when taught meaningfully (not formally) children can learn at mental ages a year or two below those found by the Committee of Seven. More significantly, cumulative evidence indicated wide ranges of difficulty in the same area (e.g., two-figure division) and, furthermore, the fact that concepts take a long, long time in their development. From all this has emerged the concept of the "stretched-out" curriculum in which the topics are thought of as strands extending over several grades. Thus almost from the start of school children can profit from a program of planned (but not formal) learning experiences.

[1] John T. Johnson, "Experiment in Grade Placement of Curriculum Units in Mathematics," Official Report of 1940 Meeting, Washington, D.C., American Educational Research Association, National Education Association, pp. 134–135.

USEFUL FRACTIONS [1]

Guy M. Wilson and Charles O. Dalrymple

[The "social utility" theory of selecting school content assumes that one way we can choose more wisely is to consider the usage people may have for the skill or information to be learned. To spend time on content that stands little chance of being needed seems wasteful when there are so many vital learnings crowding our curriculum. A dramatic illustration of this theory in action is this study by Wilson showing that most fractions are seldom if ever used outside the classroom. The reader should recall, however, that even though but few denominators may be used in teaching fractions, generalizations can be established that will enable students to deal with any novel fractions they may encounter.]

What are the useful fractions, the fractions used enough in business and life to justify teaching for mastery? School time is too precious to be spent on the useless, and, moreover, children learn most readily those things for which they see purpose.

A compilation of eight previous studies of the usage of fractions with denominators ranging from 2 to 144 included 12,613 fraction usages. Seven-eighths of these social usages involved only the denominators 2, 3, and 4. The inclusion of ⅙, ⅛, and ½₂ brought the usage total to 96.7 percent. No other fraction had as much as a half of one percent of the usage.

The present study of fractions used in business extended over a period of two years and was conducted in the large Boston metropolitan area. Analysis was made of 102,220 usages. Many busi-

nesses yielded no fractions, or fractions so few that days of observing yielded meager returns. The necessity of recording results forced the investigation into the larger and more complicated businesses to such an extent that *complicated business* usage, rather than the average adult usage, is shown in the returns. The results for nine large units (Sears, Roebuck & Co., Boston Transcript, United Drug Co., etc.) were here tabulated for comparison with the results of the previous studies. Strikingly greater usage of fourths (35.68 percent *vs.* 18.71 percent), eighths (20.37 percent *vs.* 2.24 percent), and thirty-seconds (9.47 percent *vs.* 0.02 percent) was apparent, and strikingly smaller usage of halves (31.18 percent *vs.* 60.25 percent) and thirds (1.03 percent *vs.* 8.56 percent). But the overall general-

[1] Adapted and abridged from Guy M. Wilson and Charles O. Dalrymple, "Useful Fractions," *Journal of Educational Research* (1937), 30:341–347.

ization still was obvious, that only a few fractions were doing most of the work. Fractions with the denominators 2, 3, 4, 8, and 32 accounted for 97.73 percent of the usage; the inclusion of twelfths and sixteenths brought the total to 99.60 percent. There were no "sevenths" and but seven "ninths." Large businesses add very few fractions beyond the common usage of individuals.

The data from these studies appear to be adequate for final conclusions on useful fractions. They indicate the need for thoroughgoing simplifications of the work of fractions in our schools. The operations and combinations of fractions in business are very, very simple in comparison with school practice. Have we been wasting school time on useless

fractions, and in going beyond usage on a purely manipulative basis have we not done much to confuse and defeat the child?

Needed mastery for common usage is limited to halves, thirds, fourths, eighths, and twelfths. Crossing of denominators seldom goes farther than halves with fourths. Subtraction of fractions seldom occurs. Division of a fraction by a fraction almost never occurs. This simple program of mastery can best be accomplished through an objective, non-manipulative procedure. Any further program should be purely informational. Unusual fractions should be left to learning on the job, when and if needed; they are no part of the grade task of the schools.

DEVELOPMENT OF CHILDREN'S NUMBER IDEAS [1]
William A. Brownell

[The most influential experimenter in contemporary arithmetic has been William A. Brownell. In this, his earliest important study, he set a precedent for future work. The extensive nature of his investigation, the care with which relevant hypotheses were explored (though less adequately than in later studies), and above all his concern for meaningfulness in learning have continued as primary characteristics. Only a glimpse of the total design can be presented in this abridgment.]

This monograph reports an experimental study of the development of children's number ideas in the primary grades. The children had all had at least two months of school training; it was not possible,

therefore, to deal with the earliest beginnings of number knowledge, such as knowledge of the number names; or with the earliest forms of skill in the use of number, such as the ability to

[1] Adapted and abridged from William A. Brownell, *The Development of Children's Number Ideas in the Primary Grades*, Supplementary Educational Monographs, No. 35, University of Chicago Press, Chicago, 1928.

count. The study is reported in several sections.

COMPARATIVE DIFFICULTY OF NUMBERS

Does the average child in the lower grades apprehend five visible objects more readily than he apprehends six and less readily than four? In other words, does the position of a number in the series from 3 to 12 correspond to its position in the series of degrees of difficulty in apprehension, or are some numbers inherently easy? Are odd numbers harder than even?

Six sets of exposure cards were prepared to present dot patterns corresponding to those in Table 1. First-grade children drew what they had seen on a separate sheet for each card; other children recorded in digit form the number they had seen. All were scored either right or wrong.

TABLE 1. Appearance of the Numbers from 3 to 12 in the Six Types of Arrangement

No.	Quadratic	Diamond	Domino	Triangular	Odd	Linear
3						...
4						....
5						......
6						....
7						....
8						....
9						....
10						....
11						....
12						....

The results secured in the present investigation seem to justify the conclusion that, when the factor of objective grouping is eliminated, the difficulty of apprehending visual concrete numbers is in direct proportion to the number of objects exposed. In other words, with grouping eliminated, the pupil apprehends five visible objects more readily than he apprehends six and less readily than he apprehends four. The order of difficulty of apprehension is the order of the notation system.

Furthermore, none of the numbers from 3 to 12 seems to have inherent qualities of ease or difficulty of apprehension. The odd numbers are not harder to apprehend as a class than are the even numbers; if in a given case they seem to be harder, the special difficulty is probably due to sensory causes which can be isolated. The investigation has made clear the fact that children at different grade levels employ different methods to apprehend visual concrete numbers. Some evidence has been found that the younger pupils count and that the older pupils make use of grouping.

METHODS OF APPREHENDING CONCRETE NUMBERS

Numbers may be apprehended in many ways: counting by ones or twos, the more mature method of grouping in fours, etc. (1) How do children change in their methods of apprehension during Grades 1 through 5? (2) How do methods actually used at a given grade level compare with methods theoretically theirs by reason of school training in arithmetic? (3) What are the implications for instruction in primary number?

Pupils of the various grade levels were interviewed individually so that they might show by pointing at the dots on each flash card how they apprehend numbers of various groupings. Others were carefully watched to see their methods as revealed by motor adjustments of the head, the hand, and the eye. Still others revealed their methods through their drawings from memory of what they had seen. Further groups studied cards with an exposure too short to permit counting. Finally a group of children taught at a slower number pace with much concrete experiencing during

Grades 1 and 2 were followed through Grades 3 and 4.

CONCLUSIONS

First, the pupils in the first three grades who served as subjects did not readily apprehend the visual concrete numbers exposed to them in the form of number pictures. Second, the pupils did not in general employ abstract methods, such as counting by 2's, 3's, and 4's, below the third and fourth grades although all had received training in these abbreviated forms of counting and in the additive combinations by the middle of the second grade. For pupils in the first three grades abstract and concrete numbers are apparently little related to each other and have been acquired as separate bodies of facts. So isolated are these two bodies that an opportunity for the application of abstract knowledge was not recognized. Third, a few pupils even in the fourth and fifth grades continued to use counting, the most primitive of methods, as their only means of apprehending the number pictures. Fourth, it is possible to organize early instruction in number in such a way that many of the difficulties of apprehending concrete numbers are eliminated without in any way hampering later progress with abstract numbers and their relations. In fact, effective instruction is contingent upon an understanding of the mental processes of the pupils.

The steps which children take in developing mature methods of dealing with concrete numbers are: (1) counting, a method in which each of the objects is told off until the last number name stands for the total number of objects exposed; (2) partial counting, in which a part of the total number of exposed objects is taken as a group and the rest are counted; (3) grouping, in which a number of separate groups are recognized one after the other and the total number is apprehended by adding together the subtotals; and (4) multiplication and conversion, in which the objective representation of the number is at once translated into abstract symbols and the number apprehended through these symbols without further reference to the objects themselves.

LEARNING TO ADD

Children studied in the above investigations were now analyzed for abstract operations in two-digit and in three-digit addition. For two-digit $(3 + 4)$ and later for three-digit $(3 + 4 + 2)$ addition the students were tested first with accuracy as their objective, and again with speed as their goal. Later for each type of operation the children were interviewed individually to discover their way of thinking.

The evidence gathered appears to confirm the following: First, learning to deal effectively with the additive combinations and the second additions in a three-digit example occurs in steps roughly analogous to the steps reported above for learning to deal with concrete numbers. Familiar and meaningful but immature procedures eventually lead under guidance to those that are mature and highly abstract. Each step grows out of the preceding one. Second, thorough knowledge and understanding of concrete number facilitates these learnings. Third, pupils who do not understand concrete number have difficulty with additive procedures. Fourth, two types having great difficulty are (1) pupils with only immature methods for concrete numbers who carry over and apply these methods as best they can to abstract numbers; and (2) pupils who fail to relate the new work to their earlier experiences. Fifth, even pupils who understand the processes often develop undesirable methods of using them. These can be easily detected by alert teachers and checked before becoming habitual. Finally, drill is incapable of developing in children effective methods of dealing with numbers and should be used as a valuable teaching method only during the final stages of learning.

YOUNG CHILDREN'S NUMBER ABILITIES [1]

B. R. Buckingham and Josephine MacLatchy

[At the time of this study, most arithmetic texts for third-grade children started off at an absurdly immature level and in a few pages moved to an advanced level. The assumptions apparently were that children know very little if any arithmetic until nearly eight years of age and that growth can then be fantastically rapid. This study illustrates a

[1] Abridged and adapted from B. R. Buckingham and Josephine MacLatchy, "The Number Abilities of Children When They Enter Grade One," Report of the Society's Committee on Arithmetic, Twenty-ninth Yearbook, National Society for the Study of Education, Public School Publishing Co., Bloomington, Illinois, 1930, pp. 473–524.

type of investigation that has been carried out here and there through the years to discover what arithmetic children learn prior to formal schooling. At about the same time Clifford Woody was conducting a similar and comprehensive study [2] of several thousand children that is not reported here. His findings were similar but indicated even greater competence in several areas. From these kinds of studies has also come a realization of the gradualness with which number concepts develop.]

An interview test was administered to entering first-grade children between six and six and a half years of age during their first two weeks of school and before they had been taught any number work. The 1356 school entrants tested in this Primary Investigation were selected representatively in seventeen cities and towns. The test was divided into six subtests. Test I called for rote counting by ones and by tens. Test II asked each child to count concrete objects as he touched or pointed to them. Tests III and IV tested working knowledge of numbers 1 to 10. In Test III, for example, the examiner asked a child to perform such tasks as "Give me five buttons," of the ten lying before him. In Test IV he would be asked, "How many are there here?" with reference to a group of objects lying before him.

Test V consisted of ten verbal problems, each requiring for its solution one of the ten selected number facts: "If you have _____ and get _____, how many _____ will you then have?" Test VI concerned a functional knowledge of selection number combinations presented by means of objects. For example, with buttons and combination 2 plus 2, the examiner shows two buttons and asks, "How many buttons have I

[2] Clifford Woody, "Knowledge of Arithmetic Possessed by Young Children," *Bulletin of the School of Education* (1930), 6:50–85, Indiana University.

here?" After correct response, the first two are covered by a hand, two more are shown and the same question is asked. The examiner now conceals both groups and asks, "How many are two buttons and two buttons?" The correct response is scored "4 invisible." If the child fails, the buttons are uncovered and he is asked, "See if you can tell me now how many two buttons and two buttons are." Success is scored "4 visible."

SUMMARY OF FINDINGS

1. *Rote counting.* In counting by ones about 90 percent of the children succeeded at least as far as 10 and about 60 percent of them at least as far as 20. The typical (median) child counted to 27 or 28. One in eight of the children counted to 100. Half the children counted by tens at least as far as 40, while one-quarter of them counted in this manner to 100.

2. *Counting with objects.* The test used did not require counting of this type beyond 20. The majority of the children (in fact about 60 percent) "broke the test" by counting as far as they were permitted to go. Seventy-five percent counted at least as far as 14.

3. *Reproducing numbers.* This is one of the two tests of number concepts. Practically all the children "knew" the numbers from 1 to 4. Eighty-five percent of them reproduced 5 at least once

out of three trials, and nearly two-thirds of them did so on all three trials. The numbers 6 and 7 were practically equal in difficulty. Fully 80 percent of the children reproduced them once and about 55 percent three times. The number 8 was of substantially the same difficulty as the number 10. Over 75 percent of the children reproduced each of these numbers once, and about half of them did so three times.

4. *Naming numbers.* This is somewhat more difficult as a test of number concepts than reproducing numbers, and the percents of children who succeeded are from 4 to 8 percentage points less. Yet even here the children did well. Forty-two percent of them succeeded every time on the hardest number, namely, 10. An additional 28 percent of them showed that they were "on the way" to a reliable understanding of 10 by succeeding either once or twice. Thus a total of 70 percent responded correctly at least once on the hardest number of the series. The corresponding percent for 8 was 72; for 7, 74; for 6, 75; and for 5, 81.

5. *Combinations in verbal problems.* According to the Knight-Behrens difficulty rankings, the addition combinations used in this test ranged from eleventh to eighty-first. Some of the children gave correct answers to all these combinations—in fact ninety-one, or about 7 percent, of them did so. Very nearly half the children got five combinations right, and only 11 percent of them failed to get any right. The combinations ranged in difficulty for these children from $5 + 1$, which 71.5 percent of the children answered correctly, to $4 + 5$, which only 22 percent answered correctly.

6. *Combinations with objects.* The ten addition combinations in this test ranked from tenth to eighty-eighth according to the rankings of Knight and Behrens. Half of the children answered at least five of these combinations correctly when the objects were concealed. When the objects were visible, more than half the children answered all the combinations correctly. The eighty-eighth combination $(6 + 4)$ was the hardest one for these children, as was to be expected from its placement in the Knight-Behrens list. Yet this combination was answered correctly by nearly one-third of the children (31.8 percent) when the objects were concealed and by 40 percent more of them when the objects were uncovered.

In a supplementary experiment in another city 1100 entering first-graders of the same age level were given the same test. The new findings throughout were very similar to those above but permitted further analysis to compare boys with girls, and those who had had kindergarten with those who had not. Though the differences were small, the girls consistently surpassed the boys. Furthermore, children with kindergarten experience consistently showed more number knowledge than those without kindergarten.

It is apparent from this study that children before entering school have learned a great deal of arithmetic incidentally, just in the course of living.

CONCEPT DEVELOPMENT [1]

Ned M. Russell

[Dr. Russell's study illustrates a type which used limited numbers of children to investigate certain areas more fully. From this report we see more clearly the gradualness with which concepts grow and become clear.]

Using piles of blocks with appropriate questioning the author interviewed twenty-nine children four to eight years of age to discover: (1) the responses to quantitative situations of more and less, (2) the understanding and use of words denoting *more, less, many, equal,* and *same,* (3) the limits perceptually beyond which they cannot make distinctions between quantities, and (4) the manner in which they go about the task of making distinctions between quantities.

He concluded that: (1) The child's first concept of number is *manyness,* from which the quantity and serial aspects only gradually differentiate. Data were presented to show that the differentiation is a gradual process which, at the seven-year-old level and beyond, does not reach the adult's conception of the cardinal and the ordinal ideas of number.

(2) The cardinal and ordinal number concepts develop simultaneously.[2]

Ability to count, in itself, is not a reliable measure of this development.

(3) The child four and a half to five years of age readily understands the terms *most, both,* and *biggest.* Words denoting *same* and *equal* are not comprehended. The child can compare groups of blocks up to ten with remarkable accuracy, although he has a visual notion only of three or perhaps of four.

(4) The seven-year-old child uses such terms as *many, most,* and *more.* The words *same* and *equal* are not fully comprehended. Counting by ones is a difficult method for differentiating groups and is not accurate above five. The child will form subgroups first which have unequal value mathematically. At a later stage in the differential

[1] Abridged and adapted from Ned M. Russell, "Arithmetic Concepts of Children," *Journal of Educational Research* (1936), 29:647–663.
[2] Caroline Stotlar ("Arithmetic Concepts of Pre-School Children," *Elementary School Journal* (1946), 46:342–345) made a study of nineteen children between fifty and sixty-nine months of age who were just entering kindergarten. (1) Seventy percent could count to 10 or higher by rote. (2) Seventy percent could count to 10 or above by concept. (The two processes were keeping pace.) (3) The children could learn and repeat numbers in any sequence. (4) When asked to write numbers, all showed awareness that there was such a thing as written numbers and all but one made an attempt at writing.

process, counting by ones is employed.

(5) It is not likely (as many have maintained) that the first-grade or second-grade pupil will be mature enough to master completely and understand isolated addition and subtraction facts.

Formal work such as drill over these arithmetic facts should be discouraged. The observations indicate that the initial training in arithmetic should be undertaken with the use of concrete materials.

LEARNING THE MULTIPLICATION COMBINATIONS [1]

William A. Brownell and Doris V. Carper

[All educational theorists are in agreement that it is important for children at some stage to learn the multiplication combinations. There is much disagreement, however, on when and how they should be taught. In this comprehensive monograph Drs. Brownell and Carper investigate the problem and reach important conclusions. Because the latter part of this study (though not directly a report of research) has so much value as a guide to teaching multiplication, the editors have deviated from the overall plan of the book to provide for its inclusion here in condensed form.]

This monograph is intended to serve four purposes: (1) to review previously reported research relating to the learning and teaching of the multiplication combinations: (2) to present two new and rather extensive studies on the learning of these combinations; (3) to consider critically the concept of "readiness" as this concept applies to learning the multiplication combinations and to report new data on the problem; and (4) to suggest a program of instruction, based partly on research and partly on theory, for the teaching of these combinations. [This condensation will be confined largely to purposes (2) and (3).]

A critical analysis of existing research led the authors to conclude that little is known regarding children's procedures in learning the multiplication combinations. Few data have been reported regarding the way in which children actually learn the combinations. The authors hypothesize that teaching procedures can only by accident be of the best unless they are selected and directed according to the way in which children learn. Two studies, then, were conducted in which the principal point of interest was precisely that of the changes in behavior which take place as children advance to mastery of the combinations.

[1] Adapted and abridged from William A. Brownell and Doris V. Carper, *Learning the Multiplication Combinations*, Duke University Research Studies in Education, No. 7, Duke University Press, Durham, N.C., 1943.

The same experimental procedures were attempted in both studies and the outcomes were nearly alike and corroborative of each other. The first study involved four schools, two each in Burlington and Raleigh, North Carolina, and was closely supervised by the senior author. There were 593 children with usable test data rather evenly distributed among Grades 3A, 4B, 4A, 5B, and 5A. In the second study usable data were obtained for 3026 children of the same grade levels in schools of eight states. Local teachers, principals, and supervisors had to assume responsibility for gathering data.

In both studies two techniques were used: group testing, and individual testing or interview. The group tests consisted of the eighty-one basic multiplication combinations ($\times 8$, $\times 9$, etc.), with the nineteen zero combinations omitted; they were mimeographed in nine rows, nine combinations to the row. These tests were intended to yield the two commonly used measures of mastery: (1) rate of work and (2) accuracy of answers. Interviews were then held individually with as many as possible of these children to obtain a third measure of learning, (3) the terms in which children thought about the combinations. This third measure is an uncommon research practice in arithmetic. Thus five cross-section descriptions evenly spaced during two and a half years of schooling offered insight into the way children learn the combinations. While it is common practice to expect mastery by the end of Grade 4, this study through Grade 5 pictured learning at its latest as well as at early and intermediate stages.

On the group tests, children were told to work as rapidly as possible without making errors. If they encountered combinations too difficult, they were to omit these and go on to the next, better-known combinations. In scoring, one point was allowed for each correct answer, making a possible score of 81. Rates of work were measured by having the children when told to do so (at thirty-second intervals) "mark" the combination on which they were at work, and go right on working. There was no set time limit and nearly all were allowed to finish. The "marks" then revealed how many thirty-second intervals had been required by each pupil.

All children of the local study and as many as possible representative children of the extended study were interviewed individually within two weeks of their group test. Fifteen combinations were used representing the more difficult ones of every table. They were arranged in an order to minimize the use of one combination to help solve the next. Thus 5×7 was followed by 6×9, which contained neither 5 nor 7.

In a preliminary study more than thirty children had been interviewed to secure possible categories for classifying children's thought processes. The eleven categories obtained were:

H —Habituation, meaningful: correct answer confidently given at once with every evidence of understanding.

M —Memory, rote: answer confidently given at once but with no evidence of understanding.

G —Guessing: answer, usually wrong, given promptly but guessing is apparent.

S —Solution: child starts with familiar combination and adds to or subtracts from product to get answer.

C —Counting: child adds or counts the same unit several times.

R —Reversal: child interchanges multiplier and multiplicand to get a more familiar order.

T —Tables: child starts with a lower combination of the same table and recites table to the required point.

V —Visualization: child reproduces groups in clear imagery and works with these ($4 \times 5 = ?$; $4 \times 5¢$ (nickel) $= 20¢$ or 20).

N —No attempt: child makes no attempt to state answer.

I —Indeterminate: tester cannot determine how child obtained answer given.

X —Miscellaneous: child reports process not included above or tester is uncertain of classification: child is quoted directly to be categorized later by the authors.

In each interview of the research proper, there was a preliminary interview until the tester was satisfied regarding *rapport* and the child's understanding of his task. This was especially helpful in resolving the three difficult categories, H, M, and G. Guessing caused less trouble than rote memory (M) and meaningful habituation (H) since guesses usually are wrong. Additional questioning after the fifteen had been completed usually differentiated M from H.

Figure 1 shows the progress made in speed and accuracy by showing the percent of the final (5A) median competency score that appeared as a median

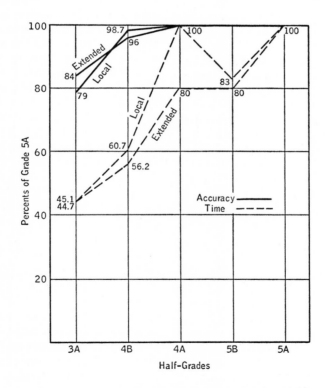

Fig. 1. Increase in Accuracy and Rate by Half-Grades Expressed in Terms of the Grade 5A Medians: Local Study and Extended Study.

at each stage. It will be noted that the greatest gain in speed occurs later than in accuracy (accuracy *should* precede speed). The later loss in speed occurred during the half-year when, with attention focused on fractions, there was little systematic work in multiplication. Accuracy persisted but quickness of response temporarily suffered.

From the accuracy data one gets the impression that learning of the combinations was about completed in Grade 4B and certainly in 4A. From the rate data one gets the impression that, except for temporary retrogression, learning was about complete in Grade 4A. But Figure 2 shows unmistakably that learning was not ended at these earlier points—in fact, not at the end of Grade 5A, where 10 to 12 percent of the answers were still obtained by processes short of the ultimately desired H. An appreciable number of children had yet to attain the final stages of abstract and mature thinking. The interview data supplement and *account* for the rate and accuracy data, showing the immature processes still operating in the earlier stages.

Grade 3A children were slow and inaccurate because they had meaningful habituations for far fewer than half of the combinations and thus had to employ immature and inefficient processes with the others. These processes, notably guessing, were prone to error and were used clumsily and none too successfully. The improvement for Grade 4B (Fig. 1) is due less to better processes than to better control over the same earlier processes. By Grade 4A, with three-fourths of the answers now obtained by H, accuracy and rate were high. By the end of the fifth grade the movement toward a mature process had continued and yet still left room for further improvement.

Children at any given stage use more than one process. Figure 3 illustrates how the same easy and difficult facts may be treated at sequential grade levels. Typically more mature processes are used with the easier facts and less mature with the harder. In Grade 3A the space occupied by H in the bar for the easy combinations is almost twice that for H in the bar for the hard combinations. The discrepancy, though growing smaller, persists through the fifth grade. *Maturity comes slowly.*

When are children ready to learn the multiplication facts? Readiness includes both neural development and the even more important preparatory experiences that make a child intellectually and emotionally ready. The older practice of teaching all the combinations in Grade 3 was not highly successful and so many if not all of them have been deferred to Grade 4. Presumably children's lack of learning at Grade 3 may have been due to intellectual immaturity but it *may* have been due to inadequate teaching methods.

In her doctoral study previously (1941) carried out, Doris V. Carper had found beginning first-graders successful in grouping objects in a row by 2's (95.2 percent success) and by 3's (83.7 percent success). They even had some skill in grouping by 4's (38.5 percent success) and by 5's (1.5 percent success), and to this extent were ready for multiplication even at the start of Grade 1. A review of other studies dealing indirectly with the question also seemed to indicate that by the middle of Grade 3 children are intellectually able to learn the multiplication combinations—in fact that many of the children had discovered some of them in their own ways. Miss Carper now conducted a further study to deal directly with the readiness of middle third-graders to learn the multiplication facts.

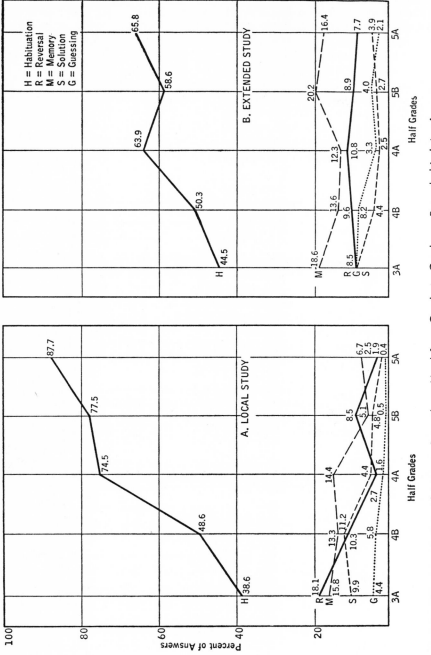

Fig. 2. Changes in Procedures Used from Grade to Grade, as Revealed in Interviews.

Eighty-six children of three schools of three small cities who had not yet been taught multiplication were tested and immediately interviewed. Their written test, administered without time limit, included twenty-four different combinations (1's, 2's, 3's, 4's, 5's, 10's), sixteen of them twice for a total of forty items. The children averaged 78.8 percent correct responses; were all correct for two 1's and two 2's; and av-eraged from 92 percent to 99 percent correct responses for two 5's, two 4's, four 2's, three 2's, and three 5's (all presented in isolated form). Fewer mistakes were made when the smaller number was multiplier (two 3's = 6 was easier than three 2's = 6). More and larger errors were made with large products, though two-thirds of the errors deviated by 30 percent or less.

The personal interviews disclosed the

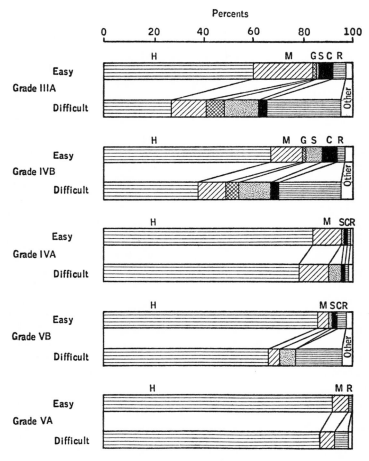

Fig. 3. Percentage Composition of Answers by Processes for "Easy" and "Difficult" Combinations, by Half-Grades, 3A to 5A.

processes used by the children to find answers for fifteen combinations which were presented by means of abstract numbers, dollar numbers, and grouped dots. Of the 1275 responses, 833 could be unquestionably classified as involving an understanding of multiplication and the ability to use the process. Four-fifths of the processes could be so classified when the number of groups (multiplier) was three instead of two. The different forms in which the combinations were presented had little effect upon the process used, from which fact it may be concluded that most of these children were able to approach the study of multiplication on an abstract basis.

All of the above facts indicated that these children were ready for the multiplication facts.

The way in which children learn facts is probably of even greater value than the facts themselves. If a child has discovered a rule or generalization for himself he is likely to apply it as needed in new situations. He is less likely to do so if this is merely a learning impressed upon him by someone else. The learning task to which one responds by rote learning has unique characteristics; to the greatest extent possible all cues, all relationships, all chances to use effectively the results of previous experiences are excluded, and the learner is left no alternative except to memorize. It is small wonder, then, that under these conditions the process of learning is seen to be that of memorizing.

There is little place for rote learning in the school. Now and then of course arbitrary associations must be set up between ideas and symbols (for example, between the names of letters and the forms in which they are written and printed, between number ideas and the figures used to stand for them); but the occurrence of such learning tasks which children meet should regularly "make

sense" to them; relationships with prior experiences should be readily identifiable, and, in a word, their learning should be meaningful.

According to "understanding" theorists, the multiplication combinations call for meaningful learning. Someone has suggested that a parrot can be taught to say, "Five 2's are 10"; but no parrot has been found able to use this "knowledge" in an intelligent way. The combination five 2's are 10 is much more than a series of sounds or of written words. To know and to be able to use the combination, the learner must: (1) understand the meanings of the numbers as groups (2, 5, 10); (2) know how to deal with successive groups of equal size in order to secure totals (the operation of multiplication); (3) recognize in the form of the statement of the particular combination that he is to combine five groups which are equal in size, each made up of 2; (4) be able to discover in many verbal and concrete situations that this relationship (of five 2's to 10) is involved; (5) be able to think the product promptly, confidently, and accurately (without recourse to roundabout procedures, "crutches," or anything of the kind).

The words in which the first four statements are couched—"know," "understand," "discover," "recognize," "meanings"—reveal how much learning in the case of the combinations transcends rote learning and how far memorizing falls short of meeting the needs of the situation. Overconcern with the fifth aspect of learning in the series above has blinded "repetition" theorists to the existence of the first four aspects. Yet, it is the first four aspects that "understanding" theorists emphasize, regarding the fifth as an end which is attained late in the course of learning. In the early stages of learning, immature processes are accepted, even encouraged, provided only that they make the learning task sensible to the learner. All possible kinds of relationships (as in tables) are furnished —or, better, are discovered by the child himself under guidance. Principles and generalizations are developed and utilized, all in the hope of aiding the child to organize the task of learning the combinations. Gradually, the child is led to adopt more and more mature procedures until finally he achieves the ability to respond quickly, accurately, and confidently to the combinations, an ability which "repetition" theorists undertake to establish almost at the outset of learning.

"Understanding" theorists regard the ability to give products glibly as not worth developing; they know the perils of accepting facility in language as evidence of sound learning; they are therefore ready to wait for such facility until it is supported by a firm basis of understanding and they know that meanings take time for their development, time which is filled with an abundance of varied experiences. For them, the teaching of the combinations consists in providing these varied experiences and in guiding children as rapidly (but only as rapidly) as they can to adopt more and more effective and mature ways of thinking of the combinations.

Some direct suggestions are offered for effectively teaching the multiplication combinations. These are four devices followed by the vital generalizations.

1. The combinations should first be written in form (a), two 4's = 8, rather than in form (b), $2 \times 4 = 8$, or in form

(c), $\frac{4}{\times 2}$. Form (a) carried its own meaning, whether read silently or stated orally: two groups of 4 each are to be combined, and this is just another way of saying the familiar "4 and 4 are 8." When forms (b) and (c) are introduced,

they should first be read, "two 4's are 8." The word "times" for "$\times$" is not meaningful and should not be used until longer multiplication examples are taught in which the combinations occur. It is easier then to say, "3 times 426" and "45 times 93" than it is to say "three 426's" and "forty-five 93's"; but the transition to "times" should be made in this way in order to preserve and extend the original meaning.

2. The tables should by all means be taught, but they should not be available at the outset and should never be "given" to children. Objections to the teaching of the tables rest upon the fact that some children recite the tables to secure answers for difficult combinations. The argument for tables is that they help the learner to organize his task and they assist in the development of important meanings and generalizations.

When a new table is started, the combinations should first be presented in random order, the purpose being to enable children to discover the corresponding products (but not then to learn them). These preliminary experiences should illustrate again and again the nature of the operation of multiplication and should reveal the relationship between factors and products. Next, children should assemble the combinations in table order, observing how each product is increased over the preceding by the amount of the multiplicand (but not of the multiplier). Still later, on this meaningful basis children should learn the tables, but mixed practice should follow soon so that they will acquire mastery over the separate facts.

3. Concrete devices should be used as needed, but the need should not be great in the middle of the third school year. Carper's data show that at this time and prior to instruction on multiplication children readily deal with small numbers as abstract groups. For them,

an occasional illustration or verification of a combination should suffice, such as for three 4's = 12.

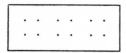

4. There is plenty of room for drill in teaching the combinations: (a) drill on the abstract formulas as the competent adult uses these, and (b) drill on the generalizations and principles which make the combinations valid and relate them to each other. The danger in connection with (a) especially lies in prescribing drill too soon. Children are not ready for drill until they have a sound basis in understanding and can readily think of the combinations in abstract terms. Then drill increases facility of recall and fixes the combinations for retention. Introduced too soon, drill on the combinations (if children do what they are supposed to do) is subversive, for it leads to a substitution of verbal glibness for understanding, and with dire consequences. On this account, drill of type (b) above should be employed liberally before drill of type (a). Children need a good deal of experience in recognizing and applying generalizations and principles in order to develop the understanding upon which to base automatic mastery of the abstract combinations.

GENERALIZATIONS

1. The meaning of multiplication as a process should be taught, and taught prior to the teaching of the first combinations and again and again along with the teaching of other combinations. Multiplication is what we do with numbers when we want to find the total of several numbers which are equal in size. It is easier to find the total of thirty-six 97's by multiplication than by addition

(which would require first the boresome writing of 97 thirty-six times before the labor of adding). Multiplication is a special case of addition, a short cut which we use in such instances as 9 + 9 + 9 + 9 + 9, but not in such instances as 3 + 6 + 9 + 7 + 8.

It follows that the multiplication combinations can profitably be developed through addition. Children readily see, as has already been stated, that two 4's are 8, because this is but a variation of the familiar 4 + 4 = 8. They can as readily see that four 7's are 28 by adding in the example, 7 + 7 + 7 + 7. The repeated discovery of products for new combinations by this device has the effect both of illustrating the meaning of multiplication and of proving the validity of products. "Repetition" theorists oppose this practice partly because they are not concerned about teaching the meaning either of multiplication or of the combinations, but more because they fear that children, once they have been exposed to the device, will always use it. This objection is not supported by our observation.

2. The principle governing reversals should be taught. Children should understand that the combinations three 4's and four 3's have the same product, and why this is so. The principle of reversals is that the order of the factors in a combination has no effect upon the product. But this principle does not mean that three 4's and four 3's are "the same." They are not, for in the first the basic group is 4 and this is taken three times whereas in the second the basic group is 3, which is taken four times. A concrete representation of the two combina-

(a)

(b)

tions brings out the difference. The principle needs to be *taught* because children may not discover it for themselves. After all, the pairs of combinations do not even sound alike, except to the sophisticated ear.

3. Two principles help to teach the nineteen combinations in which 1 is the multiplier or the multiplicand: (a) When a number is multiplied by 1, the product is that number; (b) when 1 is multiplied by a number, the product is that number. The facts covered by these generalizations are almost self-evident to children, so self-evident that there is no need to teach these combinations as such until the digit appears as part of a larger multiplier (e.g., 314) or multiplicand (e.g., 17). But though the facts are self-evident, there is value in bringing them together under covering statements.

4. Similarly, the nineteen combinations with 0 as multiplier or multiplicand may be taught through establishing two principles: (a) When a number is multiplied by 0, the product is 0; (b) when 0 is multiplied by a number, the product is 0. These generalizations are readily intelligible if developed first in the form, two 0's = 0, three 0's = 0, etc.; and no 2's = 0, no 3's = 0, and so on. There is little point in teaching the facts with 0 as the multiplicand until two- and three-place multiplicands with 0 are used in examples, and in teaching the facts with 0 as multiplier until 0 occurs as part of a two- or three-place multiplier.

5. It helps if children see that all products end in even numbers when the multiplier is 2, 4, 6, or 8.

6. It also helps if children realize that any product in which 5 is a factor must end in 5 or 0. (This relationship is usu-a very easy one for children, a fact which leads some students of arithmetic to suggest that the tables for 5 and for 5's be taught immediately after the tables for 2 and for 2's.)

7. The combinations with 9 as multiplicand have several interesting aspects: the digits in products always total 9; the first digit in products increases by 1, and the second figure decreases by 1 as the combinations are arranged in table form.

8. Except for the doubles, the multiplication combinations should be learned in pairs, e.g., five 8's = 40, eight 5's = 40. So learned, the total number of combinations is, in effect, reduced from 100 to 55. (The principle of reversals is of course the basis for understanding the pairing of facts.) Two cautions should be noted: (a) The practice of relating the paired facts should probably be postponed until after the first two or three tables. Premature introduction of the principle could overcomplicate the learning task, thus obscuring other essential relationships which are more readily grasped and which are sufficient in number and difficulty to engage the learner's full attention. (b) Care should be exercised to separate the paired facts later on for independent mastery.

9. The pace of instruction must be adapted to the rate at which learning proceeds most effectively and most healthily. Two and more decades ago it was not uncommon to teach all the multiplication combinations in a period of a few months in Grade 3, and in some of the experimental studies reviewed the learning period was cut to six and even to four weeks.

Within the last quarter of a century the practice has increasingly been to teach some limited number of combinations in Grade 3 and to postpone the rest to Grade 4. This change has resulted in part from the uncritical trend to move topics generally to higher grades, in part from the intention to encourage more thorough learning of other arithmetical skills—or to extend them further—before starting multiplication, and in part from recognition of the fact that sound learning takes time. The last reason holds especially in the case of the multiplication combinations when the teaching task is made to include, besides the verbal statements themselves, the development of generalizations, principles, and understandings of relationships. When these are taught, the period of learning must be lengthened. Some courses of study wisely introduce the concept of multiplication and some of the easiest facts in the latter part of Grade 2 and do not expect mastery of all the combinations until two years later. During this long period children are given experiences with the combinations in wide varieties of ways, so as to increase meaning as well as to secure mastery. In other words, the program in such schools leaves nothing at all to time alone, for *time is important to learning only to the degree to which it affords opportunity for experience.*

10. Once the process of division has been taught and a beginning has been made on the division combinations, the related multiplication and division facts may well be presented together. The accompanying drawing shows four different facts. Which fact one sees depends

upon the way in which one treats the groups, (a) by rows or by columns, and (b) by multiplication or by division. The four facts are: (a) four 5's = 20; (b) five 4's = 20; (c) 20 = four 5's; and (d) 20 = five 4's. The four facts together constitute "the whole story about 4, 5, and 20 in multiplication and division." Frequent experience in "telling the whole story" in multiplication and division facts has the effect of emphasizing important relationships and of increasing ease of learning. Mixed drill, instituted later on, should then establish mastery of the separate combinations.

GRADE PLACEMENT IN ARITHMETIC [1]

Carleton Washburne

[The following study reports in part upon a massive investigation involving 225 cities and towns in sixteen states and continuing for well over a decade. Criticisms of the research and replies to the criticisms ebbed and flowed during much of the period. The overall objective of

[1] Adapted and abridged from Carleton Washburne, "The Work of the Committee of Seven on Grade-Placement in Arithmetic," *Child Development and the Curriculum*, Thirty-eighth Yearbook, Part I, National Society for the Study of Education, Public School Publishing Co., Bloomington, Ill., 1939, pp. 299–324, and from Carleton Washburne, "Mental Age and the Arithmetic Curriculum—A Summary of the Committee of Seven Grade-Placement Investigations to Date," *Journal of Educational Research* (1931), 23:210–231.

the study was of the utmost importance: to discover when most children can best be taught the various parts of arithmetic. An important contemporary criticism of this study is that it was largely based upon the drill-type teaching of that time and does not necessarily reveal mental ages required for learning when taught meaningfully. An interesting corroboration of some of the findings of this study appears in the one by Brueckner and Melbye below.]

The approximate grade placement of a unit of arithmetic has been determined either by a survey of practice or by preliminary experiments in a few schools. Using this approximate placement as a "central grade" the coöperation has been secured of schools willing to teach the topic at the central grade, or one grade lower, or one or two grades higher. The spread of mental ages within each group of the coöperating three or four grades results in a distribution of mental ages in the final scores covering usually at least five or six years.

The children in the coöperating schools are given intelligence tests to determine their mental ages, are given pretests to determine their existing knowledge of the topic to be taught, and are given foundations tests to discover whether or not they have the prerequisite knowledge and skill, and in some cases the prerequisite experience and concepts, for learning the new topic. A brief teaching time is allowed after the giving of the first form of the foundations test for the teacher to attempt to bring the children to a reasonable mastery of such foundations as seem to be lacking. Then a second form of the foundations test is given, and retention-test results are later compared with the results of this second form of foundations test and those of the intelligence test.

The pretests, several intermediate "teaching tests," the "final test," given at the close of the teaching period, and the "retention test," given six weeks after the final test, are all practically equivalent forms of one test, devised to cover all the major elements and difficulties of the topic under investigation. While exact equivalence among these forms is not determined statistically (and has no bearing on the results), they correspond problem by problem as to the elements of difficulty to be tested. The pretest is used to determine (1) the degree of knowledge children have of the topic under consideration before teaching begins, and (2) which children, presumably on account of grade repetition or transfer from another school, have had so much previous instruction in the topic that their scores on the retention test should be disregarded. The teaching tests are used during the teaching period as a means of helping the teacher to determine the progress of her children. The final test is used at the close of the teaching period to determine the immediate learning of the children. And then, six weeks later, with no intervening review, the retention test is given. The Committee's recommendations are all in terms of the retention-test scores.

The results of the retention test are plotted against the results secured on the foundations test and against the scores on the intelligence test. In most experiments it is found that scores on the foundations test that fall below a certain point result in failure in learning the new topic, regardless of mental age. Children who make such low scores on foundations are therefore omitted from the final tabulation. Likewise children are eliminated whose knowledge of the topic to be taught is shown by the pretest to be so great as to indicate previous teaching of the topic. Recommendations

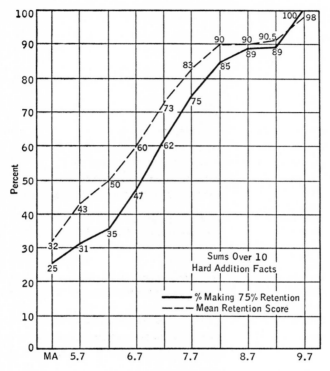

Fig. 1. This Illustrates the Similarity of Form Between Graphs Prepared on the Committee's Usual, Though Arbitrary, Standard of the Percentage of Children Making Scores of 75 Percent or Higher at Various Levels of Maturity (Shown by Solid Line) and the Graph of Mean (Average) Retention Scores, not Subject to Any Arbitrary Recommendation. This graph pertains to scores made on a test of thirty-two addition facts with sums over 10.

are therefore based upon the retention of children who have not had considerable previous knowledge of the topic but who have achieved a fairly adequate mastery of prerequisite topics and, in some cases, of prerequisite concepts.

Time and method of teaching are controlled. Using preliminary experiments in their own schools as a basis, the members of the Committee of Seven specify the number of minutes per day and the number of weeks that a topic is to be taught and prepare a general teaching outline indicating methods to be used. While unquestionably children in the experiments come from different kinds of home backgrounds and have different types of experience, while they have had their earlier arithmetical instruction in a variety of textbooks and under a variety of teaching methods and school systems, and while the teachers who attempt to follow the outlines of the Committee of Seven undoubtedly vary their methods in accordance with their own experience and ability, the number of

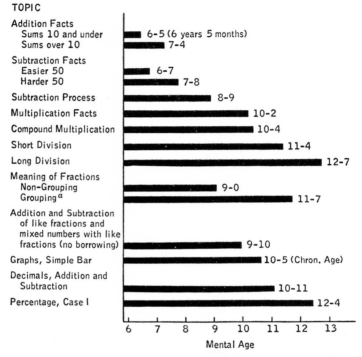

TOPIC

Addition Facts	
Sums 10 and under	6-5 (6 years 5 months)
Sums over 10	7-4
Subtraction Facts	
Easier 50	6-7
Harder 50	7-8
Subtraction Process	8-9
Multiplication Facts	10-2
Compound Multiplication	10-4
Short Division	11-4
Long Division	12-7
Meaning of Fractions	
Non-Grouping	9-0
Grouping[a]	11-7
Addition and Subtraction of like fractions and mixed numbers with like fractions (no borrowing)	9-10
Graphs, Simple Bar	10-5 (Chron. Age)
Decimals, Addition and Subtraction	10-11
Percentage, Case I	12-4

Mental Age: 6 7 8 9 10 11 12 13

[a] This involves showing 3/4 of 12 objects, 1/5 of 15 objects, etc., *by inspection* before teaching the manipulation of fractions.

Fig. 2. Minimum Mental-Age Level at Which Three-Fourths of the Children Achieved Scores of 80 Percent or More Correct.

children and teachers is such as to make these differences tend to cancel each other.

The Committee has handled the data in two ways, first by plotting the *average scores* made by children on the retention tests against their mental ages, and second by plotting the *percent of children making a score of 80 percent* (or occasionally 75 percent) on the retention test against their mental ages (see Fig. 1). Both curves usually tend to assume the S form or appear to be fragments of an S curve—relatively flat at the lower mental ages, rising with steadily increasing steepness as the mental age increases, then reaching a point of flexion and tending to flatten out again. The method of plotting average scores against mental age is free from the criticism of arbitrariness of standard, but the method of plotting percentage of children who reach an acceptable score at each mental age has seemed to the Committee to be of more practical value to classroom teachers. Actually, the point of flexion in both curves tends to occur at about the same mental age for a given topic. Some representative findings of these studies appear in the accompanying figures.

START IN GRADE SIX? [1]

L. P. Benezet

[A great controversy in arithmetic has centered on the question "When should systematic instruction in arithmetic begin?" Superintendent Benezet heaped fuel on the flames with his famous series of articles describing a city-wide tryout of an idea. He forcefully advocated "postponement of arithmetic" to Grade 7 or at least until Grade 6, though the reader will discover that he advocated postponement only of formal arithmetic. Actually he filled the early years with "meaningful" and "significant" arithmetic experiences. This study, often misquoted, has been used to support postponement of all organized arithmetic teaching.]

It seems to me that we waste much time in the elementary school wrestling with stuff that ought to be omitted or postponed until children are in need of studying it. I feel that it is nonsense to take eight years to get children through the ordinary arithmetic assignment of the elementary schools. The whole subject could be postponed until the seventh year of school, and it could be mastered in two years' study by any normal child.

For some years I had been noticing that the early introduction of arithmetic seemed almost to chloroform children's reasoning faculties. I would ask upper-grade children, "If I can walk a hundred yards in a minute how many miles can I walk in an hour at that same speed?" In nineteen cases out of twenty the answer would be "six thousand" and if I beamed approval the class settled back, well satisfied. But if I said, "I see. That means I could walk from here to San Francisco and back in an hour," they would laugh and look foolish.

In the fall of 1929, as Superintendent of Schools in Manchester, New Hampshire, I made up my mind to try abandoning all formal instruction in arithmethic below the seventh grade and to concentrate on teaching children to read,

[1] Abridged and adapted from L. P. Benezet, "Story of an Experiment," *Journal of the National Education Association* (1935), 24:241–244, and 301–303, and (1936), 25:7–8.

to reason, and to recite—my new three R's. I picked out five rooms, Grades 3 to 5 with interested young teachers in schools where not one parent in ten spoke English as his mother tongue. As anticipated, I had no parental protests.

I told these teachers that I would expect them to give the children much practice in estimating heights, lengths, areas, distances, and the like. By the end of the year there was such great growth in the children's ability to think clearly with difficult problems and to express themselves fluently that in the fall of 1930 we started six or seven other rooms along the same line. Again, results led to expansion of the experiment and by the fall of 1932 about half of the third-, fourth-, and fifth-grade rooms in the city were working under the new curriculum. During the year, 98 experimentally and 102 traditionally taught sixth-graders were selected fairly and given a series of arithmetic tests, dealing not with reasoning but only with manipulation of the four fundamental processes. One group had started formal arithmetic in the 3A, the other in the sixth grade. In the early tests the traditionally taught children excelled; by mid-April all classes were practically on a par; and when the last test was given in June it was one of the experimental groups which led the city. These children, by avoiding early drill on combinations, tables, and that sort of thing, had been able in one year to attain the level of accomplishment reached by traditionally taught children in three and one-half years of drill.

In the fall of 1933 I felt that I now had convincing evidence for the big plunge. Accordingly a committee of our principals drew up a new course of study. I would have liked to go the whole route and drop out all arithmetic until the seventh grade, but they were more cautious, and besides, I would now have to deal with the deeply rooted prejudices of the educated portion of our citizens. Through the first five grades the course calls for no formal teaching of arithmetic, and for twenty minutes increasing to thirty minutes per day of formal arithmetic during Grades 6, 7, and 8. Each of the eight grades continues and adds to the learnings of the preceding year. Always the stress is upon thoughtful analysis and reasoning.

During the first grade, in connection with reading and as the need arises, children are taught to read numbers to 100, to keep count of the date upon the calendar, and to recognize contrasting concepts like more, less; many, few; smaller, larger; etc. In the second grade, children learn to tell time, to use page numbers, to count in games, and in normal incidental fashion learn the meaning of half, double, twice, three times, penny, nickel, dollar, pint, quart, etc. In the third grade, as children come across numbers in their reading, the teacher explains the significance of their value. Before the year is over they will be taught all comparative relations of cents, nickels, dimes, quarters, halves, dollars (e.g., a dollar is 10 dimes, 100 cents, etc.). Time is told as 3:50; 2:35, etc., and they learn the number of minutes in an hour, hours in a day, days in a week or month, and months in a year. With bigger books they count farther and they play number games with license plates, house numbers, telephone numbers, etc. They also learn such relations as "half," "double," and "three times."

In the fourth grade foot rules and yardsticks help teach the meaning of inch, foot, and yard and are used to check estimates of lengths and heights. Children are taught to read thermometers and know the significance of 32, 98.6, and 212 degrees. "Square inch," "square foot," and "square yard" are introduced and they learn to make change (denomination of 5's only) with toy or real money. By walking and with automobiles they learn the meaning of mile, half-mile, and quarter-mile. Time in seconds, minutes, and days and weight in pounds and ounces are also taught concretely.

In the lower fifth grade children are asked to count *mentally* (no board, or paper, or tables), by 5's, 10's, 2's, 4's, and 3's and from this practice later learn these multiplication tables in that order. Changing money now includes the use of pennies, and work with pictured fractions leads to the generalization that the larger the denominator the smaller the fraction. Toward the end of the semester they are given the book *Practical Problems in Mental Arithmetic*, Grade 4. Those with natural number sense answer correctly; the teacher does not explain to those who do not grasp it quickly and naturally, knowing that in a year or two they will have reasoning power. The purpose is to stimulate quick thinking and to lessen the use of fingers to do headwork. The one thing avoided is that children shall believe that a fixed method or formula can be substituted for thinking.

In the upper fifth grade children count *mentally* by 6's, 7's, 8's, and 9's, leading naturally to these multiplication tables. The children are helped to build such generalizations as two 3's being the same as three 2's or that in multiples of 9 the second digit reduces by 1—18, 27, 36, etc. They now try to know the combinations in any order and are given a little idea of the meaning of ¼, ½, ⅕, ⅒. The mental problems started in the previous half-year are continued through this period, and as new terms (peck, gallon, etc.) are encountered they are explained.

Formal work in arithmetic begins in the lower sixth grade with the four fundamental processes. The Strayer-Upton arithmetic series is used as a text starting at this point with Book III and completing Book VI by the end of the eighth grade. Care is taken to avoid mechanical drill and to stress understanding of the reasons for the processes. Long numbers are avoided and accuracy rather than speed is the goal. Simple fractions and mixed numbers are also taught. Before starting any problem children are asked to estimate the answer and thus check their results.

In the upper sixth grade mutiplication tables and tables of denominate numbers are reviewed and problems requiring estimating and reasoning are continued.

Throughout the seventh grade previous learnings are reviewed, reasoning problems are continued, and in addition to the text's table of linear measure children learn the number of yards in a mile, half-mile, and quarter-mile. The stress always is upon reasoning ability rather than errorless manipulation.

The same principles continue through the work of the eighth grade. Always there is stress upon good estimates followed by measurement or computation. Children are shown reasons for the various processes (e.g., inverting the divisor and multiplying in the division of fractions). Concrete models are used in geometric problems: filling a cylinder with water from three times the contents of a cone of equal base and altitude, etc. They learn to read accurately and to attack intelligently, doing as much as possible mentally. Problems are chosen to illustrate principles and give practice in reasoning rather than in manipulation of large figures or complicated fractions.

By now the community was in a furor, with some board members demanding a return to conventional arithmetic. A committee was appointed to study the problem, and, taking a stenographer, we visited four schools in our city and three in a nearby city. The following results in a traditional and an experimental room illustrate the kinds of experiences that convinced the committee and the board. In each case an upper fifth grade was used.

In each room I drew a diagram on the board and said, "Here is a pole stuck in the mud at the bottom of a pond. There is some water above the mud and part of the pole sticks up into the air. One-half of the pole is in the mud; ⅔ of the rest is in the water; and one foot is sticking out into the air. How long is the pole?"

In the conventional room various children replied: "You multiply ½ by ⅔ and add one foot to that." "Add one foot and ⅔ and ½." "Add the ⅔ and ½ first and then add one foot." "Add all of them and see how long the pole is." "One foot equals ½. Two-thirds divided into 6 equals 3 times 2 equals 6. Six and 4 equals 10. Ten and 3 equals 13 feet." Their only thought was to manipulate numbers hoping somehow to get the right answer. I asked, "Is there anybody who knows the way to get the length?" Next child: "One foot equals ⅔. Two-thirds and ½ multiplied by 6." I asked, "Why do you multiply by 6?" Answer: "Divide."

I then gave a hint: "How much of the pole is above the mud?" Replies: "One foot and ⅔." "One foot and ⅛."

I then said, "I'll change my question. How much of the pole is in the mud?"

Answers: "Two-thirds." "One-half." "One-half." "Then how much of the pole is above the mud?" said I, thinking the answer plain. "Two-thirds." "One foot and ⅔."

"One-half of the pole is in the mud," said I. "Now how long is the pole?" and the answers given were "Two feet." "One and one-half feet." "One-half foot." "One foot." "One foot." "One foot," and I gave up.

In the experimental room: "You would have to find out how many feet there are in the mud." "And what else?" said I. Another child, "How many feet in the water and add them together."

"How would you do that?" said I to another. She, "There are 3 feet in a yard. One yard is in the mud. One yard equals 36 inches. If ⅔ of the rest is in the water and one foot in the air (one foot equals 12 inches) the part in the water is twice the part in the air so it must be 2 feet or 24 inches. If there are 3 feet above the mud and 3 feet in the mud it means that the pole is 6 feet or 72 inches long. That's 2 yards." The problem was too easy in feet; she had to use inches or yards to make it hard enough to justify my asking it.

The next child, "One-half of the pole is in the mud and ½ must be above the mud. If ⅔ is in the water, then ⅔ and one foot equals 3 feet, plus the 3 feet in the mud equals 6 feet."

The problem seemed very simple to these children, who had been taught to use their heads instead of their pencils.

START IN THE FIRST YEAR? [1]

William A. Brownell and others

[In this monograph Dr. Brownell has reached the conclusion that systematic instruction should start in the first grade. This report is included here less because it reports his own experiments with children than because of his careful analysis of the issue and his focusing of relevant research in reaching his conclusions.]

At least four approaches to arithmetic teaching (plus variations) have been advocated in Grades 1 and 2. (1) The *incidental approach* reacting against traditional formalism abolishes all systematic instruction in number. (2) The *social approach* disregards numbers as a system but plans plentiful contacts with number usage as a normal part of operating school banks, grocery stores, and the like. (3) In the *traditional program* number is systematically and abstractly presented almost from the start and with little attention to social application or psychological readiness. (4) Advocates of the fourth program (no label) want arithmetic to be socially functional like (1) and (2), and highly efficient like (3), but in addition want children to understand what they learn, to grasp the mathematics of arithmetic. Informal and planned social experiences are supplemented with learning activities deliberately designed (a) to make number and number operations sensible and (b) to encourage children as rapidly as they safely may to adopt procedures yielding

arithmetical proficiency. Before deciding among these approaches answers must be found to three crucial questions:

1. Are six- and seven-year-olds intellectually capable of profiting from systematic instruction in arithmetic? Do they have the necessary mental powers? Approach (1) says "No"; the other approaches, "Yes."

2. If the primary-grade pupil *can* learn much about arithmetic, *should he be asked to do so at this time?* Does it produce gains justifying its being given? Again approach (1) says "No" while the others reply "Yes."

3. If he *can* and *should* learn arithmetic from the start, what should be the *content and form of this teaching?* Approach (1) dismisses content and method by relying on incidental experiences while each of the others offers quite diverse solutions.

Adequate answers through research can be made to question 1, and data on the outcomes of various programs of instruction should help answer question

[1] Abridged and adapted from William A. Brownell et al., *Arithmetic in Grades I and II: A Critical Summary of New and Previously Reported Research*, Duke University Research Studies in Education, No. 6, Duke University Press, Durham, N.C., 1941.

3. In turn these should help answer the philosophical question 2. It is the purpose of this monograph to help answer these three crucial questions.

A part of answering question 1 on children's ability was to discover what arithmetic is in possession of school beginners. Entering first-grade children from thirty-two classes in twenty-four schools of four states were individually tested on: rote counting; enumeration (how many pennies do you see?); identification (put a mark on the man with four balloons); reproduction (put tails on nine of the rabbits); crude quantitative comparison (mark the largest cat); which is less, 5 or 7?; exact quantitative comparison or matching (draw as many

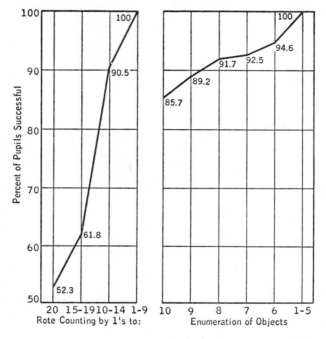

Fig. 1. Percent of Entering First-Grade Children Succeeding in Rote Counting and in Enumeration.

candles on this tree as there are on that one); addition and subtraction facts directly used in problems (Mary had 3 dolls and put 2 of them to bed. How many stayed up?) and in abstract form $(2 + 3, 4 — 3)$. The findings are reported separately for urban and rural children as well as for the total group. Wherever possible, moreover, the results are compared with those of Buckingham and MacLatchy, Woody, and others (see above).

This monograph also reports the findings of other studies in beginners' knowledge of fractions, ordinals, reading and writing numbers, recognition of geometric forms, time, U.S. money, and measures. It further reports findings of sex differences, differences between city and rural children, differences in levels of intelligence, and the effect of kindergarten instruction.

In the majority of the comparisons city children surpassed rural children, but on several the rural were more successful. Many of the findings of this study appear in Figures 1 and 2. Here are found the percentages of school beginners in Brownell's study who were able to perform various kinds of arithmetic tasks. In Figure 1 it was apparent that most were able to count by rote beyond 10 and to enumerate as many as 10 objects placed before them. Figure 2 reveals that more children knew the concept "more" than knew the concept

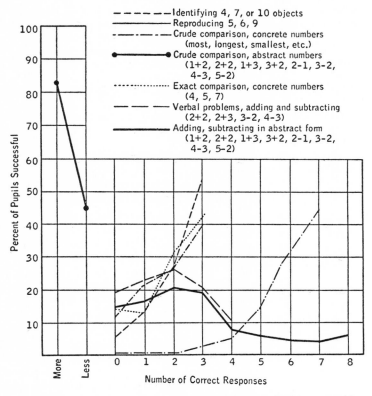

Fig. 2. Ability of Beginning First-Grade Children to Use Number in Various Contexts.

"less." All of the other tasks, even including simple abstract additions and subtractions, could be performed by many of these beginners.

Following is a summary of the findings of the many studies reviewed (in addition to Brownell's) dealing with arithmetic possessed by school beginners:

1. The following skills and concepts seem to be quite well developed by the time most children start school:

Rote counting by 1's: through 20 at least.

Enumeration: through 20 at least.

Identification: through 10 at least (the limit studied in research), and probably through 20.

Crude comparisons: (a) with objects: the concepts "longest," "middle," "most," "shortest," "smallest," "tallest," "widest"; (b) with abstract numbers: "more," with the numbers through 10.

Exact comparison or matching: at least through 5 or 7 (the limit of research).

Number combinations: (a) with objects: to sums of 10; (b) in verbal problems with easily imagined objects and situations: adding 1 and 2, and probably most facts with sums to 6 or 7.

Fractions: unit fractions through halves and fourths as applied to single objects, and perhaps halves as used with small groups in even division.

Ordinals: through sixth.

Geometric figures: "circle" and "square."

Telling time: at the hour.

U.S. coins: recognition of all coins to the half-dollar, and some understanding of relative values of pennies and other smaller coins.

2. The following skills and concepts are not so fully known to school entrants but are fairly well started among a reasonably large percentage of children of this age:

Rote counting: by 1's to 100; by 10's to 100; by 2's to 20 or 30.

Crude comparison: (a) with objects: "as long as," "fewest" (or "the smallest number"); (b) with abstract numbers: "less," with the abstract numbers to 10.

Number combinations: (a) in verbal problems: probably all the facts with sums to 9 or 10; (b) with abstract numbers: few research data available, but apparently less than 50 percent able to deal successfully even with the easiest facts (e.g., those involving the addition or subtraction of 1).

Reading numbers: only a few know the numerals to 10.

3. The following skills and concepts are possessed by less than a third of school entrants, and then in limited degrees of richness or proficiency:

Rote counting: by 3's to 30.

Crude comparison of objects: "same" or "equal."

Fractions: (a) proper fractions other than unit fractions, applied to single objects and small groups; (b) improper fractions; (c) relative size of fractions.

Reading and writing numbers: virtually no ability to read beyond 10; virtually none to write, even to 10.

Geometric figures: "triangle."

Telling time: at the half- and quarter-hour.

U.S. money: relative value of coins other than pennies.

Liquid and linear measures: relative size of units.

These findings indicate that children who already have learned so much have the capacity to learn more during Grades 1 and 2, and to that extent give a positive answer to question 1 (capacity to learn).

Additional support resulted from a second experiment, in which children in Grades 1 and 2 were taught in accordance with workbooks and readers prepared by Guy T. Buswell, Lenore John, and the author. In general the teaching plan was in accordance with approach (4) above. Group tests were administered to all experimental pupils in each half-grade (223 Grade 1 and 280 Grade 2), and individual tests were given to a representative sample. They showed that these pupils *did make substantial progress of a measurable kind.* An extensive analysis of relevant research conducted by others gives still greater support to this conclusion. Primary-grade children *can* learn arithmetic *if* "learn" does *not* mean "attain mastery in" but "make substantial progress toward the outcomes set." Mastery is best viewed as the end product of long periods of experience and practice. The answer to question 1 seems to be "Yes."

The second crucial question is not to

be answered so definitely. "*Should* primary pupils be asked to learn arithmetic?" In so far as school practice is determinable from the ability of children measurably to profit from teaching, the answer here is "Yes." But ability to learn is admittedly only one of the factors which affect policy. Other factors, sociological, philosophical, and psychological, are also involved. Indeed, according to some educational theories ability to learn is of slight importance as compared with "natural interests and needs." According to other theories, perhaps more "traditional," ability to learn is more important, especially when the thing to be learned is of demonstrable social significance. The answer to this second question is, then, largely a matter of theory and opinion. To the writer the facts argue for systematic arithmetic starting in Grade 1.

The third crucial question is, "Granted that primary pupils *can* and *should* learn arithmetic, how should the program be organized?" There is no final answer to this question. Research has not yet tested enough programs and collected enough facts. The writer's conception of an appropriate program has been outlined, but it would be the height of folly to suppose that this particular program as it stands is the final answer to the need. Instead, as teachers and research workers continue to study the way children learn and to locate and remove the sources of their difficulty, we may confidently expect steadily improved programs.

Programs were for long evaluated solely by a criterion of efficiency: speed and accuracy in computation and in conventional problem solving. This criterion is no guarantee of quantitative efficiency in affairs of life. It is incomplete, moreover, in not recognizing the importance of *meaning* and *significance*. An object or idea or skill is *meaningful*

to the degree that it is understood; is *significant* to the degree that the values are known and it is used. At every point children should see both sense (meaning) and value and usefulness (significance) in the number they encounter—or arithmetic should be deferred.

The *incidental approach* and the *social approach* present number significantly and are thus admirable; but they must perforce neglect meaning. Informal "social" encounters with number reveal value and usefulness, but, no matter how frequent, they cannot provide for the study of number elements in their intrinsic relationships—cannot develop meanings of a high order. *Drill* alone, moreover, must fail even in its one goal of efficiency. Without understanding (meaning) true efficiency is impossible, and what passes for efficiency proves to be a bag of mechanical tricks which are not susceptible to effective use and which are soon mislaid.

The authors' approach strives to make number meaningful without sacrificing significance. It uses all incidental occurrences of number and plans other experiences with number in "social" settings —guaranteeing significance. But in addition meaning is provided through studying number as number, grasping the mathematical principles which govern relationships, understanding the number system, formulating generalizations to aid organization for learning, and so on. Efficiency is not an immediate goal, though steps are taken to assure it ultimately. The procedure is not drill but the development of understanding.

In this type of systematic instruction the objections to traditional drill—formal, unpleasant, stifling—do not apply. Children are happily and intelligently studying arithmetic with full opportunity for creativeness. Moreover, children deprived of all arithmetic in their early years are robbed of the means to meet their own quantitative environment without bewilderment, and of the means to solve their number problems with greater effectiveness and peace of mind. They may later be swamped with the demands of the middle grades when they are expected to learn all that has been postponed. Readiness? Children do not merely grow into readiness by accumulating birthdays. They are ready for any phase of arithmetic when they have had the experiences which fit them to learn what is in that phase and not before. Quantitative development is slow and complex. Children approach mature forms of quantitative thinking by reorganizing at steadily higher levels their ways of dealing with number situations. They need an abundance of diversified experiences with number begun early and continued long. The problem of the arithmetic teacher is not to wait for readiness but to create it. If children are to live fully as they go along, they must continually be building meanings and must be offered the means to meet the quantitative aspects of life.

Chapter XIV

OTHER AREAS OF METHODOLOGY

Introduction

In this chapter appear studies dealing with a few types of problems in how to teach. The first, a classic study by Buswell and John, shows the degree to which adequate vocabulary and concepts may be lacking. This problem continues to be as pertinent today as when the study was made. Next is a report compiled from sixteen articles by Grossnickle dealing with his experiments in division. Should children be taught short division? How should they be taught to estimate quotient figures? What types of division errors are important? How can we best teach division of decimals? Some rather conclusive answers have been found.

Spencer's study of arithmetic errors was included as one of the first efforts to identify typical or characteristic errors so that teachers may anticipate and prevent trouble spots. Buckingham's neat little study seemed to help answer one question in teaching column addition.

The final studies offer somewhat contradictory answers to the question "Can children learn their necessary arithmetic within an activity program of unitary teaching or must there also be a planned arithmetic curriculum?" This contradiction is less true than might at first appear, since the first study reports units selected especially for their arithmetic potentialities while in the second less specific units were generally used.

CHILDREN'S KNOWLEDGE OF ARITHMETIC VOCABULARY [1]

G. T. Buswell and Lenore John

[A temptation in elementary-school teaching is to develop vocabulary deliberately only during the reading or spelling program. We are likely to take arithmetic vocabulary for granted and to assume inadequacies in arithmetic only when problems are missed. This early study called attention to the danger of such an assumption and showed the need for modifications both in teaching methodology and in the writing of arithmetic textbooks.]

The purpose of the investigation reported in this monograph was to study the nature and the development of concepts of technical and semitechnical terms in the arithmetic of the first six grades.

VOCABULARY DIFFICULTIES IN GRADES 4–6

A study was made of the general understanding of 100 arithmetical terms by a group of 1500 children selected from Grades 4–6 in twelve school systems. On the basis of the results of a group test (Test I) variations in familiarity with the words from grade to grade and from school to school were studied. Data from three additional types of tests (Tests II, III, IV) were secured for a selected list of twenty-five terms. Comparison of responses to all four tests shows the different ways in which words may be known.

Typical item in Test I, 100 terms: A *rectangle* is:
1. A figure that is round like a ball.
2. The answer to a division problem.
3. A four-sided figure with square corners.
4. A three-sided figure.

Typical item in Test II, twenty-five terms: Draw a ring around the figure that is a *rectangle*.

Typical item in Test III, twenty-five terms: A four-sided figure with square corners is called a ....

rectangle   discount   circle   triangle

Typical item in Test IV, twenty-five terms: Write the meaning of *rectangle* in arithmetic: ....

....

[1] Adapted and abridged from G. T. Buswell and Lenore John, *The Vocabulary of Arithmetic*, Supplementary Educational Monographs, No. 38, University of Chicago Press, Chicago, 1931.

DEVELOPMENT OF CONCEPTS OF WORDS IN GRADES 1–6

The growth of vocabulary in Grades 1–6 was studied more intensively by means of individual tests of 240 children, forty from each of the first six grades. Individual responses were secured from these children to thirty-three arithmetical words and phrases. These responses were studied in relation to school grade and mental level. They show both the gradual development of correct concepts and the nature of erroneous and partly correct concepts, with which the teacher must deal.

EXPLANATION OF NEW TECHNICAL TERMS IN TEXTBOOKS

The degree to which arithmetic textbooks explain technical terms in contrast with simply using them was studied by examining the initial explanations of a selected list of words in ten textbooks. The possibility of having arithmetical words taught in connection with subjects other than arithmetic was studied by comparing the 100 arithmetical terms used in the group test with the principal published vocabularies in reading and spelling.

Test I Percentage of Responses Correct (500 children each grade)

	Grade 4	Grade 5	Grade 6	Total
Mean	58.07	69.23	77.09	68.13
Standard Deviation	13.70	11.15	9.30	13.90

The results may be summarized as follows:

1. The pupils in a given grade differ widely in the size of their arithmetical vocabularies. The number of terms known increases from grade to grade, but the distributions of scores in the three grades show a large amount of overlapping.

2. The difficulty of the terms studied as indicated by the percentages of pupils responding correctly shows great variation.

3. The difficulty of the classes of terms into which the list is divided indicates that, in general, the technical terms are the most difficult and that the terms relating to time, space, or quantity are the least difficult, the terms relating to spatial figures, the terms of measurement, and the commercial terms lying between the extremes. The facts that there are more terms included in some classes than in others and that the terms in a given class are not of uniform difficulty reduce the significance of the differences between the results for the five classes.

4. The growth in the understanding of terms as indicated by the increase in the percentage of correct responses from Grade 4 to Grade 6 shows great variation for different terms, the smallest difference in percentages being 1.4 and the largest 60.2.

5. Comparison of the results for the twelve school systems represented by the pupils tested shows that for a given term the percentages of correct responses and the percentages of omissions vary widely, indicating that the course of study and the teaching procedure are probably important factors in determining the terms known by the pupils in each school system.

6. Analysis of the incorrect responses indicates that incorrect meanings are frequently associated with terms. In some cases the number of pupils who had misconceptions regarding the term was greater than the number of pupils who understood it, and the amount of misunderstanding did not decrease materially from Grade 4 to Grade 6. Such a situation presents a definite problem for teachers of arithmetic.

7. The lack of agreement between the results of Tests I, II, III, and IV suggests that ability to respond to a word correctly in one situation does not necessarily indicate that understanding is complete. Further experience with the word may be needed for complete understanding.

8. The amount of explanation of terms in textbooks is often meager and formal. Textbooks frequently fail to support the explanation of new terms with sufficient repetition to fix correct concepts of these terms in the pupils' minds.

9. A considerable number of arithmetical terms are not likely to be encountered in reading and spelling, the subjects in which new words are generally presented. If technical terms are to be taught, the obligation rests mainly on the subject of arithmetic.

SOME ISSUES IN DIVISION [1]

Foster E. Grossnickle

[The following composite report illustrates the way an individual can take an important area of learning and by carrying on experiment after experiment achieve a considerable increase in assurance. In the particular studies reported here, the author has sought evidence on four questions dealing with the teaching of division.

Should children be taught "short division"? It is fairly common practice to teach the short form of division with a one-digit divisor. All subtraction and carrying are performed in one's head rather than written beneath the dividend, with presumed increase in efficiency. The author achieved rather convincing evidence answering this question.

How should children be taught to estimate the quotient figure in long division? When the divisor contains two or more digits the selection of a trial quotient figure may be a difficult task in estimation. Any real help that children can be given on this point will reduce materially the difficulty in learning one of arithmetic's most difficult areas (note the apparent minimum mental age Washburne's study revealed for success in learning long division).

Of the ten or more ways of estimating the quotient figure in long division there are two that are most widely advocated. These are known as the "apparent method" and the "increase-by-one method." In the

[1] Adapted and abridged from the following articles by Foster E. Grossnickle:
  A. *Elementary School Journal*
    1. "How to Estimate the Quotient

Figure in Long Division" (1931), 32:299–306.
  2. "How to Estimate the Accuracy of the Estimated Quotient Figure"

former, the first figure of the divisor is used as a guide figure from which the quotient is estimated. In the latter, the first figure is used as a guide if the second figure is 5 or less; when it is 6 or more, the guide figure is increased by one. Thus if the divisor is 34 the guide figure in either method is 3; if 37, the guide figure in the apparent method is 3, but in the increase-by-one method it is 4. A variation advocated by the author at one stage in his study is to increase by one only when the second digit is 9, and otherwise to use the apparent method. What method *is* best? The author attacked the problem both by analysis of the number system itself and by studying the behavior of students. His findings are not as conclusive as in point 1 above, but nevertheless are suggestive.

What types of division errors should most concern a teacher? Children learn most readily when a rifle rather than a shotgun is used—when they focus attention on particularly troublesome points of difficulty rather than continually diffuse attention over the whole process. By identifying errors most likely to arise, a teacher can forestall many of them. This section of studies is helpful in this respect.

Trouble arises in the division of decimals. Children typically have some difficulty in becoming proficient in dividing with decimals. Here, too, an analysis of trouble spots has provided information of value to first teaching, to practice, and to testing.]

1. Should children be taught "short division"? [Based on articles 4 and 12.] Approximately 200 students of each grade level 5 through 15 (the third year of a three-year normal school) were divided into two roughly equated groups

(1931), 32:442–446.

3. "Classification of the Estimations in Two Methods of Finding the Quotient in Long Division" (1932), 32:595–604.
4. "An Experiment with a One-Figure Divisor in Short and Long Division"(1934), 34:496–506, 590–599.
5. "Methods of Estimating the Quotient in Long Division Used by Teacher Training Students" (1935), 35:448–453.
6. "An Experiment with Two Methods of Estimation of the Quotient" (1937), 37:668–677.
7. "Estimating the Quotient by Two Methods in Division with a Three-Figure Divisor" (1939), 39:352–356.
8. "Types of Error in Division of Decimals" (1942), 42:184–194.
9. "Division Facts and Their Use in Estimation of Quotient with a Two-Figure Divisor" (1945), 45:569–574.

10. "How to Find the Position of the Decimal Point in the Quotient" (1952), 52:452–457.
B. *Journal of Educational Research*
11. "Errors and Questionable Habits of Work in Long Division with a One-Figure Divisor" (1936), 29:355–368.
12. "The Incidence of Error in Division with a One-Figure Divisor when Short and Long Forms of Division Are Used" (1936), 29:509–511.
13. "Transfer of Knowledge of Multiplication Facts to Their Use in Long Division" (1936), 26:677–685.
14. "Constancy of Error in Learning Division with a Two-Figure Divisor" (1939), 33:189–196.
15. "Kinds of Errors in Division of Decimals and Their Constancy" (1943), 37:110–117.
16. "Some Factors Affecting a Test Score in Division of Decimals" (1944), 37:338–342.

totaling over 2300 students. All had been taught short division. Each group was given a comprehensive two-part test using one-digit divisors sampling all varieties and levels of difficulty. Part I consisted of easy examples; Part II of hard examples. One group used a long-

division, the other a short-division form of operation. Results were measured by the number and location of errors made and by the time required for completion. An example of the type of data obtained appears in Figure 1. This comparison of the mean number of errors

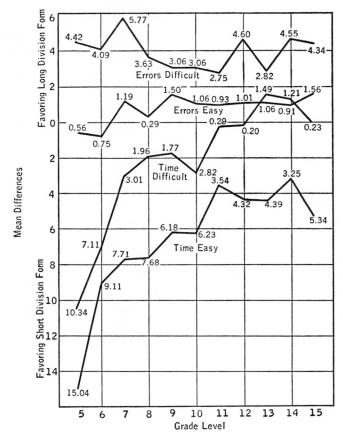

Fig. 1. Comparison of Differences in Mean Number of Errors and Mean Scores on Time Required for Easy Examples and for Difficult Examples.

made on difficult examples consistently favors the long form. Though the differences in speed of computation favored the short form for the first year or two following its teaching, these differences

soon lost size and statistical significance. The overall results were as follows:

a. In the case of both the easy and the difficult division examples, subjects using the long-division form divided

terms of a fraction may be multiplied by the same number without changing the value of the fraction.

(b) Since no particular benefit comes from the use of hard examples that is not present in easy, practice examples in division of decimals should contain easy division. [The same result was later verified in another study, article 16, footnote 1.] For review of the division process itself, integers only should be used.

A similar study [based on article 15] of errors made by 100 pupils each in Grades 6 through 9 when they repeated the same test three times in different formats showed results similar to those above, but with this additional information: An error was considered constant if it occurred on each of the three test forms. By this criterion, only one error was constant: the division of an integer by a decimal. This reinforces the need (above) to make the divisor an integer before finishing writing the example down for solution.

One additional point was discovered through analysis of test results Grades 6 through 8. Other things equal, a test is significantly more searching and difficult when the examples are arranged in a random sequence than when they are grouped according to the four possible types. Since no benefit accrues from grouping like examples, and since difficult problems are no more diagnostic than easy (see above), yet require more time, the author recommends: A diagnostic test in division of decimals should have the test items arranged in random sequence and should consist of items that are easy from the standpoint of the division operation.

STUDYING CHILDREN'S ERRORS [1]

Peter L. Spencer

[An important aspect of good teaching is the analysis of the kinds of errors made by children and of their methods of improving. In an early representative study, the author discovered that certain kinds of error characterize many children and that some children appear to make the same types of errors consistently.]

A reason for undertaking this study was to determine whether or not typical errors exist, and further, if they do exist, whether or not they are typical of the responses of the individual pupil or merely typical of the group. In other words, is a given child consistent in his pattern of errors, and are certain errors common to children in general?

The data for the study were obtained by giving an exhaustive diagnostic test in arithmetic computation (addition,

[1] Adapted and abridged from Peter L. Spencer, "A Study of Arithmetic Errors," *Stanford University Abstracts of Dissertations*, 1929–30, pp. 34–38.

subtraction, multiplication, and division) to selected sixth-grade classes in the state of Oregon. Two forms of the test were given on adjacent days to well over 400 children to determine the reliability coefficients. These ranged from .88 in multiplication to .97 in subtraction, high enough to justify the use of the data for both group and individual consideration. The number of children turning in test papers for the two forms of the four processes ranged from 550 to 623. The total number of test examples, 260, with this number of sixth-grade children gave 66,202 incorrect answers to be analyzed. They include errors with every process and from a wide sampling of the difficulties with each process.

These errors were paired to show the consistency with which various kinds of answers occurred. For example, in the problem 1000 — 825 the two testings yielded about the same percentage of error not only *in toto* (5.7 and 5.9) but in each kind of error (e.g., "Brought down left-hand 1 in minuend" accounted for 15.6 and 16.2 percent of the errors made, respectively). Typical coefficients of correlation for types of error were .74 and .84. For the most part, a relatively high positive correlation persisted throughout.

These data appear to provide conclusive evidence that errors occur which are typical of the responses of both groups of pupils and individual pupils.

A second purpose of the study was to determine whether typical errors exist in quantity. Aside from the validity of the concept of typical errors, do these errors exist in sufficient quantity to justify the use of the concept in the practical procedure of the classroom? Examination revealed that the errors so classified include from 50 to 80 percent of all the incorrect responses made. Hence the major portion falls into categories dependent upon single types of erroneous answers for their identification; they were "typical errors."

A third outcome was the determination of basal causes of typical errors: those due to the inherent qualities of our numbers system (15 inches = 1.5 ft.; zeros in quotient) and those due to defective learning of number facts and relationships. This latter in turn leads to the fourth result of the study.

A significant type of error was discovered that raises a problem relative to traditional teaching procedure. A very common type of error in addition and subtraction consisted of answers which deviated from the correct answer by one unit. These were paired with answers in multiplication and division which were due to giving the next higher or lower number in the table of primary facts instead of the correct answer. Apparently these errors are due to the teaching of the facts of each process in the form of a table.

It seems important in checking children's errors to differentiate between more wrongness and specific types of typical errors.

UPWARD VERSUS DOWNWARD ADDITION [1]

B. R. Buckingham

[This study is included for two reasons: its philosophy and its research technique. Moreover, it has been extensively referred to through the years. It well exemplifies the research of the 1920's, dominated by the drill theory of learning. The importance of meaning in learning was largely ignored. Children presumably should not be permitted to make mistakes, since these might become habitual. It was our duty to discover the "best" way to perform any process, then to teach this exclusively. People are typically most efficient in using those skills which have been reduced to habit, and habits, once established, tend to linger on unchanged. Thus it appeared to be important that the methods of computation children were expected to make habitual should be those which minimize waste motion and error. In the present study the relative merits of upward and downward column addition were examined, with the outcome slightly favoring the latter method. This is an early example of matched pair research. The reader may be interested in noting the various factors which the experimenter attempted to hold constant in the effort to permit just one variable to be at work. Any differences in outcomes might thus presumably be credited to the appropriate method of teaching. The thoughtful reader may recognize other possible variables which were not necessarily constant in this study and which might have helped to determine the outcomes.]

Previous observations by the author have indicated that there is a tendency for people to use downward addition when left to their own initiative, and that most people name the top figures first in reading $\frac{5}{3}$, saying, "Five and three are eight." This study is an experiment to see whether under controlled conditions children learn more quickly and satisfactorily by one method than by the other.

Each of seven participating classes was selected at a point when the teaching of column addition was just to begin. Each class was given a preliminary test designed to determine fitness for beginning this study and was then divided into two groups of equal ability for the diverse types of teaching. Children within the equated sections were matched as pairs for purposes of comparing the effectiveness of the two methods. The teachers were directed to de-

[1] Adapted and abridged from B. R. Buckingham, "Upward versus Downward Addition," *Journal of Educational Research* (1927), 16:315–322.

vote twenty minutes each day to the teaching of column addition. One of the groups in each class was to be taught to add upward and the other downward. The former was called the Upward Group and the latter the Downward Group. The teachers alternated the time of day at which the two recitations were scheduled. For example, if the Downward Group recited the first week from 10:10 to 10:30 and the Upward Group from 11:00 to 11:20, the groups changed places on the program the second week. They returned to the original

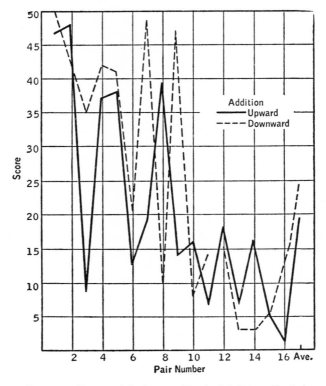

Fig. I. Scores Made on Final Addition Test by Pairs of Children in a Typical Center (Pairs Equated on Initial Test).

schedule the third week; the fourth was like the second; and so on.

All drill and review work was to be done in class and no homework was to be required. During the progress of the experiment no new topics in arithmetic were to be taken up. It was made clear that the whole purpose of the experiment was to determine the differences between teaching downward addition and upward addition. All other factors except this one were to be kept as nearly alike as possible. For example, the same columns for purposes of teaching and drill were to be employed in the two groups.

The duration of the experiment varied in different centers. As soon as the to achieve an index of less than 25 per-cent error.

4. A comparison of the figures for each major type reveals the marked dif-ferences there are among the various subtypes included in each group. This variability in difficulty should be taken into consideration in the gradation of the steps in teaching the process, and also in instructional procedure.

5. In general the mental level re-quired to achieve an index of less than 25 percent error was the same for ex-amples with either one or two quotient figures when the apparent quotient is the true quotient. In the other type there was about a year's difference in the mental-age level required to reach the index of less than 25 percent error in solving examples with one-figure and two-figure quotients. Examples with zeros in the quotients, some of which include these more difficult steps of cor-recting quotient figures, are about as difficult as examples with a one-figure quotient in which there must be a cor-rection.

6. The facts included under points 3, 4, and 5 above indicate what may be an effective sequence of instruction. It is very striking that the mental-age level required to achieve a level of less than 25 percent of error when all types of examples with one-figure quotients are combined and the mental-age level rec-ommended in the report of the Com-mittee of Seven are the same. However, in their report the Committee failed to differentiate between the level of diffi-culty of various kind of examples and did not include many types in the test of achievement used as a basis of its recommendation. The present study sup-plies this essential information.

LEARNING IN AN ARITHMETIC ACTIVITY PROGRAM [1]

Henry Harap and Charlotte E. Mapes

[In this and in a companion article appearing earlier in the *Elementary School Journal* (March, 1934) the authors describe experiments with a group of children, first with common fractions and now with decimal fractions. Tremendous interest and some controversy greeted these reports, which indicated that children taught without planned arith-metic sequence in an activity program might achieve at least as well as those taught conventionally. Critics, while strongly approving these fine experiences involving social application, believed the processes might have been developed with greater mathematical meaning if they had been less random in sequence.]

[1] Abridged and condensed from Henry Harap and Charlotte E. Mapes, "The Learn-ing of Decimals in an Arithmetic Activity Program," *Journal of Educational Research* (1936), 29:686–693.

The experimental sixth-grade class of thirty-nine pupils in a typical metropolitan school ranged in intelligence quotient from 92 to 135 with an average of 112.5. The results, however, were equally good for the lower half, averaging 104, and for the upper half, averaging 121. Materials required by the units were improvised as needed.

The thirteen activity units were selected for richness in the application of decimals and for meaning in the child's experience in school and daily life. The experiences were real and varied, including keeping accounts, making talks to classes, comparing evaporated with whole milk, making graphs, selecting a recipe, making coca, sampling tooth powders, calculating relative costs, selling glacéed apples, figuring profits, and so on. In order to provide a maximum amount of pupil participation the class was divided into about six production groups whenever the product was prepared in bulk. While most of the units were anticipated by the teacher, they were taken up willingly by the pupils because they were related to situations which were meaningful and natural to the pupils. The children were given an opportunity to communicate and associate freely as the need arose. They were given abundant opportunities for self-expression and critical judgment. Every unit had its logical and natural close. Much of the time ordinarily devoted to drill and problem solving was devoted to construction, manipulation, and other activities. Actually, therefore, much less than the customary allotment of time was used in computations.

New arithmetical steps did not occur in the order of difficulty. Each new difficulty was taken up when it arose, the explanation lasting a few minutes. No practice sheets or any other supplementary exercises were used. No tests were given other than the initial and final tests. Thus, the repetition of the twenty-seven processes was limited exclusively to their natural occurrence in the units of work. All the work of the pupils was kept in a notebook, the latter being a complete and exact record of all the computations of the pupils. No textbook or any other printed material was used in the experimental course.

The twenty-seven basic steps in decimals were kept in mind and formed the basis for the initial and final tests containing twenty-seven items of three exercises each. These tests, prepared by the arithmetic curriculum center and widely used throughout the city, were also given to a control group for comparison. The experimental group also repeated the tests on common fractions given a year earlier to discover the permanent effects of the previous experiment. Results:

1. The pupils attained a mastery of 96 percent of the twenty-seven processes. Twenty pupils mastered all steps; nine mastered twenty-six; four mastered twenty-five; four mastered twenty-four; and none mastered fewer than twenty.

2. The learning of processes in the order of their appearance in the units did not hinder the mastery of the processes.

3. The processes which occurred only a few times were learned as well as those which occurred many times.

4. The experimental group achieved a mastery of 96 percent as compared with a mastery of 67 percent for the control group.

5. Retesting the group in fractions after an interval of a year yielded a mastery of 97 percent over an attainment of about 81 percent a year ago.

6. On a test of mixed fundamentals covering fractions and decimals the experimental group achieved 90 percent accuracy.

ARITHMETIC USED IN AN ACTIVITY PROGRAM [1]
Paul R. Hanna and others

[Studies elsewhere in this volume show the vast amount of arithmetic concepts known by children before they enter school. For the most part these have been learned incidentally in the process of living, with practically no formal teaching. Moreover, normal children find few "learning difficulties" in improving roller-skating, in mastering the rules and plays of a game of checkers, or in reading and following directions for assembling the parts of an airplane. These considerations have led many to believe that arithmetic could be well learned with few pains if it were an integral and incidental part of rich daily activities lending adequate purpose. Rebelling against the isolation and sterility of existing programs, they wanted above all for arithmetic to be socially meaningful to the children and felt that this motivation would prove to be all that was necessary. Others have been equally concerned that arithmetic shall be mathematically meaningful, conceiving of it "as a closely knit system of understandable ideas, principles and processes." [2] The following study attempted to discover whether activity programs might include enough arithmetic experiences as integral parts of the units to develop the necessary skills and logical understanding.]

A survey explored the extent to which opportunities for arithmetic in the activity program were possible. Six teachers in Grade 3 and six in Grade 6 accustomed to activity teaching recorded every situation faced by individuals or by the entire class in which there was a need for quantitative thinking and manipulation. These were problems arising in the pursuit of some child-selected activity either in or out of school and they were recorded for a period of four school months.

For example, Grade 6: In a unit entitled "The Solar System—How Our Earth Became a Member Planet" there arose this problem (stated in textbook fashion): A light-year, used by astronomers as a measure of distance, is the distance light travels in one of our years at

[1] Abridged and adapted from Paul R. Hanna and others, "Opportunities for the Use of Arithmetic in an Activity Program," *The Teaching of Arithmetic*, Tenth Yearbook, National Council of Teachers of Mathematics, Bureau of Publications, Teachers College, Columbia University, New York, 1935, pp. 85–120.

[2] William A. Brownell, "Psychological Considerations in the Learning and the Teaching of Arithmetic" in *ibid.*, pp. 1–31.

the rate of about 186,000 miles per second. What is this distance in miles?

A total of 439 problems (234 for Grade 3 and 205 for Grade 6) grew out of such experiences as making hats for a dramatization, making a frieze of Old New York, planning a planetarium, etc. These reports were studied to determine:

1. How many one-step, two-step, and three-or-more-step problems do children solve in connection with their activities?

2. How many operations in each of the four fundamental processes were completed?

3. How many solutions involved integers, fractions, mixed numbers, decimals, decimal fractions, linear measure, time, calendar, etc.?

4. How many problems demanded such miscellaneous manipulations as measuring, comparison, counting, reading and writing numbers, telling time, graphing, etc.?

5. What was the general nature of the arithmetic problem arising in Grade 3? In Grade 6?

SOME ILLUSTRATIVE FINDINGS

1. Computations in division actually done by pupils in Grade 6 were: (a) fifty-one with integers ranging in size and complexity from $6 \div 3$ to $139,685,000 \div 57,255,000$ (there were far more of the latter than of the former type); (b) two with mixed numbers, $3610 \div 33\frac{1}{3}$ and $7\frac{1}{2} \div 2$; (c) thirteen with decimals ranging from $1.18 \div 3$ to $15,000,000,000 \div .03$; (d) one decimal fraction, $.10 \div 3\frac{1}{2}$.

2. A very wide range of problem situations was found in both grades.

3. A higher percentage of computational (versus noncomputational) problems is found in Grade 6 (72 percent) than in Grade 3 (56 percent).

4. Many more computations were necessary to solve the more complex problems of Grade 6.

5. Multiplication is the most frequently used fundamental process when both grades are combined.

6. Division is the least frequently used fundamental process when both grades are combined.

7. Nearly half of the computations for the two grades combined were with integers, and of the remaining computations, decimals were next most frequently used.

8. Very few problems in either grade involve fractions, mixed numbers, or decimals, other than money.

9. There is a marked increase in complexity from integer to decimal computation in Grade 6 over Grade 3.

10. Integers are fairly evenly distributed among the fundamental processes in the two grades combined.

11. Multiplication of decimals accounts for 46 percent of all computations in the two grades combined.

12. Division of decimals is seldom used.

13. Measuring, counting, and comparing are the most frequently found noncomputational problems.

14. Graphing and scale drawing seem important in Grade 6.

15. Grade 3 addition consists of all types of numbers, but in all instances simple numbers. The only fractions used are ½, ¼ and ⅛.

16. Grade 3 subtraction is almost exclusively with integers. There are some mixed numbers. The fractions include ½, ⅓, and ¼.

17. Grade 3 multiplication is confined largely to integers; the same is true of division.

18. Grade 6 addition is largely integers and decimals (money). Fractions are still simple—½, ¼, and 1⁄12.

19. Grade 6 subtraction is mostly with decimals (money).

20. Grade 6 multiplication is largely with integers and decimals.

21. Grade 6 division is largely with integers, with some large numbers.

22. Problems containing decimals were largely of money transactions.

SOME CONCLUSIONS REACHED BY
THE COMMITTEE

1. The present study is just preliminary. It considers only two grades, for much less than a year, in but a few schools in one geographic region, and with but a portion of the out-of-school number situations recorded.

2. The survey demonstrates a richness and vitality of arithmetic experiences in the activity program which may serve to give pupils significant meaning and purpose and may build readiness for the skills period. Yet these functional experiences of childhood are alone not adequate to develop arithmetic skills. The present activity program offers too few number experiences per week and relies too much upon chance to assure a comprehensive orientation in arithmetic. The 234 problems in the six third grades during four months meant an average of only ten problems per room per month, of which but five or six were computational. Similarly, the 205 problems in the six sixth grades during four months meant an average of only eight and a half problems per room per month, of which six were computational. This sparsity leads the authors to conclude that it is not possible to teach arithmetic solely through an activity program.

PART FOUR

Needed Research

The sampling of research in the three R's presented in this volume has many implications. Obviously, a great deal of careful and fruitful experimenting has been conducted through the years. Even more obviously, mere "patches of knowledge" are scattered as yet over the vast surface of the unknown. The numerous studies not reported here still leave untested most of what we need to know in education. Of those studies that are reported here, only a few are sufficiently thorough and penetrating to be considered "definitive." Most are exploratory in nature and, when finished, have reached the point of offering hypotheses to be tested further, rather than of offering truly established conclusions. This statement applies even more to most of the studies not reported here.

One effect these studies may well have upon the reader is to make him realize that he can do at least as competent experimentation as many reported here. He may develop a self-confidence that will encourage him to join the select group of "continuing researchers." By 1946, according to W. A. Brownell,[1] 1413 studies on arithmetic had been reported by 778 authors. Of these authors, 615 had reported but one study while only 53 had reported more than three. Those who have reported several more can be counted on the fingers of one hand. Yet, as can be seen, research is not an esoteric art to be performed only by an elite few. Worth-while studies can be made by almost anyone with the ability characteristic of everyday teachers and with sufficient interest and enthusiasm.

How does one start? Several of the studies presented here may have aroused a beginning itch of curiosity. "What if he had tried this?" "I

[1] Reported in G. T. Buswell, "Needed Research on Arithmetic," *The Teaching of Arithmetic*, Fiftieth Yearbook of the National Society for the Study of Education, Part II, University of Chicago Press, Chicago, 1951, Chap. XV, p. 283.

wonder if that part is really true" or "Would his results change if . . . ?" "This may be true in arithmetic; I wonder if it's true in spelling." A similar reaction when reading any report of research is likely to prove effective.

But even more effective is a tough-minded skepticism. "Is what I'm told to do in teaching this particular grade, skill, or subject based upon fact or opinion?" "What evidence does the author, supervisor, or professor have to back up the statement?" (Inquiring on this point may be a rapid route to unpopularity.) "Common sense" is not a reliable guide. It does not "make sense" that we should be blind whenever our eyes are in motion. Yet if we look in a mirror first at one eye, then the other, and attempt to watch our eyes move, we discover that common sense has betrayed us. Advances in mathematical and other research have been made by questioning accepted "truths." The educator, whether teacher, administrator, or supervisor, may make similar advances by testing our untested educational axioms.

Most fruitful of all, however, is an open mind in everyday work. "Why did that happen?" "What will happen if we do this—and why?" Encouraging children to ask "why" about any things they do not understand may be embarrassing but may lead to exceedingly rapid intellectual growth.[2] It may also sensitize adults to the unanswered educational questions that abound and that need to be answered by experimentation. Everything we are unsure of is grist for the mill of informal or formal research.

In our everyday work, trying things out and keeping careful records of what happens may be the most valuable kind of guide to new knowledge and future action. From this a person discovers what works best with the particular people and environment involved. Over a period of time important generalizations may emerge. These findings when written up for journal publication add to our professional reservoir of information to use in similar situations.

On a somewhat more formal level, many writers have suggested areas of needed research.[3] One useful bulletin, for example, suggests needed research in language expression, in reading, in speech, and in listening. Among the fifty needed areas in reading research suggested by William S. Gray are the following:

1. What is the role of imagery in interpreting what is read? How can

[2] C. W. Hunnicutt, *Answering Children's Questions*, Columbia University Press, New York, 1949.

[3] National Conference on Research in English, *Areas of Research Interest in the Language Arts*, National Council of Teachers of English, Chicago, 1952.

teachers promote the development of types of imagery essential to clear, vivid experiencing of meaning when reading?

2. What effect does training in one type of reading, such as skimming, have upon ability to engage effectively in other types of reading, such as grasping details accurately, seeing implications, and reacting critically or appreciatively to what is read?

3. To what extent can the claims made for bibliotherapy be validated for different types of personalities and through the use of different kinds of material?

4. "Will children progress faster when the vocabulary burden is kept relatively light or when it is made relatively heavy?" In attacking this problem clear distinctions should be made between progress in early and subsequent stages of reading and in different aspects of reading.

5. In what respects should the techniques used in guiding reading activities in the respective school subjects differ from those used in teaching pupils to read in reading classes?

6. How do boys and girls differ in the ease or difficulty with which they learn through different avenues—visual, auditory, kinaesthetic—and how do these differences influence the methods that should be used in teaching individuals to read?

7. What are the most effective ways of providing for individual differences among pupils when teaching reading at given grade levels?

8. What are the merits and limitations of different types of reading programs in junior high schools, senior high schools, and junior college?

9. How can the reading interests of secondary-school pupils be increased and their reading tastes elevated, and what are the conditions that make for permanence of desirable reading interests after students leave school?

10. What is the role of personal reading in the lives of children and young people who have access to and make wide use of the radio, television, and the cinema?

In the section on language expression written by Lou LaBrant, Fred Marcus, and Edwin R. Steinberg in the same bulletin, such topics as the following are suggested:

1. If the findings of Mary Katherine Smith (see pp. 224–230) and others even approximate the truth, what are the probable common elements? From, for example, 16,000 words used by each of two given youngsters, which ones are common? What determines the diversity?

2. Studies of words used in school compositions and of words *known* by school pupils point to a large unused vocabulary for the individual

child. How are the related experiences to be tapped, or are they of no importance to the progress of writing?

3. How do the vocabularies of told stories differ from the vocabularies in written compositions? Would an increase in oral composition, free as it is from spelling problems, eventually affect the range of expression in writing?

4. How long does it take the average child in second, third . . . eighth grade to copy with moderate accuracy one hundred words, two hundred, three, etc.? In the light of such physical limitations, how long a story or other composition can he write in an hour, discounting time for selection and organization of ideas? What is the effect on style, fluency, and artistic quality when a part of his composition is dictated or written on a typewriter? The whole area of the relation of ideas to physical limitations in recording has been scarcely touched. Present recording devices open a large field for research. Possibilities of combining writing and tape or wire recording have not been explored.

5. What is the effect of wide reading on use of words in composition? The statement is frequently made that reading develops vocabulary of themes.

6. What is the effect of emphasis on spelling upon fluency in writing?

7. To what extent, if any, is the frequent use of "and" to join sentences or clauses a step between the use of a series of simple sentences (relationships not expressed at all) and the complex sentence (relationships seen as involving subordination)? Piaget's work, which opened this problem twenty-five years ago, has not had adequate follow-up.

8. In what constructions do students of various age or grade levels use relative pronouns? What problems of word order are indicated?

9. At what age and by what means might they develop the ability to distinguish between facts and judgments?

10. At what age and by what means might they develop the ability to organize data into prescribed patterns or forms of written communication?

Buswell in his chapter "Needed Research on Arithmetic," referred to above, reported twenty-one proposals for research submitted by various people who had published arithmetic studies. These proposals are still highly pertinent. In each case there was a statement of the problem, its significance, some possible sources of data, suggested methods and techniques for carrying on the study, and its possible contribution to the profession. The problem statements only, for a few of these, are reported here.

1. The determination of the effectiveness of the use of manipulative materials in the teaching of arithmetic.
2. An exploration of precomputational activities with common fractions. What are the possibilities not only for developing the various concepts of fractions themselves (e.g., ratio idea) but also for formulating a program with regard to related concepts (common denominator, reduction) and to an understanding of the operations?
3. The establishment of methods of evaluating a pupil's ability to use arithmetic in functional situations. A functional situation is one that is encountered in experience and may present itself in writing, in speech, in a visual or kinaesthetic impression, or in a combination of these.
4. The value of the interview technique. As a testing procedure to help determine the thought processes of pupils this has been rather definitely established. Is it not possible that the interview technique also has diagnostic value as an instructional procedure? It is conceivable that research might determine the values of continuous day-by-day group and individual interview techniques for revealing processes of thinking in arithmetic.
5. The optimum ratio of class time to be spent on the development of understandings (meanings) and the development of computational skill or facility.

These various suggestions indicate just a few of the ideas that need to be investigated. At the request of the Carnegie Corporation, the Educational Testing Service enlisted the help of mathematician-educators to study deficiencies in mathematics education and to recommend areas of needed research. Their report [4] offers further ideas that need to be investigated. There is much to be done.

[4] Henry F. Dyer, Robert Kalin, and Frederick M. Lord, *Problems in Mathematical Education*, Educational Testing Service, Princeton, N.J., 1956.

Index